PRAISE FOR *BUILDING AN OUTSTANDING WORKFORCE*

Building an Outstanding Workforce is an accessible, concise, impressive book that covers a critical business area. This is a resource I would recommend to all those who believe tomorrow's workforce is the key to commercial success and who want an overview of the subject presented with clarity, focus and purpose. Boards inevitably give focus to financial resource but evidently businesses and organizations need equally to invest in human resource and talent management. Both as an executive search professional and a board member of a FTSE 40 business, I would warmly commend this coherent, comprehensive book to anyone looking for a professional overview of workforce management and maximization. **Baroness Virginia Bottomley, Chair, Board Practice, Odgers Berndtson**

Building an Outstanding Workforce takes us on a comprehensive and engaging journey through what it takes to run a successful organization when the surrounding context is changing fast. The narrative combines deep insight from experienced business leaders, consultants and academics together with case studies from a range of employers. The book is easy to navigate and contains practical suggestions for those grappling with how technological and societal changes will affect their business. An essential guide for all current and aspiring leaders of people. **Chris Cummings, Chief Executive, The Investment Association**

Wow! *Building an Outstanding Workforce* does an incredibly thorough and thoughtful, job of defining the workforce of the future. This book is a treasure because it summarizes so much information in useful ways, but then goes beyond to offer creative options for the workforce of the future. A neo-classic. **Dave Ulrich, Rensis Likert Professor, Ross School of Business, University of Michigan Partner, The RBL Group**

Building an Outstanding Workforce is a tour de force of the workplace psychology literature, which excellently highlights some of the great challenges in the VUCA (volatile, uncertain, complex and ambiguous) world most people work in. This is a great primer of occupational psychology as it applies to the problems and issues in business at the moment. **Professor Sir Cary Cooper, CBE, 50th Anniversary Professor of Organizational Psychology and Health at the ALLIANCE Manchester Business School**

Building an Outstanding Workforce is an excellent synthesis of the broad evidence base for what drives effective people management. It starts from the important place that, to create great workforces, it's important to understand human behaviour, and builds on this to propose a model for how people management can be organized. A great resource for Human Resources professionals and for anyone in the world of work. **Rupert McNeil, Government Chief People Officer (United Kingdom)**

Twenty years have now passed since McKinsey famously noted that organizations' main competitive advantage would be their ability to manage talent. And yet, despite a vast body of evidence on how to unlock human potential, most companies still struggle with basic talent management issues. This book digests some of the key insights from this field to provide a practical guide for leaders interested in building a high-performing organization. **Tomas Chamorro-Premuzic, Professor of Business Psychology, UCL and Columbia University**

As much as our thinking about people management over the last decades has improved, the capability of leaders and HR professionals to create a workforce outstanding in driving company performance has often not kept up with that development. *Building an Outstanding Workforce* is a deeply insightful book on the building blocks of people management that truly drive company performance. it offers a new framework for people management that hands back the responsibility for creating an outstanding workforce to the leadership of the company. Exactly where it belongs. This is a powerful book for leaders and people professionals. **Hein J M Knaapen, Chief HR Officer, ING Bank**

Businesses that are able to acquire an inspire top talent are able to do extraordinary things, winning and growing market share on a sustainable and profitable basis. *Building an Outstanding Workforce* delivers the evidence base that demonstrates the importance of the thoughtful leadership which is required to achieve this **Symon Drake-Brockman, Chief Executive, Pemberton Asset Management Group**

Anyone in business today should read this book. As we accelerate into the realities of the fourth industrial revolution this book distils important research, concepts and aspects of organizational & economic transformation, technology and the future of work into an excellent series of frameworks for understanding the impacts, the scenarios that could evolve and guidance for how to navigate them. A truly excellent and comprehensive business companion for those that need to know the big picture now! **Graham Kellen, Chief Digital Officer, Schroders Asset Management**

Building an Outstanding Workforce has comprehensively captured various aspects of people management in different cultural contexts. A must read for any leader who is deeply committed towards raising the bar on people management.
Nupur Singh Mallick, CHRO, Tata Group

Building an Outstanding Workforce takes an impressively broad yet comprehensive view of people management and workforce building across multiple academic fields and practical professional roles. The rich experience of authors allows them to insightfully investigate issues and cases across different cultural and social contexts. As such this book will be very useful for business leaders, senior organizational development professionals and researchers in China, Asia and beyond. **Ming Guo, Managing Director, EAL Consulting Shanghai**

Creating the skills and capabilities of the future is absolutely critical to surviving and thriving in this digitally disrupted world. *Building an Outstanding Workforce* provides a roadmap for HR and Learning professionals to enable and accelerate transformations. **Bill Pelster, Former Chief Learning Officer Deloitte and creator of Deloitte University**

If you want to create a higher performance work culture, while treating people with dignity, respect and developing your talent, this book is for you **Professor Jonathan Passmore, Professor of Coaching & Behavioural Change and Director of Henley Centre for Coaching & Behavioural Change, Henley Business School**

Building an Outstanding Workforce is a giant of a business book. Brilliantly researched and supported with great case studies, it provides an-depth analysis of how and why traditional approaches to organizational design need to change. Drawing on the latest business psychology insights and applying them in reality, this book delivers on its ambitious agenda **Lucy Adams, CEO of Disruptive HR and author of *HR Disrupted* and *The HR Change Toolkit***

Building an Outstanding Workforce, weaves together the perfect tapestry of current workforce research, classical business theory, technology advances, and the role of human nature and the brain. This highly useful book proves that when it comes to designing a future-proof 21st century organization, the more things change, the more they stay the same. A leader must-read. **Alexandra Levit, author of *Humanity Works***

In *Building an Outstanding Workforce*, the title speaks for itself because the book is a comprehensive guide to help readers do just that. Definitely a must read for any business professional! **Jacob Morgan, author of *The Future of Work* and Founder of the Future of Work University**

Building an Outstanding Workforce does well to cover all the key debated areas of personality and individual differences which adds useful scientific-practitioner value and meaning. It contains a good range of interesting and relevant case studies which will provoke worthwhile discussions about our psychological make up, amongst students, and practitioners alike. This book is engaging, comprehensive and will prove relevant to those interested in the aetiology of behaviours and people management per se. A well needed source indeed. **Dr Michelle Hunter-Hill, Senior Lecturer, Human Resource Management and International Business, University of Roehampton Business School**

Based on a grounding of occupational psychology *Building an Outstanding Workforce* is a thoughtful and engaging book that will appeal to both business leaders and managers and those aspiring to these positions. It is structured clearly and provides an informative insight into achieving organizational objectives through a better understanding of people at both the individual and group level. The book also benefits from a range of supporting cases on how leading organizations across different national cultures and business sectors address the challenge of successful people management. **Laurie J Mullins, author of organizational Behaviour in the Workplace 12th ed**

Building an Outstanding Workforce

Developing people to drive individual and organizational success

Paul Aldrich and
Andrew Pullman

KoganPage

First published in Great Britain and the United States in 2019 by Kogan Page Limited

2nd Floor, 45 Gee Street	122 W 27th St, 10th Floor	4737/23 Ansari Road
London	New York, NY 10001	Daryaganj
EC1V 3RS	USA	New Delhi 110002
United Kingdom		India

www.koganpage.com

© Paul Aldrich and Andrew Pullman 2019

The right of Paul Aldrich and Andrew Pullman to be identified as the authors of this work has been asserted by them in accordance with the Copyright, Designs and Patents Act 1988.

ISBNs

Hardback   9781789660173
Paperback   9780749497323
Ebook   9780749497316

British Library Cataloguing-in-Publication Data

A CIP record for this book is available from the British Library.

Library of Congress Cataloging-in-Publication Data

A CIP record for this book is available from the Library of Congress.

Typeset by Integra Software Services, Pondicherry
Print production managed by Jellyfish
Printed and bound by CPI Group (UK) Ltd, Croydon CR0 4YY

Supporting online resources for this book are available at koganpage.com/baow

CONTENTS

List of figures xiii
About the authors xiv
Foreword xv
Acknowledgements xviii

Introduction 1

PART ONE People 11

01 Evolutionary psychology and neuroscience 13
Introduction 13
Our history 14
Our brains 16
Emotions 21
Thinking 28

02 Personality psychology and intelligence 39
Introduction 39
Personality psychology 40
Beliefs, values, attitudes and interests 42
Personality traits 44
Locus of control 45
Multiple personality traits 46
Personality types 49
Socio-analytic theory 51
Social constructionism and impression management 52
The dark triad 54
Meaning and purpose 55
Personality development 56
Intelligence 58
Character 60

03   Bias, stereotypes, group culture and decision-making 66
Introduction 66
Bias and stereotypes 67
Group culture 70
In and out groups 72
Decision-making 74
System 1 and System 2 thinking 75
Procrastination 77

04   Motivation 80
Introduction 80
Overview of motivation theories 81
Need theories 82
Process theories 87
Motivation and financial reward 89
Neuroscience and motivation 91
Our human and chimp brains 92
Mindset 92
Flow 94
Motivation, job satisfaction and personality 95
Motivation and culture 97

05   Leadership 100
Introduction 100
Leadership research 102
Leadership and management 104
The future of leadership 106
Change 111
Organizational behaviour 115
Selection and development 120

Case studies 125
Smurfitt Kappa 125
Qantas 127
Tata Group 129

PART TWO The environment 131

06 Organizations 133
Introduction 133
Purpose 134
External environment 136
Strategy 140
Internal environment 144
Organization design and development 147
Social constructionism and organizational enactment 151
Organization structures 151
Practical implications 154

07 Technology and the future of work 159
Introduction 159
Changes in the pattern of work 160
The future of work: Technology impact 162
The future of work: Workforce scenarios 167
The future of work: Organizations 171
The future of work: People 174
Humanity in work 178
The future of work: Leadership challenges 181
Gender 189
On the bright side 190

08 Demographics 193
Introduction 193
Global demographic trends 194
Generational demographic trends 196
Introducing the multigenerational workforce 197
Leading the multigenerational generational workforce 204

09 Culture 212
Introduction 212
Global talent migration 213
Organization culture 224
Corporate climate 226

10   Social movements 228
Introduction 228
The social enterprise 229
Corporate and social responsibility 229
Environmental, social and governance 233
Impact of leadership 234
Stakeholder impact 236
Responsibility for CSR 238
Diversity and inclusion 238
Practical implications 244
Cultural resistance 248
Responsibility for diversity and inclusion 249

Case studies 252
Alibaba 252
Hermes 254
Oui SNCF 256
Ledcor 257
Accenture 259
Barclays Bank 262
Patagonia Inc 264

PART THREE   Workforce planning 267

11   Planning and people risk 269
Introduction 269
Strategic workforce planning 270
People risk 272

12   Human capital metrics and reporting 281
Introduction 281
Human capital strategy 282
Measuring human capital 285
People metrics 288
People management impact 290
Human capital reporting 292

13   People analytics 299
Introduction 299

People technology 299
People data 301
People analytics 302
Research design 303
Data governance 305
Social sensing technology 306
Why Moneyball? 308

14 Employee engagement and experience 310
Introduction 310
Employee engagement 311
Employee experience 316
Employer brand and the employee value proposition 322
Giving them what they want 325

15 Well-being 329
Introduction 329
Well-being and wellness 329
Workplace design 332
Psychological well-being 335
Psychological safety 336
Stress 337
Contributors to stress 338
Neuroscience and well-being 341
Meaning 342
Practical implications 344

16 The future of people development 349
Introduction 349
The future of learning and development 350
Personality 354
Mindset and belief 356
Attribution theory 358
Coaching 359

Case studies 362
Volvo 362
Monzo 364
Aramco Overseas 366

PART FOUR   The future of people management 369

17   People functions 371
Introduction 371
Strategic human resource management 372
Roles in human resource management 377
Influence in human resource management 385
The structure of human resource management 390
The importance of CEOs and senior leaders 392

18   Professional people management 396
Introduction 396
Underlying tension 397
HR in the boardroom 398
Talent management 398
Future people management 400
New framework for people management 408

PART FIVE   Creating an outstanding workforce 415

19   HR disrupted and dispersed 417
Informed by the past 417
Transformed by the future 420
The future people function 422
People advisors 424
People portfolio management 425
People specialists: Embedded 426
People facilitators 428
People enablers 429
Framework summary 429
Conclusion 430

Notes 434
References 450
Index 482

LIST OF FIGURES

Figure 1.1   Neurons 18

Figure 1.2   Synapsis 18

Figure 1.3   The brain 19

Figure 1.4   The behavioural brain 20

Figure P2.1   The people paradigm 131

Figure P3.1   The organization paradigm 267

Figure 11.1   Talent portfolio management 273

Figure 17.1   The relative influence of CEOs on people management 393

Figure 18.1   The people management framework 409

Figure 19.1   The people management framework 423

Figure 19.2   The people management framework – people advisors: advisory experts 425

Figure 19.3   The people management framework – people portfolio management: functional experts 426

Figure 19.4   The people management framework – people specializations: embedded experts 427

Figure 19.5   The people management framework – people facilitators and enablers: leaders and boundary-spanners 428

ABOUT THE AUTHORS

Dr Paul Aldrich has over 25 years' talent management experience covering banking, asset and wealth management, insurance and professional services across EMEA, APAC and the US. He started his career at Price Waterhouse in London, worked for the Chase Manhattan Bank in London and Hong Kong and is Global Head of People and Performance at Pemberton Asset Management.

Paul has a doctorate in business from Durham University, which focused on the role and influence of human resource management and talent portfolio risk management. He also has an MBA from Durham where he is a Visiting Fellow at the Business School and is a Senior Lecturer in Human Resource Management at the University of Roehampton's Business School. His current research interests focus on leadership development coaching and the impact of technology on the future of work.

Paul is a Chartered Fellow of the Chartered Institute of Personnel and Development, member of the Guild of HR Professionals, member of the Society for Human Resource Management, Fellow of the Higher Education Academy, a British Psychological Society qualified occupational test user, qualified executive coach and member of the International Coaching Federation.

Andrew Pullman is CEO and founder of People Risk Solutions, an HR consultancy working with companies in all sectors, specialising in financial and professional services. He is also founder of PeopleClear Ltd, a new company in the FinTech/RegTech sector, offering regulatory technology solutions to financial services firms. This is his first book.

As an experienced HR professional, Andrew provides strategic and tactical HR advice to a variety of clients across several industry sectors. He is particularly focused on the new Senior Manager and Certification Regime regulations for financial services in the UK. Previously Andrew was a Managing Director at Dresdner Kleinwort, the German investment bank. He was Global Head of HR for the Capital Markets business and responsible for training and talent management across the bank. Andrew has worked in financial services for over 30 years, starting in Fixed Income Sales at US bank JP Morgan following his first career as an officer in the British Army.

Andrew is a Chartered Fellow of the Chartered Institute of Personnel and Development and Co-Chair of the Organisational Design and Development Committee and SMCR Taskforces of the City HR Association. He chairs the Senior HR City Breakfast Forum and is a visiting lecturer at Cass Business School and City University. Andrew is also a member of the Guild of HR Professionals and a Freeman of the Guild of Entrepreneurs.

FOREWORD

by Peter Cheese
Chief Executive, CIPD, the professional body for HR and people development

We've all heard the phrase 'people are our most important assets'. It's certainly well worn, and doubtless is spoken with good intent. And it's true that when it comes down to it, businesses can't work or exist without people. People innovate and create, manage, oversee, produce and deliver services, they drive value and are critical to competitive advantage. But we know they also represent risk and challenge as well.

People being described as assets however points to much business thinking and behavior over the decades that seems to have treated or thought of employees as units of production, and not as whole people. Homo economicus instead of homo sapiens. We have tried to standardize and make efficient, treating and measuring people and the investments we make in them as costs, and then to manage or control people's rather inconvenient behavioural attributes and differences through rules, policies and processes, and the still familiar corporate cultures of command and control.

The world though is changing, and changing fast. We are entering what has been described as the fourth industrial revolution, powered by the rapid advances in technology, robotics, artificial intelligence and machine learning. These advances are creating very different ways in which we connect, how we learn and access knowledge, how and where we work, and the nature of jobs and skills that we need. But at the heart of all the debate about the future of work is an increasingly human agenda, a recognition of what makes people different from machines and how important that is. Klaus Schwab, the founder of the World Economic Forum and who many credit with the terminology describes our goal as to 'together shape a future that works for all by putting people first, empowering them and constantly reminding ourselves that all of these new technologies are first and foremost tools made by people for people'.

At the same time, social and political changes are happening which also impact organizations and the nature of our workforces. The shift from collectivism to individualism characterized through the rise of populism and individual voice, enabled in part by social media. And by new generations coming in to the workforce who see much more choice and ways in which they can navigate and personalize the world around them and what they experience. Regulation and policy is also increasingly focused on this changing context, trying to encourage or sometimes cajole businesses in to reporting more about their organizations and workforces, and increasing access and opportunity to good work for all.

So we are at a point of a profound need, and opportunity, to put people more at the heart of our thinking in business. To recognize everyone as whole people and as individuals, to celebrate and engage our differences and diversity, and to build the leadership, cultures, organizations and practices that help get the very best out all the people that work for us.

The positive business outcomes are clear. Most surveys today show how businesses across all sectors are increasingly struggling to fill their skills gaps, to innovate and to adapt more rapidly to change, to drive up productivity, and to show that they act responsibly in acknowledgement of all their stakeholders.

However, we have a way to go. Most indicators associated with people at work are not pointing in the right direction. We know for example that stress is the biggest source of absenteeism from work, and it's corollary of presenteeism or working when not fully fit is also growing. Many people have concerns about the future and the security of their finances and their jobs, levels of engagement can best be described as flat lining, and there are growing concerns about fairness, access to opportunity and workplace behaviours. Societally there are many questions of trust in larger businesses, whether they are only acting in self-interest, their lack of transparency and accountability beyond the relentless focus on providing returns to their financial stakeholders, and whether they are playing their part in building stronger communities and societies.

This book pulls together these questions and more and helps to point the way forwards, for business leaders, managers, HR professionals and others.

It starts appropriately with people. About understanding our differences and biases, what motivates and engages us, how we learn and what is important in our working lives.

The body of evidence and knowledge about human behavior has been growing for a long time and today is being strengthened with the advances in the field of neuroscience. This has to be the basis for the interventions and practices for good people management and development, but historically has played precious little part in actual practice and thinking in business. We can't succeed in engaging people and getting the best from them if we try to control their behaviours with rules and policies, but that seems to have been a norm from the earliest days of industrialization. Increasing automation and AI can make this worse if we are not careful.

The changing context of work, of our workforces, and our workplaces is drawn out and then goes in to the implications for organizations of all shapes and sizes. Strategic workforce planning has to be as much part of business strategy as any other element of strategy. For businesss leaders and for many organizations, this is a muscle that needs to be developed, and HR leaders and their teams need to step up to this more. Understanding of the changes in skills and capabilities needed to adapt to change and business demands, and the options in meeting these, are essential in preparing businesses for the future.

Future organizations and workforces will by fact and by necessity be much more diverse. Skills may be accessed in many different ways, from contractors, partners, contingent workforce, as well as from employees, and from many different sources or talent pools. Those skills will change as technology plays a bigger part, and we also have to be able to design jobs that are good for people and make the most of their skills. Learning and development become essential strategic capabilities for businesses so that they can readily upskill or reskill as work and skill demands change. There is no longer some kind of best practice in organizational models and cultures. These will vary and need to be understood and best fit to the context that the business operates in.

In the final two parts of the book, the focus turns to how we better manage people, the roles of leaders and managers in this changing context, and how we ultimately create outstanding workforces.

It is an extraordinary reality of so many businesses in the past as to how little we have trained leaders and managers about the essence of people management, in understanding people and all their differences, behaviours and biases. Not only have we not done enough to train them, but we also haven't done a good job of measuring and holding them to account. Perhaps it's because these are harder to measure than the tangible outputs of sales numbers, or technical expertise, or operational delivery, but without managing our teams and our people effectively, none of those outcomes can be assured. With the diverse workforces and ways of working we see now, and with the expectations of the incoming generations, it is an absolute imperative that we develop and encourage good people management and the supportive cultures that help people thrive. From the tops of organizations on down.

Finally, we need to address the overall people management practices. To move from one size fits all and the many process and policy centric views of the past, to adaptive and engaging practices, based on sound principles, evidence, and understanding of outcomes. This is the domain space and agenda for much of HR, and this is an important time for HR to step up, and as the people profession to take it's place at the heart of business thinking and practice. The book concludes with proposing a new people management framework that addresses these ideas.

Ultimately the prize goes even beyond our businesses and having outstanding workforces and the sustainable, thriving, healthy organizations we aspire to. Whether we live to work or work to live, work is such a large part of our lives. It can define us, develop and grow us, allow us to achieve our purpose and use our talents, to give us social connection and support, and to enable many other things we value in our lives. All this doesn't happen by accident and we have to work hard as leaders, managers, and as individuals to help create these outcomes as widely as possible. When we do, we create and extend wellbeing in it's widest sense. That as a goal for us all as we face in to a perhaps more uncertain future is something to aim for.

ACKNOWLEDGEMENTS

Paul Aldrich

This book is dedicated to Maria who shared me with the book for a few months but remained patient and supportive throughout; and to Tiffany, Charlotte, Alejandro and Isabela who I hope experience a more thoughtful, kinder and healthier future both in their work and in the wider world, adopt a growth mindset, are resilient, and find meaning and purpose in their lives.

Andrew Pullman

I would like to thank Alison for her valuable contributions, and dedicate this book to her, Matt and Gemma. My wider team across People Risk Solutions have been very encouraging too, and I hope that they are able to utilize some of the content to help bring best practice to a wider workforce, in many different countries and sectors.

Introduction

The people principles

This book is aimed at business leaders and managers who want to understand what excellence in people management can look like, who is responsible for it and how it can be successfully organized and delivered now and in the future.

People management is not the responsibility of a single function, whether it is called personnel, human resources, human capital or people, and while this book discusses how people management professionals can support the leadership and management of organizations through leveraging their specialist knowledge and experience, the responsibility for building an outstanding workforce sits broadly across the organization.

This book is based on four principles, which we call the *people principles*:

1 People are, and will remain, the most important factor in the establishment, development and sustainable success of organizations.

2 People, organizations and the environment in which organizations operate are complex.

3 The responsibility for people management is distributed throughout organizations, and is not the responsibility of a single function.

4 Due to their responsibility and the complexity they face, leaders and managers require access to high-quality professional people advice and execution.

These four people principles will be examined so leaders have the context they need to design an efficient and effective *people operating model*.

People

People are unpredictable. Our behaviour is driven by many factors such as: our affective state; our emotional state; and our thinking, through cognitive processes. Sometimes we are conscious of the decisions we make, and sometimes not.

As we are complicated at an individual level, the complexity that arises when we interact in groups increases significantly. In this context, leaders need to understand who they are, and what they bring and don't bring to the workplace. This includes an understanding of their own personality, including potential performance derailers, their personal objectives limiting factors. This will help them better understand the needs of their followers, improve the environment of the workplace and build an outstanding workforce.

Leadership and management

Leaders are often characterized as having a long-term vision that managers turn into short- and medium-term goals. Leaders are seen as being inspirational and skilled at influencing, while managers' focus is more conventional and directive, working within, and through, formal authority structures. Leaders are seen as catalysts for transitional and transformational change that can sometimes be disruptive, while managers maintain business-as-usual and guide developmental change. Leaders may take risks, which need to be controlled by managers, who will create target operating models and systems to support efficient and effective task execution.

However, while there maybe differences, leaders and managers both have common people-related considerations and challenges. They both need to achieve organizational objectives through people. For instance, a chief finance officer (CFO) plays a leadership role in their function that delivers financial expertise to the organization and is a key team member of the executive committee. However, the finance function will include those in management positions who should also be providing leadership within their own teams.

The interface of people and technology means the characteristics of leadership noted above are expected to spread through organizations, with the traditional role of managers diminishing, to be replaced by a more leadership-orientated approach – leader-managers. Throughout this book the term *leader* will therefore be used to include all those who are responsible for achieving organizational goals through people, and ultimately for building an outstanding workforce.

Leaders are responsible for their personal actions in attaining their stated objectives, and are also responsible for influencing the behaviour of their followers. They need to understand how to organize and motivate themselves before they can successfully organize and motivate others. Clearly, as team sizes increase, the number of individuals a leader needs to influence, directly and indirectly, increases, and teams develop their own group dynamics. When there is an interface with other teams of which the leader has no direct responsibility, or authority, the picture becomes even more complex. Leaders of global organizations with multiple lines of business and functional divisions configured across many countries and regions also have time zone and cultural issues to consider. There are additional considerations when leading virtual teams.

People management and HR

Many books and articles have been published that seek to advise human resources (HR) professionals: how to organize their function and integrate it with the strategy formulation and operating model of the organization; which HR policies and processes will deliver superior operating metrics; about the content and interface of their roles; and about the competencies required to be successful. However, there is still significant evidence suggesting that some HR professionals are not always as business orientated, proactive and strategic as their organizations need them to be and to the extent that many in their profession would aspire to be. Also, that their leadership and management colleagues in other functions and line positions are not sufficiently aware of what great people advice should look like if they are to build an outstanding workforce. This book seeks to overcome both of these shortfalls.

Environment

A number of significant factors are bringing challenges to the business environment. The main ones are considered to be: technology; regulation; demographic trends; corporate and social responsibility; and the volatile, uncertain, complex and ambiguous (VUCA) world.

Technology

Emergent technology will disrupt business models and impact the future of work. There is much debate about how developments such as artificial intelligence, machine learning, robotic process automation and blockchain, distributed ledger technology, will be utilized in the private, public and third sectors, and how business models will be adapted and organizations redesigned. This thinking extends to predict roles that will be eradicated, roles that will be created, and when and how all this will happen.

In addition to the adoption of emerged and evolving technology, leaders need be aware of how to collect, store and use available data; how to convert information into knowledge that can inform decision-making through the use of data normalization, predictive data analytics and data visualization.

Regulation

Regulation can have a fundamental impact, driving business and operating-model design. One example is the financial services sector. In the aftermath of the global financial crisis, banks have been restricted from taking significant risk positions for their own account and, in the United Kingdom, retail banks of a certain size have had to ring-fence these businesses from their capital markets and investment banking operations. In the United Kingdom, the regulator has also increased the scrutiny around people, their roles and their responsibilities which leads to a significant number of compliance-related workstreams. In response to the same crises, in the United States, amongst other provisions within the Dodd-Frank Wall Street reform and consumer protection legislation, the Volcker rule severely restricted the ability of banks to trade on a proprietary basis, effectively separating the investment and commercial functions of banks.

Demographic trends

Global demographic trends are well documented and are often summarized as increasing the importance of the East, focused on Asia-Pacific, and the Southern hemisphere, focused on Africa.

Much has been written around the generational differences in expectations around the nature of work and careers between Baby Boomers, Generation X, Millennials/Generation Y and Generation Z. However, the results of research performed to date have so far proved less than conclusive.

It has also been noted that, as people stay healthy and active for longer, and some governments extend the retirement age, the average age and number of generations represented in the workforce will increase. Leaders need to reflect upon how they can attract, train and retain people across five generational cohorts where the meaning they derive from work may vary significantly.

Corporate and social responsibility

The external context has grown more complex with the need for leaders to consider the environmental and social impact of an organization's activities and their responsibility for working towards a diverse, inclusive and healthy workforce. Leaders need to consider how they turn statements of good intention into meaningful and impactful activity that all stakeholders, including their workforce, feel is authentic.

The VUCA world

Finally, leaders are faced with a volatile, uncertain, complex and ambiguous (VUCA) world, a term originally borrowed from the American military.[1] While change has always been a constant factor, the speed of change has never been faster and the amount of information available to consider in decision-making has never been so prevalent and provisional. Leaders must find a way of negotiating this cognitive load in order to create clarity and direction for their workforce and other stakeholders. Understanding cognitive readiness, which also owes its genesis to the American military, may help in this endeavour. *Cognitive readiness* refers to the preparedness that an individual should develop to successfully perform in a complex and unpredictable environment.[2]

Book structure

This book draws on a number of sources that include: the published thinking of strategy and management consultants who are supporting leaders as they struggle to adapt quickly and successfully to change; supranational and national think tanks that produce well-researched insight that is supported and guided by practitioners; papers produced by industry and professional bodies; peer reviewed journal articles that test historical constructs and contemporary discourse, giving pragmatic guidance to practitioners; and case studies of current practice by leading organizations. Debates about the future of leadership and people management can only be fully informed when bleeding edge thinking is tested, and the results of research considered in conjunction with the perceived reality of our own experience.

Our aim was to write a book of substance that carefully builds on the thinking of experienced business leaders, consultants and academics, and provides the reader with knowledge from various domains that complement and inform each other.

Each chapter ends with a summary of *highlights*, and also *leadership impact* and *people management recommendations*. The final chapter summarizes these so readers can reflect on the extent to which their organizations are addressing each area and develop suggestions for their people operating model

Since the start of the 20th century, theories and models around the leadership and management of organizations have been dominated by research undertaken in developed, largely Western, environments, especially the United States. Research is increasingly emerging from other cultures that is testing the efficacy of the Western literature and creating culturally relevant modifications where applicable. The new framework for people management suggested in this book is *people focused* and therefore has global application for people management. In addition, the case studies have been selected to represent a breadth of sectors and cultural settings.

This book is divided into five parts. Part One focuses on *people*. It includes an introduction to evolutionary psychology, neuroscience, personality psychology, bias and stereotypes, and how these support an understanding of individual motivation, decision-making, the nature of groups and culture. Part Two focuses on *the environment*. It includes an introduction to organizations, a discussion of emerged and evolving technology, demographic changes, social movements and the future of work. Part Three focuses on *workforce planning*. It includes an introduction to planning and risk, human capital metrics and financial reporting, people analytics, employee engagement, employee experience, employee value proposition, the employer brand

and well-being. Part Four focuses on *the future of people management*, which introduces a new framework for people management in organizations. Finally, Part Five examines how this new framework for people management will support leaders in *building an outstanding workforce*.

Part One: People

Chapter 1 examines the complex nature of people by drawing on neuroscience and evolutionary psychology. What are the inherited biological drivers behind the tendency for people to behave in certain ways? What is hard-coded at birth? What develops by learning through childhood and beyond, and how can people modify their beliefs, values, attitudes and, ultimately, their behaviour?

Chapter 2 continues this theme, looking at personality psychology, how personality and intelligence are considered and assessed, and the considerations for organizational behaviour and leadership.

Chapter 3 focuses on bias and stereotypes, and how this relates to group culture and its impact on decision-making.

Chapter 4 reviews the various theories surrounding motivation and how these inform concepts of employee engagement and satisfaction, employee experience and the employee value proposition.

Chapter 5 discusses the nature of leadership, including the traits espoused for leaders, leader–follower behavioural relationships, the contingent context in which leadership takes place, leadership and change, the leader-manager debate, organizational behaviour and leadership development.

Part Two: The environment

Chapter 6 introduces the nature of organizations, their reasons for existence, and the impact of external and internal variables on organizational success including strategy and structure.

Chapter 7 examines emerged and evolving technology. What is the predicted impact of, amongst others, artificial intelligence (AI), robotic process automation, blockchain, distributed ledger technology and data analytics? It then discusses the changing nature of work and the predicted change in employment relationships. This encompasses new ways of working such as an increase in contract versus permanent roles, flexible working such as job sharing and remote working, the use of agile and virtual teams, and the interface of people and technology. It also examines the extent to which choices to build, buy or rent people resources in the future will impact the development of the workforce.

Chapter 8 looks at demographics from a global and generational cohort perspective, and the attitudes of people in their approach to work and their careers. It discusses how organizations will react to the changing priorities and preferences of the workforce and plan for multiple generation workforce composition.

Chapter 9 examines the cultural challenges faced by organizations that have stakeholders in overseas locations. Organizations may have stakeholders located outside their domestic market because they have international offices, overseas clients or employees that work virtually from other countries.

Chapter 10 discusses changing organizational attitudes towards corporate and social responsibility (CSR), which takes into consideration the importance of the social and environmental impact of an organization's activities and their responsibility for working towards a diverse, inclusive and healthy workforce. It discusses how CSR in organizations should be embraced by leaders then communicated and managed.

Part Three: Workforce planning

Chapter 11 emphasizes the importance of people in the strategic planning process. Business plans approved in isolation of people data may at best be difficult to implement and at worse doomed to failure. People planning must be integrated into the strategic decision-making of an organization to ensure that the right people are in the right place at the right time and at the right cost. Predictive analytics can be used to scenario plan the future size, composition and location of the workforce.

Chapter 12 discusses the financial implications of investing in people – how the investment in people can be accounted for and reported, and what metrics can be used to quantify the various activities that contribute to the total people cost of organizations.

Chapter 13 investigates various aspects of people risk management. This includes reputational risk, operational risk, cyber risk, and opportunity costs. A talent portfolio management approach is examined that segments the workforce and allows each segment, and the portfolio as a whole, to be risk managed using key performance indicators and data analytics.

Chapter 14 addresses the importance of employee engagement, employee experience, employee value proposition and the employer brand. Attracting and retaining people are key elements in building and outstanding workforce.

Chapter 15 importantly examines wellness and well-being, workplace design, psychological safety, stress, resilience and meaning. Organizations are increasingly acknowledging and accepting their responsibilities for the mental in addition to physical health of the people who work for them.

Chapter 16 reviews the necessity and philosophy behind the future of people development in organizations. Lifelong learning is required and governments, industry bodies and organizations need to work together to support the inclusive development of required skills.

Part Four: The future of people management

Chapter 17 outlines the challenge of people management for chief executive officers (CEOs) and the need for expert advice in this field. Given the complexity of people and their importance to organizations, it is crucial that CEOs are supported by experienced people professionals who can provide leadership in this area. Various models have been developed to demonstrate how people management should be organized within organizations, and what competencies people professionals should possess, and these are critically examined.

Chapter 18 outlines a new approach to organizing professional people support in organizations. It puts people, not processes, at the centre of complex organizations that exist and compete for resources in a VUCA environment. It emphasizes that people management is the responsibility of those leading lines of business and functions but demonstrates the professional support they must have to be successful in this endeavour. It presents a new framework for people management, a new *people operating model*.

Part Five: Creating an outstanding workforce

The final part, Chapter 19, helps the reader compare the core messages and recommendations of the book to the reality of their own organizations, enabling them to develop suggestions for changes to, and investment in, their people operating model.

For leaders to build an outstanding workforce they need support from professional people managers who understand and predict how people are likely to behave and others who can design work environments that allow the augmentation of people and technology while supporting well-being. They need functional expertise that is specific to the people domain such as talent acquisition and development, and embedded people expertise in key functions such as finance, risk and compliance and marketing. They also need the delivery of this expertise to be efficiently and effectively facilitated. Finally, they themselves need to lead from an informed position with regard to people management.

A new people management framework is discussed to include people experts, people portfolio management, people specialists embedded in functions, people facilitators and people enablers. It is a clarion call for change and delivers a new people operating model for leaders to align and integrate the purpose of people and the organizations they work for, to build an outstanding workforce for individual and organizational success.

While the people operating model is of critical importance to the effective leadership of the workforce, more important is the fundamental understanding leaders have of people, the internal and external environment within which they work and then the extent to which they are able to align individual and organizational purpose and meaning.

The aim of this book is to equip readers with a sound foundation of knowledge around people and organizations that will support them as leaders, followers and colleagues; ultimately, helping them to find purpose and meaning in their lives in a work context, and to help others find it too.

Case studies

At the end of Parts One, Two and Three we present case studies from lead-ing organizations that demonstrate how the challenge of people manage-ment is being addressed. The case studies have been selected to represent organizations' headquartered in a variety of countries and therefore cultural traditions. They represent a number of sectors and illustrate practical steps that are being taken to address many of the challenges noted in this book and demonstrate how they are addressing particular challenges in building an outstanding workforce.

PART ONE
People

Evolutionary psychology and neuroscience

01

Introduction

To build a workforce that is outstanding means building one that will support individual and organizational success. However, before embarking on this journey it is important to understand something of our individual complexity. This opening chapter reflects on our shared evolutionary past, and the impact of genes, experience and learning on our emotions, thinking and behaviour. As with the other chapters, we draw upon a wide range of research to extract key points that support the practices of leadership and management.

To appreciate the complexity of people, we need to be familiar with:

- the brain and our innate instincts;
- the nature of emotions;
- the nature of the mind and thinking;
- cultural evolutionary psychology.

The aim has been to write explanations that are scientifically accurate, based on current knowledge, but introduced in a style that is accessible. A sound knowledge of the information in this chapter is fundamental to understanding everything that follows and to being an effective leader and manager.

Chapter summary

The following subjects are discussed in this chapter:

- **our history:**
  - Big Bang to the cognitive revolution;
  - turning points from the Industrial Revolution;
- **our brains:**
  - evolution;
  - structure;

- **emotions:**
  - evolution;
  - types of emotion;
  - constructed emotions;
  - emotions and behaviour;
- **thinking:**
  - evolution;
  - cultural evolution;
  - cognitive gadgets;
  - cognitive modules;
  - theory of mind;
  - the triune brain.

Our history

Big Bang to the cognitive revolution

In *Sapiens*, Yuval Noah Harari tracks the history of earth and its human inhabitants as follows:

- About 13.5 billion years ago, matter, energy, time and space came into being in what is known as the Big Bang. The story of these fundamental features of our universe is called physics.
- About 300,000 years after their appearance, matter and energy started to coalesce into complex structures, called atoms, which then combined into molecules. The story of atoms, molecules and their interactions is called chemistry.
- About 3.8 billion years ago, on a planet called Earth, certain molecules combined to form particularly large and intricate structures called organisms. The story of organisms is called biology.
- About 70,000 years ago, organisms belonging to the species *Homo sapiens* started to form even more elaborate structures called cultures. The subsequent development of these human cultures is called history.
- Three important revolutions shaped the course of history. The *cognitive revolution* kick-started history about 70,000 years ago. The *agricultural revolution* sped it up about 12,000 years ago. The *scientific revolution* got under way only 500 years ago.[1]

Harari states that:

> from the Cognitive Revolution onwards, historical narratives replace
> biological theories as our primary means of explaining the development
> of *Homo sapiens*. To understand the rise of Christianity or the French
> Revolution, it is not enough to comprehend the interaction of genes, hormones
> and organisms. It is necessary to take into account the interaction of ideas,
> images and fantasies as well.[2]

Having quickly covered 13.5 billion years of human history with the help of
Harari, we arrive at the mid-18th century and the Industrial Revolution.

Turning points from the Industrial Revolution

In *Humans Are Underrated*, Geoff Colvin notes that most people's essential
skills remained largely the same from the emergence of agriculture 12,000
years ago to the dawn of the Industrial Revolution in the mid-18th century.
Then came a series of turning points:[3]

- **First turning point – the advent of industrial technology:** In the 18th
  century, steam-driven industrial technology devalued the work of skilled
  artisans, who handcrafted their products from beginning to end. However,
  less-skilled workers were in demand to work the new machines.

- **Second turning point – ubiquitous electricity:** In the early 20th century,
  electricity became more widely available and enabled the building of far
  more sophisticated factories, requiring better educated, more highly
  skilled workers to operate the more complicated machines. Companies
  grew much larger, requiring a larger corps of educated managers. The
  trend intensified through most of the 20th century.

- **Third turning point – ubiquitous information technology:** Starting in the
  1980s, information technology had developed to a point where it could
  displace many medium-skilled jobs, while at both ends of the skill
  spectrum the number of jobs increased and pay went up. This technology
  was not good enough to displace the problem-solving, judging, and
  coordinating tasks of highly skilled workers like managers, lawyers,
  consultants and financiers; in fact, it made those workers more productive
  by giving them more information at lower cost. At the bottom end, low-
  skill service workers were protected as technology was not good enough
  to displace repetitive manual tasks.

Colvin points out that so far, at each turning point, high-skill and low-skill
workers had both prospered, but the *fourth turning point*, which heralds
emerged and emerging technology such as artificial intelligence, robotic process automation and distributed ledger technology is encroaching *on both
ends of the skill spectrum*. The impact of technology on the future of work
is examined in Chapter 7.

However, before discussing technology and other trends that will impact work and the workplace, it is helpful to understand our shared complexity, what makes us human and therefore what sort of working lives we can hope for in the future.

Our brains

Evolution

We have evolved over millions of years, but how much of our behaviour is due to biological evolution and how much to cultural evolution?

In *Beyond Evolutionary Psychology*, George Ellis and Mark Solms write that while a number of brain modules are hard-wired, these modules exclude the whole of the neocortex and that the 'existence of innate language modules and other innate cognitive modules is not biologically plausible.'[4] They propose that key aspects of human knowledge are innate; for instance, a developing child does not have sufficient input data to deduce the rules whereby language is constructed and therefore that knowledge must be innate, the brain has

> an initial structure that is genetically determined but rather loosely prescribed
> at a detailed level, their detailed nature then being precisely determined
> through developmental processes as a consequence of learning experiences and
> interaction with the environment.[5]

The hard-wired connections

> refer to neurons where genetically based developmental programmes
> produce a fairly tightly prescribed set of connections to other neurons in a
> specific domain; they will be affected to some extent by contextual variables,
> but nevertheless the outcome is connections with a very specific set of
> predetermined functions.[6]

These hard-wired parts of the brain are responsible for emotion rather than thinking: 'there are innate modules in the brain, but they do not perform cognitive functions; they perform affective ones. A growing body of research shows the guiding role of affect (emotions) on both behaviour and cognitive development.'[7] This research suggests that 'emotion must have played a key role in evolutionary development – it must both have been selected for by evolution and affected evolution.'[8]

Our soft-wired connections

> refer to neurons where genetically based developmental programmes produce
> an initially random set of connections to other neurons in a specific domain,
> which then get pruned and altered in strength in response to experience so
> as to produce specific connections that are essentially the product of learning
> processes, with broad functions that are an outcome of this process.[9]

Our brains have therefore evolved with innate, hard-wired areas, and other areas that are soft-wired and designed for development through learning.

So far, the terms *neocortex* and *neurons* have been used, and these are explained below, along with other aspects of brain biology.

Structure

Neurons are the most important type of brain cell, and, like other cells, have a cell body, a nucleus, branch-like structures on top called dendrites and a root-like structure on the bottom called an axon. The axons of one neuron are close to the dendrites of other neurons, forming *synapses*. Neurons fire electrical signals down their axons, releasing neurotransmitters into the synapses, where receptors on the other neuron's dendrites pick them up (see Figures 1.1 and 1.2). The following neurotransmitters are associated with feelings and behaviours. Some are *monoamines*, such as noradrenaline, dopamine and serotonin, regulating emotion, arousal and memory; and others are *hormones*, such as cortisol, oxytocin and melatonin, regulating physiology and behaviour:

- noradrenalin: preparation for action;
- adrenalin: preparation for action, including breathing;
- dopamine: reward-motivation behaviour;
- serotonin: moods and social behaviour;
- cortisol: regulates stress;
- oxytocin: trust and bonding;
- melatonin: regulates sleep;
- oestrogen: female behaviours;
- testosterone: male behaviours.

In *Neuroscience for Leadership*, Swart et al note that neurotransmitters either calm or stimulate action and can affect mood, sleep, concentration, weight, and when not in balance can cause adverse symptoms. They also explain that survival emotions such as fear, anger, disgust, shame and sadness involve the release of cortisol; and attachment emotions are mediated by the effects of oxytocin, dopamine and noradrenalin. One emotion, surprise, can move response states from attachment to survival or survival to attachment. Noradrenalin intensifies the effects of many other neurochemicals and probably underlies surprise.[10]

Ellis and Solms draw a distinction between parts of the brain that serve *affective* functions and those that serve *cognitive* functions. Cognitive functions analyse, recognize patterns, make predictions and present alternative choices for selection. Affective functions assign values to events, outcomes, and memories, and guide the cognitive functions in terms of attention and reaction. Some functions are neither cognitive nor affective, for instance those responsible for physiological regulation.[11]

Figure 1.1 Neurons

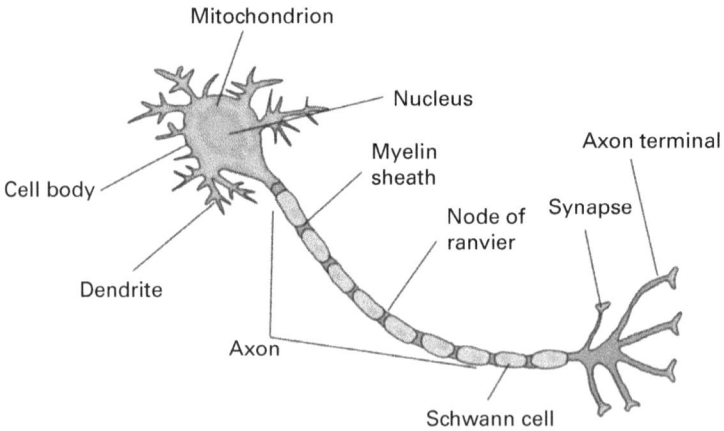

Mitochondrion

Nucleus

Axon terminal

Myelin sheath

Cell body

Node of ranvier

Synapse

Dendrite

Axon

Schwann cell

Figure 1.2 Synapsis

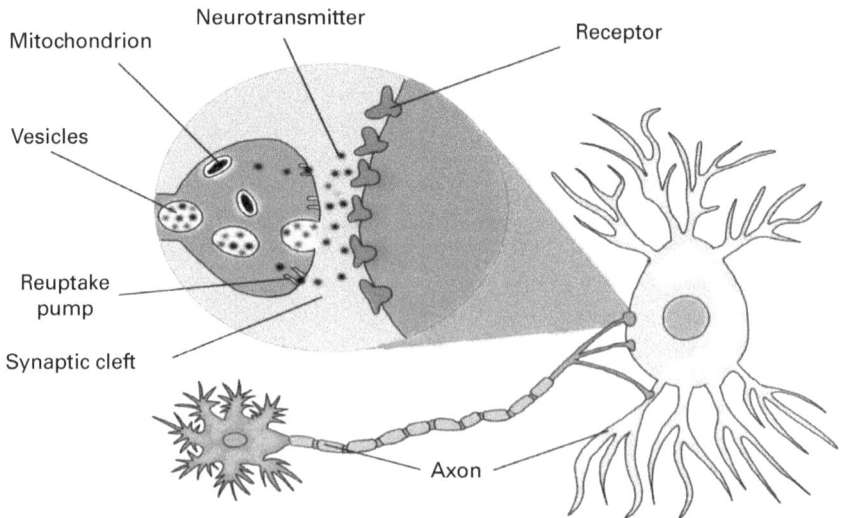

Neurotransmitter

Mitochondrion

Receptor

Vesicles

Reuptake pump

Synaptic cleft

Axon

Another way of looking at the brain's major functions is suggested by Ellis and Solms, who describe its *inner* and *outer* worlds. The inner world is the self-regulating, autonomic, body and the outer world is regulated by neurological body-monitoring nuclei, need detectors, which represent the demand for work that they body makes upon the brain by measuring functional states. Internal bodily needs are known as *drive demands*. The outer world is the environment around us, which is complex, unpredictable and is monitored by our sensory receptors, modalities of external perception: vision, hearing and somatic sensation – touch, taste and smell.[12]

Figure 1.3   The brain

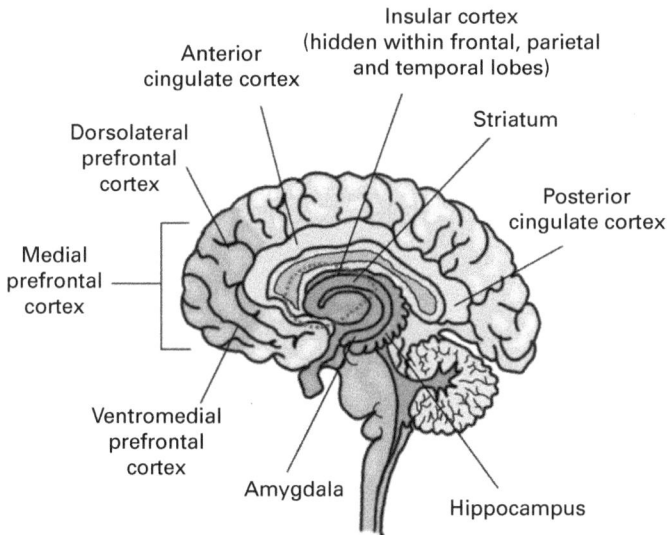

With regard to emotion and cognitive processing, the brain has been classi-fied as the reptilian brain, the limbic system, and the neocortex, which are, very broadly speaking, respectively responsible for reflex behaviour, emo-tional behaviour and symbolic behaviour.[13] A view of the major parts of the brain can be seen in Figures 1.3 and 1.4.

Descriptions that locate emotional and cognitive activity in the brain use the following terms:

- **frontal:** at the front;
- **medial:** in the middle;
- **lateral:** at the side;
- **dorsal:** back (upper), posterior;
- **ventral:** front (lower), anterior.

A classic view of the brain would be to start with the so-called reptilian brain which is located at the top of the spinal column, is attached to the central nervous system, and houses the cerebellum. It is responsible for re-flexes through motor control, unconsciously regulates our autonomic, invol-untary, physiological responses, and may be involved in some cognitive functions such as attention and language. It makes this information availa-ble to the rest of the brain.

The limbic system, which contains the amygdala, hippocampus, hypo-thalamus and the thalamus sits above the cerebellum. It is responsible for aspects of motivation, emotion, learning and memory. The amygdala is the centre for emotional responses, such as fear, anger and disgust. It is here that

Figure 1.4   The behavioural brain

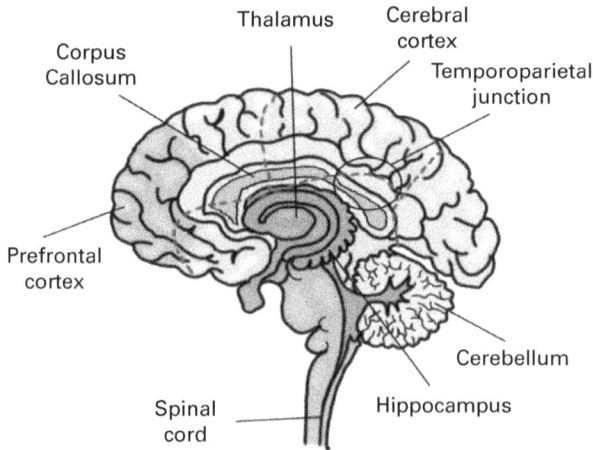

decisions to freeze, fight or flight are made in reaction to perceived threats. Humans share these with other animals. Feelings related to moral perceptions such as guilt and shame originate from the neocortex.

The limbic system also functions to capture artefacts of our experiences so that through learning we can benefit from these response memories in the future. Memories such as people and places are stored in the neocortex.

The neocortex is the most recent adaptation to the human brain. It undertakes higher-order brain functions such as sleep, memory, sensory perception, cognition, spatial reasoning and language. It is also involved in the planning, control and execution of our voluntary, somatic, movements through motor control.

The front of the neocortex contains three lobes at the back, the occipital, parietal and temporal lobes, and one at the front, the frontal lobe, also known as the prefrontal lobe, and is covered by the prefrontal cortex.

The frontal lobe, otherwise known as the executive function, receives information from other parts of the brain, analyses it against data from previous experience and makes response decisions. The back of the neocortex contains the rear lobes that receive internal data on body functioning and data from the environment through our five senses.

The neocortex, cerebral cortex lobes, divides into two hemispheres, one on the left and the other on the right, which are connected at the base by the corpus callosom. The right hemisphere is slightly bigger, controls the muscles on the left side of the body and is often more responsible for linear reasoning. The left hemisphere controls the muscles on the right side of the body and is often more responsible for reasoning functions in language. Scientific evidence suggests that low-level perceptual functions may be undertaken more in the left hemisphere, but most functions are distributed across both.

Cortical regions include the cerebral cortex, which contains the occipital, parietal, temporal and frontal lobes. Sub-cortical regions include the thalamus, basal ganglia, brainstem and cerebellum. The cerebral cortex is the outer layer of neural tissue of the cerebrum. The cerebrum contains the hippocampus and basal ganglia and is the uppermost region of the central nervous system.

Human brains are not fully formed at birth. They develop for a significant period, and much typical teenage behaviour can be attributed to the fact that the brain matures from back to front.[14] The cerebellum regulates coordination, the occipital lobe houses the visual cortex, the parietal lobe regulates movement and sensation through motor and sensory cortices. The temporal lobe includes areas that regulate emotions and sexuality, while the frontal lobe is concerned with executive functions such as judgement, insight and impulse control.

Soft-wired connections are said to exist where brain plasticity is required in order that flexibility and learning is possible; this is the case in all intrinsic cortical areas associated with cognition: the cerebral hemispheres and lobes, the cerebellum and some aspects of the limbic system – certainly the hippocampus and amygdala.[15]

Neuroplasticity is important to understand in the context of learning and in *Neuroscience for Leadership* it is noted that neuroplasticity occurs through three main mechanisms:

- **myelination:** the wrapping of a white coating around neurons to speed up transmission along them;
- **synaptic connection:** making more and/or new connections between existing neurons, and allowing the map in the brain for that particular skill to grow;
- **neurogenesis:** growing new neurons from embryonic nerve cells, which is most likely linked to developing a skill and therefore is probably the hardest to achieve.[16]

So far, we have seen how the brain has evolved, how it is structured and the difference between our hard-wired, innate and soft-wired brains. It is now time to examine our emotions and thought processes.

Emotions

Evolution

Our emotions impact our behaviour but how do they do this? Where do they come from? And can we really control them? These questions and more are considered below.

In *Emotional Intelligence*, Daniel Goleman introduces the emotional mind, which he locates in the neocortex, which developed about 100 million years ago, and describes its role in 'the subtlety and complexity of emotional life such as the ability to have feelings *about* our feelings'.[17]

In *Beyond Evolutionary Psychology*, Ellis and Solms describe the innate primary emotion command systems found in all mammals, including humans, based in the ascending activation and limbic circuits of the mammalian brain, which release neurotransmitters in the cortex. The authors suggest that these affective systems are the 'innate modules that shape both cognitive development and behaviour and are the lynchpin between evolution and psychological development.'[18] These innate modules shape the brain through developmental plasticity as the individual interacts with their physical, social and ecological environment, and thereby lead to effective modules for language and other cognitive functions.[19]

Ellis and Solms differentiate between homeostatic affects that arise from internal bodily needs and drives, and emotional affects that arise from environmental situations. They state that instincts are hard-wired, fixed patterns of behaviour in response to certain stimuli, which are designed to increase the chances of survival and reproductive success. However, both homeostatic affects and emotional affects are innate, not learned. Social emotions, such as shame and guilt, are examples of learned affects and learned responses can, over time, become more automatic. Emotions are feelings associated with instinct and intuition.[20]

In *Neuroscience For Leadership*, Swart et al distinguish between instinct, which could be misleading, and intuition, probably based on valuable experience and reflection.[21] Ellis and Solms note that 'intuition is our automatized distillation of our previous experience, packaged for fast analysis and response. It is not inherited, for how could the intuition of a fighter pilot, a brain surgeon, or a basketball player be genetically determined?'[22] Instincts play a critical role in autonomic functions, motivated behaviour and responses to threatening stimuli.

In *Minds Make Societies*, Daniel Boyer writes that:

> Intuitive representations just pop up, so to speak, as a largely automatic and fast result of being presented with the relevant stimuli. Reflective information, on the other hand, is information that has the effect of extending, making sense of, explaining, justifying, or communicating the contents of intuitive information.[23]

However, 'reflective representations can persist despite providing no explanations, poor explanations, or even incoherent explanations that conflict with our intuitions'.[24] People's minds take surface information and construct models that go beyond the information given and received.

In *Making up the Mind*, Frith states that our perception of the world is a fantasy that happens to coincide with reality,[25] that the brain reacts to sensory inputs, assigns meaning to perceptions through emotions and, in the absence of complete sensory inputs, the brain uses past experience to predict an appropriate response.

Our primary emotion command systems are hard-wired systems from our evolutionary past that provide rapid guidance as to how to act in situations of biological significance. Our feelings motivate us to act in accordance with our instincts, to survive and reproduce; we are compelled to act in ways that make us feel good, and to avoid things that make us feel bad. This is the most basic motivation principle.

Types of emotion

Various lists of primary emotions have been proposed, with seven of the basic mammalian instincts discussed by Jaak Panskepp, who capitalized each word in his list to differentiate from its common usage:

- SEEKING: desire and anticipation, also known as the wanting and reward system. Cold aggression to neutralize a threat is associated with activation of the SEEKING system.
- RAGE: Hot aggression to neutralize a threat is associated with RAGE.
- FEAR: Freeze, fight or flight.
- PANIC/GRIEF: Separation panic, distress, despair and sadness.
- PLAY: Hierarchical, rule-based, social, regulates other instincts.
- MATING: Reproduction.
- CARE: Nurture, more active in females than males.[26]

These primary emotions are still conserved in the human brain today after 200 million years and are associated with the periaqueductal gray, which is located in the cerebral aqueduct within the tegmentum of the mid-brain. The mid-brain, pons and medulla are all parts of the brainstem.

Disgust has been suggested as an additional system,[27] as an anticipatory function to protect us from harm. Panskepp acknowledges disgust but assigns it a sensory rather than emotional classification.[28]

In *Emotional Intelligence*, Daniel Goleman describes emotion as 'a feeling and its distinctive thoughts, psychological and biological states, and range of propensities to act'[29] and defines emotions as follows:

- **anger:** fury, outrage, resentment, wrath, exasperation, indignation, vexation, acrimony, animosity, annoyance, irritability, hostility, and, perhaps, at the extreme, pathological hatred and violence;
- **sadness:** grief, sorrow, cheerlessness, gloom, melancholy, self-pity, loneliness, dejection, despair, and, when pathological, severe depression;
- **fear:** anxiety, apprehension, nervousness, concern, consternation, misgiving, wariness, qualm, edginess, dread, fright, terror; as a psychopathology, phobia and panic;
- **enjoyment:** happiness, joy, relief, contentment, bliss, delight, amusement, pride, sensual pleasure, thrill, rapture, gratification, satisfaction, euphoria, whimsy, ecstasy and, at the far edge, mania;
- **love:** acceptance, friendliness, trust, kindness, affinity, devotion, adoration, infatuation, agape;

- **surprise:** shock, astonishment, amazement, wonder;
- **disgust:** contempt, disdain, scorn, abhorrence, aversion, distaste, revulsion;
- **shame:** guilt, embarrassment, chagrin, remorse, humiliation, regret, mortification, and contrition.[30]

He follows Paul Eckman[31] and others in thinking of emotions in terms of families, or dimensions, with each of these families having a basic emotional nucleus at its core, followed by moods that are muted and longer-lived, such as irritability compared to anger. Moods are partially controlled by temperaments, which is the readiness to evoke a given emotion or mood. Therefore, neuroticism (temperament) is linked to irritability (mood) and anger (emotion).[32]

It is important not to conflate emotion with affect. In *How Emotions are Made*, Lisa Feldman Barrett notes that

> affect is the general sense of feeling that you experience throughout each day. It is not emotion but a much simpler feeling with two features. The first is how pleasant or unpleasant you feel, which scientists call valence. The second feature of affect is how calm or agitated you feel, which is called arousal.[33]

To summarize the story of emotions so far, they are largely associated with the limbic system, are innate and are involved with internal physiological maintenance and our fast, instinctive reactions to our perceptions concerning the external environment. Intuition is our fast, learned response to perceptions concerning the external environment. Emotions have been categorized and associated with each category are moods, which are more muted and last longer, and temperaments, which reflect our propensity for particular moods and therefore emotions.

Constructed emotions

In *How Emotions are Made*, Lisa Feldman Barrett states, 'Emotions are not reactions to the world; they are your constructions of the world',[34] and that in classical views of emotion particular areas of the brain are dedicated to particular functions. However, research has shown that many parts of the brain serve more than one purpose. For instance, fear is created by combinations of neurons, not all of which are situated in the amygdala. This is the principle of degeneracy, meaning many-to-one. She notes that nearly 100 published studies involving nearly 1,300 test subjects across almost 20 years failed to find a brain region containing the fingerprint for any single emotion:

> large meta analyses conclude that a single emotion category involves different bodily responses, not a single, consistent response. Brain circuitry operates by the many-to-one principle of degeneracy: instances of a single emotion category such as fear, are handled by different brain patterns at different times and in different people. Conversely, the same neurons can participate in creating different mental states (one-to-many).[35]

The *classical view* states that certain emotions are inborn and universal, so everyone displays and recognizes them, while the *constructionist view* proposes that emotions are not inborn, and if they are universal it is due to shared concepts. Feldman Barrett takes a constructionist view of emotions, where individual emotional categories, such as anger, do not have a fingerprint in a particular area of the brain, and emotional experiences are not an inevitable consequence of our genes. 'Your brain invisibly constructs everything you experience, including emotions.'[36]

Feldman Barrett summarizes the elements of the constructionist view of emotion as incorporating

> all three flavours of construction. From social construction, it acknowledges the importance of culture and concepts. From psychological construction, it considers emotions to be considered by core systems in the brain and body. And from neuroconstruction, it adopts the idea that experience wires the brain.[37]

Social construction is explored later in this chapter.

Intrinsic brain activity is said to include 'dreams, daydreams, imagination, mind wandering and reveries, which we collectively called simulation. It also ultimately produces every sensation you experience, including your interoceptive sensations'.[38] The 'interoceptive network issues predictions about your body, tests the resulting simulations against sensory input from your body, and updates your brain's model of your body in the world.'[39] Affective feelings, such as pleasure and agitation, are said to be summaries of the body's physiological state, what Feldman Barrett calls our *body budget*. Interoception helps form emotion but cannot itself explain emotion; for instance, fear is more complex than a feeling of concern.

Categorization helps us construct our mental maps and this includes instances of emotion. Categories are traditionally used to group objects, events and actions that occur in the world while concepts are ideas conceived in the mind relating to categories. Goals create and maintain categories, and emotional concepts are goal-based. For instance, the emotion of enjoyment is centred on a goal and is related to how outcomes have made you feel in the past. Some concepts are learned with words, and some without. The constant predictive functioning of the brain creates simulations based on stored patterns from previous experience; 'the simulation that's closest to your actual situation is the winner that becomes your experience, and if it's an instance of an emotion concept, then you experience emotion.'[40]

Lisa Feldman-Barrett concludes that:

> The theory of constructed emotion is a biologically formed, psychological explanation of who you are as a human being. It takes into account both evolution and culture. You are born with the same brain wiring as determined by your genes, but the environment can turn genes on and off, allowing your brain to wire itself to your experiences. Your brain is shaped by the realities of the world that you find yourself in, including the social world made by

agreement among people. Your mind is a grand collaboration that you have no awareness of. Through construction, you perceive the world not in any objectively accurate sense but through the lens of your own needs, goals and prior experience.[41]

This constructionist view is aligned with thinking in evolutionary causal essentialism and social constructionism, which are discussed later in this chapter.

So far, so good. But how do we use this knowledge in building an outstanding workforce?

Emotions and behaviour

Our basic human needs include survival, involving in particular the continual search for energy, and the need for reproduction with inheritance. Our emotions impact our behaviour and so it is useful to understand that we can exert some control in this area through emotional regulation.

It can be said that interpersonal intelligence 'is the ability to understand what motivates other people, how they work, how to work cooperatively with them', while intrapersonal intelligence is the 'capacity to form an accurate, veridical model of oneself and to be able to use that model to operate effectively in life.'[42] For Howard Gardner, the core of interpersonal intelligence includes the 'capacities to discern and respond appropriately to the moods, temperaments, motivations, and desires of other people', and for intrapersonal intelligence the key to self-knowledge includes 'access to one's own feelings and the ability to discriminate among them and draw upon them to guide behaviour.'[43]

In *Emotional Intelligence*, Goleman references the work of Peter Salovey[44] who, he says, subsumes Gardner's personal intelligences in his basic definition of emotional intelligence, and expands it into the following five main domains:

- **Knowing one's emotions:** Self-awareness, recognizing a feeling as it happens, is the keystone of emotional intelligence. The ability to monitor feelings from moment to moment is crucial to psychological insight and self-understanding. An inability to notice our true feelings leaves us at their mercy. People with greater certainty about their feelings are better pilots of their lives, having a surer sense of how they really feel about personal decisions.

- **Managing emotions:** Handling feelings so they are appropriate, for instance not ruminating and perpetuating anxiety, is an ability that builds on self-awareness. People who are poor in this ability are constantly battling feelings of distress.

- **Motivating oneself:** Marshalling emotions in the service of a goal is essential for paying attention, for self-motivation and mastery, and for creativity. Emotional self-control, delaying gratification and stifling impulsiveness, being able to achieve a 'flow' state, enables outstanding performance of all kinds. People who have this skill tend to be more highly productive and effective in whatever they undertake.

- **Recognizing emotions in others:** Empathy, another ability that builds on emotional self-awareness, is the fundamental 'people skill'. People who are empathic are more attuned to the subtle social signals that indicate what others need or want. This is known as prosocial behaviour.

- **Handling relationships:** The art of relationships is, in large part, skill in managing emotions in others and drives success in all areas of life, including leadership.[45]

Goleman writes that, although the bases for our abilities in these domains are neural, because of neuroplasticity 'lapses in emotional skills can be remedied: to a great extent each of these domains represents a body of habit and response that, with the right effort, can be improved upon.'[46] Our emotions impact our behaviour, and therefore changing behaviour may be possible through *emotional regulation*, which can occur through controlling attention to the stimuli and cognitively changing the meaning of the stimuli.[47]

The amygdala is associated with attitudes, stereotyping, person perception and emotional reactions. The anterior cingulate cortex and the prefrontal cortex are also implicated in emotions. The anterior cingulate cortex sits below the cerebral cortex.

Research has found that *affect-labelling* – putting feelings into words – reduces the response of the amygdala,[48] and that 'opportunities to voice personal feeling and frustrations could lead to a form of "psychological release".'[49] Thus 'cognitive reappraisal is an emotional strategy that involves changing the way one thinks about a stimulus in order to change its affective impact',[50] and involves the use of cognitive control to modify semantic representations of an emotional stimulus.

In *Focus: The hidden driver of excellence*, Daniel Goleman draws a distinction between cognitive and emotional empathy, with cognitive empathy giving us the ability to understand another person's way of seeing and thinking, while emotional empathy operates when we are sensing what other people feel and care about. He notes that the anterior cingulate cortex, part of our attention network, tunes us to someone else's distress through accessing our amygdala, which resonates with that distress. In this sense, we actually 'feel in our physiology'[51] the emotional state of the other person and our response to their well-being.

It has been suggested that, from an epistemological, knowledge, perspective, 'empathy provides information about the future actions of other people, and important environmental properties', while from a social perspective, 'empathy serves as the origin of the motivation for cooperative and prosocial behaviour, as well as help for effective social communication.'[52]

Emotional arousal has a powerful influence over cognitive processing, and attention, perception, memory, decision-making,[53] and therefore it is useful to understand the neural basis of emotions and emotional regulation. For instance, it is explained that when people are calm, the frontal lobes guide slow and rational thinking – cold cognitions. However, when people are angry or stressed, fast, gut-thinking occurs – hot cognitions.[54]

Having examined our instincts and emotions, we now turn to examine how we think – our cognitive processes.

Thinking

Evolution

Historically, some people, such as the philosopher Descartes, believed in dualism, where mind and matter are fundamentally different, that the mind is a non-physical, non-spatial, seat of intelligence, consciousness and self-awareness that is separate from the body.[55] Modern thinking views the mind as reducible to neuronal activity, and for some the mind purely focuses on cognitive processing and therefore not emotions; however, this is debated. Hofstede calls our patterns of thinking, feeling and acting mental programs, software of the mind, developed through cultural, learning.[56] In *Mindware*, Andy Clarke discusses mindware as software of the brain 'mindware – our thoughts, feelings, hopes, fears, beliefs – is cast as nothing but the operation of the biological brain, the meat machine in our head'.[57]

The mind is therefore differentiated from our biological brain and represents our cognitive faculties, such as language, thinking, consciousness, perception, imagination, judgement and memory. The mapping of brain activity through neuroimaging, such as functional magnetic resonance imaging (fMRI), seeks to link brain activity with behaviour. The results of this endeavour, which allocates responsibility for ability and emotions to certain areas, have been criticized due to: low resolution, a relatively high number of neurons mapped into voxels which are a value on a regular grid in a three dimensional space; and that it is still imprecise, as many functions involve more than one part of the brain. However, while the conclusions of studies may be seen as provisional, we are starting to build a new awareness of what underlies our behaviour.

In *Minds Make Societies*, Pascal Boyer notes that evolutionary psychology tries to determine the connection between evolution and our mental systems because 'the best way to understand cognitive architecture, the different components of the mind and their relations, is to see how the components match specific problems we humans encountered in our evolutionary past.'[58]

In *Focus: The hidden driver of excellence*, Goleman discusses the top part of our brain, the neocortex, and the older parts of our brain and its subcortical circuitry. Cognitive science sees the neocortex monitoring and imposing its goals, top-down, on the subcortical circuitry. He notes the two directions of activity as follows:

The bottom-up mind is:

- faster in brain time, which operates in milliseconds;
- involuntary and automatic: always on;
- intuitive, operating through networks of association;
- impulsive, driven by emotions;
- executor of our habitual routines and guide for our actions;
- manage for our mental models of the world.

By contrast, the top-down mind is:

- slower;
- voluntary;
- effortful;
- the seat of self-control, which can, sometimes, overpower automatic routines and mute emotionally driven impulses;
- able to learn new models, make new plans, and take change of our automatic repertoire – to an extent.[59]

Goleman suggests that the older bottom-up system worked well for basic survival during most of human prehistory, as it favours short-term thinking, impulse and speedy decisions. However, it can lead to problems today as the top-down system needs time to analyse and deliberate and our initial gut reaction may not be a helpful one.

Beyond Evolutionary Psychology explains that cognition derives from representations of the world around us, which are derived from perception, and that representations are learnt. Although our experience suggests otherwise, the world is always filtered through previous experience. Information on the world is directed to the cortex and sub-cortical regions and the representations are selectively retained through consolidation, which also updates previous selections through transfers between short- and long-term memory systems.[60] In other words, our senses deliver information, which creates perceptions that are compared with selectively stored past experience, and the result is representations that drive our thoughts.

Cultural evolution

With regard to human nature, in *Cognitive Gadgets*, Cecelia Heyes describes the nomological view, that human nature is the 'set of properties that humans tend to possess as a result of the evolution of their species'.[61] It combines the universality proposal, that traits belonging to human nature must be typical of human beings, and the evolution proposal, that they must be products of genetic evolution. In contrast, the causal essentialist view says that 'human nature is a suite of mechanisms that underlie the manifestation of *species-typical* cognitive and behavioural regularities'.[62]

A hybrid of the resulting views, evolutionary causal essentialism, offers human nature as the suite of mechanisms suggested by the causal essentialist view but adds that humans tend to possess them as a result of the evolution of their species. This approach understands evolution to encompass all selection-based evolutionary processes, genetic, epigenetic, such as nurture, and cultural.

The historical approach to cultural evolution simply refers to any changes in time in the characteristics of a population. The populational approach takes into account time, but also suggests that cultural change is made possible by genetically inherited psychological mechanisms interacting with genetic evolution. The selectionist approach does not claim a close relationship between genetic and cultural evolution; rather, it suggests variation and selective retention and adopts the populational assumption that large-scale cultural change is the cumulative product of social learning. It includes the distinctive approach of memes, which refer to variations in culture such as ideas and beliefs that survive in their own right, not requiring reproduction by those who carry them, however, this view has not been widely developed.[63]

Changes in human behaviour over time are explained by cultural evolutionary theory, while cultural evolutionary psychology extends the analysis to the internal cognitive processes, and in *Cognitive Gadgets* Heyes states that cultural evolutionary psychology makes a

> radical departure from both evolutionary psychology and cultural evolutionary theory in proposing that distinctively human cognitive mechanisms – ways of thinking – have been built by cultural evolution. They are cognitive gadgets rather than cognitive instincts; pieces of mental technology that are not merely tuned but assembled in the course of childhood through social interaction.[64]

Heyes argues that some of the components and engines of construction are genetically inherited but we are taught thinking skills. For instance, we are taught to read, and reading has been made possible by cultural evolution. A written language emerged only five to six thousand years ago, too recently in human history for the genetic evolution of cognitive mechanisms dedicated to reading.[65]

Heyes states that the information, *culture*, that we inherit from others through social interaction, via certain kinds of social learning, ranks alongside *nature*, genetically inherited information, and *nurture*, information derived from direct interaction between the developing system and its environment, as a determinant of human development. She explains that genetic contributions to development are commonly said to be provided by nature, for example learning a language is possible if we are born hard-wired with the capability to learn a language; nurture can be illustrated by cognitive development that varies with features of the environment in which development is actually occurring; while culture can be illustrated when cognitive development varies with longer-term features of the environment, features that may not be present when a particular individual is developing and that can be acquired only via certain kinds of social learning, known as cultural learning.

She describes three possible routes of cultural inheritance:

- **vertical inheritance:** from biological parents to their offspring;
- **oblique inheritance:** from individuals of one biological generation to genetically unrelated or distantly related individuals of the next biological generation;
- **horizontal inheritance:** between individuals of the same biological generation.[66]

In *Minds Make Societies*, Boyer also believes there are many different tracks of cultural transmission. The above view can be contrasted with meme-based models of cultural transmission, which provide that one general mechanism accounts for the occurrence of similar representations in different minds. For instance, 'the existence of technology raises the question of how humans managed to create ever more complex, and ever-improving, behaviours with an unchanged brain.'[67] The reasons given include: the division of labour, communication through trade with surrounding groups with different traditions, and increasing literacy to aid the spread of technical knowledge. Therefore, 'having cumulative technology and then an accelerating technical progress does not require a special brain or a new brain but is does require new conditions in which evolved minds can interact.'[68]

Narrative theories of human development link major changes in brain structure and behaviour with climactic or demographic events during human evolution that may have been a catalyst for these changes. Evolutionary psychologists may take a cognitive instincts view that genetic evolution is the architect of the human mind and therefore that distinctively human ways of thinking are due to our genetic heritage. However, while the cognitive gadgets view is consistent with what is known about the chronology of human evolution, it is a force theory that 'is primarily concerned with the processes that have shaped the human mind and regards learning – especially social learning – and cultural evolution as dominant among these processes.'[69] It is therefore consistent with aspects of cultural evolutionary theory that suggests that 'a change in the distribution of characteristics within a population over time... can be powered not only by genetic inheritance but by cultural inheritance.'[70]

Cognitive gadgets

In *Cognitive Gadgets*, Heyes introduces mechanisms of thought

> embodied in our nervous systems, that enable our minds to go further, faster, and in different directions than the minds of any other animals. These distinctively human cognitive mechanisms include causal understanding, episodic memory, imitation, mindreading, normative thinking and many more.[71]

They are gadgets, not instincts, because they are the product of cultural and not genetic evolution. She notes that cognitive development that leads to new ways of thinking is passed from generation to generation not through our genes but through *social interaction*:

> Genetic evolution has given humans more powerful general purpose mechanisms of learning and memory, tweaked our temperaments, and biased our attention so that it is focused on other people from birth. But... it is the information we get from others, handled by general purpose mechanisms, that builds distinctively human ways of thinking.[72]

Cultural learning enables cultural inheritance, and is the cultural analogue of DNA replication.

A key difference between cultural evolutionary theory and the cognitive gadget theory concerns their differing treatment of traits. Characteristics, or traits can increase or decrease in frequency due to the extent to which genes are inherited, but also as they become more or less likely to be passed on to cultural descendants through social interaction by those who may or may not be genetically related to their cultural parents. Heyes explains the difference, in terms of cultural evolutionary theory, as focusing on the grist of the mind, what we do and make, while cognitive gadget theory focuses on the mills of the mind: cognitive gadget theory

> seeks to explain change over time in the frequency of people in a population who are capable of calculating a shortcut across unexplored territory (mental mapping), who can entertain a theory about how an instrument works (causal understanding), or who have cognitive equipment allowing them to copy facial expressions (imitation). The cognitive gadgets answer is concerned not with the grist of the mind – what we do and what we make – but with the mills, the way the mind works.[73]

To summarize, nature, through inherited genes, provides us with general-purpose starter kits for learning and memory, cognitive instincts. However, our ways of thinking are built through the course of childhood into adulthood through social, and therefore cultural, interaction.

Cognitive modules

Beyond Evolutionary Psychology states that 'affect shapes intellect through developmental processes, responding to social experiences',[74] and that there are no genetically fixed cognitive modules; 'neocortical areas are broad-purpose domains that get specialised and formed through social, physical, and ecological interactions and experiences, but are not innate in terms of cognitive content',[75] and 'after being set up as general-purpose cognitive domains, such detailed neocortical connections arise developmentally during interaction with the environment, rather than directly from genetic information; and they then continue to change throughout life, as a result of brain plasticity.'[76]

In terms of development,

> as well as being unique to us, our representations of objects and people are
> constantly being modified by experience… we aren't born with a neural
> representation of the world we live in. It takes time for our brains to develop
> the foundational neural tissue that will eventually become the scaffolding of the
> self.[77]

Evolution is said to develop the genes that create the structures that enable
the functions which are key to our survival and reproductive success, and
both our soft-wired and hard-wired central nervous system are important in
different ways. It is explained that there are no innate, genetically fixed cognitive modules; we do not inherit a mind, but the ability to develop one:

> the fertilised egg contains neither a 'language acquisition device' nor a
> knowledge of the basic tenets of folk psychology. These features come
> into existence as the mind grows. A serious examination of the biological
> processes underlying such easy terms of 'innateness', 'maturation' and 'normal
> development' reintroduces the very themes that are usually taken to be
> excluded by an evolutionary approach to the mind – the critical role of culture
> in psychological development and the existence of a plethora of alternative
> outcomes for the developing mind.[78]

This niche construction occurs when environmental conditions are significantly modified, where the modification influences selective pressures and
there is an evolutionary response caused by the modification. In *Beyond
Evolutionary Psychology*, Ellis and Solms, state that

> niche construction takes place when society creates social and physical
> structures which are extensions of the mind – indeed, the mind does not only
> organize the brain; it uses external material objects to extend its cognitive
> powers, and they become part of its daily functioning. Thus, our minds
> create contexts which then shape the development, and in the longer term the
> evolution, of our brains.[79]

To summarize, we do not inherit fixed cognitive modules. Innate modules
exist but do not perform cognitive functions. Instead, our inherited genes
deliver general purpose cognitive domains.

Theory of mind

It is suggested that that relationships between the brain, behaviour and the
world cannot be understood satisfactorily, or have predictive power, without describing those relationships at an abstract, mental level. Also, that
some of the most effective abstractions come not from folk psychology, explaining behaviour with reference to thoughts, feelings, beliefs and desires,
but from cognitive science, which explains behavioural drivers in terms of
activities of the mind.[80]

Neuroscience for Leadership notes that the *theory of mind* refers to 'our ability to distinguish between our self and others, understand that other people's behaviours are driven by their goals and beliefs, not ours, and that our knowledge and perspective is different to everyone else's'.[81] In *Minds Make Societies*, Boyer reminds us that all human beings have an intuitive psychology, theory of mind, that make sense of the intentions, beliefs and predicted behaviours of others.[82]

The difference between cognitive and emotional empathy is discussed in *The Neuroscience of Organizational Behavior*, where Beugré writes that 'cognitive empathy involves knowing people's feelings through deliberate thought whereas affect empathy involves automatic sharing in the emotional experiences of others'.[83] While empathy has been defined as the 'capacity to understand and respond to the unique affective experiences of another person'[84] it is said to have three primary components: an affective response to another person, which often, but not always, entails sharing that person's emotional state; a cognitive capacity to take the perspective of the other person; and emotion regulation.

Neuroscience for Leadership develops an article published in the *Harvard Business Review*, 'Your brain at work', which focuses on four of 15 brain networks that are particularly interesting from a leadership perspective:

- **Default network:** Engages in introspection and in imagining a different time, place or reality. Important for innovation.

- **Reward network:** Activates in response to pleasure. Important for motivation and is impacted by levels of oxytocin and dopamine.

- **Affect network:** Plays a central role in emotions. There is a significant nerve supply linking the gut and the limbic part of the brain, so gut feeling is literally a neurological occurrence that generates a physical response. Within this system, the hippocampus stores memories associated with certain emotions, with particular events or experiences being more memorable depending on their intensity, repetition and elapsed time.

- **Control network:** Involved in understanding consequences, impulse control and selective attention. It enables us to override instincts and therefore guides behaviour.

Neuroscience for Leadership Coaching notes that the ventromedial prefrontal cortex has been implicated in hot, emotional, reasoning and the lateral and dorsolateral prefrontal cortex implicated in cold, non-emotional, logical reasoning. Different neural networks have been shown to be activated when we use inductive and deductive reasoning. Inductive reasoning makes broad generalizations from specific observations, while deductive reasoning start with a hypothesis and seeks to prove or falsify the hypothesis.

Our cognitive capabilities are associated with decision-making and Chapter 4 will pick up on this when we examine bias, stereotypes, group culture and decision-making, and the associated considerations for building an outstanding workforce.

The triune brain

Before moving to Chapter Two and examining personality psychology and intelligence, it is necessary to mention that there are differing opinions on the efficacy of physician, psychiatrist and neuroscientist Paul MacLean's concept of the triune brain.

The physician, psychiatrist and neuroscientist Paul MacLean was interested in the brain's control of emotion and behaviour and his early work focused on the role of the limbic system as the brain's centre of emotions. He proposed that the limbic system had evolved in early mammals to control freeze, fight or flight behavioural responses to their environment. MacLean's early work included *Man and his Animal Brains*[85] where he argued that humans can be perceived as having three different brains in one with each 'brain' having a distinctive set of capabilities. MacLean developed his theory after further research and in 1970 he published *The Triune Brain, Emotion and Scientific Bias*[86] followed by *The Triune Brain in Evolution*[87] in 1990.

MacLean proposed that the mammalian brain had three layers that each developed at different stages of evolution: the 'reptilian brain' which is responsible for instinctive and often automatic behaviour, consisting of the midbrain, pons, medulla, and basal ganglia; the limbic system, at the centre of the 'old mammalian brain' which is responsible for emotions such as fear, love and anger; and the cerebral cortex, the 'new mammalian brain' at the top, responsible for our rational cognitive strategies and verbal and intellectual capabilities.

The Triune Brain in Evolution received critical reviews by neurobiologists in two prominent scientific journals, *Science* and *American Scientist*. In the *Science* review,[88] Anton Reiner, at the time a recent graduate in the field of neuroscience, was critical about several basic premises of the book. The *American Scientist* review by Campbell[89] was a briefer account but resembled the issues raised by Reiner. Cory subsequently defended MacLean by systematically addressing the criticisms raised in the Science review.[90, 91]

Improvements in technology have enabled neuroscientists to develop their neuroanatomical techniques for charting the circuitry of animal brains and subsequent findings have refined the traditional neuroanatomical ideas upon which MacLean based his hypothesis. For instance in *Principles of Brain Evolution,* Georg Striedter notes that: structures of the limbic system,[92] which MacLean proposed arose in early mammals, have now been shown to exist across a range of modern vertebrates; that studies based on paleontological data or comparative anatomical evidence strongly suggest that the neocortex was already present in the earliest emerging mammals; and, that although non-mammals do not have a neocortex they possess pallial regions, and some parts of the pallium mediate functions such as perception, learning and memory, decision making, motor control and conceptual thinking which occur in the mammalian neocortex. Striedler states 'Mammalian neocortex was not added to a pre-existing complement of 'old' brain regions; instead, it was radically transformed from a precursor that probably resembled the dorsal cortex of turtles'.

Streidter discusses the debate as to whether cell groups in the brain vary in size independently of each other between individuals or across species and concluded that *mosaic evolution*, where individual brain regions evolve independently of each other is less frequent in mammalian brains than *concerted evolution* where individual brain regions evolve in concert with each other due to rules of neural development

It has subsequently been noted that

> MacLean's triune brain schema, despite being incorrect in some anatomical details, remains a valid functional description of the interplay between evolutionary older and younger processes in the human mind.[93]

In addition, that

> recent results in cognitive neuroscience give critical support to the instinct-emotion-thought triunity of mental processes that dates back to James and MacLean ... yet the results also show that these three components are interconnected and hard to separate in the brain.

William James had argued in the late nineteenth century that instincts, thoughts and emotions are interconnected.[94]

To conclude our brief introduction to this debate, it is worth noting Cory's observation that competing theories may be comparable only in part, that they

> ask and respond to different questions. MacLean tries to address the larger questions of human nature and behaviour. The others how no interest in such questions but address the fine grained technical questions of anatomical and functional evolution. At the level where they meet they do not contradict each other but are largely compatible. At the point they diverge they primarily address different questions'.

Streidter admits that 'the biggest challenge in comprehending how our brains evolved is to determine how the various changes in brain size and/or structure relate to changes in behaviour'. Concluding only that 'Within *H. sapiens*, absolute brain size probably increased mainly because larger brains allowed for more sophisticated social interactions'. Cory goes on to note that while 'the triune brain concept may need modification ... as the body of neuroscience grows ... with appropriate clarifications, it is still by far the best concept we have for linking neuroscience with the larger, more generalized concepts of the social sciences'.

Highlights

The evolution and operation of our brains, emotions and thinking can be summarized as follows:

- The spinal cord and 'reptilian' brain provide background functioning such as homeostatic functions, plus reflex and instinctive functions that help protects us and aid survival in threatening situations.

- The sensory connections to the cortex feed us data about the outside world, and we use this data to respond to our environment using our motor connections.

- Some limbic system nuclei and connections, such as the hypothalamus which has a homeostatic role, monitoring and adjusting our physiological state.

- The ascending systems link limbic system nuclei diffusely to neocortical regions, which play a key role in affective activation, development and plasticity.

- The neocortex modules are broad purpose vehicles that, due to neuroplasticity, become specialized through social, physical, and ecological interactions and experiences.

  Their overall function is to generate suitable output in response to the input from the sensory stems, utilizing expectations based on internal variables, memory, and in particular to plan ahead so that the responses have a predictive character via suitable internal mental models. The output includes both physical actions and communications events.[95]

- The limbic system has been described as the seat of emotions and the neocortex the home of symbolic thought.

- The cerebellum coordinates movements and other information, and is linked to language.

- The limbic system, such as the hippocampus and amygdala and parts of the basal ganglia, has a role in learning and memory.

- Neurotransmitters play a key role in the operation of the brain.

- The mind can be thought of as operating in two different ways: bottom-up, which is quick, reactive and emotional; and top-down, which is slower, voluntary – up to a point – and effortful.
- The mind can be seen as a web of images, concepts and connections in the brain.
- Culture plays a large role in shaping the mind, alongside nature and nurture.

Having understood the emotional and thinking self, the next chapter will look at the psychology of personality and intelligence.

Leadership impact

Key themes that leaders should reflect on include:

- The complexity of people: We are all different, and an understanding some of the underlying complexities will help improve how we lead and manage.
- Emotions and how to manage them: Emotion is a key component of behaviour, and it is important to understand how to regulate our emotions.
- Cognitive capabilities: Thoughts are a key component of behaviour and so it is important to understand how cognitive processes work.
- Empathetic capabilities: Helpful in sharing experiences from an emotional perspective and understanding why from a cognitive perspective.
- Theory of the mind: We have the ability to understand the differences between our beliefs, values and behaviours, and those of others.

People management recommendations

Actions to consider:

- Occupational psychology expertise: Do you provide sufficient, or any, psychology advice for your organization?
- Development courses for leaders, leader-managers and others: What people-related development do you offer those with leadership and management responsibility? These should include elements of neuroscience and psychology.

Personality psychology and intelligence

02

Introduction

Having examined the brain, which provides the biological structure and processes to regulate our physiology, our emotional states and our cognition, in this chapter we introduce the areas of personality psychology, beliefs, values, interests, attitudes, personality traits, personality types, impression management, the dark triad, socio-analytic theory and both cognitive and social intelligence.

It is important to understand various aspects of personality for selection and development, as 'people possess a wide array of characteristics and capabilities, often referred to as individual differences, which have a direct impact on their job performance in organizations'.[1]

Personality can be defined as 'the set of psychological traits and mechanisms within the individual that are organized and relatively enduring and that influence his or her interactions with, and adaptations to, the intrapsychic, physical and social environments'.[2]

Personality and intelligence tests are becoming used more widely in the workplace, and so it is helpful to understand how the theories underlying them have developed.

Chapter summary

The following subjects are discussed in this chapter:

- **personality psychology;**
- **beliefs, values, attitudes and interests:**
  - beliefs;
  - values;
  - attitudes;
  - interests;

- **personality traits;**
- **locus of control;**
- **multiple personality traits:**
  - Eysenck;
  - Cattell's 16PF;
  - Costa and McCrae's Big Five;
  - Hogan;
- **personality types:**
  - Type A vs Type B;
  - the Myers–Briggs Type Indicator;
- **socio-analytic theory;**
- **social constructionism and impression management;**
- **the dark triad;**
- **meaning and purpose;**
- **personality development:**
  - the emergence of personality;
- **intelligence:**
  - fluid and crystallized intelligence;
  - social intelligence;
- **Character:**
  - strengths and virtues;
  - personality strengths;
  - strengths, character and coaching.

Personality psychology

In *Personality Psychology*, Randy Larsen and David Buss note that every human being in certain respects is:

- like all others: at the human nature level, the universals;
- like some others: at the level of individual and group differences, the particulars;
- like no others (the individual uniqueness level), the uniqueness.[3]

The universals of human nature include traits and mechanisms such as language skills and the psychological desire to live with others and belong to social groups.

With regard to the particulars of individual and group differences, first, people differ in their beliefs, values and motivations, and second, individuals affiliate with others in groups based on some common variables, for instance culture, generational cohort, political affiliation, faith, world view, ethnicity, gender or socioeconomic background.

When it comes to the uniqueness of individuals, no generalizations can be made, but it is possible to look at people through various different lenses. Larsen and Buss explain personality psychology within the following six domains:

- **Dispositional domain:** Examines the aspects of personality that are stable and differentiate people from others. These can be described as personality traits and abilities. Testing is quantitative and examines correlation and causal relationships.

- **Biological domain:** Based on the assumption that humans are biological systems. Mechanisms in the body that are related to personality are examined, in addition to evolutionary causal processes that created them. This approach examines biological systems that influence, or are influenced by, desires, thoughts, feelings and behaviours. Biological differences may cause personality differences; for instance, there is a biological theory relating to extraversion, or there may be biological consequences to personality traits, such as instances of heart disease being related to the Type A personality. This domain also includes research on the biological links with positive and negative emotions and with regard to behaviour driven by genetics, as it appears that our genetic make-up can influence behaviour. Personality traits are showing heritability at levels of 0.30 to 0.50. This means 30 to 50 per cent of the trait variance is due to genetic differences, leaving 50 to 70 per cent due to measurement error or environmental impact, which can be split into shared and non-shared factors. Finally, this perspective looks at us as products of evolution, examining adaptive problems and the associated psychological solutions. It acknowledges that our adaption to date has occurred over several millennia, and therefore this adaption may not serve us well in the current environment.

- **Intrapsychic domain:** Focuses on the factors within the mind that influence thoughts, emotions and behaviour. It includes defence mechanisms such as repression, denial and projection. It is assumed that there are aspects of the mind that are outside of our awareness – the unconscious mind – and that it has its own motivation, will and energy, and can be the source of psychological problems.

- **Cognitive/exponential domain:** Focuses on the factors that are related to subjective experience and other mental processes including, beliefs, desires, thoughts and feelings about oneself and others. A central concept is the self. As humans acquire sensory information, they process it and store artefacts from the instance in their memory. One approach is that humans construct their experiences. Personality could influence any stage in the cognitive process. Individuals' goals are individual expressions of social or institutional norms or standards.

- **Social and cultural domain:** Aspects of personality affect, and are affected by, experience through social interaction. It is expected that the growth of studies relating to culture and cross-cultural differences will mirror the growth of interdependence among people with different backgrounds.

- **Adjustment domain:** Personality plays a key role in how we navigate life, and is linked with health outcomes through our emotional states and behavioural choices. Positive psychology informs this domain.[4]

Given this range of viewpoints, it is clear why it is difficult to capture a discrete and holistic view of people and their behaviour. Research at the boundaries of these domains include

> collaborations among brain researchers using functional magnetic resonance imaging (fMRI) technology to conduct brain scans and psychologists studying interpersonal dispositions; collaboration between cultural and evolutionary psychologists to study the casual origins and nature of cultural differences; and collaboration between dispositional researchers and cognitive psychologists to study the information-processing mechanisms underlying stable individual differences.[5]

The difference between beliefs, values and attitudes and interests are explained below.

Beliefs, values, attitudes and interests

In *Organizational Culture and Leadership*, Schein and Schein state that individuals seen as a cultural entity can be analysed in terms of artefacts, espoused beliefs and values and basic underlying assumptions:

- **artefacts:** visible and feelable structure and processes and observed behaviour, which are difficult to decipher;

- **espoused beliefs and values:** ideals, goals, values, aspirations; ideologies; and realizations, which may or may not be congruent with behaviour and artefacts;

- **basic underlying assumptions:** unconscious, taken-for-granted beliefs and values, which determine behaviour, perception, thought and feeling.[6]

Schein and Schein also note that it is 'the degree of alignment or congruity between the three levels that determine how an individual's "sincerity" or "integrity" is judged by others'.[7]

Beliefs

An acceptance of existence without the benefit of proof is a belief. Beliefs

> are the result of an individual's attempt to make sense of a set of stimuli, a situation, or patterns of interactions between people... initiated by perceptions, beliefs result from the interpretation and organization of perceptions into an understanding of the relationship between objects, properties and/or ideas.[8]

Perception is the ability to become aware of something through sensory stimulus; perception is reality, and also the way something is understood or interpreted.

In other words, perceptions are informational cues arising from the delivery of sensory information, while beliefs are the result of cognitive processing that organizes perceptions to allow us to understand relationships based on social learning.

Leon Festinger, a social psychologist, formulated the theory of *cognitive dissonance*, which states that becoming aware of conflicts between our beliefs violates the natural human striving for mental harmony or consonance and creates an uncomfortable mental state.[9]

Values

A value is the enduring belief that a specific way of being and state of existence is more preferable than others. Once a value exists, it consciously or unconsciously guides decisions and actions, develops and maintains attitudes towards objects and situations, informs judgement of others and justifies one's own behaviours. Belief and value systems can be used to predict behaviour.

In *Cultures and Organizations*, Geert Hofstede et al suggest that collective action in society requires cultural homogeneity in its implicit values, and that

> cultural homogeneity does not allow for rapid change in values, because values are acquired. For the most part, in infancy and for life. Value system changes require generations. So, while groups with common cultural values will be good at collectively responding to circumstances, they will be slow to shift their shared value system even if changes in circumstances would give such value shifts survival advantages. Note that slow change in value systems is still very fast compared with a situation without culture, in which genetic change is the only mechanism.[10]

Values can therefore be defined as 'enduring, evaluative, but subjective and learned, standards of the preferred state of affairs which a person wishes to achieve and maintain',[11] where a preference is a greater liking for one object, event or state over others.

The Neuroscience of Leadership Coaching explains that our beliefs and values form an integral part of our sense of self, and confirming our opinions is a means of confirming our sense of self. We pay greater attention to negative than positive events in relation to our beliefs and values,[12] and once values have been acquired by individual and groups it is a slow process to modify them; it takes time to change people's minds.

Attitudes

Tendencies to react positively or negatively to classes of objects or events are known as attitudes. They have cognitive, affective and behavioural elements. Enduring attitudes are considered to be part of personality, and studies have found that some form of heritability is possible.

In *The Neuroscience of Organizational Behavior*, Beugré states that implicit attitudes are related to what is called System 1 thinking. They are rapid, automatic and comprise unconscious evaluations in response to stimuli. In contrast, explicit attitudes are related to System 2 thinking. They are relatively slower, deliberative and conscious evaluations based on contextual information.[13] System 1 and System 2 thinking are examined in the next chapter.

Interests

Interests differ from motives, a specific reason for doing something, because they have a weaker power to drive action. In a workplace context, they can be defined as 'a subset of attitudes concerning the evaluation of beliefs about occupational activities'.[14] These thoughts produce an affective desire to continue or discontinue thoughts or behaviour.

Personality traits

Traits can be defined as dimensions of individual differences in tendencies to show consistent patterns of thoughts, feelings and actions.[15]

There are many models of human traits, and in *The Psychology of Behaviour at Work* Adrian Furnham lists groups of trait theories but notes that it has been difficult to show correlation and causality between traits as independent variables and work-related outcomes. He classifies the theories as follows:

- **Biological traits:** Extraversion and sensation seeking can be seen in biological terms through physiological, genetic and/or biochemical differences.

- **Single or multiple traits:** Single traits, locus of control;[16] and multiple traits.[17]

- **Cognitive traits:** How people view the world and attribute causes of behaviour.

- **Normal vs abnormal traits:** Psychopathy, not used in the workplace, although neuroticism is common.

- **Dynamic vs stylistic traits:** Freudian and non-Freudian ideas, not used in the workplace.[18]

Personality data can be used in organizations to compare organizational outcomes to personality traits and for developing personality measures to predict organizational outcomes and assess the degree of work suitability fit, for instance Holland's model comparing realistic, artistic, investigative, social, enterprising and conventional types (RAISEC) against traits, life goals, values, identifications and aptitudes.[19]

The existence of innate biological traits and culturally adapted cognitive traits was examined in the previous chapter; single and multiple personality traits will be examined below, in addition to personality types.

Locus of control

Locus of control is a single trait theory and is related to the extent to which individuals are motivated to control the events in their lives.[20] This single trait is said to impact motivation, job satisfaction and work outcomes such as performance and turnover. Perceived behavioural control considers the extent to which an individual has control over performing a behaviour and their beliefs regarding self-efficacy related to that behaviour.[21] Self-efficacy is a belief that one can successfully undertake behaviour that will achieve a goal, and this can be influenced by modelling, which is seeing the behaviour of others successfully achieve the same goal.[22]

It has been found that those with a more instrumentalist outlook, which is related to a positive internal locus of control, are likely to be more successful than those with a fatalist, external locus of control, outlook. Furnham lists the following differences in a work context:

- '**Motivation:** Instrumentalists are more likely to believe that their efforts will results in good performance, and they exhibit stronger belief in their own competence.

- **Job performance:** Instrumentalists should be more satisfied than fatalists partly because of their success.

- **Leadership:** Instrumentalists prefer participative approaches from their supervisors, rely more on personal persuasion with their subordinates, and seem more task-oriented and less socially orientated.

- **Job perception:** Instrumentalists perceive more personal control over their environment, request more feedback on the job and perceive less role strain.
- **Turnover:** Highly job-satisfied instrumentalists exhibit the same rate of turnover, presumably low, as fatalists, whereas highly job-dissatisfied instrumentalists exhibit more turnover than fatalists.'[23]

Multiple personality traits

There are a variety of trait-based tools used to evaluate personality. We explore a few of the better known approaches below.

Eysenck

Eysenck's original theory was published in 1967,[24] and he later concluded: 'in sum, it appears that preferences for different kinds of occupation and occupational success are both determined to some extent by personality.'[25]

Eysenck suggests that there are three fundamental, unrelated, personality traits: extraversion, neuroticism and psychoticism. These can be measured or described on a continuum, are biologically based and have behavioural implications. Furnham notes that research findings on extraversion suggest that it is substantially biologically inherited and explained in terms of cortical arousal and reward sensitivity. Also, that extraverts succeed in high-pressure jobs that involve considerable interaction with strangers; are able to handle overload and stress; have task-focused coping; feelings of self-efficacy; and a good sense of well-being.[26]

With regard to neuroticism, he notes that it is also substantially biologically inherited and is associated with stress, vulnerability, sensitivity to punishment and threat avoidance. Neurotics portray highly selective biases in cognitive processes, with considerable awareness of danger, cautious decision-making, a generally negative self-concept and often depressed mood and pessimistic outlooks:

> introverts are more sensitive to pain than are extraverts; they become fatigued and bored more easily than do extraverts; excitement interferes with their performance, whereas it enhances the performance of extraverts; and they tend to be more careful but slower than extraverts.[27]

Cattell's 16PF

The 16PF test is based on Cattell's theory of personality and measures 16 dimensions of personality which are said to be independent, identifiable, and reliably and validly measurable.[28] The primary factors in his theory are warmth, reasoning, emotional stability, dominance, liveliness, rule-consciousness, social boldness, sensitivity, vigilance, abstractedness, privateness, apprehension, openness to change, self-reliance, perfectionism and tension. Although there is a technical difference in statistical analytics, the 16PF factors have been successfully mapped against Paul Costa and Robert McCrae's Five Factor Model of personality, which is introduced below.

Costa and McCrae's 'Big Five'

Paul Costa and Robert McCrae claim that there are five basic, unrelated, dimensions of personality:

- **neuroticism:** sensitive, emotional and prone to anxiety and rumination;
- **extraversion:** outgoing, assertive, active, talkative and likes groups;
- **openness to experience:** curious about the inner and outer world, open to new experiences and innovation;
- **agreeableness:** interpersonal style, compassionate, good-natured and eager to cooperate and avoid conflict, empathizing;
- **conscientiousness:** purposeful, strong-willed, determined, conscientious, well organized, has high standards and always strives to achieve goals.[29]

The NEO-PI test is used to provide information relevant to occupational performance and adjustment and provides test results against a number of facets for each of the Big Five domains.[30]

Different traits will be correlated to different behaviours in an organizational context, with extraversion and conscientiousness seen as important for jobs with a high degree of social contact, and neuroticism having a negative correlation with work success. Neuroticism is the strongest correlate to job satisfaction, followed by conscientiousness and extraversion. In terms of personality, the 'more extraverted, emotionally stable, conscientious, agreeable and open to new experiences people are, the more they will tend to engage.'[31]

While the relationship between the Big Five model and work outcomes is compelling, it was developed in a Western context, and researchers have identified a possible sixth factor related to authoritarianism.[32] Further research could be undertaken to test for cross-cultural efficacy.

Hogan

The Hogan Personality Inventory was first published in 1986.[33] The original model was the California Psychological Inventory, which was designed to assess aspects of social behaviour that are cross-culturally significant and that non-psychologists intuitively understand, and was designed to predict important social outcomes. It is based on the Five Factor model of personality and measures normal, bright-side personality characteristics that describe how people relate to others when they are at their best. Normal personality affects people's ability to get along with others and achieve their goals.

Socio-analytic theory, discussed below, specifies that personality should be defined from the perspectives of the actor and observer. Personality from an actor's perspective is a person's identity that is manifested in terms of the strategies a person uses to gain acceptance and status. Personality from an observer's view is a person's reputation and is defined in trait evaluations – the actor's characteristic ways of behaving in public.

Reputation is the perception held by others regarding the characteristics of an individual based on the accumulation of any behavioural information, acquired both directly and indirectly. Instead of trying to change reputation through changing behaviour, it is more effective to change perceived reputation first. For instance, the impression of a person's effectiveness may be changed with little or no change to actual task behaviour and performance.

The Hogan Motives, Values, Preferences Inventory, first published in 1996, describes personality from the inside – the core goals, values, drivers and interests that determine what we desire and strive to attain. Where values are assessed, motives to achieve can be understood and what type of position, job and environment and may therefore be the most productive.[34]

Values, preferences and interests are all motivational concepts and differ primarily in their generality:

- **values:** broadest and most abstract;
- **interests:** narrowest and most concrete;
- **attitudes:** favourable–unfavourable, accept or reject, orientation towards attitude objects;
- **needs and values:** importance–unimportance of the stimulus object;
- **preferences and interests:** liking–disliking the stimulus object.

The Hogan Development Survey (HDS) was first published in 1997[35] and measures items outside the Five Factor model of personality. Talented people sometimes fail because, despite competence in skill areas relevant to adequate performance in a job, various factors can limit people's ability to perform at a constantly high level. Problematic behaviours arise from any number of common dysfunctional dispositions. These dispositions reflect people's distorted beliefs about themselves, how others will treat them, and the best means to achieve their personal goals. They may also negatively influence people's careers and life satisfaction.

The HDS addresses the dark side of interpersonal behaviour, which can be strengths but, when overused, can cause problems at work and in life. It measures aspects of people's daily behaviour that may be seen at times when they are not actively managing their public image. These situations might include those involving high stress, change, multi-tasking, task saturation, poor person–job fit or when someone feels so comfortable in their work environment that no concern is given to public image.

In *The Psychology of Behaviour at Work*, Furnham has noted that in research studies Hogan tests have shown a clear relationship between successful leadership and:

- **extraversion:** dominance, sociability, surgency;
- **stability:** emotional control, self-confidence, positive mood;
- **agreeableness:** cooperativeness, diplomacy;
- **conscientiousness:** integrity, responsibility.[36]

Research has concluded that selection on the basis of conscientiousness yields effective individual performance and may therefore be reflected in organizational financial performance. It is recommended that organizations should consider variance in the traits during selection, because smaller aggregate variance on all Big Five attributes, apart from extraversion, is significantly reflected in organizational financial performance.[37]

Having looked at various trait theories of personality, we will now consider personality types.

Personality types

Personality types differ from personality traits, as they are categorizations based on reported and observed features, such as preferences. There are a number of type theories, and two examples have been selected as illustrations: Type A vs Type B and the Myers–Briggs Type Indicator (MBTI). However, it is worth noting that type-based theories have been criticized for ignoring evidence that human personality is normally distributed rather than based on grouping people, and that dividing people can be misleading; once labelled as part of a group, stereotyping may occur; it may lead to self-fulfilling behaviour and resistance to change; and that instances of pure types are rare. Despite this, MBTI, which is discussed below, remains popular for individual and team development, although, like all type based tools, it is not used for selection.

Type A vs Type B

While there is a lack of agreement about the causal components and psychological processes involved, people can be discussed in terms of Type A and Type B behaviour. In *The Psychology of Behaviour at Work*, Furnham notes research that has shown Type A individuals to be more aggressive, more neurotic, more extraverted and more anxious, as well as in greater need for control than Type B individuals, and that Type A individuals have feelings of insecurity and self-doubt, and feel depressed or anxious about their self-worth. He summarizes the results of a number of studies comparing Type A and Type B workers. Type As:

- rate themselves significantly higher on various negative traits, including complaining, conceited, cruel, dominating, selfish and unkind, and lower on positive traits including, patient, reasonable, tolerant and unselfish;

- believe themselves to be more ambitious, cold, complaining, malicious, impatient and selfish;

- are more sensitive, and therefore responsive, to rewards;

- have a sense of urgency, will work faster but produce more errors;

- tend to be aggressive and interpersonally hostile, which makes them difficult to handle, unpredictable and touchy;

- set unrealistically high performance standards of themselves and others, and hence frequently do not attain them;

- work harder, suffer more stress and ignore minor ailments such as influenza, but when they do become ill they suffer major illnesses;

- tend to be more committed to, and perform better at, organizational goals.[38]

It appears

> researchers have identified a personality variable, or more likely a cluster of variables, that predict not only stress at work but also outside it… whether a particular job characteristic is stressful depends on whether the person is Type A or B, and that intrinsic job satisfaction has the potential to moderate these effects… Type As 'fit' unambiguous environments and find ambiguous environments stressful, whereas the opposite is true for Type Bs.[39]

The Myers–Briggs Type Indicator

The MBTI personality test is based on Carl Jung's theory of personality and has enduring popularity, despite attracting the sort of criticism previously noted for type-based approaches.

Jung concluded that people have natural tendencies to behave in ways that they find satisfying and fulfilling, and this produces differences in attitudes and preferences for certain types, patterns, of behaviour. He developed a type theory around how people gather information, *perceiving*, and make decisions based on it, *judging*.

- **perceiving:** through sensing and intuition;
- **judging:** through thinking and feeling.

From this he believed there were four basic mental processes: sensing, intuition, thinking and feeling. This was his type theory. He then added the impact of extraversion and introversion to each one. This was to reflect his belief that people either preferred to locate their attention and get their energy from the outside world of objects and activities (extraversion) or from their inside world of emotions and thoughts (introversion). He believed that people had a dominant function that they preferred from the resulting eight processes, for example extraverted sensing.

Jung acknowledged that his theory was incomplete, and Isabel Briggs Myers and Katherine Briggs expanded his work by adding the orientation of energy that characterized the auxiliary process, extraversion and introversion, and adding a fourth pair, judging and perceiving. This resulted in four pairs of preference types:

- extraversion and introversion, **E** and **I**;
- sensing and intuition, **S** and **N**;
- thinking and feeling, **T** and **F**;
- judging and perceiving, **J** and **P**.[40]

Test takers agree their type from the resulting 16 possible types, for instance *ENFJ*. Only scant evidence has so far been published that demonstrates neurological validity for these types.[41]

Socio-analytic theory

Socio-analytic theory suggests that personality is defined from the perspective of the individual, their identity, and those that observe them. In *The Talent Delusion*, Tomas Chamorro-Premuzic notes that through the evolutionary and anthropological analysis of human behaviour, socio-analytic theory identifies three major elements that characterize human life from its early beginnings to current times:

- Humans have always lived in groups.
- These groups have always a hierarchy, formal and informal, which determines the allocation of power, influence and decision-making.
- No form of human civilization can exist without a system of meaning.[42]

He states that the 'significance of these three universal principles of human life is that they have shaped our fundamental needs: the need to get along with others; the need to get ahead of others; and the need to find and impose meaning.'[43] From work, people can extract affiliation with a group or groups, the possibility of achievement, and a sense of purpose.

Socio-analytic theory is additionally based on five assumptions:

- Personality is best seen in terms of human evolution.
- People emerged as group-living and culture-using animals.

- The most important human motives facilitate group living and enhance individual survival.
- Social interaction involves negotiating for acceptance and status.
- Some people are more effective at this than others.

Chamorro-Premuzic illustrates the above by drawing on Hogan's motives, values and preferences drivers outlined by socio-analytic theory:[44]

- **Getting ahead:** The main values are status drivers, recognition, power and commerce and 'explain individual differences in people's willingness to compete with others, climb up the group hierarchy to occupy positions of power, pursue financial rewards and accomplish things that may be admired and recognized by others.'[45]
- **Getting along:** The main values are social or affiliation drivers, hedonism, affiliation, altruism and tradition and 'explain why some people are particularly driven to seek joyful and pleasurable activities, connect with others and meet new people, engage in prosocial ventures to improves the lives of others, and respect established norms and traditions.'[46]
- **Finding meaning:** The main values are security, aesthetics and science, and 'explain individual differences in how people make sense of the world and find meaning. In particular, they describe the degree to which people need to minimize uncertainty and ambiguity, and to make sense of the world via more intuitive/holistic or factual/analytical means.'[47]

In *The Will to Meaning*, Viktor Frankl argues that if people can find *meaning* and *purpose* in life they can realize their potential[48]. Meaning and purpose will be examined further below.

Social constructionism and impression management

How do we experience life, and therefore our working life and how are we interpreting the environment including objects, events and other people? This is a philosophical, *ontological*, question, which means it relates to concepts of becoming, existence and reality. In terms of human interaction, social constructionism is based on the view that reality is created through interactions between people, and that the creation of a perceived social reality and meaning is both individual and provisional.

In *The Socially Constructed Organization*, David Campbell states that 'social constructionism, by its very definition, must be orientated towards the future... it is a framework that encourages people to be aware that they are continually constructing realities through conversation'.[49]

The socially constructed organization is therefore conceived as being constructed constantly through people interacting with each other and Campbell describes three domains, which each represent a different aspect of our overall experience:

- **material and scientific:** the language of facts;
- **social construction:** the language of social discourse and rhetoric;
- **political:** the language and operation of power.[50]

Organizations are experienced through these three domains.

We are judged by the impressions others form of our behaviour, and in the *Presentation of Self in Everyday Life*, Irving Goffman notes that people express themselves to convey information but the audience do not just receive the information in its narrow sense, they also assign wider meaning to the information based on past experience and current context. People make inferences and provisional judgements, which are subsequently tested.[51]

People can also manage the impression they give others. Drawing on Goffman, Schein and Schein note that human beings develop self-image and self-esteem and within society we normally seek to uphold others' claims to preserve self-esteem, even if being economical with the truth is required. He believes this is why performance appraisals have traditionally been difficult, because to be meaningful, and therefore useful, they need to explore the shared reality between reviewer and reviewee.[52]

With regard to personality testing, psychologists have often viewed all impression management as potentially distorting the results. However, given the above description of impression management in everyday life, it can be seen that while people may consciously try and answer personality tests to create a certain, usually positive, impression about themselves this form of impression management may not devalue the results.

In *The Talent Delusion*, Chamorro-Premuzic states that

> since most jobs involve dealing with people and in all those instances it is important that one creates a favourable impression, whether they are clients, colleagues, bosses or subordinates, impression management is a job-relevant skill and a relevant signal rather than 'noise'.[53]

He also notes studies which have found that impression management is positively related to a wide range of desirable workplace variables, such as employee motivation, organizational citizenship, social skills and general job competence, as well as negatively related to counterproductive work behaviours.[54]

Leadership counterproductive work behaviours are important to understand due to their impact on the well-being of the workforce and therefore the organization, and these can be discussed in relation to the so-called dark triad.

The dark triad

In *The Talent Delusion*, Chamorro-Premuzic, discusses the dark triad, which consists of narcissism, psychopathy and Machiavellianism:

- **Narcissism:** Impulsive, risky decision-making, a propensity to belittle others and take credit for their achievements, sensitivity to criticism, an inability to work well with people, self-centredness, sense of entitlement, arrogance, lack of empathy, all contribute to the delusion that they are the centre of the universe and that the world revolves around them.[55]

- **Psychopathy:** Lack of concern for both other people and social regulatory mechanisms, impulsivity, lack of guilt or remorse when their actions harm others.[56]

- **Machiavellianism:** Achievement through political machination rather than a focus on work, manipulation, engagement in counterproductive work behaviours, especially the type that concerns mistreatment and betrayal of work colleagues.[57]

In terms of narcissism, 'during early interactions, narcissists are likely to come across as confident, charming and entertaining, but as time goes by they are more likely to behave in hostile, cold and aggressive ways.'[58] They may be effective in short-term impression management for tasks that involve gaining status and persuasion and, due to their sometimes unrealistic optimism, may be entrepreneurial.

Psychopaths are also skilled at impression management, and while being charismatic may have a hands-off style and not facilitate engagement at work. 'Research has shown that psychopathic individuals may benefit from their low empathy levels: when you don't care about others, you are able to make more ruthless decisions and prioritize business interests over people issues.'[59]

Finally, Machiavellian behaviour includes manipulating and influencing others by pretending to agree with them and hiding one's true intentions. This behaviour ultimately weakens connections to others, and ultimately most struggle to achieve success in the workplace. 'Machiavellianism is also associated with higher levels of cynicism and distrust, and this is particularly useful during negotiations or when dealing with individuals who are themselves Machiavellian.'[60]

Research has established that high-involvement managerial practices can influence the willingness of an employee high in dark triad traits to engage in organizational citizenship behaviour.[61] Coaching/development discussions using Hogan's HDS can help leaders build more constructive and effective relationships and avoid habits that may derail them.[62]

Meaning and purpose

In 'Meaning in life', MacKenzie and Baumeister suggest that there are four basic needs people must fulfil in order for life to make sense and be meaningful:

- **Purpose:** 'Enables people to find meaning in present events from their relationship to possible future events. The two main types of purpose are goals and fulfilments.'

- **Values:** Or justification for one's actions. 'People want to justify their past, present, and future actions and values offer a way to do this. A particular value is usually connected to a broader, more fundamental value base. Value bases are perceived as good in and of themselves and do not require any further justification.'

- **Efficacy:** 'Gives people a sense of being in control and being capable of making a difference.'

- **Self-worth:** 'People generally like to feel that they are good and worthwhile and this is commonly accomplished by feeling superior to others.'[63]

In *The Human Quest for Meaning*, Paul Wong notes that meaning consists of 'four essential components: purpose, understanding, responsible action and enjoyment or evaluation.'[64] Functionally, these components 'entail four psychological processes for the good life: motivational (purpose), cognitive (understanding), social and moral (responsibility), and affective (enjoyment or evaluation)'.[65] Meaning can also be considered at different levels:[66]

- **Everyday:** Self-regulation, self-maintenance and self-propagation, instincts, drives, motivation and emotions. Meaning emerges to help us with sense-making.

- **Encounters:** With the unexpected, negative, threatening. Leads to feelings of frustration, anxiety, fear, guilt, anger. Meaning is adaptive to help us overcome by developing solutions.

- **Existential:** When our fundamental beliefs and reasons for existence are questioned or all our basic need are satisfied, we explore, for instance, the metaphysical, to restore meaning.[67]

According to McAdams, there are three levels of personality evolving in a complex social and cultural context:[68]

- **Dispositional traits:** Certain dispositional profiles, such as high levels extraversion, conscientiousness, openness to experience, and low levels of neuroticism, that tend to be associated with an overall feeling that life has meaning and purpose.[69]

- **Characteristic adaptations:** 'Meaning is captured in goals, projects, strategies, and other motivational, social-cognitive, and developmental facets of personality that are contextualised in time, place, and social role'.[70]

- **Integrative life stories:** From early adulthood, people construct an identity of what they believe their lives mean.

McAdams writes that 'as trait dimensions provide basic resources upon which people draw to construct a meaningful life, the characteristic adaptations at the second level of personality spell out what kinds of meanings people make and the specific areas in life wherein they make them.'[71]

Wong suggests the following overview:

> meaning is the web of connections, understandings, and interpretations that help us comprehend our experience and formulae plans directing our energies to the achievement of our desired future. Meaning provides us with the sense that our lives matter, that they make sense, and that they are more than the sum of our seconds, days and years. Comprehending our experience in this way builds the cognitive component of meaning in life thus refers to the understandings that we develop of who we are, what the world is lie, and how we fit in with and relate to the grand scheme of things.[72]

Personality development

The emergence of personality

It has been suggested that

> personality develops along three separate lines: (1) from infant temperament to the articulation of adult personality traits (personality from the standpoint of the social actor); (2) from childhood intentionality to the development of life goals and values (personality from the standpoint of motivated agent), and (3) from the emergence of episodic memory in childhood to the construction of narrative identity (personality from the standpoint of the autobiographical author).[73]

Research has shown that gene factors account for about 50 per cent of the variation in adult personality traits and attitudes, and there are three main explanations for genetic differences:

- **neutral:** random, genetic drift;
- **particular:** maladaptive deviation from the optimal trait;
- **balancing selection:** where the fitness contribution of a trait changes over time.[74]

Environmental factors account for 50 per cent variation in personality. This is impacted by both nurture and culture. However, the impact of non-shared environmental effects on personalities has still not been fully explained.[75]

With regard to the effect of people's life history, natural selection favours optimal resource allocation, which impacts our physiological and behavioural traits so, 'at the level of behaviour, individual differences in life-history strategy are reflected in patterns of self-regulation and motivation'. Unpredictable environments lead to *fast* strategies reflected in risk-taking, aggression and exploitive tendencies; and safer, more predictable environments lead to *slow* strategies reflected in risk aversion, high self-control and prosociality.[76]

Conceiving of personal goals as building blocks of personality, personality development across adulthood was studied through the concept of *personal concerns*, distinguishing between (1) *what* people typically want to achieve, maintain, or avoid at certain times in their lives, and (2) *how* they go about pursuing these goals. It would appear that the 'processes of goal setting and pursuit help to describe and predict how people interact with the world, react to internal and external age-related changes, and proactively shape who they will become in the future'[77]

In terms of neuroscience and personality traits, early research has found that 'for each of the Big-Five, and often at the level of narrow traits below them, we can point to evidence consistent with the idea that numerous biological parameters contribute to trait variation'.[78]

With regard to the stability and change in personality traits over lifetimes, research has established the following (where, N is neuroticism, E is extraversion, O is openness to experience, A is agreeableness and C is conscientiousness):

- **Late childhood to early adolescence (10–18):** All traits moderately stable and stability increases. Increase in N especially in girls, decreases in E. Initial increases followed by decreases in O, A and C.

- **Emerging and early adulthood (18–40):** All traits are stable and stability continues to increase. Decreases in N. Increases in O, A and C.

- **Middle adulthood (40–65):** All traits are very stable. Continued decreases in N, decreases in O. More pronounced increases in A. Continued increases in C.

- **Old age (65 onwards):** All traits are stable but stability decreases. Increases in N, particularly in very old age. Decreases in E, O, A and C, particularly in very old age. [79]

In terms of the impact of culture on the development of our motives, values and social selves, research has found that:

- The Big Five personality traits appear to be universal – although an additional trait, interpersonal relatedness/gregariousness, has been suggested.[80]

- We share the Big Six emotions of happiness, sadness, fear, anger, surprise and disgust but the expression of these is culturally dependent.

- Individual and collective cultures have differing concepts with regard to self-concepts and self-esteem.[81]

Research is now turning away from studying differences in national culture to studying ecological niches created by the globalized world system, such as similarities and differences between generational cohorts.

With regard to self-esteem, individual differences are relatively stable across life so are trait-like. Other findings relating to self-esteem have been noted: while there is a genetic component, environmental factors in childhood have an impact; self-esteem decreases from about 60–65; people from different generations do not differ in average levels of self-esteem; significant life events have an impact; and it is a causal force influencing life.[82]

Having looked at personality and some key areas of personality that are related to work outcomes, we turn our attention to cognitive intelligence.

Intelligence

In *Testing People at Work*, Smith and Smith define intelligence as 'the relative speed and accuracy with which the brain processes complex information'[83].

It is noted that in 1904 Charles Spearman defined intelligence as a combination of three mental processes:[84]

- **Apprehension of reality:** How a person looks at a problem and discerns the salient points.

- **Education of relationships:** Which salient elements are linked, identifying their relationships.

- **Education of correlates:** Existing relationships are extended into new situations and steps in sequences anticipated.[85]

The intelligence quotient (IQ) scale was later developed by William Stern in 1965[86] from the 1905 work of Binet and Simon in education[87] by dividing the resultant measures of mental ability (mental age) by chronological age and multiplying by 100.

In terms of its application in the workplace, a meta-analysis of research focused on cognitive intelligence and job performance found that:[88]

- The predictive validity of structured and unstructured interviews is 58 per cent, but combining structured interviews with cognitive ability tests increases this to 76 per cent.

- Reference checks on their own have a validity of 26 per cent, but when combined with cognitive ability tests the predictive validity rises to 70 per cent.

- The predictive validity of personality tests is 32 per cent, but when combined with cognitive ability tests the predictive validity rises to 68 per cent, for example with ambition and likeability for negotiators.[89]

Apart from the degree of variability in specific instances, an obvious question is the extent to which other factors account for the differences, for instance emotional intelligence (EI). Self-esteem and self-confidence are also factors that are felt to impact feelings of job satisfaction and high-performance behaviours.

Fluid and crystalized intelligence

Intelligence can be seen as fluid and crystalized.[90] Fluid intelligence represents perceiving and processing information, reasoning and learning, all independent of past knowledge. Crystalized intelligence is the ability to use acquired knowledge and skills. Fluid intelligence is said to peak in young adults and then decline due to atrophy in the right cerebellum, and lack of use may contribute to this. Crystalized intelligence increases gradually, stabilizes through adulthood and then starts to decline from around the age of 65. It will be seen in Chapter 7 that the increasing use of technology to store information and then process it quickly and accurately reduces the need of human intelligence for certain tasks.

Social intelligence

Cognitive intelligence (cognitive ability) has historically been privileged over other aspects of intelligence. In *The Social Leap*, William von Hippel notes that self-control, divergent thinking, and mental speed enables flexibility and thus should make people more socially skilled. He referenced research where people who came up with more divergent uses for an object were more persuasive, humorous and charismatic regardless of their cognitive ability measured by their IQ. Cognitive intelligence is therefore only one test of ability, and testing for broader social intelligence may be a better predictor of success in social functioning. Von Hippel notes that social skills also depend on our attitudes.[91] Social intelligence includes both emotional and cultural intelligence. Cultural intelligence is discussed in Chapter 9 and emotional intelligence is examined below.

In 'Emotional intelligence has 12 elements', Daniel Goleman and Richard Boyatzis define emotional intelligence as having four domains: self-awareness, self-management, social awareness and relationship management. Within the domains are the following twelve EI competencies:

- **self-awareness:** emotional self-awareness;
- **self-management:** emotional self-control, adaptability, achievement orientation, positive outlook;
- **social awareness:** empathy, organizational awareness;
- **relationship management:** influence, coach and mentor, conflict management, teamwork and inspirational leadership.[92]

In other research, EI has been categorized into three streams:[93]

- **Ability:** An individual's ability to perceive emotion from stimuli, use emotion to facilitate cognitive activities, understand emotion from a social perspective, and regulate emotions to allow productive functioning.[94]
- **Trait:** Behavioural dispositions and self-perceived abilities measured through self-report.[95]
- **Mixed:** Introduced by Daniel Goleman in 'What makes a leader?' – self-awareness, self-regulation, motivation, empathy and social skill.[96]

This research found that *mixed EI* has the highest association with employee job satisfaction. This was expected, as

> *ability EI* is more cognitively loaded and should have the lowest relationship with job satisfaction... mixed EI has the largest relationship with other personality traits and should thus have the strongest relationship with job satisfaction because personality is a much better predictor of job satisfaction than cognitive ability.[97]

Mixed EI alone accounts for over half of the variance in job satisfaction. It is thought that EI may cause employees to interpret their job and work performance more positively and then deduce that they have high job satisfaction.

In addition to our understanding of EI, it should not be forgotten that *emotional stability* (ES) is a personality trait found in the major approaches to personality such as those of Eysenck, Cattell, and McCrae and Costa. One study that investigated the impact of ES on organizational behaviour found that 'ES plays an important and positive trait effect on job satisfaction, job self-efficacy, and organizational commitment.'[98] Also, that leaders exhibit higher levels of ES.

It is important to remember that people learn and develop, therefore 'despite the widespread belief that intelligence is born, not made, when we really think about it, it's not so hard to imagine that people can develop their intellectual abilities'[99] and therefore an 'assessment at one point in time has little value for understanding someone's ability, let alone their potential to succeed in the future.'[100]

Character

Strengths and virtues

In their seminal 2004 text, *Character Strengths and Virtues: A handbook and classification*, Christopher Peterson and Martin Seligman write from the perspective of positive psychology which focuses on three related topics: 'the study of positive subjective experiences, the study of positive individual traits, and the study of institutions that enable positive experiences and positive traits'.[101] Character is also considered from the perspective of trait theory as: stable, general, but situationally contingent and therefore capable of change.

Peterson and Seligman suggest a classification of character strengths which allow individuals 'to achieve more than the absence of distress and disorder'. These contribute towards, rather than cause, fulfilment.

Virtues are defined as 'the core characteristics valued by moral philosophers and religious thinkers... these six broad categories of virtue emerge consistently from historical surveys'.[102] They argue that these are universal and speculate that they may have emerged through selection from an evolutionary process. Moral virtues downplay prescriptions for a good life, moral laws, and emphasize aspects of good character.

Character strengths are defined as 'the psychological ingredients – processes or mechanisms – that define virtues'.[103] The list below is not designed to be exclusive or exhaustive.

Situational themes are defined as 'specific habits that lead people to manifest given character strengths in given situations'.[104] Tonic strengths are those displayed on a consistent basis while phasic strengths are variable and situationally contingent.

Their initial step was to separate strengths and virtues and only allow strengths that meet 10 criteria. The 24 resulting strengths are categorized under six core moral virtues:[105]

- **wisdom and knowledge:** 'cognitive strengths that entail the acquisition and use of knowledge': creativity, curiosity, open-mindedness, love of learning, perspective;
- **courage:** 'emotional strengths that involve the exercise of will to accomplish goals in the face of opposition, external or internal': bravery, persistence, integrity, vitality;
- **humanity:** 'interpersonal strengths that involve tending and befriending others': love, kindness, social intelligence (includes emotional intelligence);
- **justice:** 'civic strengths that underlie healthy community life': citizenship, fairness, leadership;
- **temperance:** 'strengths that protect against excess': forgiveness and mercy, humility/modesty, prudence, self-regulation;
- **transcendence:** 'strengths that forge connections to the larger universe and provide meaning': appreciation of beauty and excellence, gratitude, hope, humour, spirituality .

Their book differentiates strengths of character from talents and abilities, examines situational conditions that enable or disable strengths, mentions the fulfilments and outcomes that flow from the exercise of character strengths. The virtues are not measured as they are too abstract, and strengths are measured through interviews and self-report questionnaires.

It is noted by the authors that in most cases reliable and valid methods exist to measure strengths as individual differences, with humility, modesty and bravery being noted as exceptions.[106]

The three-year study by 55 researchers, which culminated in *Character Strengths and Virtues: A handbook and classification*, also involved the creation of two valid measurement tools: the VIA Inventory of Strengths (VIA-IS) for adults, and the VIA Youth Survey.

Exploratory factor analysis on the results of scale scores for the VIA-IS suggests five strength factors:[107]

- **restraint:** fairness, humility, mercy, prudence;
- **intellect:** eg creativity, curiosity, love of learning, appreciation of beauty;
- **interpersonal:** eg kindness, love, leadership, teamwork, playfulness;
- **emotional:** eg bravery, hope, self-regulation, zest;
- **theological:** eg gratitude, spirituality.

The first three factors correspond to the Big Five personality factors of consciousness, openness and agreeableness, and emotional strengths may correspond to the opposite of neuroticism. However, theological strengths has no corresponding element in the Big Five.

Various research studies have tested character strengths, for instance research was undertaken on a new model of role behaviour in teams based on seven team roles theorized by the VIA Institute around character: idea creator, information gatherer, decision-maker, implementer, influencer, energizer, and relationship manager. These were found to relate positively to job satisfaction.[108] In another workplace study, which involved 686 participants, the character strength of perseverance was the strength most associated with work productivity and least associated with counter-productive work behaviour.[109]

Personality strengths

In 'Making sense of character strengths', Todd Kashdan suggests that 'Researchers and practitioners can use the term 'personality strengths' rather than character strengths to illustrate that positive psychology is simply building upon basic personality science.'[110] and that no mention of morality or virtue is needed.

He believes that:

> Strengths can be defined as dispositional qualities people possess that enable or promote well-being. The overarching category of personality traits includes Big Five traits, self-regulatory capacities, goal system orientations, and other individual differences. A subset of these personality traits, or scores on a particular pole of a personality trait (for neuroticism, lower scores reflect emotional stability), can then be classified as personality strengths.[111]

With this approach, personality strengths are derived from empirical, rather than subjective, definitions and would 'represent some combination of acquired knowledge and dispositional tendencies that act in ways to promote adjustment, adaptation, and excellence.'

Kashdan is careful to note that in some situations some personality strength traits may be maladaptive, and therefore unhelpful.

Strengths, character and coaching

In addition to the VIA inventory of strengths, other tools have been created to support individual and team development. Two examples are Strengthscope and CharacterScope.

Strengthscope enables self-awareness and supports personal development.[112] It uses a wheel with four segments:

- **emotional:** making sense of, expressing and managing emotions: self-confidence, resilience, optimism, enthusiasm, emotional control, courage;
- **relational:** establishing and maintaining productive relationships: collaboration, compassion, developing others, empathy, leading, persuasiveness, relationship building;
- **execution:** delivering results: decisiveness, efficiency, flexibility, initiative, results focus, self-improvement;
- **thinking:** gathering and using information to make decisions: strategic mindedness, detail orientation, critical thinking, creativity, common sense.

The first two clusters are people orientated and the second two are task orientated. The emotional and thinking clusters are internally orientated and the other two are externally orientated.

CharacterScope is designed to help people know themselves, develop themselves and learn to coach themselves.[113] It provides a three-step development journey for individuals to: discover their leadership strengths and gaps, decide which areas to focus their development while building the motivation and engagement required to be successful in doing so, and develop chosen strengths to focus on over a specific period.

The strengths framework combines 34 strengths into 10 factors across character and intelligence. Intelligence has four factors:

- **analytical:** quick mind, simplifies, thinks ahead, judgement;
- **practical:** sees opportunities, creates solutions, achievable, optimizes;
- **social and political:** perspective, insightful, connects, influential;
- **emotional and relationship:** self-awareness, other awareness, manages expectations, handles conflict.

The first two groups are orientated to task and the second two to people.

Character has six factors:

- **creativity:** curiosity, open-minded, originality;
- **courage:** self-belief, bravery, risk-taking;
- **energy:** zest, optimism, appetite;
- **drive:** resilience, perseverance, grip;
- **responsibility:** consistency, fairness, ownership;
- **restraint:** humility, self-regulation, prudence.

The first three groups are orientated to flow, for instance creativity, and the other three to being grounded, for instance restrained.

Mapping the 10 factors against each other gives nine leadership types. While CharacterScope can be used in conjunction with traditional coaching, an app supports self-coaching to develop selected strengths.

The importance of meaning and purpose and the developing understanding of human strengths will become increasingly critical in the workplace and beyond, as Kashdan writes: 'The study of human strengths is critically important. With psychology historically focused on deficits, weaknesses, and syndromes, there is great value in shifting to qualities that help people function well.'[114]

Highlights

The study of human beings can be undertaken at the following levels:

- ○ broad universalistic level: including our ability to learn language skills, to socialize, survive and reproduce;
- ○ individual particular level: our beliefs, values, attitudes, interests and motives;
- ○ individual unique level: our personality traits, cognitive and emotional intelligence.

- Various tools have been developed to help understand aspects of personality and intelligence for selection and development purposes.
- Socio-analytic theory suggests people try to balance getting along with others, getting ahead and finding meaning in their lives.
- A sense of meaning and purpose may be consciously important to people.
- People undertake impression management and are judged based on their reputation.
- Neuroplasticity allows us to develop our emotional and cognitive abilities.

- Character strengths are important considerations for leadership and development.

Leadership impact

Key themes that leaders should reflect on include:

- Understand the differences between beliefs, values, attitudes, interest and motives – this will help manage people in different situations.
- The differences between personality types and traits – how can you identify the various personalities of your teams?
- Impression management: Understand how people display initial impressions, how their reputations are formed, and how people actually behave.
- Socio-analytic theory: Work out the key drivers of people. How do they define meaning and purpose in their lives?
- Neuroplasticity and its impact on learning and development: Understand how your people have different and developing learning styles; this will impact the type and level of development activity within your organization.
- Understand your character strengths and select areas to develop.

People management recommendations

Actions to consider:

- Occupational psychology expertise: Ensure you have this capability either in-house or outsourced.
- Psychometric tools for selection: Not all tools are the same and therefore need to be carefully selected and used appropriately for maximum impact and effectiveness.
- Appropriately design courses for individual development: Take into account different learning styles, as well as the outcomes required from training and development.
- Coaching and mentoring: Use these to support the development of your people.
- Use a character strength tool for leadership development, consider integrating it into executive coaching.

Bias, stereotypes, group culture and decision-making

Introduction

The previous two chapters introduced the fundamental way biological and cultural evolution impact people's emotions and thoughts. In this chapter we add further elements that are key to helping you build an outstanding organization.

We look at how people think, and in particular at the faulty thinking that sometimes impacts our behaviour. We explore how this can lead to bias and stereotypes. Further, we explain how group culture evolves, and how decision-making takes place within these groups.

Understanding our faulty thinking helps us consider the efficacy and possible risks of our individual and group decision-making and is fundamental to successful leadership and management across cultures and to minimizing stereotypes that act as a barrier to building a more diverse and inclusive workforce.

Chapter summary

The following subjects are discussed in this chapter:

- **bias and stereotypes:**
  - discriminatory bias;
  - mirror neurons;
- **group culture:**
  - group development;

- in and out groups;
- decision-making;
- System 1 and System 2 thinking;
- procrastination.

Bias and stereotypes

Eric Kandel, a neuroscientist at Columbia University who received a Nobel Prize for his work on memory, estimated that 80 to 90 per cent of the work done in the mind is unconscious.[1] In *The Enigma of Reason*, Hugo Mercier and Dan Sperber write that 'human reason is both biased and lazy. Biased because it overwhelmingly finds justifications and arguments that support the reasoner's point of view; lazy because reason makes little effort to assess the quality of justifications and arguments it produces.'[2]

The brain has a range of unconscious strategies, for instance heuristics and biases, to help it work efficiently, and sometimes effectively. Some appear to be due to human evolution and others learnt from individual experience. They impact decision-making and social interaction. *Neuroscience for Leadership* explains that

> heuristics are experience-based processes for solving problems, often relying on trial and error. The term has been used in psychology for unconscious, instinctive or learned processes which are quick and tend to work in most cases but can lead to mistakes. Systematic errors are known as biases. Fallacies are mistakes in reasoning or belief, which may, in some cases, also be due to biases or heuristics.[3]

People Risk Management lists some common cognitive bias:

- **overconfidence:** overestimating positive outcomes;
- **loss aversion:** weighing losses greater than gains;
- **groupthink:** conforming to group beliefs;
- **anchoring bias:** relying to heavily on one piece of information;
- **confirmation bias:** searching for information to support existing beliefs;
- **illusion of control:** overestimating one's control over events;
- **planning fallacy:** underestimating execution problem;
- **sunk-cost fallacy:** sticking with decisions because of the cost already expended;
- **availability bias:** giving precedence to recently available information;
- **attentional bias:** focusing on prevalent and/or recurrent thoughts;

- **ambiguity bias:** dismiss alternatives if little or no information is available;
- **action bias:** tendency for action over inaction;
- **halo effect:** assigning confidence based on past success;
- **illusion of skill:** attributing poor outcomes to luck rather than lack of ability;
- **status quo bias:** wanting things to stay the same.[4]

Heuristics can be described as rules-of-thumb or educated guesses. Herbert Simon believed that people rely on heuristics because of their bounded rationality caused by the:

- amount of information they have;
- time they have to make decisions;
- cognitive limitations of their minds.[5]

This causes decisions to be pragmatic, satisficing rather than aiming to achieve an optimal decision.

In *The Enigma of Reason*, Mercier and Sperber note that humans perform a lot of inferences unconsciously and automatically, while intuitions are partially conscious. They note that in Kahneman's *Thinking Fast and Slow* intuition is contrasted with reasoning as if they are two different forms of inference, where reasoning is actually a kind of intuitive inference. They also suggest that '"reason" is a mechanism for intuitive inference about one kind of representation, namely reasons'.[6] Reason has two main functions: first, producing reasons to justify ideas and actions to build trust and cooperation; and second, to produce arguments to persuade others. Reason is both socially adapted and adaptive.

Discriminatory bias

In *Blind Spot*, Mahzarin Banaji and Anthony Greenwald document the results of various experiments undertaken using Implicit Association Tests (IAT). Over 14 million IATs had been completed by 2013, and with more than 20,000 new visitors accessing the test site each week, significant evidence has been collected that shows the 'dissociation between reflective egalitarianism and automatic preferences in attitudes involving race, sexual orientation, and age as well as skin colour, body weight, height, disability, and nationality'.[7]

In terms of ethnicity, almost 75 per cent of Americans who take the Race IAT on the internet or in laboratory studies reveal automatic White preference and this is now established as signalling discriminatory behaviour. 'It predicts discriminatory behaviour even among research participants who earnestly (and, we believe, honestly) espouse egalitarian beliefs. That last statement may sound like a self-contradiction, but it's an empirical truth.'[8] In addition, based on IAT results, 80 per cent of Americans have a strong automatic preference for the young over the old; and 75 per cent of men and 80 per cent of women display the gender stereotype of males being associated with work and females with family. Male and female respondents were both prepared to accept a reduced salary to have a male boss, and in selecting a partner nine IQ points were traded for a partner who was thinner than the higher IQ alternative.[9]

Stereotypes can evolve in ways that can be traced to changes in social and cultural circumstances. They can be implicit (unconscious) or explicit (conscious). Banaji and Greenwald discuss methods of trying to minimize the impact of hidden biases, for instance: the blinding method that seeks to remove information stimulus that may trigger bias; developing evidence-based guidelines to eliminate discretion from judgements that might otherwise afford opportunity for hidden bias; and conditioning using strong favourable associations with particular groups –although if not repeated these may only produce relatively temporary, elastic, changes.

In social categorization theory[10] it is understood that people have a tendency to categorize others along dimensions such as age, gender and ethnicity, and in that process tend to attribute certain characteristics to members of the groups and 'assume that people belonging to the same group have similar characteristics and those belonging to different groups have different characteristics.'[11] Social categorization may lead to prejudice and discrimination, as just dividing people into groups and labelling the groups is enough to trigger discriminatory behaviour. People naturally tend to associate with those who they categorize as similar to themselves and maintain social distance from those who are dissimilar.

The Neuroscience of Leadership Coaching suggests that

> unconscious bias is a consequence of the fast decision-making processes and development of a different kind of expertise. It can be described as the detection of familiar patterns and the creation of hypotheses about, for instance, events that happen repeatedly (known as schemas), types of people that we meet (our stereotypes) and tasks that we repeat regularly (our skills). This represents a form of historical expertise that we have gained partly from our own experience, but also from the experiences of our family, friends and society in general.[12]

Mirror neurons

While the focus of neuroscience research can be at the level of the individual, it is also undertaken in terms of its relevance at both group and organizational levels. At group level organizational neuroscience can help inform our understanding of biases and intergroup relationships, for instance 'the discovery of the mirror neuron system, a group of specialized neurons that mirrors the actions and behaviour of others, could help shed light on the neural basis of social interactions in organizations.'[13] At the organizational level, research can focus on structural phenomena, the social and political organization and change.

Diversity researchers have identified elements of surface diversity such as race, gender, age, and deep diversity such as education, values, personality, that differentiate people and found that 'mirror neurons could help explicate discriminatory behaviour and to some extent, they could represent the deep causes of discriminatory behaviour because they reside in the deep-brain structures of the limbic system.'[14]

Neuroscience has shown that the brain engages one cluster of neurons when we think about ourselves, the ventromedial prefrontal cortex (vmPFC), and another cluster when thinking about other people, and that when we think of those we identify with more, other in-group members, we use the cluster that relates to how we think about ourselves so that we can anticipate behaviour.[15]

People tend to show more empathy for in-group members than for out-group members. However, people can change. Therefore,

> diversity initiatives in organizations can be successful when people show empathy and refrain from dehumanizing others. Diversity in organizations implies the 'coexistence' of individuals who may perceive some members as in group members and others as out group members. Hence, the temptation for potential dehumanization of those who are perceived as out group members should not be neglected.[16]

Members of in-groups mirror the behaviour displayed by others in their group to out-group members, therefore greater personal familiarity with those who are categorized as different combined with positive behaviour towards them by in-group members help to reduce prejudice and discrimination.

Conscious and unconscious bias can lead to stereotyping and this is enacted in society by individuals and amplified by group membership. The in- and out-group effect will be explored further in the next section in relation to the culture of groups.

Group culture

It is important to understand group culture and decision-making as it impacts the ability of leaders to build an outstanding workforce in various ways. For instance, groupthink[17] and stereotyping respectively impact the quality of decisions and the ability of organizations to change organizational culture and create a more diverse and inclusive workforce.

Group development

Group development has been said to adopt the following pattern: forming, when the group comes together; storming, as the roles within the group become defined and agreed through the social interaction of group members;

norming, where the group adopts accepted behaviours; and performing, where the group starts working together.[18] A final part has been added to the pattern, adjourning, for when the group disbands, and this occurrence may be planned or unplanned.[19]

In *The Psychology of Behaviour at Work*, Furnham defines groups as having four characteristics:

- They are composed of more than two people involved in social interaction, who must be able to influence each other's beliefs and behaviours.

- They share common goals on certain issues – agreed goals, objectives and targets. Goal-sharing is an achievement of any group as much as a defining characteristic.

- They have a relatively stable structure – rules and roles that endure over time and across different social situations.

- They openly perceive and recognize themselves as being a stable group.[20]

All teams follow this definition of groups, but not all groups are teams. Groups only become teams when there is a reliance on each member to achieve a specific shared goal.

In 'Great teams are about personalities not just skills' the authors note that personality makes a difference to the role people play in teams, how they interact with the rest of the team and whether your values are aligned with the teams. These factors are psychological in nature and has a significant impact on team performance.[21]

In *The Social Psychology of Organizations*, Joanna Wilde introduces the network theory of human connection that supports collaboration. This includes three structures:

- **Bonding:** The creation of long-term connections on an individual and group basis.

- **Bridging:** Multiple, short and role-based, where membership is based on shared interests and identities but itself is not interpersonal; for instance, membership of a professional body.

- **Brokerage:** Leveraging different networks through boundary-spanning.[22]

In *Organizational Culture and Leadership*, Schein and Schein list twelve aspects of organizations and groups:

- observed behavioural regularities when people interact;
- climate;
- formal rituals and celebrations;
- espoused values;
- formal philosophy;
- group norms;
- rules of the game;
- identity and images of self;

- embedded skills;
- habits of thinking, mental models or linguistic paradigms;
- shared meanings;
- 'root metaphors' or integrating symbols.[23]

Group culture is defined as:

> the accumulated shared learning of the group as it solves its problems of
> external adaptation and internal integration; which has worked well enough to
> be considered valid and, therefore, to be taught to new members as the correct
> way to perceive, think, feel, and behave in relation to those problems.[24]

Accumulated shared learning is observed in beliefs, values and behavioural norms that become tacit in nature.

As groups grow and experience success, a common language may emerge in addition to shared cognitive and affective states and associated behaviours. Group culture can be considered in terms of group structural stability; depth of basic assumptions which may be unconscious; breadth of appearance across the group's activities; and the degree to which it is integrated.

In *The Social Leap*, Von Hippel states that 'the contents of our mind are a product of our genes, our environment, and our personal choices. Our genes nudge us in certain directions – sometimes this nudge might more aptly be described as a shove – but we make the decisions that determine the trajectory of our lives',[25] and notes that evolutionary pressure toward individualism and competition contrasts with our participation in groups. The getting ahead versus getting along.

In *The Enigma of Reason*, Mercier and Sperber note that

> in problem solving, the performance of a group tends to be much better than
> the average individual performance of the group's members and, in some cases,
> even better than the individual performance of any of its members: people can
> find together solutions that none of them could find individually.[26]

However, reason has been positioned as 'a mechanism for the pursuit of individual benefits. An individual stands to benefit from having her justification accepted by others and from producing arguments that influence others.'[27]

Decisions made in groups are often likely to produce better outcomes than those made by individuals, which is not necessarily the same as a creative process where the creative value of individuals can be significant.

In and out groups

Ethologists, who examine human behaviour and social organization from a biological perspective, have studied the acquired behavioural patterns involved in identity formation and found that there is less permanence in humans compared to other species. The 'tendency to prefer members of one's own group emerges early in infancy and is in large part based on familiarity... it serves to align the child with those who are like her and therefore more likely to offer safety.'[28] This is an early building block of identity formation, and 'identity is deeply bound to the characteristics that are true of 'us' as a group and differentiated from 'them'.[29] Once children have formed categories that allow them to identify whether someone is 'in' or 'out', the ground is laid for stereotyping to occur.

Research shows that even if the basis of group creation is meaningless, two groups will allocate resources more favourably to members of their own group. For instance, when researchers simply

> create an arbitrary connection between a person and a group and provide the mere suggestion that there are others who lack this connection to self,... the psychology of 'us' and 'them' rushes in to fill the void. Lines are drawn, whether or not the basis for the groups makes any sense, and discrimination follows.[30]

Within organizations, formal groups have defined structures, membership, reporting relationships, feedback mechanisms and goals. Informal groups come into existence for social reasons such as shared interests and friendships and develop their own norms of behaviour. The

> informal organization emerges to fulfil those needs neglected or ignored by the formal system... The composition, structure and operation of informal groups will in part be determined by the formal arrangements that exist in the company. These provide the context within which social relationships are established and can take place.[31]

In *Minds Make Societies*, it is noted that people use a social exchange heuristic to subconsciously assess reciprocal cooperation. For alliances to emerge, all participants must hold certain representations:

> First, they must represent a certain goal, such that it is better obtained through joint effort than individually. Second, each individual must expect that the other members have a roughly similar representation of the goal. Otherwise members of the alliance would not expect coordinated effort from others. Third, one must discount one's own costs in working for that common effort. Coalitional work, like all collective action, requires behaviour that may seem altruistic, that is, conferring a benefit to others at one's own cost. But the cost is offset by expected future gains from the collective venture – whether that expectation is warranted or not. Fourth, one must expect that others, too, will discount their effort. Fifth, one should expect others to have the expectation about oneself. Finally, one should represent all costs (or benefits) by the rival coalitions as benefits (or costs) to oneself so that one is motivated to increase (or decrease) them.[32]

As previously noted, the results of research suggest that the human mind uses categories to aid thinking, and that once formed categories become our framework for normal prejudgement based on prejudged attributes, this is also the case with regard to people.[33] Almost every stereotype is true to some extent but also partly false. Group stereotypes consist of traits that are more negative than those attributable to friends who are part of that particular group. Members of in-groups don't stereotype fellow members, but those who lack their societies' default characteristics are likely to be stereotyped by others and by themselves.

Unfavourable stereotypes may cause people to behave in ways that conform to the stereotype, which can be damaging. For instance, elderly people who internalize stereotypes of old age are at greater risk of declining health; women who internalize gender stereotypes are at risk of underperforming in subjects such as science, technology, engineering and mathematics; and ethnic minorities are at risk of not living up to their academic potential. In addition, research has showed that members of disadvantaged groups can play a role in maintaining their own disadvantage through accepting stereotypes that undermine them.[34]

It is noted by Mihaly Csikszentmihalyi in the *Evolving Self* that three sources of illusion stand between us and a clear perception of reality: distortions due to the genetic instructions that were once necessary to our survival, but are often in conflict with present reality; the distortions of the culture in which we were born; and the distortions that result from the emergence of the self as a separate entity making its own claims on the mind. 'Unless we understand how these forces shape the way we think and act, it is difficult to gain control over consciousness.'[35]

Understanding how we have developed as individuals helps us consider what may have impacted our culturally acquired system of beliefs and values, and how we might be constructing our unique view of the external environment and the situations and people that are present. In addition, it is important to understand that it is possible to modify our beliefs and values, thereby constructing a different view of the world. This empowers us to be ambitious in our thinking about developing ourselves and others so that our decisions are less subject to bias that creates inequality and limits individual and organizational potential.

The quality of decision-making is key to successful outcomes. However, we have already seen that various types of bias impinge on the quality of individual and group decision-making and our degree of rationality when making decisions is examined further below.

Decision-making

Our evolved mechanisms enable humans to cope with and learn from evolutionarily new situations. Successful patterns of problem-solving behaviour are repeated and become automated and deployed quickly without conscious thought.[36] Most decisions are based on our experience of previous decision-making outcomes and therefore, as our experience increases our ability to make accurate predictions increases which in turn leads to the use our fast system of thinking. This development involves neuroplastic changes in the brain.

People make decisions in a number of ways, and in *The Psychology of Behaviour at Work* Furnham summarizes some of the differences as follows: fast versus slow, risk versus risk-averse, empirical versus intuitive, rule based versus rule breaking, people versus things, individual versus group.[37]

While people may aim to make rational decisions based on full information, they often exhibit bounded rationality, where the decision is pragmatic and just good enough. Complexity, time, the availability of information, intelligence and personality traits can all impact the efficacy of decision-making. Groups are said, overall, to make better decisions than individuals and Furnham notes that:

> individual heuristics and biases appear to operate with equal force in groups; group discussion often amplifies pre-existing tendencies; groups usually perform somewhat better than average individuals, particularly if an appointed leader encourages all group members to express an opinion; the best member of a group often outperforms the group, and brainstorming is most effective when conducted by several people independently, rather than in a group session.[38]

Conscious processing has been equated with rational thought and unconscious processing with irrational thought – but this is not the case. In *The Neuroscience of Leadership Coaching*, the authors note that the difference between conscious and other-than-conscious processing is not dependent on one area of the brain that is active when we are conscious of our actions and inactive when we are not conscious of our actions:

> consciousness is not a place in the brain. Instead, it appears that activity in parts of our brains can result in conscious thought at some times but not at others... This implies that conscious and unconscious acts are based on activation in similar neural networks, and, therefore, that there is no major qualitative difference between the types of information that our conscious and unconscious behaviours can access.[39]

In addition, they state that 'It is important here to emphasize that the way that neurones code the information that is used in decision-making is the same whether the decision-making process is conscious or unconscious, slow or fast.'[40]

System 1 and System 2 thinking

In *Thinking Fast and Slow*, Daniel Kahneman describes two metaphors of thinking, System 1 and System 2. 'System 1 operates automatically and quickly, with little or no effort and no sense of voluntary control'[41] and 'System 2 allocates attention to the effortful mental activities that demand it, including complex computations. The operations of System 2 are often associated with the subjective experience of agency, choice, and concentration'.[42] Kahneman notes that people identify with System 2 'the conscious, reasoning self that has beliefs, makes choices, and decides what to think about and what to do',[43] while System 1 is 'effortlessly originating impressions and feelings that are the main sources of the explicit beliefs and deliberate choices of System 2'.[44] System 2 is creating order to the complex patterns of ideas generated by System 1. However, System 2 is not a 'paragon of rationality'.[45]

Kahneman states that the test of rationality is not whether a person's beliefs and preferences are reasonable, but whether they are internally consistent. However,

> the definition of rationality as coherence is impossibly restrictive, it demands adherence to rules of logic that a finite mind is not able to implement. Reasonable people cannot be rational by that definition, but they should not be branded as irrational for that reason. Irrational is a strong word, which connotes impulsivity, emotionality, and a stubborn resistance to reasonable argument.[46]

While people may not be irrational, they often need help to make more accurate judgements and better decisions. In their book *Nudge*, Richard Thaler and Cass Sunstein give examples of this. They discuss the libertarian paternalism that produces incentives and nudges that are consciously designed to 'move people in directions that will make their lives better'.[47] They adopt the terms Automatic System and Reflective System to describe System 1 and System 2 thinking respectively, with the Automatic System being uncontrolled, effortless, associative, fast, unconscious, skilled, a more instinctive gut-reaction and not involving word thinking; and the Reflective System being more controlled, effortful, deductive, slow, self-aware, rule-following deliberate and self-conscious.

System 1 is constantly interpreting the world and determining reactions in terms of our thoughts and actions and more often than not its intuitive guidance is accurate. Its skill is based on regular practice and feedback within a common environment but there is no warning signal when it is no longer reliable, and when passed to System 2 it cannot distinguish between a heuristic and skilled response. This is how errors and biases slip through the net.

What can be done about biases? How can we improve judgements and decisions, both our own and those of the institutions that we serve and that serve us? Kahneman says that little can be achieved without a considerable investment of effort. 'System 1 is not readily educable... I have improved only in my ability to recognize situations in which errors are likely.'[48] His suggestion is that one way to block errors is to recognize the signs that you are in a cognitive minefield, slow down, and ask for reinforcement from System 2. Unfortunately, this sensible procedure is least likely to be applied when it is needed most. We would all like to have a warning bell that rings loudly whenever we are about to make a serious error, but no such bell is available.[49]

Organizations are noted as being better at avoiding errors as the speed of decision-making is slower and 'it is much easier to identify a minefield when you observe others wandering into it than when you are about to do so. Observers are less cognitively busy and more open to information than actors.'[50]

In *The Neuroscience of Organizational Behavior*, Beugré notes that, when making a decision, if the value of the outcome is known but the risk associated with the outcome cannot be calculated there is risk ambiguity, and the ambiguity involved in a decision appears to be associated with the insula, which is located in the prefrontal cortex (PFC). He refers to research which shows that for individuals tolerant of ambiguity, their decisions involved the parasympathetic systems including the lateral anterior insula, which is associated with gut-feel. For individuals who were intolerant of ambiguity, decisions with missing information were dependent on processing in the PFC, thus activating the logical, conscious decision-making processes. In addition, individuals who are risk-averse show greater activity in the amygdala, anterior insula and anterior cingulate than individuals who are more risk-seeking. It would therefore appear that decision-making processes will differ depending on our tolerance for ambiguity.

Procrastination

Procrastination, delaying decisions or tasks, may be due to us privileging our current self over our future self. We have 'a bias that favors a short period of intense joy over a long period of moderate happiness. The mirror image of the same bias makes us fear a much longer period of moderate pain.'[51] In addition, we tend to prefer a long period of mild unpleasantness if the end will be better and to give up on an opportunity for a long happy period if it is likely to have a bad ending. *The Neuroscience of Leadership Coaching* states that:

> individual differences in delayed gratification have been associated with the degree of connectivity between neural systems – the ventromedial prefrontal cortex and the ventral striatum… this suggests that self regulation is required to reduce the discrepancy between current and future rewards.[52]

An understanding of how we think informs leadership as it gives leaders an understanding of how they and others are processing information. *Neuroscience for Leadership* lists a number of key functions of the PFC executive function:

- controlling and managing thought processes such as attention, motivation, working memory and reasoning;
- task flexibility;
- planning and execution, usually of movement;
- managing 'higher' cognitive processes like flexibility of thinking, impulse control, concept formation, abstract thinking and creativity;
- decision-making, error correction or troubleshooting;
- dealing with new situations or ones you are not well rehearsed at; that is, ones that are not habits or automatic responses underpinned by default pathways in your brain;
- responding to dangerous events and overcoming ingrained behaviour patterns or resisting temptation.[53]

Having reviewed the challenges we create for ourselves through our faulty thinking we will move our attention to motivation, which is an area of leadership that is fundamental for our understanding of organizational behaviour, for aligning individual purpose and meaning with organizational purpose and meaning, and for building an outstanding workforce.

Highlights

- Our thinking is not always as rational as we might expect and hope; biases and stereotypes can be both conscious and unconscious.
- Decision-making is fraught with bias and heuristics. It is difficult to eradicate unconscious bias.
- Mirror neurons can contribute to discriminatory behaviour.
- Group culture can encompass overt and covert bias and stereotyping.
- System 1 and System 2 are metaphors for cognitive processing that is fast and slow; they have been identified with the limbic and neocortical areas of the brain.

Leadership impact

Key themes that leaders should reflect on include:

- implications of unconscious bias, particularly during the recruitment and development processes – the impact could be costly and damaging to the organization;

- the nature and implications of decision-making errors – various types of bias can be contributory factors;
- understanding the characteristics of group dynamics can help us understand team dynamics better. This is particularly important when there are managerial and team changes and when leading agile and virtual teams.

People management recommendations

Actions to consider:

- Review the hiring process to ensure that for the points at which bias is possible, design minimizes the possibility of bias.
- Consider using additional data points during recruitment and selection; psychometric tests can be helpful, also case studies or scenarios will demonstrate individuals' skills more effectively than just relying on interviews.
- Appropriately designed courses or workshops can be used to address unconscious bias.
- Focus on key decision-making points in workflows and design gates that mitigate risks caused by heuristics and bias.
- Coaching and mentoring provision can improve management of teams.
- Teambuilding training, including group dynamics, will improve team performance.

Motivation 04

Introduction

This chapter examines historical and contemporary literature on motivation. It is important to understand what motivates people and this knowledge will inform our analysis of employee engagement, employee experience, employee value proposition and employer brand in Chapter 14. Building a motivated workforce is essential to achieving outstanding performance.

People's motivation for choosing to do something and the effort they are prepared to expend in doing it has been a source of much research and debate. For instance, where does the drive come from that compels and sustains directed action? How does this differ between one person and another, and why?

The contemporary discourse around employee engagement, employee experience and personal purpose and meaning is not based on new theory; on the contrary, our fundamental drivers have been the subject of much research and discussion. An understanding of this background is fundamental to creating an employee experience and employer value proposition that helps win the *war for talent*[1] and creates a workplace where employees can flourish.

Chapter summary

The following subjects are discussed in this chapter:

- **overview of motivation theories;**
- **need theories:**
  - Maslow's Hierarchy;
  - Alderfer's ERG;
  - Herzberg's Hygiene Factors;
  - McLelland's Need Theory;
  - McGregor's Theory X and Theory Y;

- o Self-Determination Theory;
- o Drive Theory;
- **process theories:**
  - o Reinforcement Theory;
  - o Goal Theory;
  - o Equity Theory;
  - o Expectancy Theory;
- **motivation and financial reward;**
- **neuroscience and motivation;**
- **our human and chimp brain;**
- **mindset;**
- **flow;**
- **motivation, job satisfaction and personality;**
- **motivation and culture.**

Overview of motivation theories

Many of the factors that may influence motivation make intuitive sense, for instance: positively reinforcing performance, creating supportive environments, setting clear and attainable work goals, providing appropriate resources, and making sure there is a fit between employee and employer values and motives. However, motivation is also dependent on individual aspects such as:

ability – job knowledge, skills, disposition – stable traits, beliefs and values, affective mood state; and job context, for instance 'nature of the task/job, physical environment, implicit and explicit rewards – reinforcers, wider corporate culture and social norms.[2]

There have been attempts to group theories of motivation and then assess their predictive ability around satisfaction, productivity and turnover, for instance theories around *content* – why people work, and theories around *process* – what factors influence the ongoing willingness to work. Alternatively, theories could be considered as falling into one of six types:

- **Need theories:** For example, Maslow's Hierarchy, Alderfer's Existence, Relatedness, Growth (ERG) Theory, McClelland's Achievement Theory and Herzberg's Two-Factor Theory.

- **Task characteristics theories:** Those with high-growth needs perform highly and are satisfied when they find work meaningful, feel responsible for it and receive feedback.

- **Goal setting theory:** It has been established that clear and difficult goals lead to higher levels of people productivity but does not inform levels of satisfaction, absenteeism and turnover.

- **Reinforcement theories:** These have established the impact of the quality and quantity of output, persistence of effort and levels of absenteeism, but not levels of satisfaction and turnover.

- **Equity theory:** This is strongest in its predictive capability around levels of absenteeism and turnover but weak when predicting people productivity.

- **Expectancy theory:** This has an established track record of explaining productivity, absenteeism and turnover but assumes that people have limited discretion over their decision-making.[3]

It is valuable to consider some of these major theories of motivation prior to examining the findings of literature on employee engagement and employee experience in Chapter 14.

Need theories

The need, or content, theories of motivation examined here include Maslow's Hierarchy, Alderfer's ERG Model, Herzberg et al's Hygiene Factors, McLelland' s Three-Need theory, McGregor's Theory X and Theory Y, Ryan and Deci's Self-Determination Theory and Lawrence and Nohria's Drive Theory.

Maslow's Hierarchy

Maslow's theory set out a five-level hierarchy of needs.[4] As a lower-order need is satisfied, the need for the next higher-order need is activated. This is usually represented visually as a pyramid. Starting at the base of Maslow's pyramid, these needs are as follows:

- **physiological:** the basic needs of shelter and sustenance;
- **safety:** the need for freedom from threats of physical and mental harm;
- **social:** the need to belong, to be accepted and included;
- **esteem:** self-respect ,and respect and recognition from others;
- **self-actualization:** self-fulfilment and maximization of potential.

The first three needs are known as *deficiency needs* that impact people's physical and psychological health. The last two needs are known as *growth needs* and relate to people's ability to develop and fulfil their potential.

While simple and intuitive, Maslow's theory has not found significant support from research. The theory that one need must be satisfied before the next one becomes motivational, that once a need is met it loses its motivational power, that the order of needs must be followed and that the overall model is universally applicable have not been proven. However, in *The Hope Circuit* Martin Seligman credits the work of Maslow as an original example of positive psychology[5] that was ahead of its time. He acknowledged Maslow's use of positive psychology, saying it was iconoclastic but the qualitative enquiry of the humanistic psychology movement lacked rigour.[6]

Alderfer's ERG

Alderfer[7] suggested three needs, any one of which can be triggered at any point in time:

- **existence:** aligned with Maslow's physiological and safety needs;
- **relatedness:** aligned with Maslow's social needs;
- **growth:** aligned with Maslow's esteem and self-actualization needs.

As this theory is less operationally prescriptive, it is a better fit to the results of research that suggests people seek to satisfy certain needs in a work context.

Herzberg's Hygiene Factors

Another need theory was put forward by Herzberg and others,[8] who believed that job dissatisfaction is caused by maintenance, or hygiene, factors, and job satisfaction is caused by motivation factors:

- **maintenance/hygiene:** working conditions, salary, personal life; interpersonal relations; company policies and administration, supervision, security and status;
- **motivation factors:** work itself, responsibility, growth potential, achievement, recognition, advancement.

They believe that when the hygiene/maintenance factors, which are potential dissatisfiers, are unfavourable then job dissatisfaction results. However, when they are favourable, the conditions for job satisfaction exist. While the potential dissatisfiers are related to the environmental context of work, the potential satisfiers are related to the nature of the work itself and its outcomes. If the motivators are favourable then job satisfaction occurs, and if they are absent a neutral state is experienced.

Unfortunately, there are significant doubts about the validity of the theory. Research has shown that both factors can lead to satisfaction or dissatisfaction, personality traits impact both states and some question the desirability of job enrichment and empowerment. Job enrichment refers to expanding the nature of a job, for instance through increasing variety in its content, control and responsibility, and empowerment relating to leaders sharing power and responsibility with others.[9]

McLelland's Need Theory

McLelland's Need Theory, also known as the Three-Needs Theory, focused on three motives:

- **Need for achievement (N-Ach):** The desire to excel in relation to a set of standards. It is the drive to succeed.
- **Need for affiliation (N-Aff):** The desire for close personal relationships.
- **Need for power (N-Pow):** The desire to be influential and affect an organization.[10]

His research found that those in senior management positions had a higher need for power and lower need for affiliation.

McGregor's Theory X and Theory Y

McGregor proposed contrasting views of workforce motivation, which were based on the assumptions about typical workers' approaches to their work, associated with styles of management.[11]

In Theory X, typical workers:

- have an inherent dislike of work, are lazy and avoid responsibility;
- lack intelligence, are self-interested and lack ambition;
- are individually goal oriented and work solely for a sustainable income;
- favour security over achievement.

The suggested style of management focuses on:

- individual goals;
- rewards or punishments as motivators;
- a hard approach: an 'us' versus 'them' culture, with close supervision, intimidation, and immediate punishment – this approach may breed resentment;
- a soft approach: less strict, lenient – this approach could breed entitlement.

In Theory Y, typical workers:

- feel work is a natural activity, are internally motivated, enjoys their jobs;
- do not need close supervision, may seek and accept responsibility, are self-directed – but are still required to obtain approvals;

- are one of the most valuable assets to the company;
- have potential – many not just a few.

The suggested style of management:

- lacks threats of punishment;
- is more of a personal relationship;
- encourages more discussion and more flexibility.

Some authors have looked at designing jobs so that they are motivating from a social and technical perspective, a sociotechnical systems view.[12] Job Facet Theory[13] suggests that the psychological states of experienced meaningfulness, experienced responsibility and knowledge of results are relevant to work. Also, that skill variety, task identity and task significance contribute to feelings of meaningfulness and autonomy, and that feedback, direct and frequent, respectively relate to feelings of responsibility and knowledge of results.[14]

Self-Determination Theory

Theories around intrinsic motivation appeared in 1975 in a book of the same name[15] and were discussed in *The Psychology of Self-Determination* in 1980.[16] This needs-based theory is

> particularly concerned with how social-contextual factors support or thwart people's thriving through the satisfaction of their basic psychological needs for competence, relatedness, and autonomy. Although the theory is psychological, research has also given attention to biological underpinnings of these psychological processes and places them in an evolutionary perspective.[17]

The authors of *Self-Determination Theory* believe that organizational environments should be designed to allow these innate needs to flourish.[18]

Self-Determination Theory (SDT) is

> centrally concerned with the social conditions that facilitate or hinder human flourishing. The theory examines how biological, social, and cultural conditions either enhance or undermine the inherent human capacities for psychological growth, engagement, and wellness, both in general and in specific domains and endeavours.[19]

This needs-based theory suggests that we have three universal needs:

- **competency:** efficacy, self-efficacy;
- **autonomy:** self-regulation;
- **relatedness:** belonging, self-esteem.

Organizational environments should be designed to allow these innate needs to flourish.

An extension of SDT is Cognitive Evaluation Theory, which contends that two psychological needs underlie intrinsic motivation: the need for self-determination, and the need for competence.

In *Drive: The surprising truth about what motivates us*, Daniel Pink notes a gap between what science can prove through valid and reliable research, and what business does through its carrot and stick motivators. This book suggests the introduction of Motivation 3.0, which is based on three essential elements:

- **autonomy:** self-direction;
- **mastery:** abilities are matched to challenges, to enable the experience of flow (see the explanation below);
- **purpose:** a sense of existential meaning.[20]

It builds on Motivation 1.0, based on survival, and Motivation 2.0, based on external rewards and punishments. Pink summarizes that sticks, 'traditional "if then" rewards can... extinguish intrinsic motivation, diminish performance, crush creativity, and crowd out good encourage unethical behaviour, create addictions, and foster short-term thinking'.[21] In *The Chimp Paradox*, Steve Peters writes, 'in a civilized society the stick is replaced by carrot, benchmarks and consequences'.[22]

Motivation 2.0 is said to be associated with Type X behaviour, which focuses on extrinsic rewards. The proposed Motivation 3.0 focuses on intrinsic motivation, or Type I behaviour. Autonomy gives people control over planning and delivering tasks. Mastery gives people a feeling of satisfaction as they improve their understanding, and a desire to develop despite the dedication required and difficulties faced. Purpose relates to the overall reason why an organization exists and also the fundamental purpose of the individual. Therefore, if organizations can allow employees some autonomy in their work, the opportunity to develop professionally and personally, and the purpose statement and actions of the organization are aligned with the individual's sense of purpose, the employee should be motivated to high performance.

In *The Human Quest for Meaning*, Paul Wong notes that 'the ability to integrate both humanistic–existential theories and the social–personality processes makes SDT a very powerful theory in providing the mechanisms for meaningful and authentic living'.[23] As the authors of *Motivation, Meaning and Wellness* write, 'the meaning making process is intrinsic to our nature and for us to create a coherent life course'.[24]

Drive Theory

In *Driven: How human nature shapes our choices*, Lawrence and Nohria discuss their need theory of motivation.[25] This includes four factors that drive human behaviour: the drives to acquire, defend, bond and compre-hend/learn:

- **Drive to acquire:** Refers to the natural tendency human beings have to acquire goods that improve their well-being. For example, working can be a means for people to acquire goods they value. The drive to acquire is relative, and people tend not to have enough of the goods they value.

- **Drive to defend:** Rooted in the basic fight-or-flight response. The drive to acquire and the drive to defend could be related to existence needs. For example, people strive to acquire the resources that will help them satisfy their basic needs. The drive to defend could refer to safety needs that help people protect themselves against events that could physically or psychologically harm them.

- **Drive to bond:** Similar to social needs in Maslow's Hierarchy of Needs, relatedness needs in Alderfer's ERG Theory, or the need for affiliation in McClelland's Three-Needs Theory. Human beings are social animals and strive to be included in social groups and connect with others.

- **Drive to comprehend:** Pushes humans to collect information, assess the needs of a situation, examine the environment, and make observations about explanatory ideas and theories to appease curiosity and make sound judgements. It is similar to Maslow's self-actualization needs and Alderfer's growth needs. McClelland' needs for power and achievement could be included in the drive to comprehend.[26]

Process theories

The process theories of motivation examined here include Reinforcement Theory, Goal Theory, Equity Theory and Expectancy Theory.

Reinforcement Theory

Reinforcement theories relate responses to a stimulus. Behavioural Modi-fication and Social Learning Theory are two examples.

Behavioural Modification Theory introduces contingent reinforcement and dictates that certain rewards or punishments will elicit particular behav-iours regardless of an individual's needs or values. Given the above discus-sion around need theories, it can be argued that this approach is at best simplistic.

Social Learning Theory takes into consideration individual needs, values and feelings of equity and therefore the mediating effect of cognitive pro-cesses when contingent reinforcement is introduced. The values and atti-tudes of workers perceived as role models will impact the perceptions of job satisfaction for those observing them and 'the more quickly reinforcement is given after a response, the more effective it becomes'.[27]

Goal Theory

Goal Theory relates to the impact of goal setting on job performance. Goal setting is the process of developing, negotiating and formalizing the targets or objectives that an employee is required to attain. According to Edwin Locke, goal setting has four motivational mechanisms:

- directing actions by focusing on what is relevant;
- regulating effort and motivating action;
- increasing persistence – the effort expended on a task over an extended period of time;
- developing strategies and action plans – setting goals is followed by formulating plans to attain them.[28]

The success of goal setting in motivation, and therefore behaviour, is mediated by the specificity and difficulty of the goal, acceptance and commitment to the goal, and feedback. The degree of positive impact derived from feedback is dependent on its quality, frequency and honesty.

Equity Theory

Equity Theory is based on the views of John Adams. He assumes that people make comparisons between their position and those around them, and then seek to ensure their perceived position relative to others in the organization is equitable. This comparison is likely to consider both the input of ability and discretionary effort, and the attributable outcomes in terms of financial reward, benefits, development and progression. It is a subjective process that can be influenced by personality factors.[29]

The three possible outcomes are a perception of under-reward inequity, a perception of over-reward inequity, or a perception of equitable reward. In situations of perceived inequity people will tend to respond by behaviourally increasing or decreasing inputs, raising or lowering outputs and/or psychologically modifying the perceptions of their own and/or others performance.

Research has in most cases supported Equity Theory. It is closely associated with Jerald Greenberg's Organizational Justice Theory, which looks at the decision-making process behind outcomes: procedural justice; distributive justice – the logistical process of delivering outcomes; and interactional justice – the way the outcomes are communicated.[30]

In the workplace, fairness is an important 'yardstick that employees use to assess outcome distribution, formal procedures, or interpersonal treatment in organizations'[31] and justice sensitivity can be considered at the individual level and group level. In *The Neuroscience of Organizational Behavior*, Beugré notes that neuroscientific research on fairness shows that people tend to punish those who act unfairly toward others, an altruistic punishment.[32]

Another aspect of motivation relates to the absolute value an individual derives from particular outcomes, the relative contribution of this value to a position of perceived equity or inequity and therefore the degree to which they are satisfied by outcomes relative to their colleagues.

Expectancy Theory

Expectancy Theory is based on Victor Vroom's view that people are rational in considering how much input to deliver based on their view of likely outcome scenarios. This theory suggests that motivation is the result of three different beliefs that people hold:

- **expectancy:** that one's effort will result in desired levels of performance;
- **instrumentality:** that one's performance will be rewarded;
- **valence:** the perceived value of the reward.[33]

For instance, if an employee *expects* that combining their ability and effort with the internal and external work environment will result in desired levels of performance, they will have high expectations of performance and are likely to apply the necessary discretionary effort. If they do not believe they have the requisite ability and/or that the internal and/or the external environmental conditions are supportive of the desired outcome, then discretionary effort may be withheld. Even when all conditions are favourable then it is important that the employee believes that their performance will be instrumental in obtaining an expected reward. Finally, that the reward will have valence, which must satisfy the right level of perceived value.

Motivation becomes the product of a multiplicative effect across all three factors, and as such if zero is ascribed to any one factor then perceived motivation will also be zero. The basic theory was expanded by Porter and Lawler,[34] who added intrinsic and extrinsic motivation to the concept of valence. As noted in SDT, intrinsic motivation is the satisfaction gained from undertaking work itself and extrinsic motivation is the satisfaction gained from rewards received for undertaking work. The impact of expectancy and instrumentality has been supported by research, but the contribution of valence and the multiplicative effect has not.

Extrinsic motivation includes pay and other financial benefits, and some of the thinking around the motivational power of financial reward is examined below.

Motivation and financial reward

A meta-analysis of over ninety studies found a very weak correlation between salary and job satisfaction, also that employees earning salaries in the top half of their data range reported similar levels of job satisfaction to those earning salaries in the bottom half.[35] The same result has been found by Gallup in their work on employee engagement. Employment engagement does not vary significantly by pay level.

With regard to the motivational power of money, in *The Psychology of Behaviour at Work* Furnham noted that it is a great motivator for those who need or value it enough, that it is most effective when it has noticeable impact, and that there is there is a direct link to performance. He also notes four factors that impact the power of financial reward to satisfy the recipient:

- **Adaptation:** The initial positive impact of a pay rise or bonus wears off quickly.

- **Comparison:** As wealth increases, the comparison group changes and people find there is always someone wealthier.

- **Alternatives:** As wealth increases, the marginal utility of money declines and other aspects of life become more valuable.

- **Worry:** As wealth increases, people tend to worry less about money problems and transfer their focus onto other areas of their lives.[36]

Interestingly, according to Cognitive Evaluation Theory, the introduction of an extrinsic reward for a job previously undertaken for its own sake can reduce the motivation to perform it. 'The "undermining effect'" or "motivation crowding out effect" is the tendency for external rewards to reduce the motivation to accomplish a task one does voluntarily. The undermining effect has implications for work motivation.'[37] Therefore, money may serve as a demotivator under certain circumstances

A distinction can be made between equity, equality and need relating to outcomes. Equity considers proportional distribution, equality emphasizes even distribution and need implies that the outcomes should be distributed according to recipients' needs.[38]

There are leadership implications exemplified by debates and aspirations around the gender pay gap, which does not focus on equal pay for the same role but instead looks at the average level of pay for each gender for the whole organization and notes the difference. At an organization level it is therefore an indicator of gender diversity for senior roles in combination with relative levels of financial reward.

The Neuroscience of Organizational Behavior reports that motivation is a cognitive process, and that people become less responsive to monetary incentives

> because the limbic system quickly becomes accustomed to new stimuli and reacts only to the unexpected such as a financial windfall. Unexpected rewards tend to activate the striatum more than rewards that are anticipated. Employees may respond positively to bonuses and rewards that are unexpected because they activate the brain's reward circuitry.[39]

Neuroscience and motivation

Motivation can be summarized at three levels:

- **Neural level:** The following areas of the brain are said to be involved: amygdala, interior cingulate cortex, dorsolateral prefrontal cortex, orbitofrontal cortex and ventral striatum.
- **Psychological level:** Motivation deals with goal, value, pleasure and aversion.
- **Behavioural level:** Motivation encompasses choice, duration, effort, frequency and regulation.

With regard to the psychological and behavioural levels, the desire to engage in actions is termed prosocial motivation, which is broken down into motives, behaviour and impact. The psychological and behavioural levels have been discussed above.

With regard to the neural level, three brain circuits have been identified that are involved in human motivation: the reward circuit, value-based decision-making pathway, and the self-regulation/self-control network.[40] Motivation is created in the brain when dopamine is released and takes a specific direction toward the mesolimbic pathway (the reward pathway), and then spreads to other areas in the brain like the cerebral cortex. Dopamine is the reward and punishment transmitter, and plays a critical role in positive motivation. The mesolimbic pathway connects the ventral tegmental area in the mid-brain to the ventral striatum of the basal ganglia in the forebrain.[41]

In *The Neuroscience of Organizational Behavior*, Beugré states that,

> considered simultaneously through meta-analytic regression, intrinsic motivation predicted more unique variance in quality of performance, whereas incentives were a better predictor of quantity of performance. With respect to performance, incentives and intrinsic motivation were not necessarily antagonistic and were best considered simultaneously.[42]

In other words, performance management can successfully combine both intrinsic and extrinsic motivators.

Beugré notes that human performance is said to be guided by a tonic and phasic relationship between the neural substrates of intrinsic motivation, tonic, sensory input with a longer lasting effect, and the impact of external incentives, phasic, sensory input with shorter impact. Intrinsic motivation increases activity more in the insular cortex and extrinsic motivation increases activity more in the cingulate cortex;[43]

> the results demonstrate that engagement decisions based on intrinsic motivation are determined more by weighing the presence of spontaneous self-satisfaction such as interest and enjoyment, while engagement decisions based on extrinsic motivation are determined more by weighing socially acquired stored values as to whether the environmental incentive is attractive enough to warrant action.[44]

Our human and chimp brains

In *The Chimp Paradox*, Steve Peters introduces us to a simplified representation of the mind. He illustrates our human brain (the frontal lobe), our chimp brain (the limbic lobe), and our computer brain (the parietal lobe). The human brain is said to be the real and rational you; the computer contains memory banks for reference; and the chimp is the emotional machine that thinks independently from the human brain and can make decisions.[45] His book describes how an individual would approach a task and the foundations for task success. This includes the core principle, which stands for commitment, ownership, responsibility and excellence, and differentiates commitment from motivation.

Peters suggests that, prior to commencing a task, it is wise to check that there is a real possibility of achieving it. The motivation to complete a task is an emotion that is chimp-driven, and drives us towards or away from an experience, while *commitment*, on the other hand, comes from the human brain and is not dependent on feelings. The key point here is that 'when you decide to do something, remind yourself that it is commitment not motivation that matters'.[46] A commitment screen is used to define what is required for a task and how challenges can be overcome. The key requirements to complete the task are essential, significant or simply desirable. The key challenges are seen as hurdles, barriers and pitfalls. Hurdles are obstacles that need to be addressed directly; barriers are difficulties that can be overcome with good planning; and pitfalls are derailing behaviours. While at times the goal may feel far way and challenges get in the way and cause the chimp to scream, if the goal is still possible the chimp can be subdued.[47]

The second principle, *ownership*, is about having enough control of the planning as well as the execution of a task, which drives feelings of pride and increases the chance of success. If there is not enough input into planning and decision-making during execution is limited, then this might increase feelings of anxiety driven by the chimp and decrease the chances of success.[48] *Responsibility* for the success of a task introduces accountability and discipline, and is the third principle. It is noted that organization is not the same as discipline, as even very organized people may not be disciplined enough to drive a task to completion. Having responsibility for a task and the need to report on progress increases the chances of success, as both the human and the chimp feel obligated to act.[49] *Excellence* is the final of the four principles, where it is recommended that high but achievable goals are set to increase the chances of success. The chimp will not be happy if a task is not achievable, so the best course of action is to aim for personal excellence.[50]

The other foundation for task success noted in *The Chimp Paradox* relates to the effect of carrots and sticks. It suggests that people prefer to be encouraged, supported and rewarded, receiving recognition and appreciation for their performance. If employees fail to meet employer expectations within this environment then they may need more support and development, and if they still fail they will face the consequences but not the organizational equivalent of sticks, such as public humiliation, passive-aggressive communication and the perpetuation of feelings of guilt. Examples of organizational carrots include: a variety of rewards, celebrations, recognition, encouragement and support.[51]

People's mindset about what they believe is possible is explored in Carol Dweck's book, *Mindset*, and is related to motivation and commitment.

Mindset

In *Mindset*, Carol Dweck suggests that people have *fixed* and *growth* mindsets. A fixed mindset means that personal qualities are set in stone and there is a desire, even an urgency, to continuously prove personal efficacy. A growth mindset is based on the belief that personal qualities can be added to and strengthened through application and support.[52]

Her research found that for people with a fixed mindset there was no sign of interest in information that could help them learn, even when they made mistakes. However, for people with a growth mindset learning is a priority. 'People in a growth mindset don't just seek challenge, they thrive on it. The bigger the challenge, the more they stretch. For them it's not about immediate perfection. It's about learning something over time: confronting a challenge and making progress.' In addition, 'the growth mindset allows people to value what they're doing regardless of the outcome.'[53]

Her research demonstrated that those with a growth mindset found success in doing their best, in learning and improving; while for those with a fixed mindset, success is just about establishing their superiority. Those with a growth mindset found setbacks motivating, as they are a chance to learn and improve; and people with a growth mindset take charge of the processes that brings success and maintain it.

In *Black Box Thinking*, Matthew Syed discusses an experiment that showed evidence from neuroscience relating to fixed and growth mindsets.[54] Jason Moser [55] looked at the Error Related Negativity (ERN) signal, which is largely involuntary and originates from the anterior cingulated cortex, which is situated in the part of the brain that helps regulate attention when a mistake is made. He also looked at the Error Positivity (Pe) signal, which occurs 200–500 milliseconds after a mistake, when there is a focus on the mistake. Groups with fixed mindsets and groups with growth mindsets both register strong ERN signals, while the groups with growth mindsets showed an amplitude of 15 and those with fixed mindsets showed an amplitude of 5. This would appear to indicate that those with a growth mindset were more interested in considering the mistake, and subsequent reviews indicated this correlated with an improvement in performance. Those with a fixed mindset are more likely to conceal failure, while those with a growth mindset accept occasional failure as the price of learning and development.[56]

Dweck argues that mindsets are an important part of people's personalities, that everyone has a combination of fixed and growth mindsets, that they can have different mindsets in different areas, that they can change them, and therefore that people move between mindsets.

Even with a mindset that is conducive to growth, a number of writers advocate that performance can be improved through attaining a state of *flow*, and therefore this concept is examined below.

Flow

The work of Mihaly Csikszentmihalyi[57] on flow and Albert Bandura[58] on self-efficacy suggests that 'work done well, that stretches us enough, but not too much, from which we get immediate feedback, which takes us beyond ourselves, can give the brain pleasure. It can also help us develop a sense of confidence and our own social worth.'[59]

Csikszentmihalyi suggested nine conditions for people to achieve a state of flow:

- clear goals;
- a balance between challenge and skills;
- a belief in a successful outcome;
- no self-consciousness;
- the sense of time becomes distorted;
- distractions are excluded from consciousness;
- immediate feedback;
- action and awareness merge;
- the activity becomes autotelic, a purpose in itself.[60]

In *The Evolving Self*, Csikszentmihalyi explains that flow does not happening during moments of relaxation but when we undertake activities that stretch our mental and physical ability. Our attention narrows onto our clearly defined goal and 'we feel involved, concentrated, absorbed, we know what must be done, and we get immediate feedback as to how well we are doing… We forget ourselves and become lost in the activity.'[61]

The ability to be in flow depends on external and internal conditions:

- **External:** People are given concrete goals and manageable rules, it is possible to adjust opportunities for action to people's capacities, feedback is provided, and distractions are minimized to make concentration possible.
- **Internal:** Some people can match their skills to the opportunities around them, concentrate easily and do not get distracted:

They are not afraid of losing their self, so their ego can slip easily out of awareness. Persons who have learned to control consciousness in these ways have a 'flow of personality'. They do not need to play in order to be in flow; they can be happy even as they work on an assembly line or are languishing is solitary confinement.[62]

Leaders should be aware that

to encourage and maintain motivation means putting people in the right place, so that the level of work they are asked to do is socially relevant, meaningful, challenging but not impossible, in an atmosphere of positive encouragement, with clearly articulated goals. It means timely and appropriate feedback, good delegation of autonomy and responsibility, and fair and transparent reward structures.[63]

Motivation, job satisfaction and personality

Motivation and job satisfaction are both measured by organizations. People's innate motivation is measured through personality tests for selection and development and through work-specific questionnaires that may investigate expectancy and value. Job satisfaction may be impacted by personality traits and related to overall satisfaction with life. A number of factors that relate to job satisfaction – age, gender, race, cognitive ability, personality traits, job experience, use of skills, occupational level and overall job congruence – have been researched. The results suggest that job satisfaction is likely to be determined by personal characteristics combined with two other key variables: the job itself and environmental factors.

As we understand more about personality, increasing evidence has been found that suggests personality is related to job behaviour and outcomes, where previously these were thought to be almost entirely a function of the environment. For instance, it seems that personality variables, which may be inherited, are strong predictors of job satisfaction.[64]

Research has shown that 'all genetic influences (28 per cent) on job satisfaction could be explained by its relation to personality, especially Neuroticism, Extraversion, and Conscientiousness, representing a high genetic overlap between job satisfaction and personality'.[65] Environmental influences explained the remaining three-quarters of the variance. This implies situational and dispositional determinants of job satisfaction are relevant.

There is a complex relationship between personality, ability, motivation, job satisfaction, productivity, absenteeism and turnover. In *The Psychology of Behaviour at Work*, Furnham summarizes the results of studies on the impact of personality and job motivation against process theories of motivation:

- **Goal setting:** Emotionally stable, agreeable and conscientious individuals set higher goals.

- **Expectancy motivation:** Stable and conscientious individuals have higher expectancy motivation.

- **Self-efficacy motivation:** Stable and extraverted individuals have higher self-efficacy motivation.[66]

In *The Human Capital Imperative*, Colvin suggests that motivation is seen through a transactional lens in terms of what people receive for their effort, satisfaction is related to how happy an individual is overall at work rather than their desire to maximize discretionary effort, and engagement is a proxy for a preparedness to maximize their discretionary effort. That is not to say that maximizing discretionary effort will always lead to superior performance.[67] Indeed, in *The Talent Delusion*, Chamorro-Premuzic suggests that talent can be defined by focusing on an individual's best performance, what they achieve when they are highly motivated and trying hard under optimal conditions. He notes that differences in performance are a function of ability, talent, effort and motivation, while the proportional influence varies depending on the person and the task. He also states that personality will, to a large degree, impact how frequently someone will seek to maximize their performance – for instance, ethical, self-disciplined and conscientious people and those with high recognition and achievement needs will do so more frequently.[68] 'If performance is talent plus effort, then talent is performance minus effort. In other words, talent is effortless performance.'[69] With mastery comes effortless performance and 'potential may be best conceptualised as talent plus effort. In other words, how much talent you are likely to develop depends on the talent you already have and the work you are willing to put in to develop more.'[70]

The leadership implications of motivation are discussed in *Neuroscience For Leadership*, which notes that avoidance emotions are more numerous and often stronger than approach ones, and fear focuses the mind on the perceived threat to the exclusion of anything else. Loss is felt more keenly than gain. Therefore, 'leaders who can engage the attachment emotions have a better chance of motivating people, not only towards improving individual performance and creativity but towards contributing to the community.'[71] The authors also note that:

> showing respect, genuinely listening, taking account of others' views and publicly acknowledging their contribution can also motivate engagement and cooperation... rewarding those who collaborate well by increasing status and/or autonomy can be more motivational than financial rewards.[72]

Finally, they point out that:

> a leader demonstrates fairness, who creates and maintains processes that discriminate fairly between good and bad performance, between those who work cooperatively and those who work only to promote themselves, who has processes to enable individuals to articulate their own goals as subsets of the corporate ones, creates a platform for people to work together towards the good of the whole.[73]

Motivation and culture

The above findings assume universal and constant truths across all cultures. However, in *Cultures and Organizations*, Geert Hofstede notes that culture influences motivation. He gives the following examples based on a study across 24 countries that found correlations between reward strategies and culture indexes:

- Employers in small power-distance countries more often provided onsite childcare for managers and professional and technical staff and stock options for non-managers.

- Employers in individualist countries more often paid for individual performance and provided stock options for managers.

- Employers in masculine countries more often paid commission to non-managerial employees; in feminine countries they more often provided flexible benefits and onsite childcare and maternity leave to clerical and manual workers.

- Employers in uncertainty-avoiding countries more often related to seniority and skill and less often to performance.[74]

Power-distance can be defined as 'the extent to which the less powerful members of institutions and organizations within a country expect and accept that power is distributed unequally'.[75] In small power-distance countries there is more interdependence between managers and those who work for them, and more preference for consultation.

Leaders should be aware that established theories of organizational behaviour developed in a Western context should be treated as provisional for other cultural settings.[76]

Research was undertaken to validate a motivation scale across seven languages and nine countries.[77] Three types of extrinsic motivation were discussed:[78]

- **external regulation:** performing a task to obtain reward or avoid punishment from others;

- **introjected regulation:** internal, controlling, regulation through pressuring forces such as, shame and guilt;

- **identified regulation:** volitionally undertaking an activity because of self-identification with its value or meaning. It is done for the instrumental value rather than inherent satisfaction.

Researchers merged external and introjected regulation into a controlled motivation composite score and combined identified and intrinsic motivation into an autonomous composite score.

In a study across seven languages and nine countries (Belgium, Canada, China, France, Indonesia, Norway, Senegal, Switzerland and the United

Kingdom), autonomous motivation was positively related to the need for autonomy, competence and relatedness. Also, autonomous motivation was 'positively related to important outcomes, such as vitality, emotional exhaustion, affective commitment, performance, personal initiative, effort and turnover intentions.'[79]

Due to the demographic changes discussed in Chapter 8 leaders will need to understand the cultural implications for motivation, and therefore employee engagement and experience.

Highlights

- There are many theories of job motivation and satisfaction, and some researchers have attempted to create integrated models that have greater explanatory power than individual models that look through particular lenses.

- Ultimately, people appear to value challenging work where they expect to perform at or above goals that have been set jointly with them. They prefer work that has intrinsic value and where they can have a degree of autonomy and the ability to grow. They value extrinsic rewards that are equitable.

- Personality traits that relate to motivation will impact the degree to which some people are motivated by, amongst other factors, team working, power, recognition and financial reward.

- It is important for leaders to understand the types of motivation that impact behaviour, as this will help them design a workplace environment and external brand messaging that will help them build an outstanding workforce.

Leadership impact

Key themes that leaders should reflect on include:

- links between personality and motivation;
- connections between job satisfaction and people's types, cognitive ability, personality traits and job congruence;
- goal setting and how to improve group adherence;
- performance management – how to adopt continuous feedback and de-emphasize the annual appraisal;

- employee engagement and employee experience – improving the commitment from employees to the organization, and the organization to individual employees.

People management recommendations

Actions to consider:

- Examine your reward structure and make sure it is fit for purpose. Are people being motivated in the right way to do the right things?

- Consider annual surveys to gauge employee engagement/satisfaction and, more importantly, how motivated they are.

- Consider segmenting your teams if they are undertaking significantly different tasks.

- Improve performance management by designing process to fit various people segments – one size does not fit all.

Leadership 05

Introduction

It has already been noted that the future workplace will recognize and encourage leadership at all levels of organizations and that members of the workforce may be asked to perform leadership roles in a number of different contexts and for varying lengths of time. It has also been emphasized that anyone who is required to achieve organizational goals through people should be familiar with the various approaches related to leadership.

Chapter 1 introduced the complexity of people and therefore the complexity of leaders and their followers, and this chapter adds the complexity inherent in the nature of leadership.

In *Leadership BS*, Jeffery Pfeffer questions what it will take to stop leaders failing those who work in their organizations. He points to several disconnects between what leaders say and what they do, the prescriptions of favoured traits and behaviours and the reality, the disconnect between prescriptions for what would make workplaces better and what is actually implemented. He suggests we 'explore the systematic processes that produce leaders... including the social psychology that makes traits and behaviours that cause leaders to be successful in their careers'.[1]

Much has been written about the essence of leadership, and in *Leaders*, McChrystal and colleagues describe these as *myths*, noting that the mythology of leadership is built on the relentless focus on the leader. The 'formulaic myth' is the attempt to understand the leadership process through a static checklist, while 'ignoring the reality that leadership is intensely contextual, and always dependent upon particular circumstances'; the 'attribution myth' focuses on what the leader does while neglecting the agency of followers and others that surround them; the 'results myth' sees leadership as the process of driving groups of people toward outcomes, which is true to a point, but 'productive leadership requires that followers find a sense of purpose and meaning in what their leaders represent, such as social identity or some future opportunity.'[2]

Further to the above, in *The Extraordinary Leader* it is argued that a leader's character is central to their effectiveness and success, with ethical standards, integrity, transparency authenticity all being extremely important. In addition to character, four other aspects of leadership are believed to be key to success: personal capability, focus on results, interpersonal skills and leading organizational change.[3]

It should already be clear that people are complicated and therefore leaders are complicated, with acts of leadership contingent on the complex situational context they face. An investigation into the nature of leadership should therefore be approached from various perspectives. In *Down the Rabbit Hole of Leadership*, Manfred Kets de Vries uses three lenses to study the behaviour of people in organizations: first, the *psychodynamic lens*, which examines the conscious and unconscious psychological drivers and forces that underlie human emotions, feelings and behaviour; second, *evolutionary psychology*, which 'adds to our appreciation of both the human body and the human mind, clarifying how evolutionary adaptions have affected behaviour patterns, emotions, cognition, and brain structure';[4] and finally, *neuroscience* which is 'associated with harder themes, such as physiology, neurons, hormones, receptors, and neurotransmitters, as opposed to the softer themes, such as thoughts, ideas, beliefs, emotions, and desires, that are found in more traditional psychology'.[5]

The reader has already been prepared for these views in the preceding chapters, and so like Kets de Vries, in this chapter we will consider some classic theories of leadership and associated organization behaviour while adding some recent thinking around emotions and cognitive ability, and how an understanding of neuroscience can inform leadership.

Chapter summary

The following subjects are discussed in this chapter:

- **Leadership research**
  - Fiedler's Contingency Model
  - Path–Goal Theory
  - The Managerial Grid
  - Situational Leadership Model
  - Leader–Member Exchange
- **Leadership and management**
  - Historical views of leadership and management
- **The future of leadership**
  - Leadership in a VUCA world
- **Change**
- **Organizational behaviour**
  - Methods of study
  - Male and female leaders

o   Task orientation vs people orientation

o   Transformational leadership

● **Selection and development**

o   Selection

o   Development

Leadership research

Research on leadership has included views on leadership *traits* – what leaders do, and the *styles* in which they do it.

However, trait approaches to differentiate leadership have shown an 'inability to offer clear distinctions between leaders and non-leaders and… failure to account for situational variance in leadership behaviour'.[6] Leadership research has considered what leaders do, for instance: creating a vision, decision-making, engendering cooperation, building trust and driving change. Research has also been undertaken on the style in which leadership is enacted, such as: charismatic leadership, transactional leadership, transformational leadership, servant leadership and authentic leadership.

However, the cognitive ability and personality traits of the leader and their followers, such as intelligence and emotional stability, will impact leadership efficacy. An interactional framework advocates studying leadership as a process rather than just leadership traits and considers the relationship between a leader's characteristics, followers' characteristics and situational factors.

Contingency theories of leadership acknowledge the context within which leadership is required and include: Fiedler's Contingency Model, House and Mitchell's Path–Goal Theory, Blake and Mouton's Managerial Grid, Hersey and Blanchard's Situational Leadership Model, and Graen's Leader–Member Exchange (LMX) Model.

Fiedler's Contingency Model

A contingency model of leadership and management is exemplified in *A Theory of Leadership Effectiveness* by Fred Fiedler, which states that there is no best practice leadership. Instead, the leadership style selected will be based on:

● **leader–member relations:** the extent of trust and confidence the team has in the leader;

● **task structure:** the extent to which the task is structured or unstructured;

● **leader's position-power:** the extent to which the position gives the holder more or less power to reward or punish behaviour.[7]

Fiedler suggested that the chosen leadership style would be based on the Least Preferred Co-worker (LPC) scale and select for greater task or relationship orientation. The LPC indicates the emotional reaction a person has to those they have difficulty working with and their motivation type is derived from this.

While contingency approaches look at the specific internal and external context, transformational leadership approaches focus on what is achieved through inspiration, building a shared vision, leading by example, facilitating the performance of others, facilitating learning, creating a psychologically safe environment, giving feedback in a coaching style, praising, promoting and rewarding success and a focus on the individual.

Path–Goal Theory

In House and Mitchell's Path–Goal Theory, the leader's behaviour is acceptable to followers if it is a source of satisfaction, motivational when need satisfaction is contingent on performance and where the leader facilitates and rewards performance:

- **directive path–goal clarifying leader behaviour:** sets clear objectives and tells followers how to perform their tasks;
- **achievement-orientated leader behaviour:** sets challenging goals and expects high-level performance from followers;
- **participative leader behaviour:** consultative, asking followers for suggestions;
- **supportive leader behaviour:** concern shown for the psychological well-being of followers.[8]

It assumes leaders can change their style when required and acknowledges that environmental factors and follower characteristics impact leadership success.

The Managerial Grid

Another example of the behavioural–relationship approach to leadership is illustrated by Blake and Mouton's Managerial Grid, which is based on two dimensions: concern for production and concern for people. Their combinations produce five distinct styles of leadership:

- **country club:** a strong concern for people but with little focus on production;
- **impoverished:** little concern for people and production;
- **organization person management:** a moderate concern for people and production;

- **authority–obedience:** little concern for people but a strong concern for production;
- **team:** a strong concern for employees and production orientation.[9]

While this is a much-taught model it only considers two factors, and to that extent is simplistic and of limited practical application.

Situational Leadership Model

A further example of the behavioural–relationship approach is Hersey and Blanchard's two-factor Situational Leadership Model.[10] This considers task behaviour and relationship behaviour, and establishes four behavioural leadership styles:

- **S1, selling/directing:** followers unable, motivated and confident;
- **S2, telling/coaching:** followers unable, unwilling, not confident;
- **S3, participating/supporting:** followers able, motivated, not confident;
- **S4, delegating:** followers able, motivated and confident.

The model looks at three factors associated with followers – their ability, motivation and confidence – and as such shares ground with the theories motivation considered in the previous chapter.

Leader–Member Exchange

This descriptive theory by George Graen is based on vertical dyadic linkage theory, which examined the relationships between leaders and their followers, as dyads. Leader–Member Exchange (LMX) suggests that leaders develop an exchange relationship with their followers and the quality of this relationship determines follower behaviour and organizational outcomes. The strength of the relationship varies for each follower.[11] Later research using this model focused on teams, as collections of dyads.[12]

This theory claims that leaders do not behave the same way towards each follower and that the quality of each relationship impacts work-related behaviour.

Leadership and management

Historical views of leadership and management

Leadership and management have traditionally been seen as very different. In *The Second Curve* Charles Handy discusses a traditional distinction between leadership and management, noting that 'management is a word that we properly use to describe the organization of things or systems: leadership is the word that we ought to use when we refer to people... leadership talks of vision, mission and passion, management of targets, controls and efficiency.'[13] He observes that often managers are promoted to leadership roles only to find that the task and directing strengths that had served them well in the past are no substitute for the vision and influencing skills that are now required.

Managers and leader-managers have been differentiated, with the latter sharing more of the vision, influencing and people focused roles attributed to leaders.[14] In his substantial tome *The Bass Handbook of Leadership*, Bernard Bass notes that leaders manage and managers lead but the two activities are not synonymous and acknowledges many studies that describe the diversity in how managers and organizational leaders spend their time.[15]

In *A Force for Change: How leadership differs from management*, John Kotter notes some differences between management and leadership, with management being said to involve:

- **planning and budgeting:** establishing detailed steps and timelines for achieving required results, then allocating the resources necessary to make it happen;

- **organizing and staffing:** establishing a structure to facilitate execution of the plan, staffing that structure, delegating responsibility and authority, providing policies and procedures to guide people, and a system for monitoring implementation;

- **controlling and problem solving:** monitoring results, identifying deviations from plan, then planning and organizing to problem solve;

- **producing a degree of predictability and order:** the potential to consistently produce the short-term results expected by various stakeholders (eg for customers, always being on time; for stakeholders, for being on budget).[16]

Leadership is said to encompass:

- **establishing direction:** developing a vision of the future and strategies for producing the changes needed to achieve that vision;

- **aligning people:** communicating direction in words and actions to all those required to achieve the vision to influence the creation of teams and coalitions that understand the vision and strategies and accept their validity;

- **motivating and inspiring:** energizing people to overcome major political, bureaucratic, and resource barriers to change by satisfying basic, but often unfulfilled, human needs;

- **producing change, often to a dramatic degree:** has the potential to produce extremely valuable change.[17]

In *The Human Capital Imperative*, it is noted that while middle managers understand that they undertake a key role in operationalizing firm culture and raising levels of trust, they do not always feel their role is valued or supported.[18] Research by the Chartered Management Institute (CMI) in the United Kingdom[19] found that middle managers want their leaders to reveal their thinking on important issues, admit their mistakes, encourage people to raise issues, inspire them regarding business ambition and strategy, and act consistently with the company's values.

The distinction between leadership and management may be considered less helpful in the future as organizations are designed to become more innovative and more responsive to their environment.

In *The Future of Work*, Jacob Morgan writes that:

> typically managers are focused on enforcing control. They organize oversee, supervise, delegate, and make sure things get done the right way and on time. However, often these managers may not be the best at inspiring or engaging employees, thinking outside of the box, challenging assumptions, or building trust... [These] are typically qualities that many associate with leaders.[20]

Morgan suggests that when it comes to the future of work, managers must be proficient at all these things because managers must be leaders

All leaders must have a firm grasp on the key business drivers. Any employee can demonstrate leadership, but managers who have responsibility for other people must be effective leaders. 'The bottom line is that we need fewer people who exert control and manage work and more people who inspire, engage, challenge, and lead people; this is exactly who the future manager will be.'[21]

As Kotter states,

> the negative consequences of putting people with potential into small boxes and micromanaging them will only increase. People need to be encouraged to attempt to lead, at first on a small scale, both to help the organization adapt to changing circumstances and to help themselves to grow.[22]

The future of leadership

In *Humanity Works*, Levit notes that:

> as organizations get flatter and aspects of leadership and employment become more transparent, from who is earning what salary to whether a human or a machine is more effective at a given task, cultures will increasingly emphasize accountability, efficiency and concrete contributions.[23]

This will lead to an increased level of accountability for leaders.

There are many challenges facing the future In *The Future of Work*, Morgan suggests ten principles for the future manager:

- Be a leader.
- 'Follow from the front'.

- Understand technology.
- Lead by example.
- Embrace vulnerability.
- Believe in sharing and collective intelligence.
- Challenge convention and be a fire starter.
- Practise real-time recognition and feedback.
- Be conscious of personal boundaries.
- Adapt to the future employee.[24]

These are all useful principles, in addition to being self-aware and focused on their personnel and professional development.

Leaders must understand which models are appropriate for their organizations and design them to be obsolete. They must also understand the competencies required for each role now and how they map into future scenarios, and must themselves find ways of managing increasing cognitive overload.

Leaders of remote teams are encouraged to arrange face-to-face meetings at the commencement of projects to establish relationships that can then be more easily maintained by other means.

With regard to the future of leadership, Bass predicts:

- Coaching and mentoring will be individualized and mostly delivered online.
- Most industries and businesses will be dominated by a few large multinational companies.
- Transactional bureaucratic organizations will give way to more transformational ones.
- In the developed world women will become the majority in a number of walks of life.
- Women will foster more networking, relationships and concerns for social justice, equity and fairness.
- Second careers for leaders after retirement will be commonplace, and working to the age of 85 not unusual.
- Ethical codes will be constructed empirically.
- Changes in the environment will be mirrored in changes in organizations.
- Adaptability will be essential at all levels.
- Transformational leaders will be sought after.[25]

Finally, Rob Goffee and Gareth Jones offer advice on the importance of followership, noting research that suggests followers want authenticity, significance, excitement and community from leaders, and that followers in turn need to expect and accept a degree of ambiguity and uncertainty, help leaders learn and 'encourage a process of mutual exploration as both parties cope with changing contexts and demands'[26].

Leadership in a VUCA world

Looking ahead, *Leaders Make The Future* suggests 10 skills that leaders will need in order to be resilient in the face of a volatile, uncertain, complex and ambiguous (VUCA) world:

- Exploit their inner drive to connect with others to build and grow.
- Communicate simply without being simplistic, create clarity from contradictions while being flexible to the journey.
- Improve the ability to flip dilemmas into advantages and opportunities, and succeed with challenges that cannot be solved and won't go away.
- Practise immersive learning in both physical and virtual worlds.
- Use environmental empathy to inform leadership.
- Constructively depolarize conflict where people cannot agree and bring together people from different cultures.
- Lead with a quiet transparency that shows openness and authenticity without self-promotion.
- Learn rapid prototyping, expecting and learning from failure.
- Engage, organize and nurture networks using a range of social media.
- Create shared assets with which cooperation may occur.[27]

Following from this, *The New Leadership Literacies* suggests five tools for leaders navigating today's complex and dynamic environment:

- **Looking backwards from the future:** Project into the future about ten years and then work back in, as it will help identify the direction of change, avoiding the noise around the present and developing clarity. Be clear about direction but flexible about execution, as certainty will be punished.
- **Voluntary fear engagement:** Gamify scenario testing without risk in simulated worlds, in a similar way that the military test strategy through war-gaming.
- **Leadership for shape-shifting organizations.** Learn how to thrive in distributed organizations that have less centralized authority. Technology will provide the connectivity. Reciprocity between mutually beneficial partnerships will be more important.
- **Being there when you are not there:** Learn how to engage with people who are geographically, organizationally and temporally distributed.
- **Creating and sustaining positive energy:** Learn to regulate personal energy so you have focus, stamina and resilience when required. Leaders will need spiritual, though not necessarily religious, grounding and a sense of meaning in the midst of extreme disruption.[28]

There are some useful points made above, but these should only be taken as a collection of thoughtful ideas for consideration rather than a prescriptive and exhaustive list. However, they do give an indication of the complexity faced by leaders.

One element of complexity theory relates to the ability of leaders to manage paradox, and this was examined in a study that discussed this with the CEOs of 20 organizations located in North America, Europe and India, and which had a history of sustained above-average financial performance. It focused on paradoxes in seven areas:[29]

- **location:** being present but empowering others;
- **change:** to drive change you need to be consistent;
- **creativity:** the more ideas launched the fewer will succeed;
- **diversity:** the need to be more heterogeneous, diverse, and homogeneous, inclusive, at the same time;
- **direction:** encourage independent action while maintaining direction;
- **innovation:** encourage entrepreneurial initiatives while maintaining operational excellence;
- **globalization:** become more global while respecting local differences.

This research found that CEOs advocated integrated solutions through contextual ambidexterity and did so without discussing challenges in terms of paradox. They need to find solutions without necessarily discussing that they are difficult to resolve.[30]

Leadership agility has also been discussed, with research by IMD suggesting four characteristics that distinguish agile from non-agile leaders. Agile leaders are:

- '**Humble:** They are able to accept feedback and acknowledge that others know more than they do.
- **Adaptable:** They accept that change is constant and that changing their minds based on new information is a strength rather than a weakness.
- **Visionary:** They have a clear sense of long-term direction, even in the face of short-term uncertainty.
- **Engaged:** They have a willingness to listen, interact, and communicate with internal and external stakeholders combined with a strong sense of interest and curiosity in emerging trends.'[31]

In addition, they found that agile leaders exhibited three key behaviours that helped them to successfully navigate disruptive environments:

- '**Hyperawareness:** They are constantly scanning internal and external environments for opportunities and threats.
- **Informed decision-making:** They make use of data and information to make evidence-based decisions.

- **Fast execution:** They are able to move quickly, often valuing speed over perfection.'[32]

With regard to dynamic management capabilities, specific cognitive capabilities underpin three classes of dynamic managerial capabilities – sensing, seizing and reconfiguring[33] – and these are noted as:

- **Sensing:** Attention and perception. Attention entails the selection of relevant information and perception is the construction of useful and meaningful information about a particular environment. It involves mental functions relating to pattern recognition data interpretation.

- **Seizing:** Problem solving and reasoning. Problem solving is thinking that is directed toward solving specific problems, moving from an initial state to a goal state. Reasoning is using information to determine if a conclusion is valid or reasonable

- **Reconfiguring:** Social cognition, language and communication. Language can be thought of as any system for representing and communicating ideas. 'Social cognitive capability includes the capacity to understand the point of view of others, and therefore provides the potential to influence the behaviour of others as well.'[34]

It has been suggested that:

> in highly complex and uncertain environments, cognitive heuristics may provide superior underpinnings for dynamic capabilities at the organizational level. Controlled mental processing also plays a role in problem solving, and may help to counteract potential biases that may arise in using heuristics. In addition, both automatic and controlled processing underpin cognitive capabilities of attention and perception, as well as social cognitive capabilities and language and communication.[35]

An evidence-based view of leadership, *Great by Choice* by Collins and Hansen, described the leadership traits found in commercial organizations that outperformed their sector average by ten times (10x). They found that leaders of organizations that beat their sector average performance by at least 10x

> did not have a visionary ability to predict the future. They observed what worked, figured out why it worked, and built upon proven foundations. They were not more risk taking, more bold, more visionary, and more creative than the comparisons. They were more disciplined, more empirical, and more paranoid.[36]

In addition, while the 10x companies were significant innovators, 'the evidence does not support the premise that 10x companies will necessarily be more innovative than their less successful comparisons; and in some surprise cases, the 10x cases were less innovative.'[37] They found these leaders had a passion and ambition to fulfil their organization's purpose; they accepted the VUCA environment, still planned but built in margins for error. They were disciplined and favoured empirically based creativity.[38] In *Good to Great*, Collins describes how 'Level 5' leaders 'build greatness through a paradoxical blend of personal humility and professional will'.[39]

In *The Social Leap*, Von Hippel notes that people are largely incapable of distinguishing between overconfidence and high levels of well-calibrated confidence, which can be a problem as 'overconfident leaders often make poor decisions, ignore obvious flaws in their strategies and continue with failing plans.'[40] He notes that although cultural differences play a large role in such decisions, and no doubt other contextual factors such as the economy and ability, our modern environment makes opting out of organizations and even entire communities easier than ever before. Where this is linked to a star culture, perverse incentive structures that unduly favour the stars may be seen, and this can be detrimental to the organization in both the short- and long-term.

Change

In *Flow*, the authors note that while change is pervasive,

> most leaders are secretly overwhelmed by the pace of change coming at them. And that's also why many of us who go into work each day continue to face outdated attitudes, deferential hierarchies, efficiency-busting silos, and a lack of momentum to do things differently.[41]

Changes in leaders' thinking can be caused by internal and external events or trends that influence their opinions on the reason for their organization's existence, its purpose, or at other levels its vision, mission, goals, strategies, objectives and plans.

Changes in thinking may then lead to developmental, transitional or transformational changes in organization focus and business operating models. Developmental change is the least disruptive and generally focuses on incremental improvements to the current position. Transitional change is periodic, planned and moves organizations from a current position to a new position in a controlled manner with outcomes that can be predicted with some certainty. Transformational change is episodic, may or may not be planned and moves organizations from a current position to a new position with outcomes that may not be predictable. Whatever the nature of change, there will be an impact on the workforce.

It is has been noted that change programmes often focus on the structure and technical systems over the social systems; that people are not adequately engaged in the change process; that change is becoming increasingly impacted by unpredictable and unexpected dynamics; that centralized change programmes may not capitalize on local capabilities; and that 'deeply held cultural assumptions and established behaviour patterns are impeding the growth of the "*distributed leadership*" necessary in complex change'.[42]

To lead change, a six-step change process was suggested by Beer et al:

- Mobilize commitment through joint problem diagnosis.
- Develop a shared vision of how to organize and manage.
- Foster consensus in the new vision and competence to begin and continue.
- Begin with the areas of the organization most ready for change.
- Spread the change to other areas.
- Monitor and adjust to problems that arise.[43]

As organizational change is a constant but is arguably faster and more complex than in previous decades, it is worth remembering the eight-stage process for major change offered by Kotter in *Leading Change*. He suggests:

- **Establish a sense of urgency:**
  - Examine the market and competitive realities.
  - Identify and discuss crises, potential crises or major opportunities.
- **Create the guiding coalition:**
  - Put together a group with enough power to lead the change.
  - Get the group to work together like a team.
- **Develop a vision and strategy:**
  - Create a vision to help direct the change effort.
  - Develop strategies for achieving that vision.
- **Communicate the change vision:**
  - Use every vehicle possible to constantly communicate the new vision and strategies.
  - Have the guiding coalition role-model the behaviour expected of employees.
- **Empower broad-based action:**
  - Get rid of obstacles.
  - Change systems or structures that undermine the change vision.
  - Encourage risk-taking and non-traditional ideas, activities, and actions.
- **Generate short-term wins:**
  - Plan for visible improvements in performance, or 'wins'.
  - Create those wins.
  - Visibly recognize and reward people who made the wins possible.
- **Consolidate gains and producing more change:**
  - Use increased credibility to change all systems, structures and policies that don't fit together and don't fit the transformation vision.
  - Hire, promote and develop people who can implement the change vision.
  - Reinvigorate the process with new projects, themes, and change agents.

- Anchor new approaches in the culture:
  - Create better performance through customer and productivity-orientated behaviour, more and better leadership, and more effective management.
  - Articulate the connections between new behaviours and organizational success.
  - Develop the means to ensure leadership development and succession.[44]

Kotter notes that:

> major change is never successful unless the complacency level is low. A high urgency rate helps enormously in completing all the stages of a transformation process. If the rate of external change continues to climb, then the urgency rate of the winning twenty first century organization will have to be medium to high all the time.[45]

A further model of change was suggested by the psychologist Kurt Lewin as part of his work on group dynamics and changing the behaviour of groups. It involves three stages:

- **unfreezing:** destabilizing the groups quasi-stationary equilibrium;
- **movement:** creating the motivation to learn and movement forward to a more positive place;
- **refreezing:** stabilizing the group in a quasi-stationary equilibrium, so new behaviours do not regress.[46]

One study reviewed the change management literature including Lewin and Kotter, and also discussed Hamel's eight-stage revolutionary process of change:

- **Build a point of view:** Have strong opinion and a plan.
- **Write a manifesto:** Write to inspire others.
- **Create a coalition:** Create a support team of like-minded individuals.
- **Pick your targets and moments:** Identify the key power players get the timing right.
- **Co-opt and neutralise:** Identify and convert potential supporters that will help neutralize those opposing change.
- **Find a translator:** Identify a sponsor to help promote the change agenda.
- **Win early, win small and win often:** Demonstrate success on a small scale first rather than one big, high-risk, attempt.
- **Isolate, infiltrate and integrate:** Create focus, momentum and institutionalize the change.[47]

For Hamel, change has to be a continuous cycle of 'imagining, designing, experimenting, assessing, scaling innovative ideas'.[48]

A typology of change was developed by Balogen and Hope-Hailey, who compared the nature and speed of change with the extent of change. This resulted in four generic types:

- **incremental transformation:** evolution;
- **big bang transformation:** revolution;
- **incremental realignment:** adaptation;
- **big bang realignment:** reconstruction/turnaround.[49]

Employee responses to change can be said to have eight dimensions:

- openly expressive support or resistance;
- concealed support or resistance;
- active support or resistance;
- passive support or resistance.

A wait-and-see attitude is an example of openly passive resistance, while active but concealed resistance seeks to undermine the process of change. Concealed active support is demonstrated through cooperation, while concealed passive support will be seen through compliance.[50]

In *Exploring Strategy*, it is said that leaders envisioning future strategy align the organization to deliver the strategy and embody change, and that managers implementing change act as advisors, sense-making how change is landing, reinterpreting and making changes at a local level.[51]

Leadership styles may vary depending on organizational capability and readiness:

- **collaboration:** high capability and high readiness;
- **participation:** high capability and low readiness;
- **direction (if urgent) or participation:** low capability and low readiness;
- **persuasion:** low capability and high readiness.[52]

CEO emotional stability and agreeableness has been found to have consistent effects on the initiation (positive) and performance (negative) of strategic change. However, their conscientiousness had a negative impact on initiation and a positive impact on implementation. It suggests that situational cues can activate certain relevant attributes in a trait and supress others. For instance, intolerance of ambiguity and need for structure in conscientiousness may act as a brake on strategic change, but once a strategy for change has been adopted it will promote a desire to achieve superior performance. Extraversion may fuel the imitation of strategic change due to components of excitement-seeking, adventures and risk-taking, which are not present to the same degree during later periods of implementation.[53]

If change is occurring constantly, in a more complex environment and happening faster, how can leaders use their knowledge of neuroscience and psychology to support them?

Organizational behaviour

Methods of study

In *The Neuroscience of Organizational Behavior*, Constant Beugré introduces the field of organizational neuroscience, which is informed by the domains of neuroscience, neuroeconomics, organizational science, social cognitive science and cognitive psychology as tools to study behaviour in organizations.

Beugré notes that neuroscience research includes tests of association, which involves observing or experimentally manipulating psychological states of behaviour while simultaneously measuring neural activity and examining correlations between the two. Neuroeconomics refers to the domain that studies the impact of economic decisions on the brain, for instance using game theory to examine trust, cooperation and fairness. The domain of organization science is loosely defined as including human resources management, industrial and organizational psychology, organizational behaviour, organizational theory, strategic management and management, also drawing on psychology, sociology, political science, economics and anthropology. The social-cognitive neuroscience domain seeks to understand how biological systems implement social processes and behaviour, thus giving an understanding of self, of others and the processes occurring at the interface of self and others. Finally, the domain of cognitive psychology studies how people mentally represent and process information. As such, 'it includes within its domain mental abilities such as perception, learning, memory, reasoning, problem solving, and decision-making... how people react to situations depends on how they construe them'.[54]

Cognitive psychology

> at the neural level deals with how different brain structures function and interact to influence human attitudes and behaviours... at the cognitive level, researchers are interested in knowing how brain structures affect the thought processes we experience. Such an understanding could provide clues for knowing how people process information and make decisions... The behavioural level is the observable part and can help us understand how we act or react in particular ways when faced with some environmental stimuli.[55]

What is the potential application of research produced in these domains? The field of organizational neuroscience suggests the following: training and development, job design, high performance assessment, motivating communication and conflict prevention. To these can be added creativity, team building, emotional control and regulation, the development of trust, decision-making, ethical behaviour and diversity in the workplace.[56]

For instance, Simon Sinek's *Start With Why* has received popular acclaim as a conceptual tool that gets leaders thinking about their approach to communication at both individual and organizational levels using, amongst others, Apple and Southwest Airlines as examples.[57]

Sinek proposes a model for leaders to inspire greatness, the Golden Circle. He locates *why* at the heart of the organization, the reason why the organization exists, its purpose. The middle concentric circle represents *how* they do things and how this differs from their competitors. Finally, the outer circle locates *what* the organization does – their products and/or services. To be effective it is recommended that organizations communicate internally and externally from the inside out.[58]

His model develops with a comparison to the composition of the human brain. The newest area of the human brain, the neocortex, is responsible for rational and analytical thought and corresponds to the *what* level; the middle two sections are the limbic brain, which is responsible for our feelings and decision-making but not language, and corresponds to the *how* and *why* levels.[59]

Sinek makes the point that communicating from the outside in gives people information about what we do and how we do it, but does not drive behaviour, in comparison to communicating from the inside out, which starts with the part of the brain that controls beliefs, values, motivation and decision-making but not language. Communicating organizational values is said to be hard, as language is controlled in a different part of the brain to beliefs and values. If the circle is rendered as a cone to represent an organization, the CEO at its apex represents the why, and communicates the purpose; at the next level the senior executives representing the how, translate the vision into action; followed at the bottom by the employees creating the what – the delivery of products and services. [60]

It is argued that if neuroimaging studies have a low probability to detect a true effect and are unable to precisely locate mental phenomena in the brain, then academics and practitioners should be cautious about generating new theories of leadership and management.[61] However, even if results to date are treated as provisional, extant research should still inform thinking, for instance the fact that 'a substantial body of empirical findings from research into human learning, memory, perception and cognition has led to the view that cognitive processes are constructive and regenerative'[62] that is neuroplasticity supports learning and adaptation.

It is also worth noting Paul Zak's extensive work on trust and the impact of oxytocin, which increases trust and empathy, and led to his suggested eight leadership behaviours that foster trust: recognize excellence; induce challenge, moderate stress; give people some discretion in how they work; enable job crafting; share information broadly; intentionally build relationships; facilitate whole person growth; and show some vulnerability.[63]

In addition, studies focused on personality in leaders have found a direct correlation to financial performance. For instance, it has been found that the conscientiousness of CEOs and the inner circle of leaders were directly related to lagged indicators of financial performance; and emotional stability and openness were indirectly related to organizational effectiveness.[64]

Male and female leaders

In *Neuroscience for Leadership*, leaders are seen as individuals who have sufficient status, power, dominance and influence to achieve objectives through others. They note that there is considerable evidence that high levels of testosterone and low levels of cortisol predict status and dominance in people, while separately they do not. This could be due to the fact that cortisol is linked with decreased stress and sociability. The fact that women, on the whole, appear to be less confident than men may be linked to their lower levels of testosterone; however,

> if indeed leadership is better correlated with the balance between testosterone and cortisol, and not absolute levels of testosterone, and that balance can be managed through practice, and confidence increased, then the chemistry of gender is not the barrier to leadership for women it might have been once thought to be.[65]

Indeed, with regard to risk-taking, while research shows that men and women can have a similar appetite for risk, further research shows that while oxytocin may increase levels of trust in risk simulations, testosterone has an antidote effect on oxytocin, decreasing trust in social situations and increasing the appetite for taking financial risks.[66]

Apparent differences between men and women observed through neuroscience have been debated. For instance, the brains right and left hemispheres are connected by the corpus callosum where women have up to four times the number of fibres than men, while men have more connections within the hemispheres. It has been argued that men are left hemisphere dominant and that as the left hemisphere is said to deal more with facts, logic, rational thinking and tasks, men are more adept at this than women. The right hemisphere is said to deal more with more with emotions and communication, which are both areas where some have argued women are more adept at than men. Due to the nature of their corpus callosum, women are thought to have more balance between the two hemispheres. In general, historically it has been said that women are more intuitive, better communicators, and are less task orientated.

The central nervous system consists of both grey and white matter. The outer layer of the cerebrum, the cerebral cortex, contains the grey matter containing the neuron cell bodies and below this is the white matter composed of long nerve fibres protected by myelin sheaths. It has been observed that men use more grey matter than white matter for processing, and as grey matter is associated with very specific areas of the brain it is suggested that this may be experienced as tunnel vision. In contrast, women are said to use more white matter, which connects grey matter and other processing centres and therefore may explain women's ability to quickly move from one task to another.

In addition to the difference in chemical impact of testosterone and oestrogen, men have less oxytocin, the bonding neurotransmitter, which in some circumstances may hinder building relationships. Women also have a larger limbic system and hippocampus, which it is believed respectively increase women's ability to connect with others and store memories.

In *Gendered Brain*, Gina Rippon discusses and illustrates the forward-thinking view of us constantly generating predictions based on: scripts, or stored patterns, from prior experiences; the structural differences of brains and therefore behaviour; and plasticity, meaning a path dependency creating provisional variability in brain structures.[67] However, she questions evidence that suggests[68]:

- The right side of the brain supports the emotional skills with the right supporting the logical cognitive skills.
- The size of the corpus callosum, which bridges the right and left hemispheres, mediating the volume of communication – some correlation but no causation.
- With regard to grey matter versus white matter, females have a higher percentage of grey matter – some studies have contradicted this. IQ correlations suggest men have greater correlation with grey matter and women white matter.

In addition, she states that the empathizing quotient (EQ) and systemizing quotient (SQ) are not respectively an exact proxy for female and male genders. Where EQ is associated with the need and ability to recognize and respond to thoughts and emotions of others at both a cognitive and emotional level and SQ describes the drive to analyse and be interested in rule-based processes and events.

Rippon also calls for a rethink of the role of hormones in determining behaviour. Testosterone is an androgen and is known as a male hormone. Oestradiol is known as a female hormone but occurs in both men and women, and recent studies show the levels of oestadiol and progesterone, female hormones, do not differ between women and men.

She goes on to state that the more we look at different measures from biology through the characteristics of the brain to behaviour and personality profiles, 'the less likely it is that these measures are coming from two reliably distinguishable groups of people'.[69]

Task orientation vs people orientation

In *The Neuroscience of Leadership Coaching*, it is noted that task-oriented leadership involves activating areas of the brain involved in focused attention, language, logical reasoning, mathematical reasoning and causal reasoning. These help in directing our attention to specific goals and to acting on these goals. The network of brain areas that are involved in making decisions include the dorsal and ventral attention systems, in the parietal and temporal cortex respectively, and the frontal-parietal cortex.[70]

Leadership that is socio-emotional, people oriented, will activate areas of the brain involved in emotional self-awareness, social cognition and ethical decision-making. These help creativity and insightful problem solving. The network of brain areas that are involved in this activity are collectively referred to as the default mode network and include

> the areas of the brain at the back of the midline (dorsal midline) include the medial parietal cortex and dorsomedial prefrontal cortex. These areas of the brain are associated with thinking about the mental states of others. The areas of the brain at the front of the midline, particularly the ventromedial prefrontal cortex, are associated with representing the values of external objects and are thus used when we compare options. Both these systems are activated when we make moral decisions.[71]

The activation of the network of brain areas involved in task-oriented leadership causes suppression in the socio-emotional networks and vice versa and therefore it would seem we could access either mode of thinking at any time. If some people have a preference for one mode of thinking and suppress one network most of the time they will, over time, strengthen the preferred network and weaken the other network. Importantly,

> individuals are not stuck with one style of leadership. The brain will learn from repeated experience and so the ability to develop the leadership skills that are currently under represented in an individual brain will be dependent on the willingness of the individual to gain the experiences necessary for the brain to learn.[72]

Transformational leadership

In normal business contexts, it has been found that a transformational leadership style was the dominant predictor of follower's performance, but changing to a more transactional style in extreme contexts;[73] also, that improving dimensions of transformational leadership in team leaders may improve performance by fostering greater communication and trust early in team formation.[74]

An article that compares transformational leadership to authentic, ethical and servant leadership established the following:[75]

- Transformational leadership: The leader's ability to 'to achieve follower performance beyond ordinary limits'[76] through the four Is of behaviour: idealized influence, inspirational motivation, intellectual stimulation and individualized consideration.
- Authentic leadership: Originally proposed in 2003,[77] such leaders are described as 'deeply aware of how they think and behave and are perceived by others as being aware of their own and others' values/moral perspectives, knowledge and strengths'.[78]

- Ethical leadership: This has been defined as 'the demonstration of normatively appropriate conduct through personal actions and interpersonal relationships, and the promotion of such conduct to followers through two-way communication, reinforcement, and decision-making'.[79]

- Servant leadership: 'The servant-leader is servant first. It begins with a natural feeling that one wants to serve. Then conscious choice brings one to aspire to lead'.[80]

Transformational leadership was highly valid for 'explaining behavioural, attitudinal and relational perception outcomes of followers'.[81] Research found that authentic and ethical leadership does not offer much that transformational leadership does not already provide, while servant leadership had significant utility across a wide breadth of measures.[82]

Research results found a significantly positive relationship between shared leadership and team performance. To adopt a shared leadership design 'necessitates selecting and developing employees not only to accept leadership from multiple parties (many of whom are at the same level as themselves) but who are also willing to step-up and accept leadership roles themselves'.[83]

Selection and development

Selection

In *Social Leap*, von Hippel notes that historically social groups were smaller and mobility more restricted, so leaders emerged from a group that had an understanding of leader's ability:

> This internal approach to leadership selection is less frequently used in modern organizational contexts, where candidates, especially at the highest levels of organization, are often recruited from competing organizations. External hires bring in new ideas and new energy but hiring from the outside means that people who know the candidate are rarely involved in the leadership selection process. No doubt, this is part of the reason that externally appointed CEOs usually perform worse and have shorter tenures than those recruited internally.[84]

A greater understanding of a leader's potential may help reduce failure rates through learning and development. In *Neuroscience for Leadership*, it is stated that:

> new knowledge about neuroplasticity means that interventions such as brain-based coaching, which combine psychological and physiological insights, make a profound different to the bottom line of a business through the ability of leaders to flex and adapt to evolving business demands.[85]

Understanding the brain can provide insights into improving knowledge about leadership and leadership development. For instance, the development of transformational and inspirational leaders could be approached using neurofeedback, where

> neurofeedback is a self-regulation technique providing individuals with feedback about specific levels of brain activity in conjunction with specific target behaviours. By becoming aware of how their brains function, such leaders would be able to develop the skills required to become better leaders. Brain neuroplasticity has been considered as one of the ways in which neuroscience can contribute to leadership development.[86]

Neuroscience for Leadership notes that leaders with better-developed PFCs have heightened levels of awareness, more focused attention, greater self-control and are therefore better at planning and complex problem solving.[87]

Overall, to be effective, leaders should be able to:

- focus their attention;
- change that focus when required;
- reflect critically on their thoughts, attitudes and behaviours;
- manage themselves so that they can mobilize their will power, persist in adversity and calibrate their attitude to risk and uncertainty;
- regulate their emotions and moods;
- balance their intuition with their rational thinking;
- maintain their health and energy;
- spend time and effort on developing relevant skills and knowledge for their area of activity so as to focus on the right issues, more often than not, and to have a reliable intuitive response to what comes at them, when circumstances are relatively stable;
- hone their ability to relate well to others.[88]

It is also relevant for leaders to understand well-being in terms of their own mental and physical health and that of their followers. Unfortunately, 'many organizations and leaders fail to recognize that getting maximum performance from individuals, teams and organizations is as much about emotion as it is about logic'.[89]

Development

In the 2019 Deloitte report *Global Human Capital Trends*, it was reported that in terms of leadership for the 21st century respondents felt that leaders need to have the ability to lead: through complexity and ambiguity, 81 per cent; through influence, 65 per cent; remotely, 50 per cent; an augmented workforce, 47 per cent; and more quickly, 44 per cent. They believe this is being driven by: new technologies, 75 per cent; pace of change, 66 per cent;

changing demographics and employee expectations, 57 per cent and changing customer expectations, 53 per cent. The biggest gaps are in transparency, collaboration and performance management.[90]

To support the development of leaders, a framework has been proposed based on five categories of thinking and behaviour for developing leaders 'to use as guiding principles, then adapt with new information, new experiences, new levels of complexity and new contexts'[91]

They note that leadership is contextual and temporal, and stress the importance of developing a capacity for collectiveness, shared, distributed, leadership, adaptiveness and relational emotional and cognitive complexity. Their five-part framework is as follows:

- **Learning:** Learning always and everywhere by being open-minded. Acquiring knowledge, applying it and developing further.

- **Reverence:** Acceptance, understanding and inclusion of everyone, everywhere.

- **Purpose:** Personal intentions, mission, passion, contributions and service to others through their role, work and life. Understanding the personal worldview. Understanding personal strengths, weaknesses and worldview. With will or purpose being 'the manifestation of the personality striving to accomplish its intentions'.

- **Authenticity:** 'Knowing one's self and one's beliefs, then expressing and behaving according to one's convictions and one's unadulterated, pure, true, self'. Using advanced verbal and non-verbal communication. This supports leadership in situations of complexity and paradox through its consistency.

- **Flâneur:** Notwithstanding the less favourable translations of this French word, it is applied here in terms of a leader's ability to observe, contemplate and reflect. Recognition that they have a duality as observer and participant.

Moving forward, leaders will no longer be able to rely on position power to the same extent as they might have done historically. They will need to persuade, inspire and positively motivate, exhibiting fairness and developing trust.

Goleman writes in *Emotional Intelligence*,

> imagine the benefits for work of being skilled in the basic emotional competences – being attuned to the feelings of those we deal with, being able to handle disagreements so they do not escalate, having the ability to get into flow states while doing our work. Leadership is not domination, but the art of persuading people to work toward a common goal. And, in terms of managing our own career, there may be nothing more essential than recognizing our deepest feelings about what we do – and what changes might make us more truly satisfied with our work.[92]

In *Focus: The hidden driver of excellence*, Goleman references an Accenture study, where they interviewed 100 CEOs about the skills they needed to run a company successfully. A set of fourteen abilities emerged, including thinking globally and creating an inspiring shared vision to embracing change, and being tech savvy. However, self-awareness was found to be a key 'meta' ability. 'Chief executives need the ability to assess their own strengths and weaknesses, and so surround themselves with a team of people whose strengths in those core abilities complement their own.'[93]

Leaders concludes that:

> leadership is about much more than outcomes; it is equally concerned with how complex human groups optimize their cooperation and how individuals finds symbols of meaning and purpose of life. This optimization and sense of meaning emerge from the interaction of a wide range of constantly shifting variables that include far more than the individual leader. Leadership is coproduced by leaders and followers, emerging between the influential and charismatic who crave it and the hopeful and fearful who demand it.[94]

In *Why Should Anyone Be Led by You?* Rob Goffee and Gareth Jones note that the exercise of leadership is always contextual and that effective leaders understand the complex social realities in which individuals act. They suggest three related elements to effective situation sensing: observational and cognitive skills; behavioural and adaptive skills; and the leader's ability to change the situation. Leaders are 'not passive recipients of the context. On the contrary, they work with their followers to socially construct an alternative reality'.[95] They are advised to do this at three levels: with the individuals who are key to performance; with their teams; and with the organizational constraints within which they must operate.

It is key for leaders to understand the experience, abilities and motivations of the most impactful people in their organization. Building this picture is possible from direct observation, communication, understanding their impact on the business results for which they are responsible, but also indirectly through conversations with their colleagues and reading 360 reviews. It is also important for leaders to take time to understand the group dynamics of their organization's formal groups, and to have a detailed understanding of the informal organization's networks and alliances. Teams may require task-orientated, maintenance leaders and followers for some periods, and for other periods a more creative and innovative combination.

The author of *Legacy*, James Kerr, was given access to New Zealand's rugby union team, the All Blacks, who have an 86 per cent win rate over many decades.[96] Kerr relates 15 hallmarks of the leadership philosophy that apply to every member of the team, not just the captain, and these include: character, responsibility, expectations, preparation, the ability to deal with pressure, learning and adaptation. They also include authenticity, ritual, shared language and sacrifice. The final trait described is *legacy* – being a good ancestor, planting the trees you will never see.

Maybe the best way of looking at leadership is through the leader's legacy – what can they reflect on proudly when the game ends, what will they have achieved for their stakeholders and who will they have developed to be the leaders of the future?

Highlights

- Leadership can be examined in a number of ways, including leadership traits, styles, behaviour-relationships and context including change.
- There are calls for more leader-managers and fewer managers.
- There is an expectation of more leadership emerging at all levels of organizations.
- Leadership of change has increased in importace as change has become more of a constant.
- Leadership challenges in a VUCA environment are particularly demanding.

Leadership impact

Key themes that leaders should reflect on include:

- Examine your own situation. What stage of development is your organization? What type of leadership is required? Be prepared to adapt your leadership style to suit the situation.
- What is your natural style of leadership? Have you encouraged feedback from peers and direct reports?
- In what areas do you require development? The best leaders are those that recognize the need for continuous learning.
- Have you considered the need for mentoring and coaching for you or your team?

People management recommendations

Actions to consider:

- Who can the most senior leader discuss personal and leadership issues with? Use of an external coach or mentor can be very effective.
- Consider development courses for leaders, leader-managers and others; these interventions could be achieved effectively by using a series of workshops, rather than a 'sheep dip' five-day course.
- Do you have coaching and mentoring provision available more generally? Mentoring of new managers by more senior colleagues is a very effective way of building a strong culture.

Case studies

Leadership is identified as key to the success of the business, and a clear connection is made with engagement and business performance across the organization

Location

Ireland and global.

Background

Smurfit Kappa is a FTSE 100 company and one of the leading providers of paper-based packaging in the world, with operations in 21 European countries and 12 countries in the Americas. Their experience and expertise creates new opportunities for customers and they are constantly updating their pack design and innovations to provide the optimum choice and packaging supplies.

Almost all of the raw materials are sourced from their own paper mills, so consistency is always a key attribute of their products. Because those products are 100 per cent renewable and produced sustainably, they help their customers reduce their environmental footprint.

The packaging business is going through a renaissance. A backlash to plastic packaging is countered by the popularity of online shopping. Everything from takeaways to clothing, books and a myriad of household items are delivered daily to households. The company also offers supply chain and sustainability expertise.

Smurfitt Kappa started out as an Irish paper manufacturer and has its roots in Ireland. However, the company has grown substantially, with annual revenues of over €7.5 billion and people in 370 locations globally.

People challenge

Smurfitt Kappa decided that they wanted to help their managers across the business improve and deepen their capabilities. However, they did not want to adopt the same type of training and development that traditional organizations used. They wanted an approach that was business focused, less academic and not classroom based.

The objective was a world-leading programme. In order to achieve value, the investment in leadership development needed to be substantial and also deliver a meaningful return on that investment.

Solution

The business decided to partner with the well-know business school Insead. By adapting the 'open leadership' approach and delivering a three-module programme over two years, the objective was to increase managers' self-awareness and enable them to deliver more effectively.

Situational leadership is at the core of the programme, meaning that individual managers bring their own history, corporate values and strategic competence to their daily decision-making. Smurfitt Kappa want their managers to 'lead themselves, lead their teams, lead the organization and eventually lead the market'.

The programme is run at Insead's campus near Paris, France, and coaches take participants through a journey of self-discovery, which can prove to be very revealing. It is a powerful process. Aims include empowerment, more distributive decision-making, strategic thinking and emphasis on diversity. Outcomes are focused on the individual's communication style and learning how to deliver negative feedback to their staff.

It is planned to graduate over 350 people by the end of 2020 from around the globe. The first cohort of 60 who completed the course confirmed that it had made a tangible positive difference to the way they managed the business, and also with their personal relationships.

This open leadership initiative is just part of a full programme of development to be rolled out across the firm. There is a genuine belief in the power of learning. Benefits have included high retention rates and several awards for the quality of the employee experience.

Learning points

- Leadership is the key to success for all organizations.
- Encouraging learning at the top will filter through all levels, and set the tone for all staff.
- Engagement at all levels is a major contributor to success.
- Investing in the development of people will help to create 'stickiness' to the organization and support stronger core values.

Sources

Material for this case has been adapted from the following websites:

www.smurfitkappa.com/people/talent-development

www.peoplemanagement.co.uk/voices/case-studies/smurfit-kappa-leaders-self-discovery

CASE STUDY   Qantas
Training for managing dispersed leadership teams

Location

Australia and global.

Organization

Qantas Airways is the flag-carrier of Australia and its largest airline by fleet size, international flights and international destinations. It is the third oldest airline in the world after KLM and Avianca. Having been founded in November 1920, it began international passenger flights in May 1935.

In 2018 Qantas numbered over 30,000 employees and flew more than 55 million passengers across the globe.

People challenge

Qantas Airways operates in a dynamic and highly competitive industry. Leaders are spread between on-board and on-the-ground locations, and their role is to execute change and corporate strategy that is critical to the success of the business.

Having already rolled out a global leader talent programme for on-board managers, it was decided to rebrand and expand this programme across the Qantas International Division in 2017. Objectives included:

- providing career development for high-performing individuals;
- demonstrating that their input was valued;
- using common goals and mutual understanding to connect this diverse group;
- creating a path for participants to be able to cross over to Qantas Corporate.

Solutions

The new programme was designed to be challenging, pragmatic and transformational over a five-month period and was branded Accelerate. Key features included:

- Personal and people leadership were a priority, and included senior managers sharing their own personal career journeys.
- Cadres were cross-functional, including on-board and ground managers.
- There was a two-day launch that focused on collaboration and bonding within each grouping.
- Participants were given a virtual 12-week project to complete; they were provided with coaches and a sponsor to assist, and ended with a team presentation to a senior executive.

Learning points

The first 60 participants came from Australia, Europe and Asia. Feedback was very positive and it is planned to rollout annually.

Ninety per cent of managers fed back that the programme increased their knowledge and was particularly relevant for their development needs. One quote was that the training was, 'Engaging, challenging, and enlightening. A fantastic opportunity.'

A particular learning point was the value of the syndicate projects, which brought a different perspective to some know challenges within the business. One example was the Qantas Service Promise, which ended up being improved with interactive learning and creating an end-to-end customer experience.

Sources

Material for this case has been adapted from the following websites:

www.qantas.com/gb/en/about-us/qantas-careers/more-careers.html

www.maximus.com.au/case_study/leading-virtual-workforce-qantas/

CASE STUDY   Tata Group
India's largest company and the importance of leadership

Location

India and global.

Background

Tata Group is a global enterprise founded by Jamsetji Tata in 1868. It is
headquartered in India, and comprises 30 diverse companies across 10
verticals. The group operates in more than 100 countries across six continents,
and it states its mission is 'To improve the quality of life of the communities we
serve globally, through long-term stakeholder value creation based on
Leadership with Trust'.

Leadership of people is therefore considered a critical element of the
business, and has been since its inception over 150 years ago.

In 2017–18 the revenue of Tata companies, taken together, was US$110.7
billion. These companies collectively employ over 700,000 people.

Each Tata company or enterprise operates independently under the guidance
and supervision of its own board of directors. There are 28 publicly listed Tata
enterprises with a combined market capitalization of about US$145.3 billion (as at
31 March 2018).

Challenge

In February 2017 Natarajan Chandrasekaran was installed as the new Chairman
of Tata Sons, the private holding company that controls the many companies
across the Tata Group. This followed the abrupt exit of the previous incumbent in
October 2016. The group became embroiled in a messy legal dispute, and several
companies across the group were losing money and market share due to difficult
market conditions.

Leadership would be vital to steady the ship and take the group forward in a
more positive way. Chandra himself came from relatively humble beginnings; he
grew up in a rural village in the state of Tamil Nadu and his father was a farmer.
He excelled at maths and computers and gained a masters degree at a regional
engineering college. He joined Tata Consultancy Services, India's largest IT firm,
as an intern in 1987 and was Managing Director and CEO when appointed
Chairman of the group.

Solutions

Chandra moved quickly and held a town hall meeting in April 2017 with senior managers from across the group. He told them that it was important to become united and to follow the mantra of 'One Tata'. In follow-up meetings he made it clear that there needed to be clearer line of accountability and that he would establish more detailed metrics to evaluate the performance of each of the operating companies.

He also committed to reorganize the group in order to focus on scale and growth opportunities. There were multiple companies competing in similar sectors, which did not make business sense.

Chandra also decided that he needed to hire some new talent into the group. These included some senior and experienced bankers and strategy specialists. A key change was also to reduce the number of direct reports to the chairman.

His leadership style includes a baseline of discipline and hard work, and clients describe him as affable and a good listener. As Managing Director of TCS, he would spend 200 days a year travelling in Europe, the United States and Asia, primarily to meet with customers. Now, as Chairman of the Group, he began travelling extensively to meet with all stakeholders, in India and overseas. What also stands out about his leadership style is his fascination with data and technology. In fact, one of his greatest supporters is Michael Capiraso, President of the New York Runners, who manage the New York City Marathon which TCS sponsors. Over 300,000 people have downloaded a TCS-designed marathon app that has detailed records of over 200,000 people who have run the race in the last 40 years. Chandra says that he wants to bring the same level of data focus to Tata.

Learning points

Leadership is key to the success of all organizations. Appointing the right person with the required skillset is critical. In this case, the new chairman is the first non-family member in this role.

This is also a great case of how a large traditional company is harnessing data and technology to drive itself forward, and reorganizing in a more coherent way for the 21st century.

Sources

Material for this case has been adapted from the following websites:

www.tata.com/

www.tata.com/newsroom/fit-to-lead-tata-steel-adventure-foundation

www.tata.com/newsroom/fortune-how-tata-new-chairman-pans-fix-india-biggest-company

PART TWO
The environment

Part One examined our evolution and increasing understanding of our emotions, cognitive processes, decision-making and other behaviour. We also discussed the concepts of meaning, purpose, impression management and socially constructed reality. Finally, we touched on the challenge human complexity brings for leaders. These areas are summarized in Figure P2.1.

Figure P2.1   The people paradigm

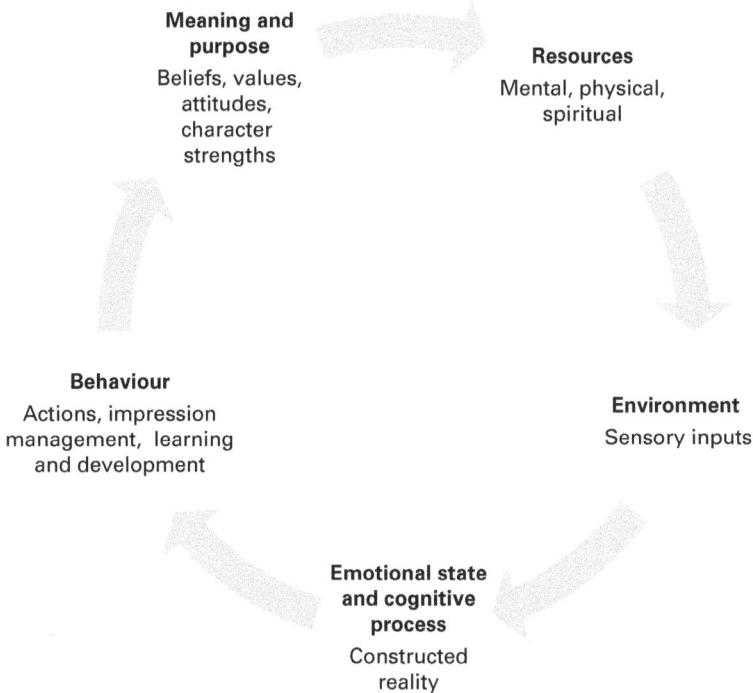

Meaning and purpose
Beliefs, values, attitudes, character strengths

Resources
Mental, physical, spiritual

Behaviour
Actions, impression management, learning and development

Environment
Sensory inputs

Emotional state and cognitive process
Constructed reality

The people paradigm summarizes five key areas of leadership focus:

- **Meaning and purpose:** Beliefs, values, attitudes, interests, motives. What are people's fundamental drivers, what is important to them? What are their character strengths? How do they define and realize meaning?
- **Environment:** Sensory inputs. How does the environment impact them?
- **Resources:** Mental, physical, spiritual. What personality traits, psychological state, cognitive ability and physical ability do people have?
- **Emotional/affective state and cognitive process:** Socially constructed reality. What is the reality they construct and navigate?
- **Behaviour:** Impression management. How do people interact with others? Learning and development. What do they learn from their experiences and how does this help them develop?

Part Two introduces the evolution in our thinking about work, workplaces and the workforce, as the second layer of complexity.

Organizations 06

Introduction

Work takes place in a complex organizational setting, and in this chapter the following aspects of organizations are reviewed: their purpose and strategies, the external and internal environment, their structure, design and associated organization behavioural considerations. It will be seen how organizational complexity is informed by, and can be compared to, the complexity of people and a parallel paradigm is developed to illustrate this.

While change is a constant, the speed and complexity of change has arguably increased significantly since Colvin's fourth turning point, which heralds emerged and emerging technology, discussed in Chapter 1. The environment within which organizations operate has become more volatile, uncertain, complex and ambiguous – a VUCA world. An increasingly VUCA world is caused by many factors, including: political and economic activity, regulation, emergent technology, sociodemographics, change and increasing expectations around corporate and social responsibility. This is challenging for the strategic decision-making, leadership, management and followership that is undertaken on the edge of chaos, a concept that is discussed later in this chapter.

Chapter summary

The following subjects are discussed in this chapter:

- **purpose;**
- **external environment:**
  - political and economic policy;
  - legal/regulation;
  - social;
  - technological;
  - environmental;
  - volatility, uncertainty, complexity and ambiguity;
  - organization ecology;

- **strategy:**
  - SWOT and Five Forces;
  - business strategy:
    - Porter on strategy;
    - Blue Ocean Strategy;
  - strategy direction:
    - Ansoff's Growth Matrix;
    - balance of business portfolio – BCG Growth Matrix;
  - integration;
- **internal environment:**
  - the Resource-Based View;
  - the Capability View;
  - models to view organizations;
    - Star Model;
    - McKinsey 7S;
  - strategy development;
- **organization design and development:**
  - organization design;
  - organization development;
- **social constructionism and organizational enactment;**
- **organization structures:**
  - Mintzberg's Organizational Model;
  - power structures;
- **practical implications.**

Purpose

Organizations are encouraged to define their purpose, vision and mission, their values and principles, and their goals, strategic plans and objectives.

The purpose of an organization describes the reason for its existence, while the vision describes where it aspires to be in the future and the mission describes how it intends to fulfil its vision.

Given the degree of uncertainty and speed of change, many organizations find themselves endeavouring to maximize their current capabilities and competitive advantage while reducing development cycles through agile working and focusing on the future by embracing innovation and disruption. While an organization's purpose may endure, its vision may flex more often and the mission may have an even shorter shelf life. This balancing act is sometimes referred to as organizational ambidexterity, where adaptability for the future occurs while alignment for the present allows for maximizing success with current products and services in current markets.

The values of an organization help define core principles that guide behaviour within the organization and in its interface with external stakeholders. There has been a lot of input in this area, such as changing societal expectations around organizations' responsibilities for environmental sustainability, diversity and inclusion, and employee well-being.

Goals are narrower and there are more specific definitions of success in executing the organization's mission. Strategic plans are the agreed approach taken to achieve goals, while objectives are measurable points on the journey to implementing the strategic plan. Shorter term plans are documented to describe how objectives will be attained. With the increased speed of change faced by organizations, shorter goal cycles are required, which in turn decreases the time horizon of each plan. It also requires organizations to have agile development teams, continuous feedback loops, a culture that embraces failure and the ability to make quick decisions.

In *Exploring Strategy*, three areas of strategic consideration are summarized:

- **strategic position:** macro-environment, stakeholders, culture, resources and industry;
- **strategic choices:** business strategy, international, acquisitions and alliances, entrepreneurship and corporate strategy;
- **strategic action:** evaluating, organizing, leadership and change and processes.[1]

This chapter will consider the external and internal positioning factors that impact strategic choices and strategic decision-making. Strategic action is examined with regard to the leadership of change. Organizational decision-making is undertaken acknowledging the potentially competing views of stakeholders. The stakeholder group includes those who are working within an organization, including those with ownership, and the following external groups: political, economic, social, technological, regulatory and owners.

Organizations are located as operating within a macro-environment which contains factors that impact many sectors, such as financial services, and industries, such as asset management within financial services. Each organization is then located in terms of its competitive positioning.

External environment

The external environment is often reviewed in terms of the political, economic, social, technological, legal and environmental/ethical (PESTLE) impact on organizations. The nature of the environment can also be considered in terms of VUCA.

Political and economic policy

Political decisions on foreign policy, trade, environmental protection, public protection, employee protection, taxation and pensions and many other areas all impact the leadership context, as does monetary policy, which impacts business growth, inflation and employment. Uncertainty regarding policy changes and the complexity of their effect increases uncertainty and may lead to market volatility. The availability and composition of labour will be directly impacted by political decisions around immigration with a supportive policy framework increasing migration, which will help limit the deceleration of global workforce growth. Political analysis can be undertaken at global societal, supranational, national and regional societal levels. Economic analysis can be examined in terms of stock cycles, investment cycles and infrastructure cycles, which have a short- to long-term perspective.

Leaders should be briefed on all likely political and economic policy decisions with an assessment of organizational, and therefore workforce, impact.

Legal/regulation

Regulation has the ability to transform or disrupt industry sectors. For instance, in the wake of the global financial crises, restrictions on the use of bank capital led to a reduction in bank lending, the growth of private debt funds, a reduction in proprietary trading by banks, and in the United Kingdom the ring-fencing of retail banking operations from capital markets and investment banking activities. Other regulations have been introduced to increase protection to customers of financial services organizations and increase consumer choice, for instance Open Banking in the UK.

More generally, the European Union's General Data Protection Regulation (GDPR) has changed the relationship between providers of data and the receivers of data. Organizations need to ensure the privacy of personal information and this creates a costly, event-driven, and ongoing compliance challenge for all organizations. In addition, it will lead to changes in customer acquisition and service provision while also impacting organizations' ability to migrate to distributed ledger systems and control cyber-crime.

In a similar way to political and economic policy decisions, leaders should be briefed during periods of consultation prior to the passing of new regulations. This allows them the opportunity to give input that informs the final statute and to prepare for its introduction. Regulatory changes that impact the workforce must be planned for to ensure compliance.

Social

Social factors can be analysed in terms of global, national and regional demographic changes, distribution of wealth, culture and networks.

The social demographic changes within countries and immigration policies will impact the availability of employees of different age groups, with different skills and different beliefs, values, interests and motivations.

The world population is expected to expand from 7.349 billion in 2015 to 9.725 billion in 2050, with more than 50 per cent of this growth occurring in Africa. However, the global increase in the population of older people will see a decrease in the growth rate of the potential workforce and there could be a 7 per cent fall in OECD countries by 2060, although labour market and pension reforms could contribute a 2.4 per cent increase in labour force participation over the same period.[2]

Labour force participation rates are falling, despite being offset by the rising participation of women. However, it has been estimated that up to 500 million new jobs will need to be created by 2020 to fulfil the demand by current potential job seekers and young people predicted to join the workforce. Youth unemployment is predicted to increase.[3]

The rise of non-standard forms of employment (NSE) is increasing and includes all forms of temporary contract work. In 2017 as much as 25 per cent of the work performed in the US was thought to be done by freelancers, and this is predicted to grow to 40 per cent by 2020. Results of a survey in 2017 suggest that by 2020 the use of contractors will increase by 37 per cent, freelancers by 33 per cent, gig workers by 28 per cent and crowd workers by 21 per cent.[4]

NSE may bring short-term cost savings and operating flexibility to employers in addition to flexible work opportunities to the workforce. However, protection for contractors is less extensive and pension provision is their responsibility. For employers it can be harder to lead and manage a workforce with a significant population of contract workers.

Social movements will also impact the organization in areas such as employee diversity and inclusion, equality and well-being. In addition, organizations are increasingly expected to behave in a socially responsible way towards their associated communities and wider stakeholder group. Corporate and social responsibility (CSR) can no longer be a statement of intent; it has to be authentic otherwise organizations will be held accountable by their employees, suppliers, customers and investors.

A 2017 study[5] found that 78 per cent of 22,000 investment professionals have increased their investments in firms with a focused CSR programme, although another study in the same year found that while 77 per cent of global respondents cited corporate citizenship as important only 18 per cent said it was a priority embedded in their organizational strategy.[6]

The need for leaders to be authentic in their approach to CSR is well supported by research. Programmes need to be aligned with their organization's purpose, integrated into the operating model and the impact monitored, measured and reported.

Technological

Technology has driven significant change since the Agricultural Revolution, through the Industrial Evolution, mass production, computer automation and now Industry 4.0, which includes cognitive computing, cloud computing, robotic process automation and the internet of things (IoT). Emerged and evolving technologies such as artificial intelligence, machine learning and distributed ledger technology will all have a transformational and disruptive impact on organizations.

One study has predicted that 60 per cent of occupations will have at least 30 per cent of their constituent work activities automated, and that by 2030 between 3 per cent and 14 per cent, or 75 million to 375 million, of the global workforce will need to switch occupational categories. They have also predicted a skill shift in the same period, with a significant decrease in the demand for physical and manual skills and basic cognitive skills, and an increase in the demand for higher cognitive skills, social and emotional skills and technological skills. Individuals will embark on a journey of lifelong learning to ensure they can adapt and survive, and employers will need to predict future needs and develop their workforce accordingly.[7]

Environmental

A specific area of concern is global sustainability. It is the responsibility of leaders to consider the impact their organizations have on the environment and what can be done to operate in a manner that increases sustainability.

Environmental damage, climate change, water shortages and conflicts are expected to increase migration. Indeed, between 2008 and 2015 it is estimated that 21.5 million people have been displaced by natural disasters.[8]

A number of organizations have adopted triple bottom-line reporting, which includes financial, social and environmental data in their annual reports.[9]

Volatility, uncertainty, complexity and ambiguity

The VUCA concept originated from the US military in the post-Cold War era. It has since been adopted by those considering the challenges of organization strategy and design and illustrated below.

Volatility, a situation that is subject to rapid change, can be illustrated in the political and economic context by changes in geopolitical relationships, immigration and employment policy, foreign exchange rate policy and the financial impact of changes to domestic fiscal and monetary policy. Leaders need to scenario plan for a number of outcomes, with global organizations facing greater uncertainty than organizations operating domestically or in their regional markets.

Uncertainty will arise where situations are unpredictable, or information is unreliable. There are known risks, and these can be calculated. Leaders can examine historic patterns of employee turnover and use predictive analytics to forecast future scenarios. Leaders may be limited in their ability to reduce levels of uncertainty where there is significant disagreement in potential outcomes, especially where complexity and ambiguity exist.

Complexity will increase uncertainty, and when trying to compare multiple variables it is a challenge to collect, store and access data that is reliable and valid. Multiple interdependent rule-based decisions are required to make a decision. Leaders trying to predict levels of employee turnover require access to data from disparate sources. When analysing multiple variables it is not always possible to have a high level of confidence in causal effects, and this can lead to ambiguity.

Ambiguity also increases uncertainty where there is more than one possible meaning, where the casual effect or effects are unclear. Where risk can't be calculated. It could be that the results of an employee turnover analysis give a number of correlations and attempts to identify causation will rely on further statistical analysis combined with qualitative research such as interviews.

The VUCA operating environment challenges the future requirements of leaders, including how their cognitive capabilities enable them to build, integrate, reconfigure and competitively reposition organizational resources. This is an important area to explore from a selection and development perspective, and another concept borrowed from the US military, cognitive readiness, is a useful framework to consider. While the antecedents of cognitive readiness have not been consistently defined, one study suggests it includes: situation awareness, memory, transfer, meta-cognition, automaticity, problem solving, decision-making, mental flexibility and creativity, leadership and emotion.[10]

Environmental uncertainty has been viewed in terms of information requirements[11] and perceived environmental uncertainty through complexity and rate-of-change:[12]

- **low complexity and low rate of change:** required information known and available;
- **low complexity and high rate of change:** constant need for new information;
- **high complexity and low rate of change:** information overload;
- **high complexity and high rate of change:** information required is unknown.

Organization ecology

In *The Demography of Corporations and Industries*, Carroll and Hannan discuss why the population of organizations changes over time, from their founding, through growth, decline, structural transformation and ultimately their demise. Organizational demography refers to processes that apply at the level of populations of organizations, population ecology refers to interactions between localized sets of organization populations and community ecology refers to the processes that follow the interactions of a full population set in a system. They look at a number of factors, including external alignment and fitness; adaptation and selection; the nature of competition; and the speed and efficiency of change processes. They note that despite increased protections for employees, either given voluntarily by employers or driven by regulation, a significant amount of employee terminations are due to corporate demographic activity such as mergers and acquisitions and organizational failure.[13] This indicates the importance of strategic planning and decision-making.

Strategy

Leaders create and execute strategic plans which should encompass a strategic workforce plan (SWP). These are discussed in Chapter 16. Leaders need to have the skills and experience to analyse their organization's situation, from an internal and external perspective, and select the most appropriate strategy.

An organization's strategic choices are said to include business strategy, strategic direction and strategic methods:

- **business strategy:** relative to competitors;
- **strategic direction:** in terms of products/services and markets;
- **strategic methods:** in terms of organic and inorganic growth, including strategic alliances.[14]

Competitive strategy is about how to create value for customers that is both superior to competitors and profitable.

When looking at an organization's strategic positioning leaders can use various tools, these include a SWOT analysis and Michael Porter's Five Forces.

SWOT and Five Forces

In reviewing the strategy of an organization, a classic tool is a SWOT analysis, which looks at internal strengths and weaknesses and compares these to external opportunities and threats. As a development of this framework, Porter established his Five Forces Framework as follows:

- **bargaining power of suppliers:** concentration, high switching costs, integration, differentiated products;
- **bargaining power of buyers:** concentration, low switching costs, integration, profitability;
- **threat of new entrants:** scale and experience, access to supply and distribution channels, expected retaliation, legislation/government action, incumbent advantages;
- **threat of substitutes:** price versus performance, switching costs;
- **intensity of competitive rivalry:** concentration and balance, growth rate, high fixed costs, high exit barriers, low differentiation.[15]

This framework suggests analysing an organization's competitive environment by looking at the micro-environment, the forces close to the organization.

Business strategy

Two approaches to developing a business strategy are noted below.

Porter on strategy

Porter's three generic strategies are base around cost, differentiation and focus:

- **cost leadership:** operating at lowest cost;
- **differentiation:** uniqueness that is priced at a premium;
- **focus:** targeting a narrow domain for products and services, based either on cost or differentiation.[16]

With simplicity always comes the criticism that models are too universal and not situationally specific, and Porter's model has not escaped these observations. Other criticisms include its rigidity and therefore that it limits the development of strategic options through blue-sky thinking

Blue Ocean Strategy

In *Blue Ocean Strategy*, W Chan Kim and Reneé Mauborgne propose and examine two theories that illustrate ways leaders can conceive of their organization's strategic options. A Red Ocean Strategy takes a structurist, environmental, *deterministic* view that assumes any industry's structural conditions are set for all competitors, In contrast, the value innovation of Blue Ocean Strategy is based on the view that market boundaries are not set and can be reconstructed by the beliefs and actions of industry players.[17] They call this the *reconstructionist* view.

In the Red Ocean, differentiation costs because firms compete with the same best practice rule. Here the strategic choices for firms are to pursue either differentiation or low cost. In the reconstructionist world, however, the strategic aim is to create new best practice rules by breaking the existing value–cost trade-off and thereby creating a blue ocean.[18]

With a Red Ocean Strategy organizations:

- compete in existing market space;
- beat the competition;
- exploit existing demand;
- make the value–cost trade off;
- align the whole system of a firm's activities with its strategic choice of differentiation or low cost.[19]

With a Blue Ocean Strategy organizations:

- create uncontested market space;
- make the competition irrelevant;
- create and capture new demand;
- break the value–cost trade off;
- align the whole system of a firm's activities in pursuit of differentiation and low cost.[20]

Kim and Mauborgne set out six principles of their Blue Ocean Strategy:

- formulation principles (4):
  - reconstruct market boundaries;
  - focus on the big picture, not the numbers;
  - reach beyond existing demand;
  - get the strategic sequence right;
- *risk factor each principle attenuates:*
  - search risk;
  - planning risk;
  - scale risk;
  - business model risk;
- execution principles (2):
  - overcome key organizational hurdles;
  - build execution into strategy;
- *risk factor each principle attenuates:*
  - organizational risk;
  - management risk.[21]

Finally, they discuss strategy execution and note four major hurdles: political opposition, resource constraints, cognitive bias to stay with the status quo and lack of motivation from employees. It is suggested that clarity and a fair process in strategy formulation will satisfy the sense of procedural justice and therefore explanation will lead to voluntary commitment and engagement.

Strategy direction

Strategy direction can be considered in a number of ways, for instance: the Ansoff Growth Matrix shows new products/services versus existing ones, and new markets versus existing ones; and the Boston Consulting Group (BCG) Growth Matrix shows products/services versus market share/market growth expectations and whether strategic integration is vertical or horizontal.

Ansoff's Growth Matrix

Ansoff's Growth Matrix suggest four directions for organizational growth with products/services aligned to existing and new markets. This leads to:

- **market penetration:** existing products and services in current markets;
- **market development:** existing products and services in new markets;
- **new products and services:** in existing markets;
- **new products and services:** in new markets.[22]

Balance of business portfolio: BCG Growth Matrix

Strategy for investment can be discussed in terms of market share and market growth to determine the relative attractive of the business portfolio:

- **high market share and high growth:** stars;
- **high market share and low growth:** cash cows;
- **low market share and high growth:** question marks;
- **low market share and low growth:** dogs.

Stars would receive continued investment, cash cows would receive throw-off funding for investment in the stars, the dogs may be divested, and question marks require decisions around resource allocation.[23]

Integration

Strategic integration can be vertical or horizontal:

- **vertical:** backwards into the value chain, suppliers; forwards into the value chain, distributors;
- **horizontal:** leveraging firm resources to produce complimentary or competing products/services.

These classic models illustrate some of the options leaders face when considering their organization's strategic direction. All have an impact on SWP. In addition to the external environment, the capability of the organization must also be established.

Internal environment

It is important to understand the internal environment of organizations as it encompasses the people operating system, and the key theory to understand here is the Resource-Based View of organizations (RBV), which is introduced below. Following this, the structural design and development of organizations will be considered.

The Resource-Based View

Jay Barney's article, 'Firm resources and sustained competitive advantage', introduced the resource-based view of organizations by focused on organizations' internal resources as a source of competitive advantage rather than how organizations are positioned in the market. To contribute to competitive advantage, resources must: be valuable, rare, imperfectly imitable, and not easily substitutable (VRIN). Organization resources include, people, knowledge and relationships.[24]

Barney later revised his theory by adding organizational support to get VRIO:

- **Value:** Address opportunities and threats, be of value to customers, must be profitable for the organization.
- **Rarity:** How unique are they?
- **Inimitability:** Difficult to create, obtain or substitute (moved from a standalone factor – previously the N): this means complexity – through connections/networks internal and external; causal ambiguity – competitors cannot understand the causes and effects; and culture – which is path dependent.
- **Organization support:** Complimentary capabilities, systems and processes.[25]

People in organizations and their relationships fit these criteria and therefore this concept is important to consider with regard to strategic human resource management and is discussed further in Chapter 16.

The Capability View

For success in the long term, an organization's capabilities must change over time and their ability to do this can be a source of competitive advantage.

David Teece introduced the concept of dynamic capabilities, which he defines as 'an organization's ability to renew and recreate its resources and capabilities to meet the needs of changing environments'.[26]

Three main types of dynamic capabilities were proposed:

- **sensing:** scanning the external environment;
- **seizing:** translating opportunity into reality;
- **reconfiguring:** changing organizational capabilities.

Dynamic capabilities are likely to have micro-foundations, that is, a starting point that is based on social relationships and interaction.[27] The concept of catalysts occurring at the micro level is associated with organizational complexity theory, which is discussed below.

Models to view organizations

A number of frameworks exist to examine the design of organizations, with the Star Model and McKinsey's 7S Model being good examples.

Star Model

The Star Model was developed by Jay Galbraith, who suggests five major areas of organizational analysis:

- **strategy:** the basic direction of the organization – goals, objectives to be achieved, values and mission to be pursued;
- **structure:** power relationships mediated by role specialization; shape – vertical and span of control; distribution – vertically, centralization vs decentralization, and laterally – movement of power to the area dealing with mission-critical issues; departmentalization – the basis on which departments are established;
- **processes:** vertical and horizontal workflows;
- **rewards:** aligning the goals of the employees with those of the organization;
- **people:** the approach to human resource management based on policy decisions.[28]

McKinsey's 7S Model

This model considers organization strategy, structure and systems plus:

- **style:** leadership behaviour;
- **staff:** talent management;
- **skills:** portable and non-portable;[29]
- shared values.

In *Chasing Stars*, Boris Groysberg looks at the relative portability of employees:

- portable (or semi-portable) human capital:
  - personal relationships with clients and outside networks;
  - innate ability, general training and education;[30]
- non-portable human capital:
  - firm's supporting capabilities and reputation;
  - routines and procedures, teammates, managers;
  - knowledge and skills gained from in-house training programmes and on-the-job experience that have no value outside the firm;
  - internal formal and informal networks that take years to develop, and a firm's capabilities, which takes years to learn how to successfully leverage.[31]

It is important to understand the segments of the people population that are more or less portable and design an employee experience that minimizes the regretted loss of talent.

Strategy development

In *Exploring Strategy*, it is suggested that deliberate strategy, based on intentional formulation and planning, is developed through the agency of strategic leadership, systematic analysis and planning, or through external intervention.

In contrast, emergent strategy, a series of decisions forming a pattern that becomes clear over time, is developed through:

- **logical incrementalism:** where, due to environmental uncertainty, strategy emerges in terms of experimentation and general goals;[32]
- **political process:** where negotiation takes place between powerful interest groups;
- **sensemaking:** which is influenced by an understanding and request for resource allocation driven by lower-level management working with structures and systems.

The importance of an organization's agility and resilience in this process has been noted:

- **agility:** any organization's ability to detect and respond to opportunities and threats quickly and easily;
- **resilience:** any organizations ability to recover from shocks.

The ability to achieve agility and resilience is impacted by organizational slack, which relates to spare resources that can be called upon to react, respond and repair. This is analogous of the situation of people in organizations who need to be physically and mentally fit to operate effectively and be resilient.[33]

Organization design and development helps leaders configure and develop their organizations, and these are defined and discussed below.

Organization design and development

To identify and analyse the resources of an organization that may contribute to its competitive advantage requires an understanding of the organization's design (ODS) and organizational development (ODV).

Organization design

ODS can be defined as 'the process of purposefully configuring elements of an organization to effectively and efficiently achieve its strategy and deliver intended business, customer and employee outcomes. The resulting configuration is the organization's design'.[34]

In *Organization Design*, Naomi Stanford defines ODS as 'arranging how to do the work necessary to effectively and efficiently achieve a business purpose and strategy while delivering high quality customer and employee experience.'[35] In this definition, arranging is seen as aligning the organization with the strategy, and creating coherent designs, while building trust among key stakeholders in the context of five organizational elements, 'the strategy, the work, the systems/processes involved in doing the work, the people who do the work, and the way in which they do it'.[36]

ODS helps organizations as they change internal structures and systems to support the adaption required to successfully anticipate and react to changes in the external environment. A number of structural models have been proposed to frame organizational reviews and these include Galbraith's Star Model and McKinsey's 7S Model, which were discussed above.

ODS is compared with ODV as follows. Organization design is

> conventionally associated with the 'technical' top-down aspects of organizational structure and system change. Its fundamental premises are about economic rationalization. It involves designing structures, networks, processes and roles to align the organization around strategy and business imperatives. Typically, ODS drives structural change and will impact on cultural change. The success factor of ODS is the extent to which organization-wide alignment is achieved.[37]

Organization development is

> about building healthy and effective organizations. It does this by improving the ways people work together and uses techniques based on behavioural science and process facilitation. ODV takes forward the design by delivering the internal changes required by the strategy. A holistic ODV approach is to define and enable the culture, capabilities and performance needed to execute strategy.[38]

Organization development

The historical base of ODV is the Tavistock Institute, based in London. It was founded in 1947 to undertake research in human relations with a primary focus on interpersonal and group dynamics. This discipline is increasingly being informed by neuroscience and interpersonal neurobiology. Stanford describes the following as having a key impact on psychological aspects of the workplace:

- Many jobs and activities undertaken by humans are now threatened by artificial intelligence and robotics.
- Increasing technology use requires workers to have high levels of technological competences and the ability to work with robots and artificial intelligence.
- Work is increasingly time-pressured by the 'always on' reality offered by mobile devices, meaning work can be done to a flexible schedule.
- Technology enables more worker mobility with less dependence on work/worker geography.
- There is a swing towards multidisciplinary team-based and collaborative work.
- Effective work performance is demanding better emotional and social skills as the workplace mix changes and 'career' patterns alter.
- The psychological contract between employer and employee is changing as job security declines and people are less interested in career advancement and more interested in 'employee experience'.
- Occupations with cognitive tasks that are not routine are adding the most jobs, although these too are increasingly threatened by technological alternatives.
- More adaptive organizations are continually redesigning around the customer to maintain or gain competitive advantage. They are also less likely to be interested in hierarchy and more interested in expertise.[39]

In *Organization Development*, the following aspects are seen as being at the heart of ODV practice, which fundamentally aims 'to improve the functioning of individuals, teams and the total organization'.[40] It is:

- a systematic process for applying behavioural science principles and practices in organizations to increase individual and organization effectiveness;
- a process (and its associated technology) directed at organization improvement;
- all the planned interventions to increase organization effectiveness and health;
- about building and maintaining the health of the organization as a total system;

- achieving organization revitalization through synthesizing individual, group and organizational goals so as to provide effective service to the client and community while furthering quality of produce and work life;
- enhancing organizational effectiveness by attending to both humans and organizational needs;
- an organizational process for understanding and improving any and all substantive processes an organization may develop for performing any tasks and pursuing any objectives.[41]

They also note that the following definitions of ODV:

- All the activities engaged in by managers, employees and helpers that are directed towards building and maintaining the health of the organization as a total system.
- A long-range effort to improve an organization's problem solving and renewal processes… with the assistance of a change agent, or catalyst, and the use of the theory and technology of applied behavioural science, including action research.[42]

ODS and ODV are informed by behavioural science and the history of organizational behaviour, which can be summarized into various periods of thinking:[43]

- **Rational economic (1910–20):** A period of mass production, driven solely by economic outcomes, universal division of labour, scientific management, Durkheim (1893),[44] Taylorism (1911),[45] classical school, Fayol (1919),[46] bureaucracy, Weber (1924).[47]) Influenced by military, engineering, classical economics, physiology. Structural.
- **Social (1920–60):** A period recognizing the social nature of people and groups where they work, human relations, Mayo (1924),[48] systems theory, somewhat contingent, socio-technical systems, Burns and Stalker (1961).[49] Influenced by sociology and social psychology. Behavioural.
- **Self-actualizing (1960–90):** A period of automating mass production, driven by economic and non-economic factors. Contingency theory, Fiedler (1967),[50] which is integrative, influenced by sociology and social psychology. Also, systems theory, Katz and Khan (1966),[51] influenced by mathematics, economics, operational research and systems engineering. Integrative.
- **Complex man (1990–):** A period of complex interactions. Stacey (2009),[52] VUCA, Whiteman (1998)[53] and Kail (2010).[54] Configurational, complex and chaotic. Flexible, agile, flow. Employee of one.

While psychologists had considered the needs of workers, it was not until Elton Mayo's research at the Hawthorne factory in America in 1924 that the human relations models of management were developed. His work researching productivity while changing the physical working environment produced results that showed social relations in the workplace had a greater impact on performance than physical conditions. From this point, social interaction and group dynamics became more of a focus and the personnel profession started to develop.

Contingency approaches, which reject universalistic best practice in favour of approaches that consider the context, were exemplified in Fred Fiedler's *A Theory of Leadership Effectiveness*, in which he argued against best practice and stated that leadership effectiveness depends on the extent of trust and confidence the team has in the leader, the task structure and the leader's position-power. Contingency approaches are recognisable through if–then statements.[55]

A systems approach to management sees organizations as open or closed systems. In *The Social Psychology of Organizations*, Katz and Khan think of organizations as receiving input from their environments, processing and then releasing outputs back into the environment.[56] Organizations that are highly impacted by the external environment are known as open systems and those that are not impacted are known as closed systems. External environments can be classified as more or less dynamic or static. Open systems facing a dynamic environment need to adapt to maintain homeostasis, which delivers not just survival but growth.

Organizations are now sometimes considered as complex adaptive systems (CAS) containing individuals, heterogeneous agents, interacting with other individuals and with the output of these interactions being discussed as emergence. People in organizations are to some extent constrained by the system they operate within, but through their actions they also modify it. Complex systems are adaptive organizations,

> like complex systems in nature are seen as dynamic non-linear systems. The outcome of their actions is unpredictable... leaders and change agents need to accept they cannot manage change; all they can do is to support the organization to move towards the 'edge of chaos' and self-manage their journey.[57]

In *Organizational Development*, it is stated that all organizations are:

> paradoxes which are... pulled towards stability by the forces of integration, maintenance controls, human desires for security and certainty and adaptation to the environment... but also pulled towards the opposite extreme of unstable equilibrium by the forces of division and decentralization backed up by the human desires for excitement, innovation and the urge to act autonomously.[58]

Any attempt to seek a stable equilibrium is doomed to failure within environments that are inherently unpredictable; instead, organizations face punctuated equilibrium. States of order are established in a non-linear and dynamic fashion and are temporary, as significant change emerges from interactions and changes occur at the micro level.

Ralph Stacey writes in *Complexity and Organizational Reality* that organizations endeavour to exist on the border between stability and instability, regular irregularity and predicable unpredictability – on the edge of chaos.[59] It is important that leaders are selected and developed to successfully manage this precarious position.

Social constructionism and organizational enactment

Social constructionism[60] encompasses the concept of intersubjectivity, or the subjective experience occurring between people compared to any objective reality that is independent of human experience. Social construction operates through three mechanisms:

- **externalization:** meaning discerned through symbols;
- **objectification:** intersubjectivity produces understandings that are not real but are objectifications;
- **internalization:** accepting the externalized, objectified, understandings as reality.[61]

Karl Weick extends this thinking through Enactment Theory,[62] by taking the view that organizations only exist in the minds of the organization's members as cognitive maps of socially constructed reality. People use these maps to navigate what they believe exists, and as such organizations are reified into existence; their conceptual map is made real. Sensemaking in organizations is therefore said to be about organizing experience in a way that makes sense, rather than finding the truth.[63]

Organization structures

In *The Management of Innovation*, Burns and Stalker differentiated between mechanistic and organic organizations.[64] Mechanistic organizations result where there are clear tasks, division of labour, expertise is held at the higher levels of the organizations structure, which is relatively fixed, and decision-making is more centralized. The culture is rule-based, innovation is either not promoted or is discouraged and change is slow to achieve. In contrast, organic organizations have a more flexible structure and culture, expertise and impact are emphasized over seniority and titles, decision-making occurs throughout the organization, innovation is encouraged, and change is more rapid.

There are three basic organization structures:

- **functional:** divides responsibilities according to primary specialist roles;
- **divisional:** separate divisions based on products, services or geography;
- **matrix:** combines different structural dimensions at the same time.

Vertical structures traditionally identify lines of control and communication; horizontal structure spans show business division and functional specialization; and national and international structures relate to the domestic headquarters. Control can be seen as more or less centralized or decentralized.

Centralization tends to produce more uniformity in the way work is achieved due to greater influence from centralized power and expertise; however, de-centralization devolves more control locally, which may better consider the local operating environment, speed decision-making and give individuals more locus of control. Structure will also reflect degrees of differentiation, standardization, formalization, specialization and integration.

The greater the organization size and geographical dispersion, the more decentralization is likely. In addition, there may be: international divisions that centralize functional decision-making; local subsidiaries containing dis-tributed divisions and functions; global product divisions to create econo-mies of scale; and transnational structures based on knowledge sharing, specialization and network management[65] which combine to deliver high local responsiveness with high global coordination.

Matrix organizations divide responsibility across divisional lines-of-busi-ness, functions and geographies. This can increase speed of decision-making, but reporting to more than one person has its inherent operational and po-litical conflicts, which must be actively managed

Mintzberg's Organizational Model

Henry Mintzberg's model generalizes that there are typically five distinctive parts to organizations, five mechanisms for coordinating activities and five configurations:

The five distinctive parts are the:

- **operating core:** those who do the work;
- **strategic apex:** the leadership/top management;
- **middle line:** the middle-management hierarchy;
- **techno structure:** those in staff roles supplying ideas;
- **support staff:** those in staff roles supplying services.

The five mechanisms to coordinate activities are:

- **mutual adjustment:** of people through informal communication;
- **direct supervision:** through hierarchical supervision;
- **standardization of work processes:** specifying details around the execution of work;
- **standardization of outputs:** specifying the desired results;
- **standardization of skills:** specifying the capabilities required to perform the work.

The five configurations are:

- **Simple structure:** The key part is the strategic apex and the coordinating mechanism is direct supervision.

- **Machine bureaucracy:** The key part is the techno structure and the coordinating mechanism is the standardization of work processes.

- **Professional bureaucracy:** The key part is the operating core and the coordinating mechanism is the standardization of skills.

- **Divisionalized form:** The key part is the middle line and the coordinating mechanism is the standardization of outputs.

- **Adhocracy:** The key part is the support staff, sometimes with the operating core, and the coordinating mechanism is mutual adjustment.[66]

This model captured the nature of very structured organizations, but organizations are now far more flexible than Mintzberg's model would suggest.

Power structures

A clear understanding of the power structures in organizations is required knowledge for the successful leader, and French and Raven have suggested five forms of social power:

- **reward power:** based on the ability of an individual to give something that is perceived as having intrinsic or extrinsic value to another;

- **coercive power:** based on the ability of an individual to enforce sanctions for non-compliance;

- **legitimate power:** based on the belief that there is the legitimate right for an individual to exert influence;

- **expert power:** based on the possession of information or expert knowledge that are needed by another;

- **personal referent power:** based on the ability of an individual to attract others because of their intrinsic qualities.[67]

Richard Emerson's Power Dependency Theory suggests that power can be exercised when someone possesses something that another person wants, and the other person cannot obtain it from someone else.[68] Social exchange theory[69] suggests that rewards and costs drive relationship decisions; that people are instinctively prepared to exchange items of value with each other. In an organizational context, a strategic contingency model of power allocates greater power to those on whom the organization depends for its survival than those who do not fulfil this role.[70]

Mintzberg's Power Theory states that three basic conditions are required for power: a source of power, the will to engage in political activity and the skill to be successful. The four sources of power noted by him are as follows:

- control of resources;
- control of a technical skill;
- control of knowledge;

- the legal prerogative to impose choices;
- access to power through those who have one or more of the first four sources of power.[71]

The first three assume critical demand for the resources, technical skill and knowledge.

Finally, there are Steven Luke's Three Faces of Power:[72]

- **open:** open participation in decision-making;
- **controlled:** the powerful subjugate the will of the less powerful, which is not hidden;
- **silent:** silent consent to norms in practices that maybe oppressive, which is hidden.

Practical implications

In a Mercer report, *Talent Trends*, they discuss changing organizational structures. Vertical hierarchies are being replaced by simpler, more horizontal organizational structures:

- 'moving support functions to shared services;
- flattening the organization structure;
- eliminating roles/departments;
- decentralizing authority;
- building internal/external networked communities;
- creating project-based units;
- forming self-driven, holarctic work teams;
- centralizing governance;
- increasing regional control;
- outsourcing parts of the business model;
- moving operations to low-cost location.'[73]

Another report made the following suggestions to effectively address the VUCA environment:

- '**Volatility:** Agility is key to coping with volatility. Resources should be aggressively directed toward building slack and creating the potential for future flexibility.
- **Uncertainty:** Information is critical to reducing uncertainty. Firms should move beyond existing information sources to both gather new data and consider it from new perspectives.

- **Complexity:** Restructuring internal company operations to match the external complexity is the most effective and efficient way to address it. Firms should attempt to "match" their own operations and processes to mirror environmental complexities.

- **Ambiguity:** Experimentation is necessary for reducing ambiguity. Only through intelligent experimentation can firm leaders determine what strategies are and are not beneficial in situations where the former rules of business no longer apply.'[74]

With this comes the need for leaders to display cognitive readiness, which is the 'mental preparation (including skills, knowledge, abilities, motivations, and personal dispositions) an individual needs to establish and sustain competent performance in the complex and unpredictable environment of modern military operations'.[75]

Certain recurrent themes can be noted:

- 'recognize patterns in chaotic situations (situational awareness, memory, transfer);

- modify problem solutions associated with these patterns as required by the current situation (metacognition, flexibility and creativity);

- implement plans of action based on these solutions (decision-making, leadership, automaticity, and channelling emotions)'.[76]

In *Flow*, Fin Goulding and Haydn Shaughnessy outline a way of collaborating and making decisions in organizations that extends agile processes and emphasizes continuous learning and adaptability. It is

> an answer to the desire of employees to engage with the same semi-gamified, challenging world they inhabit outside the workplace… people are able to take on a wider range of tasks, including the job of continuously designing how work is best done. People want to be tested at least a little each day; they want continuously to improve their abilities; and to go home with the feeling they did something novel. That means taking on new tasks and responsibilities.[77]

Gallup defines the concept of agility as

> employees' capacity to gather and disseminate information about changes in the environment and respond to that information quickly and expediently. From a strategic perspective, this combination of speed and data-driven innovation is increasingly important for many businesses to maintain a competitive advantage.[78]

Gallup measures agility by asking workers for their level of agreement with two general statements about their organizations: 'in my company, we have the right mindset to respond quickly to business needs'; and 'in my company, we have the right tools and processes to respond quickly to business needs'. Their study of employees in France, Germany, Spain and the United Kingdom points to considerable room for improvement in organizations' capacity for agility in all four countries. Only 16 per cent of respondents feel that their organizations can be categorized as agile – meaning they feel strongly that their companies have both the mindset and the right tools and processes to respond quickly to business needs. Employees who view their company as agile are significantly more likely to have confidence in its financial future and to feel it is ahead of the competition, than those who do not.

Goulding and Shaugnessy call for a new workplace environment supported by 'a new type of leadership that is comfortable with delegating power in a situation where less planning is possible and where:

- The leader has to spend less time with plans and reports and devote more to emotions and fairness.
- There has to be a commitment to making all work and all decisions visible.
- The ability to invent process, as work is broken down into its logical parts, becomes more important.
- Higher levels of personal responsibility are required in teams.
- Comfort with uncertainty is a priority.
- Decisions emerge from interaction rather than from a plan.'[79]

With *Flow*, social interaction and the transparent visualization of a provisional and contested workflow is key. Their 12-point manifesto is as follows:

- **Lead by example:** Leaders must demonstrably change; it starts in the C-suite by walking the Wall of visualized activity, and by replacing 'that'll never work' with 'interesting idea'.
- **Visualize and socialize all work:** Embrace transparency so innovation is not hidden or hoarded; make it beautiful.
- **Cycle time is a day:** All work breaks down into a day's work, or less if you can, the smaller the better.
- **Promote the pivot:** Everything is open to change on a daily basis, being able to pivot is your mantra.
- **Evangelize continuous improvement:** Every day needs to be about finding a way to do things better.
- **Promote the experimental mindset:** Work needs to be about keeping options open. What works today may not tomorrow; the search for new ways of doing things is constant.
- **Define continuous delivery goals though customer value:** The search for, and delivery of, value never stops so all project evaluation is customer-centric. Key question: will my customers share it?
- **Build in emotion:** Walls need to reflect people's desires and ambitions, humour and ingenuity, kindness and gratitude.
- **Build in belief:** Leaders need to accept responsibility for people's beliefs and the dependency that comes with that once they promise a better place to work.

- **Be holistic:** All teams should really be cross-disciplinary.

- **Promote continuous learning:** Be purposeful about creating a learning model 'in the flow' based on all the social interactions that you stimulate.

- **Co-create all processes:** Even the biggest tasks should get underway without a complete plan and be amenable to changes proposed by people doing the work.[80]

The implications for leaders of a flow approach are significant. Time frames for decision-making are condensed and the process is transparent, provisional, continuous, expectant of failures and open to input from the many not the few. It requires leaders with high levels of emotional and cognitive ability and a psychologically safe culture.

In Mercer's report *Global Talent Trends Study: Unlocking growth in a human age*, they note two key aspects of organization capability that are key to consider for organization design:

- **'Change at speed:** The ability to change, and change quickly, is emerging as a differentiating organizational competency: agile organization design, exponential learning and cultivating a lab mindset.

- **Permanent flexibility:** Flexibility is more than working wherever/ whenever; it's also rethinking what work is done, how it is done, and by whom: working in flow, the rise of adaptive working and support for digital lives'.[81]

Organization design requires agile adaptability.

Highlights

- Building an outstanding workforce begins with the leaders of organizations having great clarity on the purpose for their organization's existence and a vision for its future.

- They require an ability to plan in the context of uncertainty in an environment of continuous change, which is business as usual in the 21st century.

- Several models help conceptualize strategic thinking, and the resource-based view of the organization is vital in determining the competitive advantage that can be achieved through key people as they are valuable, rare, imperfectly imitable, and a crucial element of organizational support.

- Organization design and development expertise helps address complexity.

- Organizations have both formal and informal power networks.

Leadership impact

Key themes that leaders should reflect on include:

- Leadership is undertaken in the context of the organization's purpose.
- Leaders need to analyse the impact of internal and external factors, making sense of data as best they can, in the context of the complexity, ambiguity and volatility that drives uncertainty.
- Change is dynamic and disruptive.
- A number of significant external factors drive change, for instance: political and economic, regulatory, technological, social and environmental. What are the key factors for your organization?
- Leaders need to understand the resource-based view of their firm and the nature of their workforce within this.
- It is important to predictively map business scenarios and, in each case, consider the potential people impact through strategic workforce planning.

People management recommendations

Actions to consider:

- Strategic workforce planning must be an integral part of the strategy review process, not a separate exercise.
- Carry out a thorough review of all the key internal and external factors.
- Remember to build the organization design around the roles required, and not individuals.
- Think flexibly about organizational structure; can non-core activities be outsourced? Can expertise be accessed on a more flexible basis?
- Consider the growth in temporary, agile teams, and the use of individual consultants for short-term assignments.
- Future proof the organization through design by considering external factors such as the impact of technology on the nature and location of the workforce.

Technology and the future of work 07

Introduction

One of the biggest impacts on the future world of work is technology. The nature of work and workplaces are rapidly being transformed, and both people and organizations need to understand the future possibilities and challenges and embrace disruptive change. In this chapter we continue to build an outstanding workforce by looking at how technology is changing the future of work – what roles are under threat, what skills will be sought after and the dynamics of new employment relationships.

We start by exploring the changes in patterns of work, and then discuss the impact of technology on roles and skills. This is followed by examining a range of potential leadership challenges, including remote and flexible working, and considerations relating to individuals and teams.

Chapter summary

The following subjects are discussed in this chapter:

- **Changes in the pattern of work**
- **The future of work – technology impact**
  - Loss of jobs
  - Changing jobs
  - Changing skills
- **The future of work – workforce scenarios**
- **The future of work – organizations**
  - Top 10 at-risk organizational capabilities

- ○ Top 10 future organizational capabilities
- ○ Gaps in perceptions
- **The future of work – people**
  - ○ Cognitive technology
- **Humanity in work**
- **The future of work – leadership challenges**
  - ○ Remote and flexible working
  - ○ Remote
  - ○ Flexible
  - ○ Team impact
- **Gender**
- **On the bright side**

Changes in the pattern of work

In *The Future of Work*, which was published in 1985, Charles Handy predicted eight major changes in the pattern of work that post-industrialized countries would experience:

- a full-employment society becoming a part-employment society;
- knowledge becoming more important than manual skills;
- the service sector increasing relative to the manufacturing sector;
- hierarchies and bureaucracies increasingly being replaced by networks and partnerships;
- single-organization careers being replaced with job mobility and career change;
- the post-employment, 'third' stage of life becoming more important;
- the division of labour between home and work based on sex will becoming less rigid;
- work shifting southwards, inside and between countries.[1]

A decade later in *The Empty Raincoat*, Handy made the following predictions on the future of work:

- fewer people will work for organizations and more will work for themselves;
- many people will have shorter working lives;

- fewer people in the population will be working and therefore more will be financially dependent on others;
- there will be a greater demand for education.[2]

Alternative work arrangements were discussed by Armstrong-Stassen in 1998 as including: part-time and contingent employment, flexitime, reduced working weeks and remote tele-working.[3] In 2000, Frese listed nine trends for the future of work:

- dissolution of the unit of work in time and space;
- a faster rate of innovation;
- the increased complexity of work;
- global competition;
- development of larger and smaller units;
- changing job and career concepts;
- more teamwork;
- reduced supervision;
- increased cultural diversity.[4]

Frese also suggests that jobs of the future will involve greater self-learning, more collaboration in groups, communication with co-workers and inter-disciplinary work. Workers will need to be more self-reliant, entrepreneurial and display more personal initiative.

In *The Shift* (2011), Linda Gratton summarized three years of research that produced five major factors, or forces, that will impact the future of work:[5]

- **The force of technology:** Exponential increase in technology capability, global connectivity of five billion people, ubiquitous cloud computing, continued productivity gains with an emphasis on culture, cooperation and teamwork, increasing social participation, global knowledge becoming digitized, mega companies will dominate but millions of micro entrepreneurs and partnerships will emerge, virtual workers using avatars, cognitive assistants and technology replacing jobs.

- **The force of globalization:** 24/7 global connectivity, emerging manufacturing and trading markets, the global aspirations of Chinese and Indian domestic companies increases, developing markets succeed in lower cost innovation, India and China become large talent pools of well-educated workers – especially with STEM subjects, the proportion of the world's population living in urban centres is great than rural centres and this trend is increasing, greater economic volatility, an emergent global underclass.

- **The force of demography and longevity:** The ascendance of Gen Y whose aspirations will impact the design of work and workplaces, increasing longevity, Baby Boomers growing old poor, increasing global migration.

- **The force of society:** Families will become rearranged – smaller and less traditional, the rise of reflexivity with greater diversity and introspection, a more prominent role for women, a more balanced role for men, a growing distrust of institutions, declining happiness, an increase in passive leisure.

- **The force of energy resources:** Energy prices will increase, environmental catastrophes will displace people, a culture of sustainability begins to emerge.

Her findings are based on evidence gathered from a significant programme of research and supports the previously expressed predictions. In addition, it adds the impact of energy resources.

In *The Future of Work* (2014), Jacob Morgan noted that across all demographics and geographies the world is becoming more collaborative; new generational cohorts entering the workplace bring new beliefs, values, behaviours and expectations; technology is ubiquitous, is delivered in the cloud, collected in stacks and allows for high-speed, 24/7 connectivity; more data leads to more information but this needs to be filtered to become knowledge; and the internet of things is helping to augment our lives through digital technology.[6]

As this chapter will show, Handy, writing over 30 years ago, and subsequent writers have so far been proved accurate in their prophecies about the future of work and their key predictions are explored in this and subsequent chapters. The first area to be examined will be technology and the future of work, which includes global workforce scenarios, and individual and group impacts including flexible and remote working.

The future of work: Technology impact

Loss of jobs

In his book *Technology vs Humanity*, Gert Leonhard asks, 'How can humanness prevail in the face of exponential and all-encompassing technological change?' Humanity has been here before when the Industrial Revolution, the first machine age,[7] was seeded by the harnessing of steam power to leverage our physical ability. The second machine age is described, in the book of the same name, as leveraging our cognitive ability.[8]

Emergent technologies are reviewed annually by the Global Future Councils of the World Economic Forum (WEF).[9] This network convenes by invitation only, and for one year more than 700 of the most relevant and knowledgeable thought leaders from academia, government, business and civil society are grouped in expertise-based thematic councils. The technologies selected each year must have the ability to provide significant benefits to societies and economies in a three- to five-year timeframe, be potentially disruptive, exist in a relatively early stage of development and, ideally, be developed by more than one company. In 2018 the list included augmented reality – AI that can argue and instruct and algorithms for quantum computers.

In collaboration with Accenture, in 2015 the WEF established the Digital Transformation Initiative (DTI) to offer unique insights into the impact of digital technologies on business and wider society and it supports the WEF's broader work around the Fourth Industrial Revolution. The first industrial revolution used steam power to mechanize production, the second used electricity to allow mass production which was automated in the third by electronics and information technology. The fourth revolution, Industry 4.0, is characterized by a fusion of technologies that is blurring the lines between the physical, digital, and biological spheres. One area examined by the DTI is the digital enterprise, how to survive disruption and thrive in a digital age.

Digital disruption has been defined as 'an effect that changes the fundamental expectations and behaviours in a culture, market, industry or process that is caused by, or expressed through, digital capabilities, channels or assets'.[10] It can deliver new markets, new client segments and new business models that require digitally focused business process re-engineering.

The DTI states that incumbent businesses need to become digital enterprises and to do so must adopt digital business models, digital operating models, digital talent and skills, and digital metrics for success. The DTI have so far identified eight key technologies that are expected to have the most impact on the industries they analysed:

- AI;
- autonomous vehicles;
- big data analytics;
- cloud;
- custom manufacturing and 3D printing;
- the internet of things and connected devices;
- robots and drones;
- social media platforms.[11]

It is not a comprehensive list of emergent technologies, for instance at the time of their research blockchain, a technology base of distributed ledgers, had a small number of use cases.

A report by the McKinsey Global Institute, *Jobs Lost, Jobs Gained*, note that 60 per cent of occupations have at least 30 per cent of their constituent work activities which could be automated and that about 50 per cent of all work activities globally have the technical potential to be automated. The report estimates that across the 46 countries covered by their research, the midpoint of job displacement by 2030 is 15 per cent, 400 million people, but this varies widely across countries, from 0 per cent to 30 per cent, 800 million people, with the impact being most significant for advanced economies. In addition, the midpoint of changes in occupational categories is predicted to be 3 per cent, 75 million people, with the highest estimate being 14 per cent, 375 million people.[12]

This McKinsey report predicts that over the period to 2030 seven catalysts of workforce demand will create between 555 million and 890 million jobs. These catalysts are rising incomes, healthcare for ageing populations, investment in infrastructure, investment in buildings, investment in energy, markets for previously unpaid work and technology development. The report focuses on the United States, Germany, Japan, China, India and Mexico and predicts full or near-full employment in each by 2030. However, this is dependent on a combination of public and sector initiatives in education and training respectively to ensure a match between skill demand and supply.[13]

Using individual-level data on task composition at work, an IMF Staff Discussion Note on 'Gender, technology and the future of work' found that women, on average, perform more routine tasks than men across all sectors and occupations – tasks that are most prone to automation. They estimate that:

> 26 million female jobs in 30 countries (28 OECD member countries, Cyprus, and Singapore) are at a high risk of being displaced by technology (i.e., facing higher than 70 percent likelihood of being automated) within the next two decades. Female workers face a higher risk of automation compared to male workers (11 percent of the female workforce, relative to 9 percent of the male workforce), albeit with significant heterogeneity across sectors and countries. Less well-educated, older female workers (aged 40 and older), and those in low-skill clerical, service, and sales positions are disproportionately exposed to automation. Extrapolating our results, we find that about 180 million female jobs are at high risk of being displaced globally.[14]

They recommend:

- **endowing women with the requisite skills:** investment in early STEM education;
- **closing gender gaps in leadership positions:** proactive action, a combination of government and organizations;
- **bridging the digital divide:** close the gender gap through government support for access;
- **easing transitions for workers:** gender equality in social protection systems for displaced workers.

Over recent years, a number of technologies have been associated with transformation and disruption across public, private and third sectors. These include cloud computing, artificial intelligence, machine learning, big data and data analytics, distributed ledger technology and robotic process automation.

These technologies are predicted to make the world economy less labour-intensive and may ultimately lead to fundamental economic and social restructuring. It has also been reported that the opportunities for economic and social progress offered by the new world of work, while significant, are critically dependent on how the public and the private sector work together.

Changing jobs

In addition to the Fourth Industrial Revolution, the WEF point to a number of other factors that are set to impact business growth in the period from 2018 to 2022. These include increasing protectionism, an increase in cyber threats, shifts in government policy and economic growth, shifts in legislation on talent migration, the effects of climate change, ageing societies, and the mindsets of new generations.[15]

New jobs will be created, current jobs will be augmented by technology and a number of jobs will no longer exist. Findings of WEF's *The Future of Jobs Report*[16] encouragingly suggests that the increased demand for new roles will offset the decreasing demand for others. However, it also notes that this is not a foregone conclusion. If talent shortages, mass unemployment and a concentration of power and wealth are to be avoided, organizations need to plan for their future workforce requirements, and provide guided, continuous learning opportunities for their employees, with governments providing a supportive and enabling labour environment.

Key findings of *The Future of Jobs Report* include that by 2022 respondents will expand their adoption of technology to include the major digital disruptors noted above and expect to have undertaken business process reengineering to change the composition of their value chain, with nearly half modifying their geographical base of operations. Nearly 50 per cent of respondents expect automation to reduce their full-time workforce based on the roles that exist today, 38 per cent expect an increase in new productivity-enhancing roles and 25 per cent expect automation to create new roles. The use of contractors for specialist work is set to expand, as is the prevalence of flexible working arrangements in terms of hours and location.

The frontier between humans and machines is predicted to shift, with task hours performed by machines across 12 industries increasing from 29 per cent in 2018 to 42 per cent in 2022. For instance, the use of machines for information search and transmission and date processing will grow from 46 per cent to 62 per cent over the same period. In addition to this, tasks that would be associated with human activity will be impacted. For instance, communicating and interacting will grow from 23 per cent to 30 per cent, coordinating, developing, managing and advising, from 20 per cent to 29 per cent, and reasoning and decision-making from 18 per cent to 27 per cent.

The report also predicts that across all industries emerging roles will increase their share of employment from 16 per cent in 2018 to 27 per cent by 2022 compared to the employment share of declining roles decreasing from 31 per cent to 21 per cent over the same period. In terms of employment as a whole, one set of estimates predicts 75 million jobs will be displaced but 133 million new roles may emerge that are adapted to a workplace augmented by technology.

Established roles where demand is expected to increase in the period to 2022 include data scientists and analysts, software and application developers, and ecommerce and social media specialists. Other growth roles include those that leverage human skills, such as customer service, sales and marketing professionals, people and culture professionals – specifically organization design and training and development. New specialist roles are predicted around emerging technologies such as artificial intelligence, machine learning, advanced data analytics, blockchain, cybersecurity, robotic process automation and human–machine interaction designers.

The proportion of core skills that will remain the same is predicted to be 58 per cent over the period from 2018 to 2022, which leaves a skills gap of 42 per cent, with 54 per cent of employees requiring significant re-skilling and up-skilling. For 10 per cent this will mean courses lasting more than a year. Skills that will continue to grow in demand include analytical thinking and innovation, active learning and learning strategies, technology design, and a sharp increase in demand for technology design and programming. Innately human skills such as creativity, originality, initiative, critical thinking, persuasion, negotiation, attention to detail, resilience, flexibility, complex problem solving, emotional intelligence, leadership, social-influence and service orientation will also be in demand.

The report found that the skills gap will be addressed by hiring, automating and retraining. The likelihood of hiring new permanent staff with required skills is nearly twice that of redundancies, and between 50 and 66 per cent of respondents are likely to use contractors, temporary staff and freelancers.

Changing skills

The World Bank's *World Development Report: The changing nature of work* make a similar prognosis, noting that workers undertaking routine tasks that are codifiable are the most vulnerable to replacement, but that technology provides opportunities to create new jobs, increase productivity and deliver effective public services, with three types of skills becoming increasingly important:

- advanced cognitive skills such as complex problem-solving;
- socio-behavioural skills such as teamwork; and
- skill combinations that are predictive of adaptability, such as reasoning and self-efficacy.[17]

In *Skill Shift: Automation and the future of the work force*, the McKinsey Global Institute, published their predictions on how a range of human skills may be affected by artificial intelligence and automation. Higher cognitive skills including advanced literacy and writing, quantitative and statistical skills, critical thinking and complex information processing will be in demand, rising 9 per cent in hours worked in the period between 2016 and 2030. Social and emotional skills such as advanced communication and negotiation, empathy, the ability to learn continuously, to manage others and to be adaptable, is predicted to rise 26 per cent over the same period, and technology-related skills such as basic to advanced IT skills, data analysis, engineering and research will be highly sought after, rising 60 per cent.[18]

No matter what jobs will exist in the future, the WEF note the top 10 skills that will be required in 2022 will be:

- analytical thinking and innovation;
- active learning and learning strategies;
- creativity, originality and initiative;
- technology design and programming;
- critical thinking and analysis;
- complex problem-solving;
- leadership and social influence;
- emotional intelligence;
- reasoning problem solving and ideation;
- systems analysis and evaluation.[19]

All these are found in a similar analysis by McKinsey, who also add technology-related skills such as:

- basic digital skills;
- advanced IT skills and programming;
- advanced data analytics and mathematical skills;
- engineering;
- scientific research and design.[20]

The above lists are worth remembering when skill gaps related to the future-of-work are discussed.

The future of work: Workforce scenarios

PwC and the WEF with the Boston Consulting Group (BCG) have each prophesized workforce scenarios for the future of work and both are examined below.

PwC published *Workforce of the Future* in collaboration with the James Martin Institute for Science and Civilization and the Said Business School,

Oxford University. This stated that five major forces will shape the future of work:

- technological breakthroughs, rapid advances in technological innovation;
- demographic shifts, the changing size, distribution and age profile of the worlds population;
- rapid urbanization, significant increase in the world's population moving to live in cities;
- shifts in global economic power between developed and developing countries;
- resource scarcity and climate change, depleted fossil fuels, extreme weather, rising sea levels and water shortages.[21]

The PwC report imagines four worlds of work in 2030 based on two axes, fragmentation vs integration and collectivism vs individualism:

- **Fragmentation and collectivism:** Yellow world. Humans come first. Social-first and community businesses prosper. Crowdfunded capital flows towards ethical and blameless brands. There is a search for meaning and relevance with a social heart. Artisans, makers and 'new Worker Guilds' thrive. Humaneness is highly valued.
- **Fragmentation and individualism:** Red world. Innovation rules. Organizations and individuals race to give consumers what they want. Innovation outpaces regulation. Digital platforms give outsized reach and influence to those with a winning idea. Specialists and niche profit-makers flourish.
- **Integration and collectivism:** Green world. Companies care. Social responsibility and trust dominate the corporate agenda with concerns about demographic changes, climate and sustainability becoming key drivers of business.
- **Integration and individualism:** Blue world. Corporate is king. Big company capitalism rules as organizations continue to grow bigger and individual preferences trump beliefs about social responsibility.[22]

All four future worlds of work acknowledge the impact of automation, and PwC point to the need for organizations and individuals to be adaptable and for governments and organizations to be clear about predicted changes and provide direction to the development of technology, support for workers who need to prepare themselves for multiple careers and social solutions for those displaced from the workforce.

The WEF and BCG published *Eight Futures of Work*, which focus on three critical variables: technological change, learning evolution and talent mobility. Each one is allocated two options relating to the degree of intensity, steady/accelerated, slow/fast and low/high respectively, and this delivers eight scenarios for the future of work:[23]

- **Workforce autarkies:** Large-scale automation of simple, routine, non-cognitive, tasks through steady technological change with most medium- to high-skilled jobs largely unaffected, combined with a slow pace of learning evolution and restrictions on talent mobility.

  Talent protectionism and subsidies to protect low-skilled workers at a national, regional and city level which restricts knowledge transfer and reduces the perceived imperative for skill change of low-skilled workers. The ability for organizations to compete in the medium- to long-term is reduced and economic growth dampened.

- **Mass movement:** Large-scale automation of simple, routine, non-cognitive, tasks through steady technological change with most medium- to high-skilled jobs largely unaffected, combined with a slow pace of learning evolution and high talent mobility.

  National and international talent migration and subsidies to protect low-skilled workers at a national, regional and city level. As talent moves to compete for work urbanization increases and social cohesion becomes harder to maintain.

- **Robot replacement:** Accelerated technological change displaces lower-skilled workers first but also erodes jobs undertaken by medium- and high-skilled workers, including non-routine and cognitive tasks. This combined with a low pace of learning evolution means that the workforce is not transforming its skills at a rate fast enough to prevent a drive for further automation.

  The number of displaced workers is high and talent protectionism and subsidies are introduced to protect workers at a national, regional and city level and minimize social unrest. Policy interventions are introduced to redistribute wealth.

- **Polarized world:** Accelerated technological change displaces lower-skilled workers first but also erodes jobs undertaken by medium- and high-skilled workers, including non-routine and cognitive tasks. This combined with a low pace of learning evolution means that the workforce is not transforming its skills at a rate fast enough to prevent a drive for further automation. As online knowledge platforms have not been widely adopted, this results in national and international talent migration and subsidies to protect low-skilled workers at a national, regional and city level.

  Talent moving to compete for work gives rise to globally dispersed super economies and income inequality increases.

- **Empowered entrepreneurs:** Large-scale automation of simple, routine, non-cognitive, tasks through steady technological change, with most medium- to high-skilled jobs largely unaffected, combined with a fast-paced learning evolution and restrictions on talent mobility. Governments have ensured education systems have equipped workers with the skills they need to join organizations that have created the opportunity for continuous learning and re-skilling. However, talent mobility is restricted both nationally and internationally to minimize the loss of highly skilled talent.

Online knowledge platforms grow, and entrepreneurs start new ventures, for instance in the care economy.

- **Skilled flows:** Large-scale automation of simple, routine, non-cognitive, tasks through steady technological change, with most medium- to high-skilled jobs largely unaffected, combined with a fast-paced learning evolution and high talent mobility. Governments have ensured that education systems have equipped workers with the skills they need to join organizations that have created the opportunity for continuous learning and re-skilling. Online knowledge platforms have not been widely adopted, and learning credentials have increasingly become recognized internationally.

National and international talent migration and growing inequality between countries that have invested and adapted and those that have been slow to invest and adapt.

- **Productive locals:** Accelerated technological change displaces lower-skilled workers first but also erodes jobs undertaken by medium- and high-skilled workers, including non-routine and cognitive tasks. This is combined with a fast-paced learning evolution and high talent mobility. Governments have ensured education systems have equipped workers with the skills they need to join organizations that have created the opportunity for continuous learning and re-skilling. However, talent mobility is restricted both nationally and internationally to minimize the loss of highly skilled talent.

Online knowledge platforms grow but talent shortages continue, and livelihoods are dependent on local economies.

- **Agile adapters:** Accelerated technological change displaces lower-skilled workers first but also erodes jobs undertaken by medium- and high-skilled workers, including non-routine and cognitive tasks. This is combined with a fast-paced learning evolution and high talent mobility. Governments have ensured education systems have equipped workers with the skills they need to join organizations that have created the opportunity for continuous learning and re-skilling. Online knowledge platforms have been widely adopted, and learning credentials have increasingly become recognized internationally; this results in national and international talent migration.

The global workforce is physically and cognitively agile, but, despite global hyper-connectivity, some members of society feel a reduced sense of local identity and belonging.

The report concludes that the implications of the above scenarios suggest a need for government and private sector organizations to reform education, invest in lifelong learning and in enhance access to digital technology. Governments and other organizations should work together to provide agile social safety-nets, job protection incentives, smart-job creation incentives, positive mobility management, and governance of online platform work. There should also be support for entrepreneurs and flexible working participation incentives.

From a demographic perspective, people will want to, and often need to, work longer and this will impact the full-time and flexible workforce. The multiple-generation workforce will be more diverse and inclusive and a differing age demographic between the workforce of developed versus developing economies will need to be considered against a growing dependency ratio. The dependency ratio refers to the ratio of the economically non-productive population who are reliant on the productive population.

The future of work: Organizations

Organizations will be accountable 24/7 to all stakeholders for their corporate and social responsibilities. They will need to be innovative, agile and adaptive. They will successfully inspire a remote and flexible workforce to greatness and support their development and growth.

In *The Future of Work*, Jacob Morgan observes sixteen features of future organizations. They will:

- have employees that work in globally distributed yet smaller teams;
- become intrapreneurial;
- create a connected workforce;
- operate like a smaller company;
- focus on creating a place of 'want' instead of a place of 'need';
- adapt to change faster;
- innovate anywhere, all the time;
- build ecosystems;
- run in the cloud;
- see more women in senior management roles;
- be 'flatter';
- tell stories;
- democratize learning;
- shift from profit to prosperity;
- adapt to the future employee and the future manager;
- become globally distributed with smaller teams.[24]

Morgan's list is a leading indicator of how organizations need to adapt and in *Humanity Works* Alexandra Levit references research that predicts the following impact of technology on organizations:

- 'The industrial internet of things: More devices will be connected with each other and centralized controllers.
- Cybersecurity: The need to protect critical industrial systems and manufacturing lines from threats will increase dramatically.
- The cloud: Industry 4.0 will require increased data sharing across sites and company boundaries.
- Additive manufacturing: Additive manufacturing describes the technologies that build 3D objects by adding layer-upon-layer of material, whether the material is plastic, metal, concrete and so on. With industry 4.0, additive manufacturing methods will produce small batches of customized products that offer construction advantages like complex, lightweight design.
- Horizontal and vertical system integration: Cross-company universal data integration networks will evolve and enable automated value chains.
- Big data and analytics: The collection and comprehensive evaluation of data from many different sources will support real time decision-making.
- Autonomous robots: Robots will become more autonomous, flexible and cooperative.
- Simulation: 3D simulations of products, materials and production processes will mirror the physical world in a virtual model.
- Augmented reality: In the virtual world, operators will learn to interact with machines by clicking on a cyber-representation.'[25]

In the report *2017 Deloitte Global Human Capital Trends*, 88 per cent of respondents believe building the organization of the future is an important or very important issue, while only 11 per cent believe they know how to do this.[26] For instance, to build a new channel to market which disrupts the traditional channel may be difficult within the incumbent organization and so this may involve creating a separate entity.

Top 10 at-risk organizational capabilities

Global research by PwC surveyed more than 1,200 business and HR leaders from 79 countries, and asked them to rank 45 organizational capabilities. The subsequent report, *Preparing For Tomorrow's Workforce Today*, identifies which actions organizations know are important for their future success but which they are failing to implement. These are called at-risk activities.

The top 10 at-risk organizational capabilities relate to the use of workforce analytics and people experience are:

- data-driven people decisions using advanced analytics;
- the use of data analytics to predict skill gaps;

- data analytics to remove bias in hiring and rewards;
- HR leaders having a depth of understanding and insight into the technological landscape;
- ability to engage flexible talent when required;
- manageable workloads;
- the use of sophisticated, predictive analytics in workforce planning;
- move towards multiple career paths;
- workforce adaptability;
- a workplace ecosystem that promotes well-being.[27]

Top 10 future organizational capabilities

The same report identifies the top 10 organizational capabilities for the future:

- being trusted by society, customers and employees;
- human skills such as leadership, creativity, empathy and curiosity;
- employees' physical and mental well-being;
- a focus on output rather than hours worked;
- collaboration, teamwork and innovation;
- adaptability and agility;
- work–life balance;
- innovation culture;
- transparency in reward;
- continuous learning opportunities.[28]

Gaps in perceptions

The PwC report found that there were significant gaps between the perceptions of HR leaders and non-HR leaders around future people-related organizational capabilities. These included: an understanding by HR leaders of the impact of emergent technology; the establishment of multiple career paths; re-skilling and supporting employees displaced by technology; the establishment of wellness initiatives; and the use of workforce related data analytics.[29]

Some progress had been made in mapping tasks that are likely to be automated and using a scenario-based approach to visions of the future workplace. Progress has also been made in recognizing the value of older workers, and human abilities such as leadership, creativity, empathy and curiosity, social mobility and re-skilling.

Key results are as follows:

- While 41 per cent of HR leaders are confident the HR function has the technological capabilities they need, only 25 per cent of business leaders agree. Overall, HR leaders are more optimistic than non-HR leaders in their organization's preparation for the future of work but 55 per cent have not created a clear narrative around the future of work and automation. Indeed, mapping activities that could be automated was overall only ranked 25th, although this did vary by sector: with financial services it was ranked 15th.

- Creating the right employee experience is seen as important, but an area in which a significant number of respondents are failing. Thirteen of the top 20 at-risk areas relate to this.

- With regard to innovation, 58 per cent of respondents say they have no capability to use open innovation and crowdsourced ideas from inside the business and less than 10 per cent feel strongly they can do this. A similar number say they have the desire but not the ability to use flexible talent. Only 27 per cent use advanced data analytics, such as predictive analytics, for workforce planning.

- The digital impact on the workplace, workforce and people management includes the use of people analytics. However, with regard to people analytics, only 8 per cent of organizations survey reported that they have useable data and only 9 per cent report that they have a good understanding of the factors that drive performance.[30]

The future of work: People

Cognitive technology

Cognitive technology includes deep and machine learning, natural language processing and robotic process automation. Common tasks include analysing numbers, text and images, performing digital tasks and physical tasks. It is used in situations where access to knowledge is not evenly distributed, where the application of knowledge is too expensive, the volume and variety of data is too much for analysis by the human brain, where data needs to be processed quickly, and where there is significant repetition.[31]

Organizations are redesigning jobs to leverage cognitive systems and robots around essential human skills, and while only 17 per cent are ready to work with a technology-augmented workforce, 31 per cent are implementing and 34 per cent piloting new programs.[32] Internal technology-driven augmentation will be supported by an increasingly flexible workforce containing a 'balance of technical skills and more general-purpose skills such as problem- solving skills, creativity, social skills, and emotional intelligence'.[33]

Deloitte report that companies are using cognitive technology to augment human judgement:

> A third of the respondents to our survey are using cognitive technologies to support better decision-making. AI can improve decision-making by accurately predicting outcomes and sifting through unstructured data to find answers to questions. This is leading to better outcomes in applications as varied as loan underwriting, fraud detection, medical diagnosis, policing, and investing.[34]

They also report that in most cases, early adopters are

> using cognitive technologies to complement human intelligence, rather than replacing it outright. Analytics capabilities have been enhancing human capabilities for years now, but cognitive capabilities can improve on those efforts by making them smarter and faster – and by learning along the way.[35]

In addition to AI, other forms of augmentation include the use robotic process automation, virtual reality (VR) and augmented reality (AR) and 3D printing.

Use of AI, machine learning, robotic process automation, natural language processing, predictive algorithms and self-learning will increase. Technology will eradicate jobs, augment jobs, create new jobs and require business process redesign. A Deloitte survey found:

> twenty-two percent of respondents believe workers are likely to be displaced by cognitive technology-driven automation and 15 percent expect little change one way or the other. Many believe that machines and humans will augment each other in the workplace within three years (51 percent agreeing), although the percentages drop for the five- and 10-year time frames (36 percent and 28 percent, respectively).[36]

There is a danger that preparing those joining the workforce with the right skills and knowledge, and re-skilling those whose jobs will be disrupted, may not keep pace with technological change, leading to both skill shortages and unemployment.

In *Humanity Works*, Levit cites the results of research involving 1,000 large companies that had been using or testing AI and machine learning systems. Researchers outlined three categories of human jobs that will facilitate the use of AI in the business world:

- **Trainers:** Human workers who instruct AI systems how to perform. They help natural language processors and language translators make fewer errors and instruct AI algorithms how to mimic human behaviours. Human trainers can also help an AI system course correct when an inappropriate response is being delivered.

- **Explainers:** Bridge the gap between technologists (and their systems) and business leaders and need to have technical knowledge but be able to speak in a non-technical way.

- **Sustainers:** As machines lack a moral compass, sustainers are essential in upholding an organization's values in the face of a result that might threaten them.[37]

In *Globotics*, Richard Baldwin notes that human and physical capital face diminishing returns, while knowledge capital does not.[38] The use of technology to capture and analyse data is increasing; however, the choice of which data is useful for decision-making in highly contextualized situations and what selections to make are likely to remain human-centric for the foreseeable future.

In addition, a report by Accenture, *Judgement Calls*, discussed three categories of human judgement that will be valued:

- **Discernment:** Intelligent machines can recognize patterns and correlations, but they are less skilled in understanding the big picture behind relationships, and in determining whether a given outcome is positive or negative in the grand scheme of things. Sometimes, it takes human experience to identify that data is not exactly what it seems.

- **Abstract thinking:** Smart machines can adhere to rules set up by humans and use those rules to perform operations such as identifying classes of objects. But they cannot take the additional step of going outside those rules to generate wholly new insights.

- **Contextual reasoning:** Algorithms can provide a lot of information, but inevitably there are gaps in understanding that make it difficult to render a decision based on that data alone. In these cases, we rely on human knowledge of personal, historical and cultural context.[39]

Augmentation is discussed in *Only Humans Need Apply*, where it is seen as not just complementing humans but enhancing their capabilities, 'making humans *more* capable of what they are good at'.[40] They authors believe that with regard to human–machine augmentation governments 'will nudge enterprises to provide for it in workplaces and equip citizens to acquire and build the skills they need to thrive.'[41] For enterprises 'an augmentation agenda is the way to ensure the ongoing innovation and flexibility required to survive... only with deep human skills, well leveraged by powerful machine analysis, can they continue to offer solutions that resonate with their all-too-human customers'.[42] Finally, for individuals, 'augmentation represents the antidote to automation... the invitation to add value to what these machines do, or have the machines add value to their work'.[43] People have options:

- **stepping up:** the big-picture insights and decisions;
- **stepping aside:** non decision-making roles, creative, influencing or explaining the decisions made by machines;
- **stepping in:** monitoring and maintaining machine systems;
- **stepping narrowly:** finding a specialization that is too narrow to automate;
- **stepping forward:** creating the machines.

Augmentation will have a significant impact on professional services and *The Future of Professions* questions whether specialist knowledge should be protected and access to it controlled, or whether it should be shared widely. The authors conclude that overall 'it would be better to live in a society in which medical help, spiritual guidance, legal advice, the latest news, business assistance, accounting insight and architectural know-how is widely available, at low or no cost' to liberate this information not to enclose it. They imagine 'human beings across the world – rich and poor – having direct access to living, evolving treasure-troves of help, guidance, learning and insight that will empower them to live healthier and happier lives'.[44]

In a study by Accenture, *Reworking the Revolution*, it was reported that only 26 per cent of the workforce is ready to adopt AI, and 67 per cent of workers consider it important to develop their own skills to work with AI, with Millennials strongly supporting this view (75 per cent) and the majority of Baby Boomers agreeing (56 per cent).[45] Generational differences in confidence with regard to AI-related skills were as follows:[46]

- **Very confident:** Gen Z, 42 per cent; Millennials, 41 per cent; Gen X, 28 per cent; and Baby Boomers, 22 per cent.
- **Somewhat confident:** Gen X, 52 per cent; Baby Boomers, 50 per cent; Millennials, 47 per cent; Gen Z, 43 per cent.

Actions suggested to reimagine work include: assessing skills and tasks, not jobs, and re-allocating them between humans and machines; creating new roles, moving beyond traditional functional jobs to specialized, insight driven, multi-skilled roles; mapping skills to new roles.[47] It is suggested that the workforce should be pivoted to areas that create new forms of value by aligning them to new business models; be organized for agility, with more project teams and more autonomy and delegated decision-making; fostering a new leadership DNA; cross-functional teamwork based on courage and innovation. It is also suggested that organizations take action to scale-up in new skilling by prioritizing skills for development; taking into consideration existing skills and willingness to develop; and using digital learning tools such as VR and AR.

In Mercer's report *Global Trends 2019*, they state that aligning work to future value organizations should 'unlock growth in the new world of work by redesigning jobs and moving people to where future value will be created.' However, only 52 per cent of respondents felt their organizations had identified the gap between current and future skill requirements, and only 51 per cent had a future-focused people strategy.[48]

Deloitte asked the question 'What is work?' and state that 'in the age of artificial intelligence, the answer to a more optimistic future may lie in redefining work itself.'[49] They suggest redefining work based on the following human capabilities:

- curiosity;
- imagination;
- intuition;

- creativity;
- empathy;
- emotional and social intelligence.[50]

They suggest a new vision of human work that: focuses on creating value; is fluid rather planned; is context-specific not standardized; is not routine or processed based; but is increasingly work-group orientated.[51]

In Deloitte's *2019 Global Human Capital Trends* they found that jobs are becoming super-jobs through augmented technology: robotic process automation is used by 36 per cent of respondents, robotics by 26 per cent, AI by 22 per cent and cognitive technologies by 22 per cent. Only 26 per cent of respondents felt their organizations are ready or very ready to address the impact of these technologies. While 62 per cent of respondents are using technology to eliminate transactional work, 47 per cent are also augmenting existing work practices to improve productivity and 36 per cent are taking steps to re-imagine work. The requirement for reskilling is predicted by 84 per cent of respondents. So-called standard jobs, with specific, narrow skill-sets with low transferability will continue to give way to hybrid jobs that combine technical and soft skills, and super jobs will emerge that will combine the content of multiple standard jobs using technology augmentation and combining domain, technical and human skills. Job descriptions and people profiles will be replaced by a job canvas, which focuses on the purpose of the workforce, the relationships required for success, the tools and technologies that support the role, the integration of learning and development[52] and presumably also the skills and abilities required of the workforce.

The competitive advantage of people can be examined using the resource-based view. To what extent are people: valuable – philosophically yes but situationally this depends; rare – we are individually unique, but some traits are held by many; imperfectly inimitable – philosophically this is true but not for many basic tasks; non-substitutable – philosophically yes but situationally this depends.

Expand Research, which delivers business intelligence services, notes that 'having the right people on board to deliver the firm's strategy is vital; this requires increasingly more sophisticated skillsets and strategies, as technology advances and individuals grapple with the implications this has on business culture and role requirements'.[53]

Humanity in work

In *Humans are Underrated*, Colvin states that

> figuring out what computers will never do is an exceedingly perilous route to determining how humans can remain valuable... a better strategy is to ask: what are the activities that we humans, driven by our deepest nature or by the realities of daily life, will simply insist be performed by other humans, regardless of what computers can do?[54]

These include:

- creating a hypothesis for investigating heavily context-laden problems in organizations;
- undertaking qualitative research;
- interpreting the results of both qualitative and quantitative research to understand the situational context, especially the social context;
- non-rational decision-making;
- activities that require fine dexterity;
- creativity;
- encouragement and motivation;
- mentoring and coaching;
- caring and compassion.

Certain tasks are more efficiently carried out by people, and there are other tasks where a human touch is preferred,

> even if machines become super-intelligent, they won't master human persuasion anytime soon. It's hard to believe that a robot leader will be able to identify the exact combination of words that will motivate an employee to take a job he or she doesn't want for the same amount of money.[55]

While in *Heart of The Machine*, Richard Yonck notes that affective computing may lead to the manipulation of human emotions by computers and social robots.[56]

Typical workplace tasks that draw on social intelligence are negotiation, persuasion, providing care and emotional support. The least automatable activity is managing and developing people, and the next least automatable activity is applying expertise.[57]

Colvin writes that 'as knowledge increases, people must specialize in narrower slices of it to achieve mastery'[58] and it is becoming clear that people are capable of lifelong learning and can modify their thinking around beliefs and values, and learn new skills. They just need the motivation to do so.

In *Globotics*, Baldwin suggests that 'we should invest in building soft skills like being able to work in groups and being creative, socially aware, empathic and ethical. These will be the workplace skills in demand because globots aren't good at these things.'[59] In fact, 'jobs that thrive in the face of AI competition will be those that stress humanity's great advantages centred around social cognition.'[60]

Uniquely human skills such as empathy, social and emotional intelligence and the ability to set context and define business problems will see increased demand. There will also be demand for general abilities rather than specific occupational skills[61] and the need for *stempathy*, the mix of science, technology, engineering and maths ability with empathy.[62]

While people have varying abilities in social cognition, Baldwin believes everyone has an advantage over AI as we need to recognize what others are thinking and feeling, how we feel about them and them about us, and how they feel about each other.[63] While this is true, we would argue that we also need to understand how we feel about ourselves.

Ultimately, machine learning is restricted by the need to work with data logic through code. It is therefore constrained by the availability of data, speed and the inability to mirror social cognition. In *Globotics*, Baldwin lists people's advantage over AI as follows:

- **Teamwork:** Empathy and reciprocity.

- **Trust:** Detection of cheating and building trust.

- **Pattern recognition:** 'Robots trained by machine learning do not have a capacity to think; they cannot reason, plan, or solve problems they have not seen before; and they cannot think abstractly or comprehend complex ideas that are more than patterns in data'.[64]

- **Hypothesis and results:** In many social situations the questions and answers are unclear.

- **Black box problem:** Algorithms are unable to explain why they came to a particular answer.

- **Lucas critique:** Algorithms only work as long as the correlations that exist in their training data continue to be valid. 'AI-trained robots do not understand the world. They just understand patterns in their training data sets. This reliance on correlation rather than causation will inevitably lead to very systematic mistakes when underlying factors change.'[65]

The skills that will become more valuable in the future of work include 'empathizing, collaborating, creating, leading, and building relationships',[66] and it would appear that some people will have a better starting point than others. However, these skills can be taught and should be a focus of education in schools and organizations.

In *Rise of the Robots*, Martin Ford writes that 'we are running up against a fundamental limit both in capabilities of the people being herded into universities and the number of high-skill jobs that will be available for them if they manage to graduate',[67] that 'the skills ladder is not really a ladder at all: it is a pyramid' and 'it is becoming increasingly clear that robots, machine learning algorithms, and other forms of automation are gradually going to consume much of the base of the jobs skills pyramid'.[68]

In terms of the impact on society, he writes that 'despite all the rhetoric about "job creation" rational business owners do *not want* to hire more workers: they hire people only because they have to'.[69] Therefore unconditional basic income or guaranteed minimum income combined with nudge incentives are likely and should be embraced. He recommends continued education to a certain level in areas that will benefit society, and higher levels of basic income to those who volunteer for services to their communities.

As technology takes over the repetitive, mundane, mechanical tasks that machines have previously been unable to undertake, replacing humans in these processes, humans will be able to spend more time understanding their humanity and sharing it with others.

The future of work: Leadership challenges

Remote and flexible working

Remote and flexible working is gathering pace across all types of organizations, it is therefore important to explore its impact on the nature of the workplace.

In Mercer's 2018 *Global Talent Trends Study* it is reported that most companies have a degree of flexibility based on bilateral arrangements with their manager, but among employees who requested a flexible work arrangement 36 per cent were turned down. Mercer recommend:

> shifting the emphasis from an individual's need for flexibility to an evaluation of a role's degree of flexibility is changing the conversation. Yet only 13 per cent of companies systematically assess whether, and to what extent, a job can be done flexibly... establishing a policy that allows for structured variability minimizes the need for ad hoc requests and reduces the complexity for individuals needing to negotiate arrangements.[70]

In Deloitte's 2019 *Global Human Capital Trends* they found that the alternative workforce is now mainstream: freelancers paid by unit of time, gig-workers paid by task, and crowd workers compete for participation in projects. Only 8 per cent of respondents feel their organizations are effective in sourcing and managing the alternative workforce. Respondents felt that organizational performance is positively impacted as follows: outsourcing/managed services, 53 per cent; freelancers, 49 per cent; gig workers, 30 per cent; and crowd, 17 per cent.[71]

Remote

Organizational culture incorporates meaning and purpose[72] and there will be cultural challenges surrounding the use of technology for remote working and virtual teams and the contingent or composite workforce.

A Deloitte report looked at four combinations of remote and contract employment relationships. The alternative workforce may be viewed as follows:

- **on-campus and on-balance sheet:** traditional worker – culture absorbed by direct contact, costly to maintain, relatively homogeneous environment;
- **on-campus and off-balance sheet:** outside contractor – outsider mentality, often lacks formal onboarding and training;
- **off-campus and off-balance sheet:** tenured remote worker – culture hard to absorb, isolated from the office, reliant on digital communication;
- **off-campus and on-balance sheet:** low-quality touch points, interaction through app or third-party platform, can have high interaction with stakeholders without much oversight.[73]

In *Globotics*, Richard Baldwin notes that remote working is being supported by improved telecommunication like telepresence and augmented reality and the use of software platforms to aid collaboration. Service workers are subject to remote intelligence (RI) threats from external markets and competition from artificial intelligence, which is 'zero-wage competition from thinking computers... designed to replace workers.'[74] The existence of tele-migrants and cognitive computers will undermine wages, benefits and workplace protections.

Baldwin also notes that the nonverbal signals we send are more authentic, and thus more trustworthy, exactly because they are more innate and far more deeply embedded in our brains than are words. Human verbal communication didn't occur until about 50,000 to 200,000 years ago, despite *Homo sapiens* being around for over 300,000 years, and experiments show when people are face-to-face in the same room, only 7 to 30 per cent of the information exchanged is verbal.[75] Our non-verbal skills therefore appear to disproportionately help us assign trust. Baldwin lists five non-verbal cues:

- 'body language (kinesics);
- touching (haptics);
- voice quality (vocalics);
- physical proximity and relative positioning of speakers and listeners (proxemics);
- timing (chronemics, for example, how long different speakers speak).'[76]

This gives co-location an advantage over those working remotely. Another obvious advantage of local people over remote people is local knowledge.

Therefore, jobs that will survive competition from RI will be those requiring face-to-face interactions and, with regard to AI, uniquely human abilities such as social sensing, judgement and empathy, aspects of social cognition, and teamwork and collaboration are hard to replace. One outcome may therefore be that our working lives will be 'filled with far more caring, sharing, understanding, creating, empathizing, innovating, and managing people who are actually in the same room',[77] although for some workers this may not be a frequent occurrence.

In *The Second Curve*, Charles Handy likens organizations to shamrocks, where the central leaf is the workforce who between them own the intellectual and skill capital of the firm; the secondary leaf is the organizations to which some work is outsourced; and the third leaf is a combination of specialist contract professionals and lower-skill part-time workers. The stem is the management holding the three leaves together.[78] He writes that offices are becoming more like clubs and will continue to be needed to provide social interaction, serendipity, cohesion and shared meaning. Also, that there will be a growth of individual specialists selling their services to larger organizations from home or from the office clubs.[79]

It has been noted that organizations aspire to provide a flexible physical and virtual working environment in terms of:

- **social flexibility:** location, hours, environment;
- **social resilience:** interactions and relationships;
- **social adaptability:** expect that change is part of business as usual and give opportunities for continuous learning, delivering innovation, internal mobility and multiple careers;
- **social responsibility:** inside and outside the organization.[80]

Humanity Works references a Knoll report that shows co-working, which brings together different types of employees from a variety of organizations in a common workspace, has increased and leads to higher levels of engagement and motivation; a *New York Times* article that reports that almost 45 per cent of US workers spend at least some time working remotely; and the American Sociological Association that has found higher levels of job satisfaction and reduced burn-out and psychological stress for those participating in flexible working programs.[81] Levit reports:

> Knoll found that companies have adopted co-working in a variety of ways including satellite offices or incubators at existing co-working spaces, and encouraging their remote or work-from-home employees to join co-working spaces to experience enhanced collaboration, built in peer accountability and job satisfaction.[82]

However, organizations will need to address 'the lack of a cohesive company culture and loyalty to fellow employees, inconsistent communication, security risks and the tendency for overcrowding'.[83]

Levit notes that organizations will integrate virtual teams into most departmental operations and defines a virtual team as 'any group of employees in different geographic locations who leverage technology to work together on a project or series of projects.'[84] She also discusses the traits of highly effective virtual teams:

- **Highly effective virtual teams are comprised of employees with the 'Three A's' – assertiveness, accountability and ability to work independently.** Team members take responsibility for getting their work done and know when and how to speak up with concerns and suggestions. Solid results lead to a certain degree of flexibility.
- **Highly effective virtual teams comprehend expectations.** Roles and responsibilities, as well as team rules and protocols, are tightly defined. Feedback is clearly communicated. Assumptions do not exist.
- **Highly effective virtual teams are infused with relevant technology.** Team members have access to the most sophisticated collaboration tools so that project work is efficient and seamless. They make use of instant messaging, video-conferencing and social networks to converse in real time.
- **Highly effective virtual teams are familiar with the in-person dynamic.** Ideally team members have met each other in person more than once in

both a business and social setting. Although not always feasible, a single in-person gathering makes it much more likely that employees will trust and like each other.

- **Highly effective virtual teams have a visible manager.** Team members are more engaged, more productive and less stressed when they are co-located with their manager from time to time. They are well informed about how team activities impact the organization's bottom line.

- **Highly effective virtual teams build and maintain solid relationships.** Team members understand how important it is to talk through conflicts, and to familiarize themselves with their virtual colleagues as people. With a new team or new hire, a buddy and/or mentoring system helps fast and lasting integration.

- **Highly effective virtual teams run great meetings.** Agendas are sent out in advance. Team members are punctual. Discussion time is built in to allow for input and consensus. Ground rules are adopted, such as respecting time-zone differences and reducing ambient noise.[85]

In *Leading Virtual Teams*, researchers suggest the following:

- 'Establish and maintain trust through the use of communication technology:
  - focusing the norms on how information is communicated;
  - revisiting and adjusting the communication norms as the team evolves ("virtual get-togethers");
  - making progress explicit through use of team virtual workspace;
  - equal "suffering" in the geographically distributed world.

- Ensure diversity in the team is understood, appreciated, and leveraged:
  - prominent team expertise directory and skills matrix in the virtual workspace;
  - virtual sub-teaming to pair diverse members and rotate sub-team members;
  - allowing diverse opinions to be expressed through use of asynchronous electronic means (eg electronic discussion threads).

- Manage virtual work-cycle and meetings:
  - all idea divergence between meetings (asynchronous idea generation) and idea convergence and conflict resolution during virtual meetings (synchronous idea convergence);
  - use the start of virtual meeting (each time) for social relationship building;
  - during meeting – ensure through 'check-ins' that everyone is engaged and heard from;
  - end of meeting – ensure that the minutes and future work plan is posted to team repository.

- Monitor team progress through the use of technology:
  - closely scrutinize asynchronous (electronic threaded discussion and document postings in the knowledge repository) and synchronous (virtual meeting participation and instant messaging) communications patterns;
  - make progress explicit through balanced scorecard measurements posted in the team's virtual workspace.
- Enhance external visibility of the team and its members:
  - frequent report-outs to a virtual steering committee (comprised of local bosses of team members).
- Ensure individuals benefit from participating in virtual teams:
  - virtual reward ceremonies;
  - individual recognition at the start of each virtual meeting;
  - making each team member's "real location" boss aware of the member's contribution'.[86]

Ensuring traditional face-to-face meeting interaction at the start of projects is thought to increase the effectiveness of teams, help attain a tighter network, as well as taking steps to ensure focus during virtual meetings. This would suggest that using physical meetings to enhance technology-based relationships will be required to create bonds between team members.

In *Globotics*, Baldwin predicts that jobs that remain will be those that require face-to-face interactions, and this will make communities more local, and probably more urban. If people have to go into the office every day, then it is beneficial to live near to places of employment. He believes that

> in the not-too-distant future, AI and RI will allow smart, dedicated, in-place, and flexible teams of generalists sitting in the same building to direct more larger teams of tele-migrants and white-collar robots. This combination of in-person, remote and synthetic workers will allow the teams to react quickly to new opportunities and quickly retreat from failures.[87]

A final prediction on the future of organizations is as follows:

> the nomadic and yet technologically interconnected lives enabled by new and emerging technologies will move organization toward the virtual, perhaps one day disappearing the need for this concept, replacing it with completely fluid and flexible organizing practices that can no longer be identified as an organization.[88]

Flexible

In *Humanity Works*, Levit notes the growth of the contract workforce and defines it as a 'provisional group of workers who work for an organization on a non-permanent basis, also known as freelancers, independent professionals, temporary contract workers, independent contractors or consultants'[89] and a gig economy as 'an environment in which temporary positions are common and organizations contract with independent workers for shorter term engagements.'[90]

Results of a 2016 study showed that the contract workforce in US was 10.7 per cent of the employee base in 2005 and had grown to 16 per cent in 2015, although only 0.5 per cent of the workforce undertook gig work online.[91] A study by the IBM Smarter Workforce Institute, which compared independent workers to regular employees in a sample of over 33,000 workers across 26 countries, found that independent workers are more engaged than most full-time employees and have greater pride and satisfaction than even high-potential, full-time employees.[92]

Integrating contract employees in the workplace will be an important leadership challenge, but inclusion can be enhanced in a number of ways: as far as possible contract workers should be interviewed by those who will manage them as well as other potential future colleagues; once employed there should be regular, at least weekly, check-ins to include video as well as voice and text-based communication; and they should be invited to both informal and formal organizational gatherings.

Flexible working will include flexible careers, and Levit summarizes potential new career experiences as:

- **Sideways:** Workers are much more likely to make sideways or 'lateral' moves in their careers to gain additional functional or industry experience. If employees can find these sideways opportunities within their current organizations, they are far less likely to leave in search of greener pastures.

- **Customization:** Research has found that career customization enhances employee engagement over time and is related to higher commitment, and that career customization participants obtain higher performance ratings than non-career customization participants.

- **Tours of duty:** Involves working full time in consecutive roles within an organization, working full time in consecutive organizations for upskilling purposes or taking breaks or dialling down from a full-time role in an organization.

- **Cross-functional expertise:** Knowing how to do work across a variety of areas holds greater value for employers than ever before. Leaders can encourage broader expertise in their workforces through rotations and exposure to external resources.

- **Monitoring:** By 2030, most professionals will wear a badge that does a lot more than track steps. Future advancements will allow for a total customization of every employee's role to maximize productivity every moment of every day.[93]

Levit also predicts the following impacts of flexible and remote working:

- The value of sharing resources, offering competitive and useful amenities, and providing flexible workspaces that employees can access on demand are already being recognized.

- As flexwork becomes more pervasive, the one-size-fits-all model increasingly does not apply but you need clear guidance on how it can be utilized.

- Virtual teams will become more prevalent, but these must be managed in a thoughtful way to enhance the employee experience and ensure shared purpose.

- Work teams will be temporary in addition to virtual, but teamwork will still be valued and rewarded.

- Distributed teams will be supported by telepresence, virtual and augmented reality.[94]

In *The End of the Traditional Manager*, the authors note the changes to work, working and the workplace: flexible workspaces are on the rise, with 74 per cent of employees having the ability to move to different areas to do their work; working hours are more flexible, with 52 per cent of employees saying they have some choice over when they work; there is more remote working, with 43 per cent of employees reporting that they work away from their team at least some of the time; and there are more matrixed teams, with 84 per cent of employees matrixed to some extent.[95]

The 2017 Deloitte Millennial Survey reports that globally two-thirds of Millennials say their employers have adopted flexible working arrangements as follows:[96]

- flexible time: 69 per cent;
- flexible role: 68 per cent;
- flexible contract: 67 per cent;
- flexible location: 64 per cent.

Research examined job satisfaction relating to formal and informal arrangements for flexible working. Informal arrangements for flexibility over working hours were found to be negatively associated with performance, but also a source of greater job satisfaction; informal remote working arrangements have positive indirect effects via organizational commitment and job satisfaction on worker performance.[97]

Research found that employees who perceive more flexible work arrangements (FWA) available to them 'have higher job satisfaction and organizational commitment especially in organizations that report offering fewer formal FWA policies.'[98] The authors note that 'flexible scheduling is more positively associated with job satisfaction than flexible location and hours, and both flexible scheduling and location are more positively associated with organizational commitment than flexible number of hours.' However, they also found that employees who actually use flexible scheduling have lower job satisfaction and organizational commitment than those who have it available but do not use it.[99]

Flexible working will, at least in the short term, lead to a reduction in employment stability and benefits but there will be gains in flexibility and a larger and more diverse network.

In *The Future of Work*, Morgan suggests seven principles for future employees who will:

- have a flexible work environment where they can work any time and anywhere;
- be able to shape and define their own career paths instead of having them predefined for them;
- share information internally in an open and transparent way in real time;
- have the opportunity to become leaders without having to be managers
- collaborate and communicate in new way;
- shift from being knowledge workers to learning workers;
- learn and teach at will.[100]

Team impact

Teams will increasingly become transient as well as virtual, forming for the period of projects and then disbanding. 'The growth of contract work and the specialization of organizations will spell the end for stable groups that work together a long time. Teamwork will still be valued and rewarded, but the teams themselves will form and disband with lightning speed'.[101] The research and consulting firm Gartner has called this process *swarming*.

Teams with varying degrees of planned permanence are likely to be working together on a network basis, perhaps reflecting better the social organization than more traditional hierarchies and require clear accountability for success. A Deloitte survey found tools to aid collaboration are being used in 73 per cent of respondent organizations. One tool is organizational network analysis (ONA), which uses patterns in emails, instant messages and other data to identify communication nodes and patterns of communication activity between them. Only 8 per cent of respondents use it but 48 per cent are experimenting with it, and while 94 per cent report that 'agility and collaboration' are critical to success only 6 per cent report being highly agile today.[102]

Research has concluded that groups are often more effective at solving problems than individuals, a fact that does not detract from the uniqueness and value of individual creativity. Group performance could not be predicted by the average cognitive ability of the group, or the level of cognitive ability of the cognitively most capable member. However, it was found to be influenced by social sensitivity, which mediates the flow of ideas within groups through increased collaboration.[103] It has also been found that people who grow up in larger families tend to be more prosocial, cooperate more, try to maximize positive outcomes for others as well as themselves and seek greater equality.[104]

In *Emotional Intelligence*, Goleman writes that

> the overall performance of harmonious groups was helped by having a member who was particularly talented; groups with more friction were far less able to capitalize on having members of great ability. In groups where there are high levels of emotional and social static – whether it be from fear or anger, from rivalries or resentments – people cannot offer their best. But harmony allows a group to take maximum advantage of its most creative and talented members' abilities.[105]

Gender

In *The Gendered Brain*, Gina Rippon discusses the research of psychologist Simon Baron-Cohen, who has found that in general women score higher than men on measures of social sensitivity, with the best-performing teams in his research tending to be those with the most women. Fundamentally, he believes that men's brains are *systemizing*, understanding the rules of systems, and women's are *empathizing*, understanding the affective state of another person and generating an appropriate affective response.[106] In *Humans are Underrated*, Colvin summarizes some of the evidence presented by Baron-Cohen:

- 'Starting at age one, girls are more likely to respond empathically to the distress of others. By age three, they're better than boys at figuring out the thoughts and intentions of others, and they never lose their advantage.

- Women are better than men not just at reading eyes but also at nonverbal communication generally, such as reading tone of voice and facial expressions.

- Women value reciprocal relationships more highly than men do. Men value power and competition more highly than women do.

- Empathy disorders, such as psychopathic personality disorder, are far more common among men.

- The way girls talk is much more cooperative and collaborative than the way boys talk, and girls can keep a conversation going longer than boys can.

- Girls show more concern for fairness than boys do. Boys share less than girls.'[107]

The above evidence positions women well for a world that will increasingly value these skills in the workplace. In addition, in *Humans are Underrated*, Geoff Colvin notes brain imaging research that has found that in problem solving women take a broader view than men, who tend to have a narrower focus.[108] Taking a more inclusive view of people's contributions and a broader view of problem solving should help lead to more effective decision-making in groups.

Despite the positive messages of Baron-Cohen and Colvin, Rippon believes that psychology will increasingly be informed by the results of neuroscience research and this will equip us with knowledge that will modify and extend our thinking around the place of gender in the debate around individual differences,[109] and therefore differentiating competencies based on gender may become a thing of the past.

On the bright side

In *The Mind is Flat*, Nick Chater writes that computational intelligence has so far focused on activities that can be reduced to processing large amounts of data at lightning speed and that routine and well-defined processes currently undertaken by people will continue to be automated. However, while

> the rise of digitization and big data can create an ever more frictionless and more precisely defined world in which computers can operate far better than we can... the secret of human intelligence is the ability to find patterns in the least structured, most unexpected, hugely variable of streams of information... to find mappings and metaphors through the complexity and chaos of the physical and psychological worlds. All this is far beyond the reach of modern artificial intelligence. To those who fear the march of the machines, this should be of some comfort. If imagination and metaphor is the secret of our intelligence, then that secret may, perhaps, be safely locked away in the human brain for centuries and perhaps for ever.[110]

Nearly 50 years ago Michael Argyle wrote *The Social Psychology of Work* and identified the following problems: alienation and low job satisfaction; lack of motivation; difficulties in communication; conflicts between groups and problems of technological change; the number of workers needed; and the levels of skill required. Sounds familiar? He concluded with his view on the future of work, recommending the modification of 'the character of work so that it provided maximum satisfaction, and incorporated as many of the properties of leisure as possible'.[111] He notes that in medieval village communities 'there was little distinction between work and leisure; work was intermingled with social, religious and other activities and met a variety of needs'.[112] He believes that people will seek activities, whether called work or leisure, because they deliver the 'conditions for human satisfaction: completing interesting and meaningful tasks, which use basic skills and abilities, giving adequate recognition and social-status, performed under considerate and democratic-persuasive supervision (or no supervision) in cohesive groups'.[113] This theme is echoed in discussions around employee experience in Chapter 14.

In the *Second Machine Age*, Erik Brynjolfsson and Andrew McAfee note that we 'need to think much more deeply about what it is we really want and what we value, both as individuals and as a society.'[114] As Richard Baldwin writes in *Globotics*, 'the globotics revolution could mean soaring productivity that could finance a breakthrough to a new nirvana, a better society that offered fulfilling work and fostered more caring-and-sharing attitudes.'[115]

Highlights

- The impact of technology will be significant on the future of work.
- Specific types of roles are at risk and there is a need to hire and train for skill gaps in the workforce.
- The roles most at risk include those that involve processing data with limited value-added by the person involved.
- Jobs that require the interpretation of a variety of data, decision-making that is highly contextual or where people demand the human touch, will be safe for the foreseeable future.
- Lifelong learning and development are key to lifelong work, although the way people work and where they work is also changing. Career experiences will also change.
- Overall leaders will need to adapt quickly to their new future.
- Operating models must redesign for speed and flexibility, more easily sharing information, failing fast, adapting and changing.

Leadership impact

Key themes that leaders should reflect on during this chapter include:

- A critical exercise will be to heat-map organizations to establish areas of skill deficits.
- The results will provide input into skill-based strategic workforce planning.
- Understanding the predictions and strategy scenario planning will be important.

- Leaders should develop themselves, and ensure that learning and development minimizes the skills gap across the workforce.

- New ways of working should be explored, including use of virtual teams, flexible working arrangements and, where appropriate, the outsourced workforce.

People management recommendations

Actions to consider:

- Carry out a strategic workforce planning exercise in order to future proof the organization.

- Develop, design and implement learning and development programmes to re-skill and up-skill the workforce.

- Form skills alliances within government, and with industry sector groups – all organizations will be facing the same types of challenges.

- Experiment with remote and flexible working – there are often significant cost savings if staff can work remotely more often.

- Assess the need and benefit of using the alternative workforce.

- Get advice on the latest technology developments in communication and collaboration solutions.

Demographics   08

Introduction

While emerged and evolving technologies will have a significant impact on the future of work, demographic trends must also be considered. In this chapter, global and generational demographic trends are examined.

Global population trends see an aging workforce in the West and a growing dependency ratio, but a supply of labour from developing markets. With regard to the question of a five-generation workplace, Baby Boomer managers express despair and concern in relation to managing Gen Y/Millennial and Gen Z cohorts. However, it is vital that each generation understands the differences, similarities and the strengths of others in order to create an outstanding workforce. This chapter will discuss the major themes and suggest ways to make the most of a diverse team.

Chapter summary

The following subjects are discussed in this chapter:

- **global demographic trends;**
- **generational demographic trends;**
- **introducing the multigenerational workforce:**
  - GenY/Millennials;
  - Gen Z;
  - Baby Boomers;
- **leading the multigenerational workforce:**
  - the more things change the more they stay the same;
  - leading multiple generations;
  - narcissism.

Global demographic trends

In *Inclusive Talent Management*, Stephen Frost and Danny Kalman note that we are facing three demographic megatrends that should be considered in strategic workforce planning: a rising population in Africa and Asia; decreasing birth rates to below replacement levels; and ageing populations in the West and parts of Asia. The global supply of graduates from emerging countries will increase from 54 per cent in 2015 to 60 per cent in 2025; the global share of people aged 60 years or more will increase from 11.7 per cent in 2013 to 21.1 per cent in 2050; and birth rates will decline significantly, with Europe's population falling from 739 million in 2011 to 709 million by 2050, and Japan's population from 66 million in 2013 to 40 million in 2040. China and South Korea will decline by about 18 per cent.[1] However, the Pew Research Centre projects the US population will increase from over 312 million in 2010 to over 400 million in 2050, an increase of 28 per cent.[2]

A working paper published by the International Labour Office notes the key megatrends in the world of work as technology, climate change, globalization and demography. The report defines the future of work along five dimensions:

- the future of jobs;
- the quality of jobs;
- social protection systems;
- wage and income inequality;
- social dialogue and industrial relations.[3]

First, workforce availability will be impacted by demographic changes. The world population is predicted to expand from 7.349 billion in 2015 to 9.275 billion in 2050, with more than half this growth happening in Africa. The report predicts a global increase in the share of older people and lowering participation rates for young people in emerging and developing countries due to longer time spent in education. The fall in working age population is expected to be highest in OECD countries, possibly falling 7 per cent by 2060, while labour market and pension reforms may compensate this by 2.4 per cent over the same period, although delaying the retirement age will increase the share of workers with disabilities. Rising female labour force participation is also expected to help mitigate the fall in the workforce, as women are underrepresented in the labour market.[4] In developed markets, the dependency ratio, which compares the difference between those not in the labour force with those who are working, will increase. International labour migration is expected to mitigate global differences in demographic transitions, with an increase helping to limit the deceleration of labour force growth. However, the report warns that there may be a greater supply of young migrants than high-income countries can absorb and that it has a negative impact on the sending countries' human capital stock. In addition, permanent migration will start to decline from about 2050, while temporary migration will increase to meet the shortfall in skills in developed countries. Environmental factors will increase migration, especially from geopolitically volatile regions. Despite falling global workforce participation rates, the World Economic Forum[5] predicted that 500 million new jobs will need to be created by 2020 to provide work for the current workforce and those joining the workforce.

Second, workforce conditions will be impacted by the growth of new business models utilizing flexible and temporary work among other forms of non-standard employment (NSE). The International Labour Office report predicts lower wages, reduced social protection and greater work insecurity while noting that the possibility of flexible and remote work will allow participation by marginalized workers and those with carer responsibilities. The gig economy increases precariousness, uncertain employment, and occupational health and safety concerns while reducing collective bargaining power and legal protections.

Third, workforce protection will be subject to a number of challenges. Contributions to social protection will fall as participation in the gig economy increases and labour supply decreases. At the same time, ageing populations will require more access to pension and care services, inbound migration may put more pressure on systems of social protection and low interest rates are predicted to continue for the foreseeable future. Universal basic income has been discussed as a potential solution for the under- and unemployed workforce.

Fourth, workforce wage and income inequality is an increasing problem, with implications for social justice and therefore political decision-making. It is exacerbated by a decrease in union representation, automation, globalization, the rise of so-called superstar firms such as Facebook, Apple, Amazon, Netflix, Google (FAANG) and an increase in rent-seeking and protectionism by large and powerful firms seeking to increase economic gain without increasing societal wealth. In addition, while traditional middle-class jobs will decline there will be an increasing polarization between high-risk jobs and high-value jobs while there will still be an income dividend for children whose parents have participated in higher education.

Finally, workforce relations will see continued reduction in union participation unless trade unions are successful in gaining members from the growing non-traditional labour force.

A 2017 report by the United Nations Population Fund states that the populations of the world's least developed countries will double by 2050, and in some countries may even triple.[6] The population in industrialized nations will be supported by immigration and the workforce will become more diverse. In addition, Levit states that in the United States there will be virtually no growth in the working age population between 2018 and 2030, which puts increasing pressure on organizations that are already finding it hard to attract and retain workers for key roles.[7]

Two-thirds of the global population is expected to live in cities by 2050 and already an estimated 800 million people in more than 570 coastal cities are vulnerable to a sea-level rise of 0.5 metres by 2050; and the intensifying impact of sea-level rise on coastal cities and plains will render an increasing amount of land uninhabitable or economically unviable. This is likely to lead to population movement within and from large cities. More people will be crammed into shrinking tracts of habitable urban space, and more are likely to move to other cities, either domestically or in other countries. These movements have the potential to cause spill-over risks; for example, they could result in heightened strain on food and water supplies and in increased societal, economic and even security pressures. In 2017, 18.8 million people were newly displaced by weather-related causes, including floods and coastal storms.[8]

Generational demographic trends

There are now five generations in the workplace: Traditionalists, Baby Boomers, Gen X, Gen Y/Millennials and Gen Z, and while this provides opportunities for organizations, it also poses a number of questions with regard to work-related preferences. Much has been written in the popular press regarding the nature of GenY/Millennials and Gen Z but research studies with conclusive results to confirm these generalizations are sparse.

A review of theory and evidence around generational differences in work values[9] noted 17 studies and found that for:

- **Baby Boomers:** Start dates could be 1943, 1945 or 1946 and end dates 1960, 1961 or 1964. The range of the period was between 15 and 20 years.

- **Gen X:** Start dates could be 1961, 1962 or 1965 and end dates 1977, 1979, 1980, 1981 or 1982. The range of the period was between 12 and 20 years.

- **Gen Y:** Start dates could be 1977, 1978, 1980, 1981, 1982, 1983 and end dates of 1994 and 2000. Many of these studies do not have an end date for Gen Y, so a comparative range is less relevant.

The US Census Bureau[10] and Pew Research Centre[11] use the following: Baby Boomers (1944–64); Gen X (1965–80); and Gen Y (1981–95). The differences in start and end dates and era ranges is one limitation on our ability to build consistent evidence for generational differences in work values.

Another significant factor when considering the degree to which generational research is helpful in examining work values is the distinction between generational, cohort and maturation effects.[12] First, research considered the differences between cohorts and generations:

> the approach adopted when considering cohorts is first to define the cut-off points of birth date for those being considered and then test where 'outcomes' (including values and attitudes) from this group exhibit particular differences from other cohorts. In contrast, with the theory of generations, one begins from

a social, political or economic event; change in resource, demography or other social characteristic and, from this, we need to search for appropriate cut-off points to define a generation.[13]

Second, it considered the differences between age and period effects:

age effects are changes that affect people as they 'mature', regardless of when they were born, whereas period effects are caused by the fact that people's values will be affected by the influences that exist at any particular point in time.[14]

Life stages have also been suggested as another way of explaining behaviour rather than simply their generational cohort.[15]

Most research has been cross-sectional, that is, across generational co-horts at a single point in time, and have not been longitudinal. One longitudinal study compared work-related values between Baby Boomers and Gen X in 1974 and 1999 and found evidence to support the proposition that work values differ due to generational experience rather than age and maturation.[16] However, as this research was not panel based it is difficult for this evidence to be conclusive.

In addition, it has been noted that individual differences exist within each generational cohort. For instance, gender- and ethnicity-based experiences may vary, with some studies finding gender-based variations within generational cohorts.[17] Deloitte research, 'Talking about *whose* generation?', illustrates the different experiences and influences experienced by the same generational cohort but in different countries.[18] The experiences of different generations vary based on national cultural contexts driven, for instance, by social, political and economic factors, and while increasing globalization may begin to reduce these differences[19] this is unlikely to occur in the short-term.

It has been noted that as Millennials inherit senior leadership roles from Baby Boomers and Gen X, more should be understood about their personality traits, motivational drivers and levels of organizational commitment.[20] Therefore, having considered some of the issues around evidence-based research that has been undertaken to date, it is now instructive to look at the contribution from consultancy firms.

Introducing the multigenerational workforce

A report by Roffey Park, *Talent and the Generations*, use broadly the same eras, only extending Millennials/Gen Y to 1999 with Gen Z being born from 2000[21] and concludes that:

- **Baby Boomers:** Are characterized as being hierarchical, conservative, measured, sharing, and having wisdom and a collective mindset. The leaders are recognized as visionary, having regard and respect for authority, and a focus on governance and rigour in their approach to the process of change.

- **Gen X:** Are characterized as fair, hard-working, competent, straight-forward, collaborative, experimental within boundaries and having a reluctant respect for authority. The leaders are recognized as being inspiring and pace setting.
- **Gen Y:** Are characterized as innovative, individualistic, fast-paced, challenging of authority, short-term focused, ambitious and narcissistic. The leaders are recognized as driven, pace setting, decisive, trusted, charismatic, coaches.[22]

Gen Y/Millennials

The 2011 PwC report, *Millennials at Work: Reshaping the workplace*,[23] presented findings of an online survey of 4,364 graduates across 75 countries who were under 31 and had graduated between 2008 and 2011. Their definition of Millennial encompasses those born between 1980 and 2000. This report was published three years after PwC's earlier research *Millennials at Work: Perspectives of a new generation*[24] and while many features of Millennials identified in the original report are confirmed, the 2011 report states that 'the attitude and expectations of Millennials have changed as a result of the economic downturn in many parts of the world',[25] specifically:

- **Loyalty:** In 2008 75 per cent expected to have between two and five employers in their lifetime but this had fallen to 54 per cent by 2011.
- **Compromise:** 72 per cent felt they had made compromises in their ideal role to get a job, 38 per cent were actively looking for another job, and only 18 per cent expected to remain with their employer for the long term.
- **Development and flexibility:** Personal development and working flexibility as benefits rank above cash bonuses.
- **Overseas postings:** 71 per cent want and expect to experience an overseas assignment during their career.
- **Unkept promises:** 95 per cent report that work–life balance is important to them but 28 per cent felt that work–life balance was worse than expected and over half felt their organizations did not 'walk the talk' with regard to diversity, and opportunities were not equal for all.
- **Technology:** 78 per cent believe that technology makes them more effective at work, 59 per cent say that the employer's provision of state-of-the-art technology was important to them when considering a job but still use their personal technology alongside their work technology and 41 per cent prefer to communicate electronically at work than face-to-face or by telephone.

- **Progress:** Career progression is the top priority, with 52 per cent saying it was the main attraction to their employer, with competitive salaries coming in second with 44 per cent.

- **Employer brand:** In 2008, 88 per cent were looking for corporate and social responsibility (CSR) values matching their own and 86 per cent said they would consider leaving an employer that did not have the values they expected of them. In 2011 the numbers had fallen to 50 per cent and 56 per cent respectively.

- **Generational tensions:** Millennials say they are comfortable working with older generations, valuing mentors in particular, but 38 per cent say that older senior management do not relate to the younger workforce and almost 50 per cent felt older senior management sometimes do not understand how to use technology.

It is interesting that as the environment changed, the views of Millennials modified, which may indicate the need to separate potential changes in aspects of personality with those associated with those driven by choices available that had not previously been a possibility, for instance technology-supported flexible working and overseas postings.

The PwC report also compared the factors that make an organization an attractive employer and the reasons why respondents accepted their current jobs. These cluster as follows:

- **Career and development:** Opportunities for career progression came top of factors that are attractive, 52 per cent; with excellent training/development programmes third, 35 per cent; and international work experience sixth, 20 per cent.

- **Financial and non-financial benefits:** Competitive financial incentives ranked second of the factors which are attractive, 44 per cent; good benefits packages fourth, 31 per cent; and flexible working arrangements fifth, 21 per cent.

- **Employer brand/values:** Reputation for ethical practices, corporate values that match the respondents and reputation as hiring the best and brightest ranked equally seventh in terms of factors that are attractive, 15 per cent. Employer brand ranked tenth with 10 per cent, and diversity eleventh with 8 per cent. The sector also ranked eleventh with 8 per cent.

In terms of the actual career decisions made, the opportunity for personal development came top, 65 per cent, and employer reputation second, 36 per cent. Following this was a cluster of quite practical factors: the role came third, 24 per cent; salary fourth, 21 per cent; sector, work location and long-term financial rewards fifth, 20 per cent; and the need to get a job quickly, sixth, 19 per cent. Corporate ethics and corporate responsibility came twelfth and thirteenth with 7 per cent and 5 per cent respectively. Clearly Millennials are willing to be pragmatic when it comes to accepting a role, with more idealistic factors ranking low in both expectation and actual decisions made.

A report by Deloitte, *The 2016 Millennial Survey: Winning over the next generation of leaders*, collected responses from nearly 7,700 Millennials from 29 countries, split between emerging, 4,300, and developed, 3,392, markets, all of whom were born after 1982 and had graduated with a college or university degree and were predominantly employed in large, private sector, organizations, with at least 100 employees.[26] They identified as important a number of factors relating to loyalty, corporate responsibility, business success and employer attractiveness.

In 2016, 44 per cent of respondents said they would leave their employer within two years and 66 per cent within five years. Overall, the numbers were higher in emerging markets, averaging 69 per cent, and lower in developed markets, averaging 61 per cent, although some developed markets where higher, the UK, 71 per cent, and US, 64 per cent, and some lower, Spain at 52 per cent. Indonesia and Russia were lower than the emerging market average at 62 per cent and 61 per cent respectively. Those with children were less likely to leave their jobs within five years than those with no children, 32 per cent versus 24 per cent, and slightly more women than men expect to leave over the same period, 67 per cent versus 64 per cent.

In terms of social responsibility, 58 per cent believe their organizations behave in an ethical manner, 57 per cent felt their leaders were committed to helping society but 64 per cent felt that businesses focus on their own agenda rather than society as a whole. These were improvements on the 52 per cent, 53 per cent and 75 per cent reported for the same areas in 2015. A high proportion, 87 per cent, believe that the success of a business should be measured in terms other than financial performance.

With regard to long-term success of a business, 26 per cent feel this is driven by workforce satisfaction, 25 per cent that it is driven by ethics and 19 per cent by customer focus. Interestingly, only 6 per cent selected innovation. When asked about the factors that influence their own decision-making, personal values/morals ranked first, impact on clients/customers came second and personal goals and ambitions third. Overall, Deloitte concluded that Millennials would prioritize the sense of purpose around people rather than business growth or profit maximization. However, while Millennials believe in stakeholder satisfaction, they are still aligned with senior leadership on the need for investment and innovation to ensure the long-term future of the organization.

Finally, in terms of employer attractiveness, financial compensation was the top-ranked influencing factor across all 29 countries, but when this was excluded work–life balance came top, followed by career opportunities, flexible working, sense of meaning from work, professional development, societal impact, quality of products/services, strong sense of purpose, opportunities for international travel, a fast-growing business, a leading company that people admire, investment in and use of technology and reputation of its leaders.

A 2017 KPMG report, *Meet the Millennials*, examined the five generations who are already working together: Traditionalists/Matures (born before 1946); Baby Boomers (1946 to 1964); Gen X (1965 to 1979); Millennials/Gen Y (1980 to 1995); and Gen Z (1996 to 2010).[27] They characterize Millennials as:[28]

- curious, wanting to know their purpose, why they are doing something before they do it and a desire for learning and mentoring;
- open, honest and challenging in communication, confident in questioning why things are done in a particular way;
- expecting positive feedback but in search of new challenges, wanting security but in roles for a maximum of three years;
- tech savvy;
- inclusive, with an expectation of diversity and focus on social impact;
- seeking flexibility and work–life balance.

The 2017 Deloitte Millennial Survey obtained responses from 8,000 Millennials almost equally split between developed and developing markets. In terms of their predictions about economic, social and political situations improving in the next 12 months, those in mature/Western countries were more pessimistic than those in developing countries, 75 per cent versus 52 per cent. Compared to 2016, global uncertainty had reduced. The number who say they will leave their employer within two years fell from 44 per cent to 38 per cent and the number who believe they will stay for more than five years increased from 27 per cent to 31 per cent.[29]

The 2018 Deloitte Millennial Survey obtained responses from 36 countries and included data from10,455 Millennials (January 1983 and December 1994), and from 1,844 Gen Z (January 1995 and December 1999).[30] Compared to previous years, perceptions of business motivation and ethics fell, good pay and positive cultures are strong attractors, but diversity and work flexibility are important in maintaining happiness; they are concerned about whether they are skill-set ready for industry 4.0, and the integration of physical and digital technology with work and the workplace, especially with regard to soft skills. Consistent with previous years, 'companies and senior management teams that are most aligned with Millennials in terms of purpose, culture and professional development are likely to attract and retain the best millennial talent and, in turn, potentially achieve better financial performance.'[31]

Millennials are more likely than previous generations to agree that they are unique, highly intelligent and would make the world a better place if they ruled it. They have higher levels of self-esteem, assertiveness, competitiveness and self-resilience and care less about conforming to social norms.[32]

Gen Z

Another Deloitte report, *Generation Z Enters the Workforce*, notes that while Gen Z, otherwise known as digital natives, bring technological skills, they express concern around their interpersonal skills and explore what organizations should consider in designing entry-level roles.[33]

They specifically note that tacit knowledge is hard to transfer digitally and therefore apprenticeships and mentoring will remain important, also that entry-level roles have become increasingly sophisticated as basic tasks are automated and that there may be a shortfall in highly cognitive social skills such as problem solving, critical thinking and communication. In the book, *Meet Generation Z* the author also points to challenges for Gen Z around their interpersonal communication, critical thinking and decision-making and another study added problem solving to the list.[34]

An article which examined possible adaptations that might be useful in working with Gen Z stated that they were entrepreneurial, aspirational, motivated by causes and clarity of purpose and a desire for continuous feedback and learning.[35] It concludes by recommending a hiring process that is more inclusive, not focusing unduly on university degrees, and jobs that provide personal and professional development opportunities. With regard to Gen Z, the Deloitte report recommends a re-evaluation of traditional approaches to workforce acquisition, cultural integration and development.[36]

The KPMG report *Meet the Millennials* adds that, compared to Millennials, Gen Z:

- are less focused;
- expect continuous updates;
- process information faster;
- are better multi-taskers, early starters;
- have a preference to opt out of traditional paths of higher education;
- tailor ongoing learning experiences to their specific preferences;
- are more cautious, having grown up in a turbulent economic and political environment;
- are more entrepreneurial.[37]

In *The Gen Z Effect* the authors state that individual and organizational perceptions of boundaries between generations should be rethought, that the year of birth should not be seen as the principle identifier of behaviours and attitudes and that the Gen Z effect compresses and eliminates many generational boundaries. The Gen Z effect is said to be

> the big shift we are all part of... a new set of behaviours that finally allows us to work across generations, and which is driven by technologies that are increasingly shared across all ages, promoting an awareness of the world and a collective engagement in economic and social institutions.[38]

The authors state that hyper-connectivity delivered by technology democratizes access to information and integrates various aspects of life. Connectivity creates transparency in relationships, which makes trust an earned rather than accepted status and online and offline worlds are seen as complementary and integrated. 'Slingshotting' is positioned as the accelerating force of innovation where technological laggards can skip multiple iterations of development but still arrive at the same destination as those who experienced the full journey. This happens as the user experience becomes simplified, connectivity becomes ubiquitous, and the availability of data increases utility to the user.[39]

Move over, Gen Z. Generation Alpha, those born since 2010, are the next generation to attract comment. 'What does the future hold for Generation Alpha?'[40] suggests that they will be fully augmented with technology, better off than Gen Y and Gen Z and will do everything later: leaving education, joining the workforce and having children. They will be demanding customers, employees and active, global, social citizens. They will also be better at dealing with complexity and managing risk, and will be adaptable to learning and re-learning.

Baby Boomers

In *Humanity Works*, Levit notes that nearly 20 per cent of Americans who are 65 and older are now working,[41] that the United States has the largest number of older workers in its history and according to her research

> 50 per cent of currently employed Millennials already meet our definition of a leader, meaning that they have decision-making authority and at least two direct reports. Forty four per cent of them have only three to five years of experience, yet forty one per cent have four or more direct reports.[42]

It is estimated that in the UK one in three workers will be aged over 50 by 2020, and by 2024 there will be 18 million people aged 60 and over, which is 3.1 million more than today and will equate to more than one in four workers being over 60 years old.[43]

Mercer's report, *Global Talent Trends 2019: Connectivity in the human age*, noted that 75 per cent of employees intend to keep working post retirement age,[44] and the *Age in the Workplace* report estimates that as many as 1 million people age 50–64 want to return to the UK workplace.[45] This would be useful, as the Government Office for Science in the UK predicts that 12.5 million people will retire from work between 2012 and 2022, with only 7 million currently available to potentially fill those posts.[46]

In terms of the ageing workforce, Levit notes that almost half of ageing US workers were experiencing money problems that keep them working. This is because for some the global financial crisis devastated their savings, while others hadn't saved enough and healthcare costs are increasing. On a positive note, others extend their working lives or return to work because they are physically fitter than previous generations at the same age, and Baby Boomers are bored and enjoy working.[47]

In terms of strategic workforce planning, organizations should determine which segments of their employee population will be retiring and what essential skills and knowledge they will take with them. Organizations may benefit from introducing phased retirement plans and flexible working by the transfer of knowledge through mentoring.

Leading the multigenerational generational workforce

The more things change the more they stay the same

A critical review of the theoretical and empirical evidence for generational differences in work values by Emma Parry and Peter Urwin found methodical challenges in studies using cross-sectional research, confusion between the definition of a generation as opposed to a cohort and problems caused by not considering differences in gender, ethnicity and national contexts. The authors note that while the suggestion that 'different groups of employees have different values and preferences, both based on age and other factors such as gender, remains a useful idea for managers... a convincing case for consideration of generation as an additional distinguishing factor has yet to be made'.[48] While the theoretical foundation for generational research has some validity, the existence of generational differences has not yet been validly tested.

One article concluded that 'stereotypes about generational differences in the workplace are unfounded and ill advised... there is little solid empirical evidence supporting the existence of generationally based differences'.[49] It suggests that organizations should 'focus on real, impactful, and actual differences among workers and should strongly resist the temptation to implement management and HR strategies that are based on unsupported and ill-founded ideas about characteristics of groups of people'.[50]

A 2016 article in the Harvard Business Review, 'Generational issues', states: 'conventional wisdom holds that Millennials are entitled, easily distracted, impatient, self-absorbed, lazy, unlikely to stay in a job for long. On the positive side they're also looking for purpose, feedback and personal life balance in their work'.[51]

However, it goes on to note that these views are often presented as self-evident with scant empirical research available to support them. Studies have found small differences between attitudes and values that have always existed between younger and older workers. For instance, a multigenerational study of 1,784 employees from companies across 12 countries and six industry sectors based on 10 long-term career goals found minimal differences between Baby Boomers, Gen X and Millennials. The largest difference was reported for 'becoming an expert in my field' where Baby Boomers returned 15 per cent and Gen X and Millennials both returned 20 per cent. Interestingly, Baby Boomers returned 24 per cent for 'helping to solve social and/or environmental challenges' while Gen X and Millennials returned 20 per cent and 22 per cent respectively.[52]

The article goes on to quote a CNBC survey which found that Millennials are variously more satisfied with the development they receive and promotion opportunities than the non-Millennial population, and a KPMG engagement survey that found that Millennials were almost identical to the non-Millennial population for measures of overall engagement such as pride in the organization and trust in leadership. In addition, a KPMG survey found that employees under the age of 35 were less likely to leave the firm than those of the same age in past surveys.[53] The author concludes that four key factors impact attraction and retention across gender, race and age:

- Is this a winning organization I can be proud of?
- Can I maximize my performance on the job?
- Are people treated well economically and personally?
- Is the work fulfilling and enjoyable?

These seem to echo factors that positively impact motivation that were discussed in Chapter 4.

Leading multiple generations

The 2011 PwC report, *Millennials at Work*, concluded that whether Millennials are entirely different to previous generations is not particularly important, but the demographic challenge is real, and the following areas should be addressed:

- segmenting the workforce;
- design of total reward;
- personal and professional development;
- clarity of purpose and objectives;
- flexibility in working arrangements;
- feedback frequency and delivery;
- progress based on contribution not time in role;
- expectation of higher turnover.[54]

Notwithstanding the 'dubious nature of applying generational thinking to the study of leadership',[55] researchers have recommended that the retention of Millennials will be improved by a culture of open communication with frequent performance appraisals that:

- link individuals' contributions directly to specific organizational outcomes;
- identify individuals' contributions to team success;
- focus on individuals' impact, not time taken on tasks;
- focus on successes and frame failures positively as knowledge acquisition;
- document innovative ideas and problem-solving success.

The 2016 Deloitte Millennial Survey suggested that retention can be supported by organizations identifying, understanding and aligning their purpose with Millennials' values; satisfying Millennials' financial and non-financial, demands; and supporting Millennials' professional development. The report notes that employees who expect to remain for more than five years are more likely than those who expect to leave within two years to:

- identify with the organization's sense of purpose, 88 per cent vs 63 per cent;
- have aligned values, 82 per cent vs 62 per cent;
- enjoy a variety of experiences, 86 per cent vs 68 per cent;
- make use of their skills, 86 per cent vs 62 per cent;
- experience professional development, 83 per cent vs 58 per cent, and mentoring, 81 per cent vs 61 per cent;
- receive personal recognition, 81 per cent vs 61 per cent;
- experience cross-team collaboration, 74 per cent vs 59 per cent.

The gaps are widest, 25 per cent, for sense of purpose, professional development and personal recognition. In addition, those intending to stay more than five years are more than twice as likely to have a mentor, 68 per cent versus 32 per cent. Only 56 per cent of those expecting to leave within two years report having a mentor.[56]

The Gallup report *How Millennials Want to Work and Live* provides guidance for leading Millennials:[57]

- **Purpose vs pay-check:** For Millennials, work must have meaning, and they want to work for organizations with a mission and purpose. Compensation is important and must be fair, but it's no longer the driver.
- **Development vs job satisfaction:** 'Most millennials don't care about the bells and whistles found in many workplaces today – the ping-pong tables, fancy latte machines and free food that companies offer to try to create job satisfaction. Giving out toys and entitlements is a leadership mistake, and worse, it's condescending. Purpose and development drive this generation.'[58]
- **Coaches vs bosses:** 'Millennials care about having managers who can coach them, who value them as both people and employees, and who help them understand and build their strengths.'[59]
- **Conversations vs formal annual reviews:** Millennials want ongoing feedback conversations and so relying on annual reviews no longer works.
- **Strengths vs weaknesses:** 'Gallup has discovered that weaknesses never develop into strengths, while strengths develop infinitely. This is arguably the biggest discovery Gallup or any organization has ever made on the subject of human development in the workplace'.[60] Organizations should minimize weaknesses and maximize strengths and in doing so build a strengths-based culture.
- **Life vs job:** Millennials see their work as an integral part of their life and so the fit must be a good one.

In addressing the impact of Baby Boomers, Gen X and Gen Y, a Roffey Park report notes: 'what is clear is that the psychological contract for each generation is subtly different with implications for sourcing and retention of talent and leadership development'.[61] It suggests Baby Boomer talent is attracted by title, status and salary while Gen X value the overall package including work–life balance and development opportunities. Millennials put lower weight on the salary and higher weight on undertaking challenging and meaningful work that is supported by strong development that supports their career plans. Flexibility of working arrangements is important for both, while Gen X and Gen Y have less tolerance for poor management.

Research has shown no significant differences in the work values of pre-career and working Millennials, which is contrary to similar research on Baby Boomers and Gen X. The significant differences that were noted suggested that financial incentives, working conditions and continuous learning and career advancement become more important once Millennials enter the workforce, while the importance placed on being engaged in interesting work, achievement, their coworkers and helping others reduces.[62] In terms of work ethic, consistent with the results of previous surveys,[63] researchers found that individuals' level of work engagement was higher for older people than younger people.[64]

An article in the *Harvard Business Review*, 'Managing people from 5 generations', suggests leading a multi-generational workforce may involve experimenting with mixed-age teams, reverse mentoring, and tailored total reward plans to reflect employees' stage of life. It stresses the importance of regular feedback and warns against establishing generation-based affinity groups to avoid reinforcing stereotypes.[65] Leadership development implications include:

- the moral dimensions, including inclusive, ethical and humble leadership;
- self-awareness, an understanding of personality types and traits and how this impacts leadership styles and the development of emotional intelligence;
- a coaching approach to feedback.

Research has suggested that societal changes impacting Baby Boomers, Gen X and Gen Y may have resulted in differing values and behaviours with regard to work–home balance for each generation. Understanding these differences is important when designing an attractive work environment.[66]

Career success has also been examined to establish if national experiences were different for the same generation. The countries selected were the United Kingdom, USA, China and South Africa and the sample included those under 30 and those over 50 to compare the youngest and oldest in the workforce. The most important influencing factors on career success were work context and personal history for both groups, and traits and skills for the older and younger groups respectively. The researchers also found that younger employees in all four countries actively managed their social capital, career and skill development. Finally, they concluded that the relative pace of economic and political change between countries provides a more reasonable explanation for generational differences between countries than national culture.[67]

Research into the approach of Gen Y professional couples to dual careers has also been undertaken and concluded that 'within this generation and this particular cohort "new" career patterns are evolving to reflect changes at a societal and demographic level as well as individual agency in how careers are enacted for "lifestyle and family" reasons as well as work and career reasons.'[68] Dual career issues are being discussed and negotiated early in relationships with an eye on future phases of life and organizations are advised to consider cultural and structural changes to enable dual career families to manage the work–life interface effectively.[69]

The speed of technological change and adoption drives the need for reverse mentoring where mastery of new technology is often passed to those who may have more life and work experience. This is seen to work best where 'the protégé suspends her authority and seniority, accepts that her life experience is not a proxy for disproving the radically different experiences of her mentor and puts up with the level of discomfort required to gain a new, and likely very disruptive, perspective'.[70]

Deloitte research asked respondents to select phrases that were the best match with their organization's culture and compared the results for those expecting to stay for more than five years versus those expecting to leave within two years. The gap was widest, 16 per cent, for organizations with open and free-flowing communication. This was followed by a number of factors with a 14 per cent gap: a strong sense of purpose beyond financial success; strong commitment to equality and inclusiveness; a culture of mutual support and tolerance; idea generation actively encouraged across generations; and the ambitions of younger employees are understood and supported.[71]

Narcissism

In *The Talent Delusion*, Chamorro-Premuzic notes three trends to be considered for the future.

- **Millennial mindset:** Scientific evidence for increasing levels of narcissism among Gen Y, and what that implies for organizations in terms of how they are managed and how they will lead others.

- **Three critical competencies:** Self-awareness, 'to help people make better career decisions and develop their talents; curiosity, to navigate the sea of information we live in, never ceasing to be learning animals and to handle the challenges of a global and complex world; and entrepreneurship, to turn stagnant ideas into innovative products and services, and to exploit opportunities in the face of crisis.'[72]

- **Reputation economy:** Where each member of the workforce is worth only as much as their reputation, the collective and public impression we have of their talent and capabilities.[73]

The increasing prevalence of narcissism has been noted in studies that have found that Millennials are more likely than previous generations to agree that they are unique, highly intelligent and would make the world a better place if they ruled it. They have higher levels of self-esteem, assertiveness, competitiveness and self-resilience and care less about conforming to social norms.[74]

Research compared archival data from different generational groups at different points in time to establish differences in personality by generation and age or maturation. They found Gen Y had increased self-esteem, narcissism, anxiety and depression, a lower need for self-approval and higher external locus of control compared to other generations.[75]

Chamorro-Premuzic writes that 'generational increases in narcissism will harm our ability to work in teams, and since every significant accomplishment of civilization is the results of coordinated team effort, the prospect of a more narcissistic and individualistic society is indeed rather bleak.'[76] However, he notes that if leaders, Millennials and males are more likely to be narcissistic, interventions to build awareness, curiosity and entrepreneurship may help recipients better understand their limitations.

Roffey Park's report, *Talent and the Generations*, point out that 'a productive narcissistic personality could be very useful for organizations' as they bring passion and innovation to leadership in the workplace.[77] Organizations should therefore inspire and engage them.

In *Leaders Eat Last*, Simon Sinek states that 'growing up in a world of instant gratification has its liabilities. It also offers a huge advantage. Millennials are comfortable with change and quicker to pivot than older generations.'[78] He suggests that leaders should:

- mentor and support them;
- lead by example;
- talk about your failures;
- give them the opportunities to develop 'human' skills;
- help them love themselves;
- take a chance on them;
- they are the leaders of the future, but we are the leaders right now;
- solve your own problem;
- push to completion;
- beg for criticism;
- sacrifice credit.[79]

In *Mindset*, Carol Dweck writes that younger generations in the workforce appear to require ongoing reassurance and that this may be limiting in a VUCA environment where both challenge and resistance are ubiquitous, therefore

> instead of just giving employees an award for the smartest idea or praise for a brilliant performance, they would get praise for taking initiative, for seeing

a difficult task through, for struggling and learning something new, for being undaunted by a setback, or for being open to and acting on criticism… Maybe it could be a praise for not needing constant praise.[80]

She concludes by questioning where leaders will come from if organizations do not develop a more mature, robust and growth-focused workforce.

Highlights

- A working paper published by the International Labour Office, 'The future of work', notes the key megatrends in the world of work as technology, climate change, globalization and demography. The report defines the future of work along five dimensions:
  - the future of jobs;
  - the quality of jobs;
  - social protection systems;
  - wage and income inequality;
  - social dialogue and industrial relations.
- There are long-term global demographic trends that will impact the availability of people to organizations.
- In the United States and Europe populations are ageing and there are now five generations in the workplace for the first time.
- New generations entering the workforce are said to have different beliefs, vales, attitudes and interests, which deliver different motives for work.

Leadership impact

- Clearly understand the makeup of your workforce and the needs of each generational cohort.
- Consider making better use of more experienced staff, as people work longer.
- Take into account the demographic changes in relevant specific regions and sectors.
- Understand the predictions and carry out strategy strategic workforce scenario planning accordingly.

- Ensure the employer brand, employee experience and employee value proposition support attracting and retaining people across all relevant generations.

People management recommendations

Actions to consider:

- Carry out a generational review of the organization.
- Train staff to understand the dynamics of the various demographics in the organization, as well as any cultural issues.
- Review and segment benefit provision to ensure they are relevant as the work population evolves.
- Review the recruitment process to ensure that appropriate channels are being used.

Culture

09

Introduction

It is important to understand culture from both a global as well as an organizational perspective, as it has direct implications for leading and managing across borders and building an organizational culture that positively impacts the employee experience and firm performance. It should also have a positive impact on the employee value proposition and employer brand.

Many organizations have global stakeholders, because they have global operations, global customers, global suppliers or employ people who grew up in a different cultural environment. With regard to organizational culture, all organizations have them, but they tend to be path dependent, developing over time, and hard to change. In fact organizations don't just have one culture, they have many sub-cultures and it is important to understand their impact when building an outstanding workforce.

International and organizational culture introduce an additional layer of complexity wrapped around people and organizations.

Chapter summary

The following subjects are discussed in this chapter:

- **global talent migration:**
  - global talent considerations;
  - cultural anthropology:
    - Hofstede;
    - the GLOBE project;
  - organizational implications;
  - eight-scale culture guide;
  - expatriates;
  - culture and the Big Five;
- **organization culture;**
- **corporate climate.**

Global talent migration

Global talent considerations

If globalization and talent migration continue, leaders will increasingly interact with stakeholders from different cultures and lead multinational workforces. Cultural anthropology has informed our knowledge of cultures in other countries, and as leadership is undertaken in a cross-cultural environment research has studied cultural knowledge and sensitivity in an organizational context as well as the impact of national and corporate culture on teams.

A number of research projects have been undertaken to try to identify differences in global cultures, including Hofstede's study, *Cultures Consequences*,[1] and the GLOBE (Global Leadership and Organizational Behaviour Effectiveness) project *Culture, Leadership and Organizations*.[2] Hofstede's cultural dimensions theory is a framework based on extensive research with IBM and describes the effects of culture on its members and how this may be used to predict behaviour. The GLOBE research programme is a multi-phase, multi-method, multi sample research project, where researchers spanning the world have examined the interrelationships between societal culture, societal effectiveness and organizational leadership.[3]

For the GLOBE project, culture is defined as: 'shared motives, values, beliefs, identities, and interpretations or meanings of significant events that result from common experiences of members of collectives that are transmitted across generations.'[4] Cultural practices define cultures as they exist now and cultural values define what societies desire in the future.[5]

In *Cultures and Organizations*, Edgar Schein notes that

culture is always a collective phenomenon, because it is at least partly shared with people who live or lived within the same social environment, which is where it was learned. Culture consists of the unwritten rules of the social game. It is the collective programming of the mind that distinguishes the members of one group or category of people from others.'[6]

Schein also notes that culture is learned, not innate, as it is derived from a person's social environment rather than their genes.

Lastly, Alfred Kroeber and Clyde Kluckhohn define culture as

patterns, explicit and implicit, of and for behaviour acquired and transmitted by symbols, constituting the distinctive achievement of human groups, including their embodiment in artefacts; the essential core of culture consists of traditional (ie historically derived and selected) ideas and especially their attached values; culture systems may, on the one hand, be considered as products of action, on the other as conditioning elements of further action.[7]

As explained in Chapter 1, human nature describes our common inheritance, which determines our ways of interpreting the world and our associated instincts. How we express our instincts through emotions, cognitive processes and behaviour are impacted by personalities and learned behaviour developed in a cultural context. In this chapter the results of studies from cultural anthropology will be examined with a view to influencing leadership behaviour when building an outstanding workforce.

Cultural anthropology

Hofstede

Hofstede's study was conducted within IBM and the results suggested four cultural dimensions that impact the way people work together. These were compared across 40 nationalities.

- **Power distance:** Refers to the manner in which power is distributed in organizations. Decentralized cultures are flatter, with fewer levels of supervision. They allow for greater independence, and more discussion and debate vertically. There is more informal consultation, fewer symbols of rank and a belief that all members of the workforce have a strong work ethic.

- **Uncertainty avoidance:** A lower tolerance of ambiguity means a greater need for structure and rules, a desire for expert opinions and need for consensus. This may lead to in-group favouritism, high levels of stress and displays of emotion.

- **Individualism–collectivism:** Contrasts differences that can be identified between Western and Eastern societal values. Low individualistic Eastern societies have a higher external locus of control, extended organizational families that give protection in exchange for loyalty, primacy of organization needs over those of the individual, an emotional dependency on organizations and belief in group decision-making.

- **Masculinity–femininity:** Relates to values that historically have been associated with male versus female leaders. These include success, extrinsic reward, empathy and quality of life, and of the four dimensions it has less cross-cultural impact.[8]

Following Hofstede, Trompanaars outlined seven dimensions that impact cross-cultural leadership:

- **Universalism–particularism:** Organization needs are universally more important than the needs of individuals, or the particular needs of organizations are more important than those of individuals.

- **Individualism–communitarianism:** Individuals are responsible for their decisions and success rather than teams, or the organization as a whole is seen as being responsible for the security and success of an individual in exchange for loyalty.

- **Specific–diffuse:** Individuals form close relationships with others, are specific in there messaging and understand what can be shared, or remain remote and more diffuse in their communication.

- **Neutral–affective:** Individuals are reluctant to show how they feel and remain outwardly neutral and stoic, or individuals display spontaneity and high emotional intelligence.

- **Achievement–ascription:** The status of an individual is determined by their portfolio of achievements, or is determined by their genealogy, sex, age or wealth.

- **Time orientation:** Past-orientated organizations base future success on past events, while future-orientated organizations base future success on the present. Individuals work on tasks sequentially and schedules and the ordering of tasks are important, or individuals multi-task, see commitments as provisional and are flexible.

- **Internal–external:** Individuals feel an internal locus of control, or an external locus of control.[9]

However, these dimensions were not based on empirical research but on conceptual distinctions derived from American sociologists that were not designed as a framework for examining national cultures.

The GLOBE project

In the first phase of the GLOBE project, over 17,000 middle managers in 62 cultures participated in the study and researchers established nine dimensions of societal culture:

- **'Performance orientation:** The degree to which a collective encourages and rewards (and should encourage and reward) group members for performance improvement and excellence.

- **Assertiveness:** The degree to which individuals are (and should be) assertive, confrontational, and aggressive in their relationship with others.

- **Future orientation:** The extent to which individuals engage (and should engage) in future-oriented behaviours such as planning, investing in the future, and delaying gratification.

- **Humane orientation:** The degree to which a collective encourages and rewards (and should encourage and reward) individuals for being fair, altruistic, generous, caring, and kind to others.

- **Institutional collectivism:** The degree to which organizational and societal institutional practices encourage and reward (and should encourage and reward) collective distribution of resources and collective action.

- **In-group collectivism:** The degree to which individuals express (and should express) pride, loyalty, and cohesiveness in their organizations or families.

- **Gender egalitarianism:** The degree to which a collective minimizes (and should minimize) gender inequality.

- **Power distance:** The extent to which the community accepts and endorses authority, power differences, and status privileges.

- **Uncertainty avoidance:** The extent to which a society, organization, or group relies (and should rely) on social norms, rules, and procedures to alleviate unpredictability of future events. The greater the desire to avoid uncertainty, the more people seek orderliness, consistency, structure, formal procedures, and laws to cover situations in their daily lives.'[10]

A further GLOBE study was undertaken to determine leadership behaviour across cultures. Leadership profiles across 410 culture clusters followed from their development of culturally implicit leadership theory (ILT), which relates to the beliefs people hold about the attributes, personality characteristics, skills and behaviours that impact outstanding leadership. They extended ILT to the cultural level based on the argument that the structure and content of belief systems will be shared among individuals in common cultures.

With regard to leadership attributes and its relationship to societal culture, they identified 21 primary and six global leadership dimensions. The six global leadership dimensions differentiate cultural profiles of desired leadership qualities and are briefly defined as follows, including the 21 primary leadership dimensions:

- 'Charismatic/value-based leadership: Reflects the ability to inspire, motivate, and expect high performance outcomes from others based on firmly held core values. It includes the following *six primary leadership dimensions*: (a) visionary, (b) inspirational, (c) self-sacrifice, (d) integrity, (e) decisive and (f) performance oriented.

- **Team-oriented leadership:** Emphasizes effective team building and implementation of a common purpose or goal among team members. It includes the following *five primary leadership dimensions*: (a) collaborative team orientation, (b) team integrator, (c) diplomatic, (d) malevolent (reverse scored), and (e) administratively competent.

- **Participative leadership:** Reflects the degree to which managers involve others in making and implementing decisions. It includes *two primary leadership dimensions*: (a) nonparticipative and (b) autocratic (both reverse-scored).

- **Humane-oriented leadership:** Reflects supportive and considerate leadership and includes compassion and generosity. This leadership dimension includes *two primary leadership dimensions*: (a) modesty and (b) humane orientation.

- **Autonomous leadership:** Refers to independent and individualistic leadership attributes. It is measured by a *single primary leadership dimension*: autonomous leadership, consisting of individualistic, independence, autonomous, and unique attributes.

- **Self-protective leadership:** Focuses on ensuring the safety and security of the individual and group through status enhancement and face saving. It includes *five primary leadership dimensions*: (a) self-centred, (b) status conscious, (c) conflict inducer, (d) face saver, and (e) procedural.'[11]

Among the six global dimensions of CEO leadership behaviour, charismatic leadership behaviour is consistently the most impactful regarding top management team dedication and firm performance. CEO team-oriented behaviour is the next most important global leadership behaviour, followed by humane-oriented leadership. Participative leadership is moderately related to top management team dedication but not firm performance. Autonomous and self-protective leadership were found to be generally ineffective.[12]

Of the 21 primary leadership dimensions, the research identified universally desirable, universally undesirable, and culturally contingent attributes of leadership:

- **universally desirable:** integrity, charismatic-visionary, charismatic-inspirational, team builder;
- **universally undesirable:** self-protective, malevolent, autocratic;
- **culturally contingent:** self-sacrificial, status conscious, internally competitive, face-saver, bureaucratic, humane orientation, autonomous.[13]

In 2014, GLOBE researchers published further research which was designed to determine how a society's culture influences leadership behaviours expected in that culture and whether leadership success depends on a CEO matching their leadership style to these societal expectations. More than 70 GLOBE researchers collected data from over 1,000 CEOs and over 5,000 senior executives in corporations in a variety of industries in 24 countries.

Their findings reinforce the importance of CEOs to organizational outcomes, the considerable influence of culture on societal leadership expectations, and the importance of matching CEO behaviours to the leadership expectations within each society. *Star* CEOs scored close to six on a seven-point scale and *superior* CEOs between five and five-and-a-half.

Seven *mission-critical* competencies were identified for star and superior CEO performance:

- '**Visionary:** Star leaders anticipate possible future events and prepare for them. They create and communicate a clear vision of the future, articulating a clear picture of where the organization will be in 5 years, and make plans and take actions to achieve it.
- **Performance oriented:** Superior leaders strive for excellence for themselves and their teams and set high standards and goals. They communicate high performance expectations, work hard, and seek continuous performance improvement.
- **Decisive:** Star leaders offer high levels of intuition and insight. They make decisions firmly and quickly based on logic and intuition.

- **Inspirational:** Superior leaders are positive, energetic, enthused, and optimistic. They mobilize their teams by giving courage, confidence, hope, and praise. They emphasize the importance of being committed to values and beliefs.
- **Administratively competent:** Star leaders are able to manage complex administrative systems and are highly organized and methodical. They clarify priorities and plan, organize, and coordinate the work of others. They explain the rules and procedures that employees are expected to follow.
- **Integrity:** Superior leaders deserve to be trusted because they mean what they say and can be relied upon to keep their word. Their actions are always ethical. They articulate a strong sense of values and purpose and act accordingly.
- **Diplomatic:** Star leaders have a strong world outlook. They have high levels of interpersonal skills through effective negotiation skills and by identifying solutions that satisfy diverse interests.'[14]

A second set of five competencies were identified as *important* leadership competencies, but these are not required to be performed at the same high level as the first set of activities. The average score of top-performing CEOs is significantly higher than the bottom-performing CEOs, but the difference is not as large as in the case of the mission-critical competencies:

- '**Self-sacrificial:** Star leaders are willing to forgo their own self-interest to serve the interest of the organization and their team members. As a result, they are viewed as persuasive by their teams.
- **Collaborative:** Superior leaders have good relations with subordinates, are concerned about the welfare of the group, and are supportive in the face of difficulty or conflict.
- **Participative:** Star leaders share critical information with subordinates and allow them a high degree of discretion in performing their work. They seek advice and recommendations from their team members and allow them to have influence on important decisions.
- **Team integrator:** Superior leaders communicate frequently, openly, and effectively with their subordinates, clarifying what is expected of each team member. They work hard at getting team members to work together and integrating them into a cohesive team.
- **Bureaucratic:** Star leaders act according to established rules, guidelines, norms, and conventions. They use a common standard to evaluate all who report to them and administer rewards in a fair manner.'[15]

The seven mission critical leadership competencies and the five important leadership competencies constitute their general theory of strategic leadership where leaders have to perform at a high level in each but with an understanding of what this means in each country context.

The frameworks of Hofstede and GLOBE are built on extensive research, and while inevitably each have their critics they are an excellent starting point for contemplating cultural implications in organizations.

Organizational implications

Cultural competency joins cognitive and emotional ability as a consideration for hiring decisions and people management throughout organizations. The authors of *Leading Across New Borders* believe

> cultural competency reflects the degree to which differences are understood and effectively bridged and is demonstrated through both cognitive and behavioural adaption. Cognitive adaption is the ability to see the world through the cultural frameworks of diverse stakeholders, customers, or colleagues. Individuals with such a mind-set displace an unthreatened acceptance of cultural difference as natural and other cultural practices as legitimate and multifaceted in their own right.[16]

Research has emphasized the need for thought around the selection and development of those who perform well across cultures and those who may be more suitable for particular cultural environments. Considerations for selection include observed personal experiences, personalities, values and cognitive styles,[17] and for development the provision of high-contact cross-cultural experiences.[18]

Leaders' ability to build their cultural competency and create inclusive organizations can be learned, but for learning to bring about deep and sustainable change it should consist of more than: expecting others to adapt, employing universal techniques, practising dos and don'ts, and being submerged in contemporary culture.[19]

In *Organizational Cultures and Leadership*, Schein and Schein note that getting multicultural organizations and teams to work together effectively is a much larger cultural challenge than within a single macro culture. They suggest that learning about norms and assumptions of multiple cultures can be too time-consuming and abstract, while improving *cultural intelligence* allows for an educated lens to be more effectively applied to multiple cultures, and state that

> the concept of cultural intelligence introduces the proposition that to develop understanding, empathy, and the ability to work with others from other cultures requires four capacities: (1) actual knowledge of some of the essentials of the other cultures involved, (2) cultural sensitivity or mindfulness about culture, (3) motivation to learn about other cultures, and (4) behavioural skills and flexibility to learn new ways of doing things.[20]

In addition to the international work on culture, Hofstede et al suggest the following variables that impact organization culture:

- **Regional, ethnic, and religious cultures:** Account for differences within countries and ethnic and religious groups; often transcend political country borders.

- **Gender differences:** Are not usually described in terms of cultures, although it can be revealing to do so.

- **Generation differences:** Symbols, heroes, rituals and values are associated with different generational cohorts and are evident to most people, but their impact is often overestimated.

- **Social classes carry different class cultures:** Social class is associated with educational opportunities and with a person's occupation or profession. Education and occupation are in themselves powerful sources of cultural learning. The criteria for allocating a person to a class are often cultural.

- **Symbols:** These play an important role, and include manners, accents in speaking the national language, and the use and non-use of certain words.[21]

The results of research regarding national cultures and their dimensions have only proved to be partially useful for understanding organizational cultures. Hofstede notes that cultural norms of power-distance can be used to examine who has the power to make decisions about what cultural norms of uncertainty avoidance can be used to examine the processes and regulating mechanisms that are followed.

Research by Owen Stevens is referenced by Hofstede to describe the culture of various organization structures and lines of reporting:[22]

- **Pyramid of people:** Exemplified by a French model of organization with the most senior manager at the top. This is consistent with Fayol's view that authority is found in the person and the rules.[23]

- **Well-oiled machine:** Exemplified by a German model of organization where, because of a strong rule-based system, management intervention is only necessary in exceptional cases. This is consistent with Weber's view that authority resides in the rules.[24]

- **Village market:** Exemplified by a British model of organization where neither hierarchy nor rules but rather the demands of the situation determine what will happen. This is consistent with the views of Taylor and Follet, who privilege the situation over the person and the rules.[25] It is market driven.

- **Family:** Exemplified by the Indian and Indonesian model of organization, which is quite paternalistic. This is consistent with Ouchi's view of clans led by elders.[26]

Hofstede states that all other 'factors being equal, people from a particular national background will prefer a particular organizational configuration because it fits their implicit model.'[27] He superimposes Mintzberg's five configuration types with the quadrant formed by power-distance and uncertainty-avoidance, and suggests matches to preferred coordination mechanisms: mutual adjustment fitting the market model of organizations; standardization of work process fitting the French concept of bureaucracy; and direct supervision corresponding to Chinese organizations, including those outside mainland China, which emphasize coordination through personal intervention of the owner and their family.[28]

Organizations that expand internationally will continue to be strongly influenced by their domestic headquarters mediated by control systems developed at the centre and by the presence of expatriates.

Eight-scale culture guide

As noted by Erin Meyer in *The Culture Map*, identity develops from childhood and the culture in which we grow up has a significant impact on how we perceive the world:

> in any given culture, members are conditioned to understand the world
> in a particular way, to see certain communication patterns as effective or
> undesirable, to find certain arguments persuasive or lacking merit, to consider
> certain ways of making decisions or measuring time 'natural' or 'strange'.[29]

Our perceptions, cognitions and actions are impacted by cultural patterns of behaviour, and in *The Culture Map*, Meyer has created eight scales to guide management in an organizational context where culture sets a range, and within that range each individual makes a choice. For her, it is not a question of culture *or* personality, but of culture *and* personality. Also, it is not the absolute position on the scales that matters but the relative position of the cultures that interact:

- **communicating:** low context vs high context;
- **evaluating:** direct negative feedback vs indirect negative feedback;
- **persuading:** principles-first vs applications-first;
- **leading:** egalitarian vs hierarchical;
- **deciding:** consensual vs top-down;
- **trusting:** task-based vs relationship-based;
- **disagreeing:** confrontational vs avoids confrontation;
- **scheduling:** linear-time vs flexible-time.[30]

Meyer writes that 'it is only when you start to identify what is typical in your own culture, but different from others, that you can begin to open a dialogue of sharing, learning, and ultimately understanding.'[31]

Breaking down cultural barriers can be achieved through hiring for cultural diversity, the rotation of team members to give increased exposure to cultural diversity, international postings for immersion in other cultures and in *Humanity Works*, Levit suggests that when hiring in a new talent market an organization should:

- 'Understand the intricacies involved with hiring in a new market: Regulations involving everything from global mobility and migration policies to permits and the management of contract labour vary from country to country.

- **Leverage experts in the talent market:** Understand the risks and opportunities of setting up shop and then hiring there, and to promote effective integration once you get started.

- **Seek advice for translating your culture, values and policies:** Be sure they make sense in the nomenclature of the new market, and that they encourage collaboration among a diverse workforce.

- **Set up digital talent communities:** Online properties showcase your knowledge of the local workforce and offer an opportunity for real time interaction with potential full time and/or freelance hires in the new market.

- **Consider sending people from headquarters on short term assignments:** Stints of three to six months in the new region will ensure that there are reliable connections between the centre and spokes of your wheel.'[32]

Leading Across New Borders notes that, during the past century, American and European leadership and business models have largely dominated multinational corporate cultures. However the economic shift toward markets such as China and India means that cultural norms from other countries will increasingly mediate the manner in which business is undertaken, and 'the harsh reality is that many emerging leaders working for Western multinationals are being evaluated on a set of implicit leadership expectations that are so culturally embedded that they are often not even *articulated*, much less measured.'[33]

Expatriates

Expatriates, or expats, can be defined as people living in a country other than their native country on a temporary or permanent basis. Expatriate postings may be necessary to fill skill-gaps, for developmental purposes, and to strengthen cross-border relationships. In *The Psychology of Behaviour at Work*, Furnham lists key areas to consider with regard to expat moves: distance from the normal location; destination country; the job; the degree of social support received; length of posting; dynamics around repatriation; and the degree to which choice exists.[34]

A model has been developed based on how expatriates see themselves on two dimensions, their allegiance to the parent firm and their allegiance to the local operation:

- **dual citizens:** strong on both dimensions;
- **free agents:** weak on both dimensions;
- **left behind:** low local and high parent;
- **going native:** high local and low parent.[35]

Difficulties in expat postings are often described as 'culture shock' and can be seen as a

> stress reaction where salient psychological and physical rewards are generally uncertain hence difficult to control or predict... an individual's lack of points of reference, social norms and rules to guide their actions and understand others' behaviour.[36]

Culture shock is seen as a transitional experience with three theoretical perspectives: cultural learning; stress, coping and adjustment; and social identity and inter-group relations.[37]

Four factors have been suggested as crucial to the success of foreign assignments: environmental briefings; culture assimilation; language; and sensitivity training and field experiences.[38]

Leading Across New Borders notes that organizations that have an increasingly global footprint should increase the frequency of international assignments, using them more strategically and less as a temporary stop-gap measure. Organizations should ask themselves whether global rotations consider local needs and whether they have a positive or negative impact on motivation locally. They should also improve their focus on improving the repatriation experience to reduce subsequent turnover.[39]

Culture and the Big Five

In *Cultures and Organizations*, Hofstede states that 'systematic individual differences in perceptions of organizational cultures are most likely based on personality ... and individual perception dimensions can be associated with Big Five personality dimensions as follows:

- alienation with neuroticism;
- workaholism with extraversion – includes active and energetic;
- ambition with openness to experience;
- machismo negatively with agreeableness;
- orderliness with conscientiousness'.[40]

However, no personality factor is available to associate with authoritarianism. Previously, Hofstede and Robert McRae[41] had found that mean personality scores correlated significantly with all four IBM culture dimensions but not long-term orientation, so Hofstede considered whether the Five-Factor Personality Model, which was conceived by Western minds, might miss a personality dimension that relates to a long- versus short-term orientation. Subsequently, research evidence from studies in China and the Philippines offered a sixth personality factor relating to interpersonal relatedness, or gregariousness. Gregariousness and authoritarianism may be seen as two facets of a sixth personality factor relating to dependence on others, which itself might correlate with a long-term orientation.

Having examined culture and its impact on organizations, we can look at the difference between corporate culture and corporate climate.

Organization culture

In *Exploring Strategy*, organization culture is defined as the 'taken-for-granted assumptions and behaviours of an organization's members'.[42] Culture is conceived in four layers: beliefs, values, behaviours and a paradigm, which is a set of assumptions held in common and taken for granted.[43]

It is suggested that every organization has a cultural web that 'shows the behavioural, physical and symbolic manifestations of a culture'.[44] Central to this is the paradigm of taken-for granted assumptions, which contains artefacts of stories, symbols, power structures, organizational structures, control systems, rituals, routines and stories.[45]

An organization's identity is what members believe and understand about who they are as an organization. Within organizations, sub-cultures will exist, for instance in teams, divisions and geographies.

Organization culture has been given four designations by Kim Cameron and Robert Quinn:

- **Collaborate (clan) culture:** Open, transparent and friendly place to work. Feels like an extended family. Leaders are considered to be mentors or even parental figures. Group loyalty and sense of tradition are strong. A premium is placed on teamwork, participation and consensus.

- **Create (adhocracy) culture:** Dynamic, entrepreneurial, creative and disruptive. A creative place to work. Innovation and risk-taking are embraced by both employees and leaders. Psychologically safe environment. Commitment to experimentation and thinking differently unifies the organization.

- **Control (hierarchy) culture:** Rule-based, highly structured and formal. Maintaining an efficient and effective functioning organization is critical. Consistent, predictable, performance and efficient operations are the long-term goals.

- **Compete (market) culture:** Results-driven organization focused on job completion. Competitive and goal-oriented.[46]

In addition, Schein presents seven dimensions of organizational culture, arguing that they can reveal some of the more implicit social aspects of corporate culture:

- **Group versus individual:** The extent to which the organization on-boards new employees, is it a mass process or more individually tailored.

- **Formal versus informal:** The extent to which the process is formalized and institutionalized or more apprentice-based through close mentoring and coaching.

- **Self-destructive and reconstructing versus self-enhancing:** The extent to which the process seeks to replace aspects of individuality with group cognition and behaviour.

- **Serial versus random:** The extent to which mentoring and other support is provided or are deliberately withheld to uncover coping behaviour and levels of success.

- **Sequential versus disjunctive:** The extent to which there is a planned, predictable, process or a more open and therefore less certain journey.

- **Fixed versus variable:** The extent to which there are specified times for each stage of a training process or whether progress to the next stage depends on performance reviews.

- **Tournament versus contest:** The extent to which each stage might lead to termination or a longer-term game.[47]

He writes that the

> strength and degree of internal consistency of a culture are… a function of the
> stability of the group, the length of time the group has existed, the intensity
> of the group's experiences of learning, the mechanisms by which the learning
> has taken place (ie positive reinforcement or avoidance conditioning), and the
> strength and clarity of the assumptions held by the founders and leaders of the
> group.[48]

In a Gallup report, *Building a Culture That Drives Performance*, they state that 'culture is unique to every organization. Every organization has a unique purpose and brand. Organizations that want to create or sustain a strong culture can only do so by understanding the ways in which purpose, brand and culture interact.'[49] For Gallup, the five drivers of culture are:

- leadership and communication;
- values and rituals;
- human capital;
- work teams and structures;
- performance.

Gallup believe that 'culture attracts world-class talent to your organization… helps align teams and improves performance'.[50]

In culture change projects, leaders need to modify beliefs, values and behaviour. Culture change through behaviour will only occur if the behaviour is perceived to improve the culture and if it becomes internalized and stable. Culture change through cognitive redefinition of beliefs and values is hard to achieve unless preceded or accompanied with specific behavioural change.

In *Mindset*, Carol Dweck notes that people who work in growth-mindset organizations have 'far more trust in their company and a much greater sense of empowerment, ownership, and commitment',[51] while 'employees in fixed-mindset companies not only say that their companies are less likely to support them in risk-taking and innovation, they are also far more likely to agree that their organizations are rife with cutthroat or unethical behaviour.'[52]

Corporate climate

A corporate climate, examined through a psychological lens, can be seen as a part of corporate culture, examined through a sociological and anthropological lens, which mediates performance and job satisfaction and is in turn impacted by leadership behaviour.

In *The Psychology of Behaviour at Work*, Furnham notes that

> culture researchers have been interested in the evolution and stability of organizational social systems over time, while climate researchers have been more interested in the impact of systems on individuals and groups. Culture researchers look at the underlying assumptions, values and meaning, while climate researchers look more at 'surface' factors that are more easily observable.[53]

Denison explores this as follows:

> Culture refers to the deep structure of organizations, which is rooted in the values, beliefs, and assumptions held by organizational members. Meaning is established through socialization to a variety of identity groups that converge in the workplace. Interaction reproduces a symbolic world that gives culture both a great stability and a certain precarious and fragile nature rooted in the dependence of the system on individual cognition and action. Climate, in contrast, portrays organizational environments as being rooted in the organization's value system, but tends to present these social environments in relatively static terms, describing them in terms of a fixed (and broadly applicable) set of dimensions. Thus, climate is often considered as relatively temporary, subject to direct control, and largely limited to those aspects of the social environment that are consciously perceived by organizational members.[54]

The distinction between organizational climate and organizational culture may be summarized as follows. 'Climate refers to a situation and its link to thoughts, feelings, and behaviours of organizational members.'[55] It is provisional, subjective, and often subject to direct manipulation by people with power and influence. In contrast, culture refers to an evolved, path-dependent, context within which a situation may be embedded. Culture is 'rooted in history, collectively held, and sufficiently complex to resist many attempts at direct manipulation.'[56]

Organizational climate may be seen as an independent variable that directly impacts work outcomes such as motivation, productivity, satisfaction and turnover or as a dependent variable such as index of an organization's health or a moderating factor.

Highlights

- It is important for leaders to understand the additional complexity driven by international and organizational culture as it impacts leadership and management choices.

- Cultural anthropology studies have given guidance relating to differences in beliefs, values and attitudes exhibited by people that have grown up in different cultures.

- Cultural evolutionary psychology in Chapter 1 gives an understanding of how these changes come about. In addition to societal differences in culture, organizations have developed cultures and sub-cultures in functions, divisions and teams.

Leadership impact

Key themes that leaders should reflect on include:

- Leaders should understand the implications of cultural diversity in their organizations, particularly if they operate internationally.

- Expatriate postings should be well-planned and managed, including training around cultural awareness and repatriation.

- The impact of culture should be considered when using remote workers who are not immersed in the organization's culture day to day; this is particularly relevant as working becomes more flexible and agile.

- Leaders set the cultural tone for their organizations through their words and actions.

People management recommendations

Actions to consider:

- Reinforce organizational culture by ensuring that all staff are aware of core values and that these are lived by the organization's leaders.

- Design and develop training for cultural diversity, and to reinforce organizational culture.

- Ensure that the employer brand has broad cultural appeal to support talent acquisition and the employee experience supports a strong cultural employee value proposition.

- Ensure that the cultural diversity of the market is reflected in the organization.

Social movements

10

Introduction

Social responsibility is an increasingly important factor for organizations, both internally and externally. This chapter explores various aspects, including corporate and social responsibility (CSR), the emergence of economic, social and governance (ESG) for investment and the increased focus on diversity and inclusion (D&I).

Organizations are not only expected to demonstrate their commitment to stakeholders such as suppliers and clients, it is an important factor for the employer brands, the employee experience, and employee value proposition. The whole issue has moved beyond whether it is morally the right thing to do and has become a commercial imperative.

Chapter summary

The following subjects are discussed in this chapter:

- **the social enterprise;**
- **corporate and social responsibility:**
  - corporate sustainability;
  - transformative, civil, philanthropy;
- **economic, social and governance;**
- **impact of leadership;**
- **stakeholder impact;**
- **responsibility for CSR;**
- **diversity and inclusion:**
  - diversity and inclusion management;
  - leadership impact;

- **practical implications:**
  - implementation;
- **cultural resistance;**
- **responsibility for diversity and inclusion.**

The social enterprise

A 2018 Deloitte report, *The Rise of the Social Enterprise*, discussed the premise that commercial organizations are transforming themselves from *business* enterprises to *social* enterprises. They define a social enterprise as: 'an organization whose mission combined revenue growth and profit-making with the need to respect and support its environment and stakeholder network'.[1]

Stakeholder theory suggests that organizations have responsibility to stakeholders other than the organization's owners, which for commercial organizations may be shareholders or partners. Stakeholders have been defined as 'any group or individual who can be or is affected (positively or negatively) by the achievement of the organization's objectives.'[2]

In their report, Deloitte noted that governments can often be slow in legislating on societal issues that are largely domestic in nature. However, this is compounded when governments need to collaborate on solutions to problems with global consequences, where progress can be glacial. It is felt that the private sector can play an important role in helping to effect societal change and three areas where this is the case are examined in this chapter: CSR, ESG and D&I.

Organizations with a poor track record in societal issues will be held to account by their workforce, suppliers and investors and the report card is increasingly becoming a public and global one. On the other hand, an increasing number of studies show that an investment in the above areas have a positive impact on organization performance.[3]

Corporate and social responsibility

In the introduction to *Strategic Corporate Social Responsibility: Tools and theories for responsible management*, Haski-Leventhal noted that 'strategic CSR is not about doing less harm or giving some money to charity but it is focused on a holistic business approach that demonstrates responsibility in its strategy and core operations, while working from a multi-stakeholder perspective and long-term focus.'[4] Other definitions include 'business decision-making linked to ethical values, compliance with legal requirements, and respect for people, communities, and the environment around the world'[5] and 'CSR refers to the integration of an enterprises social, environmental, ethical and philanthropic responsibilities towards society into its operations, processes and core business strategy in cooperation with relevant stakeholders'.[6]

Corporate sustainability

Corporate sustainability (CS) is seen as representing an organization's continuity and long-term orientation, its adaptability to the environment, and the consideration of interests of the stakeholders that to a great extent represents the triple bottom line (TBL). Simply put, corporate sustainability means 'meeting the needs of the present without compromising the ability of future generations to meet their own needs'.[7]

In triple bottom line, it is suggested that the term sustainability maybe preferred over CSR as some feel it gives equal importance to the benefits enjoyed by organizations in addition to other stakeholder groups. It notes that TBL is a reaction to a growing demand 'for new ways of measuring business value that take environmental, social and economic factors into account'[8] and that 'the TBL captures the essence of sustainability by measuring the impact of an organization's activities on the world'.[9]

In *Talent, Transformation and the Triple Bottom Line*, Savitz notes that sustainability:

- begins with your own employees;
- can serve as a talent magnet;
- alters traditional job requirements;
- strategies often have important human resource implications;
- affects talent management processes;
- increases employee engagement.[10]

Studies have found that leadership behaviour supporting CS was similar to normal effective leadership practices but also exhibits an additional task of boundary-spanning between the organization's CS activities and its environment. Promoting CS requires an energized workforce who operate in a positive, trusting and cooperative social climate and who are inspired by ethical executives who lead by example.[11]

Transformational civil philanthropy

Despite 77 per cent of the respondents to Deloitte's study citing citizenship as important, only 18 per cent said it was reflected in their organizational strategy and 56 per cent said it was not a focus or not well developed or invested in.[12]

Organizations may have various motivations to participate in CSR: a moral sense of duty to the society that support its existence; maintaining good stakeholder relationships; and economic and therefore instrumental motivation.[13] Indeed, research has shown that commercial organizations have a mix of responses, from simple adherence to regulation, to a response focused on business return and finally a response that is altruistic. They may move through various stages of adoption from having positive impact in the short term to a positive impact in the long term:

- **defensive:** deny there is a problem, don't take responsibility;
- **compliance:** with social norms and legislation;
- **managerial:** embedding CSR in management processes;
- **strategic:** integrated into business and core processes;
- **civil:** sector leadership.[14]

Three seminal papers were published by Porter and Kramer in the *Harvard Business Review* in 2002, 2006 and 2011. The first argued that companies that were not beneficial to society would lose their competitive advantage, and promoted the importance of strategic philanthropy and the positive impact in can have on society.[15] The second encouraged a proactive corporate social agenda that does more than be responsive to stakeholder concerns and expectations.[16] The third proposed the creation of shared values, which were defined as 'policies and operating practices that enhance the competitiveness of a company while simultaneously advancing the economic and social conditions in the communities in which it operates'.[17]

In *Corporate Social Responsibility: Strategy, communication, governance*, organizations are categorized into one of five business strategies for sustainability.

- **Denial:** Sustainability and CSR are highly irrelevant to organization strategy.
- **Defensive:** Organizations admit and accepts responsibility for social and environmental impact.
- **Isolated:** Sustainability begins to make a substantial impact on organization strategy and operations.
- **Embedded:** Strategically, operationally and culturally embedded.
- **Transformative:** The sustainability strategy results in positive impact on the environment.[18]

Studies have found that socio-environmentally proactive firms have higher than mean dividend return, earnings per share growth and cumulative sales growth but lower than mean earnings before interest, tax, depreciation and amortization (EBITDA) than their sector peers.[19] They tend to have lower short-term liquidity than their sector peers and while their total leverage is significantly lower their long-term leverage is significantly higher. High social responsibility and environmental sustainability (SRES) companies are also found to have higher managerial efficiency ratios such as return on assets, equity and investment (ROA, ROE and ROI).[20] CEO ethical leadership and firm performance can have a positive relationship, but it needs support from a strong programme of corporate ethics that together enhance firm ethical culture. [21]

A pyramid of business responsibilities was proposed by Carroll:

- **economic:** required by society – invest, create jobs, pay taxes;
- **legal:** required by society – comply with legislation and regulations;
- **ethical:** expected by society – do the right thing, voluntary codes of governance an ethics;
- **philanthropic:** desired by society – donate money to charities, corporate volunteering, CSR projects.[22]

This was modified by Haski-Leventhal, who added environmental and social responsibilities, and saw ethical as forming the base of the pyramid, followed by legal, economic, social, environmental and philanthropic.[23] Ultimately, 'to be professionally ethical means to act in accordance with the accepted principles of right and wrong that govern the conduct of a professional, while being unethical is defined as not conforming to approved standards of social or professional behaviour'.[24] Ethical guidance can be normative, rule-based, or descriptive, context-based, narrative guidance.

It has been said that

> people evaluate their actions against moral thresholds held by their referent groups. The existence of a code of ethics may also lead employees to expect others to see them as following the ethical guidelines prescribed by the organization. Consequently, they may want to be seen as ethical and moral agents.[25]

Research has shown that when ethical leadership is strong, CSR has an indirect and positive impact on firm performance via firm reputation, but not when ethical leadership is weak.[26] Research also suggests that perceptions of CSR impact a variety of employee attitudes and behaviours, including trust in organizational leadership,[27] and all four of Carroll's variables reduce employee cynicism indirectly through employee trust.[28]

From an external stakeholder perspective, organizations' signals to stakeholders around their CSR activity are communicated in the context of other information, which may suggest an instrumental, commercial, rather than moral driver for CSR activity[29] and that the degree to which a CEO is perceived as an ethical leader has an impact on this. Other research notes the importance of the executive group in CSR decision-making[30] and the extent to which a board is independent also impacts the promotion of CSR activity.[31]

An extension of CSR is the adoption of ESG by investors, which has become an increasingly significant consideration for leaders of organizations from a financing perspective.

Environmental, social and governance

Socially responsible investing has been defined as follows: 'sustainable, responsible and impact investing (SRI) is an investment discipline that considers environmental, social and corporate governance (ESG) criteria to generate long-term competitive financial returns and positive social impact'.[32] ESG investing has been defined as 'the research and investment strategy framework that evaluates environmental, social, and governance factors as non-financial dimensions of a security's valuation, performance, and risk profile.'[33]

There has been significant growth in ESG investing, and in early 2014 assets managed by US-based firms considering corporate ESG practices as investment criteria had grown to US$4.8 trillion from US$1.4 trillion in 2012,[34] and 'even though there is no convincing evidence that SRI funds outperform the market in the long term, most academic studies published in the last decade found that these investments are competitive with non-SRI strategies.'[35]

In 1992 corporate social performance was measured against seven pillars:

- community issues;
- diverse workplace;
- employee relations;
- environmental performance;
- international;
- product and business practice;
- other, eg governance.[36]

These pillars became the foundation of the ESG rating system for investments, and third-party rating agencies now advise institutional investors on ESG factors such as: accounting standards, pollution, sustainability practices, brand reputation, cyber security and data management, CSR activity, board and management team diversity, employee relations and practices, health and safety, and human capital development and compensation.

In 2006 the United Nations released the *Principles for Responsible Investment* containing six core principles for making investment decisions:

- Incorporate ESG issues into investment analysis and decision-making.
- Be active owners and address ESG issues as an organization.
- Seek appropriate disclosure of ESG issues by investee organizations.
- Promote acceptance and implementation of ESG policies in the investment industry.
- Work together to enhance effectiveness of implementing ESG principles.
- Report activities and progress on ESG as an organization.[37]

These are a voluntary and aspirational set of investment principles that offer guidance for incorporating ESG issues into investment practice.

Four common methods of approaching responsible investing have been suggested by Sherwood and Pollard:

- **Exclusion-based:** Where certain organizations' securities would explicitly not be considered or may be divested from portfolios.
- **Integration-based:** Where certain organizations' securities would explicitly be included.
- **Impact-based:** May be driven by the investor's desire to meet social and environmental objectives while still receiving a desired target return.
- **Engagement-based:** Describes the type of communication and potential collaboration or hostile activism associated with investors.[38]

Increasingly, CEOs will find the sustainability, CSR and D&I activities undertaken by their organizations will impact their access to capital and the cost of capital. They will also affect the degree of investor engagement.

Impact of leadership

Leadership is often noted as influencing, motivating and enabling others to contribute to the success of organizations. In *Strategic Corporate Social Responsibility*, Haski-Leventhal rightly points out that this can be very challenging; 'they are expected to demonstrate strong values and work with all stakeholders to lead sustainable organizations. In an era of fast changes, globalization, technology and social media, the business leadership challenges are greater than ever'.[39]

She considers a number of leadership types that have increasingly been discussed in conjunction with CSR:

- **Sustainable:** A focus on environmental impact emphasizing purpose and values.
- **Responsible:** Making decisions taking into consideration the interests of all stakeholders, emphasizing respect, service, justice, honesty and community.
- **Ethical:** Display honesty, openness, integrity and a desire to do the right thing without compromise.
- **Purpose-driven:** A focus on the higher order raison d'être for an organization's existence. Why do we do what we do, how do we do it, and at the individual level what is our purpose?
- **Value-based:** Having strong values that are focused on stakeholders helps to create a strong culture of trust and social responsibility.
- **Transformational:** Successful agents of change, driving change through communicating a vision and inspiring action.
- **Servant:** A focus on followers, putting their needs first based on the belief that this will support a high-performance workforce.

- **Authentic:** Visibly and consistently behaving in a way that is true to the inherent moral values of the leader.
- **Shared:** A view that anyone in the workforce can share the responsibility of leadership
- **Conscious:** A combination of transformational, responsible, purpose-driven, servant and authentic leadership.[40]

Virtuous leadership traits include, humility, gratitude, forgiveness and altruism. However, there are elements of overlap between many of these styles, and as such they are not mutually exclusive.

One study investigated the relationship between integrity and transformational leadership behaviour, transformational leadership and CSR and the mediating effect of transformational leadership between integrity and CSR. Its findings reinforce the premise that transformational leaders have a moral dimension, act as role models of ethical behaviour and contribute to an ethical climate in the organization.[41]

Another study found that middle management positively impact environmentally favourable behaviour in the cascading process of CSR activity[42] and an exponentially positive relationship between perceived CSR and organizational pride impacts levels of job satisfaction and affective commitment.[43]

Little empirical evidence has been found when considering the competencies of sustainability leaders who 'integrate social, environmental, ethical human rights and consumer concerns into their business operations and core strategy in close collaboration with their stakeholders'.[44] However, the results of research that utilized critical behavioural competencies from Saville Consulting's Wave Professional Styles questionnaire have been used to create a competency framework for effective leadership for sustainability. It suggests that leaders should be:

- **results driven:** the most critical competency is developing expertise;
- **inclusive operators:** the most critical competency is establishing rapport;
- **change agents:** the most critical competency is generating ideas;
- **ethically orientated:** the most critical competency is interacting with people;
- **visionary thinker:** the most critical competency is exploring possibilities.[45]

Overall, the most important competencies were found to be:

- developing expertise;
- impressing people;
- establishing rapport;
- articulating information;
- interacting with people;
- valuing individuals;
- exploring possibilities;

- generating ideas;
- challenging ideas;
- understanding people.

Narcissistic CEOs are seen to care more about CSR than hubristic CEOs. When narcissistic CEOs observe the behaviour of competitors with regard to CSR they will respond in the opposite manner, while hubristic CEOs will only invest less.[46] Narcissistic CEOs have been found to have higher profile in corporate philanthropy and maintain successful programmes.[47]

Research has found similarities and differences between genders and leadership styles around CSR. Overall, a *dominant* style of leadership was found to be the worse style for deploying a CSR strategy.[48] Other studies support the belief that conducting business in accordance with norms that integrate economic, social and environmental principles is a strategy that increases shareholder value,[49] that the presence of women on boards has an indirect impact on financial performance with CSR possibly acting as a mediating factor,[50] that male CEOs with gender diverse boards are more likely than other firms to have a strong environmental record,[51] and that firms with women CEOs and female interlinked board members are less likely to be challenged by environmental concerns.[52] Overall, gender diverse leadership teams are more effective than other firms at pursuing positive environmental strategies[53] and the presence of female directors is associated with a stronger firm-level commitment to CSR. This is true even if there is only one woman on a board.[54]

Stakeholder impact

Research has examined the role of organizational trust in relation to perceptions of CSR activity and employee cynicism, and organizational cynicism has been defined as having three dimensions:

- **Cognitive:** Employees think the firm lacks integrity.
- **Affective:** Employees develop a negative feeling towards the firm.
- **Behavioural:** Employees publicly criticize the firm. CSR activity may contribute towards a positive working environment, which in turn helps to reduce cynicism.[55]

It is recommended that CSR communication should start with employees who need to be convinced about the genuine motives underlying CSR activity,[56] with leaders choosing between an instrumental or integrative style.[57] They are more likely to be advocates for the organization and feel more affective attachment when the underlying reasons are genuine and not instrumental.[58]

To encourage the workforce to engage in CSR activity, organizations should not treat CSR as an add-on activity to their traditional business model but something that should be carefully planned and integrated into organizational strategy and culture.[59]

Organizations should ensure corporate and employee social responsibility congruence, in conjunction with internal, external and relational contingent factors,[60] to help increase the authenticity of their CSR activities.[61]

Stakeholders' perception of CSR authenticity can be summarized as authentic, inauthentic, disingenuous and misguided:

- **Authentic:** Distinctive and socially connected. It acknowledges stakeholder goals, which are reflected, in firm values and tailored CSR activities.

- **Inauthentic:** Generic and socially disconnected, it engages in superficial activities that ignore stakeholder goals.

- **Disingenuous:** Occurs when firms relate to their stakeholder goals but do not live this in their own values and activities. There is a lack of value congruence.

- **Misguided:** Exemplified where firms have strong values, but these are disconnected from the firm's social context and stakeholders.[62]

Corporate Social Responsibility summarizes the key stakeholder challenges faced by organizations in an age of digital communication and social media:

- Stakeholders groups can form more easily, more quickly and more globally than before and create a stronger voice.

- Stakeholders and stakeholder managers are identifiable, and campaigns are more personal, with a 'names and faces' approach that creates a more emotional response.

- Stakeholders can access corporate data and their personal data more easily, and organizations are scrutinized constantly, with many encouraging a more public dialogue than has previously been seen.

- Boundaries between stakeholder groups have become blurred and communication between stakeholder groups has increased without the coordination of the organization.[63]

Corporate social responsibility incorporates ethical people management, which includes the concept of fairness and differentiates between equality, which is about everyone being treated in the same way, and equity, which means that people are given the same opportunity to succeed. This in turn encompasses the concept of diversity and inclusion, which is examined below.

CSR is often linked to organizational citizenship behaviour (OCB), which is defined as 'individual behaviour that is discretionary, not directly or explicitly recognized by the formal reward system, and that in aggregate promotes the effective functioning of the organization'.[64] OCB is not bounded by role specifications or tasks. Higher levels of OCB have been linked to higher levels of employee performance, promotions and higher customer satisfaction.[65] CSR activities are seen as not only enhancing firm performance and reputation, but also influencing employees' OCB under conditions of high task significance.[66] Performance also increases when employees believe organizations perceive moral consistency with CSR activity and the nature of the organization and also that it is strategically beneficial to the organization.[67]

Neuroscience For Leadership notes that 'leaders who can engage the attachment emotions have a better chance of motivating people... working towards the greater good, towards helping others, can be not only motivational, but also capable of reducing stress and increasing our resilience and sense of well-being.'[68]

Responsibility for CSR

While the CEO should drive and remain involved in CSR activity, the responsibility for directing an organization's policy on CSR may rest with one or more functions, for instance marketing, compliance and human resources. Where CSR has moved beyond a defensive, compliant and instrumental mindset then the impact will be far-reaching and involve the developing culture and employer brand. It is therefore suggested that the human resource function may be the best location for functional experts to reside. Like diversity and inclusion, there are a number of public policy considerations to understand and engage with. In *Talent, Transformation and the Triple Bottom Line*, the human resource function is seen as playing a central role in the success of corporate and social responsibility.[69]

Diversity and inclusion

Diversity and inclusion (D&I) initiatives are increasingly an integral part of organization strategy and strategic workforce planning. It is now seen as less about compliance, less about the commercial benefits and more as a responsibility to society.

The terms diversity and inclusion are often conflated, but one distinction is that while 'diversity can be mandated and legislated... inclusion stems from voluntary actions'.[70]

One definition of diversity is as follows:

> workforce diversity refers to the division of the workforce into distinct
> categories that (a) have a perceived commonality within a given cultural
> or national context and that (b) impact potentially harmful or beneficial
> employment outcomes such as job opportunities, treatment in the workplace,
> and promotion prospects – irrespective of job-related skills and qualifications.[71]

Inclusion can be defined as follows: 'in inclusive organizations and societies, people of all identities and many styles can be fully themselves while also contributing to the larger collective, as valued and full members'.[72] Optimal distinctiveness theory (ODT) is an area of research that examines the balance between individuals finding social cohesion with others while maintaining their unique identity.[73]

Inclusion is seen as a multilevel system of practices,[74] with fully inclusive organizations not only considering diversity for themselves but also extending this to a local, regional, national and global context.[75]

Organizations may find it difficult to be inclusive. As Helen Turnball states in *Illusion of Inclusion*, 'Companies hire for diversity and manage for similarity. We hire people for their difference and then teach them directly and indirectly what they have to do to fit in to the corporate culture.'[76]

Diversity and inclusion initiatives are important in helping to establish a society where everyone feels their participation is valued, and the economic case is becoming increasingly compelling. For instance, an IMF Staff Discussion Note, 'Economic gains from gender inclusion: New mechanisms, new evidence', found that 'obstacles to women entering the labor force are even more costly than initially thought, and benefits from closing gender gaps are likely to be larger than initially thought.' Their analysis of economic data suggests that

> women and men complement each other in the production process. The implication is that there is a value to diversity: adding more women to the labor force should induce larger gains than an equal increase in male workers. These higher gains are preserved even when considering that home production would decline when women work in the market economy.[77]

Their findings also suggest that greater gender diversity is likely to boost male incomes, which 'makes discrimination against women in labor markets not only economically inefficient but also directly costly to men.'[78]

Diversity and inclusion management

Diversity management practices have mainly been focused on gender, disability, age, race and ethnicity, as well as members of other marginalized groups in the workplace, while inclusion practices 'have sought to create equal access to decision-making, resources, and upward mobility opportunities for these individuals'.[79]

In *Inclusive Talent Management*, Frost and Kalman state that the historic approach by organizations to diversity is said to have fallen into three types:

- **Diversity 101:** Diversity for diversity's sake, with programmes designed to raise awareness of difference.

- **Diversity 2.0:** Diversity for social responsibility, with programmes designed to draw out the benefits of difference.

- **Inclusion 3.0:** Diversity as a business strategy, with integrated systems designed to embed the benefits of difference.[80]

It is suggested that Diversity 101 was driven by civil rights and affirmative action movements in the United States and equal opportunities programs in the United Kingdom that largely focused on gender and ethnicity and were sometimes seen as problematic due to non-merit-based selection. Diversity 2.0 is said to have been driven by shareholder pressure and embraced greater breadth in diverse groups but was sometimes seen as doing little more than managing reputational risk mitigation. Finally, Inclusion 3.0 is driven by the recognition of unconscious bias and leadership deficits; a recognition that attaining a diverse workforce is not enough and therefore promoting a truly inclusive culture.

Quotas are seen as problematic, as some quotas, for instance gender, may lead to the underrepresentation of ethnic and/or socioeconomic groups; they may restrict the free flow of talent and bring into question whether appointments and promotions are merit-based. These may lead to out-group members feeling a loss of equity and that in-group members care more about their success than that of the wider organization. However, quotas may be adopted, at least in the short term, to address cognitive imbalance and create role models to promote diversity at lower levels in organizations.

In *Inclusive Talent Management*, Frost and Kalman note that collective ability is more important to organizational success than individual ability within teams, and that while diversity may relate to an individual's physical traits there are also other considerations such as cultural, linguistic, faith and socioeconomic factors.[81]

Although a diverse workforce can lead to positive organization outcomes, there may also be negative impacts, such as increasing conflict, higher turnover, less cohesion and poorer performance.[82] For instance, targeting diversity initiatives specifically towards women instead of all employees may lead to the anticipation of bias by both women and men.[83]

Diversity intelligence (DQ) is a tool promoted as contributing to more D&I in the workplace and it is suggested that DQ assessments need to be created for hiring and development.[84] This is based on research that suggests individuals possess multiple intelligences that reflect our social environment, and which are therefore all important to leadership.[85] Indeed, both authentic and servant leadership are thought to create 'long-term, positive relationships based on mutual trust'[86] and this in turn promotes positive dialogue across a diverse workforce.

Inclusion is seen as helping to reap the potential rewards of diversity. An examination of the literature on inclusion identifies a number of themes:

- **safety:** the need to feel safe, both physically and psychologically;
- **work group involvement:** a sense of belonging and access to critical information and resources;
- **feeling respected and valued:** appreciated by the team and the organization;
- **influence on decision-making:** a sense that their ideas and perspectives are valued, that they are listened to;

- **authenticity:** where employees can share valued identities that differ from the pervading organizational or team norm without fear of negative outcomes;
- **recognizing, honouring and advancing diversity:** the senior leadership team demonstrate that they value diversity through their words and actions.

Building a diverse and inclusive workforce is one of the most significant challenges for leaders, and their role is examined below.

Leadership impact

In 2016 Deloitte published a report entitled *The Six Signature Traits of Inclusive Leadership: Thriving in a diverse world*, which suggests that diversity comes in four types:

- **diversity of markets:** for instance, emerging markets;
- **diversity of customers:** changing demographics and attitudes;
- **diversity of ideas:** with various agents of disruption highlighted including technology and hyper-connectivity; and,
- **diversity of talent:** socio-demographic factors combined with expectations of equality and equity.[87]

This idea can be extended to incorporate the diversity of all stakeholders.

The Deloitte research defines the elements that are required for an inclusive culture. These are about creating an atmosphere of fairness and respect, where people feel valued for who they are, their uniqueness, but also have a sense of belonging and the confidence and inspiration to share their ideas without fear of negative outcomes. The results of their research suggest that in addition to the traits and competencies traditionally associated with successful leadership, six signature traits are now required of a leader is to be inclusive. These are:

- **commitment:** aligned with personal values and belief in the business case;
- **courage:** speak up and challenge the status quo, humble about strengths and weaknesses;
- **cognizance:** mindful of personal and organizational blind-spots and self-regulate to aid fairness;
- **curiosity:** open mindset, desire to understand how others view the world and tolerance for ambiguity;
- **cultural intelligence:** confident and effective in cross-cultural interactions;
- **collaboration:** empower individuals as well as creating and leveraging the thinking of diverse groups.[88]

In addition to each trait, the authors note 15 specific elements, all of which can be developed.

In the same year as the Deloitte report, the research institute of the world's largest executive search firm, Korn Ferry, published a report entitled *The Inclusive Leader*, which looked at the traits and abilities required for leaders to be inclusive in their 'thoughts, perceptions and actions – and to inspire an inclusive mindset in others'.[89] Their research included the analysis of two and a half million leadership assessments and determined that the key traits for successful inclusive leadership are flexibility, adaptability, openness and authenticity.[90] The report also stated that a 21st century leader is by definition an inclusive leader, as for organizational success they must think globally and therefore have cultural agility. Leaders must: be innovative and therefore be open to diverse points of view; be able to drive change and therefore be able to motivate diverse teams; and, in growing a business, be aware of the opportunity to service underrepresented customer segments.

The results of a McKinsey report showed that companies in the top quartile for racial and ethnic diversity were 35 per cent more likely to perform better financially than their sector medians, and for gender diversity this was 15 per cent.[91] However, in 2012 the average percentage of women in the UK and US on executive teams was respectively 12 per cent and 16 per cent, and when considering the overall population the proportionate lack of representation for ethnicity/race was 78 per cent and 97 per cent respectively.[92]

An article by David Rock and Heidi Grant, 'Why diverse teams are smarter', cited a report by the global investment bank Credit Suisse, which reported that a global analysis of 2,400 organizations showed that those with at least one female board member achieved higher returns on equity and higher income growth. Heterogeneity delivers superior results, as 'diverse teams are more likely to constantly re-examine facts and remain objective. They may also encourage greater scrutiny of each member's actions... and you allow your employees to become more aware of their own potential biases'.[93]

A study by Gallup found that having gender diverse teams improved financial outcomes for business units in two independent companies. The combination of employee engagement and gender diversity resulted in 46 per cent and 58 per cent higher financial performance with respect to comparable revenue and net profit, respectively, for business units above the median on both engagement and gender diversity, compared with those below the median on both.[94]

Research into LGBT policies and firm performance concluded that the presence of LGBT-supportive policies is associated with higher firm value, productivity and profitability.[95]

The results of a McKinsey report, *Diversity Matters*, showed that companies in the top quartile for racial and ethnic diversity were 35 per cent more likely to perform better financially than their sector medians, and for gender diversity this was 15 per cent.[96] Also, that a more diverse workforce and leadership team are likely to make more informed and robust decisions that better reflect their social context, and this in turn leads to a more engaged employees and higher performance.

Indeed, other research has found that context plays a moderating role in the relationship between leader gender and team performance. The findings suggest that teams led by women are more effective than teams led by men when:

- **Team size increases:** They report more cohesion, cooperative and participative learning.
- **The team is geographically dispersed:** They report more cooperative and participative learning.
- **Functional diversity increases:** They report more cohesion.[97]

It appears that when the need for coordination is high, women may have a more positive impact on team performance than men.

Research has pointed to the paradox of inclusion, that 'working towards inclusion in diverse organizations and societies can often be experienced as polarizing and presents many challenges and tensions'.[98] One paper explores three core dilemmas of inclusion and suggests how each one can be managed:

- **the paradox of self-expression and identity:** contrasts an emphasis on belonging and absorption vs distinctiveness and uniqueness;
- **the paradox of boundaries and norms:** contrasts an emphasis on stable and well-defined standards vs shifting and flexible standards;
- **the paradox of safety and comfort:** contrasts an emphasis on comfort and 'my way' vs discomfort and openness to change.[99]

In *Diversity at Work: The practice of inclusion*, Bernardo Feldman suggests that inclusion is about: both everyday behaviour and organizational and social systems; both structures and processes; both comfort and discomfort; and both deriving practical benefits and doing what is right and just.[100] It is also argued that 'inclusion goes far beyond merely developing *soft skills* of caring and compassion, to a need for courage and making tough decisions.'[101]

Inclusion research undertaken in a Chinese context drew on inclusion literature that was based on Western perspectives of inclusion practices adopted by organizations and perceptions of inclusion by organizational members.[102] This research found seven factors of inclusive management:

- inclusive teamwork;
- inclusive communication;
- inclusive decision-making;
- fairness in treatment;
- inclusive leadership;
- tolerance;
- inclusive adaptation.[103]

Tolerance is seen as unique in the Chinese context and maybe driven by cultural norms. In a Chinese context, inclusion is defined as having reciprocity between the organization and its workforce, and inclusive adaption is therefore not simply considered from an organization to its workforce, as it is also believed that employees need to adapt to the organization policies.[104]

Having understood the background philosophy of diversity and inclusion, and the results of research that has been undertaken, it is useful to consider the practical implications.

Practical implications

Implementation

In *Inclusive Leadership*, a guide to developing an impactful D&I strategy, Charlotte Sweeney and Fleur Borthwick offer a framework for mapping the extent to which it is embedded and how engaged leaders and managers are around D&I in their thoughts and actions:

- **low embedding and low engagement:** produces inertia and no lasting progress;
- **high engagement and low embedding:** produces a lot of initiatives with limited impact;
- **low engagement and high embedding:** will result in imposed change, which may not carry the hearts and minds of the workforce; and,
- **high engagement and high embedding:** creates inclusion, which will result in sustainable change.[105]

D&I practitioners are recommended to have the following seven competencies:

- **change management:** organization development, corporate communication and critical interventions;
- **diversity, inclusion and global perspective:** cultural competence, negotiation and facilitation, continuous learning, complex group dynamics, judgement, subject matter expertise;
- **business acumen:** D&I ROI;
- **strategic external relations:** CSR/government/regulatory, strategic alliances, diverse markets/supplier diversity and brand/reputation management;
- **integrity:** ethics, resilience, influence, empathy, communication;
- **visionary and strategic leadership:** diversity and inclusion future state, pragmatism and political savoir faire;
- **HR competencies:** total rewards, talent management, organizational development, work–life balance, training, compliance, employee relations.[106]

Understanding the impact of bias, both conscious and unconscious, is another important competence; however, knowing about bias does not automatically result in changes in behaviour by managers and employees. Even if unconscious bias training has the theoretical potential to change behaviour, lasting positive change will depend on a number of factors, including individual starting points, their desire to change, programme design, repetition and practice.

Everyone has bias and so it is important to raise awareness and ensure there are compensating factors for key decisions such as selection, promotion and reward. Bias can occur through implicit stereotypes, in-group favouritism and out-group homogeneity bias.[107]

McKinsey suggests overcoming bias by education and development, changing organizational decision-making, providing salient information about peer achievements, and positive imagery and diversity messages from respected thought and opinion leaders, all with a strategic context.[108]

Deciding whether to have a dedicated D&I team or one that is integrated into other roles is subject to the same pros and cons as other specialist roles, such as CSR. Dedicated teams are very focused on mission, goals and objectives; they are specialists in their field and are a clearly symbolic of the organization's commitment to D&I. However, care needs to be taken to ensure others in the organization understand and embrace their own part in delivering the D&I programme. Integrating responsibility into other roles addresses this issue may result in lack of visibility, limited exposure to specialist knowledge and slower roll-out.

In *Lean In*, Sheryl Sandberg notes that when members of a group are made aware of a negative stereotype they are more likely to perform according to that stereotype, and women are susceptible to this.[109] Many men believe they can have both a successful professional and family life, while many women assume that doing both is either difficult or impossible.[110] In addition, women tend to be more susceptible to the 'imposter syndrome' than men and are more limited by it.[111] According, to Carol Dweck in *Mindset*, a fixed mindset, stereotyping and women's trust in other people's assessments of them all contribute to the gender gap in those studying maths and science subjects.[112] Also, women have a higher bar to negotiate when it comes to perception of personality and ability; 'if a woman is competent, she does not seem nice enough. If a woman seems really nice, she is considered more nice than competent. Since people want to hire and promote those who are both competent and nice, this creates a huge stumbling block for women'.[113]

Goleman writes in *Emotional Intelligence* that the culture of an organization must change to foster tolerance, even if individual biases remain, and that

since prejudices are a variety of emotional learning, relearning is possible – although it takes time and should not be expected as the outcome of a one-time diversity training workshop. What can make a difference, though, is sustained camaraderie and daily efforts toward a common goal by people of different backgrounds.[114]

In *Inclusive Talent Management*, Frost and Kalman believe that nudges to address unconscious bias and proactive leadership are required to embed inclusive talent management (ITM) and suggest the following model:

- **Purposeful planning – who do we want?**
  - Create a strategic workforce plan and redesign jobs.
  - Mobilize data and set targets.
  - Change selection criteria and job descriptions.
- **In the moment measures – nudges and leadership:**
  - Reduce bias through awareness and nudges.
  - Demand a balanced slate for all shortlists.
  - Use mixed panels for interviews.
  - Hire teams, not just individuals.
  - Apportion accountability for decision-making.
- **Time efficient ways to go ever further:**
  - Use technology and algorithms.
  - Consciously take risks to widen your portfolio.
- **Proactive marketing – create the new norm:**
  - Make your employee value proposition inclusive.
  - Purposefully widen the talent pool.
  - Target under-represented groups.
- **Establish concrete talent pathways:**
  - Establish a guaranteed interview scheme.
  - Set up a returners programme.
  - Make use of apprentices.
  - Establish recruitment action plans with partners.
- **Manage your stakeholders' transparently and assertively:**
  - Benchmark your recruiters and push them hard.
  - Take advantage of government incentives.
  - Communicate and set the norm.[115]

They also recommend using the conscious ladder of competence, which provides a four-step framework for considering leadership in diversity and inclusion. At first, leaders may not know they are biased, and are unconsciously incompetent. Then, through discussion and taking IATs, they become aware of their bias and become consciously unskilled. Through development and practice, leaders can consciously reduce their bias, and eventually, through habit, this can become an unconscious skill.[116]

Leading Across New Borders states that improvements in race and gender diversity can also impact additional diversity such as generational cohort and/or socioeconomic background.[117] They identify five areas of consideration for D&I in a global context:

- **Race and gender:** Progress has been made but continued attention is required.

- **Shared principles, local relevance:** Incorporate shared underlying principles and implement solutions with local relevance.

- **Generational differences:** The characteristics and terminology best used to define each generation are linked to important historical events within certain countries and regions and therefore it is essential to avoid assuming that the characteristics of age cohorts in one country will be consistent with those in another.

- **Functional differences:** Stereotypical differences across job functions can seem to be even more significant than the differences between people from various countries.

- **Technical versus non-technical:** Awareness of the biases toward others held by people in different functions can be a first step toward increasing their ability to collaborate effectively.[118]

In their 2018 report *Diversification: Is there a NEET, not in employment or training, solution to the workforce crises?* Mercer suggest a five line of defence model to address workforce shortage:[119]

- **Regroup:** Review the strategic workforce plan.

- **Move work:** Relocate jobs as required, including the use of virtual solutions.

- **Invest in automation and productivity:** What can be automated or augmented?

- **Enhance the EVP:** Review and upgrade the employer brand and employee value proposition.

- **Diversify the talent pool:** In the United Kingdom, in terms of inclusion of women, accessing 5 per cent of NEETs in the 20–50 age range would add 400,000 employees; for older workers, increasing participation in the 55–65 age range by 5 per cent and in the 6–65 per cent age range by 10 per cent would add 900,000 to the workforce; and including 6.4 per cent of those with some form of long-term sickness or disability would add another 475,000.[120]

With regard to disability, a 2018 Accenture study, *Getting to Equal: The disability inclusion advantage*, found that only 29 per cent of Americans of working age with disabilities participated in the workforce, which suggests an untapped talent pool of 10.7 million people. If 1 per cent more people with disabilities joined the workforce it is estimated that gross domestic product (GDP) would increase by US$25 billion. They looked at the Disability Equality Index (DEI), which is curated by Disability:IN, and found 45 organizations that excelled in categories that are specific to disability employment and inclusion make up 32 per cent of the companies covered by the DEI. These organizations were twice as likely to have higher total shareholder returns than those of their peer group.[121]

Addressing the talent shortage and improving performance through improving inclusivity is becoming easier through the use of technology, and in *Global Talent Trends 2019*, Mercer report that technology platforms now enable companies to connect with former employees and future candidates, helping them tap into diverse candidate pool including those who:

- have in-demand industry skills or know-how, but have been displaced;
- need to temporarily leave the workplace but still want to keep their skills up to date to ease re-entry;
- are nearing retirement and want project-based or part-time work.[122]

Cultural resistance

In a *Harvard Business Review* article, 'Diversity is useless without inclusivity', Christine Riordan described a number of factors that can derail attempts to promote an inclusive culture and some suggestions to help boards and CEOs:

- **People gravitate toward people like themselves:** Unconscious bias attracts us to people that we identify with and leaders will therefore often hire and promote those who share their own attitudes, behaviours and traits. This limits cognitive diversity and is unhelpful for promoting inclusion. To counter this, leaders are encouraged to study metrics around diversity and inclusion and check to see whether they are spending time talking with and listening to those who do not appear to share their traits.
- **Subtle biases persist and lead to exclusion:** When minority-group employees are hired, they may face conscious and/or unconscious exclusion from formal and informal groups and maybe judged more harshly in performance reviews. To guard against exclusion, leaders should proactively review the composition of formal teams, committees and informal groups. Development opportunities should also be available to all employees and training should be undertaken to address unconscious bias in the review feedback process.
- **Out-group employees sometimes try to conform:** Coping strategies for minority-group employees may include downplaying their differences and even mirroring the characteristics of the majority in an attempt to fit in. Leaders are encouraged to highlight differences within a positive narrative.
- **Employees from the majority group put up resistance:** Those in the majority group may perceive a sense of injustice regarding diversity

initiatives such as promotions that are not merit-based. Leaders are encouraged to ensure that diversity and inclusion programmes include input from the majority group so that they understand the objectives and are part of framing the solution.[123]

Responsibility for diversity and inclusion

The success of diversity and inclusion starts with the CEO and board driving the agenda, remaining actively involved and holding all leaders and managers accountable for progress. In *Inclusive Leadership*, Sweeney and Borthwick discuss the organization of D&I. A dedicated functional team brings focus and expertise, and demonstrates organizational commitment. However, they may get siloed and may need to work hard at eliciting collaboration with others abdicating responsibility to the specialists. Alternatively, if it is integrated into other roles it becomes the responsibility of a wider leadership team who increase their knowledge as well as bringing fresh perspectives. However, D&I activity may compete for attention, depth of knowledge will be not be as great and the visible expression of its importance may be lower.[124]

It has been suggested that responsibility for supporting D&I falls to the human resource function, while ownership is not always located there. The processes and compliance aspects of D&I may be with them, but a separate function may take responsibility for the organizational culture and climate or it may be more widely distributed. It has been recommended that the human resource function plays a more strategic role as change agents and policy experts.[125]

Highlights

- In 2018 Deloitte entitled its annual report on human capital trends *The Rise of the Social Enterprise*, and discussed the premise that commercial organizations are transforming themselves from business enterprises to social enterprises.

- Stakeholder theory suggests that organizations have responsibility for societal issues to stakeholders other than the organization's owners.

- Deloitte noted that governments can often be slow in legislating on societal issues that are largely domestic in nature. However, this is compounded when governments need to collaborate on solutions to problems with global consequences, and progress can be glacial.

- It is felt that the private sector can play an important role in helping to effect societal change, and three areas where this is the case are examined in this chapter: CSR, ESG and D&I.

- Organizations with a poor track record in these areas will be held to account by their workforce, suppliers and investors, and the report card is increasingly a public and global one. An increasing number of studies show that investment in these areas has a positive impact on organization performance.

Leadership impact

Key themes that leaders should reflect on include:

- Corporate and social responsibility has become an important consideration for organizations.

- An organization's philosophy regarding the content and enactment of its CSR strategy will become a major determinant of stakeholder relationships and interactions.

- D&I has become an important consideration for organizations; it has moved beyond gender to incorporate ,amongst other areas, ethnicity, educational background and attainment, social background and disability.

- While having a diverse and inclusive workforce has gradually become seen as the right thing to do, the positive impact on business is also being researched and discussed.

- Unconscious bias has become part of D&I training, but it is also an important consideration where artificial intelligence is used in workforce selection.

- Economic, social and governance factors are central to measuring the sustainability and ethical impact of an investment in organizations.

- Understanding the nature of ESG considerations for investors is important to organizations, as it may determine the degree to which capital is accessible and the cost of capital.

- CSR and D&I activities need to be authentic, and internally and externally congruent.

People management recommendations

Actions to consider:

- Expertise is required in all relevant areas of social and environmental public policy.
- Stakeholder views and expectations need to be monitored and actioned.
- Leaders must be briefed on the implications for the organization and how it should respond.
- This expertise needs to be applied in leadership and management training.
- Internal and external stakeholder communication should positively impact the employee value proposition and employer brand.

Case studies

Becoming a global Smart business

Location

China and global.

The organization

China's largest ecommerce company presides over a collection of online platforms – including Tmall, Taobao (similar to eBay) and the payment service Alipay – that together create one of the most sophisticated and lucrative online retail ecosystems in the world.

Alibaba is therefore not just an online ecommerce company. It has developed a huge combination of retail links and coordinates them online into a massive, data-driven network of sellers, marketers, service providers, logistics companies and manufacturers. In fact, Alibaba does what Amazon, eBay, PayPal, Google, FedEx, wholesalers, and a good portion of manufacturers do, with a dash of financial services to top everything off.

Revenues in 2018 were almost US$40 billion, with a total workforce of over 65,000. The market cap is more than US$500 billion.

Business challenge

The key challenge for Alibaba has been to create a technology-centric business across many different business sectors simultaneously. This concept of a 'Smart' business entails harnessing machine-learning technology to leverage data; this allows companies to adapt rapidly and dynamically, as market conditions and customer preferences change.

Drivers for this business model are massive computing power and digital data. This allows sophisticated algorithms to produce powerful output. Information is produced during real time so that market decisions can be made instantly. A result is machine learning on a huge scale, which in due course replaces human decision-making.

Solutions

So, how did Alibaba create a Smart business?

First, they automated as many operating decisions as possible using live data. Then, applying a four-step process, decision-making was transformed as follows:

1 Every customer exchange must be 'Datafied': In order to ensure that machine learning can take place, it is essential to capture live data. This is then fed back into the loop and the process is improved.

2 Every activity is applied to software: All activities, including management and client relations interactions, are automated. The initial step is to build models that replicate how humans make decisions.

3 Data must start flowing: This means improving and harnessing communication, typically between suppliers and customers. As data starts flowing across the network, the smarter it becomes and the more value is created.

4 Finally, algorithms must be applied: Models and algorithms need to be created to deal with the increase in data that is produced. This is a growing requirement for data scientists and economists, in addition to the many other new skills that are required.

Learning points

Leaders of Smart companies must mobilize huge networks to realize their goals and mission. These leaders have to be inspiring as well as visible and are often outspoken. Examples of these people include Elon Musk and Steve Jobs, as well as Jack Ma, CEO of Alibaba – not many people know who the leaders of traditional firms are.

Another key skill for these leaders is to visualize the future, but not necessarily with a set of concrete steps. More likely, they will be able to describe what the future looks like, and how their industries will evolve in response to technological and society changes.

Overall, companies like Alibaba have a distinct advantage in the digital age – they have been born online and so can adapt quickly to new business models and do not find technology intimidating or restricting.

Sources

Material for this case has been adapted from the following websites:

www.alibabagroup.com/en/global/home

https://hbr.org/2018/09/alibaba-and-the-future-of-business

CASE STUDY   Hermes
A gig economy company tackling the important issue of values and communication to grow the business and differentiate itself from competitors

Location

UK and global.

The organization

Hermes UK has a wide range of specialized companies along the retail value chain, supplying comprehensive logistical services to meet global demands. Whether for businesses or consumers, domestically or internationally, on your doorstep or in ecommerce, over 12,000 highly trained employees work towards a single goal: fully dedicated with all of the experience for their clients' success.

It begins with sourcing, all around the world. This is followed by product testing and quality assurance. Hermes also offers sea and air transport logistics, and, beyond that, the development and operation of online shops. Their portfolio also features comprehensive fulfilment services, including warehousing and returns management. Rounding it all off is the distribution of all shipment types to end customers.

This makes Hermes one of a few service providers worldwide to offer such a complete, full-service portfolio. As the partner of a constantly growing number of internationally operating companies, Hermes distinguishes itself not only through its traditionally close collaboration with retailers, but also by its ability to realize individually tailored solutions on demand.

People challenge

In the United Kingdom, the reputation of gig economy firms generally has been poor in recent years. Typical complaints have centred around ill-treatment of staff, irregular earnings due to zero hours contracts and livelihoods being taken away without any warning.

Trying to build a people business that delivers high-quality service in this environment is difficult. In the UK in 2017, Hermes employed 2,500 permanent employees at its head office, and a further 14,500 self-employed couriers.

Despite problems in other firms, Hermes' length of service of couriers within the company was over 10 years for 12 per cent of the staff, more than five years for 33 per cent and more than two years for 66 per cent.

So the challenge was to ensure that the Hermes business continued to differentiate itself and maintain good employee relations.

Solutions

A key way to tackle these challenges was to ensure strong communications and relationships with all staff. By using field managers to interact daily with couriers it is possible to keep a finger on the pulse of the business, as well as managing the people effectively. This is in contrast to companies like Uber, which interacts with its people via a digital platform.

Hermes also operate helpdesks that can deal with day-to-day queries, and quarterly booklets are produced to update staff and keep them informed about new clients and how the business is performing. This type of engagement helps to keep staff motivated to provide services to clients.

Another important element has been to create stable and predictable earnings for couriers by giving them their own, established rounds that are of a stable and predictable size.

The HR team work closely with the business and try to keep away from the traditional HR ivory tower. The 'to do' list includes health and well-being initiatives, apprenticeships and leadership development programmes. Also vitally important has been the use of technology to improve HR processes so that the business can be better supported.

A very practical initiative has been the introduction of 'Peak Treats', which includes massages, fruit and pizza deliveries, discounted gym memberships and employee of the week awards for depot staff.

Learning points

- Engage with staff to align them with business objectives.
- Harmonize client needs with staff motivational requirements.
- HR to work closely with the business, rather than sitting in an ivory tower, and be viewed as business people.
- Make use of new ideas and technology.

Sources

Material for this case has been adapted from the following websites:

www.hermesworld.com/en/about-us/hermes-group/

www.peoplemanagement.co.uk/voices/case-studies/hermes

CASE STUDY   Oui SNCF
Setting up a gaming room and team as an interesting way
to attract and retain Generation Y employees.

Location

France.

Organization

Oui SNCF is the official French Railways website that sells tickets for train
journeys in France and for international journeys to or from France, at the correct
SNCF price with no booking fees and a range of seating options. In 2017 the
company changes names from Voyages SNCF. The parent company SNCF is the
French national railway operator.

There are approximately 1,000 employees of this digitally based organization.

People challenge

All organizations are under pressure to attract and retain high-quality staff.
Traditional firms find the problem particularly difficult when targeting members of
Generation Y who are typically not understood by management teams.

Oui SNCF, as a digital company, decided to launch a new initiative as part of
their retention and attraction strategy. The organization already had a successful
well-being programme ('I feel good') that included teleworking arrangements, job
role exchanges, meditation sessions, kids-at-work days and hobby course in
cooking and photography.

Solution

A novel solution was to set up a state-of-the-art gaming room at its head office,
and to encourage staff members to take part in e-sport competitions. They set up
a team, Team Loco, and staff joined from across Voyages SNCF and the parent
company. Staff played FiFa, Overwatch and League of Legends on a competitive
basis. The company supported a team of 17 including paying registration fees for
competitions and travel expenses for e-sport competitions.

Not only was a strong team spirit created, but also new skills were gained in
coding and understanding the social elements of e-sport.

Learning points

- Think about creative ways to attract and retain staff. A good way is to consult with the current team and ask for ideas.
- Be prepared to put resources behind the ideas.
- Identify ways to measure return on the investment.

Sources

Material for this case has been adapted from the following websites:

https://en.oui.sncf/en/

www.voyages-sncf.eu/

www.employeebenefits.co.uk/issues/march-online-2017-2/voyages-sncf-introduces-office-e-sport-gaming-room/

CASE STUDY   Ledcor
A great company to work for

Location

Canada and North America

Organization

The Ledcor Group of Companies was established in 1947. It is based in Vancouver and operates in such places as San Diego, Honolulu and Nevada. It is one of North America's most diversified construction companies, serving the civil and infrastructure, oil and gas, pipeline, building, mining, power, and telecommunications sectors. Ledcor also owns operations in property investment, forestry, aviation, and marine transportation services. Ledcor is a privately held, employee-owned company with over 800 employee shareholders. Ledcor employs over 7,000 people across 20 offices and has an annual revenue of over US$2 billion.

Ledcor was identified by Forbes as one of Canada's best companies in 2019. Forbes partnered with market research company Statista to identify the companies liked best by employees in their annual ranking of Canada's best employers. The list, compiled by surveying 8,000 Canadians working for businesses with at least 500 employees, ranks the 300 employers that received the most recommendations.

People challenge

The leadership of Ledcor Group was radically impacted in 1980. Bill Lede was Mayor of Leduc and also a well-liked local entrepreneur. He had successfully built up Ledcor following the big Leduc oil strike in 1947. As he was inspecting a work site with his sons Cliff and Dave, Bill was suddenly and unexpectedly buried by a high bank of gravel and clay that collapsed. This tragic incident changed the company in a significant way.

Solutions

First, safety became the major priority for the construction business, and still is to this day. The accident also propelled Dave, Bill's eldest son, into the CEO role. As Cliff Lede says, ' My father taught my brother and me the importance of having good people and treating them right'. As a result, Ledcor is well known for the quality of its people and the responsibility placed on smart unit managers who run fairly large businesses on their own.

The goal for the business became to diversify well beyond earth moving and road building. The company name was changed to Ledcor, which reflected the desire to grow beyond the home town of Leduc. New business lines were started, including pipeline trenching for companies like TransCanada, and mining, civil construction, office building and other areas. Operations moved to Vancouver, British Columbia while the COO was based in Edmonton, Alberta.

In the 1990s the company spotted an important opportunity. Having started to lay the new glass-fibre networks across Canada, one of their managers, Bernie Stene, and a few colleagues recommended that instead of just laying fibres, perhaps the firm should build its own networks.

The new 'Goldrush' in fibre networks across the world threw up the massive requirement for expanded broadband services. A new business, 360Networks, was born and started to go from strength to strength. Expansion included global projects such as laying the Atlantic network between Halifax in Canada and Liverpool in the United Kingdom. However, the competition was growing as well, and the market was not ready for so many players. 360Networks was hit by the dot.com bubble and collapsed in 2001. Ledcor was sufficiently diversified and so avoided too much damage to the overall business, and quickly switched focus to the oil sands boom in northern Alberta, which is still successful today.

The roots of Ledcor's business are still strong today, as evidenced by their vision, mission and values:

- **Our vision:** Forward. Together.
- **Our mission:** Committed to building Ledcor Lifetime Clients through accountability, innovation, quality and sustainability.

- **Our values – these are our values and we live by them:**
  - safety: zero accidents through best practices;
  - quality: continuous measurements and improvement;
  - integrity: ethical, honest, consistent, highly regarded;
  - sustainability: balancing people, planet and profit;
  - success: client and employee satisfaction, shareholder value.

Learning points

Core values and culture are not just words on a poster, or some sort of new idea. They are born of experience and should reflect the type of organization people want to work for. In this case, the core values have been carried forward through generation to generation over 70 years in the same company.

Leadership is key to the success, and direction of travel, for organizations. In this case a family ran the business and over time has handed over to control to new managers.

Treating people with respect and bringing them on the journey with you is very effective and ultimately will pay dividends – including getting their votes for best company to work.

Sources

Material for this case has been adapted from the following websites:

www.ledcor.com/

www.theglobeandmail.com/report-on-business/from-digging-in-the-oil-patch-to-toiling-in-the-vineyard/article573392/

CASE STUDY   Accenture
Diversity and inclusion

Location

Global.

Background

Accenture is a global management consulting and professional services firm that provides strategy, consulting, digital, technology and operations services.

A Fortune Global 500 company, it has been incorporated in Dublin, Ireland since 1 September 2009.There are almost 400,000 employed by the firm global, of whom 12,500 are in the United Kingdom and Ireland.

The firm strives to be at the forefront of workplace diversity and inclusivity. Its significant commitment to providing a supportive environment for its employees has received external recognition, such as a 2015 European Diversity Award for Outstanding Employee Network Group of the Year for its African Caribbean Network, and successive recognition as a Star Performer on Stonewall's Top 100 Employers list.

However, the firm is not satisfied with being complacent about these successes. It wants to keep moving the dial and making even more strides forward.

People challenge

The Head of Human Capital and Diversity in the UK and Ireland said in 2017 that 'we have an aspiration to be the most inclusive and diverse organization on the planet, not just within professional services, by 2020.' The rationale is that diversity will make the firm smarter. Research shows that diverse organizations and leaders typically outperform their competitors. Recruitment therefore needs to target people from diverse talent pools.

The reasons for more diversity are not limited to pure business ones; it can also encourage better camaraderie, which in turn will lead to better outcomes, as well as for society and moral improvements. Ultimately, the firm should reflect its client base and the communities it operates in if it wants to grow and succeed.

Over 70 per cent of Accenture's employees are made up of Millennials, and so it is critical to hire the best talent and keep up with competitors, and diversity forms a core element of that strategy.

Solutions

Accenture, like many of its competitors, already has a network of various diverse groups such as gender and ethnic background. However, there has been a move to update the approach in order to make the networks less siloed and exclusive. For instance, the women's network has been renamed 'Accent on Gender' to focus more on the challenges around gender diversity, rather than just women's issues. Equally, the family network has been refocused to capture the fact that not all parents are women, and not all women are parents.

Training is another area where more progress has been made. All new joiners receive some diversity training, anyone who has been promoted attends a one-day 'immersion training' on this topic, and there is a mentoring programme thath has been significantly expanded. Even the CEO put out a video about gender equality, and included a focus on the opportunities he wanted his daughter to benefit from in the future.

Events are run throughout the year to celebrate inclusivity and diversity. These range from activities to mark calendar events such as Pride Week and International Women's Day, to educational events in-house from external experts. One example was a talk about Mermaids, a charity designed to help parents support children with gender identity issues. Much of this is also available online for those unable to attend.

Policies have been adapted and improved to support these initiatives. In the UK, for instance, Accenture offers enhanced parental leave of up to 32 weeks on full pay to both mothers and fathers. This policy also offers support to staff before, during and after parental leave in order to help them thrive following significant life changes.

Learning points

Diversity and inclusion policies can make a difference to not only attract and retain talented staff, but also reflect more closely the client base the business is serving. More and more organizations are making these changes and their productivity is improving.

Often it is not just a question of putting in place seemingly sensible networks, based on previous thinking. It is vital to refresh the approach to take into account the changing nature of the workforce, and the changing expectations and needs of your staff.

It is clear that diversity and inclusion is no longer just a fad; the concept is evolving into the fabric of how organizations do business and there are strong links to customers and clients. The approach adopted by the organization will much more closely dictate the success or failure to attract and retain talent.

Sources

Material for this case has been adapted from the following websites:

www.accenture.com/gb-en/company-diversity

www.changeboard.com/article-details/16644/focusing-on-inclusion-at-accenture/

www.peoplemanagement.co.uk/voices/case-studies/accenture

CASE STUDY   Barclays Bank
Disability and mental health

Location

Global – focusing on the United Kingdom, United States and Asia.

Background

An example of a global organization tackling the important issues of disability
and mental health. These are relevant themes for businesses in the 21st century,
as organizations increasingly try to reflect their diverse client base and
incorporate disability and mental health at the top of the business agenda.
Barclays is on a journey to becoming an accessible and inclusive business.

Organization

Barclays is a global bank, headquartered in London, that moves, lends, invests
and protects money for customers and clients worldwide. The landscape has
been challenging for banks in the UK and globally following the financial crisis
from 2008.

Despite these challenges, the company has responded by creating a common
purpose that it describes as: 'Creating opportunities to rise. We are a company of
opportunity makers working together to help people rise – customers, clients,
colleagues and society. By creating opportunities for people to rise, we
recognize that Barclays rises too. We'll measure and reward our people, not just
on commercial results, but on how they live our values and bring them to life
every day.'

People challenge

One challenge that has been tackled rigorously is to improve the ways the bank
has approached building disability and mental health confidence. This has been
led from the top by Ashok Vaswani, CEO of Barclays UK. He has stated that
'Being a disability confident leader is important to Barclays, because it enables
us to broaden our understanding of the needs of all stakeholders – customers,
clients and colleagues – and, as a result, work to create opportunities and
improve life for everybody.'

Vaswani has made it clear that, as the Executive Sponsor of the agenda, he is
committed to driving change and levelling the playing field for disabled people
and people with mental health conditions.

As many as 1 in 5 people live with some form of disability or mental health condition – that is 20 per cent of the population. With the gradual lifting of the stigma and taboo of these issues in society, it is important for large institutions to take the lead in tackling ways to improve the situation.

Solutions

One of the first steps has been for Barclays to create opportunities across the bank for people of all abilities. Three examples of successful initiatives were in the UK, US and Asia:

- In the UK, Barclays' award-winning programme, Able to Enable, supports people whose careers may have been held back by stigma surrounding disability and mental health conditions. The programme offers a three-month paid internship. At the end of the programme, they can move onto an apprenticeship or into a permanent position as a full-time employee.

- For six years Barclays in the US has partnered with Integrate Autism Employment Advisors, which helps businesses identify, recruit and retain qualified professionals on the autism spectrum. Students or graduates with autism profiles take part in work experience and learn how to prepare to enter the world of work.

- In Singapore, a number of employees became mentors as part of the 'Singapore Business Network on Disability'. Working with SG Enable, a specialist agency, they have been helping to run a 12-week mentoring programme to help students with special needs transition into the workforce.

The bank knows that it is not enough just to recruit more people with disabilities and mental health; it is equally important to support every individual and to provide the adjustments and inclusive environment that can help them succeed. Examples of initiatives have included:

- providing mental health awareness training for all colleagues: over 12,000 staff completed the programme in the first year;

- sharing experiences: 250 members of staff have shared their personal stories of disability, mental health and well-being as part of the 'This is Me' campaign.

Learning points

Barclays have learnt, and are continuing to learn, about how to incorporate disability and mental health confidence into their business. They have suggested seven steps as insights for other firms to follow in their footsteps:

1 Make a commitment: Being prepared to be accountable has helped orientate the business, individuals, teams, networks and partners.

2 Be courageous: Despite the sensitivity of this subject, having the courage to try something for the first time really drives positive change.

3 Build competency: It is important to continually develop competency across the business, as no individual can be an expert.

4 Combine the approach and effort: A most effective way to make change is to encourage and empower colleagues to 'own' and drive initiatives.

5 Communicate clearly: It is vital to communicate regularly and clearly.

6 Be consistent: Take a long-term, consistent approach in order to change attitudes, cultures and behaviours.

7 Be willing to collaborate: A wider impact on disability and mental health can be achieved by collaborating with external partners.

Sources

Material for this case has been adapted from the following website/source:

https://home.barclays/who-we-are/our-strategy/diversity-and-inclusion/
disability/

Barclays Group Media Relations

CASE STUDY   Patagonia Inc

Taking corporate and social responsibility to new levels:
'We're in business to save our home planet'

Location

North America.

Organization

Patagonia Inc is a private benefit corporation and appreciates that the Earth is under threat of extinction. Their aim is to use the resources they have – their business, their investments, their voice and their imaginations – to do something about it.

Set up in 1973 by Yvon Chouinard, Patagonia grew out of a small company that made tools for climbers. Alpinism remains at the heart of a worldwide business that still makes clothes for climbing, as well as for skiing, snowboarding, surfing, fly fishing, mountain biking and trail running.

Staying true to their core values during over forty years in business has helped them create a company that they are proud to run and work for. There are over 1,000 staff. Their journey has not been without problems, and in 1989 the original company went bankrupt after a series of legal case. However, it has risen from the ashes and is well known for its environmental focus – Patagonia commits 1 per cent of its total sales to environmental groups.

People challenge

Corporate and social responsibility has become a popular and recognized element of organizations today. Patagonia tackled this important issue many years before it became 'a thing'. The challenge has been to develop a profitable business and remain true to their environmental values.

The people challenge is both internal and external. Internally, staff need to be true to environmental values and source products that meet those criteria; externally, customers need to be persuaded to buy the products because they trust the environmental credentials and because they are good products.

Solutions

Patagonia has built the business using CSR as the driver for all activities. The company has donated over US$185 million to environmental and conservation efforts since 1973. Additionally, they have invested over US$38 million into socially responsible companies and ventures.

The company has adopted a series of values that reflect those of a business started by a band of climbers and surfers, and the minimalist style they promoted. The approach they take toward product design demonstrates a bias for simplicity and utility:

- **Build the best product**
  Our criteria for the best product rests on function, repairability, and, foremost, durability. Among the most direct ways we can limit ecological impacts is with goods that last for generations or can be recycled so the materials in them remain in use. Making the best product matters for saving the planet.

- **Cause no unnecessary harm**
  We know that our business activity – from lighting stores to dyeing shirts– is part of the problem. We work steadily to change our business practices and share what we've learned. But we recognize that this is not enough. We seek not only to do less harm, but more good.

- **Use business to protect nature**
  The challenges we face as a society require leadership. Once we identify a problem, we act. We embrace risk and act to protect and restore the stability, integrity and beauty of the web of life.

- **Not bound by convention**
  Our success – and much of the fun – lies in developing new ways to do things.

Additionally, the company is transparent and genuine about its CSR credentials. They provide 'Footprint Chronicles', which is an interactive map showing where their textile mills, factories and farms are located. They also publish a regular environmental and social initiative report, which outlines a breakdown of campaigns, grants, material selections and events. As a result, they have grown a strong social media following.

An example of a counterintuitive route to market, Patagonia not only promise to 'make great stuff, fix it when it breaks and recycle it when you're done with it' free of charge, but they have also asked customers not to buy their products; in 2011 they ran a campaign entitled 'Don't Buy This Jacket' – customers were prompted not to buy their clothes if they truly did not need them, and went on the discuss the environmental cost of producing the products. The following year revenue grew by 30 per cent and an additional 6 per cent the following year.

Learning points

By taking CSR seriously Patagonia have been able to attract new business and grow. It shows that doing the right thing can actually improve the organization, and not just act as a side issue, or something done to 'tick the box'.

Patagonia is an extreme example of what can be achieved, but in most organizations today both customers and staff have an expectation that ethical and sustainable behaviour will happen.

Sources

Material for this case has been adapted from the following websites:

www.patagonia.com/actionworks/about/

https://acasestudy.com/case-study-228/

www.chuckjoe.co/patagonia-corporate-social-responsibility/

PART THREE
Workforce planning

Part Two examined the development of management and organization behaviour thinking. This illustrated the move from superficial rationality at the start of the 20th century through systems and contingency views to the resource based view of organizations, organizations as complex adaptive systems, social constructionism and enactment theory. These areas have been summarized in Figure P3.1.

The organization paradigm summarizes five key areas of leadership focus:

- **Meaning and purpose:** Mission, vision, goals, objectives. The fundamental reason for the organization's existence.

Figure P3.1   The organization paradigm

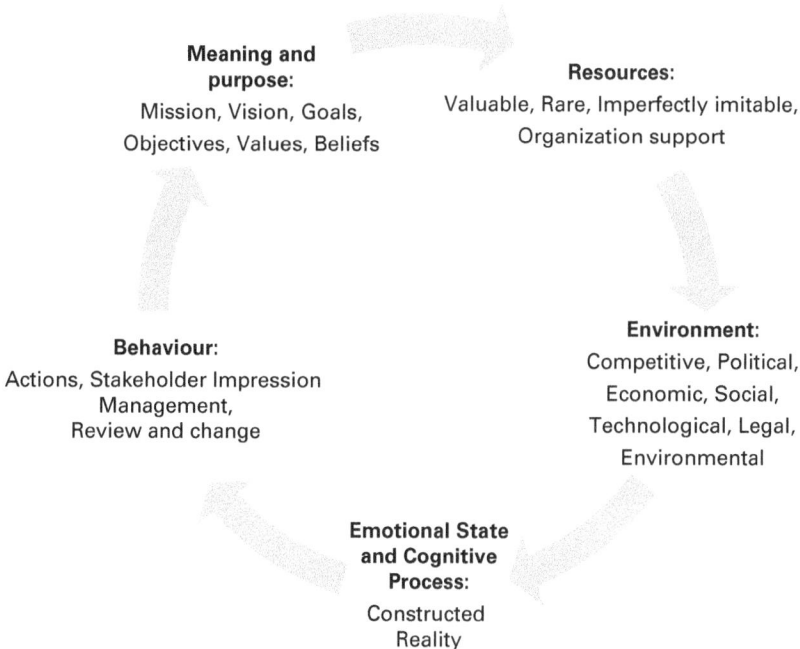

Meaning and purpose:
Mission, Vision, Goals,
Objectives, Values, Beliefs

Resources:
Valuable, Rare, Imperfectly imitable,
Organization support

Behaviour:
Actions, Stakeholder Impression
Management,
Review and change

Environment:
Competitive, Political,
Economic, Social,
Technological, Legal,
Environmental

**Emotional State
and Cognitive
Process:**
Constructed
Reality

- **Resources:** Intangible and tangible – valuable, rare, inimitable and organizationally supportive.
- **Environment:** Competitive, political, economic, social, legal, technological, environmental/ethical.
- **Strategy:** Constructed reality. Using models and data to formulate a response.
- **Behaviour:** Stakeholder impression management.

Review and change. In this context, and considering the impact of technology, demographic changes, culture and social movements, Part Three introduces important areas of strategic workforce planning. These include people risk, human capital metrics and reporting, the use of people analytics, the importance of employee engagement, the employee experience, employee value proposition and employer brand. Finally, it considers various aspects of employee development.

Planning and people risk

11

Introduction

This chapter focuses on strategic workforce planning and people risk. Until recently, people risk was rarely identified as a separate risk, normally being captured as part of general operational risk within enterprise risk management. However, organizations have increasingly realized that their human capital is critical to success, and that the risks surrounding the largest part of the cost base should be more effectively managed.

Workforce planning has always been a key senior management activity; however, it is often more tactical, short-term focused, rather than also capturing long-term, strategic imperatives. It is fundamental that strategic workforce planning is integrated into strategy deliberations, as people are key to its implementation.

Chapter summary

The following subjects are discussed in this chapter:

- **strategic workforce planning:**
  - key factors;
- **people risk:**
  - people portfolio management;
  - risk management:
    - risk;
    - control;
    - risk of key talent loss.

Strategic workforce planning

In *Strategic Workforce Planning*, Ross Sparkman defines strategic workforce planning (SWP) as 'an activity or process relating to the workforce that an organization, team or function takes part in to develop, optimize or enhance that entity's ability to contribute to positive business outcomes.'[1] He notes that a good SWP should consider how individuals and teams throughout organizations contribute to current organization success, the organizational strategy, and the associated people requirements needed to successfully execute the strategy. This in turn will raise questions around future workspace requirements from a location and design perspective, and, amongst other things, technology support, the composition of the talent acquisition team, required learning and development initiatives and the total reward strategy.

International Standard ISO 30409 has been developed in response to worldwide demand for workforce planning. It provides a framework to support all organizations 'to advance their workforce planning capabilities and to respond more effectively to the current and projected demands of the labour market, the dynamic international business environment and its increasing complexity.'[2]

The International Standards Organization (ISO) is an independent, non-governmental international organization with a membership of 164 national standards bodies. Through its members, it brings together experts to share knowledge and develop voluntary, consensus-based, market-relevant international standards that support innovation and provide solutions to global challenges.

Organization design is too often considered a one-off activity rather than a continuous process. Implementation of new design is often incomplete and is not evidence based and data driven. In *Data-Driven Organization Design*, Rupert Morrison states that organization design does not harness the potential of human capital:

> too many employees are unable to fulfil their potential owing to siloed functional, geographic, customer or product areas... The right resources are not allocated in the right proportions to the priority areas because the priorities are not agreed nor the means for determining the 'right proportions' established.[3]

ISO30409 states that

> workforce planning generates business intelligence to inform business of the current and future impact of the external and internal environment on the organization, enabling the organization to be resilient to structural and cultural change to better position itself for the future. These influences can be complex and comprehensive, and include the following:

- **external influences:** local, regional, national and international economic, political, social and demographic labour market environment, industry and government regulation, compliance, legislation, technology;

- **internal influences:** varying market conditions, local and global economic cycle, workplace policy and practices, workforce mobility, amalgamations, upsizing, downsizing, closures, new entities, cost reduction, competition, productivity, new products and services, retaining talent, building business resilience, capability building.'[4]

A number of key factors need to be considered during the planning process.

Key factors

Strategic Workforce Planning discusses the demand side. Internal demand 'refers to the short and long-term demand for skills, experience and education that the organization requires to accomplish its core goals and strategy',[5] while external demand 'refers to those same skills, experience and education, but on an aggregate (global and regional) level. It can be useful to think of external demand as the demand for the entire universe of skills, experience and education across all sectors, industries and competitors.'[6] The importance of including contractors and contingent workers in the workforce strategy will only increase as gig and freelance arrangements account for increasingly larger proportions of the workforce.

Sparkman notes that, when it comes to SWP, workforce segmentation is critical. Various attributes may cause one particular category of the workforce to be of central importance, including:

- segments where skills are in short supply and/or high demand;
- segments that have a disproportionate impact on the success of the organization by their impact in the value chain;
- segments that have a disproportionate impact on positive business outcomes.[7]

The workforce can also be segmented based on geographical location, generational cohort, level of seniority and myriad other factors. *Play to Your Strengths* suggests that key workforce characteristics have three dimensions:

- **workforce capabilities:** knowledge skills and competencies, what it can do;
- **workforce attitudes:** psychological propensities, what it believes and values;
- **workforce behaviours:** specific actions, what it does.[8]

One helpful planning tool is the Internal Labour Market (ILM) model, which focuses on causal links between employee events and behaviours over time, looking at turnover, promotions, lateral moves, compensation and individual performance. It focuses on:

- **employee attributes:** demographic, personality, psychological, employment history;

- **organizational attributes and practices:** the internal environmental factors;
- **external influences:** characteristics of external environmental factors.[9]

In addition to the talent portfolio, *Strategic Workforce Planning* looks at the importance of decision criteria around workforce location. These include:

- current and future state talent scenario analysis;
- talent supply and availability in the location's market;
- full-time employment (FTE) and contingent employee growth forecasts for the location;
- competitor talent intelligence in location
- space-planning optimization for positive employee experience at the location;
- quality of life and cost of living information for the location
- infrastructure considerations such as transportation links
- government policy around immigration, work permits for foreign nationals and tax incentives.[10]

Sparkman suggests that, associated with workforce location, workplace design will include:

- employee workplace expectations;
- workplace productivity;
- open versus closed concept;
- comfort;
- meeting rooms;
- workspace amenities and perks;
- workspace technology.[11]

Workplace design is examined in more detail in Chapter 14 in terms of its impact on employee experience and well-being.

People risk

People portfolio management

Strategic workforce planning is an important exercise in people risk management. One way of considering this exercise is through people portfolio management. There are fundamentally two types of human capital risk:[12]

- volatility in cash flow related to changes to human capital and/or how it is managed;

- threats to shareholder value stemming from an unanticipated loss of value in the organization's human capital assets.

A number of studies support the approach of conceiving the talent pool of organizations as an investment portfolio, for instance a 'pool of human capital under the firm's control in a direct employment relationship'.[13] As noted above when discussing segmentation, the portfolio, or pool, does not contain fungible assets 'in most businesses, not all employees are created equal. A sub-set... always plays a disproportionate role in creating value'.[14] Developing the theme of segmentation,

> the human resource function should begin its transformation by applying tools of segmentation... Just as marketing systematically segments customers to target investments strategically, the human resources function needs to segment talent to deploy human capital strategically.[15]

Further to this, management consultants McKinsey state that talent management should not be limited to top talent but instead should follow a more inclusive approach by thinking of employees as 'a collection of talent segments',[16] and therefore rather than being prescriptive organizations could use the term 'talent' both in relation to a subset of their workforce and to capture all employees whether full time or on flexible contracts.

Research undertaken in the capital markets and investment banking sector concluded that, not withstanding the global financial crises, businesses undertake a sophisticated approach to their risk management of assets and that the management of a segmented workforce is analogous to this. A model of talent portfolio management (Figure 11.1) was proposed to conceptualize the importance of managing people risk in this sector.

Figure 11.1   Talent portfolio management

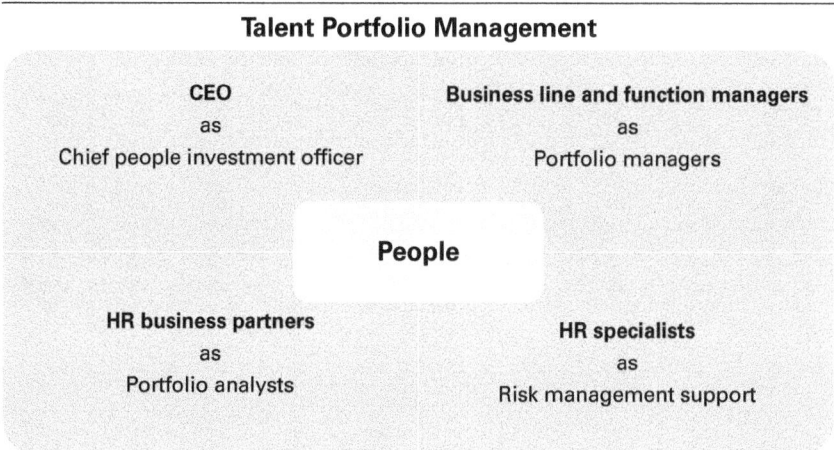

Talent Portfolio Management

CEO
as
Chief people investment officer

Business line and function managers
as
Portfolio managers

People

HR business partners
as
Portfolio analysts

HR specialists
as
Risk management support

SOURCE Adapted from Aldrich, 2007

In the IFR Market Intelligence publication *Talent Portfolio Management: Leveraging human assets in capital markets and investment banking*, this model of talent portfolio management sees the CEO playing the role of chief people investment officer, with senior leaders of business lines and functions as the portfolio managers of talent for each segment of the workforce; and people management professionals as portfolio analysts, advisors and risk managers. It was noted that

> a talent portfolio management approach to managing human resources requires advanced skills, for example in organizational analysis and statistical modelling, which may not currently be part of the core competencies of professionals in the human resource function and therefore this approach, though straightforward to conceive, may require a radical change in thinking by business line managers and the human resource professionals that support them.[17]

The implications include:

- a strategic approach to management of the talent portfolio, led by the CEO. This involves an understanding of the fundamental links between leadership and management competency as it relates to the human resource environment; talent portfolio management; and better firm performance;
- an integrated and strategic working relationship between the human resource function and business line managers;
- stronger numerical, analytical and commercial skills in the human resource function;
- greater measurement around talent, building up to sophisticated human capital metrics; and
- the identification and active management of people-related risk.[18]

It was suggested that the above required the creation of functional human resource roles that focus on human capital metrics, human resource portfolio modelling and people risk management; and people management professionals acting as stakeholder champions.

Just as certain capital markets activity involves the management of asset portfolios, such as foreign exchange, equity, loans bonds and commodities, talent portfolio management involves taking an investment based, strategic approach to the management of human resources. Organizations can segment their overall workforce into different human asset groups to ensure that the organization can consistently deploy the right people, in the right place, at the right time, for the right cost and for the workforce to be fully engaged and effective.

The same principles behind talent portfolio management apply today across all sectors, but in the new framework of people management proposed in this book it is not envisaged that the risk management and data analytics specializations that support it would be part of the people function.

Instead, it is recommended that these roles are undertaken within enterprise-wide risk management.

While people risk should be a key focus for risk management functions, 'although many firms and consultancies talk about enterprise risk management, few have actually embedded human capital risk identification and measurement in their risk management functions',[19] therefore having looked at people risk from the perspective of SWP other aspects of people risk are examined.

Risk management

Risk

People risk is defined in *People Risk Management* as 'the risk of loss due to the decisions and non-decisions of people, inside and outside of the organization',[20] with loss being defined as directly financial but also indirectly financial, for instance people and reputational. In this definition, people include individuals who are paid to undertake work for the organization and other stakeholders.

The risks associated with human decision-making are infinite but include: breaches in data governance, legal claims due to faulty or mis-sold products and environmental disasters. From a workforce perspective this might include, legal claims for discrimination, lawsuits for breaches in health and safety provision, and a poor working environment that may lead to mental health problems such as anxiety and depression, which might have fatal consequences.

If risk management is defined as 'coordinated activities to direct and control an organization with regard to risk',[21] depending on the nature of the organization a number of areas will support this, for instance legal, compliance, human resources, operational risk, underwriting, market and credit risk, and cysbersecurity.

Risk management frameworks can be created with reference to ISO 31000, which states that managing risk considers the external and internal context of the organization, including human behaviour and cultural factors,[22] in addition to being informed by whatever guidance from regulators that is specific to the nature and location of the business being conducted. This framework describes the combined role of corporate governance, risk governance and risk processes and is operationalized through assigning and aligning key responsibilities, resources and reporting requirements.

A few models of people-related risk exist and are summarized in *People Risk Management*. These include Cressey's Fraud Triangle, which consists of motivation, opportunity and rationalization,[23] and Adam's Risk Thermostat, which examines propensity for risk and rewards, incidents and losses and perceived danger. The first two aspects increase risk-taking behaviour and the other two decrease risk-taking behaviour.[24]

The authors of *People Risk Management* expand Cressey's work, adding two sub-elements to each dimension with:

- **motivation:** specific *or* ambiguous;
- **opportunity:** intended *or* unintended;
- **rationalization:** being individual *or* collective.[25]

Volatility, complexity and ambiguity lead to uncertainty, and both visible and invisible variables, which maybe internal or external, will increase risk in decision-making, for instance:

- the information available;
- knowledge of information that is missing;
- peer pressure;
- conflicts of interest;
- heuristics;
- conscious and unconscious cognitive bias;
- the time given to make decisions;
- cognitive ability.[26]

In addition to individual aspects of risk-taking, groupthink/teamthink and organization culture may have an impact on risk-taking. The risk culture of an organization will be driven by its espoused and acted values. For instance, in Kim Cameron and Robert Quinn's Competing Values Framework internal and external focus are mapped against stability and flexibility, resulting in four types:

- **hierarchy:** internal with stability – doing things right;
- **clan:** internal with flexibility – doing things together;
- **market:** external with stability – doing things fast;
- **adhocracy:** external with flexibility – doing things first.[27]

It is instructive to consider what sort of culture exists within organizations so controls can be tailored accordingly. For instance: with hierarchy, decisions may take too long; with clan, there is a danger of groupthink; and with market and adhocracy, decisions may be made too quickly and may be biased.

Control

In order to control risk, a six-line of defence model has been proposed:

- individual;
- business management;
- risk management;
- internal audit;

- board;
- stakeholders.[28]

To this could be added external audit, by audit firms and regulators.

This six, or seven, line defence approach is an extension of the basic three lines of defence model for people risk:

- **first line:** business line managers and operational HR managers, follow the appropriate control framework;
- **second line:** control functions such as risk and compliance, monitoring compliance with the control frameworks;
- **third line:** internal and external audits.[29]

In *Managing People Risk in the Financial Sector*, the authors suggest a simple four-step approach to managing people risk.

- HR practitioners in conjunction with other functional experts identify the adverse events that could impact the business.
- Once risks are identified, they must be continually assessed to monitor trends and their impact.
- Risk acceptance takes place where senior management – perhaps at a risk committee meeting – will set both what levels of the risk can be tolerated because key processes that deliver products and services are sufficiently under control and also what levels should prompt review and potential action.
- Risk and control monitoring will continue thereafter.[30]

Managing People Risk in the Financial Sector notes that monitoring risk might include a number of management actions:

> it is important to spot trends and to provide commentary to explain what might be happening to cause an indicator to vary over time particularly where there is a clear trend. As an indicator trends to dangerous levels, senior management are likely to question controls and to require further action to mitigate the chance of a serious event. Selecting effective actions to mitigate risk can then reverse a trend so that the chance of a serious event reduces. This might happen quickly or with a time delay, depending on the risk and the mitigating actions.[31]

In *People Risk Management* it is proposed that the people management function should coordinate the communication, learning, feedback and re-ward flows that impact the efficacy of the line of defence models. Whether this should be a role for the people management function is debated in the final chapter of this book; however, there are uniquely people-related controls that can be implemented in different stages of the employee lifecycle. For instance:

- **Recruitment:** Avoid bias in communication positioning and content.
- **Selection:** Avoid bias and unconscious bias when screening CVs and in interviews, including in the use of AI. Use of psychometric tests for predictive purposes and fit to team.
- **Onboarding and leaving:** Consider well-being during social events.
- **Organization design and reporting:** Compliance with regulation.
- **Learning and development:** Training that is that is both compliance and values-driven.
- **Total reward:** Design a total reward and performance management methodology that that drives appropriate behaviour.

People risk can be thought of at individual, team and organization culture levels and factors influencing the risk environment can be internal, external, visible and invisible.

Risk of key talent loss

With regard to the risk of turnover of key talent, in *Chasing Stars*, Boris Groysberg states that general human capital is understood to be portable between one firm and another, for instance, relationships with contacts, clients and external networks. In contrast, firm-specific human capital is, by definition, not portable from an economic standpoint:

> dependence on general human capital has consequences for firms. Competing firms tend to bid up wages for high performing workers whose skills are not firm specific. Thus highly skilled knowledge workers can extract most of the value they contribute to their firms; in other words, the profits on their work, flow largely to themselves rather than their employers.[32]

However, with regard to firm-specific human capital, 'firm specific mastery of the idiosyncrasies of a particular work setting is an essential condition of high productivity but the set of skills that constitutes such mastery has no value outside the firm.'[33]

Human capital theory

> ascribes efficacy to firm specific training and employee development programs, and empirical studies in turn have found a link between such training and productivity. Researchers have also found that job specific investment (on the part of both employees and employers) increases dramatically with job tenure, seniority and rank.[34]

Groysberg identified some factors that have a decisive impact on portability of performance:

- the relative quality of the two firms matters – those moving to a superior firm maintain performance, otherwise there is a sharp decline;
- the orientation of the employee's firm of origin matters – those leaving portability orientated firms did better than those that didn't;

- the hiring and integration capacities of the new firm matter – it achieves faster target performance;
- the function an analyst is hired to perform matters – start up, major upgrade or strengthening and established platform;
- leaving solo or with a team matters – team moves become productive faster;
- gender matters – women's post-move performance surpassed men's.[35]

Non-portability organizations, those where human capital value is more integrated into the resource-based value of the organization, use more qualitative and discretionary performance management and compensation policies combined with greater management discretion and utilize metrics to understand employee behaviours. It is important that these areas are transparent and fair.

There have been many calls to increase the sophistication of metrics and reporting around human resource management and the capabilities available to do so:[36]

> the human resource function cannot just declare themselves to be a business partner, rather, they have to earn this partnership by acquiring the necessary skills and demonstrating to the customer-partner that they have something of value. When operating in this way, they build visible links between human resource work and the bottom line of the company.[37]

The nature of metrics and reporting around people management is examined in the next chapter.

Highlights

- The importance of strategic workforce planning has been introduced and linked to the portfolio risk management of people.
- Segmentation of the workforce is key to this.
- Other people-related risks have been identified related to decision-making and where this can go wrong.
- Issues around decision-making related to the unconscious vs conscious, fast vs slow, irrational vs rational, heuristics and bias, are examined in Chapter 1 and organizational culture is discussed in Chapter 9.
- Risk management controls for various stages of the employee lifecycle have been illustrated.
- One aspect of segmentation is the relative degree of human capital portability.

Leadership impact

Key themes that leaders should reflect on during this chapter include:

- The nature of risks associated with people in their organizations – it is not simply the potential loss of critical employees.
- Implementation of a people portfolio management approach.
- Designing people risk management into the structures, systems and processes across the organization in order to manage this key risk.
- Decisions are required regarding who is responsible for people risk management and how this relates to enterprise-wide risk management.

People management recommendations

Actions to consider:

- Carry out an exercise to identify key people risks across the organization.
- Be clear about the differences between strategic and operational people risks.
- Agree responsibility for people risk management, monitoring and enforcement.
- Agree key risk indicators.
- Set up controls and control indicators in order to mitigate or manage the risks.
- Ensure that people risk is linked to the management of all other key business risks.
- Set people risk thresholds, and adapt as required.
- Receive a regular flow of risk management information.

Human capital metrics and reporting 12

Introduction

This chapter introduces the concept of human capital, its measurement and reporting. It examines the value of metrics in building an outstanding workforce. This is important because the value of organizations is partially driven by the reports of equity analysts whose recommendations consider the intangible assets of organizations including certain metrics relating to people management.[1]

Human capital metrics are also key to managing workforce performance, the efficiency and impact of people management systems and processes, and ultimately the success of human capital strategies.

Chapter summary

The following subjects are discussed in this chapter:

- **human capital strategy:**
  - human capital;
  - structural capital;
- **measuring human capital:**
  - Watson Wyatt Human Capital Index;
  - Human Capital Monitor;
- **people metrics:**
  - ROI, MBOs and OKRs;
- **people management impact;**

- **human capital reporting:**
  - 10 core human capital reporting areas;
  - the future of human capital reporting;
  - investor impact;
  - human capital metrics.

Human capital strategy

In *High Impact Human Capital Strategy*, Jack Phillips and Patricia Phillips state that 'the most admired companies, the most innovative organizations, the best places to work, and the most successful businesses all attribute their success to how their employees are engaged and drive value for the organization.'[2] Human capital is the key differentiator and 12 goals are suggested for a human capital strategy:

- 'setting the optimal investment level for human capital and reviewing this expenditure periodically;
- aligning the HR programs to the business as they are initiated, developed and implemented;
- managing critical talent in the organization, ensuring that the appropriate number and quality of talented employees are available, addressing skills shortages, and ensuring that talent remains in the organization;
- pursuing a program of employee satisfaction, commitment, and job engagement, so that employees are fully involved in their work, remain loyal to the organization, and help attract others to the organization;
- creating a performance and innovation culture to achieve results in the organization with proper direction, roles and motivations;
- ensuring that employees are healthy and safe with proper healthcare and wellness opportunities;
- addressing the current demographics and societal issues to ensure that a proper employee mix is available and included in processes to enhance productivity and innovation;
- using technology to its fullest extent to unleash the creativity and potential of employees, while ensuring that it is driving productivity, innovation, customer satisfaction;
- addressing globalization in terms of how it affects employees in the present and will affect employees in the future, by having them actively engaged in every part of the process;

- addressing environmental and energy issues as they relate to jobs, the organization and society;
- developing effective leaders who can operate successfully in a global, diverse environment;
- implementing a system for accountability, including measuring success with analytics and big data, and delivering value that will be credible to top executives, including the chief financial officer'.[3]

They define human capital within any organization as relating to the capabilities of individuals. Organizations have tangible assets such as plant and machinery, financial capital, sometimes classed as tangible assets, and intangible assets. Intangible assets include intellectual capital and intellectual capital includes human capital and structural capital.

Human capital

People loan their human capital to organizations, which provide an environment for them to create value for all stakeholders; 'human capital is what people take home with them and structural capital is what they leave behind'.[4] A further view of human capital points to the opportunity for people to develop their skills and abilities over time; human capital is defined as 'people, their performance and their potential in the organization'.[5] This is informed by Gary Becker's Human Capital Theory,[6] which suggests that, on the whole, investments in education and training will improve productivity. It should be noted that this theory has been criticized for not considering ability and experience, and that some skills are industry-specific.

A human capital view is based on systems thinking, decisions based on facts and a focus on value. Human capital has two essential forms: one is generalized employee attributes and qualities that are of value to any organization; the other is firm-specific, where employee value is unique to a single firm and grows with tenure. 'Human capital is the accumulated stock of skills, experience and knowledge that resides in an organization's workforce and drives productive labor'.[7] Since human capital is an asset, it follows that 'human capital strategy is a form of asset management: a plan for securing, managing and motivating a workforce capable of achieving business goals'.[8]

Structural capital

In *The Human Value of the Enterprise*, Andrew Mayo notes that structural capital consists of:

- **external:** customer capital;
- **internal:** organizational capital, contracts, networks and reputation.

Mayo also introduces other forms of capital:

- **emotional capital:** including beliefs, values, interests and motivations;
- **relationship capital:** including both internal and external relationships;
- **knowledge capital:** including both explicit knowledge and tacit knowledge.

Knowledge-based resources are said to be 'resources that are rare, scarce, without complementary products and without substitutes, are sources of sustained competitive advantage for companies and organizations'.[9]

Intellectual capital includes all knowledge assets, while intellectual assets are part of intellectual capital and intellectual property is the legally protected part of intellectual assets.[10] It has been noted that 'an important function of knowledge management is to convert the human capital of an organization into its structural and relational capital'[11] and that knowledge management is about 'knowledge preservation, knowledge creation and knowledge diffusion'.[12]

Structural capital can also be defined as 'the supportive infrastructure, processes and databases of the organization that enable human and social capital to function'.[13] Innovation capital has also been added to this category. Social capital can be defined as the value of 'the relational networks in actual and potential capital based on individual or social units'.[14]

Following the resource based view (RBV) of organizations, which was discussed in Chapter 6, the knowledge based view (KBV) has appeared as a subset of the RBV where knowledge has been described as 'the most strategically important of the firm's resources'.[15]

Further to the above, human capital strategy was defined in a six-factor framework by Mercer as including: people, work processes, managerial structure, information and knowledge, decision-making, and rewards[16] and now includes talent strategy and leadership.[17] In their HC Scan, Mercer state that critical questions for leaders include:

- What are we spending/investing and what value is derived?
- Is the human capital strategy aligned with business design?
- What can we change in the way we manage people to generate greater returns?[18]

Barriers to human capital orientated strategic thinking include:

- seeing people as an operating cost versus generators of value;
- lack of clarity in who owns the human capital issue;
- policies and processes that are not considered as a whole; and,
- a lack of internal measures.[19]

The considerations around measuring human capital are examined below.

Measuring human capital

Measurement of human capital is inherently difficult and has seen many approaches. Early ones included:

- Baruch Lev:[20] discounted future remuneration;
- Dr Karl-Erik Sveiby, *The Invisible Balance Sheet*:[21] customer capital, structural capital and human capital;
- Leif Edvinsson, Goran Roos and Johan Roos:[22] human capital as competence, attitude and intellectual agility;
- Thomas Davenport:[23] human capital in terms of ability – knowledge and skill, behaviour including attitude and personality, and effort – the application of ability.

Various attempts to measure human capital have been reviewed and key ones include the: cost-based approach, market value approach, accounting approach, value-added approach, and human resource indicator approach. In *The Human Value of the Enterprise*, Mayo considers the following categories:[24]

- creating an index of practices and relating them to business results:
  - Watson Wyatt HCI, and later the HC Scan (examined below);
- statistical analysis of productivity based on workforce variables and the efficiency of the HR function and ROI of initiatives and interventions:

  The Saratoga Institute founded by Jac Fitz-enz published *The ROI of Human Capital: Measuring the economic value of employee performance* in 2000:[25]
  - enterprise level: revenue value, intellectual capital value, financial value added and economic value added;
  - process/function level: contribution to structural capital using performance metrics;
  - human capital level: effectiveness of six HRM functions;
- people-related measures integrated into a system of performance management:
  - the Kaplan and Norton Balanced Scorecard:[26] financial, customer, business process and learning and growth, with leading measures, performance drivers, and lagging measures, outcome;
  - the Becker, Huselid and Ulrich HR Scorecard:[27] HR deliverables, high performance work system (HPWS), HR system alignment and HR efficiency measures;
- attempts to value people as assets:
  - Mayo's Human Capital Monitor (examined below);

- ○ human resource accounting: values assets based on cost, market value, associated income on an NPV basis;
- ○ Flamholz:[28] conditional value is a combination of performance, flexibility of skills and promotability, and the result is multiplied by the future length of service adjusted for probability.

Watson Wyatt Human Capital Index

Prior to the change in organization to Towers Watson, Watson Wyatt developed its Human Capital Index (HCI). Five-year total returns to shareholders of 750 publicly listed companies were analysed, and those with a low composite score on the human capital index had a 21 per cent return, those with medium composite scores had 39 per cent and those with high composite scores had 64 per cent. The conclusion was that shareholder value would be increased by:

- **achieving recruiting and retention excellence:** mission-critical hires to hit the ground running, build a positive employer brand, get the basics right in the messaging;
- **creating a total reward and accountability orientation:** link rewards to performance, encourage CEO, top leadership ownership, benefits are important;
- **establishing a collegial, flexible workplace:** focus on employee satisfaction, minimize status distinctions, be flexible, tailor development, manage change well;
- **opening up communication between management and employees:** communication open and candid, be careful implementing 360 reviews, ask for feedback but be prepared to implement;
- **implementing focused HR technology:** use technology to create efficiencies, consistent, high-quality, delivery, and data analytics.[29]

The HCI was a predictive tool, and in comparing correlations between HCI and financial performance over a three-year period Watson Wyatt found that human capital practices were a leading rather than lagging indicator of business success:

> our analysis demonstrates that HR practices are not only associated with business outcomes, but also create them… a careful inspection of all the data shows that for every available correlation calculated over time, the relationship between past HR practices and future financial performance is stronger than the relationship between past financial outcomes and future HR practices.[30]

Willis Towers Watson have since established *The Human Capital Framework* where an organization's business strategy is delivered through human capital dimensions that include:[31]

- desired culture;
- human capital strategy;
- employee value proposition: people, purpose, work, total rewards.

The outcomes include:

- customer experience;
- business performance;
- employee performance;
- employee retention;
- employee engagement;
- employee attraction.

There has been increasing interest in examining the non-physiological and non-cognitive factors that impact the value of human capital. These include beliefs, values, attitudes, interests and socio-emotional skills.[32] Indeed, it is suggested that strategic human capital practice could start 'moving away from the use of proxy-orientated measures at the macro level, to using psychological concepts and measurement at the individual level'.[33]

Human Capital Monitor

In the Human Capital Monitor, Andrew Mayo identifies people as assets using the following framework:

- **people as assets:** employment costs x individual asset multiplier (IAM), human capital maximized through acquisition, retention and growth;
- **IAM:** a function of capability, potential, contribution and values alignment;

  +

- **people motivation and commitment:** leadership effectiveness, practical support, the workgroup, learning and development, and rewards and recognition;

  =

- **people contribution to added value:** financial and non-financial today and in the future.[34]

This model is based on the premise that assets have intrinsic value and help to generate value; people lend their personal human capital because they will receive value in return; and the value they receive will drive their motivation and commitment and the value they deliver to other stakeholders.[35]

People metrics

It has been stated that 'systematically quantifying the worth of individuals and their contribution to shareholders has generally neither been a priority or an aspiration'.[36] However, people rent their human capital to organizations, which provide an environment in which they can contribute value to all stakeholders.

In *Accountability in Human Resource Management*, the authors outline approaches to people accountability as follows:

- **early:** MBO, employee attitude surveys, HR case studies, HR audits;
- **value-add:** HR KPIs, HR cost monitoring, HR reputation, HR benchmarking;
- **leading edge:** ROI, effectiveness index, human capital measurement, HR as a profit centre.[37]

To this can be added objectives and key results (OKRs), which are discussed below.

ROI, MBOs and OKRs

The authors of *Accountability in Human Resource Management* favour measuring results through the ROI methodology, but acknowledge that 'confusion sometimes exists concerning ways to allocate specific costs, overall program costs can usually be pinpointed. The difficulty lies in determining program benefits'.[38] The 10 recommended strategies to do this are:

- use of control groups;
- trend line analysis;
- forecasting methods;
- participant estimates;
- supervisor estimates;
- management estimates;
- customer input;
- expert estimates;
- subordinate input;
- calculating the impact of other factors.

Management by objectives (MBO) was first outlined by Peter Drucker in his 1954 book, *The Practice of Management*,[39] to help improve the performance of an organization by clearly defining objectives that are agreed to by both management and employees. He felt that sharing goal setting and the development of action plans should encourage participation and commitment among employees, and align objectives of all stakeholders. However, it has since been argued that MBO can privilege the setting of goals over the plan required to achieve the goals and may not adequately consider the context within which the objectives and goals are being set.

The development of objectives and key results is attributed to Andy Grove, who introduced the approach at Intel.[40] Objectives are what is to be achieved, and should be action-orientated and inspirational. Key results describe how the objective is achieved and should be specific, measurable, time-bound, aggressive but realistic. They share the same attributes as SMART goals (specific, measurable, assignable, realistic and time-bound). Completion of all objectives must result in the attainment of the objective. There are four superpowers of OKRs: to '(1) focus and commit to priorities (2) align and connect for teamwork (3) track for accountability (4) stretch for amazing'.[41]

Key performance indicators (KPIs) may measure the key results of OKRs. However, while KPIs may be used over a long period, the objectives part of OKRs will often exist for a short period and the selected KPIs will change as the OKR changes. Doerr states that 'we need a new HR model for the new world of work. That transformational system, the contemporary alternative to annual reviews, is continuous performance management'.[42] This should be implemented by conversations, feedback and recognition (CFRs), which, 'like OKRs, champion transparency, accountability, empowerment and teamwork, at all levels of the organization':[43]

- **conversations:** authentic, coaching orientated discussions between the leaders and contributing colleague;
- **feedback:** bilateral and network communication to reflect on contribution and guide future behaviour;
- **recognition:** appreciation shown privately and publicly for service and contribution.[44]

AI will increasingly augment the work undertaken by people and therefore objective setting and performance indicators will need to adapt to this. What part of the value chain is impacted by people and how will success be measured? To focus on people, a new set of terminology can be envisaged. MBO thinking could change to being LTP thinking, leadership through people, KPIs should still exist, but for some with P standing for people not performance, and OKR can be modified to OKPR, objectives and key people results.

While the concept of eradicating annual reviews sounds attractive to some, a more balanced approach is maybe more appropriate. Annual, biannual or quarterly check-ins are not mutually exclusive with continuous feedback. If designed for brevity and delivered in a coaching style they can be seen as opportunities to discuss the performance of the organization and the team and progress against development objectives. Indeed, Doerr writes, 'I'm not proposing that performance reviews and goals should be completely severed'.[45]

Whatever methods of organizational goal and objective setting are used, they should form an evidence base for the goals and objectives agreed with employees in building an outstanding workforce.

In *Evidenced-Based Management*, Eric Barends and Denise Rousseau state that in many domains, and 'extensively documented in the subject area of human resource management',[46] managers don't use evidence in implementing policies and practices. The objective of evidence-based management is to 'increase the likelihood of favourable outcomes',[47] it is about 'making decisions through the conscientious, explicit and judicious use of the best available evidence from multiple sources by:[48]

- **asking:** translating a practical issue or problem into an answerable question;
- **acquiring:** systematically searching for and retrieving the evidence;
- **appraising:** critically judging the trustworthiness and reliance of the evidence;
- **aggregating:** weighting and pulling together the evidence;
- **applying:** incorporating the evidence into the decision-making process;
- **assessing:** evaluating the outcome of the decision taken.

Evidence-based management is needed due to: frailties in personal judgement, which is subject to bias and heuristics; issues with groups where decisions are affected by group conformity; and calls to seek out and implement best practice, which is often a flawed concept given organizational contingency and the resource-based view of the firm.

Business impact can only be identified if it is measured and reported. However, this has not historically always been achieved due to a lack of metrics focused on the impact of people management initiatives; the lack of systems to capture data; and poor people analytics capability within the human resource function. Ulrich and Dulebohn argue that 'it is no longer possible to sidestep data, evidence, and analytics that bring rigor and discipline to HR'.[49]

As will be seen in the next chapter, advances in technology, data capture and data analytics capabilities have addressed a number of these issues. However, the right metrics still need to be measured.

People management impact

The importance of people management can be considered through the lens of both cost and value. Often, people-related expenditure is the most significant cost to an organization and people can also be the major source of sustainable competitive advantage. Therefore, people-related inefficiency and underperformance have significant financial and economic implications for organizations. The people function therefore needs to demonstrate its direct and indirect contribution to the organization through measurement of efficiency and impact.

Ulrich has campaigned for human resource functions to provide human resource professionals who should learn to create value, not as they perceive it, but as the managers and other clients perceive it, and has noted that 'the absence of a value proposition leaves the human resources profession to justify itself through anecdotes, perceptions, goodwill, and the instincts of senior managers.'[50] The challenge of demonstrating value is noted by those who believe that as CFO the human resource function has neither been traditionally viewed as, nor empirically demonstrated to be, contributing to organizational performance it is not considered to be important or effective.[51]

Unfortunately, many human resource professionals are still struggling to be respected by CEOs and senior line business managers as senior contributors when they still cannot 'talk the language of business'.[52] It would help if they could 'build visible links between human resource work and the bottom line of the company'[53] for 'in many respects the "Holy Grail" for HR functions is the ability to show the bottom-line impact of their activities. This is a powerful way to increase HR's influence on company business decisions and future business strategies.'[54]

A 2012 survey by the Economist Intelligence Unit, *CFO Perspectives: How HR can take on a bigger role in driving growth*, found that:

- '25 per cent of CFO respondents say that their head of HR does a good job in succession planning (compared with 43 per cent of CEOs) and merely 14 per cent say the same of global sourcing decisions (compared with 34 per cent of CEOs)'.[55]

- 'More than one-half (58 per cent) believe their head of HR is not of the same calibre as other C-level executives. And two-thirds (67 per cent) say that they don't understand the business well enough'.[56]

- 'Although only 30 per cent of CFOs think that the head of HR is a key player in strategic planning, a much greater proportion (75 per cent) wants them to be a key player'.[57]

It has been noted that 20 per cent of CFOs report that they don't have a sound grasp on their organization's investment in human capital[58] because:

- employees and investment in the workforce have been treated as costs;

- ownership of the investment in human capital has been unclear;

- the impact of human capital investment has been unclear;

- appropriate measurement relating to human capital has not been undertaken.[59]

This situation needs to change. In *Talent Wins*, the authors recommend elevating the human resource function to the same level as finance and creating a G3 of CEO, CFO and CHRO.[60] They state that modern CHROs must have a 'deep understanding of the business, as well as expertise at linking it to people'[61] and the capacity and willingness to discuss talent-related capital decisions.[62]

Thankfully, this seems to be the trend. In 2014, EY published *Partnering for Performance: The CFO and HR*.[63] It reported the results of a global survey of CFOs and CHROs and found that 80 per cent of the CFO and CHRO respondents stated that their relationships had become more collaborative since 2011. This was caused by the high cost and scarcity of talent, elevation of the human resource function's organizational status as business and people strategies become more closely aligned; changes to strategy and creation of new products and services; and changes to operating models. The organizations with much higher levels of collaboration reported higher EBITDA growth and improvements in a range of human capital metrics including engagement and productivity. The CFO involvement in human capital investment decisions was significantly higher in the better performing organizations:[64]

- scenario planning: 58 per cent vs 16 per cent;
- predictive workforce analytics: 54 per cent vs 13 per cent;
- bridging the gap between SWP and execution: 52 per cent vs 13 per cent;
- skill gap analysis: 49 per cent vs 14 per cent.

Collaboration was also significantly higher in the following key areas:[65]

- structure and operating model: 62 per cent vs 42 per cent;
- strategic planning and decision-making: 58 per cent vs 22 per cent;
- data analytics to improve the performance of the HR function: 49 per cent vs 23 per cent;
- involvement of CFO in people-related metrics: 51 per cent vs 10 per cent.

Clearly, human resource professionals need to support their value proposition by documenting links between specific aspects of people management and the financial bottom line, not just through the efficient cost-effective delivery of human resource support processes, but through business impact. Evidence also suggests the need for the CFO and head of the people function to collaborate more closely and to use people analytics as an evidence base for decision-making.

Human capital reporting

Investor interest in the impact of people in meeting firm objectives is increasing, and questions a CEO should be able to answer include:

- What is the actual size of our investment in human capital?
- How is human capital managed as an asset?
- Which attributes of our people and which of our people practices impact business results and by how much?
- Are the returns acceptable?

- Can investors see evidence of your approach to investment in human capital?
- Are metrics available to demonstrate the impact of this investment?
- Are metrics available that indicate employee well-being?
- Are metrics available that demonstrate sustainability impact?

In 2018, ISO 30414, 'Human resource management: Guidelines for internal and external human capital reporting', was published to provide guidance for human capital reporting (HCR) to internal and external stakeholders, and to consider and make transparent the human capital contribution to the organization in order to support sustainability of the workforce.[66] ISO 30414 is guided by the principles of human rights at work and is coupled with the human governance standard ISO 30408. See Chapter 11 for an explanation of ISOs.

Human capital is defined by ISO 30414 as including 'the cumulative knowledge, skills and abilities of an organization's people and the impact on an organization's long-term performance, as well as competitive advantage through optimizing organizational outcomes',[67] and notes that the

> measurement of human capital facilitates the ability of an organization to manage one of its most critical resources and risks, people. Research shows that organizations that do not manage their human capital may damage the ability and opportunity for the business to create long-term and sustainable value achieved through their people.[68]

With rising investment in human capital and its impact on financial performance, these guidelines acknowledge the diverse interests of multiple internal and external stakeholders, for instance employees and shareholders, and consist of a common set of metrics.

ISO 30414 states the benefits of a standardized approach to HCR as including:

- 'the use of standardized and agreed data, which describes organizational value in a broadly comparable sense;
- the improvement of HRM processes that support good practice in establishing and maintaining positive employment relations;
- greater understanding of the financial and non-financial returns that are generated as a result of investments in human capital;
- accessible and transparent reporting of human capital data and insights that enhances internal and external understanding and assessment of an organization's human capital and its present and future performance'.[69]

10 core human capital reporting areas

ISO 30414 provides guidelines on 10 core areas of HCR with 23 reportable metrics noted. The 10 core areas are as follows:

- 'ethics: number and type of employee grievances filed; number and type of concluded disciplinary actions; percentage of employees who have completed training on compliance and ethics;
- **costs:** total workforce costs;
- **workforce diversity:** with respect to age, gender, disability, and "other indicators of diversity"; and diversity of leadership team;
- **leadership:** "leadership trust" (to be determined by employee surveys);
- **organizational safety, health, and well-being:** lost time for injury; number of occupational accidents; number of people killed during work;
- **productivity:** EBIT/revenue/turnover/profit per employee; human capital ROI, or the ratio of income or revenue to human capital;
- **recruitment, mobility, and turnover:** average time to fill vacant positions; average time to fill critical business positions; percentage of positions filled internally; percentage of critical business positions filled internally; turnover rate;
- **skills and capabilities:** total development and training costs;
- **succession planning:** to be confirmed;
- **workforce availability:** number of employees; full-time equivalents'.[70]

It is intended that these guidelines and associated metrics result in better organizational performance and there is a recognition that some organizations do not have the objective or the capacity to use the entire set of metrics and therefore additional recommendations for their use by SMEs are provided. The guiding principles of ISO 30414 are noted as the:

- importance of HC contribution to organizational success;
- focus on metrics that are in consonance with the organization's leadership direction, proportionate, practicable and material to an organization's business and operating model, regulatory, political, and social contexts;
- relevance for organizations in all sectors, of all types and sizes, and internationally;
- transparency of reporting in terms of opportunity and risk for internal and external stakeholders.[71]

The primary focus of HCR and disclosure is to determine the long-term health of an organization, thus mitigating the risk for the shareholder. An HCR framework will disclose financial and social value creation in the organization thus providing 'evidence of underlying strengths or risks that might otherwise be overlooked in traditional headcount reporting'.[72]

The future of human capital reporting

In addition to the guidance given by ISO 30414 on HCR, a number of initiatives are being discussed to improve the quality and consistency of human capital reporting and some of these address sustainability :

- **Valuing Your Talent:** a collaborative project supported by the UK Commission for Employment and Skills (UKES). Participants include the Chartered Institute for Personnel and Development (CIPD), Investors in People (IP), the Chartered Institute of Management Accountants (CIMA) and Chartered Management Institute (CMI). It reviews the human capital narrative reporting for Finanacial Times Stock Exchange (FTSE) 100 companies under four main categories: knowledge, skills and abilities (KSAs); human resource development (HRD); employee welfare/stability (EW); and employee equity (EE). It showed an increase in reporting between 2013 and 2015 in all four categories: KSA 15 per cent, HRD, 26 per cent, EW 6 per cent and EE 23 per cent. Over the same period workforce risk was established by additionally looking at The Economist, Financial Times and BBC websites. This had risen 29 per cent. [73]

- **Global Reporting Initiative (GRI) (2002):** Includes around 80 per cent of the world's largest 250 companies. Conceived by sustainability not-for-profit Ceres in 1997, it focuses on the triple bottom line (TBL), and it is the ambition of some to merge GRI with generally accepted accounting principles (GAAP).

- **International Accounting Standards Board (2010):** Gives guidance on materiality relating to the omission or misstatement of information. However, the concept of materiality is not universally defined so the International Integrated Reporting Council (IIRC) has developed a statement of common principles.

- **International Integrated Reporting Council (IIRC) (2010):** Focuses on the creation of value over time and the alignment of capital allocation and corporate behaviour to financial stability and sustainability. In *Creating Value*, it is noted that there is 'sufficient evidence of human capital materiality to warrant inclusion in standard investment analysis'.[74] They take a systems approach to value creation, viewing the business model as inputs, activities, outputs and outcomes. The International Framework for Reporting includes six capitals:[75]

  - financial;
  - manufactured;
  - intellectual;
  - human;
  - social and relationship;
  - natural.

- **Sustainability Accounting Standards Board (SASB) (2012):** A not-for-profit organization that attempts to reflect TBL impacts in corporate accounts.

- **Financial Reporting Council (2014):** Regulation determining the content of strategic reports and directors' reports that require items relating to business development, performance and positioning to be stated. These include matters related to the environment, employees, society, community and human rights.

Investor impact

Creating Value states that 'people's talent, skills, personal attributes and creativity affect current organizational performance and shape its future. Human capital is therefore an essential building block for creating value.'[76]

Mainstream investors have traditionally made only limited demands on organizations to report on human capital matters, but there are signs that this is changing. A major institutional investor in the United States has stated:

> interest in human capital data continues to increase. CalPERS has added human capital as a dimension of their investment philosophy and organizations are disclosing more than ever. The question is, what makes the most sense to disclose for a particular company? That's where time is well spent in HR.[77]

The Human Capital Management Coalition is a cooperative effort among a diverse group of influential institutional investors, representing over US$3 trillion in assets, to further elevate human capital management as a critical component in company performance. The coalition engages organizations with the aim of understanding and improving how human capital management contributes to the creation of long-term shareholder value.[78] In 2017 they petitioned the US Securities and Exchange Commission urging it to adopt standards that would require listed companies to disclose human capital related information.

The Chair of the Investment Association, Helen Morrissey, shines further light on the direction of travel:

> human capital is increasingly central to value creation and competitive advantage in many organizations' business models. Investors need to ensure they place a higher emphasis on human capital in investment appraisal and decisions. It is therefore essential that organizations provide more information on people, including strategy and performance metrics, in their reporting. We welcome initiatives that help to facilitate more consistent data and information on this important capital.[79]

Research is ongoing that seeks to understand the relationship between human capital reporting disclosures, equity analyst views and stock market performance.[80] For instance, qualification and competency-related disclosures have been linked to mid- to long-term increases in share price.[81]

Human capital metrics

The EY report *Partnering for Performance* noted that higher performing companies used workforce analytics to better understand the impact of human capital management on organizational performance. Five key areas were suggested as being particularly powerful:[82]

- managing attrition;
- fraud prevention;
- identifying hidden potential;
- identifying process deficiencies;
- strengthening the talent acquisition process.

The higher performing companies were significantly more likely to measure the return on investment of human resource related projects, 56 per cent vs 31 per cent, and measure engagement, 56 per cent vs 34 per cent.[83]

There is sometimes a sense of disquiet with regard to assigning value to people and using metrics to monitor their performance. Some may feel that people should not be reduced to assets. However, remembering motivation theory, achievable goal setting and continuous feedback are positive factors in supporting employee engagement. So too is the congruence of person–role fit, the opportunity to have some control of tasks, fairness, justice with regard to reward, and the ability to tailor working arrangements and employee benefits. Indeed, research has demonstrated that investors have achieved above-normal returns on investment by investing in a portfolio of companies with above-average levels of training.[84]

Leaders are able to make better-informed decisions that have a positive impact on employees when armed with evidence provided by accurate data. Surely it is better to think of people in terms of value creation than cost and to imagine that technology and data analytics can be used to improve the employee experience. Indeed, 'at the heart of value creation lie factors such as quality and stability of leadership, depth of talent, employee engagement, learning culture and other drivers of productivity, innovation and the employer brand.'[85]

The use of people analytics is examined further in the next chapter.

Highlights

- The value of people has been of increasing interest to investors and other stakeholders and it is argued that human capital should be accounted for, and reported as an intangible asset.

- The value of people is either general and portable, or firm-specific and non portable, and it contributes to the resource based value of organizations.

- People metrics should be utilized to measure the impact people have on the organization.

- Metrics should also be used to monitor the impact, and effectiveness, of people management. For instance, around people portfolio management, and the efficiency of people workflows.

Leadership impact

Key themes that leaders should reflect on include:

- the demands of shareholders, and therefore equity analysts, for human capital reporting;
- reporting guidance given by ISO 30414;
- the increasing importance of reporting related to corporate and social responsibility activity, and specifically ESG reporting for asset managers;
- how the required data can be captured and reported;
- what metrics related to peoples performance can be used in goal setting, and performance management conversations.

People management recommendations

Actions to consider:

- Update people portfolio management metrics and reporting.
- Integrate the performance management system into business planning through goal setting.
- Establish metrics for people workflows so that their cost and ROI can be measured accurately.
- Review the impact and effectiveness metrics for people management across the organization.

People analytics 13

Introduction

Terms such as human capital, human assets, people metrics and people analytics have their detractors. However, using a combination of quantitative and qualitative analysis to establish an evidence base for decision-making seems like a smart way of approaching leadership.

The more that the complexity of people, and their behaviour, is understood, the better hypothesis can be proposed to initiate and support quantitative analysis. Although, the results often still need to be interpreted using qualitative methods.

Chapter summary

The following subjects are discussed in this chapter:

- **People technology**
- **People data**
- **People analytics**
- **Research design**
- **Data governance**
- **Social sensing technology**
- **Why Moneyball?**

People technology

A 2018 report by Mercer, *Global Talent Trends Study*, found executives saying that the most valuable talent analytics are those that determine: whether it's better to build, buy, or rent talent; what causes people to leave/stay with the organization; what drives engagement, which characteristics are unique to high-performing teams; and which training programmes are most effective.[1]

Overall, people activities that will be impacted by emerged and evolving technology include:

- **recruitment:** employer brand supported and monitored by digital-based marketing; selection and review of talent acquisition channels; selection of employees using AI to screen CVs, interview and to gamify selection tests including psychometric assessments; more effective systems supporting organization design and internal mobility;

- **employee engagement:** real-time feedback on satisfaction and engagement both internally and using external data sources; sentiment analysis; predicting turnover using disparate data analytics;

- **employee safety and wellness:** wearable technology and sensors, and use of the internet of things to ensure safe working environments and practices and to monitor physical and mental health;

- **learning and development:** adaptive programme design and monitoring; tailoring the content, timing and learning methods to meet the requirements of the individual, for instance short bursts of 'micro' learning and blended learning using a mix of online and classroom delivery; virtual classrooms, virtual reality and augmented reality tools for the delivery of technical courses through to mentoring and coaching;

- **performance management:** real-time analysis of activity using AI and sensors; data analytics to measure and predict performance and to create more efficient and effective working environments and workflows;

- **administrative self-service:** employees access benefits, make enquiries and choose outcomes using AI enabled that augment human interaction.

Much is promised, but much has yet to be delivered. An ambition to find actionable insights from people analytics has not yet been fulfilled for most. A 2017 Mercer report said that 'very few respondents are able to translate data into predictive insights, and nearly 1 in 4 are still only able to produce basic descriptive reporting and historical trend analysis.'[2]

In Gartner's 'Reimagine HR 2018', the hype-cycle of human capital management (HCM) technology showed:[3]

- **cloud-based systems and talent management suites:** reaching a plateau of productivity within two years;

- **onboarding applications:** sitting between a trough of disillusionment and a slope of enlightenment;

- **workforce planning, workforce analytics and video interviewing, and candidate relationship management applications:** descending from the peak of inflated expectations into the trough of disillusionment;

- **machine learning, platform-as-a-system voice of the employee, worker engagement platforms, virtual assistants and internal talent marketplace:** are all on the curve rising from innovation trigger to the peak of inflated expectations, with internal talent marketplace at the lowest point on the curve.

With technology being used extensively, more data will be available than ever before. The use of data analytics to support strategic workforce planning and evidence-based decisions around people management choices will continue to increase.

People data

There has been significant growth in the use of data and analytics tools to identify insights and people that enable faster, more accurate, and more confident decision-making. Data analytics empowers business teams to leverage granular data from across their organizations to support proactive scenario testing and workforce planning, In *Data-Driven HR*, Bernard Marr states:

> HR teams can use data to make better HR decisions, better understand and evaluate the business impact of people, improve leadership's decision-making in people-related matters, make HR processes and operations more efficient and effective, and improve the overall well-being and effectiveness of people, which all can have a significant impact on a company's ability to achieve its strategic aims.[4]

Organizations store a significant amount of data on the people that work for them and the outcomes of their activity, but: what data is relevant, where does it reside, who owns it, how can it be accessed, how will it be processed, how will the data be presented and to what audience? There is a need to consider data sources, data storage, data analysis, data output and the different categories of data:[5]

- **internal:** data owned by the organization;
- **external:** publicly available data, and data held privately by other organizations;
- **structured:** data that can be arranged in rows and columns;
- **unstructured:** text-heavy, audio and video;
- **semi-structured:** some shared structural characteristics combined with unique content.

In *Data-Driven HR*, Marr outlines the different types of data relevant to people activities which will fall into one or more of the above categories:

- **activity data:** a record of actions undertaken by an employee;
- **performance data:** employee outcomes and feedback;
- **relationship data:** communication activity;
- **photographic and video data:** still and moving images;
- **sensor data:** physical and mental well-being.[6]

To this can be added personal data, some of which may require regular, episodic or periodic updates.

Text in emails can be used to analyse levels of stress, satisfaction, engagement and sentiments such as the propensity to leave. Images may be used for security and internal and external communication, while video can be analysed for selection purposes for interviews and to determine levels of stress. Voice data can also be analysed for levels of stress, satisfaction and engagement.

People analytics

The development of a people analytics capability tends to be an evolutionary process, from simple operational reporting through to predicative analytics:

- **operational reporting:** reactive, ad hoc, non-repeatable, manual and time-consuming. Disparate data sources, difficult to develop coherent datasets;
- **advanced reporting:** increased data sophistication – drawing together data from multiple disparate data sets. Multi-dimensional reporting – using dash-boarding solutions to allow drill down/through capabilities;
- **advanced analytics:** development of advanced statistical pattern analysis. Incorporate a wide variety of internal and external data sources;
- **predictive analytics:** development of predictive models and what-if scenario analysis. Scenario analysis allows more effective resource planning and risk mitigation.

Defining the approach to people analytics demands an assessment of internal capabilities, and the complexity–impact matrix provides a useful mechanism for assessing the optimal balancing ease of implementation with impact:

- **trivial endeavour:** low complexity and low impact;
- **quick win:** low complexity and high impact;
- **pet project:** high complexity and low impact;
- **big bet:** high complexity and high impact.

It is suggested that the optimal approach uses agile data analytics to deliver quick wins that allows teams to build a track record of delivery without significant investment.[7]

Defining key metrics to be analysed via people analytics will be dependent on a number of factors, driven primarily by the availability of data. In *Data-Driven HR*, Marr considers critical people analytics to include:

- **capabability:** skill resource;
- **competency acquisition:** hiring;
- **recruitment channel:** success of channel strategies;
- **capacity:** matching people resource to demand;

- **employee churn:** turnover;
- **corporate culture:** climate, engagement;
- **leadership analytics:** communication style;
- **performance analytics:** organization impact.[8]

For instance, people analytics has typically leveraged data available to human resource teams to assess the following key metrics:

- **turnover:** regretted hires and volume: find patterns and use qualitative research to find out why;
- **talent acquisition costs:** time taken, fees paid, internal vs external, retention rates: find patterns and use qualitative research to find out why;
- **intervention returns:** relationship between employee engagement, customer satisfaction, revenue: find patterns and use qualitative research to find out why;
- **workforce planning:** current composition, scenario predictions for segments, eg roles to be eradicated due to emergent technology such as AI, responsive robotics, distributed ledger technology.

As people analytics becomes more established, the demand to collect, collate and leverage additional data sets is likely to drive the growth of new and more sophisticated analytics outcomes to risk manage the segmented people portfolios and use predictive data using disparate data sets. Ultimately, people analytics 'offers an opportunity to get better HR for less; link HR practices with business outcomes and value; challenge beliefs through data; educate practitioners on what works and what does not; improve decision-making through sound predictions'.[9]

Research design

The Power of People notes that research design will involve decisions around: experiments, quasi-experiments, correlational studies and qualitative studies, with the objectives of quantitative analysis being to explore, associate, predict, classify, reduce and segment; and the objectives of qualitative analysis to hypothesize, interpret and contextualize.[10]

Research design for any business problem where people analytics is considered should consider the following methodology:

- **Define problem statement:** determine the challenge that the data analytics is looking to resolve and obtain stakeholder buy-in to confirm the problem statement.
- **Build hypothesis:** Statements developed to frame the research.
- **Data discovery:** Identify data attributes required to address the problem statement, assessing internal data sources to determine if required attributes available, identify gaps.

- **Source, load and normalize data:** Typically, data resides in disparate sources with inconsistent formats/structures, so use data analytics tooling to source, load and normalize data.

- **Construct analytics logic:** Leverage data analytics tooling to construct, test and validate logic, and utilize agile analytics technology which allows logic to be developed in process.

- **Test hypothesis:** An agile approach enables hypothesis to be tested throughout the solution development, with continued testing until the solution addresses initial problem statement.

- **Visualize results:** Using business information modelling, build visualization levels to display analytics outputs, as business information tooling enhances storytelling, making analytics outcomes accessible to stakeholders.

- **Productionization process:** Development of repeatable data analytics logic allows outcomes to be monitored through time, which allows quantification of impact of the solution.

Business impact modelling is a people analytics approach that uses statistical tools to identify the effects of specific human capital practices and attributes on business performance.

The Power of People recommends that the delivery of people analytics solutions requires six skills for success:

- business acumen;
- consulting;
- data science;
- communications;
- work psychology;
- human resources.[11]

It will involve individuals from a number of complimentary disciplines, such as organization design, organizational development and ergonomics as well as other functions such as finance and marketing.

Internal stakeholders include those who provide data, those who analyse data, those who receive data and those whose work experience will be impacted by the data. It is important to understand everyone's perspectives, discuss and resolve any concerns, communicate well and demonstrate value. In terms of enabling analytical thinking, *The Power of People* match perspective and enablement:

- perspective:
  - **analytically savvy:** formally trained, numerate, data-driven;
  - **analytically willing:** open-minded, potentially hesitant, prepared to learn;
  - **analytically resistant:** unwilling to support, rely on gut feel, sceptical;

- enablement:
  - **analytically savvy:** advanced training, user groups and forums, professional affiliations and conferences;
  - **analytically willing:** clarify what analytics is and is not, analytics training on tools and data, participation in relevant analytics projects;
  - **analytically resistant:** identify the reasons for resistance, collaboration to solve a problem they are facing, use of analytics to potentially boost their success.[12]

The Power of People highlights demands for the human resource function to deliver more information to run the business and the desire from employees for more personalized services and experience[13] – the 'employee of one'.

Research has found strong support for the hypothesis that human resource professionals 'with higher analytical skills have higher overall individual performance… results show that they create more value both for external and internal stakeholders of the business.' The results are believed to be the case across geographies and contexts.[14]

It is therefore suggested by Marr that human resource teams are divided between those focused on people analytics, using data analytics to support insights, and those focused on people support, such as development, engagement and well-being, with administrative tasks being outsourced or automated.[15] However, our framework for people management introduced in Chapter 17 takes a different approach.

It has been questioned whether the human resource function will 'lose the battle over analytics',[16] which suggests that human resource functions aspire to *own* people analytics. The choice appears to be a reporting line to the enterprise-wide analytics function or into the human resource function. In *The Power of People* a global director of HR strategy and analytics is quoted as saying that workforce analytics does not need to be separate from the analytics function and that she would like her team to be integrated within enterprise-wide analytics.[17] There have also been calls to keep ownership and accountability of people analytics with line managers.[18]

It is argued in Chapter 17 that people-related activities should be domiciled within the functional domains that hold the relevant core expertise, for instance people analytics as part of enterprise-wide analytics.

Data governance

There are a number of important considerations when using people-related data. Legislation may impose statutory responsibilities on the storage and use of data. For instance, General Data Protection Regulation (GDPR) from the European Union (EU), which covers EU citizens. Organizations may only use personal data with consent and only for the express purpose given.

Employers must therefore be transparent about what data they require and why. If they then wish to use it for another purpose they must get further permission. There should be a clear business case for gathering and using the data. Employees also have the right to withdraw consent and ask for data to be deleted. This applies to all data types noted above.

Data governance is clearly a significant concern in terms of collecting, storing and utilizing data, as is the security of the data to guard against its loss, unapproved disclose and fraudulent use. Minimizing and anonymizing data within a secure environment will help to safeguard data and help prevent financial and reputational loss due poor data governance.

There are also the issues of bias and fairness to consider in relation to algorithms.

Social sensing technology

Social sensing technology that could help transform social interaction and well-being in the workplace is examined by Ben Waber in *People Analytics*. First, social network analysis enables a quantitative view of relationships between people and groups. They show communication and its frequency pictured using nodes of different shades or colours and lines of different colours and also thickness. Each relationship is called a degree. Complex relationships can be shown in a matrix. Other concepts include the amount of cohesion, which measures the amount that people at an individual level communicate with each other, and the concept of centrality, betweenness centrality, which identifies nodes that are conduits for information to move between groups.[19]

The extent to which groups are tightly connected, cohesive, or whether there is a diverse network is dependent on the needs of the role. Cohesive groups create and leverage psychological trust, which is built on shared experiences and understanding, both within the work environment and perhaps socially as well. They share tacit knowledge and may even develop their own language. While it is hard to hire laterally into very cohesive groups and also hard to effect change, studies have shown that increasing cohesion can have a positive impact on performance and a reduction in turnover.[20]

Social network analysis can also be used to analyse the impact of proximity on performance. Studies have shown that remote teams who never meet in person perform worse than those that meet and then work remotely, and that the best performing teams are ones that are co-located. Also, teams that work with each other, but from separate locations, work more productively when the teams are a similar size or one team is much larger than the other. Where there is a small difference in team size, the slightly smaller team may resent their position, feel threatened, and this may lead to conflict and a negative impact on performance.

Office design and the use of communication technology also impact behaviour and performance. Whether teams that need to collaborate are located on campus or within single office buildings makes a difference, as does the design of desks. Working through ideas with other people in the same group will help problem solving, as well interaction between people in different groups. These can be planned, or unplanned serendipitous meetings. Office layout will become increasingly important and 'bring a strategic approach to office design, one where political concerns take a backseat and collaborative considerations… drive decisions'.[21]

Organizational boundaries occur between teams that are reliant on each other in the value chain as their members report upwards within the team. This can be resolved with shared reporting or by appointing individuals or teams to coordinate between teams.

The power of data gathered through the use of sociometric badges, and other technology, is championed by Waber. He believes they can:

- help identify the natural variation in the way that people work and communicate to ascertain what will make people safe, happy and effective;
- capture, analyse and visualize individual and team activity and communications, which can lead to greater efficiency and effectiveness and increased exploration and innovation;
- monitor individual well-being and the health of the organization's social system.

It is explained that augmented social reality uses sensor data to layer social context over everyday interactions. For example, introducing people in an organization whose collaboration could be impactful. While face-to-face communication is shown to be important for working with complex information, innovation and stress reduction, there is a trend towards flexible working that includes remote working, and so the adoption of augmented social reality and holography will become critical to enhancing the remote experience.

People Analytics concludes that people used to live in villages and small towns, they knew each other and built communal bonds. In the global 24/7 marketplace, the

> future consists of connection, collaboration and data, a future where we are
> judged not solely on our deeds, but by that of our entire community. It's a future
> where age-old practices of relationship building and trust are married with
> the new age of data gathering that the world of sensors and data streams has
> brought forth.[22]

The method of collecting data for sociometric studies relies on members of the workforce giving their permission for their written and verbal communication to be captured and analysed, also for the monitoring of their mental and physiological states. The data captured can be used in a supportive way to design for higher levels of well-being in work environments, which of course will be also beneficial to organizations. This is considered further in the next chapter, which examines the employee value proposition and includes well-being.

Why Moneyball?

Bill James started publishing baseball statistics in 1977 and was quoted by Michael Lewis in *Moneyball*: 'When the numbers acquire the significance of language they acquire the power to do all of the things which language can do: to become fiction and drama and poetry'.[23] He challenged the traditional views of the game by questioning the relevance of the statistics that were used by fans, team management and coaches.

In 1997 Billy Bean became the Oakland As general manager, and hired Paul de Podesta, who used 'sabermetrics', a term coined by Bill James, to collect and summarize relevant data from in-game activity that could be used to select players. In 2002 the As became the first team in the hundred years of American League baseball to win 20 consecutive games. They also became one of the most cost-effective teams in baseball and in the Major League Baseball 2006 season ranked 24th of 30 major league teams in player salaries.

The use of data and data analytics to second-guess the experienced baseball coaches did not meet with universal approval, and likewise the use of human capital terminology and data analytics for people management has its detractors. This is sometimes because experienced leaders want to solely trust their gut-feel and sometimes because some object to the human asset and human capital discourse being applied to people. However, it is clear that by adopting human capital thinking and people analytics, organizations can maximize employment opportunities, improve the employee experience and improve employee well-being. After all, a number of the players recruited by Billy Bean were supposed 'misfits' that other teams did not value and had rejected. People analytics identified their value and matched them to roles where they were able to contribute to team success.

Highlights

- People-related data analytics gives organizations the ability to reduce or eradicate the use of spreadsheets to capture and manipulate data relating to people.

- It allows disparate sets of data to be compared, correlations identified and causation investigated.

- People analytics also supports predictive analysis and impacts the design of the work environment.

Leadership impact

Key themes that leaders should reflect on include:

- the importance of evidence-based management;
- types and frequency of people-related data captured by their organization;
- different ways of analysing people data – operational, performance, advanced and predictive;
- different ways of visualizing data and the use of dashboards;
- a methodological approach to building a people analytics capability – starting with quick wins;
- be mindful of governance issues around data, in particular GDPR where relevant;
- be clear about who owns and has access to the required data.

People management recommendations

Actions to consider:

- Agree who is responsible for people analytics.
- Review current data and reports.
- Plan for the introduction of more sophisticated analytics. Learn from the experience of other organizations.
- Agree priorities.

Employee engagement and experience

14

Introduction

In this chapter, employee engagement and experience are examined, followed by the employee value proposition and employer brand.

Potential employees are interested in a potential employer's brand, and current employees in their employee experience. With a wide range of employment opportunities on offer, it is vital to create an environment that attracts and retains high-quality people. Organizations need to be aware of the issues that motivate people to join, stay and productively apply maximum discretionary effort while they are at work.

Chapter summary

The following subjects are discussed in this chapter:

- **employee engagement:**
  - engagement surveys:
    - Gallup's Q12;
    - Towers Watson's Three Core Elements;
  - unlocking employee engagement;
- **employee experience:**
  - the three contracts and trust;
  - employee experience vs employee engagement;
  - employee feedback;
- **employer brand and the employee value proposition:**
  - employer brand;
  - employee value proposition;

- ○ employee segmentation;
- ○ responsibility for employer brand management;
- **giving them what they want.**

Employee engagement

The 2017 Gallup *State of the Workplace* report shows that the global aggregate from data collected in 2014, 2015 and 2016 across 155 countries indicates that just 15 per cent of employees worldwide are engaged in their job. Two-thirds are not engaged, and 18 per cent are actively disengaged. Worryingly, only 10 per cent of Western European employees are engaged at work, while the vast majority, 71 per cent, are not engaged, and 19 per cent are actively disengaged.[1] In the book *Build It*, these are known as engagement gaps.[2]

Unfortunately, these numbers are quite stable, so what can be done by organizations to increase levels of engagement?

It is understood that people enjoy their jobs more when they are treated fairly, when they are challenged and when they have some freedom in meeting their challenges. In *The Talent Delusion*, Chamorro-Premuzic notes that this means finding the right people for the right roles is not just a matter of matching them in terms of ability, but also in terms of their values and interests.[3] He draws a distinction between job satisfaction and engagement, with job satisfaction being an attitude or mental concept about your job while engagement additionally involves an emotional and behavioural component – how your job makes you feel and what you do.

High levels of engagement increase positive outcomes for both individuals and organizations; 'interventions designed to boost employee engagement are mainly focused on increasing the fit between employees and the organization, in particular its culture and climate.'[4] However, Chaamorro-Premuzic warns that that the relationship between engagement and job performance is far stronger in individualistic than in collectivistic cultures.

Engagement surveys

There are many surveys that show the positive link between employee engagement and business performance. For instance, those of Gallup and Towers Watson.

Gallup's Q12

Gallup suggest that 'engaged employees produce better business outcomes than do other employees across industry, across company size and nationality, and in good economic times and bad.'[5] They measure employee engagement using a 12-element survey (Q12) that is based on employees' performance management needs. When those needs are met, employees become emotionally and psychologically attached to their work and workplace and their performance increases. The Q12 is based on four types, or levels, of employees' performance development needs:

- basic needs;
- individual needs;
- teamwork needs;
- personal growth needs.[6]

The 12 elements are as follows:

- **Know what's expected:** I know what is expected of me at work.
- **Materials and equipment:** I have the materials and equipment I need to do my work right.
- **Opportunity to do my best:** At work, I have the opportunity to do what I do best every day.
- **Recognition:** In the last seven days, I have received recognition or praise for doing good work.
- **Cares about me:** My supervisor, or someone at work, seems to care about me as a person.
- **Development:** There is someone at work who encourages my development.
- **Opinions count:** At work, my opinions seem to count.
- **Mission/purpose:** The mission or purpose of my company makes me feel my job is important.
- **Committed to quality:** My associates or fellow employees are committed to doing quality work.
- **Best friend:** I have a best friend at work.
- **Progress:** In the last six months, someone at work has talked to me about progress.
- **Learn and grow:** This last year, I have had opportunities at work to learn and grow.[7]

Towers Watson's Three Core Elements

Towers Watson have developed a model of engagement which is based on three core elements:

- **discretionary effort and commitment to achieving work goals – being engaged:** belief in organization goals and objectives, emotional connection – pride and employer advocacy, willingness to invest additional effort to support success;

- an environment that supports productivity in multiple ways – being enabled: freedom from barriers to achieve success at work, the availability of resources to perform well, the ability to meet work challenges effectively;

- a work experience that promotes well-being – feeling energized: the ability to maintain energy at work, a supportive social environment, feelings of enthusiasm and accomplishment at work.[8]

The results of employee engagement surveys can be depicted in scorecards and heat-maps, and while people analytics may identify correlations with the antecedents of engagement and also with performance, causation will need to be explored using qualitative research such as interviews.

Unlocking employee engagement

The book *Magic: Five keys to unlock the power of employee engagement* suggests that five key elements are required to create employee engagement:

- **meaning:** work transcends instrumentality and is aligned with employee values and interests;

- **autonomy:** control and flexibility in decision-making;

- **growth:** professional personal development;

- **impact:** clarity in the relationship between people's work and organizational outcomes;

- **connection:** engagement with internal and external stakeholder relationships and sense of belonging.[9]

The authors note that leaders don't decide if engagement happens, employees do, and in a later book state that 'because success starts with talented people, your most important role as a leader is to give them a reason to join your cause, a reason to stay, and a reason to engage'.[10] The above elements can be compared to Self-Determination Theory (SDT) and the conclusions of Daniel Pink in *Drive*.

- **meaning and impact** → purpose in *Drive* → autonomy in SDT;

- **autonomy** → autonomy in *Drive* → autonomy in SDT;

- **growth** → mastery in *Drive* → competency in SDT;

- **connection** → relatedness in SDT.

It has been said that when people are engaged they are so immersed in their roles that the psychological distance between their work personae and themselves is minimized.[11] This is similar to the concept of 'flow' in positive psychology.

In *Build It*, Glenn Elliot and Debra Corey define someone as being engaged if they: understand and believe in the direction the organization is heading, its purpose, mission and objectives; understand how their role affects and contributes to these; and genuinely want the organization to succeed. They believe that engaged employees help to be build strong, resilient and more successful organizations through their innovation, superior decision-making and greater productivity. They also differentiate between happiness and engagement, noting that they have 'found companies that have quite happy employees based on a combination of good working conditions, low ambition and low accountability for results'.[12]

Their model for leaders to conceptualize employee engagement has 10 elements that between them contribute to an employee engagement culture. They call this the engagement bridge. The following three elements underpin and support the bridge; they are key factors that must be in place:

- **Pay and benefits:** These must be equitable and transparent, and benefits can help build the employee value proposition and are less expensive than cash rewards.

- **Workspace:** Physical and virtual workspaces must enhance the employee experience but also be fit for purpose.

- **Well-being:** Employers must focus on physical, mental and financial well-being.[13]

The seven supported elements are as follows and none of the seven is privileged over the others:[14]

- **Open and honest communication:** Overly and unduly selective communication and under-communication erode trust. Encouraging diversity of opinion and debate helps build trust.

- **Purpose, mission and values:** Must be authentic, embedded and lived.

- **Leadership:** Must consistently live the organization's values, nurture their followers, and deliver results.

- **Management:** Must be aligned with organizational values and not block the cascading of what leadership say will be done.

- **Job design:** Design jobs that are demanding and give control over how the results are achieved.

- **Learning:** Support tailored learning, encourage ambition and a culture that accepts, even embraces, failure.

- **Recognition:** Must be personal, meaningful, fair and timely.

In *The Talent Delusion*, Chamorro-Premuzic notes that 'engagement has been negatively associated with turnover intentions, actual staff turnover, counterproductive work behaviours (eg bullying, antisocial behaviour, abusive management, loafing) and burnout.'[15]

In terms of more positive outcomes,

they range from motivation and well-being to actual performance and productivity. For example, engaged individuals are generally healthier, report better work–life balance (even when they work harder!) and are more persistent and driven at work. This is reflected not just in better individual performance and higher productivity rates, but also in more positive organizational citizenship behaviours. In other words, engaged employees are not just more valuable to their employers because of their work-related output, but also because they are better colleagues and have a more favourable impact on other employees.[16]

In *Leading Organizations*, Meaney and Keller state that organizations need to focus on more than employee engagement and distil a set of cultural measures that have been empirically proved to improve performance:

- **direction:** clarity of destination and journey;
- **leadership:** creating inspiration;
- **work environment:** quality of interactions;
- **accountability:** clarity of task, delegated authority, accepted responsibility;
- **coordination and control:** joint evaluation of performance and risk and problem solving;
- **motivation:** enthusiasm driving extraordinary efforts and results;
- **external orientation:** quality of stakeholder engagement;
- **innovation and learning:** quality and flow of new ideas and organizational flexibility.[17]

In *Organization Development*, the authors state:

> the changing workforce mix, and in particular expectations of the 'connected' generations for immediacy of response, shared information and opportunities to contribute are driving a greater emphasis on employee voice... As labour markets become more fluid, people will only stay and give of their best of they feel that they are key stakeholders, are informed and involved in what is happening in their organizations.[18]

In addition, 'HR must make efforts to understand what engages and disengages key parts of the workforce and put in place actions to improve engagement and commitment. Creating emotional commitment goes beyond the tangible elements of the employee "deal" or psychological contract.'[19]

They note that people want to experience a shared purpose, meaningful work, flexibility in work and work organization, feeling empowered and valued, and be given the opportunity to develop. Evidence from Gallup supports this view, with one-third of global employees strongly agreeing with the statement 'the mission and purpose of my organization makes me feel my job is important.'[20] They increasingly want to feel that *their* experience is an individual rather than standardized one.

Employee experience

The Employee Experience: How to attract and retain top performers and drive results defines employee experience as 'the sum of perceptions employees have about their interactions with the organization in which they work'[21] and starts with the following statement: 'every important business outcome lies downstream from the experience and engagement of the people who make the organization go'.[22] The authors believe that employee experience (EX) is about 'creating an operating environment that inspires your people to do great things'[23] and a high-quality sustainable customer experience (CX) is not possible without high-quality EX.

The experience of any employee encompasses their perceived reality, how this compares to their expectations and feelings of equity; this is expectation alignment (EA). If perceived reality is not aligned with expectations there is a lack of congruence, which could be positive or negative. However, even if the experience is positive, feelings of inequity may still occur when comparisons are made with the others in the organization. It is noted that employee expectations are influenced by:

- implicit promises of the employer brand;
- implied promises of leaders;
- rumours and conjecture from colleagues and peers;
- external news.[24]

To this can be added explicit leader promises. They go on to suggest that secrecy, lack of clarity, inconsistency, asymmetrical expectations and over-promising create a lack of EA and cognitive dissonance. Where information vacuums occur, conspiracy theories fill the void and rumours describe the latest perceived reality.[25]

Six factors, or pillars, are suggested which, it is believed, create EA: fairness, clarity, empathy, predictability, transparency and accountability. The authors found from research that at least four of these need to be present to create EA and that organizations with four or more in place showed employee engagement at levels 25 per cent to 30 per cent higher than those organizations with fewer than four.[26]

Tracy Maylett and Paul Warner's book, *Magic: Five keys to unlock the power of employee engagement*, showed that managing employee expectations and building trust were key factors in driving employee engagement and therefore the three critical components of winning EX are: expectation alignment; transactional, psychological and brand contracts; and trust.[27] As noted above, EA is the extent to which an employees expectations and perceived actual experiences are in line with each other.

The three contracts and trust

The *transactional contract* is the 'mutually accepted, reciprocal and explicit, agreement between two or more parties that defines the basic operating terms of the relationship'.[28] An employment contract is a legally enforceable transactional contract, and may refer to other documents such as an employee handbook. The presence and length of an employee handbook may be linked to the employer brand. Maylett and Wride believe that transactional contracts are compliance focused, setting the default position for tangible factors focused on conformity, and should be: promissory, reciprocal and bilateral, mutually beneficial, fair and only changed through mutual agreement.

The *psychological contract* is the 'unwritten, implicit set of expectations and obligations that define the terms of exchange in a relationship'.[29] The existence of a psychological contract based on employees' perceived expectations of what equitable outcomes may look like has been debated but a belief that rights exist that are not part of transactional contracts, or may even conflict with them, has been documented.[30] It is noted that psychological contracts may fill the void left by an absence of transactional and brand contracts, and are built around feelings of perceived fairness. They are therefore belief-based, implicit, unilateral, subject to interpretation, open-ended, dynamic and flexible in the short term.[31]

The *employer brand contract* is the sum of all the promises made to an organization's stakeholders who are aware of it and so it is important to be specific about its construction and to test perceptions of it both within and outside the organization. As noted above, it impacts employee expectations and therefore EA and the employee value proposition (EVP), which is one part of the employer brand and is defined as being 'the value – tangible, intangible and reputational – that an employee receives from an organization in exchange for his or her work'.[32] The employer brand and employee value proposition are explored further below.

The fourth key factor that impacts EX is trust and, further to this, how employees, and therefore organizations, behave in moments of truth (MOT).[33] These MOTs are said to test the perceived validity of the three contracts discussed above. Will the reaction of leaders and other colleagues reinforce trust or erode it? Maylett and Wride believe that the implication of trust being breached is dependent on whether it is accidental or deliberate, the frequency and the response.

In 2019 the Edelman Trust Barometer found that 'people have low confidence that societal institutions will help them navigate a turbulent world, so they are turning to a critical relationship: their employer' and employees' expectation that prospective employers will join them in taking action on societal issues, 67 per cent, is nearly as high as their expectations of personal empowerment, 74 per cent, and job opportunity, 80 per cent.[34] Companies are also trusted to take specific actions that both increase profits and improve economic and social conditions.

It is noted that people who work in growth-mindset organizations have 'far more trust in their company and a much greater sense of empowerment, ownership, and commitment'[35] while 'employees in the fixed-mindset companies not only say that their companies are less likely to support them in task-taking and innovation, they are also far more likely to agree that their organizations are rife with cutthroat or unethical behaviour.'[36]

In a further model, Deloitte suggested a model for positive employee experience underpinned by cross-organizational collaboration and communication:

- **meaningful work:** autonomy, select to fit, small, empowered teams, time for slack;
- **supportive management:** clear and transparent goals, coaching, investment in management development, agile performance management;
- **positive work environment:** flexible work environment, humanistic workplace, culture of recognition, fair, inclusive, diverse work environment;
- **growth opportunity:** training and support on the job, facilitated talent mobility, self-directed dynamic learning, high-impact learning culture;
- **trust in leadership:** mission and purpose, continuous investment in people, transparency and honesty, inspiration.[37]

A strong employee experience drives a strong customer experience and the traditional view of organizations of shareholders first, customers second and their people last is being reversed.

According to Gallup, 'the employee experience is the journey an employee takes with your organization. It includes all the interactions an employee has with your organization before, during and after their tenure'[38] and the employee lifecycle defines the critical stages that employers must get right as they have the most influence during the employee experience. Interactions at these points shape employees' perceptions and directly affect employee performance and employer brand – employees have become 'consumers of the workplace'.[39] Gallup suggest that 'purpose, brand and culture are foundations that determine how you customize elements of the employee life cycle and employee experience to represent your organization's unique identity.'[40]

Employee experience vs employee engagement

In his book *The Employee Experience Advantage*, Jacob Morgan differentiates employee experience from employee engagement, noting that 'employee experience is something that creates engaged employees but focuses on the cultural, technological and physical design of the organization to do that'.[41]

It is conceptualized as the intersection of employee expectations, needs and desires and the organization's ability to meet these expectations, needs and desires. There is either an absolute match, some degree of overlap or a complete miss. From his perspective, engagement surveys have become like annual review results, not frequent enough and too long. They measure from engaged downwards, look at the outcome but not the cause and lead to short-term measures to boost engagement but with no sustainable impact.

Morgan creates a framework for employee experience that is divided into 17 attributes between the three environments of physical space, technology and culture.[42]

The physical environment is allocated a weighting of 30 per cent for its contribution to employee experience. Studies have shown that it mediates the relationship between the organization and employee satisfaction and well-being.[43] Morgan suggests that physical environments should be places: where people choose to bring their friends and visitors; that offer flexibility of use; which reflect organizational values; and leverage multiple workspace options.

Studies have shown that flexible job design decreases stress and absenteeism, increases employee health and trust, decreases costs and increases productivity.[44] For instance, supervisor support, control and flexibility in roles had a beneficial effect both for the employees and the organization.[45]

The physical and virtual spaces in which people interact should facilitate communication and be a pleasure to use. People want to feel proud of the places where they live, their homes, and also the places where they work and it is therefore important that the work environment reflects the employer brand. They should also be thoughtfully designed to support agile, flexibly designed workspaces to support the many different work activities.

A technological environment designed to enhance the employee experience should focus on its availability to all and consumer-grade technology, and consider employee needs over business requirements. It is important to roll out new technology as fast as possible and to all employees that can benefit from it. Slow roll-outs may be seen as favouring certain individuals, teams or organizational levels and cause resentment. Technology that is not intuitive or attractive will negatively impact employee experience, as will solutions that are designed to instrumentality deliver on the business case but are not designed with the users in mind. This environment has a 30 per cent weighting.[46]

Finally, the cultural environment is allocated a weighting of 40 per cent and said to be created by ten elements:

- a legitimate sense of purpose;
- a positive stakeholder view of the company;
- employees referring potential colleagues;
- everyone feeling valued, through reward, recognition and voice;
- employees are treated fairly;
- executives and managers act as coaches and mentors;
- employees feel like they are part of a team;

- there is the ability and support to learn new things and progress;
- there is a dedication to employee health and wellness;
- there is a belief in diversity and inclusion.[47]

Moments that matter (MTM) for employees are meaningful and influential, and therefore obvious areas of focus where attention to the employee experience is important.[48] All MTMs are examples of the MOTs, noted above. They can be ongoing relationship moments; moments that are created by the organization; and moments of specific importance to employees such as family events, qualifications, promotions and work anniversaries.

Morgan used his framework to categorize 256 organizations based on their experience score (ExS) in each of the three environments. This delivered nine types of organization:

- **inexperienced:** 20 per cent not actively investing in any of the three environments;
- **technologically emergent:** only focused on the technological environment, 3 per cent;
- **physically emergent:** only focused on the physical environment, 6 per cent;
- **culturally emergent:** only focused on the cultural environment, 20 per cent;
- **engaged:** a focus on the physical and cultural environments, 14 per cent;
- **empowered:** a focus on the technological and cultural environments, 4 per cent;
- **enabled:** a focus on technological and physical environments, 4 per cent;
- **pre-experential:** investing in all three environments but not amazing at any of them, 23 per cent;
- **experiential:** only 6 per cent of the 252 organizations analysed scored highly for ExS in all three environments.[49]

Organizations were then analysed to ascertain whether those that have a high ExS outperform those that have a lower ExS. For the purpose of this analysis Morgan chose independent measures of performance: customer service, innovation, employer brand, admiration and respect. Following this he looked at headcount, headcount growth, turnover, pay, average revenue, average profit, revenue per employee and profit per employee. Finally, he measured stock growth from January 2012 to September 2016. It was found that organizations with a higher ExS outperform those with lower scores.

Experential organizations were 2x more highly rated for customer service compared to all the other categories combined and 4.5x more for innovation. For employer brand it was 2x, admiration 2x and respect 2x.[50]

When it comes to business metrics and financial performance, experiential organizations had 20 per cent lower headcount and '40 per cent lower turnover, 1.5x the employee growth, 2.1x the average revenue, 4.4x the average profit , 2.9x more revenue per employee, and 4.3x more profit per employees when compared with nonExperential organizations.'[51]

His extensive research provides an evidence base for leaders to consider their approach to employee experience.

Employee feedback

Deloitte reported employee experience as being very important by 80 per cent of executives but 59 per cent felt they were not ready or only somewhat ready to address this challenge.[52] Many have not yet made this a priority and the use of technology in the workplace needs to catch up to support this as people expect the same user experience with work-related technology as the best they experience outside of a work context. Technology and data will be used to apply analytical rigour, seek to remove bias and personalize the people experience for the employee of one.

People's experience of their relationship with organizations is being re-considered and employer value propositions redesigned. Engagement is being measured by net promoter scores (NPS) borrowed from marketing, which in this context is the extent to which someone would recommend an organization as an employer – promoters score 9 out of 10, detractors, 0 to 6, and passives 7 and 8. Employer brand messaging not only needs to be internally consistent across media but also with the experience of people in the organization and other stakeholders.

Employees want more regular feedback as individuals but also as teams and opportunities for continuous learning and Glassdoor has published data that suggests for Millennials the ability to learn and progress is the principal brand factor for organizations, and 42 per cent say they are likely to leave as they are not learning fast enough. Lifetime learning is expected, while people will learn in different ways. It will be more interdisciplinary and different methods of learning will include, virtual universities, massive open online courses and short-courses. Employers are not going to be able to provide well-defined career paths, and more responsibility for learning will fall to employees.[53]

In *Humanity Works*, Levit discusses aspects of performance management and development. She predicts that an agile approach will become the norm and performance management will include frequent feedback, crowdsourcing, strengths management, social recognition and skill building. She suggests that key action steps include:

- connecting business philosophy to performance philosophy and linking individual goals to organizational goals;
- establishing a growth mindset;
- increasing feedback frequency;
- doing the 'rounds' to ensure connectivity;
- practising the mechanics of good feedback;

- separating performance from compensation;
- including the tough-to-measure;
- understanding how technology can help;
- careful adoption of agile performance for other leaders.[54]

Gallup advocate a strength-based approach to management, noting that employees who use their strengths on the job are more likely than others to be intrinsically motivated by their work and therefore

> employees who say they use their strengths every day are 8 per cent more productive and 15 per cent less likely to quit their job. Moreover, managers in strengths-based organizations waste little time trying to wring adequate performance out of employees who are unsure if what they can contribute is making a difference.[55]

Continuous performance management is predicted by 91 per cent of respondents to the Deloitte survey who feel they will benefit from better data on which to base people decisions.[56] Leaders should be evaluated based on the quality and frequency of their feedback. They need to think, act and react differently, and as such need to be aware of their emotional, cognitive and behavioural implications.[57]

The following section will discuss how employer brand and employee value proposition are different but must operate together.

Employer brand and the employee value proposition

Employer brand

In *Employer Brand Management*, the employer brand is said to include: a promise of a particular kind of employment experience,[58] an aspiration for the organization's image and reputation[59] and a set of holistic benefits delivered by the organization that are functional, economic and psychological.[60]

If an employer brand is defined in terms of perception and associations, it provides realistic measures of its status and value. It is 'ultimately shaped by what people hear about you, and how they experience you, and not simply by your intended brand messages, however powerfully they may be conceived and executed.'[61]

Employee value proposition

The employer brand defines reputation in terms of qualities and related benefits that are associated with an organization as an employer, while the employee value proposition (EVP) 'describes the defining qualities you most want to be associated with in the future'.[62] It should not be seen as an exhaustive list of all that is offered to employees but the most defining elements of the brand.

Employer brand management describes the 'tools and techniques you apply to ensuring people recognize, experience and believe in the key qualities defined by your EVP'.[63]

The benefits of having a strong employer brand are noted in *Employer Brand Management* as:

- targeting the right potential candidates through careful research;
- having a focused creative spend;
- benefiting from brand awareness that becomes stronger and more differentiated over time;
- the receipt of more inbound applications;
- reducing the conversion premium required to attract mid-career candidates;
- reducing attrition due to poor hiring matches.[64]

In addition to reducing costs, other benefits are associated with enhanced revenue: it is easier to attract higher performers, onboarding is more effective, employee engagement is improved, and there is enhanced effectiveness in communication and change management. Ultimately, 'research shows that building both engagement and performance factors into your EVP and delivering them consistently will lead to higher levels of customer satisfaction and sales than high engagement is capable of delivering alone'.[65]

An employer brand should support the overall business strategy, via the people element of this, and be linked to the organization's core values and purpose. The EVP 'serves to translate the corporate values into the employment context, clarifying their "value" to employees and highlighting those aspects of brand ideology, culture and future aspiration that are of greatest relevance to talent attraction and engagement'.[66] The employer brand contract in *The Employee Experience* includes:

- **Brand wake:** With the impact determined by a combination of the EVP and time.
- **Perceptions of leadership:** The message conveyed by the words and actions of the CEO and senior leadership team.
- **Customers:** Organizations are partly defined by their customers/clients.
- **Values:** What does the organization stand for?
- **Culture:** What does it feel like to work in the organization?
- **Communication:** All digital and non-digital content.
- **Openness:** Transparency in failures as well as successes.
- **Authenticity:** Is the brand real and lived?[67]

To this could be added all relationships, including advisors, as organizations are partly defined by the company they keep.

The employer brand is one facet of the overall organization brand directed at current and future employees rather than current and future customers/clients and as with customers, current and future employees can be segmented and receive a tailored EVP. The employer brand and its value, brand equity, is significantly impacted by the image of the overall sector in which the organization operates, the organization's relative standing against peer group competitors, organization-specific views and the elements of attraction for each employee segment.[68]

Employee segmentation

Employee segmentation should be clear for brand-building and communication. Demand-side segmentation focuses on capabilities and supply-side segmentation defines the qualities different target groups require from an employer. Segments maybe defined in a number of ways, for instance by function, geography, by level of experience, or be diversity and inclusion related. Major employers work with no more than 5 to 10 segments.[69]

In *Employer Branding*, the authors write that

> the attractiveness of an organization to an employee is an important predictor of the ability to recruit and subsequently retain them, so for several years now human resource management (HRM) functions have adopted the marketing concept of brand management and applied this marketing thinking to their HR strategies under the label of employer branding.[70]

Responsibility for employer brand management

In *Employer Brand Management*, Richard Mosley writes that the 'key components of employer brand management (employer branding, recruitment, on-boarding and talent management) deliver a greater impact on revenue and profit growth than any other HR discipline'.[71] Mosley suggests that the core development team should include 'representatives from HR, Talent Management, Marketing and Communications, and where possible line management'.[72] The team is usually led by the human resource function with support from the corporate brand team which for him makes sense, as despite their lack of brand knowledge the human resource professionals involved 'have accountability for most of the processes that shape the employer brand experience'.[73]

Successful employer brand management requires close collaboration between marketing, the human resource function, and research has 'revealed that EB is no more the exclusive sphere of the HR function – previously seen as the conventional guardian. Progressively, HR, marketing and communication professionals are all managing the EB strategy.'[74] Other research reports that employers who make talent the highest priority are no longer making it the sole responsibility of HR.

It was noted that 'EB targets should be shared between HR and marketing directors for HR marketing philosophies to become part of organizational cultures, but EB is still seen more the responsibility of HR with input from marketing as opposed to a shared responsibility with common targets.'[75]

Giving them what they want

In *Respect: Delivering results by giving employees what they really want*, Jack Wiley and Brenda Kowske published research covering over 200,000 employees across some of the world's major economies including the United Kingdom, the USA, China, France, Germany and Japan. They summarized that the fundamental desires of employees can be broken down into seven parts – RESPECT:

- **recognition**: private and public praise from managers and colleagues;
- **exciting work:** a job that is interesting, challenging and fun;
- **security of employment:** job security;
- **pay:** compensation that is equitable;
- **education and career growth:** opportunities to develop their skills, abilities and ultimately their career;
- **conditions at work:** a workplace environment that is well designed ergonomically and for social interaction;
- **truthful:** leadership that is transparent and honest.[76]

In Mercer's report *Talent Trends*, the biggest concerns for all respondents in all geographies and across all generations were health, 61 per cent, wealth, 23 per cent and career, 16 per cent.[77] People are asking for work that works for them holistically, taking them as a whole person:[78]

- **flexible working:** four-day working week, sabbatical, unlimited unpaid time off, work four years at 80 per cent and get a year off for 80 per cent pay;
- **time off:** summer Fridays, more paid holiday;
- **fitness and well-being:** fitness facility access, well-being services, onsite relaxation room;
- **other:** financial advice, company volunteering.

In one article it is suggested that designing the employee experience needs to start with a needs-based segmentation and review of the employee journey map and then undertake research to help understand what the journey feels like from an employee's perspective,[79] and in 2019 Deloitte's *Global Human Capital Trends* suggests that:

- **Employee experience should become a more human experience:** The report suggests that organizations should move beyond thinking about experience in terms of rewards and instead focus on job fit, design and meaning. Some 41 per cent of respondents felt that their organizations were not effective or only somewhat effective in creating a positive work environment; 46 per cent of respondents felt that their organizations were not effective or only somewhat effective in creating meaningful work; and 57 per cent of respondents felt that their organizations were not effective or only somewhat effective in creating growth opportunities. The report proposes that by adding a focus on the meaning of work to employee experience it translates into human experience.[80]

- **There should be more agile models for measuring and rewarding performance:** Fewer than 50 per cent of respondents felt that the rewards strategy was aligned or highly aligned with overall organizational goals, and 72 per cent felt that it was not effective in addressing the diverse needs of alternative workers.[81]

- **Brand resonance should be developed:** 'Listen carefully and learn from data to create a brand proposition that attracts the talent you want'.[82]

It has been reported that half of all employees rated their application and hiring process as average or below average. The line manager's role in shaping how employees experience the organizational culture is pivotal to delivering the brand promise:[83]

- **executives:** culture, 50 per cent; brand recognition, 40 per cent; business model, 28 per cent; reward, 14 per cent; benefits, 10 per cent; diversity and inclusion, 9 per cent;

- **employees:** reward, 33 per cent; benefits, 30 per cent; culture, 22 per cent; diversity and inclusion, 16 per cent; brand recognition, 13 per cent; business model, 9 per cent;

- **human resource function:** interestingly reported higher percentage than executives and other employees for reward, benefits and diversity and inclusion and significantly lower for brand recognition, 9 per cent.[84]

In terms of an employee value proposition, 54 per cent of employees said managing their work–life balance is one of the top five things their company can do to help them thrive at work, compared to 40 per cent in 2018 and 26 per cent in 2017. This sentiment is also reflected in 82 per cent of employees saying that they would be willing to consider working on a freelance basis.[85]

It was found that career support most sought by employees included: clearly defined skills for advancement, future-focused training, transparent pay, regular career conversations, onboarding for success, best in class learning and development tools.

From an employer's perspective, in *The Talent Delusion*, Chamorro-Premuzic challenges recently published thinking, writing that

the idea that organizations are ultimately interested in making their employees happy is hardly realistic. What employers care about, even in the case of non-profit organizations, is productivity, performance and organizational effectiveness. It is only because employee engagement enhances these variables that they are interested in boosting it; not for the sake of making people happy.[86]

However, in *Dying for a Paycheck*, Jeffrey Pfeffer states:

work environments matter. We know they matter for people's engagement, satisfaction, turnover intentions, and performance – findings that constitute a vast research literature in the domain of organizational behaviour. Work environments matter also for people's physical and mental health, and well-being. It follows that concern for life and human sustainability, as well as focus on costs and productivity, needs to include a focus on the workplace and its effects.[87]

Organizations should approach their response carefully; as Chamorro-Premuzic writes in *The Talent Delusion*,

from the late 1960s onwards, with the rise of humanist and positive psychology, HR began to focus on employee well-being, creating a significant shift in how people regard work. We are now living in the aftermath of this era, the age of the spiritual workaholic.[88]

In *Exceptional Talent*, it is noted that 'the employers who are currently winning the battle for exceptional talent are those who understand that they must have long-term human-centric relationships with this talent, from attention to retention and beyond.'[89]

An increasingly important area of employee experience and engagement relates to various aspects of well-being and these are examined below as key tools in attracting and retaining people.

Highlights

- Employee engagement has been examined in relation to the theories of motivation introduced in Chapter 4.

- The importance of employee experience has been discussed in terms of various environments that impact people when they are working.

- These ideas have been linked to the importance of the employer brand and employee value proposition, especially with regard to attracting and retaining people.

Leadership impact

Key themes that leaders should reflect on include:

- the drivers of employee engagement, and links to motivation theory;
- how to design an employee experience that supports high levels of satisfaction and performance;
- link the employee experience to the culture and values of the organization;
- how to use the employee value proposition to attract and retain people.

People management recommendations

Actions to consider:

- Consider using an employee survey; action and feedback on ideas that are generated.
- Focus on employee engagement and monitoring.
- Create and maintain an employer brand – ensure it is communicated internally as well as externally.
- Create and maintain an employee value proposition; include input from employees to ensure relevance for all.

Well-being   15

Introduction

In this chapter, various aspects of well-being are discussed including workplace design and psychological well-being. There is a focus on stress, resilience and the concept of psychological safety.

Finally, we revisit meaning and explore how organizations can help provide a working environment where the people who work for them have the opportunity to do so in a positive and meaningful way.

Chapter summary

The following subjects are discussed in this chapter:

- **well-being and wellness:**
  - frameworks for well-being;
- **workplace design;**
- **psychological well-being;**
- **psychological safety;**
- **stress:**
  - contributors to stress;
  - resilience;
- **neuroscience and well-being;**
- **meaning;**
- **well-being.**

Well-being and wellness

Our health is impacted by our genes and our environment, and the World Health Organization (WHO) defines health as 'a state of complete physical, mental and social well-being, not merely the absence of disease or infirmity'.[1] The National Wellness Institute in the UK defines wellness as a 'conscious, self-directed and evolving process of achieving full potential'[2] while the Oxford Dictionary defines wellness as being well or in good health.

The Oxford Dictionary considers well-being as the state of being that encompasses happiness, good mental and physical health, prosperity and environmental factors, including relationships, that impact our health and wellness. Well-being therefore implies a more holistic view when describing a state of being at a point of time experienced by an individual or group. Wellness, on the other hand, can be seen as a more personal, emotional and, for some, spiritual endeavour.

The National Wellness Institute promotes six dimensions of wellness:

- **emotional:** awareness of feelings and self-regulation, resilience;
- **occupational:** personal satisfaction through work, intrinsic;
- **physical:** physical wellness through exercise and nutrition;
- **social:** an active participation in social life and community;
- **intellectual:** stimulation and growth;
- **spiritual:** contentment in our search for meaning and purpose.

The Healthy Workplace Nudge suggests providing healthy buildings, changing the environment by designing working environments with inbuilt 'nudges' to make healthy choices as easy as possible. The authors note that well-being comes before wellness, that we must care for people before we can help them; that people should undertake work that plays to their natural strengths and build social capital; and that a focus on balancing cost and wellness has ended.[3]

In *Wellbeing at Work*, Ian Hesketh and Cary Cooper describe well-being as either being Eudaimonic, positive ways we identify with our life experience, self-acceptance and a sense of purposeful meaning, or Hedonic, which relates to feelings of pleasure and happiness. They note various types of well-being:

- **psychological well-being:** free from stress, anxiety and depression;
- **physiological well-being:** free from injury or physical ailment;
- **societal well-being:** the quality of life experienced by people in that particular area;
- **financial well-being:** financial stress can very quickly have a huge impact on the other spheres of well-being.[4]

Frameworks for well-being

The National Institute for Health and Care Excellence (NICE) has issued a quality standard, QS147, for employers in relation to the improvement of the mental and physical well-being of workers. The four quality statements cover:

- making health and well-being an organizational priority;
- the role of line managers;
- identifying and managing stress;
- employee involvement in decision-making.[5]

The UKs Health and Safety Executive have established six 'management standards that define the characteristics or culture, of an organization where the risks from work related stress are being effectively managed and controlled':[6]

- **demands:** workload, work patterns and work environment;
- **control:** the degree of decision-making autonomy in how work is completed;
- **support:** encouragement and support from managers and colleagues in addition to the resources required to achieve goals;
- **relationships:** the promotion of psychological safety in general communication and performance feedback;
- **role:** the degree to which roles are clear, non-conflicting and congruent with the experience, abilities and desires of the incumbent;
- **changes:** the way organizational change is managed.[7]

In *The Human Capital Imperative*, Alan Coppin considers the following model to be definitive for organizational well-being strategies. An outer wheel includes business benefits and an inner wheel includes employee actions, while five inner segments are the broad cultural areas that organizations need to address for well-being. The author states that addressing all elements of the model will increase employee well-being, engagement, and business productivity through:

- '**better physical and psychological health:** creating a safe and pleasant work environment by promoting a psychically safe working environment and promoting healthy behaviours, both psychical and mental;
- **better work:** creating a happy, engaging environment of good work, which is underpinned by good job design, autonomy, variety, employee voice, talent management, employee security, and a management style and culture that promotes mutual trust and respect;
- **better relationships:** promoting better communication both inside and outside the workplace, to ensure employees maintain the social capital they need for good mental health well-being;
- **better specialist support:** ensuring teams manage health issues at work in a proactive way, and facilitate a more efficient return to work for those off work, by equipping specialist teams, line managers and all employees with information and skills to maintain their own health and support others;

- **working well:** positioning employee well-being as a boardroom issue, creating a culture of well-being where employees feel trusted, respected, with a strategic proactive approach to well-being, underpinned by strong governance and reporting arrangements.'[8]

It is worth remembering the statement in *Wellbeing at Work*, that 'without doubt, the relationship that workers have with their immediate line manager is the one that can impact most on their well-being.'[9]

A report by the British Psychological Society, *Psychology at Work: Improving wellbeing and productivity*, gives guidance on building a psychologically healthy workplace, supporting those who have difficulty at work and supporting people into appropriate work.[10] The report recommends that jobs are thoughtfully designed, and guidance from NICE and the HSE on improving psychological well-being at work is implemented. It is suggested that this includes regular discussion of employee well-being and psychological safety at board level.

The report highlights neurodiversity, which describes differences in people's skills and abilities and encompasses a range of conditions including dyslexia, affecting up to 10 per cent of the UK population, attention deficit hyperactivity disorder (ADHD), affecting up to 2 per cent of the UK population and autism, which affects up to 1.5 per cent of the population. Not everyone wishes to disclose these conditions and they may not be immediately observable to colleagues. There is risk that inconsistent performance caused by these conditions is blamed on a poor attitude or lack of ability, instead of recognizing that workplace adjustments may be required.

It also discusses a change in approach in considering reasons for ill health from a biological medical model to a biopsychosocial approach that is more holistic and inclusive as it also considers circumstantial social and psychological elements which may contribute to ill health.

In addition to this, an important aspect of employee experience is the work environment, which also has a significant impact on mental and physical health. We therefore now turn to workplace design.

Workplace design

The Healthy Workplace Nudge reported that CBRE experienced a business and cultural transformation with wellness at its core and received the first WELL certification for commercial office space from the International Well Building Institute. The more recent WELL v2 includes 10 concepts that impact well-being: air, water, nourishment, light, movement, thermal comfort, sound, materials, mind and community.[11] *The Future Office* lists three key 'hygiene' factors, remember Herzberg, that can have an impact on well-being and productivity:[12]

- **noise:** sounds that are loud, sharp, unpredictable and uncontrollable, although for some too little noise can impact concentration;
- **light:** prolonged periods of exposure to artificial light and lack of control over glare or access to daylight;
- **indoor climate:** an environment with extreme temperatures and/or humidity, and lack of control over it.

The workplace environment must be designed while considering environmental, physiological and psychological dimensions, and if done well, this can lead to improved work practices, higher productivity, greater innovation and lower stress. In *The Future Office*, Nicola Gillen focuses on six facets of well-being 'through which well-being at work can be understood, supported and improved, truly holistically':[13]

- **Physiological health:** Physiological health allows us to feel fit and get through our daily activities without undue fatigue or physical stress.
- **Psychological health:** Psychological health incorporates mental health and emotional well-being, which includes job-related happiness, satisfaction and a positive-negative emotional balance.
- **Social health:** Being socially well means one is well connected with others at work, feels part of a community or communities, and has access to support networks.
- **Intellectual health:** People who are intellectually well at work have the ability to use their knowledge and skills to perform well and are given the right input and stimulation to develop their skills further. Intellectual well-being refers to the level of satisfaction with the intellectual challenge that their work provides.
- **Spiritual health:** Feeling spiritually well refers to the match between an individual's personal values and ethics and those inherent in their work activities and the organization.
- **Financial health:** Material well-being relates to financial rewards, such as income or other remunerations. People who feel materially well are satisfied with the quality or quantity of rewards they receive for their work and experience a sense of fairness around the distribution of rewards.[14]

Gillen references a research project which was designed to test how environmental facets of the workplace, assessed objectively through quality standards, and subjectively, through perception, as well as through work-related factors, such as job design and management culture, predict 'physical, mental, social, intellectual, spiritual and material dimensions of well-being, performance and satisfaction.'[15] The author summarizes the findings as follows:

- **Manager capability is a key indicator for satisfaction and well-being:** People who feel supported by their managers experience higher levels of mental, social, intellectual and spiritual well-being, and report better job satisfaction.

- **Protocols as vehicles to objective conversation – agreeing on ways of sharing workplace:** Adherence to protocols, objective norms of behaviour, is positively associated with mental, social and spiritual facets of well-being, as well as workplace satisfaction.

- **People want to be proud of their workplace:** Employees report being more satisfied with their workplace when the office creates a strong, positive experience for visitors through an appealing look and ambience. The workplace is a significant contributor to the brand, and an important contributor to staff satisfaction levels.

- **Choice and control as drivers of well-being:** A crucial indicator of well-being at work is the degree to which people feel autonomous, and that they have freedom over how and where they do their work.[16]

The Future Office concludes by predicting how technology, human uniqueness, new ways of working and delivery of the environment will impact the workspace in the near future and beyond:[17]

- **Impact of technology:** The digitization of work provides mobility and flexibility; the use of voice instructions will require noise regulation through design; the modular design and 3D printing of workspaces; augmentation of robotics.

- **Impact of human uniqueness:** The office will remain a place for social interaction and collaboration; we will continue to add value with creativity, communication, empathy and data interpretation; Generation Z, otherwise known as 'centennials' will multitask at work; the accommodation of four generations in the workplace and the increase in mentoring; driven by the need for whole-life learning, workplaces will become places for development as much as innovation and production; robot taxes to subsidize caring jobs, or those displaced from work, in the form of universal income.

- **New ways of working:** The widespread adoption of agile and remote working, workplaces will become valued spaces for meaningful and serendipitous interaction; organizations will occupy less space but the space they do inhabit will be higher quality and will promote higher quality interaction and innovation; mega-corporations will exist in campus-style city districts attracting people from all over the world and delivering exemplary, and stimulating, well-being environments; independent, free spirits will support these large organizations.

- **Delivering the workspace environment:** Wearable devices, controllable environment and the internet of things; modular construction, shorter lead-times and reusable material; the use of AI and robotics in the design and construction process; new skills for architects; the centricity of people in the design process.

Psychological well-being

In *The Social Psychology of Organizations*, Joanna Wilde notes that initially work on stress at work focused on the individual and how they were dysfunctional. However, the psychological environment of the workplace is now a focus and 'there is consistent evidence that high job demands, low control and effort–reward imbalance are risk factors for mental and physical health problems'.[18]

Stress is linked to heart disease, bronchitis and musculoskeletal disorders,[19] with the annual cost to Europe of work-related depression estimated at €617 billion.[20]

Wild has developed a model that shows: sources of workplace toxicity, the overall workplace psychological environment and the micro-processes that mitigate or maximize toxicity:

- sources of workplace toxicity:[21]
  - **structural:** formal design, informal – control, communication;
  - **cognitive:** bias, heuristics, stereotyping;
  - **behavioural:** bullying, exclusion, harassment;
  - **symbolic:** includes rituals, performance reviews, dispute resolution, work–life balance;
- workplace psychological environment:[22]
  - **contributing/justice disorders:** contribution is not fairly enabled and appreciate;
  - **belonging/attachment disorders:** no sense of belonging, inability to build relationships in or out of group, over-attachment;
  - **meaning making/accountability disorders:** dissonance between what is said and done on multiple levels;
- micro-processes that mitigate or maximize toxicity:[23]
  - accountability;
  - compassion;
  - appreciation;
  - growth.

In *The Fearless Organization*, Amy Edmondson writes that today's employees, at all levels, spend 50 per cent more time collaborating than they did 20 years ago, in the mid 1990s, and

> for an organization to truly thrive in a world where innovation can make the difference between success and failure, it is not enough to hire smart, motivated people... For knowledge work to flourish, the workplace must be one where people feel able to share their knowledge! This means sharing concerns, questions, mistakes, and half-formed ideas.[24]

Psychological safety

Psychological safety is seen as a key antecedent of organizational success, and a 'crucial source of value creation in organizations operating in a complex, changing environment'.[25] It is described as:

> a climate in which people are comfortable expressing and being themselves. More specifically, when people have psychological safety at work, they feel comfortable sharing concerns and mistakes without fear of embarrassment or retribution. They are confident that they can speak up and won't be humiliated, ignored, or blamed. They know they can ask questions when they are unsure about something. They tend to trust and respect their colleagues.[26]

An individual's willingness to share, experiment, learn and innovate is to some degree related to their feeling of psychological safety, and research has shown that those lower down organization hierarchies generally feel less safe than those with higher status.[27]

In *Well-Being: Productivity and happiness at work*, Ivan Robertson and Cary Cooper note that people with higher levels of psychological well-being (PWB) perform better than those reporting lower levels of PWB, with the results predicting job performance more effectively than job satisfaction. A one-point increase on their PWB scale predicted an 8.8 per cent rise in productivity.[28]

A 2017 Gallup poll found that only 30 per cent of employees strongly agreed with the statement that their opinions count at work, and Gallup calculated that by 'moving that ratio to six in 10 employees, organizations could realize a 27 per cent reduction in turnover, a 40 per cent reduction in safety incidents and a 12 per cent increase in productivity'.[29]

In *The Fearless Organization*, Edmondson notes that psychological safety and performance standards are two separate but related dimensions:[30]

- **Apathy zone:** When both psychological safety performance standards are low, people go to work, but their hearts and minds are elsewhere and they choose self-protection over exertion.

- **Comfort zone:** When there is high psychological safety but low performance standards, people generally enjoy working with one another, are open and collegial but not challenged by the work.

- **Anxiety zone:** When performance standards are high but psychological safety is low employees are anxious about speaking up, and both work quality and workplace safety suffer.

- **Learning zone:** When performance standards and psychological safety are both high, this is also the high-performance zone where people can collaborate, learn from each other, and deliver complex, innovative work.

In *Black Box Thinking*, Mathew Syed writes that when it comes to mistakes, the more unfair the culture, the greater the punishment for the honest mistakes and the faster the rush to judgement, the deeper this information is buried. This means that lessons are not learned, so the same mistakes are made again and again, leading to more punitive punishment, and even deeper concealment and back-covering.[31]

When a culture is unfair and opaque, it creates multiple perverse incentives. When a culture is fair and transparent, on the other hand, it bolsters the adaptive process.[32]

In *The Neuroscience of Leadership Coaching*, Bossons et al differentiate between exploitation and exploration behaviours. When we perceive a situation to be positive it can be associated with feelings of choice, which we exploit; however, where we perceive a situation to be working less well, we may feel the need to change and therefore increase our level of risk-taking. They note that neuroscientists have identified the cingulate cortex, where risk is assessed, as being involved in controlling the point at which we are prepared to move between exploitation to exploration. This area of the brain is responsible for self-regulation, error detection and conflict monitoring.[33]

Emotional dissonance is the conflict originating from expressed and experienced emotions.[34] Regardless of emotional dissonance, employees are expected to display the situationally required emotions, which involves emotional labour, and in *The Neuroscience of Organizational Behavior* Constant Beugré states that 'emotional labour includes two components: surface acting and deep acting. Surface acting consists of modifying one's behaviour to be consistent with expected emotions while continuing to hold different internal feelings'[35] and 'deep acting consists of modifying one's behaviour to match the required emotions'.[36]

Stress

In *Wellbeing at Work* the authors note that some stress is good for us, if it is moderate, short-lived and increases energy, as it can bring about challenge and stimulation.[37]

However, *Do We Need HR?* states that when stress is severe and enduring there is a serious impact on our health. Mental health problems come at great cost to individuals, organizations and society as a whole. The costs of depression are estimated at one per cent of Europe's GDP; globally, mental ill health is estimated to account for a cumulative output loss of US$16 trillion global output in the 20 years from 2011.[38] In the United States, workplace stress is said to cost employers nearly US$200 billion every year in healthcare costs,[39] while studies have shown a positive link between organizational health and performance. In one case, for instance, shareholder returns were three times higher for healthy companies than unhealthy ones.[40]

For individual organizations in the most developed economies, mental health is now often the most common cause of sickness absence, accounting for 30–50 per cent of all new disability benefit claims in OECD countries, and for up to 40 per cent of time lost with 'presenteeism' (lost productivity while present at work), adding at least 1.5 times to the cost of absenteeism.[41]

In *Corporate Emotional Intelligence*, Gareth Chick writes that while fear is a natural and helpful emotion related to actual or perceived threats, anxiety is an unhelpful emotion related to the expectation of a future threat and is associated with rumination which inhibits problem-solving ability.[42]

In *The Psychology of Behaviour at Work*, Furnham notes that stress has a variety of cognitive, physiological and behavioural symptoms and consequences:

- An individual will cognitively evaluate the situation and their perceived coping skills.
- The associated physiological symptoms are linked to the innate fight-or-flight response when faced with a stressor, including fear, anxiety, and defensive attitudes and behaviour.
- Job-related behavioural symptoms of stress include problems with concentration and judgement, sickness, absenteeism and lack of cooperation.[43]

He also states that some people are more susceptible to the adverse consequences of job pressures than others because of their personality, for instance, Type A behaviour, which is associated with impatience and hostility, and an external locus of control. Three major signs of burnout at work are emotional exhaustion, depersonalized relationships and lower personal accomplishments.

Contributors to stress

Furnham suggests various elements that contribute to stress:

- **role conflict:** stress resulting from conflicting demands within the work place;
- **role ambiguity:** stress resulting from uncertainty and ambiguity in role, responsibilities and situation;
- **role imbalance:** stress from having too little or too much to do;
- **responsibility for others:** stress resulting from a sense of duty to others and the need to regulate behaviour and performance;
- **lack of social support:** stress from being socially isolated or ignored, not having a supportive ear to listen and/or provide guidance;
- **lack of participation in decisions:** stress from helplessness and alienation, loss of input and control over decisions that have significant impact;

- **poor performance appraisal:** stress from the absence of feedback, feedback that is perceived to be biased or in some way unfair, and negative feedback that is surprising but undisputed;

- **working conditions:** stress from poor working conditions, such as extremes of temperature, loud noise, crowding, poor lighting, poor equipment and poor ergonomics;

- **organizational change:** stress that comes from adaption, such as the speed, type and amount of organizational change;

- **career development:** stress from feeling stuck or constrained in their career;

- **home–work interface:** stress from conflicts over the time and commitment allocated between home and work.[44]

In terms of work-related behaviour, it has been reported that the average manager has less than six and a half hours per week of totally uninterrupted time to get work done,[45] and a CMI study, *The Quality of Working Life*, on out-of-hours email usage found that:

- Sixty-one per cent of managers said that technology has made it difficult to switch off from work.

- One in five managers say they now check their emails all the time outside of working hours; over half check them frequently.

- Nearly 40 per cent of managers are looking to employers to restrict out-of-hours email access, including 43 per cent of those who check emails all of the time.

Those who struggle to switch off from work report lower levels of personal productivity and job satisfaction and higher levels of stress.[46] It is important for leaders to understand that this is often mirrored in those who work for them.

Neuroscience for Leadership refers to a number of studies that have shown that certain personal characteristics are all conducive to managing responses to stress, and that they appear to correlate with the Big Five personality traits. These include:

- openness to new tasks and new people;
- a greater tendency towards attachment emotions;
- feeling in control;
- not having high levels of anxiety;
- being secure in one's status;
- realistic optimism;
- the ability to adapt by reframing stressful events and situations;
- close, supportive personal relationships.[47]

As it is important to develop our resilience and ability to manage stress, a three-pronged strategy for stress management in organizations has been suggested:[48]

- **primary prevention:** through stress reduction;
- **secondary prevention:** through stress management;
- **tertiary prevention:** through employee assistance programmes and workplace counselling.

Given the pressures of daily life in both personal and professional realms, it is helpful to understand the concept of resilience and its practical implications for managing anxiety, stress and other mental health challenges.

Resilience

Resilience can be defined as 'the ability of an individual or organization to expeditiously design and implement positive adaptive behaviours matched to the immediate situation, while enduring minimal stress'[49] or the 'positive psychological capacity to rebound or bounce back from adversity, uncertainty, conflict, failure or even positive change, progress and increased responsibility'.[50]

It is explained in *The Neuroscience of Leadership Coaching* that the amount of stress that is perceived at any given time is called the allostatic load, and that resilient people are less easily stressed. They reference studies showing that resilience is related to positivity, and note that people who are more positive about their experiences are less stressed and more resilient.[51]

In *Wellbeing at Work*, Hesketh and Cooper state that people who are highly resilient have up to thirty times more activation in the left prefrontal area than those who are less resilient.[52] Key elements that impact resilience include:

- facing fears with a positive attitude;
- cognitive flexibility;
- coping skills and supportive networks;
- role models;
- physical well-being;
- moral compass.[53]

In *Developing Resilience*, Michael Neenan notes that resilience comprises a set of 'flexible, cognitive, behavioural and emotional responses to acute or chronic adversities which can be unusual or common place'.[54] These responses can be learnt and so are available to everyone. To achieve and retain resilience Neenan suggests:

- learning and practising skills in everyday life;
- not rushing to bounce back – instead glide/soar;

- having sturdy but flexible attitudes and acting on them;
- acknowledging emotions but changing your thinking for more positive outcomes;
- focusing on what is within your control;
- believing in and accepting yourself.[55]

Furnham outlines methods of stress management that can be adopted by individuals and these include: changing their thinking about situations through physical exercise; improved patterns of nutrition and sleep; mindfulness; cognitive self-coaching; and cognitive behavioural therapy. Organizations can help by: assessing the role–person fit; assessing goals; improving work-based relationships; and providing a healthy physical and mental work environment.[56]

A thoughtful approach to workforce well-being is effective. In 2008, PricewaterhouseCoopers assessed 55 wellness programme interventions in UK companies across a range of industries and sizes. They reported finding an average 45 per cent reduction in sickness absence, 18 per cent reduction in staff turnover, 16 per cent reduction in accidents/injuries, an increase in productivity and a drop of 7 per cent in health and employer liability insurance claims.[57]

Neuroscience and well-being

In *The Neuroscience of Leadership Coaching*, Bossons et al state that the neural response to stress is widely distributed within the brain. The authors reference research that identifies the key structures involved and these include:

> the hypothalamus (hormonal response), the amygdala (response to threat), the nucleus accumbens (response to reward), the orbital and ventromedial frontal cortex (self regulation, identity, risk and reward) and hippocampus (memory for stressful events), the dorsolateral and dorsomedial prefrontal cortex (dmPFC) (executive functions including working memory, attention and inhibition) and the cingulate cortex (error detection).[58]

They also note that studies have demonstrated decision fatigue can impair our ability to trust others. Leaders need to exert self-regulation to work through decision fatigue, and subsequently they are unable to address important decisions that arise after this depletion. It is therefore important to budget the use of decision resources.[59]

The authors describe the mechanisms that link our feelings to our health:

- chemical or hormonal, from the endocrine system;
- nervous, from the central nervous system comprising of your brain and spinal cord or peripheral nervous system;
- psychological, from thoughts and perceptions.[60]

Stress triggers various neurotransmitters such as adrenalin, a short-term re-action to perceived threats, and cortisol, a longer term harmful chronic stress response which can damage the hippocampus, which is important for memory retention, and reduces our immunity.[61]

They cite the results of research that found people in higher positions of authority have lower levels of cortisol and reported anxiety:

> Leadership is thus associated with lower levels of stress. This counters the conventional wisdom that the higher up you are in a hierarchy, the more stressed you are. The researchers make it clear that the lower stress levels of leaders may either be a contributory factor to their high position, and/or a result of it. They proposed that a key factor in the lower stress levels is the greater sense of control, a psychological resource known to have a stress-buffering effect.[62]

With regard to anxiety, Bossons et al note, 'The fact that different people become anxious in different situations suggests that it is our perception of the situation, rather than anything about the situation per se, that causes the anxiety. Change the perception and you will change the response in the amygdala.'[63] They also explain that our emotional state, created by the pattern of activity in the prefrontal cortex and amygdala, can also be changed relatively easily, and that

> If the right prefrontal cortex (avoidance emotions) is more active than the left (approach emotions), and the amygdala is active, it is likely that your mood will be sad. If, by contrast, your left prefrontal cortex is active and the amygdala is inactive, it is likely that you will feel happy or maybe even angry.[64]

Importantly, they explain that 'when we imagine or remember an emotional state, we recreate a similar pattern of activity in the brain – our brain does not differentiate fully between felt, remembered or imagined emotions.'[65] This means that it should be possible to change our approach to anxiety.

Meaning

At the foot of a chestnut-tree, Sartre's character Roquentin had a clear vision that the feeling of nausea that increasingly came upon him was due to his perception of life as random, absurd and meaningless which itself confirmed and defined his existence.[66] In *The Will to Meaning*, Victor Frankl believed that the root cause of many modern psychological disorders originates from a lack of recognition of meaning in life situations, which creates an existential vacuum[67] and it is therefore helpful to understand how meaning and purpose are considered in the workplace.

In *The Why of Work*, the Ulrichs consider that the underlying cause of many presenting problems in business today is a deficit of meaning and that:

- 'Employees' ability to find meaning in their work leverages and sustains their competencies and commitment.

- The collective competence and commitment of employees creates organization capabilities.
- These capabilities address the presenting problems facing organizations today, leading to sustained organizational success.'[68]

They suggest that leaders should help employees find meaning at work by learning and applying the following seven drivers of meaning:[69]

- **increasing clarity about identity and signature strengths:** evolving their identity by using their personal values and strengths at work;
- **gaining a sense of purpose to understand better what motivates us:** staying grounded in a purpose and a direction that connects personal drives to a common good;
- **managing work complexity through teamwork:** enjoying satisfying relationships where they feel respected and attached;
- **replacing social isolation with positive work settings:** creating positive work environments that sustain their productivity;
- **identifying and responding to challenges that we care about and engage us:** tackling challenges that invite growth and innovation;
- **growing from change by learning and becoming resilient:** finding value even in setbacks as they learn and bounce back;
- **building sources of delight and civility into our work routines:** appreciating the daily delights of civility, creativity, humour, playfulness, and pleasure.

This will help address the following problems:

- declining mental health and happiness: through positive psychology;
- increased environmental demands that shape social responsibility, organization purpose, and individual motivation: through social responsibility, organization purpose, and individual motivation;
- increased complexity of work: through high-performing teams;
- increased isolation: through a positive work environment, organization culture;
- low employee commitment: through employee engagement;
- growing disposability: through growth, learning and resilience;
- greater hostility and enmity: through civility and happiness.[70]

In *The Hope Circuit*, Martin Seligman writes that

people who prefer meaning, *eudemonia*, to pleasure, *hedonia*, have distinguishable genetic profiles and the pursuit of meaning and engagement is much more predictive of life satisfaction than the pursuit of pleasure; externalities together account for no more than 15 per cent of variance in life satisfaction.[71]

Practical implications

Thriving at Work: The independent review of mental health and employers (also known as the Farmer review) in the United Kingdom estimates that the impact of poor mental health costs the UK economy up to £99 billion every year.[72] From a survey of 674 managers, 35 per cent of respondents felt work was a contributing factor to their mental ill health, but only 17 per cent felt their organizations were supportive.[73] On a positive note, 72 per cent felt they could discuss mental health issues with colleagues, vs 63 per cent in 2017, 67 per cent felt they could discuss them with their managers compared to 56 per cent in 2017 and 58 per cent felt their organizations culture is open and accepting of mental health issues, up from 46 per cent in 2018.[74]

Another UK report on mental health in the workplace, *Mental Health at Work Report 2017*, found that 60 per cent of employees have experienced mental health issues due to their work or where work was a related factor; and almost one in three employees have been diagnosed with a mental health issue. Consistent with the 2017 findings of the Roffey Park research, 53 per cent of employees feel comfortable talking about mental health issues at work. While 91 per cent of managers agree that what they do affects the well-being of their staff, less than 24 per cent of them have received any training in mental health and, somewhat worryingly, only 49 per cent would welcome such training.[75]

In *Talent Trends*, Mercer suggest organizations should build thriving organizations. A thriving organization experiences business success, is resilient and adaptive and has a positive social impact; a thriving workforce is diverse and inclusive, energized and focused and is committed to health and wellness; a thriving employee grows and contributes, is empowered and connected and is healthy and energized.[76] However, only 41 per cent of organizations focus on physical wellbeing, and only 37 per cent on psychological and 35 per cent on financial wellbeing.[77]

Those who say they thrive at work tend to be higher in the organization: middle managers, 68 per cent; first-line supervisors, 49 per cent; and individual contributors, 29 per cent. The 'individual contributors rate their company lower on pay equity, purpose, and fostering an inclusive culture. They also report that they are rewarded only for performance against financial or activity metrics; not for their other contributions.'[78] Mercer differentiate between loyalty contracts, engagement contracts and thrive contracts:[79]

- **Loyalty contract:** The deal: basic needs: pay, benefits, security. Basic assumption: workers are assets to be retained. Value proposition: pay and benefits for time and output. Main concern: turnover.

- **Engagement contract:** The deal: psychological needs: achievement, camaraderie, equity. Basic assumption: employees are assets to be acquired and optimized. Value proposition: a broader set of rewards in exchange for organizational engagement. Main concern: motivation.

- **Thrive contract:** The deal: growth needs, purpose, meaning, impact. Basic assumption: people and machines are value creators to grow and leverage. Value proposition: individualized rewards in exchange for a wide range of contributions. Main concern: stagnation.

A thriving work environment promotes psychological investment and a growth mindset and supports this by moving from a culture of wellness to one of well-being:[80]

- **physical:** energy, health risk, awareness, prevention, nutrition, exercise, sleep;
- **emotional:** resilience, mindfulness, stress management, learning, social engagement;
- **financial:** security, life planning, retirement, debt, management, insurance;
- **social:** belonging, inclusion, togetherness, community, trust.

With regard to one item, sleep, in *Why We Sleep*, Walker notes that a study on lack of sleep undertaken with US companies found insufficient sleep cost between US$2,000 and US$3,500 per employee per year in lost productivity and that individuals sleeping for fewer than seven hours a night reduce GDP by 2.9 per cent in Japan, at a cost of US$138 billion, and 2.3 per cent in America at a cost of US$411 billion.[81] He also reports that low-quality sleep negatively impacts leaders' personal effectiveness and can lower team engagement. NASA discovered that 'naps as short as 26 minutes in length still offered a 34 per cent improvement in task performance and more than 50 per cent increase in overall alertness'.[82]

One study synthesized research evidence concerning the most popular leadership conceptualizations and their associations with major mental health-related outcomes and job performance. The conclusions were as follows:

- **Destructive leadership behaviours:** 'The consistent associations of destructive leadership behaviours and poor mental health should induce organizations to prevent all forms of aggressive or abusive leadership behaviours, because destructive leadership seems not only to deteriorate mental health but also to reduce the levels of positive mental health states.'[83]
- **Motivational leadership behaviours:** 'Although motivational and inspirational leadership, intellectual stimulation, shared vision, encouragement and empowering leadership, at least as captured to some extent by the concept of transformational leadership, are usually evaluated regarding their contribution to leader effectiveness, they may also act as instruments of an overall occupational health strategy fostering positive mental health and reducing the risk of mental health symptoms. Leaders may thus motivate followers by providing the necessary tools for increasing job self-efficacy and a higher sense of personal accomplishment.'[84]

- **Task and relational leadership:** 'It is desirable that the well-known conceptualizations of task-oriented and relations-oriented leadership are appropriately combined in order to increase the positive effects resulting from each class of behaviours. For instance, whereas task-related behaviours may increase well-being and psychological functioning by means of a well-designed assignment of work tasks and a transparent planning and monitoring of work processes, a relations-oriented leadership may be enacted to reduce negative mental health states associated with followers' socio-emotional needs.'[85]

- **Leadership communication:** 'Communicative processes such as feedback, availability of information, and communicative support may reduce role, task, and interpersonal conflicts and contribute to the formulation of efficient problem-solving strategies.'[86]

- **Leadership EI:** 'Emotion-related processes such as leaders' emotional intelligence skills and appraisal of emotions are also important to enhance, because they may play a fundamental role in emotion regulation, stress coping, and fostering of positive affect experiences in occupational contexts.'[87]

The role of managers is to

> act as talent advocates for the enterprise, facilitating movement and understanding individuals' career goals; hold 'career conversations with purpose' to help identify learning opportunities as part of team members' professional growth plans; and monitor workload, complexity, and change fatigue, especially with remote workers, to support the team's physical and emotional well-being.[88]

The results of a Deloitte survey with nearly 10,000 respondents in 119 countries suggests five design principles for social enterprises to support their workforce:[89]

- giving individual and organizational purpose and meaning;
- leveraging technology to increase levels of ethics and fairness;
- designing jobs, work and organizational missions to nurture personal growth and sense of personal impact;
- facilitating collaboration and personal connections and relationships that move beyond digital;
- transparency and openness in a psychologically safe environment with a growth mindset.

Embedding a higher sense of purpose into the employee value proposition unlocks individual potential and spurs people to be change agents: the thrive contract, careers people crave, commitment to health and well-being.[90] As Jefferey Pfeffer notes,

> giving people more control over their work life and providing them with social support fosters high levels of physical and mental health. A culture of social

support also reinforces for employees that they are valued, and thus helps in a company's efforts to attract and retain people. Job control, meanwhile, has a positive impact on individual performance and is one of the most important predictors of job satisfaction and work motivation, ranking as more important even than pay.[91]

Personal growth is impacted by the learning and development opportunities provided to people in organizations. Development is discussed in the following chapter.

Highlights

- Wellness and well-being have been examined with regard to preventing physical and mental harm, especially stress. This included thinking around workplace design and the future workplace.
- Psychological well-being is a key component.
- Stress has been explored.
- Resilience and having meaning at work were also examined.
- Neuroscience and practical implications were discussed.

Leadership impact

Key themes that leaders should reflect on include:

- the importance of work and workplace design to support well-being;
- putting psychological health on the same footing as physical health;
- how to spot stress in the workplace, and then how to deal with it;
- building resilience across the workforce, particularly during change;
- leaders need to think about their own mental health and well-being; ensure that they are fit to lead.

People management recommendations

Actions to consider:

- Make use of ergonomics expertise to optimize the work environment.
- Ensure access to occupational psychology expertise as required.
- Train staff to be mental health first-aiders, as well as physical health first-aiders.

- Ensure you have appropriate support available to assist those who may be experiencing stress.
- Provide resilience training for all staff.
- Messaging about the importance of mental well-being as well as physical well-being.
- Consider use of employee assistance programmes from experienced outsourced providers.

The future of people development

Introduction

Developing individuals is key to developing organizations, and contributing to the success of both in achieving purpose and meaning.

Given the complex needs of individuals, including leaders, to hone their current abilities and develop new ones, leaders must focus on learning and development in new ways. Its importance should be obvious by now, but how will it be conceived and delivered? These questions are examined in this chapter.

Chapter summary

The following subjects are discussed in this chapter:

- **the future of learning and development:**
  - skills;
  - high-impact learning that lasts;
  - lifelong learning;
- **personality;**
- **mindset and belief;**
- **attribution theory;**
- **coaching.**

The future of learning and development

In the *2018 Deloitte Millennial Survey: Millennials disappointed in business unprepared for industry 4.0*, they found that over 50 per cent of Gen Z and most Millennials feel that industry 4.0 will augment their jobs and free time to be more creative, human and value added. Only 36 per cent of Millennials and 29 per cent of Gen Z feel they are ready for it. While 41 per cent of men and 52 per cent of senior team members believe they are ready, only 30 per cent of women and 28 per cent of junior team members feel they are ready. Only 36 per cent of Millennials and 42 per cent of Gen Z feel they are being supported in preparing for industry 4.0. However, for those intending to stay for five years 46 per cent feel supported, and for those intending to leave within two years only 28 per cent feel supported. Around 80 per cent of Millennials feel on-job training, continuous professional development, self-directed learning and formal training and development courses provided by employers are important for their performance. The Deloitte report concludes that the 'role of employer as educator will take on even greater significance'.[1]

The World Economic Forum's white paper, *Realizing Human Potential in the Fourth Industrial Revolution*, outlines key action areas for a responsive education ecosystem that can meet the needs of both today's and tomorrow's labour market. It is aimed at policy makers, education specialists and the private sector, and sets out eight areas of collaboration: early childhood education; 'future ready' curricula; professionalized teaching workforce; early exposure to the workplace and ongoing career guidance; digital fluency; robust and respected technical and vocational education; a new deal on lifelong learning; and an openness to education innovation.[2]

Mercer believe that, given the speed of technological change, individuals must embrace learning and organizations need to consider how they create a lab mindset environment that is a catalyst for innovation. One role of managers is therefore to 'clarify direction and build change readiness; champion change; embrace the new; and model lifelong learning; and promote transparency and objectivity in feedback to encourage learning for the future.'[3]

In *Creating Impact Through Future Learning*, Filip Dochy and Mien Segers note that, to achieve sustainable employability, 'in addition to professional expertise in terms of knowledge and skills as a basic condition, a great deal of flexibility to deal with change, and to anticipate it, is necessary for individual employees as well as for the organization.'[4]

All employees need to learn and continuously develop. It is critical for their future, for the future of their organizations and for society as a whole; there is a need for frequent learning opportunities, knowledge and skills should be updated and sustainable workforces created that are less interested in turnover and that are able to fulfil future competence needs.[5] Personal growth through development has also been noted as a significant motivator for employees from various generational cohorts.

Skills

In 2019, the OECD published a list of skills for the future:[6]

- **foundation skills:** numeracy, literacy, digital literacy;
- **transversal cognitive and meta-cognitive skills:** critical thinking, complex problem solving, creative thinking, learning to learn and self-regulation;
- **social and emotional skills:** such as conscientiousness, responsibility, empathy, self-efficacy and collaboration;
- **professional, technical and specialized knowledge and skills:** to meet the demands of specific occupations but with transfer potential.

The above list should be considered together with the results of studies discussed in Chapter 7 relating to future skill requirements and skill gaps.

In Mercer's report *Global Talent Trends 2019*, respondents identified a variety of learning methods to keep their skills relevant: 59 per cent employee-directed learning; 55 per cent formal reskilling programmes; and 50 per cent informal hands-on learning. A large majority, 83 per cent, of employees see keeping their skills up to date as primarily their responsibility, rather than the organization they work for.[7] Employees are split, with 56 per cent expecting their company to provide learning based on their level and career aspirations, and 44 per cent asking for a learning budget to spend as they see fit with the top technical skills, future readiness skills and power skills being listed as follows:[8]

- **top technical skills:**
  - machine learning;
  - blockchain for business;
  - deep learning;
- **making your organization future ready:**
  - digital leadership;
  - digital transformation;
  - agile project management;
- **essential power skills:**
  - inclusive leadership;
  - critical thinking and problem solving;
  - business model innovation.

In a Deloitte report, *Global Human Capital Trends*, the top-rated trend in the survey was the need to improve learning and development, with 86 per cent of respondents saying this was important or very important. They advocate learning in the flow, where it is suggested that learning and knowledge management is integrated into workflows, tailored to individuals in terms of content and timing but also designed to support teams.[9]

High-impact learning that lasts

In *Creating Impact Through Future Learning*, Dochy and Segers describe high-impact learning that lasts (HILL), which occurs when 'the learners enriches effectively his or her body of knowledge, skills and attitudes (KSAs) in such a way that the learner's professional functioning changes and consequently influences future situations in her/his working context.'[10] They list the key areas of HILL as follows:

- '**Collaboration and coaching:** Learning in well coached teams brings you into the state of flow.
- **Hybrid learning:** Variation between online learning and offline face to face learning keeps the process going
- **Action and knowledge sharing:** When doing things and sharing know how, you feel that learning happens.
- **Flexibility:** Formal and informal learning: when your own learning track is flexible, not overloaded and provides spaced informal moments and formal training, you will like learning.
- **Assessment as learning:** If you get frequent feedback as assessment, and this is either used as a start or as a way of monitoring what you do, your drive to learn will remain.
- **Urgency, gap, problem:** If you feel the urgency to know something, you will spend the time to learn it.
- **Learner agency:** The more people can decide themselves and the more choices they can make, the more they are motivated to learn'.[11]

Dochy and Segers note that HILL:

- builds on what learners find urgent;
- uses learner agency;
- focuses on teams and appropriate coaching;
- uses well-thought-out hybrid learning;
- is based on action and takes knowledge sharing as key;
- uses formal and informal learning in a flexible way;
- promotes feedback, feedback seeking and assessment as learning.[12]

Lifelong learning

Lifelong learning can be described as 'learning that is pursued throughout life: learning that is flexible, diverse and available at different times and in different places'.[13]

Traditional learning, involved group learning in formal classes or individual tuition, lifelong learning calls for a blended learning approach which combines:

- different modules into one programme;
- different media and tools in an e-learning environment;
- different didactic methods or approaches, such as instruction, video, group assignments;
- traditional learning and web-based online approaches;
- different modes of assessment.[14]

This helps support those who have completed their formal education and:

- do not have the time and/or other resources to participate in formal traditional learning programmes;
- wish to learn specific parts of learning materials instead of completing an entire learning trajectory;
- differ in the degree of difficulty in knowledge or skills they wish to obtain due to varying levels of pre-knowledge.[15]

Learning provision should therefore be focused on individual requirements and allow for flexibility. However, technology enabled remote learning has so far not been an unqualified success. Research on one MOOC found that 154,000 registered students created 230 million student interactions but 'participants who attempted over 5 per cent of the homework represented only one-fourth of all participants, but accounted for 92 per cent of the total time spent in the course; indeed 60 per cent of the time was invested by the 6 per cent who received certificates'.[16] Another study found that out of 1 million students, only 4 per cent completed the course.[17]

Another study, which examined 39 courses, found that completion rates varied between 0.9 per cent and 36.1 per cent, with a median value of 6.5 per cent. However, the completion rates of active students varied between 1.4 per cent and 50.1 per cent with a median value of 9.8 per cent, which suggests work could be done to examine factors that increase student engagement.[18] Other research examined how and what non-completing participants in MOOCs, invisible learners, learn. It found that they use courses for inspiration and to update them on practice. They choose what is relevant for their purpose and may not wish to take assignments or follow specific learning objectives.[19] Therefore, non-completion statistics do not on undermine the potential value of MOOCs.

The rapid disruptive change in the technology sector is driving the need for lifelong learning. Lifelong learning should be 'individual, on demand and just in time in order to be practical; this implies investment in hybrid learning.'[20] This requires collaboration between government, educational institutions and business. Organizations need to be better informed and hire people with the most suitable abilities and learning potential. They will move away from generic job descriptions and instead focus on the competences that their current and future employees need.

In *Creating Impact Through Future Learning*, Dochy and Segers write that

> the concept of lifelong learning can only reach its maximal impact when it is mutually reinforced by three key players: educational institutions, businesses and the government. The more these three key stakeholders reinforce each other, the greater the chance that lifelong learning initiatives will become successful.[21]

Human capital development at the individual level includes 'tools that promote self-awareness and strengths development and mentoring programs such as those on career development or financial health'.[22] Unlocking human potential through personal development and a focus on individuals' innate strengths requires commitment by both employers and individuals.

Greater levels of support are required for new business start-ups and education–workforce ties such as internships, and there is a need for government an business to engage on public policy matters involving education.

In the future, organizations may wish to hire for curiosity, creativity, innovation and people who are entrepreneurial. Chamorro-Premuzic believes that, while the key jobs of the future are hard to predict with any certainty, some individuals stand a much higher probability of being prepared for it than others. He notes that

> when organizations hire curious individuals, they acquire employees who are dispositionally inclined to seek out challenging activities, as well as more interested in absorbing knowledge. This disposition is not only a key determinant of learning and expertise, it is also linked to higher levels of engagement and subjective well-being for curious people are more intrinsically motivated and able to find meaning in complex and challenging work roles.[23]

It has been noted that 'training, capacity building and learning are key enabling factors for sustainability, which is seen as a long-term ability of individuals and organizations to produce innovation as a reaction and adaptation to changes in external conditions.'[24]

However, in *The Second Curve*, Charles Handy predicts that

> the real inequality and unfairness in modern capitalism is going to be the lack of meaningful work for the less skilled and less talented among us, and there are many millions of them... To remedy it we need a massive injection of funds to provide better education and training, including the encouragement of self-employment and apprenticeships.[25]

Personality

In *The Talent Delusion*, Tomas Chamorro-Premuzic suggests that any notion of talent is ultimately a social construction of sorts, artificially created in order to make a future prediction about an individual's performance on a task, job or role. Yet at the same time, in order to be accurate, that prediction should not be based on an arbitrary notion of talent but on key individual differentiators.[26]

These differentiators are seen in people's personality, which he defines as 'an individual's typical tendencies or default predispositions, including his values, interests, skills and usual behavioural patterns – in other words, everything we normally mean we talk about what a particular person is like.'[27]

Chamorro-Premuzic discusses talent in terms of: how *rewarding* they are to deal with; their *ability* to do the job, their expertise and intelligence; and their *willingness*, their general level of motivation. These factors are abbreviated to RAW.

How rewarding it is to work with someone can be demonstrated through their organizational citizenship behaviour (OCB), their positive interpersonal and intrapersonal skills, and is linked to their emotional intelligence. With regard to ability, expertise includes domain-related knowledge, experience and skills, while intelligence captures learning ability and reasoning potential. Finally, willingness includes levels of motivation and work ethic.

In terms of attaining senior leadership positions, narcissism appears to be a positive trait:

> for all the talk of humility and altruism as essential ingredients of leadership, the truth is that people are generally perceived as being leadership material when they display confidence, rather than competence, as self belief. Extraversion and charisma are generally perceived as solid indicators of leadership potential. In reality, however, these attributes only help individuals emerge as leaders; they have little to do with actual leadership effectiveness.[28]

A point that supports Pfeffer's views in *Leadership BS*.[29]

We have seen that personality theories describe each person as having a profile of traits that allow an assessment to be made about their likely behaviour; however, 'as they tell us very little about the psychology behind people's behaviour, they tell us very little about how people can change.'[30] In fact, Chamorro-Premuzic concludes that those who are deluded about their abilities are better able to fake competence to others and hide their insecurities from others; 'when you think you are really talented, it is easier to fool others into believing that you have some talent.'[31]

Even when mistakes may be obvious to people, Matthew Syed writes in *Black Box Thinking*, cognitive dissonance occurs 'when mistakes are too threatening to admit to, so they are reframed or ignored. This can be thought of as the internal fear of failure: how we struggle to admit mistakes to ourselves.'[32]

Those who are realistic about what they know and don't know are more likely to achieve their goals and not miss deadlines and let others down. However, those with a knowledge illusion may have higher levels of self-confidence; 'many great human achievements are underwritten by false belief in one's own understanding. In that sense, the illusion may have been necessary for the development of human civilization.'[33]

Syed discusses the concept of marginal gains, identifying and isolating problems, gathering evidence and agreeing a plan to make improvements. The identification of testing until failure is transformed into success requires a growth mindset, a psychologically safe environment, discipline and resilience.[34] He argues that organizational success is not simply dependent on intelligence and talent, for instance, it includes identifying where a strategy is going wrong and adapting and evolving.[35]

In *Self Theories*, Carol Dweck refers to Martin Seligman who defines optimism in terms of how people explain to themselves their successes and failures. Those who are optimistic see a failure as learning that contributes to ultimate success while pessimists believe failure is due to lasting characteristics they are helpless to change.[36] It is easy to see how these differing views are analogous to growth and fixed mindsets.

Mindset and belief

In *Mindset*, Carol Dweck notes that fixed mindset managers believe employees are not capable of development and are not interested in receiving or giving feedback that doesn't confirm pre-set notions. However, growth mindset managers are committed to the development of others and themselves and seek and value feedback even when challenging.[37]

Dweck states that leaders should aspire to create a growth mindset environment in which people can thrive and this involves:

- 'presenting skills as learnable;
- conveying that the organization values learning and perseverance, not just ready-made genius or talent;
- giving feedback in a way that promotes learning and future success;
- presenting managers as resources for learning'.[38]

Feedback is an important element of growth but as Chamorro-Premuzic notes, we don't naturally seek feedback as we tend to overrate our ability and it can be perceived as a sign of weakness.[39] In *The Talent Delusion*, Chamorro-Premuzic notes that

> what people need is honest feedback on their potential, rather than confirmation of their talent delusion. When employees are made aware of their limitations, they have a chance to close the gap between their actual and ideal selves and improve. When they are told that they are more talented than they actually are, they risk making overly ambitious decisions.[40]

Leaders can take help here, as research has found, that 'managers with stronger feedback orientation engage in coaching behaviours, encourage favourable relationships with their subordinates and foster a favourable feedback environment'.[41]

Dweck states that an entity theory view contains fixed traits and therefore a tendency to see global and stable trait attributions for actions and outcomes. On the other hand, an incremental theory view leads people to focus on more dynamic, specific, unstable processes as the mediators of behaviours and the causes of outcomes. She also states that ability has two meanings, 'a fixed ability that needs to be proven, and a changeable ability that can be developed through learning.'[42]

In terms of learning, in *Emotional Intelligence*, Daniel Goleman notes that

> developing a competency of any kind strengthens the sense of self-efficacy, making a person more willing to take risks and seek out more demanding challenges and surmounting those challenges in turn increases the sense of self-efficacy. This attitude makes people more likely to make the best use of whatever skills they may have – or to do what it takes to develop them.[43]

In *The Knowledge Illusion*, Steven Sloman and Philip Fernbach, note that there is too much complexity in the world for any individual to master. Even the use of analytics to examine data and help create knowledge will deliver more knowledge than one person can process. The Dunning-Kruger effect states that 'those who lack skills also lack the knowledge of what skills they're missing. So they think they're pretty good. Those who have skills have a better sense of what the terrain looks like: they know what skills they could improve on.'[44]

Albert Bandura, who has undertaken much of the research on self-efficacy, writes that

> people's beliefs about their abilities have a profound effect on those abilities. Ability is not a fixed property; there is a huge variability in how you perform. People who have a sense of self-efficacy bounce back from failures; they approach things in terms of how to handle them rather than worrying about what can go wrong.[45]

In *Self-Theories*, Carol Dweck states that people develop beliefs that organize their world and give meaning to their experiences, and these can be called meaning systems. Some people believe that their intelligence is a fixed trait that can't be changed and she calls this entity theory. Entity theory suggests an inherent capacity or potential, a system that requires easy success and sees challenge as a potential threat to self-esteem. This may lead to people passing on learning opportunities and disengaging from tasks when the going gets tough even if they were succeeding to that point. However, Dweck believes that intelligence, skills and knowledge are not fixed traits but can be increased through effortful learning. This is known as the incremental theory. She notes that many entity theorists don't grant people the potential to grow, while incremental theorists see failures as problems to be solved.[46]

We all have belief systems that give structure to our world and meaning to our experiences and the sense that we can predict what will happen.

These beliefs are also an integral part of people's motivational systems in that they can strongly influence the goals people choose to pursue, how intrinsic versus extrinsic their motivation tends to be, the interest they maintain in an activity over time, the vigour with which they pursue the tasks in their lives, and much more.[47]

Research has found that beliefs and goals can change, that the beliefs people hold have a significant impact on their adaptive functioning, and that, while some temperaments make it easier to learn adaptive skills, under the right circumstances virtually everyone can.[48]

Attribution theory

In *Focus: The hidden driver of excellence*, Daniel Goleman argues that when our mind is not focused on decision-making it is wandering, navigating our complex world, learning, generating future scenarios, incubating creative ideas and organizing memories. He notes that this facilitates unexpected insights and creativity and states that 'in a complex world where almost everyone has access to the same information, new value arises from the original synthesis, from putting ideas together in novel ways, and from smart questions that open up untapped potential'[49] and

> in a world characterized by information overload, ignoring information
> may be as adaptive as paying attention to it. In that sense, the capacity
> to translate information into valuable knowledge may require the ability
> to suppress one's appetite for empty and meaningless (but also addictive)
> information.[50]

Attribution theory examines how people make sense of their world, how they explain the things that they observe and experience and 'the attributions people make for their successes and failures (ie, the way they explain them) will determine the impact of those successes and failures. Some explanations leave you with a greater hope of success than do others.'[51]

Individual differences in the kinds of causal explanations that people tend to make for negative events in their lives have been examined by Seligman, who called these explanatory styles. Dweck found that

> some people tend to focus on more pessimistic explanations for negative
> events, blaming more global and stable factors, while others tend to focus
> on more optimistic explanations, blaming more specific and temporary ones.
> They then went on to dramatically demonstrate the power of a helpless,
> pessimistic explanatory style to predict such things as depression, and the
> power of an optimistic explanatory style to predict mental health and physical
> health.[52]

Coaching

In *The Talent Delusion*, Chamorro-Premuzic notes that personality is not supposed to change as it represents all the attributes that make us systematically different from other people. However, if personality is the sum of a person's behaviours, then changing their behaviours should eventually produce a 'new' personality.

> A person's personality, intelligence and values, which are the major markers of dispositional individual differences and key determinants of talent, are remarkably stable from early adulthood onwards. Major changes in these attributes are possible, but improbable, particularly when they involve going against the direction of inherent predispositions.[53]

Therefore, when someone who is predisposed to be introverted and uncreative becomes more extroverted and more creative it is likely to be the result of significant interventions such as coaching and regular practice over an extended period.

It has been stated that leaders are both born and made, and that this implies the need for all leaders to develop skills in both technical and soft skills. While there is some evidence to suggest that EQ can be developed through traditional training, it is recommended that executive coaching is also considered. Executive coaching can be seen as 'a customized development relationship between a leader and coach to facilitate performance-enhancing behavioural changes'.[54]

Jonathan Passmore has developed a model of executive coaching that incorporates six areas:

- **developing:** the coaching partnership by establishing empathy, positive self-image, openness and honesty, focus on and positive regard for the coachee;
- **maintaining:** the coaching partnership through self-awareness, awareness of coach and behaviour adaptation;
- **behavioural focus:** problem-solving and planning behaviour;
- **conscious cognition:** deepening understanding of the relationship between thoughts and behaviours;
- **unconscious cognition:** deepening awareness of self;
- **the cultural context:** which surrounds the model.[55]

This leads to a deeper understanding of self, improved self-regard, stronger motivation to act and more effective behaviour.

The domain of leadership and executive coaching (LEC) includes the:

- **intrapersonal domain:** the beliefs, values, attitudes, interests, preferences of the leader;

- interpersonal domain: how the leader engages and interacts with stakeholders;
- environment: complex system with dependencies and interdependencies.[56]

In terms of coaching, 'good psychological tests used appropriately can be useful tools for coaches to support their clients in building awareness through self-exploration and understanding'[57] and developing self-awareness and an appreciation of how their behaviour impacts others means that leaders can be more effective in building high-performance teams that operate in a psychologically safe environment.

Highlights

- The potential future of learning and developments was examined through high-impact learning that lasts.
- Lifelong learning was also examined and compared to traditional learning.
- This chapter related the possibilities of learning and development to personality traits, mindsets and beliefs discussed in Chapters 1 and 2, including the action of neuroplasticity.
- Coaching is a key development tool.

Leadership impact

Key themes that leaders should reflect on include:

- how different personality traits, mindsets and beliefs can affect learning;
- the importance of closing skills gaps and creating new skills;
- what learning and development is necessary for themselves;
- learning and development needed for others;
- whether the organization can evolve into one of continuous learning;
- ensure that sufficient budget is set aside for learning;
- consider coaching for themselves and train to deliver coaching-style feedback to others.

People management recommendations

Actions to consider:

- Ensure that all learning is aimed not just at developing people, but that it also supports the organization's objectives.

- Look at creative ways to deliver tailored learning and development.
- Ensure that there is robust policy to support all learning activities.
- Use expertise internally and externally to design and develop learning programmes.
- Make use of technology, as well as offering a blended learning approach in order to satisfy the different learning styles found across the organization.
- Try to measure the return on the learning investment.
- Consider establishing a coaching programme and coaching feedback training.

Case studies

CASE STUDY   Volvo
Using hiring to reinvent the business

Location

Sweden and global.

Organization

The first Volvo car rolled off the Gothenburg production line in Sweden in 1927. Since then, Volvo Car Group has been a world-leader in safety technology and innovation. Today, Volvo is one of the most well-known and respected car brands in the world with sales in about 100 countries.

The company's corporate and brand strategy, 'Designed Around You', puts people at the centre and is a foundation and a guide for the business, the products and the corporate culture.

Volvo cars are marketed and sold by regional market companies and national sales companies through approximately 2,300 local dealers in about 100 countries. Most of the dealerships are independent companies. As of December 2017, Volvo Cars had around 38,000 full-time employees around the globe.

People challenge

Many large traditional companies would like to transform themselves into more agile and talent-driven organizations. However, often many of the current staff do not necessarily have the required skillset or the appetite for change that is required.

Developing a 'strategy for talent' is one way to overcome this challenge. Volvo was a brand in a difficult place; its cars were not top luxury brands like Mercedes, BMW and Audi, yet the company could also not compete head-to-head with mass-market leaders like Toyota and General Motors.

Under new ownership, the Swedish car maker decided to transform its business by becoming a premium player. CEO Stefan Jacoby and CHRO Björn Sällström carried out a detailed review of Volvo's existing workforce. The result was clear: to move into the premium-brand tier, Volvo needed new people with different skills. For instance, there was a need for more software engineers, because cars are increasingly dependent on computers. Also, in order to achieve more entrepreneurial culture there was a need for some fresh talent across the board.

Solutions

Volvo decided to adopt three critical steps to ensure that its outside-in transformation would work.

- **The first step was to appoint thechief human resources officer (CHRO) to lead the initiative**. The CHRO needs to be at the centre of any hiring of talent. This is also true for more traditional M&A, where CHROs are too often sidelined, rather than being central to driving strategy. Today's talent-driven companies know that talent is what drives value. That's why they deploy financial and human capital together, aligning the two for maximum impact. At these companies, the CHRO plays a central role in any kind of acquisition. While Volvo didn't acquire companies as it went looking for outside talent, the CEO relied upon HR to find what the company needed, sometimes in places it had never hired from before.

- **The second step was to look beyond the traditional hiring routes**. To get the skills and change agents it needed, Volvo looked outside the automotive industry. The CHRO mapped various industries, identifying people with relevant skills. Volvo became very creative and, in some cases, counterintuitive. They hired salespeople and marketers from Google, who transformed Volvo's use of technology and social media in those disciplines. They hired Nokia engineers, who were used to thinking about what digital approach appeals to consumers and to redesign radio and navigation systems. Between 2011 and 2015, the company added 3,000 new people in engineering and development.

- **Finally, the third step; the company developed a robust system for integrating the new talent**. Communication was critical: the CEO described the strategy shift to Volvo's key 300 employees and held regular live meetings with employees. Training was very important: a range of initiatives were implemented to shift the staff into a more entrepreneurial mindset, and each of the 300 key leaders were given a personal coach. A 30 person 'catalyst group' mainly made up of younger employees was charged with showing others in the organization that work could be done differently. For example, the question was asked as to why every design change in a car required a dozen signatures, and they managed to cut that number in half. Changing small things starts to send a clear message across the whole organization.

After two years of getting the company to think more entrepreneurially, the catalyst group disbanded – further proof of a policy of keeping overheads under control.

Outcome

Making such transformational changes takes time to take effect. The financials are already showing improvements – net revenue hit an all-time high in 2017, and profits rose for the third consecutive year. The company sold 571,000 cars in 2017, up from 373,000 in 2010.

Culture change takes longer, but the signs are positive, and Volvo is going from strength to strength.

Learning points

- Think laterally to solve people problems. The sourcing of new talent from unconventional industries and businesses is a good example.
- HR needs to work closely with the business. Having a place at the top table is essential to add most value and align the people strategies with the business.
- Evolve the people strategy as the business situation develops. In this case, the focus was on integrating the new talent and not just on hiring.

Sources

Material for this case has been adapted from the following websites:

www.volvocars.com/intl

https://hbr.org/2018/03/how-volvo-reinvented-itself-through-hiring

CASE STUDY   Monzo
Making mental health a priority

Location

United Kingdom.

Organization

Monzo bank is one of a new breed of challenger banks in the UK with the headline of: 'We're building a new kind of bank'. Founded in London in 2015, the bank has grown using technology via mobile apps and the use of debit Mastercards.

Monzo is a bank that lives on your smartphone and is built for the way we live today. By solving financial problems, treating you fairly and being transparent, it believes it can make banking better.

The bank had about 775 employees in 2019, and is renowned for raising £1 million in just 96 seconds via crowdfunding in 2016.

People challenge

The bank believes that physical health and mental health are linked, and that the two do not exist in isolation. In the UK, one in four adults face a mental health challenge every year, and so it makes sense not to ignore up to 25 per cent of the client base and staff.

The key challenge has been to not only design products that support those with mental health issues amongst their customer base, but also to implement policies internally for their staff. Mental health is a spectrum and so it would be incorrect to try to solve one need for one set of people. Everyone, at one point or another, has to deal with stress, anxiety about their finances and lack of confidence about where their money is going.

Solutions

One of the important solutions has been to give customers real time updates on their money. This is in stark contrast to the more traditional banks and what people are used to. The power of visibility can be overlooked, and it does have a very positive impact about anxiety over money. There have also been straightforward explanations, avoiding confusing jargon, about the processes. Finally, strong and positive customer support means that customers know they have someone they can talk to at any point.

Another feature has been the ability to block transactions related to gambling, following discussions with customers. This relatively straightforward feature came about as a result of one of the regular 'Monzo Time' sessions; these occur every fourth Friday. This is time set aside for all staff to work on projects that they are passionate about exploring. In this case a group of engineers, a designed and members of the customer team collaborated to bring this feature to the table.

A solution brought in for staff in 2018 was the creation of a 'Slack channel' exclusively for the topic of mental health. The channel was made public so that anyone could join in the discussions. Once staff found that it was a safe environment, regular chats started to take place daily.

Finally, in the same way that physical first-aiders have been trained, Monzo ensured that 45 mental health first-aiders were trained to deal with any mental health issues that cropped up during working hours.

Learning points

A key learning point has been to make mental health part of the culture of the business, rather than just a specialist subject for a few people. It was also important to make this a positive mental health environment, removing any stigma or taboo as far as possible.

Other features of the culture in support of this initiative have been a focus on flexible hours, the promotion of walking meetings to get people out of the office, and the creation of different types of workspaces – even being dog-friendly in the office!

All staff also have access to a mediation app, Headspace and Spill, which lets individuals speak to a counsellor on a daily basis.

Sources

Material for this case has been adapted from the following websites:

https://monzo.com/about/

https://monzo.com/blog/2018/05/18/mindfulness-and-wellbeing/

CASE STUDY Aramco Overseas
Introducing coaching as a way of empowering its people

Location

Netherlands and other European locations. HQ in Saudi Arabia.

Background

Aramco Overseas is a subsidiary of Saudi Aramco – the state-owned oil company of the Kingdom of Saudi Arabia, and a fully integrated global petroleum and chemicals enterprise. The network of experts provide a vital link between Saudi Aramco, the world's leading energy company, and our operations within Europe and other parts of the world. Services include: research and technology, engineering, procurement, local content, contracting, quality, management, logistics, staffing services and professional development.

Aramco Overseas has 350 staff across Europe and is headquartered in the Netherlands.

People challenge

Staff training was offered across the business following the establishment of a learning and development function in 2014. However, it soon became clear that offering coaching would not only help to accelerate learning, but would also bring a new focus onto professional development.

Previously when training was undertaken, it was not certain if new skills were being optimally applied when staff returned to their jobs. It was clear that there needed to be more conversations between managers and staff in order to unlock more potential from them.

Solution

Coaching training began with the HR team, and was led by the Chartered Institute of Personnel and Development (CIPD), with the aim of showing managers how to move conversations from being instructive to being empowering.

A range of coaching options were introduced including career, peer and team coaching through to executive coaching and upskilling for managers.

To date, more than 100 staff have joined the programme. There are already many signs that there is a shift in behaviours across the organization in a positive way. Whereas before HR were seen as the function to handle difficult conversations, now managers are taking much more responsibility and feel much more empowered to take the lead. Surveys have confirmed that managers are using their new coaching skills in day-to-day activities. More internal moves are taking place and communication has improved across the organization.

Most importantly, employees are taking more responsibility for their own careers and development. Also, coaching is now perceived as part of the way the firm does business, rather than just a remedial activity.

Learning points

- It is important to remove the stigma that coaching is just for remedial support for poor performers.
- Communication is critical to ensuring the best practice spreads across organizations.
- The HR function can act as a catalyst for change, and allow managers to take on responsibility for managing their people.

Sources

Material for this case has been adapted from the following websites:

www.aramcooverseas.com/

www.peoplemanagement.co.uk/voices/case-studies/coaching-shifted-culture-aramco-overseas

PART FOUR
The future of people management

It was noted in the Introduction that this book is based on four principles, which we call the *people principles*:

- People are, and will remain, the most important factor in the establishment, development and sustainable success of organizations.
- People, organizations and the environment in which organizations operate are complex.
- The responsibility for people management is distributed throughout organizations and is not the responsibility of a single function.
- Due to their responsibility and the complexity they face, leaders and managers require access to high-quality professional people advice and execution.

The first two of these principles have been examined in previous chapters and the final two are now discussed so leaders have the context they need to design an efficient and effective *people operating model* to ensure that people management of the future is the foundation on which an outstanding workforce can be built.

People functions 17

Introduction

This chapter introduces the research and theories that have informed the human resource management structures, policies and processes that are found in many organizations today.

It is instructive to do this, as it gives the reader a view of the complexity, ambiguity and conflicts that surround decisions undertaken to align and integrate people management. By doing so, the logic of the suggested framework for people management is given important context.

In the following pages human resource management (HRM) and people management are both used to describe the management of people in organizations. The terms human resource professionals and people professionals are used to denote those employees with functional responsibility for supporting human resource management.

Human resource management has been become synonymous with the term human resources, which is unhelpfully used to describe the people that work in organizations as well as the HR function, or HR, as it is often known. This is a problem as it conflates the two and potentially confuses who is responsible for people management. Is it HR or is the leadership of organizations, including those in the function termed HR?

The first area to be examined is the growth of strategic human resource management. This is followed by exploration of the roles and influence associated with the management of human resources. The importance of the CEO and senior leadership team in mediating the effectiveness of human resource management is reviewed. Finally, the conception of talent portfolio management is discussed. This is the precursor of people portfolio management, which is found in the new framework for people management that is discussed in the final chapter.

Chapter summary

The following subjects are discussed in this chapter:

- **strategic human resource management:**
  - universalistic, contingency and configurational approaches;
  - complexity;
  - internal environment;

- **roles in human resource management:**
  - relative roles;
  - frameworks for human resource functional roles;
  - the Ulrich Model;
  - integrated roles;
- **influence:**
  - relative influence;
  - integrated influence;
- **the structure of human resource management:**
  - shared services;
- **the importance of CEOs and senior leaders.**

Strategic human resource management

Universalistic, contingency and configurational approaches

During the last 30 years of the 20th century a number of writers focused on the importance of human resource practices, with a call[1] for a link between strategic planning and human resource planning giving birth to the field of strategic human resource management. The fundamental premise underlying strategic human resource management is that any organization's human resource practices should be aligned with the business strategy of the firm and that these practices will be different to the ones used by firms pursuing different business strategies. This premise also assumes that the variation in human resource practices between firms can be explained by a variation in strategy, and that between those organizations following the same strategy, the ones that show greatest congruence between their human resource practices and their business strategies should show superior performance.[2]

Strategic human resources management has largely drawn on three approaches: universalistic, contingency and configurational.[3]

A normative, universalistic, best-practice, approach has been taken by those who believe that all organizations should adopt certain human resource practices all the time.[4] However, in addition to discussions regarding strategic fit, there has also been research on the concept of strategic flexibility which states that organizations 'faced with complex and dynamic environments require flexibility to adapt to diverse and changing requirements'.[5] Human resource flexibility has been defined as 'the capacity of HRM to facilitate the organization's ability to adapt effectively and in a timely manner to changing or diverse demands from either its environment or from within the firm.'[6]

A second group of writers adopted a contingency perspective to human resource management, arguing that to be effective, any organization's human resource policies and practices must be internally consistent with other organizational capabilities. Contingency arguments are more complex than universalistic arguments as they imply interactions rather than linear relationships. The behavioural perspective of strategic human resource management, which focuses on employee behaviour as the mediator between strategy and firm performance, has its roots in contingency theory. For instance, research based on the contingency perspective of strategic human resource management concludes that human resource management systems influence employee attitudes and behaviour, and therefore organizational outcomes, through employee interpretations of work climate.[7]

A third group of human resource management theorists have developed arguments that are consistent with a configurational approach. These theories are different to traditional contingency approaches as they are based on typologies of ideal situations; adopt systems of equifinality,[8] where the same goal can be reached in many ways; and have informed studies on strategic human resource management that explore high-commitment management.

In *Human Resource: Rhetorics and realities*,[9] Karen Legge observed that the language of hard versus soft human resource management[10] had been replaced by the US alternatives of high-commitment management (HCM).[11] HCM utilizes high-performance work systems (HPWS) where each element of the human resource system is designed to maximize the overall quality and impact of human capital throughout the organization. A HPWS has been conceived as a strategy implementation system, embedded within the firm's larger strategy implementation system and that intersects with the larger strategy implementation system at many different points and perhaps with multiple elements at the same point.[12] It is believed that understanding how to identify those points of intersection in a firm and how to align the human resource system accordingly is the key to knowing how to measure the human resource impact on value creation and to securing a strategic role for human resource professionals.

The configurational view was extended as writers begin to discuss human resources in terms of bundles of competencies[13] and pools of human capital.[14] However, in terms of a configurational approach, one review concludes that 'while logic supports the notion of bundling human resource practices, theoretical and empirical attempts to define the components and measure the contents and prevalence of bundles, while individually impressive, are collectively deficient and confusing.'[15] Indeed, others found there to be little coherence among the empirical results of the field.[16] Even proponents of human resource–firm performance link research, such as Mark Huselid, have noted that the measures used cannot differentiate between the presence of operationally appropriate human resource practices and the quality of their implementation.[17] A best-practice human resource policy poorly implemented may be less effective than other policies that are well implemented.

The universalistic, contingent and configurational approaches discussed above have sought to link the management of human resources to organizational performance and have reached conclusions that, due to their methodology and methods, researchers in the field have found to be problematic. Criticisms include their quantitative approach, the problem of single-respondent errors and the lack of clear causality in their results. These issues have been addressed by Barry Colbert who believes that the basic precepts of strategic human resource management have a natural affinity with the resource-based view of competitive advantage.[18] As we saw in Chapter 6, this view contends that competitive advantage develops through a process that is impacted by path dependency, social complexity and causal ambiguity,[19] and therefore explains why it has been difficult to identify causation in this field.[20] Indeed, others believe that a human resource system deeply embedded in the organization is hard to imitate because it is difficult to identify the precise mechanisms by which human resource practices interact and create value.[21] For instance, studies have found that management philosophy with regard to managing human resources has an important influence on the people environment.[22]

The significance of management philosophy in the management of human resources has been discussed and strategic human resource management is noted as having four meanings:

- the use of planning;
- matching human resource management activities and policies to some explicit business strategy;
- seeing the people of an organization as a strategic resource for the achievement of competitive advantage;
- a coherent approach to the design and management of personnel systems based on an employment policy and manpower strategy and often underpinned by a 'philosophy'.[23]

It would appear that, while it is believed more successful organizations align and integrate their business strategy with their human resource strategy, research does not address how the various roles and influence of human resource management maybe critical to this. Ultimately, while the configurational view comes closest to modelling the complexity of organizations it still reduces complex organizational systems to a few possible configurations for the sake of analytical manageability.

Organizational complexity impacts the people environment and this is examined further below in terms of the extent to which organizational culture and symbolism is perceived by human resource professionals and business line managers as having an impact on people management.

Complexity

In an attempt to address organizational complexity, Colbert extends the configurational approach by proposing an integrated framework for strategic human resource management. In his model, levels of abstraction in the human resource system are noted as: principle, policy, practice and product. These are set against four modes of theorizing: universal, contingency, configurational and complex.

With regard to the levels of abstraction Colbert notes that:

- **HR principles:** can be exemplified by the thought that 'employee participation is critical to our success';
- **HR policies:** alternative methods of enacting the guiding principles, examples in this case include 'team-based work systems' and 'comprehensive communication processes';
- **HR practices:** the specific tools that are available to execute the policies. Examples here include: 'TQM teams', 'team-based reward systems';
- **HR products:** the metric that describes the effect of behaviour, induced by the practices, for instance, team productivity could be measured before and after implementing the practices.[24]

In the same year as Colbert's helpful contribution, a study was published that looked at the strength of the HRM system.[25] It described the meta-features of a human resource management system that results in a strong organizational climate and concluded that the strength of the human resource management system can help explain how individual employee attributes accumulate to affect organizational effectiveness. It proposed that a strong human resource management system can enhance organizational performance owing to shared meanings in the promotion of collective responses that are consistent with organizational strategic goals, assuming the appropriateness of these goals. While this study supports findings that firm performance is related to employee engagement and HPWS, it does not address the roles and relative influence of human resource professionals and business line managers in contributing to a strong human resource environment.

In terms of management influence on the human resource environment, strategic models tend to share a 'somewhat rational, proactive decision-making process as the major influence on the development and alignment of various HRM practices.'[26] It is argued that to predict and understand the decision-making process surrounding the formulation of human resource practices, 'it is necessary to understand non-strategic determinants of HRM practices... the determinants that are not the result of rational strategic decision-making processes, but rather derive from institutional and political forces in the firm.'[27]

This rejection of rational decision-making was extended by a number of propositions:

- There is no single human resource strategy in a firm.
- Business strategy may be an important influence on human resource strategy but it is only one of several factors and the relationship is not unilinear.
- Implicit, if not explicit, in the mix of factors that influence the shape of human resource strategies is a set of historical compromises and trade-offs from stakeholders, that is, management may seek to shift the historical pattern of human resource strategy significantly in response to major contextual change, but not all management will respond in the same way or equally effectively.
- The strategy formation process is complex, and excessively rationalistic models that advocate formalistic linkages between strategic planning and human resource planning are not particularly helpful to our understanding of it.
- Descriptions of the dimensions that underpin human resource strategies are critical to the development of useful typologies but remain controversial as no one set of constructs has established an intellectual superiority over the others.[28]

Internal environment

Following this rejection of rational decision-making, positions are examined that contend that human resource practices are developed in the context of socially constructed reality; and that this process is constrained by an organization's history and the internal and external environments within which it exists. When taking an international perspective, the challenge of managing human resources becomes even more complex.

One study focused on integrated power, politics and social construction theory in an empirical investigation of how human resource functions as a whole gain influence. It found that symbolic actions such as image and importance-enhancing behaviours were the strongest predictors of power and influence for human resource functional management.[29] Another study examined how human resource functions as a whole actively engage in the process of self-justification and develop a perception of their importance to the organization.[30] Others discuss symbolic issues in human resource management, how to understand the power and influence of human resource functions as a whole and the implementation of progressive human resource practices.[31] These studies acknowledge and address the social complexity of the human resource environment in association with the relative influence of human resource professionals.

The informal organization is thought to have significant influence on the human resource environment and a number of authors have emphasized the importance of human resource professionals acknowledging and understanding the impact of social capital.[32] With regard to the migration of terminology in the United Kingdom from personnel management to human resource management, the importance of organizational culture was noted 'as an influence shaping the direction of change and adoption of human resource management designation and policy within particular organizations.'[33] It was found that moves towards a human resource management designation were linked to aspects of organization needs, politics and power but David Guest warns that 'it is important to bear in mind that a change in title may be no more than a symbolic gesture and a possible statement of intent, in many cases the policies will stay much the same.'[34]

In other words, just changing the designation from personnel to human resources, human capital or people will not in itself change how people management is delivered or the quality of the relationships required to deliver it.

To fully understand the role of human resource practices on organizational performance, researchers explored factors that impact organizational capabilities and one study quantitatively examined how human resource practices effect organizational and social climate conditions which in turn positively, but indirectly, impact organization performance.[35] They found that commitment-based human resource practices were positively related to organizational social climates of trust, cooperation, shared codes and language, and that these measures of an organization's social climate were related to its performance. This is consistent with the results of research that shows higher levels of employee engagement positively impact organizational performance. While the study addressed organizational complexity and speaks to the importance of trust and cooperation, which is relevant to relationships within the people environment, including those between business line managers and people management professionals, it does not directly address the roles and relative influence that impact the efficacy of people management.

Indeed, while a number of writers believe more successful organizations align and integrate their business strategy with their human resource strategy, extant literature does not fully address how the roles and relative influence of human resource management, as enacted through people professionals and business line managers, amongst others, maybe critical to this.

Roles in human resource management

Relative roles

The developing roles, status and power of personnel managers and subsequently human resource managers is a longstanding and recurrent debate. Back in 1929 Donald and Donald published 'Trends in personnel administration' in the *Harvard Business Review*, summarizing the changing responsibility of the personnel man from taking a very central and dominant role in all areas that impacted the management of people in the organization, to a facilitating and advisory role. Management teams, from foreman to president, were seen by the authors as regaining the responsibility for managing people and looking to the personnel professionals for support.[36] This trend continued and 72 years later it was noted that as line management began to take more responsibility for industrial relations and other human resource issues, many new initiatives had been directed from the CEO, senior line and functional management teams.[37]

The roles of human resource professionals and senior business line managers have been examined in relation to organizations that are most likely to adopt a strategic approach to human resource management. This research concluded that these organizations have:

- a strong, visionary leadership;
- a closely knit team at the top;
- a coherent and clearly articulated business strategy;
- a personnel director on the board who is actively involved as a 'business partner' and who is supported by personnel specialists who also take the business-partner role;
- line managers who 'own' the human resource strategies.[38]

Another study examined the extent to which human resource management has developed and overcome three challenges highlighted by Karen Legge:[39]

- how far senior managers accept and act upon the arguments about the central role of human resources;
- whether the focus on outcomes, and specifically the relationship between human resource management and performance, has entered the consciousness of senior management;
- how far the advent and influence of human resource management has affected the role of personnel departments and personnel specialists.

One finding of the study was a wider acceptance that line managers have primary responsibility for managing human resources, although many CEOs and operational managers were critical of business line managers' acceptance of this responsibility.[40]

Frameworks for human resource functional roles

The question of the roles played by senior business line managers and human resource professionals in the management of human resources has been the subject of a number of frameworks.

Three models of human resource management were suggested by Shaun Tyson in 1987:[41] the clerk-of-works model, the contract-manager model and the architect model. The clerk-of-works model focuses on administrative support and process functions. The contract-manager model focuses on trade union interface responsibilities. The architect model focuses on strategic input with the human resource function represented in the senior management of the organization.

In 1990, Randall Schuler[42] discerned a shift from human resource professionals being part of a solely staff function. Instead, they were seen as becoming part of the management team with roles that included: being a business person with influence on strategy formulation and implementation; a change agent; a talent/assets manager; and a cost controller. These changes were also noted by Stephen Caroll in 1991,[43] who saw a greater requirement for human resource professionals to contribute to organizational effectiveness through more significant links with business management and suggested three roles as taking on increased importance: delegator, technical expert and innovator. The delegator role sees business line management being the primary implementers of human resource management systems. The technical expert role reflects the need for human resource professionals to be competent across a range of human resource specific skills such as compensation and benefits. The innovator role involves human resource professionals finding new solutions to human resource challenges.

In 1992, John Storey developed a model based on action orientation that contrasted human resource roles as being either interventionary or non-interventionary and strategic or tactical.[44] Four different roles for the human resource function were developed from this: advisors, handmaidens, regulators and change-makers. The *advisor* role sees human resource professionals acting as internal consultants to business managers and other functional management. The *handmaiden* role, later referred to by Raymond Caldwell[45] as service-provider, emphasizes a more subservient relationship to line management. The *regulator* role illustrates the development and enforcement of rules, driven by internal decisions or external legislation, and interface with trade unions. Finally, the *change-maker role* focuses on activity that helps align employee behaviour with business needs.

In 2003, Caldwell found that in the eleven years since this model was proposed, the strategic and change-agent elements of the human resource professionals role had increased, while the regulator role had declined and the service-provider role had become more about the effective delivery of the human resource functions services.[46]

The Ulrich Model

In 1997 Dave Ulrich published his seminal *Human Resource Champions*,[47] in which he developed an influential model for the delivery of human resource management. Some of his key points can be summarized as follows:

- Business line managers are primarily responsible for human resource management in any firm.

- Partnerships between business line managers and human resource professionals are important for sustaining competitive advantage.

- Human resource professionals should seek to define value in terms of how the receivers of their services, such as business line managers, perceive it.

- The delivery structure of the human resource function should contain four mechanisms: service brokers, service centres, centres of expertise and integrated solutions.

- Value creation should occur through four steps: customer requirements, satisfied through a customer interface, delivering shared services through appropriate processes.

- The delivery process should contain at least five delivery channels: business line managers; business dedicated human resource professionals; shared service located human resource professionals; information technology; and outsourcing.

- The four roles identified for human resource professionals are developed from people versus process and strategic versus operational dimensions. They are strategic partner, administrative expert, employee champion and change agent.

- Business-dedicated human resource partners may adopt multiple roles.

- In order to undertake the various roles noted above, human resource professionals should have four competencies: business mastery; human resource mastery; change and process mastery; and personal credibility.

Having started in 1987 with three of the four competencies noted above, credibility was missing.[48] These were modified in 1997 to include culture[49] and again in 2003 by Wayne Brockbank and Ulrich when they became: strategic contribution, which includes change management; delivery of human resource practices, which includes processes and information technology; business knowledge; and credibility.[50] These competencies were updated once more in 2007[51] with HR professionalism spanning people and business, supported by competencies at three levels:

- **relationships:** credible activist;

- **systems and processes:** operations executor and business ally;

- **organization capabilities:** talent management/organizational design, culture and change steward and strategy architect.

The credible activist is explained as follows: credible as in respected, admired, and listened to; and active as in offering a point of view, taking a position, and challenging assumptions. Credible activists share information, deliver results with integrity, and execute their roles with attitude.

In other research, antecedents of credibility were examined and in order of importance found to be:

- the business line managers trust in, and personal empathy, with the business partner;

- the business partner's knowledge of the external environment;
- the track record of the individual business partner in delivering HR services and their part in business plan execution;
- the track record of the HR function in delivering HR services to the business manager;
- the business partner's technical knowledge of HR practices and procedures;
- the business partner's knowledge of the internal, political, environment;
- the availability and effective use of valid methodologies and metrics to analyse the impact of HR initiatives;
- membership of a professional body;
- academic qualifications.[52]

The first item, trust and empathy, was ranked first by both business line managers and their human resource directors, while the second item, knowledge of the external environment, was ranked joint first by business line managers but fourth by their human resource directors. Interestingly, knowledge of technical HR expertise was ranked higher by business line managers than their human resource directors.[53]

Business-dedicated human resource professionals have become known as business partners who may adopt multiple roles and trade a narrow technical specialism for a broader, generalist position. In *HR Business Partners* the requirements of a business partner are seen as: credibility, alignment with and integration with the business management team, deep influencing and change skills and access to the required HR resources for delivery. It is seen as a difficult role that has been hard to successfully implement because:

- Organizations appoint too many without clarity on roles expectations for the business partner, their internal client and HR functional colleagues.
- People are appointed to the roles without the competencies noted above.
- Senior business line management are not committed to, or not trained, to support this model.
- Not enough support is provided to the business partner and they don't feel part of the business line or HR functional teams.
- Tensions may exist between the business partner and HR functional colleagues.
- Business partners focus too much on the tactical to the detriment of the strategic.
- There is insufficient focus on accountability and measurement.[54]

In 2001 research examined the effectiveness of human resource professionals in performing various roles. These were based on Ulrich's 1997 typology and include the following:

- a strategic partner role that participates in, and has influence over, the formulation of strategy rather than just aligning human resource and business strategies;
- tailoring human resource practices as part of strategy implementation;
- providing the basic human resource services noted above;
- supporting business line managers to implement change initiatives;
- and identifying and/or developing critical organizational core competencies or capabilities.

It concluded that human resource professionals and business line managers differ in their perceptions of the effectiveness of the human resource professionals in their roles, with business line managers rating their effectiveness lower than human resource professionals for every role.[55]

A review of Storey's 1992 typology and Ulrich's 1997 model for adding value and delivering results was undertaken by Caldwell in 2003, who concluded that

> Storey's typology has lost much of its empirical and analytical veracity, while Ulrich's model ends in prescriptive overreach by submerging issues of role conflict within a new rhetoric of professional identity. Neither model can adequately accommodate the emergent tensions between competing role demands, ever-increasing managerial expectations of performance and new challenges to professional expertise, all of which are likely to intensify in the future.[56]

He notes significant role changes and role complexity since the above typologies were published and sees human resource professionals as a relatively weak occupational group facing challenges relating to inherent role ambiguities that have characterized their functional position. These include:

- issues of 'powerlessness' or marginality in management decision-making processes, especially at a strategic level;
- an inability to maintain or defend the boundaries of their specialist expertise from encroachment or control by managerial intervention;
- lack of clarity or accountability in specifying the goals, business outcomes, or the contribution of the personnel function;
- tensions in sustaining an ethos of mutuality in the face of the opposing interests between management and employees.[57]

Caldwell found that the advisor role is seen as intrinsically weak if human resource professionals are used as internal consultants reacting to short-term problems rather than being involved with longer-term, strategic matters. There was considerable customer-driven emphasis on human resource professionals acting as service providers and monitoring and controlling the efficient delivery of HR activities. One manager said, 'My credibility depends on running an extremely efficient and cost-effective administrative machine... If I don't get that right, and consistently, then you can forget about any big HR ideas'.[58] The regulator role was still thought to be important although not simply in reference to industrial relations: 'there are more and more areas of the business where HR has to act as policeman and ethical guardian'.[59] Finally, it was felt that the change agent role could be undertaken with human resource professionals operating as reactive pragmatists, positively facilitating change initiatives as they arose from the line or the interventions of outside consultants. The need to deliver on administrative and operational matters was made clear, as was the internal policing role.

Caldwell drew four tentative inferences from his study:

- Personnel roles and the process of role change are much more complex than either existing empirical research or prescriptive models suggest.
- Greater organizational complexity and flexibility may not only be challenging the conventional occupational self-identity of the personnel function, it may also be undermining, in the long run, the foundations of the expertise, status and credibility necessary to sustain a new HR professional identity.
- Old and newly intensified patterns of role ambiguity and conflict may have combined to become an intrinsic feature of personnel or HR roles in a context of constant organizational change.
- Although personnel and HR professionals may have little control over the forces driving role change, they appear to demonstrate a remarkable ability at present to cope with the challenges of intensified role ambiguity and conflict.[60]

Complexity and inherent conflict in the roles played by human resource professionals were acknowledged by this study, which concludes that Ulrich's depiction of the multiple and often-conflicting roles of human resource professionals as proactive business partners, with the success of all four roles dependent on collaborative partnerships, may often remain as rhetoric rather than existing in reality.

One aspect of complexity is the integration of roles. This is discussed below with regards to partnerships between business line managers and human resource business partners.

Integrated roles

With regard to the integration of roles, it has been found that there were greater strategy–HR linkages in above average performing companies[61] and with regard to decision-making, that higher performing organizations made much greater efforts to involve human resource executives in planning and decision-making processes.[62]

Further support for these conclusions is given by others who believe that for human resources strategies to be integrated with business strategies, it is necessary for there to be consistency between the human resource strategy, the business strategy and other functional strategies, and that a critical management task is to align formal structures and human resource systems so that together they drive the strategic objectives of the organization.[63] However, it has also been noted that integration is easier said than done for various reasons: because there is often diversity of strategic processes, levels and styles between businesses and that the strategy formulation process is

> a complex, interactive process heavily influenced by contextual and historical factors; because of the emergent nature of strategy in both the business and human resource domains, compounded by its lack of articulation; and the qualitative nature of human resource issues.[64]

Thus integrated decision-making with regard to human resource management is felt to have a positive impact on firm performance, but the socially complex nature of the human resource environment makes this difficult to achieve and observe.

An integrated – team – approach to the management of firm human resource has been recommended where senior human resource management professionals understand the internal and external factors that affect the human resource environment and know the needs of all stakeholders that are impacted by business decisions, and are therefore fully involved by senior business line managers with relevant business decision-making. For this approach to be successful it is believed that human resource professionals should be

> part of the top management team; involved in corporate/business planning and the integration of human resources plans with corporate/business plans; well placed to exert influence on the way in which the enterprise is organized, managed and staffed... professionally competent in personnel techniques... able to convince others of the need for change and act as effective change agents; and to be involved in shaping corporate culture and values.[65]

The interaction between business line managers and human resource professionals was discussed by Ulrich, who believes that if the management of human resources is to be seen as increasingly important for gaining and sustaining competitive advantage, then both human resource professionals and business line mangers must become human resource champions and partners. Strong and productive partnerships between human resource professionals and line managers

> imply mutual respect, with partners working together towards common goals in a process enriched by varied perspectives... A true partnership exists where observers at a staff meeting cannot readily tell the human resource executive from the line manager, because both clearly focus on business results.[66]

For human resource professionals to achieve this position, Ulrich believes that they need both technical business and technical human resource knowledge; the ability to partner with line in a real and effective way; and to deliver advisory and process related services from the human resource function that supports the short-term and long-term business goals of the organization. Despite the above, he also notes that business line managers

> are primarily responsible for the HR practices within a firm. Line managers have ultimate responsibility for both the outcomes and the processes within a firm. They are accountable to shareholders for delivering economic value, to customers for product or service value, and to employees for work place value.[67]

Therefore, Ulrich calls for: an integrated, seamless, partnership between human resource professionals and business line managers; for human resource professionals that deliver both process support and tactical and strategic advice to business line managers; and for business line managers that take ultimate responsibility for the management of firm resources to maximize stakeholder value. This view is supported by research which concludes that the human resource function has legitimacy in the organizations studied because the contribution of the human resource function to business effectiveness is perceived to centre on the business imperatives of performance and results; that human resource management strategies are rooted in business necessity; and that they are integrated with business strategy.[68]

The need for business line managers to embrace their responsibility for the management of firm human resources is emphasized by those who believe that, given the significant financial impact, people management needs to be a core operational process and not solely a support function run by human resource professionals. Even slight changes in employee productivity have a significant impact on shareholder returns, therefore human resource management should no longer be seen as a support function but rather a core process for business line managers.[69]

The above review identifies prescriptions for integrating business strategy and human resource strategy and notes that, while business line managers should take ultimate responsibility for the management of human resources, this is more likely to occur where human resource professionals and business line management relationships are themselves integrated through partnerships. In other words, strategy integration needs to be preceded by partnerships at a divisional-functional and individual level.

The complex relationship between business line managers and human resource professionals has often been examined in the context of their relative influence on decision-making and this is examined in more detail below.

Influence in human resource management

Relative influence

Like shared roles, the relative influence of senior line managers and human resource professionals on the human resource environment is a long-standing and recurrent debate, with Donald and Donald noting that the influence of the personnel professional is not only dependent on 'the personality and promotive qualities of the director of personnel activities, but also... scientific management in the field of personnel management'.[70] In other words, the ability of the personnel function to facilitate and advise line management is dependent on the personal attributes of individual personnel professionals and their technical knowledge of their field. This can be seen as an early indication of competencies that impact the credibility of human resource professionals.

A historical lack of influence on decision-making was noted which characterized personnel managers as being, 'reactive, passive, risk-averse, not business orientated, unable to shape management thinking, not involved in business decisions, lacking influence and operating in a vacuum.'[71] Results of a study on functional management found that the personnel function lacked influence in any type of decision-making and exerted almost no influence on strategic decisions. Other findings indicated that the power bases that provide departments with their influence in the administrative area of decision-making are: formal position authority; access to resources; and the scanning of administrative and regulatory trend; and that while the personnel function showed some influence in administrative decision-making, it displayed the least influence of any functional department.[72]

Given this historic lack of influence, it is interesting to note comments with regard to the type of relationship between human resource professionals and business line managers that underpins the influence of human resource professionals in the decision-making process:

> Whatever the structural arrangement, integration was more complete when key line, planning, and human resource executives shared a true appreciation for the strategic importance of people in the organization and, further, when these executives had mutual respect for each others knowledge and skills. These conditions contributed to a sense of partnership in the strategic management of the business.[73]

The influence of human resource professionals in the strategic management of the organization is therefore thought to be derived from partnerships that develop due to an appreciation of the importance of firm human resources by key management and mutual respect between human resource professionals and business line managers based on each other's competencies.

One study that investigated the organizational influence of functional departments, drawing on contingency and institutional theories of intra-organizational power, examined where the marketing function had higher levels of influence. The results indicated that influence is determined not only by adaptation to the organizational environment but also by unique historical aspects that become institutionalized. This finding supports the resource-based view of the firm in terms of its focus on complexity, causal ambiguity and path dependency and indicates that human resource professionals need to build partnerships with consideration to the historical context of the people environment.[74]

With regard to future influence, the development of human resource systems has tended to lag behind developments in strategy and structure and two short-term actions are suggested to increase the value of human resource functions as a whole to the organizations they serve. First, perceptions of senior business line and functional management need to change. They must believe that human resource functions as a whole and their leaders are competent in all aspects of human resource management and quickly follow this by appropriately funding and staffing the human resource function. Second, human resource functions themselves must not only possess human resource professionals with the knowledge and skill required to perform the full range of services commonly expected from such functions; they also need to substantially improve their capability to develop and implement management systems that complement different business strategies.[75] It was predicted that the personnel department would in the future 'continue to perform all of the services traditionally needed to acquire, develop, and allocate human talent. Moreover, it will act as an in-company consultant to top management on issues of organization design and development.'[76]

In terms of the relative influence of the senior business line management team, one study examined the links between top management values, philosophies, and business strategies and human resource management. It concluded that senior management shape the internal culture of organizations by clarifying the values at work within the firm and that not all companies successfully create a culture that facilitates effective human resource management policies. Their work emphasizes the role and responsibility of CEOs and senior business line management in determining the nature and resulting effectiveness of the human resource environment.[77]

Research has concluded that business and human resource strategy integration is more likely to occur where human resource professionals and business line management relationships are based on partnerships. However, even where these partnership-based relationships exist it would appear that CEO and top management influence on the people environment is significant and therefore their influence on decision-making is discussed further below.

Integrated influence

A study of professional services firms describes a number of cases where decisions made in conjunction with human resource professionals had significant impact on the survival of organizations. The importance of a strong CEO and top management team is noted and also that 'the fundamental strategic priority of those who are charged with responsibility for HRM in a firm is to ensure that management takes those ongoing HR actions that are vital for securing and maintaining industry membership.'[78] However, this assumes that human resource professionals have the ability to influence decision-making with regard to significant human resource related issues.

Creating an environment of integration and influence is not straightforward, especially when it involves the devolution of certain human resource management responsibilities to business line managers. Indeed, resistance to the devolution of responsibilities to business line managers has been identified by a number of writers.[79] It has been found that promoting an integrative culture of human resource management through the devolution of human resource responsibilities to line managers can create a tension between line mangers and the personnel function, with little evidence to show that there is an increase in influence of the personnel function after devolution has occurred.[80] It has also been found that some business line mangers resist formally delegated responsibility for human resource management[81] and that the success of devolvement varies by country.[82]

Research was undertaken to explore the possibilities of linking corporate and human resource strategy and one emergent issue with regard to organizational context is the style through which power is managed in organizations and its positive, or negative, impact on the performance of an organization's human resources. Another key factor is the extent to which human resource related issues are owned by the human resource function relative to business line management, or jointly by both. It was found that if a corporate strategy department exists but only focuses on formulating strategy without specifically considering human resource implications, then human resource strategic planning may well not occur at all and if it does, it will not be approached in an integrated way. This research concluded that the relative success of any organization's strategy is very likely to be determined by the extent to which the human resource function is well positioned and perceived as genuinely value-adding and relevant by the top levels of management within the organization. In the bank that was studied, the personnel function was not perceived as being particularly influential and therefore human resource strategy was marginalized.[83]

Despite its importance, strategic human resource management may not have fulfilled its initial promise due to a number of factors. First, the complexity and diversity of, sometimes emergent and intangible, linkages may undermine attempts to operationalize and implement strategy. Second, it may not be appropriate to give the human resource strategy its own identity without also ensuring that it is linked back into the firm's core business and functional strategies. Finally, while any organization's politics and turbulence may prevent linkages from developing, this process can be improved if adequate attention is paid to who should own human resource strategy and where it should sit in an organization's structure.[84]

It has been argued that human resource strategy integration requires support from broad constituencies within the organization with representation on the board and/or on senior management committees; direct access to the CEO through a formal reporting mechanism; and the success of informal networks that human resource professionals develop with key senior executives. However, the results of a study by Cathy Sheehan indicate that,

> although HR representation on the senior committee, a direct reporting
> relationship with the CEO and good informal relationships provide appropriate
> access for HR to make a contribution, other factors such as the business
> credibility of the HR manager, the level of CEO HRM commitment and the
> level of corporate cultural support for HRM, were stronger determinants of
> strategic integration.[85]

Sheehan found that if human resource professionals are to become credible, attitudinal changes that demonstrate an acceptance of a business-orientated approach and the rebranding of the function and specific positions have to be accompanied by changes in competencies. In terms of the devolution of human resource management responsibilities, it was found that business line managers were 'often frustrated by HRM initiatives that may interfere with production pressures' but that this can be mitigated by 'the business credibility of the HR manager, the actions of the CEO, or the presence of a supportive HRM corporate culture'.[86] The results of her study indicate that while at a superficial level human resource management integration involves structural changes, the rebranding of the human resource function and roles that reflect changes in expectations and responsibilities within organizations must also be supported by 'more substantial underlying adjustments to complex sets of beliefs, values and learned ways of coping.'[87] CEO and organization commitment to human resource management were both found to be important drivers behind the realization of expected human resource management outcomes.

Ultimately, there is less impact if there is less influence, less influence if a limited partnership exists between the CEO, business line managers and human resource professionals, and there is no partnership without credibility. Sheehan explored the relationship between the human resource function's access to avenues of political influence and perceived organizational performance through individual human resource professionals. It was found that while access to political influence does not impact firm performance, CEO support and organizational support for the human resource function predicts perceived organizational performance. Representation on the board of directors appears only to have symbolic value.

CEO support is noted by a number of commentators as important in terms of influencing management responses to their human resource management responsibilities, and a triangle of best-practice is proposed with CEO recognition at the apex and integrated human resource and business strategies at the lower corners, leading to business effectiveness.[88]

Further research found that strategic decision-making can take place at CEO and board level, so board membership is not necessary to influence decision-making; that both informal and formal routes of influence are important; and that business focus is more important than advocacy of a specialist function in strategy formulation. It also found a separation between strategy formulation and the implementation of policies and practices due to differences in the understanding of, and commitment to, human resource policies and practices by human resource professionals and business line mangers.[89]

It can be seen that social complexity impacts the strategy-making process and the implementation of its results due to a less than universal acceptance of devolved responsibility for human resource management by business line managers.

A place on the management team does not automatically mean a strategic role or comprehensive involvement. Instead, the presence of trusting relationships between human resource professionals and business line managers is emphasized alongside the human resource business partner's ability to show the importance of human resource related issues. Technical and professional human resource knowledge combined with knowledge and experience of the business are seen as most important for the involvement of human resource professionals in decision-making along with the need for human resource professionals to be active and use initiative, and for business line managers to be trained to see the importance of human resource related issues.[90]

It is believed that the capabilities and activities of human resource professionals are connected to their interpersonal skills, their ability to establish relationships based on trust appearing to be of significant importance to business line management. Trust is established by combining functional specialist knowledge with business savvy and has been associated closely with the concept of credibility.[91] The role of human resource professionals is partly determined by the status of the human resource function as a whole[92] and day-to-day human resource management has to work well before involvement in more strategic activities is granted.[93]

Having looked at the nature of strategic human resource management and the associated roles and influence of those delivering it we now turn to the structure of the human resource function.

The structure of human resource management

In terms of organization structure, Ulrich develops a framework within which the influence of human resource professionals might be delivered. He advocates shifting to a debate that concerns *value creation* where 'HR professionals as administrative experts must learn to create value, not as they perceive it, but as the managers and other clients perceive it.'[94] This involves adding four mechanisms to the delivery structure of the human resource function:

- service brokers;
- service centres;
- centres of expertise;
- integrated solutions.[95]

He defines the value creation process in terms of four steps of customer requirements that are satisfied through customer interface as the relational part of the process that delivers shared services. In this model the needs of the internal client drive the delivery process, and the delivery process includes at least five delivery channels:

- business-dedicated HR professionals;
- shared service located HR professionals;
- line managers;

- information technology;
- outsourcing.[96]

The business-dedicated human resource professionals of Ulrich can be thought of as a development of Donald and Donald's facilitating and advisory role, where the management team were seen as regaining the responsibility for managing people while looking to personnel professionals for support; of Tyson's architect model, which focused on strategic input; of Storey's internal consultants; and of Fitz-enz confidents.[97] Ulrich accepts the necessity for process roles within the human resource function, which in his model are provided by shared service HR professionals utilizing information technology and outsourcing.

Shared services

Four major drivers behind the adoption of shared services have been noted:[98]

- **cost reduction:** reduce headcount, increase procurement leverage, increase efficiency;
- **quality improvement:** identify and implement improvements, better accuracy more consistently;
- **organization change:** structural flexibility, reconfiguration of the organization supported by a firm platform, benefits from organizational learning, repositioning HR;
- **introduction of technology:** the support of new technology platforms.

With 'increased devolution of people responsibilities to the line and administrative work outsourced or automated out, senior management in some organizations has started to question what value the function can add. If it cannot demonstrate its worth, then managers will wonder what the point of having an HR function is.'[99]

Adopting a shared service model was seen as helping to reposition the human resource function, which was seen as:[100]

- short-term vs long-term;
- operational vs strategic;
- reactive vs proactive;
- compliant vs confident;
- traditional vs innovative;
- business inhibitor vs business facilitator.

These perceptions needed to be addressed, in addition to the difficulties relating to the boundaries of responsibilities within the human resource function; for instance, how responsibilities were divided between the operational and administrative staff, business partners and centres of excellence.

Ultimately, it is believed that human resource professionals will add value by:[101]

- getting the basics right;
- excellence in the people-centric role and advice on the people aspect of all decisions;
- deciding what non-people specialists are responsible for;
- recognizing where the human touch is valued, necessary and required.

Human resource professionals need to understand how they must adapt to more integrated role structures, including working as human resource business partners,[102] and this includes understanding how the activities undertaken by the human resource function, through human resource professionals, fits with and supports the organization's mission, strategy and basic business processes.[103]

The resources and performance of the human resource function as a whole impact the influence of individual human resource professionals. In addition, people management is seen to be more effective where:

- the orientation of the CEO and senior business line to managing firm human resources is deemed to be high;
- CEO influence regarding the management of human resources is significant
- personal relationships with CEOs appear to have greater importance than membership of committees which have more symbolic value.[104]

The importance of CEOs and senior leaders

The ability of the most senior human resource professional to add value in determining the strategic direction of the corporation, with particular focus on the human resource issues, is important. However, their degree of input 'depends mostly on the CEO and President's view of what a human resource function can contribute to the development and achievement of business plans and results, and on the credibility and performance of the person in the human resource executive position.'[105]

It has been proposed that strategic human resource planning and strategic business planning should be integrated. However, it has also been noted that CEOs and senior business line management will have greater influence on whether this occurs than human resource professionals. This is illustrated by comparing CEO and senior business line manager competency in strategic human resource management and influence over the human resource environment, in operation with the credibility of human resource professionals (Figure 17.1):[106]

Figure 17.1 The relative influence of CEOs on people management

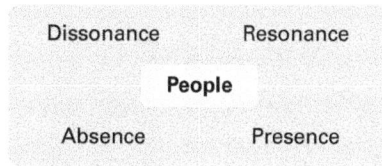

Dissonance	Resonance
People	
Absence	Presence

SOURCE Adapted from Aldrich, 2009

- **Resonance:** Where there is high CEO competency in strategic human resource management and influence on the human resource environment; high senior business line manager understanding of what contributes to a high-performance human resource environment; and high human resource credibility with high influence. The relative competitive advantage of the organization gained through people will be *maximized*.

- **Dissonance:** Where there is high CEO competency in strategic human resource management and influence on the human resource environment; high senior business line manager understanding of what contributes to a high-performance human resource environment; and low human resource credibility with low influence. The relative competitive advantage of the organization gained through people will be *high*.

- **Presence:** Where there is low CEO competency in strategic human resource management and influence on the human resource environment; low senior business line manager understanding of what contributes to a high-performance human resource environment; and high human resource credibility with high influence. The relative competitive advantage of the organization gained through people will be *low*.

- **Absence:** Where there is low CEO competency in strategic human resource management and influence on the human resource environment; low senior business line manager understanding of what contributes to a high-performance human resource environment; and low human resource credibility with low influence. The relative competitive advantage of the organization gained through people will be *minimized*.

For the sake of clarity, extreme positions are described above. However, in reality the picture is much more complex. Organizations will display multiple positions on the grid; for instance, the credibility of human resource professionals, and therefore influence, will vary by individual relationship, by business unit, by division, by function and therefore, in combination, across an organization as a whole. In addition, credibility, and therefore influence, may be institutionalized, for example in decision-making relating to compensation and benefits, or contingent on individual partnerships between human resource professionals and business line managers.

While in certain respects CEOs are expected to exert greater influence over the human resource environment than human resource professionals, this will only be beneficial to the competitive advantage of the firm where they are competent in human resource management. If the CEO does not think strategically about talent issues or is not aware of how to capture the maximum discretionary effort from their employees then their ability to influence will not be fully utilized, and in the worst case their influence may have a negative impact on people management.

Of course, CEOs may be highly competent in human resource management but may not have the influence to drive initiatives down through the organization for successful implementation. Similarly, CEOs with a low competency in human resource management may have high influence and be able to drive poor human resource initiatives down through their organization that then have a negative impact on the human resource environment and the competitive advantage gained through people.

It has been found that the degree of human resource business partner influence is contingent on the degree of human resource business partner credibility. It is therefore argued that if human resource professionals have no credibility, CEOs and senior business line managers are unlikely to include them in significant decision-making. Without credibility there is no influence, and without influence there is no impact.[107]

Credibility can be both individual and institutional. Where credibility is based on bilateral relationships between individuals then credibility can be seen as transient, while if it is attributed to the function it is institutionalized and thus more resilient.[108] Indeed, it has been reported that:

> sources for [human resource business partners'] credibility can be both individual and institutional, yet the reported lack of position power felt by most [human resource business partners] in our study suggests that, in the banking sector at least, the HR function's influence is determined by the strength of individual interpersonal relationships. It is rarely institutionalized for its own sake. This renders the HR function's status rather precarious and transient, reliant on fragile trust, the highest-ranked determinant of credibility.[109]

Highlights

- This chapter has examined the discussion and debate that has surrounded people management, starting with an HBR article in 1929. It highlighted suggested management approaches that were universalistic, contingent, configurational and ultimately those that acknowledge complexity. Not surprisingly, these tracked approaches to general organizational management theory.

- Following this, the role and influence of people management professionals and non-people management professionals were discussed in terms of their impact on the people environment in organizations.

- It is clear that an integrated approach to people strategy and implementation is more effective than situations where there is limited integration.

- The degree to which this is possible depends on a number of complex relationships, but most significantly on the philosophy and capabilities of the CEO and senior leadership team. Also, the capabilities and credibility of people management professionals, as well as the historical context of people management and the current and future challenges.

- In the next chapter we focus on the design and implementation of an effective people operating model that reflects our understanding of people, organizational and environmental complexity.

Leadership impact

Key themes that leaders should reflect on include:

- knowledge they have around people and organizational complexity;
- the role they are expected to play in leading and managing people;
- the importance of the CEO philosophy towards people management;
- ownership of the people strategy;
- investment in, and development of, the support they need to implement the people strategy effectively;
- a boundary-spanning role, currently performed by human resource business partners.

People management recommendations

Actions to consider:

- Identify the competencies that lead to credibility, influence and impact within your organization.
- Integrate strategic workforce planning between business line managers and HR professionals.
- Review organization design from a people management perspective.
- Human resource professionals should engage with business line managers early in the strategy process in order to influence the process.

Professional people management

18

Introduction

So far, we have been on a journey to understand the complexity of people and how they construct and negotiate their reality. We have also looked at organizations and how they, through their people, also construct and negotiate the reality of their environment. A number of significant environmental trends that impact organizations have been identified and discussed.

In the previous chapter the contested nature of the roles and responsibilities relating to human resource management were examined, and the importance of an integrated approach established. In this chapter some underlying tensions are explored, and the future people management challenges summarized. Finally, a new framework for people management is introduced.

Chapter summary

The following subjects are discussed in this chapter:

- **underlying tension;**

- **HR in the boardroom;**

- **talent management;**

- **future people management:**

  - leadership challenges;

  - people management challenges;

  - organizing for people management;

- **new framework for people management:**
  - people advisors;
  - people portfolio management;
  - people specializations – embedded;
  - people facilitators;
  - people enablers.

Underlying tension

In *The Talent Delusion*, Chamorro-Premuzic opines on the role of the human resource function:

> with the emergence of HR as a regulatory employee protection body in the 1950s, the average experience of employees began to improve, but the relationship between employers and employees was still merely transactional and extrinsic from a motivational perspective. This turned HR into a bureaucratic procurement entity and employees into instrumental salary-men, or *Homo economici*: rational and pragmatic minds focused on the pursuit of extrinsic rewards and the avoidance of losses.[1]

In terms of strategy, in *HR in the Boardroom*, Lance Wright notes that

> the continued use of the term 'HR strategy' helps perpetuate the subliminal idea that the HR function and the true operation of the business are separate. Somehow, unlike manufacturing strategies, or marketing strategies, or financial strategies, which easily fit under the umbrella of business strategies, HR strategies seem to continue to occupy a space of their own. It is as if there is something called 'the business' that exists as an entity that is separate and distinct from the people of an organization. In reality, there is only the business.[2]

The business and HR discourse is unhelpful in perpetuating the situation where 'business leaders know a lot less than they should about basic human resource management and human resource professionals... know a lot less than they should about business.'[3]

The authors of *Human Resource Management in a Business Context* note an underlying tension between human resource professionals and business line managers who see human resource professionals as:

- out of touch with business realities, pushing through policies like work–life balance that they feel may conflict with their business goals;
- constraining their authority to take decisions;

- unresponsive and slow to act;
- idealistic, pushing policies that are fine in theory but hard to execute.[4]

The authors of *Do We Need HR?* state that HR

> spend time specifying how to parcel up its expertise, thinking about clarity of the proposition and the governance of this expertise. It has created questions about the availability of expertise, as well as the level of skill and the level of business acumen needed within these centres.[5]

Senior line managers could take more responsibility for aspects of people management, either directly or in combination with an HR business partner and this would increase the line's ownership of these activities. However, HR is viewed as a cost centre and the following other challenges have been noted: a lack of impact metrics to assess the value of HR driven programmes which anyway have difficulty in establishing causation; poor historical collaboration with HR who show an inconsistency in their approach; the line managers' lack of HR knowledge, relevant skills and competencies; and their lack of time.[6]

HR in the boardroom

With regard to the efficacy of the human resource function, in *HR in the Boardroom*, Wright acknowledges the familiar criticism that HR is administrative, reactive and not strategic and asks whether or not after 'many years of essentially the same criticism should prompt rethinking about HR'.[7] His vision is for

> a new breed of business leader in C-Suites who understands that it really is all about people. Regardless of what we call it, each senior executive will be a human resource management expert in their own right. The roles of CEO and Chief human resource officer will essentially be one.[8]

In *Reinventing Talent Management*, Edward Lawler recommends that each board has at least one member who has expertise in people management and states that disruptive technology, multiple generations in the workplace, changing views of work and working by new generational cohorts, a focus on CSR, globalization and the growing complexity of work are driving the need for changes in the delivery of professional people support in organizations. He adds that 'talent management should become increasingly strategy driven, skills based, performance focused, agile, segmented, and evidence based.'[9]

Talent management

In *The Talent Management Handbook*, it is stated that talent management is an important function that is usually situated within the human resource management function and is the responsibility of all leaders and managers. It is described as the systematic design, integration and proactively implemented programmes that build and sustain a high-performance workforce.[10] For Lawler, all human resources of an organization are described as talent.[11]

Talent management originally emerged in workforce planning and then became focused more specifically on the acquisition, development and retention of high-potential talent pools. Heads of Talent emerged, and talent management teams increased in size. In *Do We Need HR?* four philosophical approaches to talent management are outlined: people, practices, positions and pools.

The *people* philosophy focuses on identifying and segmenting 'employees with unique skill sets... assumed to be rare, hard to find, difficult to replace, and to add a disproportionate amount of value to the organization compared to other employees.'[12] However, it is noted that this approach can lead to the use of A, B and C categories of employees, an over-reliance on compensation to retain A players, and an elitist view of the few stars, which limits expectations regarding the effectiveness of development for C players. It is argued that organizations need a balance of capabilities and potential.

The *practices* philosophy focuses on ensuring the presence of highly effective and impactful bundles of talent management practices and emphasizes the following seven key components:

- **identifying and recruiting talent:** analysis of labour pools, benchmarking competitor strategies, decentralizing or centralizing recruitment strategies, coordinating preferred suppliers and establishing brand and reputation amongst key employee segments;

- **attracting talent to the organization:** creation of employee value propositions, management of an employer brand;

- **minimizing attrition through engagement and retention:** effective onboarding, aligning rewards and recognition structures, improving line management skills and engagement with talent, retention initiatives;

- **identifying key internal talent:** systematic and effective approaches to affirm individuals with the status of talent, high potential identification systems, identify the roles are most talent-dependent, and the use of assessment instruments and frameworks;

- **managing talent flows:** developing effective succession systems, creating flexibility in internal mobility, career management and planning systems, succession management;

- **developing employees:** coaching and mentoring, flexible portfolios of development activities, learning opportunities and options for employees, team learning processes, strategic and operational leadership development programmes;

- **delivering performance:** organization talent review processes, linking data on organizational performance to the selection of talent, stretching the performance of talented individuals, managing underperformance.[13]

The practices philosophy states that talent management is only effective if managed as an overall architecture which must be strategically aligned.

The *position* philosophy focuses on identifying and segmenting key positions for organizational success. It is said to facilitate strategic focus and execution with regard to value creation, value protection and leverage.[14]

The *strategic pools* philosophy focuses on investment and return choices from a human capital and segmentation perspective. The hiring, development and retention of talent are seen as an investment not a cost.[15] Returns are monitored where value is created through the:

- identification and translation of the organizational capabilities articulated in the strategy into specifications for talent;
- the creation of insight into the relative value of specific talent to the execution of strategy;
- the assessment of the consequences or feasibility for build or buy talent strategies;
- the use of frameworks to segment the existing or target talent population in different ways against strategic considerations.

Future people management

Leadership challenges

A second way of considering the future of people management is to look at the key areas of leadership challenges that must be supported.

Leading Organizations offers lessons from a review of leadership articles and McKinsey's assignment database, and summarizes ten areas of leadership focus:[16]

- **Talent attraction and retention:** Talent attraction and retention are the first areas of leadership focus because superior talent is eight times more productive, great talent is scarce and most companies are not getting it right. They recommend three- to five-year workforce planning, focusing on the 5 per cent of employees that deliver 95 per cent of the value, creating a magnetic employer proposition, and delivering on it, linking company meaning to personal meaning, leveraging technology and people analytics and removing non value-added activities from jobs.

- **Talent development:** The second key area of leadership focus is talent development, as in organizations that can't acquire enough talent skills will become obsolete faster, and most companies struggle to do it well. They recommend making it personal, involving business leaders in the design, focusing on the capabilities required to deliver the strategy, stretching strengths, understanding the efficacy of new approaches and linking learning to retention.

- **Performance management:** The third key area of leadership focus is performance management, as done well it delivers results, there is a greater understanding about what works than before; and what most companies are doing isn't working. They recommend understanding the strengths and weaknesses of current systems, making explicit design choices harmonizing company and employee motivations, focusing on skills, including capability and mindset interventions, ensuring an equitable process, making business leaders accountable for implementation and monitoring business outcomes.

- **High-performance teams:** The fourth key area of leadership focus is creating high-performance teams as teamwork beats individual talent, but few teams achieve greatness and the future will be more demanding for teams. They recommend focusing the team on work only it can do, not to let structure dictate who is on the team, and measuring progress through alignment of shared goals, quality of abilities and interaction, and an environment that promotes risk-taking.

- **Decision-making:** The fifth key area of leadership focus is decision-making. Decision quality can have a significant impact on the organization; it impacts talent retention and poor decision-making is rampant. They recommend recognizing and addressing biases, ensuring dialogue as well as data, differentiating three types of decisions: infrequent, high-stakes, repetitive that can be delegated and repetitive cost-cutting. Prioritizing decisions based on value and 'pain', fully understanding the causes in problem areas, institutionalizing continuous improvement, and testing solutions with stakeholders before implementation.

- **Organization design:** The sixth key area of leadership focus is organization redesign, as it is inevitable, it can have profound impact and only 23 per cent get it right. They recommend thinking beyond structure boxes and lines, achieving stability to allow for agility and rapidly iterate agile design elements, safeguarding business continuity from the start, and solving strategic needs not just pain points.

- **Cost reduction:** The seventh key area of leadership focus is cost reduction as value creating companies keep costs under control. If done badly it undermines growth and more talent is often lost than is planned for.

- **Culture:** The eighth key area of leadership focus is culture. Culture drives performance, it is hard to copy and not managing it can prove fatal. They recommend using four high-impact levers: having a compelling story, role modelling, developing confidence and skills, and reinforcing mechanisms. Making change personal for a critical mass of leaders and engaging with them early in any change programme, focusing on more than employee engagement and reframing limiting mindsets that drive behaviours, measuring key outcomes, and infusing desired shift into people-related processes.

- **Transformational change:** The ninth key area of leadership focus is change. As transformational change is a path to greatness, there is a proven way to double the chance of success and the old adage 'adapt or die' is true. They recommend engaging a broad leadership coalition from day one, applying the five frames approach: aspire, assess, architect, act and advance.[17] Tap into sources of meaning for employees, being rational about irrationality, focusing equally on strengths and weaknesses, placing equal focus on performance and health and upskilling next generation leaders.

- **Leadership transitions:** The tenth and final key area of leadership focus is leadership transitions, as they are high-stakes events. Nearly half of transitions fail, mostly because of the soft stuff, and transition frequency is increasing. They recommend taking stock in five areas simultaneously: business, culture, team, stakeholders, myself. Putting in place no-surprises review systems, acting early on no-regret changes, being clear on what you will and will not do, focusing on impact rather than the first 100 days, creating a powerful, integrated, change story, and co-creating the aspiration with the team.

People management support is required in each area, but how should this be organized? Having looked at key areas of leadership focus we examine the key challenges for people management.

People management challenges

A third way of looking at the future of people management is to look at its key objectives and in *High-Impact Human Capital Strategy*, twelve objectives for people management are suggested:

- **investment:** setting the optimal investment level for human capital and reviewing this expenditure periodically
- **aligning people management:** aligning HR programs to the business as they are initiated, developed and implemented
- **critical talent:** managing critical talent in the organization, ensuring that the appropriate number and quality of talented employees are available, addressing skills shortages, and ensuring that talent remains in the organization
- **engagement and satisfaction:** pursuing a program of employee satisfaction, commitment, and job engagement, so that employees are fully involved in their work, remain loyal to the organization, and help attract others to the organization
- **performance and innovation:** creating a performance and innovation culture to achieve results in the organization with proper direction, roles and motivations
- **well-being:** ensuring that employees are healthy and safe with proper healthcare and wellness opportunities

- **demographics:** addressing the current demographics and societal issues to ensure that a proper employee mix is available and included in processes to enhance productivity and innovation

- **technology:** using technology to its fullest extent to unleash the creativity and potential of employees, while ensuring that it is driving productivity, innovation, customer satisfaction

- **globalization:** addressing globalization in terms of how it effects employees in the present and will affect employees in the future, by having them actively engaged in every part of the process

- **csr:** addressing environmental and energy issues as they relate to jobs, the organization and society

- **development:** developing effective leaders who can operate successfully in a global, diverse environment

- **data analytics:** implementing a system for accountability, including measuring success with analytics and big data, and delivering value what will be credible to top executives, including the chief financial officer.[18]

The above objectives have all been covered in the preceding pages with one exception, the alignment of people management. This is addressed in the final chapter of this book.

Organizing for people management

In *Towards a New HR Philosophy*, Peter Allen suggests that where executives and managers focus on business results and not managing people, the human resource function fills the gap and when it acts as 'manager, mediator and nurturer, it further separates managers from their employees'[19] and calls for a change in approach.

One suggested change has been to the human resource business partner role. McKinsey published 'The CEOs guide to competing through HR', where the authors suggest the reinvention of the human resource function, with four key areas of focus: talent value leaders (TVLs) to transform the human resource business partner role, helping manage the talent pool to maximize positive outcomes for employees and the organization; the use of people analytics in decision-making and process re-engineering; the use of digital technology to transform the delivery of people operations; and combining analytics with an agility.[20]

Another approach also focuses on impact and value creation but takes a broader view. In *Transformational HR: How human resources can create value and impact business strategy*,[21] Perry Timms focuses first on the key areas of business impact where the human resource function already makes an impact: brand, recruitment and selection, job profiles, rewards and benefits, well-being, employee engagement, performance management, diversity and inclusion, culture and values, change and organizational development and learning and talent development.[22]

Timms proposed a four-zone framework to deliver transformational HR which is interpreted below:[23]

- **people and programme support:** employer brand, talent acquisition and leaving, employee experience, learning and development, total reward, transformation governance and support, HR information systems;
- **people strategy and partnerships:** collaborative intelligence conduit feeding into strategic as well as tactical decision-making;
- **people performance and development:** delivering guidance on organization design, structure, behaviour and development;
- **people and organizational transformation:** episodic and flexible delivery of transformational activities.

He also believes that transformational HR leads and delivers fundamental changes in how people and organizations work.[24] At a strategic level this requires:[25]

- **external vigilance:** external environment scanning;
- **contextual intelligence:** people analytics and qualitative data;
- **design artistry:** organization and employee experience;
- **stewarding a just organization:** wellness and corporate sustainability;
- **application of science:** philosophy and psychology.

In *Winning With Your Talent Strategy*, McKinsey undertook a global survey that received response from 1,820 participants representing all regions, industries and functions.[26]

They looked at the relationship between various talent-management practices and their overall effectiveness. The three practices with the highest statistical relationship, using standardized regression coefficients, with talent-management effectiveness, that is effectively or very effectively improving organization performance, were as follows:[27]

- **rapid talent allocation:** quickly moving talent to address strategic priorities (0.32);
- **positive employee experience:** facilitating employee experience (0.30);
- **strategic HR team:** the HR team understands strategy and business priorities (0.23).

The resulting effectiveness delivered by these three practices drove financial outperformance versus peers (0.40).

Rapid allocation of talent led to a 1.4 times greater likelihood of outperformance and 39 per cent of respondents felt they were fast or very fast at re-allocating talent when required.

The involvement of human resource management helped improve the employee experience when teams of experts could be assembled quickly to support business priorities and where they were able to deploy talent with skills that matched business requirements. This led to a 1.3 times greater likelihood of outperformance and 37 per cent of respondents felt that the human resource function facilitates a positive employee experience.[28]

The presence of a strategic human resource team gave a 1.4 times greater likelihood of outperformance. The authors write that:

> the factor that most supports this practice, according to the results, is cross-functional experience. When HR leaders have experience in other functions – including experience as line managers – they are 1.8 times more likely to have a comprehensive understanding of strategy and business priorities. Also important is close collaboration among the organization's chief HR officer, CEO, and CFO. Fewer than half of all respondents say those executives work together very closely at their organizations, but those who do are 1.7 times likelier to report a strategy-minded HR function.[29]

In *Talent Wins*, it is proposed that the talent agenda should be driven by a tripartite, G3, consisting of the CEO, CFO and CHRO focused on the critical 2 per cent of the organization who create the most value. Also, that the G3 should work with the chief information officer (CIO) to leverage technology for talent transformation[30] and 'the Board should be familiar with the work around talent, focus on items such as diversity, CEO succession and the critical 2 percent of talent, and it is important to dispel any misconception that the CHRO is "just a people person"'.[31]

- The compensation committee should be renamed the 'talent and rewards committee'.
- There should be a focus on the employer brand.
- The vertical hierarchy structure approach to talent management should be replaced with an internal market view of talent mobilization.
- Work should be meaningful.
- There is a need to understand, measure and monitor the social, informal organization.

In *Reinventing Talent Management*, it is recommended that the board should help make informed decisions about the organization's talent management operating model and should therefore have at least one member who is an expert in this field. It is also recommended that the CHRO regularly attends board meetings. In terms of input by the executive team it is stated that

> the top executive team of every corporation needs to be involved in the making of key talent decisions. It needs to understand the design of the talent management systems, assure that design is operating effectively and in the case of key appointments be sure that the right individuals are chosen.[32]

It is suggested that a chief human resource officer with expertise in HR and talent management should be part of the executive team drawing on the expertise of chief talent officers when required and also that one option might be splitting the HR function into operational and strategic functions, with the operational HR reporting to the COO and strategic HR reporting to the CEO. Another option discussed sees the adoption of a chief organizational effectiveness officer who is responsible for the HR function, organization design, organization development, business strategy and talent management.[33]

In terms of the *HR Function*, Lawler gives the following advice:

> if you want an HR department that contributes far more than administrative support, you and your CHRO need employees with business savvy. Your HR staffers should be as adept at understanding the complex needs of your business as they are at understanding the needs of your complex employees. Creating a staff filled with these kinds of strategic thinkers is likely to involve a slow and painful transformation. Many HR workers have grown up in a service culture centred around explaining benefits, salary increases, and workplace behavioural norms to company employees. It may well be that they haven't had to think strategically, to see themselves as leaders who can contribute as much value to forward-looking discussions, as say, leaders from manufacturing or marketing. Some of your existing HR people will be able, perhaps with training, to make the transition. Others will not.[34]

It is envisaged by. Charon that the HR function may split into two entities, one that focuses on strategy and talent management and one that focuses on operational, transactional functions:[35]

- **strategic:** includes talent strategy, organizational diagnosis, learning and development, recruiting, performance management, compensation strategy, leadership coaching;
- **transactional:** includes payroll, compensation and benefits administration, legal and compliance.

The transactional work should be streamlined through the operating model by focusing on process improvements, automation and outsourcing.

With regard to the continued use of human resource business partners, in *Do we Need HR?* the authors note that

> it has taken HR many years to build its cadre of business partners, and to get there, it has had to solve problems of capability (upskilling, building business acumen, cultural insight and relational skills), expectations (selling the proposition, educating the line about how to use this expertise and building the line capability to actually do it), aligning the resources behind the business partners (aligning them to the business, avoiding role overload and providing necessary support), regulating the relationships they have so that they can be aligned to potential differences between business unit and corporate agendas, thinking about the line management decisions over HR resources, avoiding role drift back into more reactive, operational or residual transactional work, and managing the boundaries between the business partner relationships and their connections back to work in centres of expertise and service centres.[36]

In terms of centres of expertise, the authors view them as 'an organizational unit that embodies a set of capabilities that has been explicitly recognized by the firm as an important source of value creation, with the intention that these capabilities be leveraged by or disseminated to other parts of the firm'[37] and 'small groups of individuals recognized for their leading-edge strategically valuable knowledge and mandated to leverage and/or make that knowledge available throughout the... firm.'[38] They argue that centres of expertise should only be established inside organizations if they are preceded by 'an accepted intention to derive value from the unit's capabilities for the broader organization, and an explicit recognition and declaration that, through its role, the unit can truly add value.'[39]

It has been suggested that the future success of the human resource function will require accepting diverse definitions of the role, incorporate other disciplines and require boundary-spanning within the organization. In some organizations activity around communications and corporate and social responsibility may lead to expanded roles that incorporate responsibility for all these areas, while in other organizations 'it might mean that things like strategy, process excellence and employment branding are primarily driven out of functions such as corporate strategy, operations or marketing'.[40]

In *Talent Wins*, to draw the human resource closer to the business it is suggested that human resource professionals spend time outside of the function in other parts of the organization and that non-human resource professionals spend time in the human resource function. From a development perspective, 'it is concerning that HR professionals do not appear to gain benefits from contacts in other functions'.[41] CEOs should announce that

> anyone who expects to have a senior HR position in our talent-driven company should gain experience in line jobs and in functions such as finance, to build better business-strategy capabilities. Line managers intent on becoming senior leaders should see stints in HR as a normal part of their career path.[42]

It is also suggested that the traditional advisory business partner role is replaced by one that can drive strategic talent decisions and they call this a talent value leader (TVL) who is part of a business unit G3. In this model, TVLs will be held accountable and judged on the portfolio management and performance of talent, will have strong influence on decision-making, but will not make the final decision on people-related matters. 'The TVL plays the role you wish your HR business partners were playing today' and 'exemplifies what HR should be in the twenty-first century'.[43]

In 2015, Josh Bersin contributed to a collection of thought pieces by the CIPD. In 'A modern HR operating model: The world has changed',[44] he notes that the core of high-impact HR today is creating more specialists and locating them closer to the business, where they can drive the most value. His recommendations include:

- **More specialists and fewer 'generalists':** High-impact human resource containing almost 65 per cent specialists compared to less than 40 per cent for non-optimized teams – the role of 'generalist' almost going away.

- **Networks of expertise not 'centres of expertise':** They maybe be assigned or embedded in the business and are all connected to each other by leveraging technology. Centres of expertise reduce in size and focus on quality and consistency, not centralized service delivery.

- **VPs of HR:** Senior human resource business partners are 'often operating as "VPs of HR" in the business', partnering directly with local business line leaders as consultants designing and helping to deliver solutions. These roles require strong business knowledge and broad people management experience and expertise. 'Many of our clients tell us the title "business partner" is now obsolete, so these are essentially "people leaders" or "talent managers" – to denote their direct responsibility for results.'

- **CHROs not just delivering efficient HR services:** '35–40% of all CHROs we now interview and work with are coming from the business' and are focused on delivering effective and impactful business outcomes.

Less than 8 per cent of all organizations have a professional development team for the people professionals that work in the human resource function.

In 'Implications for the function formally known as HR', Kay Foster-Cheek and Eva Sage-Gavin describe the roles that remain once transactional elements are stripped out by automation and outsourcing.[45] These include trend forecasting and supporting culture and relationship building. Activities will be decentralized, distributed, and talent from other functions will be leveraged, for instance marketing and finance, to help with workforce segmentation and business impact reporting. Indeed, Ian Ziskin suggests that the human resource function, or whatever it is called in the future, should act as an 'orchestra conductor' to help organizations successfully address complex problems that are multi-disciplinary and cross-functional in nature.[46]

In *The Future Office*, it is predicted that 'a specialist HR professional will act as a coach, mentor, manager and career-development guide. A key reason for workers to come to the office will be to interact with these specialists.'[47]

New framework for people management

To address the various views expressed relating to the future organization of human resource management a new framework has been designed that is people-centred and therefore flexible in terms of its application in different cultural environments and size of organization, from the largest global business to small and medium-sized enterprises who can source expertise on a flexible basis. It addresses the concerns of Caldwell and others noted above by removing role ambiguity, focusing on core expertise to support credibility and allowing for flexibility in its implementation and development.

A new people management framework is proposed with five roles: people advisors, portfolio management, embedded people specializations, people facilitators, and boundary spanners (Figure 18.1).

People advisors

- Mental:
  - psychologists;
  - neuroscientists;
  - mental health first-aid;
  - external support.
- Physical:
  - exercise physiologists;
  - organizational ergonomics;
  - safety marshal/first-aid;
  - external support.
- Corporate sustainability and social responsibility:
  - public policy engagement – supranational, national and local;
  - employee relations, voice and mediation;
  - diversity and inclusion – including multi-faith expertise;

Figure 18.1 The people management framework

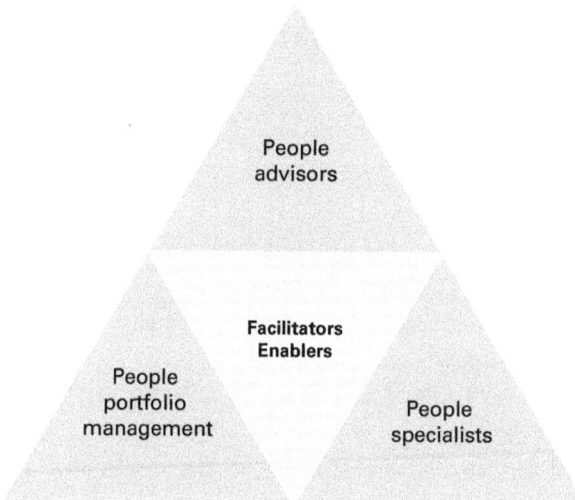

- cultural anthropology;
- financial advice support by an external advisor;
- internal communications

People portfolio management

- Strategic workforce planning:
  - workforce strategy and planning;
  - organization design and development;
  - segmented employee value proposition.
- Acquisition and transition:
  - employer brand manager;
  - recruitment and selection;
  - onboarding;
  - transitioning – internal and external moves, voluntary and otherwise;
  - alumni network.
- Talent development:
  - continuing personal and team development;
  - coaching and mentoring;
  - careers advice and mobility.
- Funding and reporting:
  - compensation and benefits design;
  - people metrics and internal reporting.

People specializations: Embedded

- **Marketing:** employer brand and employee value proposition, with the CPO as brand manager;
- **finance:** investment and public reporting, payroll and expenses;
- **technology:** people systems;
- **data analytics:** data management and analytics;
- **legal and compliance:** contracts, compromise agreements and compliance with regulation regarding conduct and governance;
- **operational risk:** people risk assessment around target operating models and processes with regard to physical safety and areas of high-impact decision-making;
- **operational service delivery:** to ensure the quality of people-related services, shared services/service-centres.

People facilitators

- To avoid leaders having multiple touch points for people-related advice and services this could be located within the divisional COO function or where none exists the leader will have a dedicated person in this boundary-spanning role.

- The boundary-spanning role would be used as a rotation for leadership training for CPOs as well as for other executive positions

- In small and medium-sized businesses the picture is different, as all functional professionals need to cover more waterfront with certain expertise outsourced.

People enablers

- The only people generalists in an organization will be the ones with no specialist people advisory expertise, no people portfolio management expertise and no embedded people specialization. Leaders of business lines and functions are people generalists but must be more than this, they must be well-informed employee champions, as enablers, coaches, and facilitators of employee success.

- The link between business divisions and functions and the people advisory and people portfolio management teams will vary. As previously discussed, many functions will contain embedded people specialists who report within the function and will represent their function on joint, ongoing, flow projects. For business divisions the divisional COOs team would be the natural link.

- How the people management knowledge and expertise maps across the divisional and geographic organization and who reports to who will depend on the context. There is no best practice here. However, given everything discussed in this book, is there any reason why the most senior people function leader should not be part of the executive committee?

This new framework is developed and discussed in the concluding chapter.

Highlights

The new model of people management organization delivers:

- **focus on people**: informed CEO and senior leadership who influence on people management;

- **integrated approach to strategy**: integration of workforce planning in firm strategic planning;

- **focus on people expertise**: employment of subject matter experts;
- **relocation of non-core people-related activities**: distributed cross-functional roles;
- **reduction of administrative activities**: use of AI where appropriate;
- **relocation of operational activities**: leveraging operations for service delivery;
- **removal of policing functions**: leveraging legal, risk and compliance.

Leadership impact

Key themes that leaders should reflect on include:

- importance of the CEO philosophy towards people management;
- new framework for distributed professional people management support;
- the personal development support they need to do this effectively;
- the professional people management they need to do this effectively;
- operational and developmental importance of the boundary-spanning role;
- the organizational development and design expertise required;
- the change management leadership required.

People management recommendations

Actions to consider:

- Review the people operating model.
- Be aware of role ambiguity and conflict that have been designed into the model.
- Identify people advisors and functional talent portfolio management experts.

- Identify areas where core functional expertise is held by another function and review cross-functional operations; consider embedding a people expert within the other function.

- In conjunction with lines of business and other functions, identify people facilitators who can become part of their leadership team.

- Review the development required for all who have people management responsibility, especially the business enablers.

PART FIVE
Creating an outstanding workforce

HR disrupted and dispersed 19

Informed by the past

This book commenced with an introduction to neuroscience and evolutionary psychology, followed by a quick tour through the fields of cognitive psychology, personality and organizational behaviour. Having examined people through these various lenses, the scene was set for the rest of the book – the context of organizations in which people work, the complex environment within which organizations operate and how the provision of professional people management functional support is delivered within organizations.

Organizational leadership has been explored with a focus on key trends, disruptive technology, demographic change and social movements. Each trend has been examined with regard to the leadership impact and people management recommendations, and here we conclude by exploring a new framework for people management.

Previous thoughts on 'personnel' management

Personnel management has evolved. In *The Practice of Management*, Peter Drucker wrote the following about personnel administration, as the human resource function was still termed in 1955, 'it is partly a filing clerk's job, partly a housekeeping job, partly a social workers job and partly fire-fighting to head off union trouble or to settle it'.[1] He continues by noting that 'the constant worry of all personnel administrators is their inability to prove their contribution to the enterprise. Their preoccupation is with a search for a gimmick that will impress their management associates. Their persistent complaint is that they lack status.'[2]

However, in *Understanding Organizations*, published in 1985, Charles Handy listed the many roles that are variously performed by the personnel function, as the human resource function was still often called at that time, and wrote that 'contemplating this list, it is not surprising to find that the major problems facing personnel departments are role conflict; role ambiguity'.[3] He suggests that this is because it can easily find itself carrying out more than one of the following roles in its interaction with other departments:

executing, negotiating and counselling; servicing, recruitment and training; auditing, performance and compensation reviews; advising, organizational behaviour through behavioural science; and coordinating, internal mobility. This creates ambiguity and conflict where supportive advisory and counselling activities are accompanied by process and policing activities. Handy also writes that, to avoid conflict, all advisory, coordinating and auditing relationships should ideally be backed by expert power but that this 'expert power has to be earned, given by the recipient of influence to the department exerting influence'[4] and that often this power is not given to personnel departments as they have not proved their expertise through delivery or accepted professional qualifications. Personnel functions therefore have to rely on position power backed up by a strong power base which encourages control over resources and processes, and which leads to the growth of the function. Handy questions the wisdom of boxing all people problems in one function and suggests various components could be differentiated and restructured to avoid conflict and ambiguity.[5]

In *Management and Organizational Behaviour*, also published in 1985, Laurie Mullins writes that 'people and organizations need each other. Organizations can only achieve their aims and objectives through the coordinated efforts of their members. This involves effective management of human resources and the role of management as an integrating activity'.[6]

A review of subsequent literature undertaken in 2009 established that the structure of human resource management will change over time and the human resource function's institutionalized influence is likely to depend on the:

- historic and current environmental context;
- philosophy of the CEO with regard to the management of firm human resource;
- adoption of this philosophy by senior line business managers;
- nature of the business decision and the need for boundary-spanning, where boundary-spanning is communication and cooperation between different teams with different formal lines of reporting;
- personality and competencies of individual human resource professionals – ultimately their credibility;
- success of their human resource function colleagues in delivering human resource services.[7]

It concluded that the roles and relative influence of people management professionals are impacted by:

- the path dependence and complexity of the human resource environment;
- their business awareness and boundary-spanning capabilities;
- their human resource technical skills;
- their interpersonal skills, including political awareness;
- their visibility;

- the creation of partnerships between human resource professionals and business line managers to provide a platform for influence;
- the importance of credibility in building partnerships in the first instance.[8]

Current positions on HR management

The current structure of leaders' advice and support for people management is embodied within the much-maligned function of HR. On the one hand, HR is asked to step up to the plate and have a sound grasp of their organization's purpose and strategic challenges, a detailed understanding of organizational performance, and for commercial organizations understand the key drivers behind the stock price and the levers that can impact this. On the other hand, it is the repository of all people-related issues that materialize in the organization and the author of employee handbooks which contain policies that are meant to encompass every possible vagary of human behaviour and are designed more to prevent lawsuits than support people and organizations to mutually fulfil their respective purposes.

This multifaceted demand to have a view on all things to do with human resources has led to the development of centres of excellence in traditional and emergent HR expert disciplines, generalist HR professionals who mediate the business line or functional manager domains with regard to the delivery of HR expertise, HR shared services and HR operations. The function has expanded, the opportunity for role ambiguity and conflict has increased, and recently there have been ever more frequent suggestions to transform the provision of people management advice and support in organizations.

In 1996, 'Taking on the last bureaucracy' suggested that human resource functions should be eliminated as they had failed to prove their value;[9] in 1999, Keenoy questioned the meaning and reality of HRMism;[10] and in 2009, 'Picking over the bones of human remains: A resource that business does not need' predicted the demise of human resource functions.[11] In 2014, Ram Charan wrote 'It's time to split HR' and suggested that the human resource function is divided into HR-A, for administration, to primarily manage compensation and benefits and report to the CFO, and HR-LO, for leadership and organization, to focus on improving the people capabilities of the business and report to the CEO;[12] in a 2015 article, 'People before strategy: A new role for the CHRO', it was suggested that to make the CHRO a true partner, the CEO should create a triumvirate at the top of the corporation that includes both the CFO and the CHRO;[13] another 2015 article asked 'Why we love to hate HR…and what HR can do about it?', and suggested re-imagining HR as evidence-based and creating value;[14] finally, in 2019, 'The HR generalist is dead' examined the demise of this role and questioned its very existence.[15]

The authors of *Flow* write that, in their experience, 'in enterprises of all sizes, HR departments sustain the dysfunctional systems that slow work and waste effort'[16] and in *Reinventing Talent Management*, Edward Lawler states that overall, a new design of the HR function is clearly needed for talent management to operate effectively. The traditional organization design of the HR function was never intended to have talent operate as a strategic driver of the business nor to respond to a rapidly changing world of work, workers, and organizations. Merely giving HR a 'seat at the table' is not the answer; it must be a major force in developing and implementing talent management principles and practices that are major drivers of organizational effectiveness.[17]

The authors of *Do We Need HR?* comment that in its ongoing quest for significance the human resource function risks becoming an opportunistic 'collection of the incidental, peripheral and unrelated activities. It risked creating activities that would be perceived as an expensive and dispensable overhead.'[18] A trash-can function.[19]

Importantly, in terms of structure, it was noted in 2015 that

most of the problems for which organizations need HR support (that is, those that have a significant people element) are increasingly cross-functional, by which we mean that they not only involve, but also need, joint input from expertise from other disciplines, such as operations, internal communications, marketing and information systems; and the solution to these problems requires cross-functional (by which we now mean across the sub-functions of HR) expertise. No longer can people dedicated to organization design, employee engagement or talent management work as separate centres; they need to have their expertise 'mixed and matched' and aligned much more flexibly with the business needs and with the major change projects of the day.[20]

In reviewing the above it can be seen that there have been many calls to transform the human resource function: improving relationships at the top of organizations with the board and executive colleagues; rationalizing its areas of direct responsibility; and increasing the effectiveness of cross-functional relationships.

Transformed by the future

In 1955 Drucker commented that organizations create personnel management functions that do not deal with the work of people, and are not management.[21] The good news is that functional people management has moved forward a long way since then. However, the human resource function is still haunted by its administrative genes and cultural inheritance. Outside of the human resource function, too many senior leaders have reached their positions without seeing the positive impact of appropriate people management advice and support, they don't know what good looks like, they don't know what is possible. In addition, the human resource function has increased its breadth of functional coverage while still trying to balance its people-centric and organizational responsibilities.

Given the criticisms, questions and potential adaptations noted above, this book suggests a new people management framework for organizations that locate people as the central focus rather than policies and processes that need to be policed. It calls for expertise in people and a distributed cross-functional model of people management with better-informed leaders playing their part. The centricity of people means it is flexible and is applicable across cultures.

The future context of work has been discussed by academics, consultants and popular business writers and the themes are clear, even if the timing of what awaits us is not. We stand at the beginning of a new revolution of human endeavour with regard to working life and the leadership required in this emergent context. For some, the journey has already started, while others may feel they are still preparing to set off. In reality the future is already transforming their environment, but how prepared are organizations to support their leaders from a people management perspective?

In *Do We Need HR?* it is noted that business line managers are more concerned with cross-functional issues than HR processes and therefore it is suggested that HR stops focusing on its processes and contributes to the building of centres of expertise around fundamental strategic capabilities and distributes other strategically people-related activities to other functions. It concludes that

> the good news for HR... is that on nearly every business issue, other management functions are now framing the problems in ways that recognize the centrality of people management issues to the solution. The bad news for HR... is that on nearly every business issue, other management functions are now framing the problems in ways that recognize the centrality of people management issues to the solution! In other words, general management will encroach on HR's aspired turf. They will take responsibility for many of these issues themselves.[22]

The authors therefore conclude that HR should think about breaking up and re-combining its expertise in a constellation model that emphasizes the growing importance of new interfaces between previously separate centres of excellence and other management functions. HR functions may or may not be dismantled but they will reconfigured.

HR Disrupted also looks to the future, with Lucy Adams writing, 'I can foresee chief executives of major companies shedding their HR functions, transferring the compliance and policy elements to their legal and finance teams, and outsourcing the transactional processing to a self-service model'[23] and also noting that

> our CEOs want our employees to be able to cope in a disrupted world but that will only come through HR's ability to understand how human beings behave and are motivated. In today's knowledge economy, in which 70 per cent of our assets are intangible, it's all about the people. And unfortunately, HR hasn't really been about the people but about operational efficiency.[24]

She advocates removing some of HR's compliance role, because

> if we believe we're here to sit on top of people by creating rules and enforcing them, our minds will stay log jammed with parental thinking. We

have to be prepared to give away some control and become comfortable with doing so. Our new mindset needs to be one of enabling our employees to do the best work of their lives; it's not about us, our processes, or our status in the organization; it's about them... But as long as we see our role as that of making employees do what they don't want to do rather than enabling them to become the people we need them to be, we'll be doomed to irrelevance.[25]

The future people function

Given our familiarity with the complexity of people, organizations and the environmental challenges they face, it is clear that leaders and their followers deserve people management support that delivers expert advice related to emotional states, cognitive processes and mental and physical health in addition to engaging in socially responsible activity. This is not an easy endeavour and requires a change of thinking. There is a need to ensure leaders do not abdicate responsibility for people-related issues to HR.

Ultimately, it is the leaders who have followers and who must own the issues relating to their people, both good and bad. However, they need professional advice to help them maximize success and people professionals must deliver this. As stated in *HR Disrupted*, people management professionals 'need to become the go-to people for insight into employees: who they are, how they think and feel, why they behave as they do, and how they relate to one another.'[26] This will include support from those who have expertise in occupational psychology.

The human resource function should be transformed. The term HR carries negative connotations for many, including people professionals who work in the function who may have to invest significant time in building personal credibility when no institutional credibility exists. It has been described in *HR Disrupted*, by Lucy Adams, an experienced human resource director, as 'the most hierarchical, process driven, and least well equipped for the modern world of work out of any (department) in the business'.[27]

In *Organization Development*, the human resource function is encouraged to exercise leadership and 'create a people and organizational mission for the business, not an HR agenda'.[28] It is suggested that the HR function needs to show leadership on the people front to positively impact organizational health and sustainable success, and looking ahead 'it's vital HR practitioners develop some organizational design understanding and/or capability if they are to help organizations achieve flexibility and sustainable high performance.'[29] This includes support from those who have expertise in organizational design and development.

In *Reinventing Talent Management*, it is noted that

HR functions are required that differ from those traditional bureaucratic organizations in how they are structured, staffed, and operated. Important changes in how the top management and boards of organizations operate and are staffed, are also needed. Organizations need to be able to make talent management decisions that fit their overall structure and strategy and that are based on date and talent management expertise.[30]

In terms of the future, in 'Are we there yet? What's next for HR?' Dave Ulrich and James Dulebohn propose that what the human resource function does inside an organization is guided by the external environment and stakeholders. In its drive to add value, people professionals need to advise on: the impact of globalization; people risk management; and sustainability. Additionally, they need to help people find meaning in their work.[31]

People have always been, and will continue to be, the most complex contributor to the success of organizations, and the future of work may give us an opportunity to focus on our uniquely human attributes. Neuroscience and technology are delivering a significant amount of knowledge to help leaders of organizations align individual purpose with organizational purpose, while managing the impact of factors which can frustrate this relationship.

Figure 19.1   The people management framework

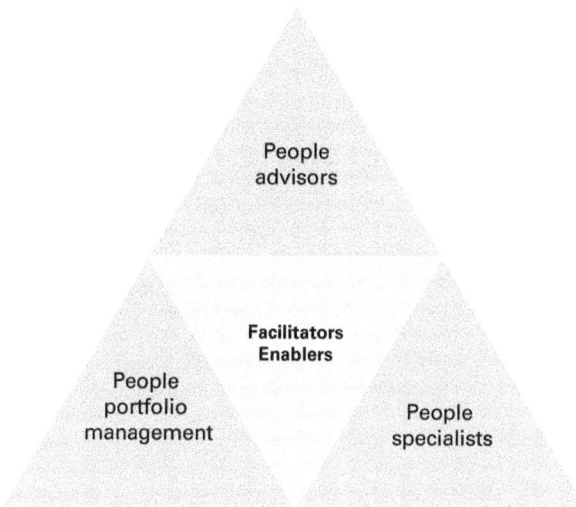

The proposed framework of people management contains five elements: people advisors, people portfolio management, people specialists – embedded in other management functions, people facilitators and people enablers (Figure 19.1).

The framework in Figure 19.1 builds on Ulrich's thinking, the suggestions of Bersin and of Charan, Barton and Carey, and the predictions of *Do We Need HR?* and *HR Disrupted* as it designs for expert, distributed, cross-functional, processing and policing light, people-centred, people management.

As people are complex, so too is the knowledge required to become a professional in the fields that are relevant to supporting those who lead them. It is therefore suggested that a people function contains people advisors, that focus on the mental and physical aspects of people and on corporate and social responsibility (Figure 19.2), and professionals who are focused on people portfolio management: strategic workforce planning, acquisition and transition, talent development and talent funding and reporting (Figure 19.3).

In addition to the people function, which contains advice and activities that are uniquely related to people, other functions may employ professionals that major on areas that are people specific, for instance marketing, finance, technology, data analytics, legal and compliance, operational risk and operational service delivery. The people specialists embedded within, and reporting to, their functions will interface with various colleagues in the people function to design, monitor and modify people-related services.

People advisors

People advisors deliver expert advice relating to the emotional, cognitive and physiological impact of the work environment on people's behaviour and well-being. People advisors also provide specialist expertise in areas of societal impact such as diversity and inclusion, sustainability and skill development – domains that impact purpose and meaning.

All these areas of expertise are people-centred and people-specific. The people advisors study and gain experience to acquire the relevant level of competence. There is legitimacy in the expertise, and their roles are not ambiguous or conflicting.

Mental:

- psychologists;
- neuroscientists;
- mental health first-aid;
- external support.

Physical:

- physiologists;
- organizational ergonomics;
- safety marshal/first-aid;
- external support.

Corporate sustainability and social responsibility:

- public policy engagement – supranational, national, regional and local;
- employee relations, employee voice and mediation;
- diversity and inclusion – including multi-faith expertise;
- cultural anthropology;
- financial advice support by an external provider;
- internal communications.

Figure 19.2 The people management framework – people advisors: advisory experts

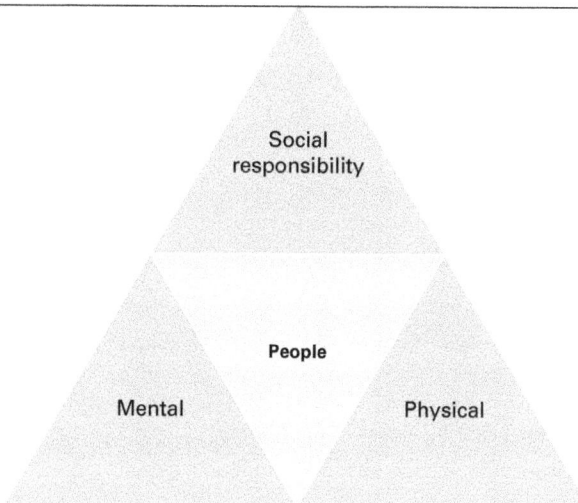

People portfolio management

The people portfolio management professionals deliver expertise in areas that are people-centric and people-specific. The areas of acquisition and transition and talent development could not easily exist within another function and arguably strategic workforce planning, funding, compensation and benefits, and reporting, internal not public, require close proximity to the other two. There is legitimacy in their expertise, their roles are not ambiguous or conflicting.

Strategic workforce planning:

- workforce strategy and planning;
- organizational design and development;
- segmented employee value proposition.

Figure 19.3   The people management framework – people portfolio management:
functional experts

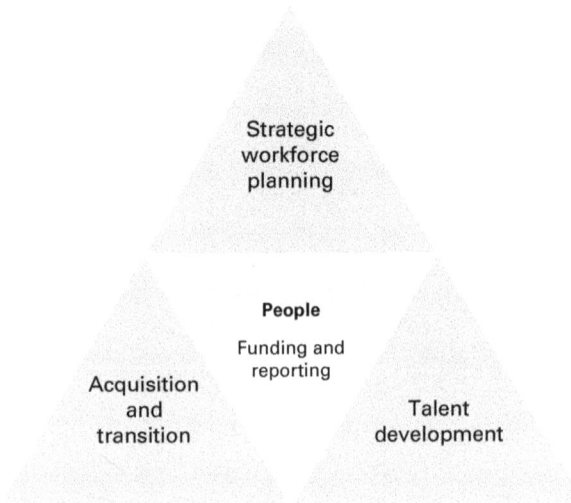

Strategic
workforce
planning

People

Funding and
reporting

Acquisition
and
transition

Talent
development

Acquisition and transition:

- employer brand manager;
- recruitment and selection;
- onboarding;
- transitioning – internal moves and all external moves, voluntary and otherwise;
- alumni network.

Talent development:

- continuing personal and team development;
- coaching and mentoring;
- careers advice and mobility.

Funding and reporting:

- compensation and benefits design;
- people metrics and internal reporting.

People specialists: Embedded

People specialists embedded within other functions focus their functional expertise on people. They report within their functions but interface cross-functionally on a daily basis with colleagues in the people function. There is legitimacy in the core expertise, their roles are not ambiguous or non-conflicting. One exception is employer brand where the chief people officer can be seen as the brand manager and also responsible for internal communication.

- **Marketing:** employer brand and employee value proposition, with the Chief People Officer (CPO) has brand manager;
- **finance:** investment and public reporting, payroll and expenses;
- **technology:** people systems;
- **data analytics:** data management and analytics;
- **legal and compliance:** contracts, compromise agreements and compliance with regulation regarding conduct and governance;
- **operational risk:** people risk assessment around target operating models and processes with regard to physical safety and areas of high-impact decision-making;
- **operational service delivery:** to ensure the quality of people-related services, shared services/service centres.

Figure 19.4   The people management framework – people specializations: embedded experts

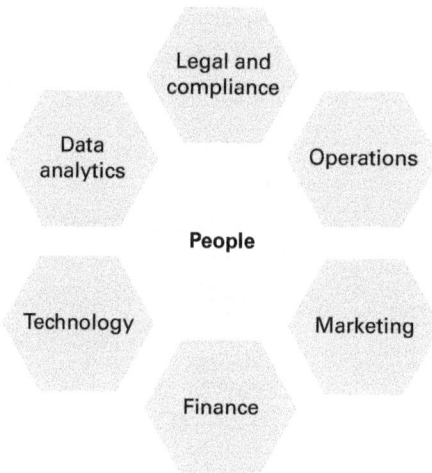

This framework is not prescriptive in terms of how the advisory role and functions are staffed, or their operating models and normative workflows. However, these should be flexible and quickly adaptable. People professionals must provide an evidence base for their proposals, the principles driving them, and also the quantitative and qualitative results of their activities.

Those in human resource functions with relevant experience and expertise can be redeployed, embedded in other functions or given people facilitator roles, with those that remain in the people function as experts focusing
on specific aspects of people and organizational growth. However, research
found that only 20 per cent of the 5,000 HR professionals who provided
data are willing and able to meet the challenges laid down by Ulrich and
Dulebohn. Of the rest, 20 per cent are either unwilling or unable, and there
is therefore a question mark for 60 per cent where competence and commitment needs to increase.[32] Ultimately, it may not be possible, or indeed advis-
able, to retain or redeploy in some cases.

People facilitators

To avoid leaders having multiple touch points for people-related advice and
services, people facilitators provide a boundary-spanning role (Figure 19.5).
This role links functional and divisional teams and could be located within
the divisional COO function, or where none exists the functional or divisional leader will have a dedicated person in the role. This will go some way
in addressing some of the problems that have been associated with the HR
business partner role (see Chapter 17), especially issues around role ambiguity and role conflict.

Figure 19.5   The people management framework – people facilitators and enablers:
leaders and boundary-spanners

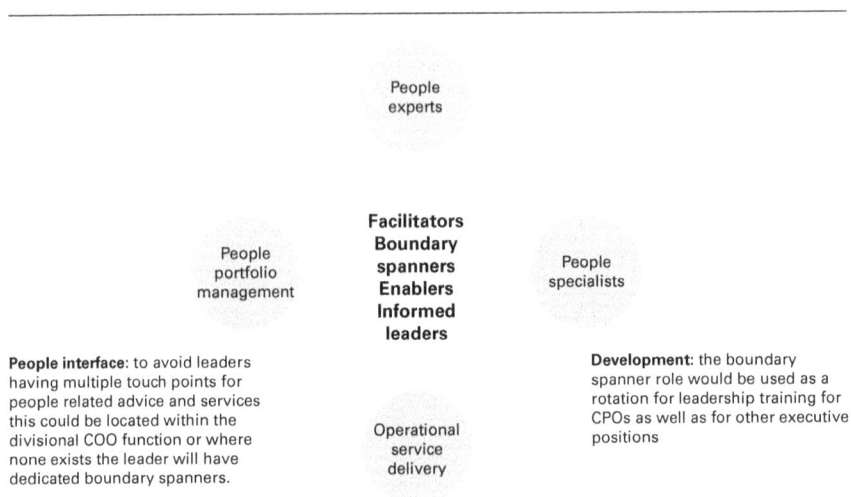

People
experts

**Facilitators
Boundary
spanners
Enablers
Informed
leaders**

People
portfolio
management

People
specialists

People interface: to avoid leaders
having multiple touch points for
people related advice and services
this could be located within the
divisional COO function or where
none exists the leader will have
dedicated boundary spanners.

Operational
service
delivery

Development: the boundary
spanner role would be used as a
rotation for leadership training for
CPOs as well as for other executive
positions

The current HR generalist role took shape in HR business partner roles, which conceptually showed promise, but have often been poorly implemented. The time has come for HR generalist roles to be reconceived and the incumbents redeployed into new boundary-spanning roles or roles where they can build specific professional expertise.

This role is consistent with the Talent Value Leader (TVL) of Charan, Barton and Carey and Bersin's 'VP of HR' but reports within the business line or function it supports.

The boundary-spanning role would be used as a rotation for leadership training for chief people officers (CPOs), as well as for other executive positions.

In small and medium-sized businesses, the picture is different, as all functional professionals often need to wear several hats. Therefore, when an organization reaches the size where it requires dedicated internal people leadership expertise, they should hire a people professional who has a clear understanding of leadership, management, occupational psychology and operational talent acquisition experience. They can be supported in specialist areas through outsourced advice and delivery; for example, for learning and development, reward, legal and compliance, well-being and diversity and inclusion. Operational service delivery is one area of embedded people-related specializations but is also shown in Figure 19.5 to emphasize the importance of a high-quality operations platform, whether internal or external, to the delivery of people-related services.

People enablers

The only people generalists in an organization will be the ones with no specialist people advisory expertise, no people portfolio management expertise and no embedded people specialization. Leaders of business lines and functions are people generalists, but must be more than this; they must be well-informed employee champions, as enablers, coaches and facilitators of workforce, and therefore organizational, success (Figure 19.1).

Framework summary

The link between business divisions and functions and the people advisory and people portfolio management teams will vary, and, as previously discussed, many functions will contain embedded people specialists who will represent their function on cross-functional projects. For business divisions, people facilitators within the divisional COO's office would be the natural link.

How the people management knowledge and expertise maps across the divisional and geographic organization and who reports to who will depend on the context. There is no best practice here. However, it is important that the most senior people function leader, the CPO, should be part of the executive committee.

This new framework for people management is people-centred and as such the basic needs of people are addressed at a level of universality that has global application. It supports their mental, physical and societal needs, through people advisors. The people portfolio management function represents a generic, systems view of employee journeys but is not prescriptive in terms of its implementation. The embedding of people specialists within other functions will vary in its application by organizations but the philosophy driving this change is to strip out roles from the HR function, which on balance are informed more by technical expertise in another functional area. Finally, the fact that leaders should be people enablers of their workforce has universal application, as does the need for people facilitators that coordinate the delivery of people-related advice and services.

There are considerations for implementation in other cultures. The culture map suggests one consideration as the difference between task and relationships on a scale of trust. For example, in the United States, Germany and the United Kingdom, trust is more task-based and grown through business-related activities; trust may build quickly but also may be transient. In contrast, in Japan and also Brazil, Russia, India and China (BRIC), trust is more relationship-based and is built slowly over the long term. The culturally endorsed leadership theory and CEO behaviour suggested by the results of the GLOBE study suggest that US CEOs will be more charismatic and participative and less autonomous and self-protective than Chinese CEOs; and, compared to US CEOs, Japanese CEOs credit subordinates for organizational accomplishments while de-emphasizing their own roles. India scores higher than these other countries for humane orientation, Brazil scores higher on team orientation and Russia higher on autonomy. The transformation of the human resource function will demand an approach that varies based on national and organizational cultures.

Conclusion

Decades of research and advice have pointed to the difficulty of providing leaders with an efficient and effective people operating model. Early indications were documented by Donald and Donald in 1929, Drucker in 1955 and Handy in 1985, and the level of complexity and accompanying dissatisfaction has continued to increase.

It should be obvious by now that the function has often been set up to fail organizations, and its collective self, with too much inherent role ambiguity and role conflict designed into it.

One function cannot hope to be entirely successful as the organizational housekeeper and super-nanny engaged to nurture people, set and police boundaries of behaviour, reward, rebuke and clear up every possible mess people could make as individuals and teams. Indeed, it says much for the professionalism and vision of human resource functional heads who have, against the odds, successfully overcome these challenges.

People professionals should locate their core area of knowledge and experience and develop their expertise in this field. Those aspiring to leadership roles should ensure they gain experience in various areas of people advisory, people portfolio management and embedded people specialization, while ideally gaining operational experience as COOs of key business divisions. Follow the advice in *HR Disrupted* and 'do something different'. Become the people experts.

Leaders of business divisions and other functions should continually develop their understanding of people and organizational behaviour as it is fundamental to their success. At the time of writing this book, industry bodies for finance, legal, technology and marketing professionals either do not provide any continuing professional development on leadership or have limited provision. However the Chartered Institute for People and Development (CIPD) in the UK and Society for Human Resource Management (SHRM) in the US both have a suite of courses available on many of the areas discussed in this book which could form the basis for divisional and cross-functional leadership development.

Indeed, the CIPD's purpose statement is 'Championing better work and working lives', which sums up what all leaders should be delivering. They have published a new professional map that challenges its members to be principles-led, evidence-based and outcomes-driven. These are critical values which are supported by the people management framework proposed here. Principles that support the purpose of better work and working lives include the following: ensuring a deep understanding of people's mental and physical nature and therefore well-being; basing decisions not just on gut-feel but on evidence; and reviewing outcomes through quantitative analysis, remembering that creating hypotheses and searching for causation may largely be qualitative endeavours. The SHRM similarly aspires to advance people management through research that provides evidence-based insights and recommendations to improve the employee experience and positively impact business performance in organizations. In addition to these professional bodies, two other valuable sources of thinking around people management include the Josh Bersin Academy, which features online programmes that cover the most important people management issues with members having access to future-focused people-related topics, curated resources and a global community of HR professionals and experts, and Dave Ulrich's RBL Institute, which offers training courses globally and online access to his thought leadership which, along with his many books, is both prolific and prophetic.

With regard to professional people management advice, it is argued that this should be delivered on a distributed basis using nodes of expert knowledge and cross-disciplinary teams. Leaders should be given master classes in the evolving research that underpins the people advice they are being given. They should be provided with dashboards that visualize the key people-related data that represents the composition of the workforce, the well-being of the workforce and relates this data to the performance data of the organization.

Many of the various knowledge domains and trends discussed in this book will be familiar to readers, but here they have been examined together for the first time with a view to informing practitioner action. Readers who are not functional people professionals have been shown what is needed and what is possible both from the people professionals that support them and from themselves.

People are, and will remain, the most important factor in the establishment and sustainable success of organizations, and therefore fully addressing the decades of debate around the roles and responsibilities concerning the leadership and management of people in organizations is long overdue. People are complex, organizations are complex, and the environment in which organizations operate is complex. The responsibility for people management is distributed throughout the organization and is not the responsibility of a single function. Leaders need to own this responsibility but require high-quality professional people expertise to support them. People professionals need to deliver this expertise and by doing so will naturally build individual, and ultimately institutionalized, credibility for doing so.

What are the key lessons from this book to take into your organization?

Key lessons

The people context

- Acknowledges the complexity of people – as leaders, followers and other stakeholders;
- establishes the links between the biological brain, the mind, emotions, cognitive, personality and organizational behaviour;
- examines the impact of nature, nurture and cultural evolution;
- acknowledges the provisional individual social construction of reality from philosophy and from neuroscience;
- establishes the innately human skills required to lead;
- acknowledges the ongoing need for learning and the possibilities for learning based on mindset and neuroplasticity;
- acknowledges the need for purpose and meaning at a personal level.

The organizational context

- Acknowledges the complexity of organizations;
- establishes the resource-based view of organizations;
- acknowledges the formal and informal organization;
- acknowledges the impact of culture and in–out groups;
- acknowledges the provisional corporate social construction of reality;
- acknowledges the ongoing need for change – developmental, transitional and transformational;
- acknowledges the need for purpose and meaning at an organizational level.

The environmental context

- Acknowledges the volatile, uncertain, complex and ambiguous environment;
- examines current themes;
- establishes the societal obligations of organizations;
- acknowledges the need for purpose and meaning at a societal level.

Deconstructing people management

- Introduces a focus on people;
- deemphasizes the focus on people-related organizational principles, policies and processes;
- suggests expert roles for a new People Function that focus on peoples mental, physical and existential needs;
- suggests expert roles for a new people function that focus wholly on people-centric functional activities;
- suggests embedded roles that deliver the expertise of other functions for people management related projects;
- suggests facilitator roles to integrate people-related activities across the organization;
- emphasizes the importance of enabler roles;
- removes role ambiguity in people management;
- removes role conflict in people management;
- develops position-related expertise.

Our suggestion to transform people management starts with a thorough review of your current organization and how your people are organized and managed. Creating an outstanding workforce is predicated on the design and development of an excellent people operating model, so take the first steps now for the benefit of all stakeholders – not forgetting that this includes you.

NOTES

Introduction

1 Whiteman, 1998; Kail, 2010a, 2010b, 2010c, 2011.
2 Morrrison and Fletcher, 2002.

1 Evolutionary psychology and neuroscience

1 Harari, 2011, p 3.
2 Ibid, p 37.
3 Colvin, 2016, pp 15–17.
4 Ellis and Solms, 2018, p ix.
5 Ibid, p ix.
6 Ibid, p 8.
7 Ibid, p 3.
8 Ibid, p 3.
9 Ibid, p 8.
10 Swart et al, 2015, p 12.
11 Ellis and Solms, 2018, pp 17–18.
12 Ibid, p 19.
13 MacLean, 1989.
14 Jensen and Nutt, 2015, p 37.
15 Ellis and Solms, 2018, p 9.
16 Swart et al, 2015, pp 24–25.
17 Goleman, 1996, p 12.
18 Ellis and Solms, 2018, p 4.
19 Ibid, p 9.
20 Ibid, pp 27–29.
21 Swart et al, 2015, p 33.
22 Ellis and Solms, 2018, p 148.
23 Boyer, 2018, p 257.
24 Ibid, p 257.
25 Frith, 2007.
26 Panskepp, 1998.
27 Toronchuk and Ellis, 2007.
28 Panskepp, 1998.
29 Goleman, 1996, p 289.
30 Ibid, pp 289–90.
31 Eckman, 1992, p 175.
32 Goleman, 1996, p 290.
33 Fedman Barrett, 2018.
34 Ibid.
35 Ibid.
36 Ibid.
37 Ibid.
38 Ibid.
39 Ibid.
40 Ibid.
41 Ibid.
42 Gardner, 2006.
43 Gardner and Hatch, 1989.
44 Salovey and Mayer, 1990, pp 185–211.
45 Goleman, 1996, p 43.
46 Ibid, p 43.
47 Ochsner and Gross, 2005.
48 Lieberman et al, 2007.
49 Beugré, 2018, p 162.
50 Buhle et al, 2014.
51 Goleman, 2013, p 104.
52 De Vignemont and Singer, 2006.
53 Le Doux, 2000.
54 Beugré, 2018, p 160.
55 Cottingham, 2017.
56 Hofstede et al, 2010, p 5.
57 Clark, 2016, p 7.
58 Boyer, 2018, p 22.
59 Goleman, 2013, pp 25–26.
60 Ellis and Solms, 2018, pp 22–23.
61 Heyes, 2018, p 214.
62 Ibid, p 214.
63 Ibid, p 35.
64 Ibid, p 22.
65 Ibid, pp 19–20.
66 Ibid, p 39.
67 Boyer, 2018, p 269.
68 Ibid, p 269.
69 Heyes, 2018, p 13.
70 Ibid, p 13.
71 Ibid, p 1.
72 Ibid, p 24.
73 Ibid, pp 13–14.
74 Ellis and Solms, 2018, p 104.
75 Ibid, p 104.
76 Ibid, pp 104–05.
77 La Cerra and Bingham, 1998.
78 Grffiths and Stotz, 2000.

79 Ellis and Solms, 2018, p 143.
80 Heyes, 2018, p 10.
81 Swart et al, 2015, p 79.
82 Boyer, 2018, p 25.
83 Beugré, 2018, p 122.
84 Decety and Jackson, 2006.
85 MacLean, PD (1964) Man and his animal brains, *Modern Medicine*. 32, pp95–106
86 MacLean, PD (1970) The triune brain, emotion, and scientific bias. In FO Schmidt et al (eds.). *The neurosciences: Second study program*. pp336–49. Rockefeller University Press
87 MacLean, PD (1990) *The Triune Brain in Evolution*. Plenum Press
88 Reiner A. (1990) An explanation of behavior review of MacLean's *The Triune Brain in Evolution. Science*. 250, pp 303–5.
89 Campbell CBG. (1992) Book review MacLean's *The Triune Brain in Evolutio. American Scientist*. 80. pp 497–8.
90 Cory , GA (1999) *The Reciprocal modular brain in economics and politics*. New York: Plenum Press pp13–27.
91 Cory, GA (2002) Reappraising MacLean's triune brain concept. In: Cory GA Cory, R Gardner R (eds). *The evolutionary neuroethology of Paul MacLean*. Westport (CT): Praeger Publishers; pp. 9–27.
92 Striedter, GF (2005) *Principles of Brain Evolution*. Sunderland (MA): Sinauer Associates.
93 Levine, DS (2017) Modeling the instinctive-emotional-thoughtful mind. *Cognitive Systems Research*. 45, pp 82-94.
94 James, W (1890/1891) The principles of psychology (Vol. Vols. 1 and 2). New York.
95 Swart et al, 2015.
96 Ellis and Solms, 2018, p 110.

2 Personality psychology and intelligence

1 Goldstein et al, 2017.
2 Larsen and Buss, 2018, p 4.
3 Ibid, p 10.
4 Ibid.
5 Ibid, p 632.
6 Schein and Schein, 2017, p 18.
7 Ibid, p 28.
8 Rousseau, 1988, p 142.
9 Bananji and Greenwald, 2016, p 59.
10 Hofstede et al, 2010, p 56.
11 Smith and Smith, 2005, p 64.
12 Bossons et al, 2015, p 50.
13 Beugré, 2018, p 169.
14 Smith and Smith, 2005, p 67.
15 Ibid, p 37.
16 Rotter, 1966.
17 Eysenck, 1967; Cattell, 1971.
18 Furnham, 2005, p 164.
19 Holland, 1985, p 5.
20 Rotter, 1966.
21 Ajzen, 1991.
22 Bandura, 1982.
23 Furnham, 2005, p 251.
24 Eysenck, 1967.
25 Eysenck and Eysenck, 1985, p 329.
26 Furnham, 2005, p 172.
27 Ibid, p 172.
28 Cattell, 1971.
29 Costa and McCrae, 2018, p 9.
30 Ibid, pp 12–17.
31 Chamorro-Premuzic, 2017, pp 108–09.
32 Hofstede and McRae, 2004.
33 Hogan and Hogan, 2007.
34 Hogan and Hogan, 2010b.
35 Hogan and Hogan, 2010a.
36 Furnham, 2005, p 575.
37 Schneider and Bartram, 2017, p 461.

38 Furnham, 2005, p 195.
39 Ibid, p 195.
40 Briggs-Myers, 2015, pp 2–3.
41 Nardi, 2011.
42 Chamorro-Premuzic, 2017, pp 90–91.
43 Ibid, p 91.
44 Hogan and Hogan, 2010b.
45 Chamorro-Premuzic, 2017, p 94.
46 Ibid, p 94.
47 Ibid, p 95.
48 Frankl, 2014.
49 Campbell, 2000, p 34.
50 Ibid, p 29.
51 Goffman, 1959.
52 Schein and Schein, 2017, p 171.
53 Chamorro-Premuzic, 2017, pp 75–76.
54 Ibid, p 76.
55 Ibid, p 151.
56 O'Boyle et al, 2012.
57 Chamorro-Premuzic, 2017, p 159.
58 Ibid, p 153.
59 Ibid, p 170.
60 Ibid, p 169.
61 Webster and Smith, 2018.
62 Fico et al, 2012.

63 MacKenzie and Baumeister, 2014, pp 32–33.
64 Wong, 2012.
65 Ibid.
66 Peterson, 1999.
67 Wong, 2012, p xxxii.
68 McAdams, 2012, pp 107–115.
69 Wong, 2012, p xxxvii.
70 McAdams, 2012, p 119.
71 Ibid, p 119.
72 Wong, 2012, p xxxv.
73 McAdams, 2012, p 16.
74 Del Guidice, 2019, p 29.
75 Ibid, p 30.
76 Ibid, p 31.
77 Freund et al, 2019, p 324.
78 De Young and Allen, 2019, p 95
79 Bleidorn and Hopwood, 2019, p 245.
80 Hofstede and McRae, 2004.
81 Gregg, 2019, p 380.
82 Orth and Robins, 2019, p 338.
83 Smith and Smith, 2005, p 23.
84 Spearman, 1904.
85 Smith and Smith, 2005, p 23.

86 Stern, 1965.
87 Binet and Simon, 1914.
88 Schmidt, 2016.
89 Sharma et al, 2018.
90 Cattell, 1971.
91 Von Hippel, 2018.
92 Goleman and Boyatzis, 2017
93 Miao et al, 2017.
94 Mayer et al, 2004.
95 Petrides and Furnham, 2001.
96 Goleman, 2004.
97 Miao et al, 2017, pp 194–95.
98 Ahlstrom and Li, 2016, p 22.
99 Dweck, 2017, p 67.
100 Ibid, p 29.
101 Peterson and Seligman, 2004, p 5.
102 Ibid, p 13.
103 Ibid.
104 Ibid.
105 Ibid, pp 29–30.
106 Ibid, p 626.
107 Ibid, p 633.
108 Ruch et al, 2016.
109 Littman-Ovadia and Lavy, 2016.
110 Kashdan, 2018.
111 Ibid.
112 Strengthscope, 2019.
113 CharacterScope, 2019.
114 Kashadan, 2018.

3 Bias, stereotypes, group culture and decision-making

1 Ayan, 2008.
2 Mercier and Sperber, 2017, p 90.
3 Swart et al, 2015, p 101.
4 Blacker and McConnell, 2015, p 47.
5 Simon, 1976.
6 Mercier and Sperber, 2017, p 7.

7 Banaji and Greenwald, 2016, p 69.
8 Ibid, p 47.
9 Ibid, pp 117–18.
10 Tajfel, 1970.
11 Beugré, 2018, p 168.
12 Bossons et al, 2015, pp 48–49.
13 Beugré, 2018, p 18.
14 Ibid, p 170.

15 Banaji and Greenwald, 2016, p 138.
16 Beugré, 2018, p 176.
17 Janis, 1982.
18 Tuckman, 1965.
19 Tuckman and Jensen, 1977.
20 Furnham, 2005, p 478.

21 Winsborough and Chamorro-Premuzic, 2017.
22 Wilde, 2016, pp 152–54.
23 Schein and Schein, 2017, pp 3–5.
24 Ibid, p 6.
25 Von Hippel, 2018, p 14.
26 Mercier and Sperber, 2017, p 333.
27 Ibid, p 333.
28 Banaji and Greenwald, 2016, p 130.
29 Ibid, p 130.

30 Ibid, p 136.
31 Furnham, 2005, p 484.
32 Boyer, 2018, p 43.
33 Allport, 1954.
34 Jost et al, 2004.
35 Csikszentmihalyi, 1993, p xvii.
36 Ellis and Solms, 2018, p 149.
37 Furnham, 2005, pp 531–32.
38 Ibid, pp 559.
39 Bossons et al, 2015, p 44.
40 Ibid, p 47.
41 Kahneman, 2012, p 20.

42 Ibid, p 21.
43 Ibid, p 21.
44 Ibid, p 21.
45 Ibid, p 415.
46 Ibid, p 411.
47 Thaler and Sunstein, 2009, p 6.
48 Kahneman, 2012, p 417.
49 Ibid, p 417.
50 Ibid, p 417.
51 Ibid, p 409.
52 Bossons et al, 2015, p 54.
53 Swart et al, 2015, pp 20–21.

4 Motivation

1 Michaels et al, 2001.
2 Furnham, 2005, p 277.
3 Robbins, 1991.
4 Maslow, 1954.
5 Seligman and Csikszentmihalyi, 2000.
6 Seligman, 2018, p 268.
7 Alderfer, 1969.
8 Herzberg et al, 1959.
9 Furnham, 2005, p 335.
10 McClelland, 1961.
11 McGregor, 1960.
12 Burns and Stalker, 1961.
13 Hackman and Oldham, 1980.
14 Furnham, 2005, 314.
15 Deci, 1975.
16 Deci, 1980.
17 Ryan and Deci, 2017, p 3.
18 Ryan and Deci, 2017.
19 Ibid, p 3.
20 Pink, 2009.
21 Pink, 2009, p 59.
22 Peters, 2012, p 263.

23 Wong, 2012, p xxxiv.
24 Weinstein et al, 2012.
25 Lawrence and Nohria, 2002.
26 Beugré, 2018, p 77.
27 Furnham, 2005, pp 302–03.
28 Locke, 1976.
29 Adams, 1965.
30 Greenberg, 1987.
31 Beugré, 2009, p 129.
32 Ibid, p 119.
33 Vroom, 1964.
34 Porter and Lawler, 1968.
35 Judge et al, 2010.
36 Furnham, 2005, p 280.
37 Beugré, 2018, p 87.
38 Deutsch, 1975.
39 Beugré, 2018, p 84.
40 Kim et al, 2016.
41 Beugré, 2018, p 77.
42 Ibid, p 86.
43 Ibid, pp 87–88.
44 Ibid, p 89.
45 Peters, 2012.
46 Ibid, p 251.
47 Ibid, p 251.
48 Ibid, p 258.

49 Ibid, p 259.
50 Ibid, p 260.
51 Ibid, pp 261–66.
52 Dweck, 2017.
53 Ibid, p 21.
54 Syed, 2015.
55 Schroder et al, 2014.
56 Syed, 2015, p 276.
57 Csikszentmihalyi, 2008.
58 Bandura, 1982.
59 Swart et al, 2015, p 91.
60 Ibid, p 180.
61 Csikszentmihalyi, 1993, pp xviii–xiv.
62 Ibid, pp xiv–xv.
63 Swart et al, 2015, p 91.
64 Ilies and Judge, 2003.
65 Hahn et al, 2016, p 217.
66 Furnham, 2005.
67 Colvin, 2017, pp 65–66.
68 Chamorro-Premuzic, 2017, pp 39–42.
69 Ibid, p 47.
70 Ibid, p 65.
71 Swart et al, 2015, p 90.
72 Ibid, p 91.

73 Ibid, p 88.
74 Hofstede et al, 2010, p 331.

75 Hofstede et al, 2010.
76 Hofstede, 1980.

77 Gagne et al, 2015.
78 Ibid, p 179.
79 Ibid, p 191.

5 Leadership

1 Pfeffer, 2015, p 3.
2 McChrystal et al, 2018, p 8.
3 Zenger and Folkman, 2009, pp 12–14.
4 Kets de Vries, 2019, p 12.
5 Ibid, p 13.
6 Beugré, 2018, p 91.
7 Fiedler, 1964.
8 House and Mitchell, 1974.
9 Blake and Mouton, 1985.
10 Hersey and Blanchard, 1982.
11 Graen, 1976.
12 Graen and Canedo, 2016.
13 Handy, 2015, p 124.
14 Gardner, 1993.
15 Bass, 2008, p 654.
16 Kotter, 1990.
17 Ibid.
18 Colvin, 2017, p 31.
19 Chartered Management Institute, 201.
20 Morgan, 2014, pp 92–93.
21 Ibid, p 94.
22 Kotter, 2012, pp 174–75.
23 Levit, 2019, p 150.
24 Morgan, 2014, p 91.
25 Bass, 2008, p 1208.
26 Goffee and Jones, 2015.
27 Johansen, 2012.
28 Ibid.
29 Fredberg, 2014, p 180.
30 Ibid, p 185.
31 IMD, 2017, p 3.
32 Ibid.
33 Teece, 2007.

34 Helfat and Peteraf, 2015, p 844.
35 Ibid, p 845.
36 Collins and Hansen, 2011, p 9.
37 Ibid.
38 Ibid, pp 36–38.
39 Collins, 2001, p 39.
40 Von Hippel, 2018, p 179.
41 Goulding and Shaughnessy, 2017, p 17.
42 Cheung-Judge and Holbech, 2015, p 151.
43 Beer et al, 1990.
44 Kotter, 2012, p 23.
45 Ibid, p 170.
46 Lewin, 1958.
47 Kotnour and Al-Haddad, 2015.
48 Hamel, 2000.
49 Balogen and Hope-Hailey, 2008.
50 Bovey and Hede, 2001.
51 Johnson et al, 2014, pp 470–71.
52 Ibid, p 476.
53 Nadkarni and Herrmann, 2014, p 1336.
54 Beugré, 2018, p 16.
55 Ibid, pp 17–18.
56 Ibid, p 21.
57 Sinek, 2009.
58 Ibid, p 37.
59 Ibid, p 56.
60 Ibid, p 137.
61 Jordan and Lindebaum, 2014, p 905.
62 Ibid, p 905.
63 Zak, 2017.
64 Colbert et al, 2014.
65 Swart et al, 2015, p 47.

66 Ibid, p 68.
67 Rippon, 2019, pp 120–141.
68 Ibid, pp 327–40.
69 Ibid, p 340.
70 Bossons et al, 2015, p 64.
71 Ibid, p 64–65
72 Ibid, p 65.
73 Geier, 2016.
74 Boises et al, 2015.
75 Hoch et al, 2018.
76 Bass, 1985, p xiii.
77 Luthans and Avolio, 2003.
78 Avolio et al, 2004, p 802.
79 Brown et al, 2005. p 120.
80 Greenleaf, 1970, p 13.
81 Hoch et al, 2018, p 523.
82 Ibid.
83 D'Innocenzo et al, 2016, p 1986.
84 Von Hippel, 2018, p 184.
85 Swart et al, 2015, p 161.
86 Beugré, 2018, p 102.
87 Swart et al, 2015, pp 45–46.
88 Ibid, pp 51–52.
89 Roebuck, 2014, p 222.
90 Deloitte, 2019a.
91 O'Connell, 2014, p 183.
92 Goleman, 1996, p 149.
93 Goleman, 2013, p 235.
94 McChrystal et al, 2018, p 9.
95 Goffee and Jones, 2015, p 89.
96 Kerr, 2013.

6 Organizations

1   Johnson et al, 2014, p 12.
2   Balliester and Elsheikhi, 2018, p 4.
3   Ibid, p 6.
4   Ibid, p 19.
5   Deloitte, 2018b, p 58.
6   Ibid, p 60.
7   Bughin et al, 2017, p 2.
8   Balliester and Elsheikhi, 2018, p 6.
9   Savitz and Weber, 2014.
10 Morrison and Fletcher, 2002.
11 Hatch, 2018, p 84.
12 Duncan, 1972.
13 Carroll and Hannan, 2000, p xix.
14 Johnson et al, 2014, p 206.
15 Porter, 1980.
16 Ibid.
17 Kim and Mauborgne, 2005
18 Ibid.
19 Ibid.
20 Ibid.
21 Ibid.
22 Ansoff, 1988.
23 Henderson, 1979.
24 Barney, 1991, pp 91–120.
25 Barney, 1997.
26 Helfat et al, 2007.
27 Johnson et al, 2014, p 122.
28 Galbraith, 1973.
29 Pascale and Athos, 1981.
30 Groysberg, 2010.
31 Ibid.
32 Quinn, 1980.
33 Johnson et al, 2014, pp 460–61.
34 Morhman, 2003.
35 Stanford, 2018, p 6.
36 Ibid.
37 Cheung-Judge and Holbeche, 2015, p 296.
38 Ibid.
39 Stanford, 2018, p 21.
40 Cheung-Judge and Holbeche, 2015, p 10.
41 Ibid.
42 Ibid, p 11.
43 Furnham, 2005, pp 68–69.
44 Durkheim, 2013.
45 Taylor, 1911.
46 Fayol, 1919.
47 Weber, 1924.
48 Roethlisberger and Dickson, 1939.
49 Burns and Stalker, 1961.
50 Fiedler, 1967.
51 Katz and Kahn, 1966.
52 Stacey, 2009.
53 Whiteman, 1998.
54 Kail, 2010.
55 Fiedler, 1967.
56 Katz and Kahn, 1966.
57 Cheung-Judge and Holbeche, 2015, p 38.
58 Ibid, p 39.
59 Stacey, 2010, p 65.
60 Berger and Luckmann, 1966.
61 Hatch, 2018, pp 39–40.
62 Weick, 1995, pp 30–38.
63 Hatch, 2018, pp 40–41.
64 Burns and Stalker, 1961.
65 Johnson et al, 2014, pp 446–48.
66 Mintzberg, 1983.
67 French and Raven, 1959.
68 Emerson, 1962.
69 Emerson, 1976.
70 Salancik and Pfeffer, 1977, p 3.
71 Mintzberg, 1983.
72 Hatch, 2018, p 315.
73 Mercer, 2017b, p 3.
74 Bennett and Lemoine, 2014, p 313.
75 Fletcher, 2004, pp 1–2.
76 Ibid.
77 Goulding and Shaughnessy, 2017, p 16.
78 Gallup, 2018b, p 3.
79 Goulding and Shaughnessy, 2017, p 79.
80 Ibid, pp 76–77.
81 Mercer, 2018b, p 7.

7 Technology and the future of work

1   Handy, 1985a.
2   Handy, 1995.
3   Armstrong-Strassen, 1998.
4   Frese, 2000.
5   Gratton, 2011.
6   Morgan, 2014.
7   Leonhard, 2016.
8   Brynjolfsson and McAfee, 2014.
9   World Economic Forum, 2018a.
10 www.gartner.com/ it-glossary/ digital-disruption (archived at https:// perma.cc/GSC8-KAPT).

11 World Economic Forum, 2018b, p 7.
12 Bughin et al, 2017, p 2.
13 Ibid, p 14.
14 Brussevich et al, 2018.
15 World Economic Forum, 2018d, p 6.
16 World Economic Forum, 2018d.
17 World Bank Group, 2019, p 6.
18 McKinsey Global Institute, 2018, pp 1–19.
19 World Economic Forum, 2017, p 12.
20 McKinsey Global Institute, 2018, p 16.
21 PwC, 2018b.
22 Ibid, p 10.
23 World Economic Forum, 2018c.
24 Morgan, 2014, p 145.
25 Levit, 2019, pp 30–31.
26 Deloitte, 2017a, p 19.
27 PwC, 2018a, p 10.
28 Ibid, p 12.
29 Ibid, pp 5–7.
30 Ibid, pp 11–12.
31 Deloitte, 2017c, p 113.
32 Deloitte, 2017a, p 119.
33 Deloitte, 2016a.
34 Deloitte, 2017b, p 8.
35 Ibid, p 8.
36 Ibid, p 10.
37 Levit, 2019, p 55.
38 Baldwin, 2019, p 28.
39 Shanks et al, 2016, p 4.
40 Davenport and Kirby, 2016.
41 Ibid.
42 Ibid.
43 Ibid.

44 Ibid.
45 Accenture Strategy, 2018, p 9.
46 Ibid, p 36.
47 Ibid, p 16.
48 Mercer, 2019.
49 Deloitte, 2019b, p 113.
50 Ibid, p 116.
51 Ibid, p 117.
52 Deloitte, 2019a.
53 Expand, 2019.
54 Colvin, 2016, pp 41–42.
55 Levit, 2019, p 57.
56 Yonck, 2017.
57 Baldwin, 2019.
58 Colvin, 2016, p 122.
59 Baldwin, 2019, p 268.
60 Ibid.
61 Deloitte, 2017c, p 56.
62 Ibid, p 103.
63 Baldwin, 2019, p 236.
64 Baldwin, 2019, p 241.
65 Ibid, p 244.
66 Colvin, 2016, p 212.
67 Ford, 2015, p 251.
68 Ibid.
69 Ibid, p 254.
70 Mercer, 2018b, p 20.
71 Deloitte, 2019a.
72 Hesketh and Cooper, 2019.
73 Deloitte, 2017c, p 168.
74 Baldwin, 2019, p 4.
75 Ibid, p 253.
76 Ibid, p 255.
77 Ibid, p 13.
78 Handy, 2015, p 117.
79 Ibid, p 59.
80 TBC
81 Levit, 2019, pp 82–86.
82 Ibid, p 83.
83 Ibid, p 85.
84 Ibid, p 92.

85 Ibid, pp 92–93.
86 Malhhotra et al, 2007, p 62.
87 Baldwin, 2019, p 270.
88 Hatch, 2018, p 188.
89 Levit, 2019, p 106.
90 Ibid.
91 Katz and Krueger, 2016.
92 Levit, 2019, p 109.
93 Levit, 2019.
94 Ibid, pp 102–03.
95 Hickman and Pendell, 2018.
96 Deloitte, 2017e.
97 De Menezes and Kelliher, 2017, p 1051.
98 Chen and Fulmer, 2018, p 381.
99 Ibid.
100 Morgan, 2014, p 31.
101 Levit, 2019, p 95.
102 Deloitte, 2017a, p 19.
103 Colvin, 2016, pp 124–27.
104 Ibid, p 190.
105 Goleman, 1996, p 161.
106 Rippon, 2019, pp 239–41.
107 Colvin, 2016, pp 182–83.
108 Colvin, 2016, p 185.
109 Rippon, 2019, pp 351–53.
110 Chater, 2018, p 219.
111 Argyle, 1972, p 261.
112 Ibid.
113 Ibid, 262.
114 Brynjolsson and McAff, 2014, p 257.
115 Baldwin, 2019, p 262.

8 Demographics

1 Frost and Kalman, 2016.
2 Pew Research Centre, 2014, p 40.
3 Balliester and Elsheikhi, 2018, p 29.
4 Ibid, pp 4–5.
5 World Economic Forum, 2016, pp 55–58.
6 United Nations, Department of Economic and Social Affairs, Population Division, 2017.
7 Levit, 2019, p 17.
8 World Economic Forum, 2019, pp 55–62.
9 Parry and Urwin, 2011, p 89.
10 Stewart et al, 2017, p 46.
11 Ibid.
12 Parry and Urwin, 2011, pp 82–83.
13 Ibid, pp 82–83.
14 Ibid, pp 83–84.
15 Polach, 2007, p 9.
16 Smola and Sutton, 2002.
17 Parry and Urwin, 2011, p 89.
18 Hole et al, 2010, p 86.
19 Parry and Urwin, 2011, pp 90–91,
20 Stewart et al, 2017, p 48.
21 Jenkins and Swarbrick, 2012.
22 Ibid, p 4.
23 PwC, 2011.
24 PwC, 2008b.
25 PwC, 2011, p 3.
26 Deloitte, 2016b.
27 KPMG, 2017.
28 Ibid.
29 Deloitte, 2017e.
30 Ibid.
31 Ibid.
32 Jenkins and Swarbrick, 2012, p 8.
33 Deloitte, 2017c.
34 White, 2017.
35 Gibbons, 2018.
36 TBC
37 KPMG, 2017.
38 Koulopoulos and Keldsen, 2014, p xviii.
39 Ibid, p 78.
40 Nellis, 2017.
41 Levit, 2019, p 11.
42 Ibid, p 10.
43 Hesketh and Cooper, 2019.
44 TBC
45 Business in the Community, 2016, p 33.
46 Government Office for Science, 2016, p 29.
47 Levit, 2019, pp 11–16.
48 Parry and Urwin, 2011.
49 Constanza and Finkelstein, 2015, p 321.
50 Ibid.
51 Pfau, 2016.
52 Ibid.
53 Ibid.
54 PwC, 2011.
55 Rudolph et al, 2018, p 52.
56 Deloitte, 2016b.
57 Gallup, 2016, pp 3–4.
58 Ibid.
59 Ibid.
60 Ibid.
61 Jenkins and Swarbrick, 2012, p 4.
62 Kuron et al, 2014.
63 Towers Perrin, 2005.
64 Kim and Kang, 2017, p 740.
65 Knight, 2014.
66 Sok et al, 2014, p 63.
67 Unite et al, 2014, pp 222–23.
68 Clarke, 2015, p 574.
69 Ibid.
70 Koulopoulos and Keldsen, 2014 p 67.
71 Deloitte, 2016b, p 23.
72 Chamorro-Premuzic, 2017, p 173.
73 Ibid.
74 Jenkins and Swarbrick, 2012, p 8.
75 Twenge and Campbell, 2008.
76 Chamorro-Premuzic, 2017, p 181.
77 Jenkins and Swarbrick, 2012, p 9.
78 Sinek, 2017, p 295.
79 Ibid.
80 Dweck, 2017, p 137.

9 Culture

1 Hofstede, 1986.
2 House et al, 2004.
3 House et al, 2014.
4 Ibid, p 11.
5 Ibid, p 6.
6 Hofstede et al, 2010, p 6.
7 Kroeber and Kluckholm, 1952.
8 Hofstede, 1986.

9 Furnham, 2005.
10 House et al, 2014, p 367.
11 Ibid, p 368.
12 Ibid, p 299.
13 Javidan et al, 2006, p 75.
14 House et al, 2014, p 360.
15 Ibid, p 361.
16 Gundling et al, 2015, p 36.
17 Wang et al, 2012, p 578.
18 Caliguri and Tarique, 2012, p 620; Javidan et al, 2006, pp 85–86.
19 Gundling et al, 2015, pp 41–43.
20 Schein and Schein, 2017, p 108.
21 Hofstede et al, 2010.
22 Ibid, pp 302–11.
23 Fayol, 1919.
24 Weber, 1924.
25 Taylor, 1911.
26 Ouchi, 1980.
27 Hofstede et al, 2010, pp 302–13.
28 Ibid, pp 302–14.
29 Meyer, 2014, p 252.
30 Ibid, p 16.
31 Ibid.
32 Levit, 2019, pp 24–25.
33 Gundling et al, 2015, p 30.
34 Furnham, 2005, p 703.
35 Black, et al, 1992.
36 Furnham, 2005, p 706.
37 Ward et al, 2001.
38 Tung, 1981.
39 Gundling et al, 2015, p 172.
40 Hofstede et al, 2010, p 367.
41 Hofstede and McRae, 2004.
42 Johnson et al, 2014, p 171.
43 Ibid.
44 Ibid, p 175.
45 Ibid.
46 Cameron and Quinn, 2006.
47 Schein, 1990, p 116.
48 Ibid, p 11.
49 Gallup, 2018a, p 2.
50 Ibid, p 13.
51 Dweck, 2017.
52 Ibid.
53 Furnham, 2005, p 636.
54 Denison, 1996, p 624.
55 Denison, 1996.
56 Ibid, pp 644–45.

10 Social movements

1 Deloitte, 2018b, p 2.
2 Freeman, 1984.
3 Miralles-Quiros et al, 2017, p 26; DiSegni et al, 2015, pp 131–48.
4 Haski-Leventhal, 2018, p xxvii.
5 Aaronson, 2003, p 310.
6 Rasche et al, 2017b, p 6.
7 World Commission on Environment and Development, 1987.
8 Savitz and Weber, 2014, p 283.
9 Ibid, p 5.
10 Savitz and Weber, 2013.
11 Haski-Leventhal, 2018, pp 161–79.
12 Deloitte, 2018b, p 59.
13 Aguilera et al, 2007.
14 Zadek, 2004.
15 Porter and Kramer, 2002.
16 Porter and Kramer, 2006.
17 Porter and Kramer, 2011.
18 Rasche et al, 2017a, p 93.
19 DiSegni et al, 2015, p 140.
20 Ibid, p 131.
21 Eisenbeiss et al, 2015, p 647.
22 Carroll, 1991.
23 Haski-Leventhal, 2018, p 36.
24 Ibid, p 93.
25 Beugré, 2018, p 156.
26 Zhu et al, 2014, p 940.
27 Archimi, 2018, p 917.
28 Ibid, p 907.
29 Ogunfowora et al, 2018, p 537.
30 Reimer et al, 2018, p 977.
31 Aguinas and Glavas, 2012.
32 Forum for Sustainable and Responsible Investment, 2019.
33 Sherwood and Pollard, 2019, p 3.
34 SIF Foundation, 2014.
35 Derwall et al, 2011 in Tonello, 2015.
36 Sherwood and Pollard, 2019, o 12.
37 UNPRI, 2019.
38 Sherwood and Pollard, 2019.
39 Haski-Leventhal, 2018, p 162.
40 Ibid, pp 163–78.
41 Verissimo and Lacenda, 2015, p 47.

42 Vlachos et al, 2014, p 1011.
43 Zhou et al, 2018, p 339; Ng et al, 2019.
44 European Commission, 2011.
45 Knight and Paterson, 2018, pp 567–69.
46 Petrenko et al, 2016, p 275.
47 Tang et al, 2018, p 1370.
48 Alonso-Almeida et al, 2017, p 157.
49 Miralles-Quiros et al, 2017, p 1026.
50 Sial et al, 2018.
51 Glass et al, 2016, p 507.
52 Ibid.
53 Ibid, p 495.
54 Cook and Glass, 2018, p 917.
55 Dean et al, 1998.
56 Vlachos et al, 2017, p 1125.
57 Maak et al, 2016, p 484.
58 Ibid.
59 TBC
60 Haski-Leventhal et al, 2017, p 47.
61 Mazutis and Slawinski, 2015, p 147.
62 Ibid, p 144.
63 Rasche et al, 2017b, p 93.
64 Organ, 1988, p 4.
65 Ong et al, 2018, p 45.
66 Ibid, p 56.
67 Storey and Neces, 2014, pp 120–22.

68 Swart et al, 2015, p 90.
69 Savitz and Weber, 2013, pp xxi–xxiv.
70 Winters, 2014, p 206.
71 Mor Barak, 2014, p 136.
72 Ferdman, 2017, p 235.
73 Brewer, 1991.
74 Ferdman, 2017, p 239.
75 Ibid, p 238.
76 Turnball, 2016.
77 Ostry et al, 2018, p 21.
78 Ibid.
79 Shore et al, 2018.
80 Frost and Kalman, 2016, p 39.
81 Ibid, pp 21–23.
82 Ibid, p 42.
83 Cundiff et al, 2018, p 759.
84 Sims, 2018, p 325.
85 TBC
86 TBC
87 Dillon and Bourke, 2016, p 1.
88 Ibid, p 2.
89 Tapai and Lange, 2016, p 1.
90 Ibid, p 4.
91 Hunt et al, 2014, p 3.
92 Ibid, p 5.
93 Rock and Grant, 2016.
94 Badal and Harter, 2013.
95 Pichler et al, 2018, p 283.
96 Hunt et al, 2014.
97 Post, 2015, p 1167.
98 Ferdman, 2017, p 235.

99 Ibid, p 241.
100 Ferdman, 2014, pp 45–47.
101 Gallegos, 2014, p 179.
102 Tang et al, 2015, p 856.
103 Ibid, pp 865–66.
104 Ibid, p 867.
105 Sweeney and Bothwick, 2016, pp 8–9.
106 Ibid, pp 59–65.
107 Hunt et al, 2014, p 15.
108 Ibid, pp 16–17.
109 Sandberg, 2015, p 22.
110 Ibid, p 23.
111 Ibid, p 29.
112 Dweck, 2017, p 79.
113 Sandberg, 2015, p 43.
114 Goleman, 1996, p 159.
115 Frost and Kalman, 2016, p 120.
116 Ibid.
117 Gundling et al, 2015, p 78.
118 Ibid, pp 210–11.
119 Mercer, 2018a, p 10.
120 Ibid, p 23.
121 Accenture, 2018, pp 6–7.
122 Mercer, 2019.
123 Riordan, 2014.
124 Sweeney and Borthwick, 2016, p 85.
125 Offerman and Basford, 2014, p 253.

11 Planning and people risk

1 Sparkman, 2018, p 3.
2 ISO 2016, p vi.
3 Morrison, 2015, p 7.

4 ISO, 2016, p 4.
5 Sparkman, 2018, p 50.
6 Ibid, p 51.
7 Ibid, p 82.

8 Nalbantian et al, 2004, p 76.
9 Ibid, p 251.
10 Sparkman, 2018, p 118.

11   Ibid, p 137.
12   Nalbantian, 2017, p 3.
13   Wright et al, 1994.
14   Agrawal et al, 2003.
15   Boudreau and Ramsted, 2005, pp 23–24.
16   Guthridge et al, 2008, p 56.
17   Aldrich, 2007.
18   Ibid.
19   Nalbantian, 2017, p 14.
20   Blacker and McConnel, 2015, p 19.
21   ISO, 2018b, p 1.
22   Ibid, p v.
23   Blacker and McConnel, 2015, p 21.
24   Ibid, p 29.
25   Ibid, p 31.
26   Ibid, pp 126–27.
27   Quinn and Cameron, 2011.
28   Blacker and McConnel, 2015, p 205.
29   Ibid, p 206.
30   City HR Association, 2013, p 11.
31   Ibid.
32   Groysberg, 2010.
33   Ibid.
34   Ibid.
35   Ibid.
36   Lawler et al, 2004, p 29.
37   Fitz-enz, 2002.

12 Human capital metrics and reporting

1   Bassi and McMurrer, 2007.
2   Phillips and Phillips, 2015, p 15.
3   Ibid, p viii.
4   Mayo, 2001, p 31.
5   Thomas et al, 2013, p 3.
6   Becker, 1964.
7   Nalbantian et al, 2004, p 79.
8   Ibid.
9   Ordonez de Pablos, 2015, p xv.
10   Lee and Yip, 2015, p 170.
11   Ibid, p 167.
12   Ibid, p 168
13   Bourdieu, 1986.
14   Ordonez de Pablos, 2013, p 125.
15   Grant, 1996, p 10.
16   Nalbantian et al, 2004, p 4.
17   Mercer, 2017a.
18   Nalbantian et al, 2004, p 8.
19   Ibid, p 9.
20   Lev and Scwartz, 1971.
21   Sveiby, 1990.
22   Roos et al, 1997.
23   Davenport, 1999.
24   Mayo, 2001, p 47.
25   Fitz-enz, 2000.
26   Kaplan and Norton, 1996.
27   Becker et al, 2001.
28   Flamholz, 1999.
29   Warosn Wyatt, 2002, p 3.
30   Ibid, p 4.
31   Willis Towers Watson, 2016a, p 2.
32   Kautz et al, 2014.
33   Boon et al, 2017, p 56.
34   Mayo, 2001, p 65.
35   Ibid, pp 12–13.
36   TBC
37   Phillips et al, 2016.
38   Ibid, p 29.
39   Drucker, 2011, pp 54–75.
40   Doer, 2017, pp 20–34.
41   Ibid, pp 16–17.
42   Ibid, p 176.
43   Ibid.
44   Ibid.
45   Ibid, p 181.
46   Barends and Rousseau, 2018, p xvi.
47   Ibid, p 2.
48   Ibid.
49   Ulrich and Dulebohn, 2015, p 202.
50   Ulrich, 1997, p 247.
51   Wright et al, 1998, pp 17–29.
52   Phelps, 2004.
53   Fitz-enz, 2002, p 19.
54   Lawler et al, 2004, p 29.
55   EIU, 2012, p 4.
56   Ibid.
57   Ibid.
58   Durfee, 2013.
59   Phillips, and Phillips, 2015, pp 11–12.
60   Charan et al, 2018, p 11.
61   Charan et al, 2018, p 20.
62   Ibid, p 83.
63   EY, 2014, pp 8–9.
64   Ibid, p 14.
65   Ibid, p 22.
66   ISO, 2018a.
67   Ibid, p v.
68   Ibid.
69   Ibid.
70   Ibid.
71   Ibid.
72   Ibid.
73   Valuing Your Talent, 2016, pp 6–7.
74   Intergrated Reporting, 2016, p 10.

75 Houghton and Spence, 2016, pp 17–18.
76 Intergrated Reporting, 2016, p 6.
77 Bassie et al, p 12.
78 Human Capital Management Coalition, 2019.
79 Intergrated Reporting, 2016, p 19.
80 Krausert, 2018; Abdolmohammadi, 2005; Vafaei et al, 2011.
81 Gamerschlag, 2013.
82 EY, 2014, p 19.
83 EY, 2014, p 22.
84 Bassi and McMurrer, 2005.
85 Bassie et al, 2014, p 18

13 People analytics

1 Mercer, 2018b.
2 Mercer, 2017b, p 12.
3 Gartner, 2018.
4 Marr, 2018, p 2.
5 Ibid, p 59.
6 Ibid, p 54.
7 Guenole et al, 2017, p 126.
8 Marr, 2018, p 79.
9 Van der Togt et al, 2017, p 131.
10 Guenole et al, 2017, p 44.
11 Ibid, p 170.
12 Ibid, pp 228–35.
13 Ibid, p 7.
14 Kryscynski et al, 2018, p 732.
15 Marr, 2018, p 222.
16 Monbaeva, 2018, p 711.
17 Guenole et al, 2017, p 209.
18 Ulrich and Dulebohn, 2015, p 202.
19 Waber, 2013, pp 50–55.
20 Ibid, pp 59–60.
21 Ibid, p 197.
22 Ibid, p 201.
23 Lewis, 2003, p 67.

14 Employee engagement and experience

1 Gallup, 2017.
2 Elliot and Corey, 2018, p 4.4
3 Chamorro-Premuzic, 2017, p 89.
4 TBC
5 Gallup, 2017.
6 Ibid.
7 Ibid, 2017.
8 Willis Towers Watson, 2016b.
9 Maylett and Warner, 2014.
10 Maylett and Wride, 2017.
11 TBC
12 Elliot and Corey, 2018, p 6.
13 Ibid, p 12.
14 Ibid, p 13.
15 Chamorro-Premuzic, 2017.
16 Ibid.
17 Meaney and Keller, 2017.
18 Cheung-Judge and Holbeche, 2015.
19 Ibid.
20 Gallup, 2018c, p 2.
21 Maylett and Wride, 2017.
22 Ibid.
23 Ibid.
24 Ibid.
25 Ibid.
26 Ibid.
27 Maylett and Warner, 2014.
28 Maylett and Wride, 2017.
29 Ibid.
30 Ibid.
31 Ibid.
32 Ibid.
33 Ibid.
34 Edelman, 2019, p 3.
35 Dweck, 2017.
36 Ibid.
37 Deloitte, 2017a, p 55.
38 Gallup, 2018c, p 2.
39 Ibid, p 2.
40 Ibid, p 2.
41 Morgan, 2017.
42 Ibid.
43 Ibid.
44 Ibid.
45 Ibid.
46 Ibid.
47 Ibid.
48 Ibid.
49 Ibid.
50 Ibid.
51 Ibid.
52 Deloitte, 2017a, p 51.
53 Ibid, p 29.
54 Levit, 2019, pp 167–68.
55 TBC
56 Deloitte, 2017a, p 66.
57 Ibid, p 80.
58 Mosley, 2014.
59 Ibid.
60 Ibid.

61 Ibid.
62 Ibid.
63 Ibid.
64 Ibid.
65 Ibid.
66 Ibid.
67 Maylett and Wride, 2017.
68 Mosley, 2014.
69 Ibid.
70 Sparrow and Otaye, 2015, p 2.
71 Mosley, 2014, p 8.

72 Ibid, p 126.
73 Ibid, p 126.
74 Minchington, 2015, pp 14–17.
75 Vishwas Maheshwari et al, 2017, p 754.
76 Wiley and Kowske, 2011.
77 Mercer, 2017b.
78 Ibid.
79 Lee, 2016.
80 Deloitte, 2019a.
81 Ibid.

82 Ibid.
83 Mercer, 2017b.
84 Ibid.
85 Deloitte, 2019a.
86 Chamorro-Premuzic, 2017.
87 Pfeffer, 2018a.
88 Chamorro-Premuzic, 2017.
89 Dinne and Alder, 2017.

15 Well-being

1 World Health Organization, 2019.
2 The National Wellness Institute, 2019.
3 Miller et al, 2018, p 59.
4 Hesketh and Cooper, 2019.
5 National Institute for Health and Care Excellence, 2019.
6 Coppin, 2017.
7 Ibid, p 89.
8 Ibid, pp 90–91.
9 Hesketh and Cooper, 2019.
10 British Psychologicial Society, 2017.
11 International Well Building Institute, 2019.
12 Gillan, 2019, p 76.
13 Ibid, p 77.
14 Ibid.
15 Ibid, pp 77–78.
16 Ibid, pp 78–80.
17 Ibid, pp 170–72.
18 Wilde, 2016.
19 Ibid, p 98.
20 Ibid, p 100.
21 Ibid, p 110.
22 Ibid, p 145.
23 Ibid, p 128.
24 Edmondson, 2019, p xiv.

25 Ibid, p xvi.
26 Ibid, p xvi.
27 Ibid, p 15.
28 Robertson and Cooper, 2011.
29 Gallup, 2012, p 112.
30 Edmondson, 2019, pp 18–19.
31 Syed, 2015, p 243.
32 Ibid, p 250.
33 Bossons et al, 2015.
34 Abraham, 1998.
35 Beugré, 2018, p 161.
36 Ibid, p 161.
37 Hesketh and Cooper, 2019.
38 Sparrow et al, 2015, p 155.
39 Pfeffer, 2018b, p 1.
40 De Smet et al, 2014, p 2.
41 Sparrow et al, 2015, p 155.
42 Chick, 2018, p 71.
43 Furnham, 2005, pp 372–73.
44 Ibid, pp 365–68.
45 Worrall et al, 2016, p 5.
46 Ibid, p 5.
47 Swart et al, 2015, p 163.
48 Ibid, pp 156–58.
49 Hesketh and Cooper, 2019.
50 Ibid.

51 Bossons et al, 2015, p 59.
52 Hesketh and Cooper, 2019.
53 Ibid.
54 Neenan, 2018, p 17.
55 Ibid, pp 174–78.
56 Furnham, 2005, pp 372–75.
57 PwC, 2008a, pp 22–23.
58 Bossons et al, 2015, p 58.
59 Ibid, p 57.
60 Swart et al, 2015, p 154.
61 Ibid, p 154.
62 Ibid, pp 162–63.
63 Bossons et al, 2015, p 61.
64 Ibid.
65 Ibid, p 62.
66 Sartre, 1965, pp 182–93.
67 Frankl, 1988.
68 Ulrich and Ulrich, 2010.
69 Ibid.
70 Ibid.
71 Seligman, 2018, p 267.
72 Farmer and Stevenson, 2017.
73 Lucy et al, 2018, p 44.
74 Ibid.
75 Business in the Community, The

Prince's Responsible Business at Work, 2017, p 7.
76 Mercer, 2017b, p 25.
77 Ibid, p 24.
78 Mercer, 2018b, p 10.
79 Ibid, p 11.
80 Mercer, 2018c, pp 14–15.
81 Walker, 2018, p 298.
82 Ibid, p 305.
83 Montano et al, 2017, p 343.
84 Ibid, p 344.
85 Ibid.
86 Ibid.
87 Ibid.
88 Mercer, 2018b, p 11.
89 Deloitte, 2019a, p 4.
90 Mercer, 2018b.
91 Pfeffer, 2018b, p 7.

16 The future of people development

1 Deloitte, 20118a.
2 World Economic Forum, 2017, p 13.
3 Mercer, 2018b, p 7.
4 Dochy and Segers, 2018.
5 Ibid.
6 OECD, 2019, p 61.
7 Mercer, 2019.
8 Ibid.
9 Deloitte, 2019.
10 Dochy and Segers, 2018.
11 Ibid.
12 Ibid.
13 Ibid.
14 Ibid.
15 Ibid.
16 Seaton et al, 2014.
17 Cusumano, 2016, p 110.
18 Jordan, 2014, pp 147–49.
19 Dalsgaard and Gislev, 219.
20 Dochy and Segers, 2018.
21 Ibid.
22 Gallup, 2017, p 16.
23 Chamorro-Premuzic, 2017, p 185.
24 Dixon and Gorecki, 2010.
25 Handy, 2015, pp 160–61.
26 Chamorro-Premuzic, 2017, p 35.
27 Ibid, p 49.
28 Ibid, p 167.
29 Pfeffer, 2015, pp 2–3.
30 Dweck, 2000, p 133.
31 Chamorro-Premuzic, 2017, p 16.
32 Syed, 2015, p 137.
33 Sloman and Fernbach, 2017, p 263.
34 Syed, 2015.
35 Ibid, p 156.
36 Dweck, 2000, p 140.
37 Ibid, p 141.
38 Ibid.
39 Chamorro-Premuzic, 2017, p 136.
40 Ibid, p 224.
41 Steelman and Wolfed, 2018, pp 51–52.
42 Dweck, 2017, p 15.
43 Goleman, 1996, p 89.
44 Sloman and Fernbach, 2017, p 258.
45 Bandura, 1997.
46 Dweck, 2000.
47 Ibid.
48 Ibid.
49 Goleman, 2013.
50 Ibid.
51 Dweck, 2000.
52 Ibid.
53 Chamorro-Premuzic, 2017, p 136.
54 Conger, 2004.
55 Passmore, 2007, p 69.
56 Ellam-Dyson et al, 2019.
57 Allworth and Passmore, 2012, p 22.

17 People functions

1 Walker, 1978.
2 Guest, 1997; Huselid, 1995.
3 Delery and Doty, 1996.
4 Huselid and Becker, 1996; Guest and Conway, 1998.
5 Wright and Snell, 1998.
6 Millman et al, 1991.
7 Bowen and Ostroff, 2004.
8 Doty and Glick, 1994.
9 Legge, 2005.
10 Storey, 1987.
11 Becker and and Huselid, 1998.
12 Becker et al, 2001.
13 Teece et al, 1997.
14 Wright et al, 1994.
15 Dyer and Reeves, 1995.
16 Boselie et al, 2005.

17 Huselid et al, 1997.
18 Colbert, 2004.
19 Barney, 1991; Wright et al, 1998.
20 Boselie et al, 2005.
21 Ferris et al, 1999.
22 Hendry and Pettigrew, 1990.
23 Ibid.
24 Colbert, 2004.
25 Bowen and Ostroff, 2004.
26 Wright and McMahan, 1992.
27 Wright and McMahan, 1992.
28 Boxall, 1993.
29 Galang and Ferris, 1997.
30 Russ et al, 1998.
31 Ferris et al, 1999.
32 Wright and Snell, 1999.
33 Gennard and Kelly, 1994.
34 Guest, 1990.
35 Collins and Smith, 2006.
36 Donald and Donald, 1929.
37 Strauss, 2001.
38 Armstrong and Long, 1994.
39 Legge, 1978.
40 Guest and King, 2004.
41 Tyson, 1987.
42 Schuler, 1990.
43 Caroll, 1991.
44 Storey, 1992.
45 Caldwell, 2003.
46 Ibid.
47 Ulrich, 1997.

48 Ulrich et al, 2008, p 24.
49 Ibid.
50 Ibid.
51 Ibid, p 37.
52 Aldrich, 2009.
53 Ibid.
54 Hunter et al, 2006.
55 Wright et al, 2001b.
56 Caldwell, 2003.
57 Ibid.
58 Ibid.
59 Ibid.
60 Ibid.
61 Gitzendanner et al, 1983.
62 Glass, 1988
63 Guest, 1989b.
64 Armstrong and Long, 1994.
65 Ibid.
66 Ulrich, 1997.
67 Ibid.
68 Guest et al, 2003.
69 Barber and Strack, 2005.
70 Donald and Donald, 1929.
71 Guest and King, 2004.
72 Hegarty and Hoffman, 1987.
73 Buller, 1988.
74 Wernerfelt, 1984; Barney, 1991; Wright et al, 2001a.
75 Miles and Snow, 1984.
76 Ibid.
77 Kochan and Borocki, 1985.
78 Boxall and Steenveld, 1999.

79 Guest and King, 2004.
80 Cunningham and Hyman, 1999.
81 Guest and King, 2004.
82 Larsen and Brewster, 2003.
83 Grundy and Brown, 2003.
84 Ibid.
85 Sheehan, 2005.
86 Ibid.
87 Ibid.
88 Antila and Kakkonen, 2008.
89 Kelly and Gennard, 2007.
90 Antila and Kakkonen, 2008.
91 Pfeffer, 2002.
92 Truss et al, 2002.
93 Antila and Kakkonen, 2008.
94 Ulrich, 1997.
95 Ibid.
96 Ibid.
97 Fitz-enz, 2002.
98 Reilly and Williams, 2003, p 11.
99 Ibid, p 1.
100 Ibid p 19.
101 Ibid, p 145.
102 Beer, 1997.
103 Dyer, 1999.
104 Aldrich, 2009, p 195.
105 Borucki and Lafley, 1984, pp 75–76.
106 Aldrich, 2009, p 200.
107 Ibid.
108 Ibid, p 162.
109 Aldrich et al, 2015.

18 Professional people management

1 Chamorro-Premuzic, 2017, p 227.
2 Wright, 2015, pp 47–48.
3 Ibid, p 48.
4 Kew and Stredwick, 2016, p 476.
5 Sparrow et al, 2015, p 220.
6 Phillips et al, 2016, pp 59–61.
7 Wright, 2015, p 224.
8 Ibid, p 229.
9 Lawler, 2017, p 3.
10 Berger and Berger, 2017, p 3.
11 Lawler, 2017, p ix.
12 Sparrow et al, 2015, p 186.
13 Ibid, p 196.
14 Ibid, p 198.
15 Ibid, p 199.

16 Meaney and Keller, 2017, pp 3–4.
17 Ibid, p 5.
18 Phillips and Phillips, 2015, p viii.
19 Allen, 2015, p 2.
20 Bafaro et al, 2017, p 3.
21 Timms, 2018.
22 Ibid, pp 45–65.
23 Ibid, pp 222–31.
24 Ibid, p 210.
25 Ibid, p 211.
26 Andrianova et al, 2018.
27 Ibid, p 5.
28 Ibid, p 7.
29 Ibid, p 8.
30 Charan et la, 2018.
31 Ibid, p 55.
32 Lawler, 2017, p 110.
33 Ibid, pp 112–13.
34 Charan et al, 2018, pp 86–87.
35 Ibid, pp 87–88.
36 Sparrow et al, 2015, p 6.
37 Frost et al, 2002.
38 Moore and Birkinshaw, 1998, p 81.
39 Sparrow et al, 2015, p 217.
40 Ziskin and Boudreau, 2011, p 257.
41 Gubbins and Garavan, 2016, p 253.
42 Charan et al, 2018, p 92.
43 Ibid, p 97.
44 Bersin, 2015, pp 5–7.
45 Foster-Cheek and Sage-Gavin, 2018.
46 Ziskin, 2018.
47 Gillen, 2019, p 170.

19 HR disrupted and dispersed

1 Drucker, 2007, p 238.
2 Ibid.
3 Handy, 1985b, p 285.
4 Ibid, p 286.
5 Ibid.
6 Mullins, 1985, p 321.
7 Aldrich, 2009.
8 Ibid.
9 Stewart and Woods, 1996.
10 Keenoy, 1997.
11 Sanghera, 2009.
12 Charan, 2014.
13 Charan et al, 2015.
14 Cappelli, 2015.
15 Brandl et al, 2019.
16 Goulding and Shaughnessy, 2017, p 51.
17 Lawler, 2017, p 116.
18 Sparrow et al, 2015, p 17.
19 Ibid.
20 Ibid, p 6.
21 Drucker, 2007, p 238.
22 Sparrow et al, 2015, p 220.
23 Adams, 2017, p 205.
24 Ibid.
25 Ibid, pp 214–15.
26 Ibid, p 213.
27 Ibid, p 214.
28 Cheung-Judge and Holbeche, 2015, p 281.
29 Ibid, p 298.
30 Lawler, 2017, p 116.
31 Ulrich and Dulebohn, 2015, p 201.
32 Ibid, pp 201–03.

REFERENCES

Aaronson, SA (2003) Corporate responsibility in the global village: The British role model and the American laggard, *Business and Society Review*, **108**(3), pp 309–38

Abdolmohammadi, MJ (2005) Intellectual capital disclosure and market capitalization, *Journal of Intellectual Capital*, **6**(3), pp 397–416

Abraham, R (1998) Emotional dissonance in organizations: Antecedents, consequences and moderators, *Genetic, Social, and General Psychology Monographs*, **124**(2), pp 229–46

Accenture (2018) *Getting to Equal: The disability inclusion advantage*, Accenture

Accenture Strategy (2018) *Reworking the Revolution*, Accenture

Adams, JS (1965) Inequity in social exchange, in *Advances in Experimental Social Psychology*, ed L Berkowitz, Vol 2

Adams, L (2017) *HR Disrupted*, Practical Inspiration

Agrawal ,V, Manyika, JM and Richards, JE (2003) Matching people and jobs, *The McKinsey Quarterly, Number Two: Organization*

Aguilera, RV, Rupp, DE, Williams, CA and Ganapathi, J (2007) Putting the S back into corporate social responsibility: A multi-level theory of social change in organizations, *Academy of Management Review*, **32**(3) pp 836–63

Aguinas, H and Glavas, A (2012) What we know and don't know about corporate and social responsibility: A review and research agenda, *Journal of Management*, **38**, pp 932–68

Ahlstrom, D and Li, Y (2016) Emotional stability: A new construct and its implications for individual behavior in organizations, *Asia Pacific Journal of Management*, **33**, pp 1–28

Ajzen, I (1991) The theory of planned behaviour, *Organizational Behaviour and Human Decision Processes*, 50, pp 179–211

Alderfer, CA (1969) An empirical test of a new theory of human needs, *Organizational Behaviour and Human Performance*, **4**(2), pp 142–75

Aldrich, P (2007) *Talent Portfolio Management: Leveraging human assets in capital markets and investment banking*, IFR Market Intelligence, Thomson Financial Group

Aldrich, P (2009) The role and influence of human resource management in the capital markets and investment banking sector, DBA Thesis, Durham University

Aldrich, P, Dietz, G, Clark, T and Hamilton, P (2015) Establishing HR professionals' influence and credibility: Lessons from the capital markets and investment banking sector, *Human Resource Management*, **54**(1), pp 105–30

Allen, PL (2015) Towards a new HR philosophy, *McKinsey Quarterly*, April

Allport, GW (1954) *The Nature of Prejudice*, Addison-Wesley

Allworth, E and Passmore, J (2012) Using psychometrics and psychological tools, in *Psychometrics in Coaching: Using psychological and psychometric tools for development*, ed J Passmore, Kogan Page

Alonso-Almeida, MDM, Perramon, J and Bagur-Femenias, L (2017) Leadership styles and corporate social responsibility management: Analysis from a gender perspective, *Business Ethics: A European Review*, **26**, pp 147–61

Andrianova, S, Maor, D, Schaninger, B (2018) *Winning With your Talent-Management Strategy*, McKinsey & Company

Ansoff, I (1987) *Corporate Strategy*, Penguin

Antila, EM and Kakkonen, A (2008) Factors affecting the role of HR managers in international mergers and acquisitions: A multiple case study, *Personnel Review*, **37**(3)

Archimi, CS, Reynaud, E, Yasin, HM and Bhatti, ZA (2018) How perceived corporate social responsibility affects employee cynicism: The mediating role of organizational trust, *Journal of Business Ethics*, **151**, pp 907–21

Argyle, M (1972) *The Social Psychology of Work*, Penguin Books

Armstrong, M, and Long, P (1994) *The Reality of Strategic HRM*, Institute of Personnel and Development

Armstrong-Strassen, M (1998) Alternative work arrangements: Meeting the challenge, *Canadian Psychology*, **39**, pp 108–23

Avolio, BJ, Gardner, WL, Walumbwa, FO, Luthans, F and May, DR (2004) Unlocking the mask: A look at the process by which authentic leaders impact follower attitudes and behaviors, *The Leadership Quarterly*, 15, pp 801–23

Ayan, S (2008) Speaking of memory: Q&A with neuroscientist Eric Kandel, *Scientific American Mind*, October

Badal, S and Harter, JK (2013) Gender diversity, business-unit engagement, and performance, *Journal of Leadership & Organizational Studies*, **21**(4), pp 354–65

Bafaro, F, Ellsworth, D and Gandhi, N (2017) The CEO's guide to competing through HR, *McKinsey Quarterly*, July

Baldwin, R (2019) *The Globotics Upheaval*, Weidenfeld & Nicolson

Balliester, T and Elsheikhi, A (2018) The future of work: A literature review, Working Paper No 29, Research Department, International Labour Office

Balogen, J and Hope-Hailey, V (2008) *Exploring Strategic Change*, Prentice Hall

Banaji, MR and Greenwald, AG (2016) *Blind Spot*, Bantam

Bandura, A (1982) Self-efficacy mechanism in human agency, *American Psychologist*, **37**, 122–47

Bandura, A (1997) *Self-Efficacy: The exercise of control*, WH Freeman

Barber, F, and Strack, R (2005) The surprising economics of a people business, *Harvard Business Review*, June, pp 81–80

Barends, E and Rousseau, D (2018) *Evidence-Based Management*, Kogan Page

Barney, J (1991) Firm resources and sustained competitive advantage, *Journal of Management*, **17**(1), pp 99–120

Barney, J (1997) *Gaining and Sustaining Competitive Advantage*, Addison-Wesley

Bass, BM (1985) Leadership and Performance Beyond Expectations, Free Press

Bass, BM (2008) *The Bass Handbook of Leadership: Theory research and managerial applications*, Free Press

Bassi, L and McMurrer, D (2005) Developing measurement systems for managing in the knowledge era, *Organizational Dynamics*, **34**, 185–96

Bassi, L and McMurrer, D (2007) Maximising your return on people, *Harvard Business Review*, March, 115–23

Bassi, L, Creelna, D and Lambert, A (2014) *The Smarter Annual Report: How companies are integrating financial and human capital reporting*, McBassi & Co

Becker, GS (1964) *Human Capital: A theoretical and empirical anlaysis with special reference to education*, Columbia University Press

Becker, BE and Huselid, MA (1998) High performance work systems and firm performance: A synthesis of research and managerial implications, in *Research in Personnel and Human Resource Management*, ed KM Rowland and GR Ferris, JAI Press, pp 53–101

Becker BE, Huselid, MA and Ulrich, D (2001) *The HR Scorecard: Linking people, strategy and performance*, Harvard Business School Press

Beer, M (1997) The transformation of the human resource function: Resolving the tension between a traditional administrative and new strategic role, *Human Resource Management*, **36**(1), pp 49–56

Beer, M, Eisenstat, RA and Spector, B (1990) Why change programs don't produce change, *Harvard Business Review*, **68**(5), pp 158–66

Bennett, N and Lemoine, GJ (2014) What a difference a word makes: Understanding threats to performance in a VUCA world, *Business Horizons*, **57**, pp 311–17

Berger, LA and Berger, D (2017) *The Talent Management Handbook*, McGraw-Hill Education

Berger, P and Luckmann, T (1966) *The Social Constructionism of Reality: A treatise in the sociology of knowledge*, Doubleday

Bersin, J (2015) A modern HR operating model: The world has changed, in *Changing HR Operating Models*, CIPD, www.cipd.co.uk/knowledge/strategy/hr/operating-models (archived at https://perma.cc/B3MQ-L28U)

Beugré, CD (2009) Exploring the neural foundations of organizational justice: A neurocognitive model, *Organizational Behaviour and Human Decision Processes*, **110**(2), pp 129–39

Beugré, CD (2018) *The Neuroscience of Organizational Behavior*, Edward Elgar

Binet, A and Simon, TH (1914) *Mentally Defective Children*, Edward Arnold

Black, J, Gregerson, H and Mendenhall, M (1992) *Global Assignments*, Jossey-Bass

Blacker, K and McConnel, P (2015) *People Risk Management*, Kogan Page

Blake, R and Mouton, J (1985) *The Managerial Grid III*, Gulf

Bleidorn, WB and Hopwood, CJ (2019) Stability and change in personality traits over the lifespan, in *Handbook of Personality Development*, ed DP McAdams, RL Shiner and JL Tackett, The Guildford Press

Boises, K, Fiset, J and Gill, H (2015) Communication and trust are key: Unlocking the relationship between leadership and team performance and creativity, *The Leadership Quarterly*, **26**, pp 1080–94

Boon, C, Eckardt, R, Lepak, DP and Boselie, P (2017) Integrating strategic human capital and strategic human resource management, *The International Journal of Human Resource Management*, **29**(1), pp 34–67

Borucki, CC and Lafley, AF (1984) Strategic staffing at Chase Manhattan Bank, in *Strategic Human Resource Management*, ed CJ Fombrun, NM Tichy and MA Devanna, Wiley

Boselie, P, Dietz, G and Boon, C (2005) Commonalities and contradictions in research on human resource management and performance, *Human Resource Management Journal*, **15**(3), 67–94

Bossons, P, Ridedell, P and Sartain, D (2015) *The Neuroscience of Leadership Coaching*, Bloomsbury

Boudreau, JW, and Ramstad, PM (2005) Where is your pivotal talent? *Harvard Business Review*, April, 23–24

Bourdieu, P (1986) The forms of capital, in *Handbook of Theory and Research for the Sociology of Education*, ed JG Richardson, Greenwood

Bovey, WH and Hede, A (2001) Resistance to organizational change: The role of cognitive and affective processes, *Leadership & Organization Development Journal*, **22**(7/8), pp 372–82

Bowen, DE and Ostroff, C (2004) Understanding HRM–firm performance linkages: The role of the 'strength' of the HRM system, *Academy of Management Review*, **29**(2), pp 203–21

Boxall, PF (1993) The significance of human resource management: A reconsideration of the evidence, *International Journal of Human Resource Management*, 4(3), pp 645-664

Boxall, P and Steenveld, M (1999) Human resource strategy and competitive advantage: A longitudinal study of engineering consultancies, *Journal of Management Studies*, **36**(4), pp 443–63

Boyer, P (2018) *Minds Make Societies*, Yale University Press

Brandl, J, Dreher, J and Schneider, A (2019) 'The HR generalist is dead': A phenomenological perspective on decoupling, *Research in the Sociology of Organizations*, forthcoming

Brewer, MB (1991) The social self: On being the same and different at the same time, *Personality and Social Psychology Bulletin*, **17**(5), pp 475–82

Briggs Myers, I (2015) *Introduction to Myers–Briggs Type*, CPP

British Psychological Society (2017) *Psychology at Work: Improving wellbeing and productivity*, British Psychological Society

Brown, ME, Treviño, LK and Harrison, DA (2005) Ethical leadership: A social learning perspective for construct development and testing, *Organizational Behavior and Human Decision Processes*, **97**(2), pp 117–34

Brussevich, M, Dabla-Norris, E, Kamunge, C, Karnane, P, Khalid, S and Kochhar, K (2018) Gender, technology, and the future of work, IMF Staff Discussion Note, SDN/18/07, pp 21–26

Brynjolfsson, E and McAfee, A (2014) *The Second Machine Age*, Norton

Bughin, J, Manyika, J and Woetzel, J (2017) *Jobs Lost, Jobs Gained: Workforce transitions in a time of automation*, McKinsey Global Institute

Buhle, JT, Silvers, JA, Wager, TD et al (2014) Cognitive re-appraisal of emotion: A meta- analysis of human neuroimaging studies, *Cerebral Cortex*, **24**(11), 2981–90

Buller, PF (1988) Successful partnerships: HR and strategic planning at eight top firms, *Organizational Dynamics*, Autumn, pp 27–43

Burns, T and Stalker, J (1961) *The Management of Innovation*, Tavistock

Business in the Community (2016) *Age in the Workplace: Retain, retrain, recruit*, Business in the Community

Business in the Community, The Prince's Responsible Business at Work (2017) *Mental Health at Work Report 2017: National Employee Mental Wellbeing Survey Findings 2017*, Business in the Community

Caldwell, R (2003) The changing roles of personnel managers: Old ambiguities, new uncertainties, *Journal of Management Studies*, **40**(4), pp 983–1004

Caliguri, P and Tarique, I (2012) Dynamic cross-cultural competencies and global leadership effectiveness, *Journal of World Business*, **47**, pp 612–22

Cameron, K and Quinn, R (2006) *Diagnosing and Changing Organizational Culture: Based on competing values framework*, Jossey-Bass

Campbell, D (2000) *The Socially Constructed Organization*, Karnac

Cappelli, P (2015) Why we love to hate HR... and what HR can do about it, *Harvard Business Review*, July–August

Caroll, SJ (1991) The new HRM roles, responsibilities and structures, in *Managing Human Resources in the Information Age*, ed RS Schuler, Bureau of National Affairs

Carroll, AB (1991) The pyramid of corporate and social responsibility: Evolution of a definitional construct, *Business & Society*, **38**(3), pp 268–95

Carroll, GR and Hannan, MT (2004) *The Demography of Corporations and Industries*, Princeton University Press

Cattell, R (1971) *Abilities: Their structure, growth and action*, Houghton-Mifflin

Cattell, R (1971) *The Scientific Analysis of Personality*, Penguin

Chamorro-Premuzic, T (2017) *The Talent Delusion: Why data, not intuition, is the key to unlocking human potential*, Piatkus

CharacterScope (2019) The guide, https://characterscope.com/blog-the-guide/?et_fb=1 (archived at https://perma.cc/4MR9-KT95)

Charan, R (2014) It's time to split HR, *Harvard Business Review*, July–August

Charan, R, Barton, D and Carey, D (2015) People before strategy: A new role for the CHRO, *Harvard Business Review*, July–August

Charan, R, Barton, D and Carey, D (2018) *Talent Wins*, Harvard Business Review Press

Chartered Management Institute (2016) *The Middle Manager Lifeline: Trust and communication in the heart of your organization*, Chartered Management Institute

Chater, N (2018) *The Mind is Flat*, Allen Lane

Chen, Y and Fulmer, IS (2018) Fine-tuning what we know about employees' experience with flexible work arrangements and their job attitudes, *Human Resource Management*, **57**, pp 381–95

Cheung-Judge, MY and Holbech, L (2015) *Organization Development: A practitioner's guide for OD and HR*, Kogan Page

Chick, G (2018) *Corporate Emotional Intelligence: Being human in a corporate world*, Critical Publishing

City HR Association (2013) *Managing People Risk in the Financial Sector: A guide for HR and risk practitioners*, City HR Association

Clark, A (2016) *Mindware: An introduction to the philosophy of cognitive science*, Oxford University Press

Clarke, M (2015) Dual careers: The new norm for Gen Y professionals? *Career Development International*, **20**(6), pp 562–82

Colbert, BA (2004) The complex resource-based view: Implications for theory and practice in strategic human resource management, *Academy of Management Review*, **29**(3), pp 341–58

Colbert, AE, Barrick, MR and Bradley, BH (2014) Personality and leadership composition in top management teams: Implications for organizational effectiveness, *Personnel Psychology*, **67**, pp 351–87

Collins, J (2001) *Good to Great*, Random House

Collins, J and Hansen, MT (2011) *Great by Choice*, Random House

Collins, CJ and Smith, KG (2006) Knowledge exchange and combination: The role of human resource practices in the performance of high-technology firms, *Academy of Management Journal*, 49(3), pp 544–60

Colvin, G (2016) *Humans are Underrated*, Nicholas Brearley

Conger, JA (2004) Developing leadership capability: What's inside the black box? *Academy of Management Executive*, **18**, pp 136–39

Constanza, DP and Finkelstein, DP (2015) Generationally based differences in the workplace: Is there a *there* there? *Industrial and Organizational Psychology*, 8(3), pp 308–23

Cook, A and Glass, C (2018) Women on corporate boards: Do they advance corporate and social responsibility? *Human Relations*, 7(7), pp 897–924

Coppin, A (2017) *The Human Capital Imperative: Valuing your talent*, Palgrave Macmillan

Costa, PT and McCrae, R (2018) *NEO-PI-3*, Hogrefe

Cottingham, J (2017) *Descartes: Meditations on First Philosophy: With selections from the* Objections *and* Replies, Cambridge University Press

Csikszentmihalyi, M (2008) *Flow: The psychology of optimal experience*, Harper Perennial

Cundiff, JL, Ryuk, S and Cech, K (2018) Identity-safe or threatening? Perceptions of women-targeted diversity incentives, *Group Processes & Intergroup Relations*, **21**(5), pp 745–66

Cunningham, I and Hyman, J (1999) Devolving human resource responsibilities to the line: Beginning of the end or a new beginning for everyone? *Personnel Review*, **28**(1-2), pp 9–27

Cusumano, MA (2016) The high costs of 'free' online education: Some observations and policy suggestions, www.portlandpresspublishing.com/sites/default/files/Editorial/Wenner/PPL_Wenner_Ch09.pdf (archived at https://perma.cc/3L2L-SGAX)

Dalsgaard, C and Gislev, T (2019) Embracing Dropouts in MOOCs: Exploring potentials of invisible learners, *Journal of Interactive Media in Education*, **1**(3), pp 1–12

Davenport, TH and Kirby, JK (2016) *Only Humans Need Apply*, Harper Collins

Davenport, TO (1999) *Human Capital*, Jossey-Bass

De Menezes, LM and Kelliher, C (2017) Flexible working, individual performance and employee attitudes: Comparing formal and informal arrangements, *Human Resource Management*, November–December, **56**(6), pp 1051–70

De Smet, A, Schaninger, B and Smith, M (2014) The hidden value of organizational health – and how to capture it, *McKinsey Quarterly*, April

De Vignemont, F and Singer, T (2006) The empathetic brain: How, when and why? *Trends in Cognitive Sciences*, **10**(10), 435–41

De Young, CG and Allen, TA (2019) Personality neuroscience: A developmental perspective, in *Handbook of Personality Development*, ed DP McAdams, RL Shiner and JL Tackett, The Guildford Press

Dean, JW, Brandes, P and Dharwadkar, R (1998) Organizational cynicism, *Academy of Management Review*, **23**(2), pp 341–52

Decety, J and Jackson, PL (2006) A social-neuroscience perspective on empathy, *Current Directions in Psychological Science*, **15**(2), pp 54–58

Deci, EL (1975) *Intrinsic Motivation*, Plenum

Deci, EL (1980) *The Psychology of Self-Determination*, Lexington Books

Del Guidice, M (2019) The evolutionary context of personality development, in *Handbook of Personality Development*, ed DP McAdams, RL Shiner and JL Tackett, The Guildford Press

Delery, JE and Doty, DJH (1996) Models of theorizing in strategic human resource management: Tests of universalistic, contingency, and configurational performance predictions, *Academy of Management Journal*, **39**, pp 802–35

Deloitte (2016a) *Talent for Survival: Essential skills for humans working in the machine age*, Deloitte LLP

Deloitte (2016b) *The 2016 Deloitte Millennial Survey: Winning over the next generation of leaders*, Deloitte Touche Tohmatsu Limited

Deloitte (2017a) *2017 Deloitte Global Human Capital Trends: Rewriting the rules for the digital age*, Deloitte University Press

Deloitte (2017b) *Bullish on the Business Value of Cognitive: Leaders in cognitive and AI weigh in on what's working and what's next, The 2017 Deloitte State of Cognitive Survey*, Deloitte Development LLC

Deloitte (2017c) *Generation Z Enters the Workforce*, Deloitte Insights, Deloitte Development

Deloitte (2017d) Navigating the future of work, *Deloitte Review*, **21**, July, Deloitte University

Deloitte (2017e) *The 2017 Deloitte Millennial Survey: Apprehensive Millennials: Seeking stability and opportunities in an uncertain world*, Deloitte Touche Tohmatsu

Deloitte (2018a) *The 2018 Deloitte Millennial Survey: Millennials disappointed in business unprepared for industry 4.0*, Deloitte Touche Tohmatsu

Deloitte (2018b) *The Rise of the Social Enterprise*, Deloitte Insights, Deloitte Development

Deloitte (2019a) *Global Human Capital Trends: Leading the social enterprise: Reinvent with a human focus*, Deloitte Insights, Deloitte Development

Deloitte (2019b) What is work? *Deloitte Review*, **24**, pp 112–20

Denison, D (1996) What is the difference between organizational culture and organizational climate? *Academy of Management Review*, **21**, pp 619–54

Derwall, J, Koedjijk, KCG and Horst, JT (2011) A tale of values-driven and profit-seeking social investors, *CFA Digest*, CFA Institute, **41**(3), August

Deutsch, M (1975) Equity, equality and need: What determines which value will be used as the basis of distributive justice? *Journal of Social Issues*, **31**(3), pp 137–49

Dillon, B and Bourke, J (2016) *The Six Signature Traits of Inclusive Leadership: Thriving in a diverse world*, Deloitte University Press

D'Innocenzo, L, Mathieu, JE and Kukenberger, MR (2016) A meta-analysis of different forms of shared leadership–team performance relations, *Journal of Management*, **42**(7), pp 1964–991

Dinnen, M and Alder, M (2017) *Exceptional Talent: How to attract, acquire and retain the very best employees*, Kogan Page

DiSegni, DM, Huly, M and Akron, S (2015) Corporate and social responsibility, environmental leadership and financial performance, *Social Responsibility Journal*, **11**(1), pp 131–48

Dixon, P and Gorecki, J (2010) *Sustainagility: How smart innovation and agile companies will help protect our future*, Kogan Page

Dochy, F and Segers, M (2018) *Creating Impact Through Future Learning*, Routledge

Doer, J (2017) *Measure What Matters*, Penguin

Donald, WJ and Donald, EK (1929) Trends in personnel administration, *Harvard Business Review*, 7(2), pp 143–55

Doty, DH and Glick, WH (1994) Typologies as a unique form of theory building: Toward improved understanding, *Academy of Management Review*, **19**, pp 230–51

Drucker, PF (2011) *The Practice of Management*, Routledge

Duncan, RB (1972) Characteristics of organizational environments and perceived environmental uncertainty, *Administrative Science Quarterly*, **17**, pp 313–27

Durfee, D (2013) *Human Capital Management: The CFO's perspective*, CFO Publishing

Durkheim, E (2013) *The Division of Labour in Society*, ed S Lukes, Palgrave

Dweck, CS (2000) *Self-Theories: Their role in motivation, personality and development*, Routledge

Dweck, CS (2017) *Mindset: Changing the way you think to fulfil your potential*, Robinson

Dyer, G (1999) Training human resource champions for the twenty-first century, *Human Resource Management*, **38**(2), pp 119–24

Dyer, L and Reeves, T (1995) Human resource strategies and firm performance: What do we know and where do we need to go? *The International Journal of Human Resource Management*, **6**(3), pp 656–70

Eckman, P (1992) An argument for the basic emotions, *Cognition and Emotion*, 6(3–4), pp 169–200

Edelman (2019) *Edelman Trust Barometer, 2019: Annual global survey*, Edelman Inc

Edmondson, AC (2019) *The Fearless Organization: Creating psychological safety in the workplace for learning, innovation, and growth*, Wiley

Eisenbeiss, SA, van Knippenberg, D and Fahrbachh, CM (2015) Doing well by doing good? Analyzing the relationship between ethical leadership and firm performance, *Journal of Business Ethics*, **128**, pp 635–51

EIU (2012) *CFO Perspectives: How HR can take on a bigger role in driving growth*, The Economist Intelligence Unit

Ellam-Dyson, V, Graifoner, D, Whybrow, A and Palmer, S (2019) Leadership and executive coaching, in *Handbook of Coaching Psychology: A guide for practitioners*, ed S Palmer and A Whybrow, Routledge

Elliott, G and Corey, D (2018) *Build It: The rebel playbook for world-class employee engagement*, Wiley

Ellis, G and Solms, M (2018) *Beyond Evolutionary Psychology*, Cambridge University Press

Emerson, R (1962) Power dependence relations, *American Sociological Review*, **27**, pp 31–40

Emerson, RM (1976) Social exchange theory, *Annual Review of Sociology*, **2**, pp 335–62

European Commission (2011) *Communication from the Commission to the European Parliament, the Council, the European Economic and Social Committee and the Committee of the Regions: A renewed EU strategy 2011–14 for corporate social responsibility*, European Commission

Expand (2019) Asset management operations and IT member roundtable, May

EY (2014) *Partnering for Performance: The CFO and HR*, Ernst & Young Australia

Eysenck, HJ (1967) *The Biological Basis for Personality*, Thomas

Eysenck, H and Eysenck, M (1985) *Personality and Individual Differences: A natural science approach*, Plenum

Farmer, P and Stevenson, D (2017) *Thriving at Work: The independent review of mental health and employers*, Department for Work and Pensions and Department of Health and Social Care

Fayol, H (1965) *General and Industrial Management*, Pitman

Feldman Barrett, L (2018) *How Emotions are Made: The secret life of the brain*, Pan

Ferdman, BM (2014) The practice of inclusion in diverse organizations: Toward a systematic and inclusive framework, in *Diversity at Work: The practice of inclusion*, ed BM Ferdman and BRD Deane, Jossey-Bass

Ferdman, BM (2017) Paradoxes of inclusion: Understanding and managing the tensions of diversity and multiculturalism, *The Journal of Applied Behavioural Science*, **53**(2), pp 235–63

Ferris, GR, Hochwater, WA, Ronald Buckley, M, Harrell-Cook, G and Frink, DD (1999) Human resources management: Some new directions, *Journal of Management*, **25**(3), pp 385–415

Fico, JM, Brady, R and Hogan, R (2012) Identifying potential derailing behaviours: Hogan Development Survey, in *Psychometrics in Coaching: Using psychological and psychometric tools for development*, ed J Passmore, Kogan Page

Fiedler, FE (1964) A contingency model of leadership effectiveness, *Advances in Social Experimental Psychology*, **1**, pp 149–90

Fiedler, F (1967) *A Theory of Leadership Effectiveness*, McGraw-Hill

Fitz-enz, J (2000) *The ROI of Human Capital: Measuring the economic value of employee performance*, Amacom

Fitz-enz, J (2002) *How to Measure Human Resources Management*, McGraw Hill

Flamholz, EG (1999) *Human Resource Accounting: Advances in concept, methods and applications*, Kluwer

Fletcher, JD (2004) Cognitive readiness: Preparing for the unexpected, Institute of Defence Analysis, IDA Document D-3061, Log: H 06-000702

Ford, M (2015) *The Rise of the Robots*, OneWorld

Forum for Sustainable and Responsible Investment (2019) www.ussif.org/sribasics (archived at https://perma.cc/KR4D-428Q)

Foster-Cheek, K and Sage-Gavin, E (2018) Implications for the function formally known as HR, in *Black Holes and White Spaces: Reimagining the Future of*

Work and HR with the CHREATE project, ed J Boudreau, C Lavelle Rearick and I Zoskin Black, Society For Human Resource Management, Loc 1792–1834

Frankl, V (1988) *The Will to Meaning: Foundations and applications of logothereapy*, Meridian

Frankl, V (2014) *The Will to Meaning*, Plume

Fredberg, T (2014) If I say it's complex, it bloody well will be: CEO strategies for managing paradox, *The Journal of Applied Behavioural Science*, 50(2), pp 171–88

Freeman, RE (1984) *Stakeholder Management: Framework and philosophy*, Pitman

French, J and Raven, B (1959) The basis of social power, in *Studies in Social Power*, ed D Cartwright, University of Michigan Press

Frese, M (2000) The changing nature of work, in *Introduction to Work and Organizational Psychology*, ed N Chmiel, Blackwell

Freund, AM, Napolitano, CM, Rutt, JL (2019) Personality development in adulthood: A goal perspective, in *Handbook of Personality Development*, ed DP McAdams, RL Shiner and JL Tackett, The Guildford Press

Frith, C (2007) *Making up the Mind*, Blackwell

Frost, S and Kalman, D (2016) *Inclusive Talent Management: How business can thrive in an age of diversity*, Kogan Page

Frost, A, Birkinshaw, JM and Prescott, CE (2002) Centres of excellence in multinational corporations, *Strategic Management Journal*, 23(11), pp 997–1018

Furnham, A (2005) *The Psychology of Behaviour at Work: The individual in the organization*, Psychology Press

Gagne, M et al (2015) The multidimensional work motivation scale: Validation evidence in seven languages and nine countries, *European Journal of Work and Organizational Psychology*, 24(2), pp 178–96

Galang, MC, and Ferris, GR (1997) Human resource department power and influence through symbolic action, *Human Relations*, 50, pp 1403–26

Galbraith, JR (1973) *Designing Complex Organizations*, Addison-Wesley

Gallegos, PV (2014) The work of inclusive leadership: Fostering authentic relationships: Modelling courage and humility, in *Diversity at Work: The practice of inclusion*, ed BM Ferdman and BRD Deane, Jossey-Bass

Gallup (2012) *State of the American Workplace Report*, Gallup

Gallup (2016) *How Millennials Want to Work and Live*, Gallup

Gallup (2017) *State of the Global Workplace, Untapped Human Capital: The next great global resource*, MINE

Gallup (2018a) *Building a Culture That Drives Performance*, Gallup

Gallup (2018b) *The Real Future of Work*, Gallup

Gallup (2018c) *Designing Your Organization's Employee Experience*, Gallup

Gamerschlag, R (2013) Value relevance of human capital information, *Journal of Intellectual Capital*, 14(2), pp 325–45

Gardner, H (2006) *Multiple Intelligences*, Basic Books

Gardner, H and Hatch, T (1989) Multiple intelligences go to school, *Educational Researcher*, **18**(8)

Gardner, JW (1990) *On Leadership*, Free Press

Gartner (2018) Reimagine HR 2018: Key takeaways, www.gartner.com/en/human-resources/trends/reimagine-hr-keytakeaways-2018 (archived at https://perma.cc/59YB-ZQ2M)

Gartner (2019) Digital disruption, www.gartner.com/it-glossary/digital-disruption (archived at https://perma.cc/L3ND-ABLB)

Geier, TG (2016) Leadership in extreme contexts: Transformational leadership performance beyond expectations, *Journal of Leadership & Organizational Studies*, **23**(3), pp 234–47

Gennard, J, and Kelly, J (1994) Human resource management: The views of personnel directors, *Human Resource Management Journal*, **5**(1), pp 15–32

Gibbons, S (2018) How to adapt to working with The Gen Z Talent Pool, www.forbes.com/sites/theyec/2018/04/09/how-to-adapt-to-working-with-the-gen-z-talent-pool/ (archived at https://perma.cc/ZA5M-8RXF)

Gillan, N (2019) *Future Office: Next-generation workplace design*, RIBA

Gitzendanner, C, Misa, K and Stein T (1983) Management's involvement in the strategic utilization of the human resource, *Management Review*, **72**(10), pp 13–17

Glass, H (1988) *Handbook of Business Strategy: 1988/1989 Yearbook*, Warren, Gorham, and Lamont

Glass, C, Cook, A and Ingersoll, AR (2016) Do women leaders promote sustainability? Analysing the effect of corporate governance composition on environmental performance, *Business Strategy and the Environment*, **25**, pp 495–511

Goffee, R and Jones, G (2015) *Why Should Anyone Be Led By You? What it takes to be an authentic leader*, Harvard Business Review Press

Goffman, E (1959) *The Presentation of Self in Everyday Life*, Penguin

Goldstein, HW, Pulakos, ED, Passmore, J, Semado, C (2017) *The Wiley Blackwell Handbook of the Psychology of Recruitment, Selection and Employee Retention*, Wiley Blackwell

Goleman, D (1996) *Emotional Intelligence: Why it can matter more than IQ*, Bloomsbury

Goleman, D (2004) What makes a leader? *Harvard Business Review*, January

Goleman, D (2013) *Focus: The hidden driver of excellence*, Bloomsbury

Goleman, D and Boyatzis, RE (2017) Emotional intelligence has 12 elements: Which do you need to work on? *Harvard Business Review*, February

Goulding, F and Shaughnessy, H (2017) *Flow: A handbook for change-makers, mavericks, innovation activists and leaders*, Flow Academy

Government Office for Science (2016) *Future of an Aging Population*, Government Office for Science

Graen, G (1976) Role-making processes within complex organizations, in *Handbook of Industrial and Organizational Psychology*, ed MD Dunette, Rand McNally

Graen, GB and Canedo, J (2016) The new workplace leadership development, *Oxford Bibliography on Management*, Oxford University Press

Grant, RM (1996) Toward a knowledge-based theory of the firm, *Strategic Management Journal*, 80(2), pp 117–24

Gratton, L (2011) *The Shift: The future of work is already here*, Collins

Greenberg, J (1987) A taxonomy of organizational justice theories, *Academy of Management Review*, **12**(1), pp 9–22

Greenleaf, RK (1970) *The Servant as Leader*, Robert K Greenleaf Center

Gregg, GS (2019) Culture and the development of motives, values and social selves, in *Handbook of Personality Development*, ed DP McAdams, RL Shiner and JL Tackett, The Guildford Press

Grffiths, PE and Stotz, K (2000) How the mind grows: A developmental perspective on the biology of cognition, *Synthese*, **122**, pp 29–51

Groysberg, B (2010) *Chasing Stars: The myth of talent and the portability of performance*, Princeton University Press

Grundy, T and Brown, L (2003) *Value-Based Human Resource Strategy: Developing your consultancy role*, Butterworth-Heinemann

Gubbins, C and Garavan, T (2016) Social capital effects on the career development outcomes of HR professionals, *Human Resource Management*, March–April, **55**(2), pp 241–60

Guenole, N, Ferrar, J and Feinzig, S (2017) *The Power of People*, Pearson Education

Guest, DE (1989) Personnel and HRM: Can you tell the difference? *Personnel Management*, **21**, pp 48–51

Guest, DE (1990) Human resource management and the American dream, *Journal of Management Studies*, 27(4), pp 377–97

Guest, DE (1997) Human resource management and performance: A review and research agenda, *International Journal of Human Resource Management*, 8(3), pp 263–76

Guest, DE and Conway, N (1998) *Fairness at Work and the Psychological Contract*, London, Chartered Institute of Personnel Directors

Guest, D and King, Z (2004) Power, innovation and problem solving: The personnel managers' three steps to heaven? *Journal of Management Studies*, **41**(3), pp 401–23

Guest, DE, Michie, J, Conway, N and Sheehan, M (2003) Human resource management and corporate performance in the UK, *British Journal of Industrial Relations*, **41**(2), pp 291–314

Gundling, R, Caldwell, C and Cvitkovich, K (2015) *Leading Across New Borders*, Wiley

Guthridge, M, Komm, AB and Lawson, E (2008) Making talent a strategic priority, *The McKinsey Quarterly*, August, pp 49–59

Hackman, J and Oldham, G (1980) *Work Redesign*, Addison-Wesley

Hahn, E, Gottschling, J, Koning, CJ and Spinath, FM (2016) The heritability of job satisfaction reconsidered: Only unique environmental influences beyond personality, *Journal of Business Psychology*, **31**, pp 217–31

Hamel, G (2000) *Leading the Revolution*, Harvard Business School Press

Handy, C (1984) *The Future of Work*, Blackwell

Handy, C (1999) *Understanding Organizations*, Penguin Books

Handy, C (1994) *The Empty Raincoat*, Arrow

Handy, C (2015) *The Second Curve: Thoughts on reinventing society*, Random House

Harari, YN (2014) *Sapiens: A brief history of human kind*, Vintage

Haski-Leventhal, D (2018) *Strategic Corporate and Social Responsibility*, Sage

Haski-Leventhal, D, Roza, L and Meijs, LCPM (2017) Congruence in corporate and social responsibility: Connecting the identity and behaviour of employers and employees, *Journal of Business Ethics*, **143**, pp 35–51

Hatch, MJ (2018) *Organization Theory: Modern, symbolic and postmodern perspectives*, Oxford University Press

Hegarty, WH and Hoffman, RG (1987) Who influences strategic decisions? *Long Range Planning*, **2**(2), pp 76–85

Helfat, CE and Peteraf, MA (2015) Managerial cognitive capabilities and the micro foundations of dynamic capabilities, *Strategic Management Journal*, **36**, pp 831–50

Helfat, C, Finkelstein, S, Mitchell, W, Peteraf, M, Singh, H, Teece, D and Winter, S (2007) *Dynamic Capabilities: Understanding strategic change in organizations*, Wiley-Blackwell

Henderson, BD (1979) *Henderson on Corporate Strategy*, Abt Books

Hendry, C, and Pettigrew, A (1990) Human resource management: An agenda for the 1990s, *International Journal of Human Resource Management*, **1**(1), pp 17–44

Hersey, P and Blanchard, K (1982) *Management of Organizational Behaviour*, Prentice-Hall

Herzberg, F, Mausner, B and Snyderman, B (1959) *The Motivation to Work*, Wiley

Hesketh, I and Cooper, C (2019) *Wellbeing at Work: How to design, implement and evaluate and effective strategy*, Kogan Page

Heyes, C (2018) *Cognitive Gadgets: The cultural evolution of thinking*, Belknap Press

Hickman, A and Pendell, R (2018) The end of the traditional manager, *Business Journal*, May

Hoch, JE, Bommer, JH and Wu, D (2018) Do ethical, authentic, and servant leadership explain variance above and beyond transformational leadership? A meta-analysis, *Journal of Management*, **44**(2), pp 501–29

Hofstede, G (1980) Motivation, leadership, and organization: Do American theories apply abroad? *Organizational Economics*, **9**(1), pp 42–63

Hofstede, G (1984) *Culture's Consequences: International differences in work-related values*, Sage

Hofstede, G and McRae, RR (2004) Personality and culture revisited: Linking traits and dimensions of culture, *Cross-Cultural Research*, **38**(1), pp 52–88

Hofstede, G, Hofstede, JH and Minkov, M (2010) *Cultures and Organizations*, McGraw-Hill

Hogan, J and Hogan, R (2007) *Hogan Personality Inventory Manual*, Hogan Assessment Systems

Hogan, J and Hogan, R (2009) *Hogan Development Survey Manual*, Hogan Assessment Systems

Hogan, J and Hogan, R (2010b) *Motives, Values, Preferences Inventory Manual*, Hogan Assessment Systems

Hole, D, Le Zhong, Schwartz, J (2010) Talking about *whose* generation? Why Western models can't account for a global workforce, *Deloitte Review*, **6**, pp 84–97

Holland, J (1985) *The Self-Directed Search*, Psychological Assessment Resources

Houghton, E and Spence, P (2016) *People Measurement and Reporting: From theory to practices*, CIPD

House, R and Mitchell, T (1974) Path-goal theory of leadership, *Journal of Contemporary Business*, **3**, pp 81–99

House, RJ, Hanges, PJ, Javidan, M, Dorfman, PW and Gupta, V (2004) *Culture, Leadership and Organizations: The GLOBE study of 62 societies*, Sage

House, RJ, Dorfman, PW, Javiden, M, Hanges, PJ and Sully de Luque, MF (2014) *Strategic Leadership Across Cultures: The GLOBE study of leadership behaviour and effectiveness in 24 countries*, Sage

Human Capital Management Coalition (2019) http://uawtrust.org/hcmc (archived at https://perma.cc/9LYT-RSQ6)

Hunt, V, Layton, D and Prince, S (2015) *Diversity Matters*, McKinsey & Co

Hunter, I, Saunders, J, Boroughs, A and Constance, S (2006) *HR Business Partners*, Gower

Huselid, MA (1995) The impact of human resource management practices on turnover, productivity and corporate performance, *Academy of Management Journal*, **38**, pp 635–72

Huselid, MA and Becker, B (1996) Methodological issues in cross-sectional and panel estimates of the human resource–firm performance link, *Industrial Relations*, **35**(3), pp 400–22

Huselid, MA, Jackson, SE and Schuler, RS (1997) Technical and strategic human resource effectiveness as determinants of firm performance, *Academy of Management Journal*, **40**, pp 171–88

Ilies, R and Judge, T (2003) On the heritability of job satisfaction, *Journal of Applied Psychology*, **88**, pp 750–59

Integrated Reporting (2016) *Creating Value: The value of human capital reporting*, International Integrated Reporting Council

International Well Building Institute (2019) https://v2.wellcertified.com/v/en/ overview (archived at https://perma.cc/5CL6-28S9)

ISO (2016) ISO 30409:2016(E) Human resource management: Workforce planning

ISO (2018a) ISO 30414(E) Human resource management: Guidelines for internal and external human capital reporting

ISO (2018b) ISO 31000:2018(E)

Janis, I (1982) *Groupthink*, Houghton Mifflin

Javidan, M, Dorfman, PW, de Luque, MS and House, RJ (2006) In the eye of the beholder: Cross cultural lessons in leadership from Project GLOBE, *Academy of Management Perspectives*, 20(4)

Jenkins, M and Swarbrick, A (2012) *Talent and the Generations*, Roffey Park Institute

Jensen, FE and Nutt, AE (2015) *The Teenage Brain*, Harper Thorsons

Johansen, B (2012) *Leaders Make the Future*, Berret-Kohler

Johansen, B (2017) *The New Leadership Literacies*, Berret-Kohler

Johnson, G, Whittington, R, Scholes, K, Angwin, D and Regnér, P (2014) *Exploring Strategy*, Pearson

Jordan, K (2014) Initial trends in enrolment and completion of massive open online courses, *International Journal of Research in Open and Distance Learning*, 15(1), pp 133–60.

Jordan, PJ and Lindebaum, D (2014) A critique on neuroscientific behaviour methodologies in organizational behaviour and management studies, *Journal of Organizational Behaviour*, 35, pp 898–908

Jost, J, Banaji, M and Nosek, B (2004) A decade of system justification theory: Accumulated evidence of conscious and unconscious bolstering of the status quo, *Political Psychology*, 25, pp 881–919

Judge, TA, Piccolo, RF, Podsakoff, NP, Shaw, JC and Rich, BL (2010) The relationship between pay and job satisfaction: A meta-analysis of the literature, *Journal of Vocational Behaviour*, 77, pp 157–67

Kahneman, D (2012) *Thinking Fast and Slow*, Penguin

Kail, EG (2010a) Leading in a VUCA environment: V is for volatility, *Harvard Business Review*, 3 November, *Harvard Business Review*

Kail, EG (2010b) Leading in a VUCA environment: U is for uncertainty, *Harvard Business Review*, 10 November, *Harvard Business Review*

Kail, EG (2010c) Leading in a VUCA environment: C is for complexity, *Harvard Business Review*, 3 December, *Harvard Business Review*

Kail, EG (2011) Leading in a VUCA environment: A is for ambiguity, *Harvard Business Review*, 6 January, *Harvard Business Review*

Kaplan, RS and Norton, DP (1996) *The Balanced Scorecard*, Harvard Business School Press

Kashdan, TB (2018) Making sense of character strengths, www.psychologytoday.com/us/blog/curious/201810/making-sense-character-strengths (archived at https://perma.cc/9PGE-TGEW)

Katz, D and Kahn, RL (1966) *The Social Psychology of Organizations*, John Wiley & Sons

Katz, L and Krueger, A (2016) The rise of alternative work arrangements in the United States, 1995–2015, NBER Working Paper No 22667, National Bureau of Economic Research

Kautz, T, Hackman, JJ, Diris, R, Terweel, B and Borghans, L (2014) Fostering and measuring skills: Improving cognitive and non-cognitive skills to promote lifetime success, NBER Working Paper No 20749, National Bureau of Economic Research

Keenoy, T (1997) Review article: HRMism and the languages of re-presentation, *Journal of Management Studies*, **34**(5), pp 825–41

Kegan, R (1993) *The Evolving Self*, Harper Collins

Kelly, J and Gennard, J (2007) Business strategic decision-making: The role and influence of directors, *Human Resource Management Journal*, **17**(2), pp 99–117

Kerr, J (2013) *Legacy: What the All Blacks can teach us about the business of life*, Constable

Kets de Vries, MFR (2019) *Down the Rabbit Hole of Leadership: Leadership pathology in everyday life*, Palgrave Macmillan

Kew, J and Stredwick, J (2016) *Human Resources in a Business Context*, CIPD

Kim, N and Kang, SW (2017) Older and more engaged: The mediating role of age linked resources on work engagement, *Human Resource Management*, September–October, **56**(5) pp 731–46

Kim, WC and Mauborgne, R (2005) *Blue Ocean Strategy*, Harvard Business School Press

Kim, SI, Reeve, J and Bong, M (2016) Introduction to motivational neuroscience: Recent developments, in *Neuroscience Research on Human Motivation: Advances in Motivation and Achievement*, vol 19, ed SI Kim, J Reeve and M Bong, Emerald Group Publishing

Knight, R (2014) Managing people from 5 generations, *Harvard Business Review*, https://hbr.org/2014/09/managing-people-from-5-generations (archived at https://perma.cc/3LR9-AKZQ)

Knight, B and Paterson, F (2018) Behavioural competencies of sustainability leaders: An empirical investigation, *Journal of Organizational Change Management*, **31**(3), pp 557–80

Kochan, TA and Borocki, TA (1985) *Human Resource Management and Industrial Relations*, Little Brown

Kotnour, T and Al-Haddad, S (2015) Integrating the organizational change literature: A model for successful change, *Journal of Organizational Change Management*, **28**(2)

Kotter, JP (1990) *A Force for Change: How leadership differs from management*, Free Press

Kotter, JP (2012) *Leading Change*, Harvard Business Review Press

Koulopoulos, T and Keldsen, D (2014) *The Gen Z Effect: The six forces shaping the future of business*, Bibliomotion

KPMG (2017) *Meet the Millennials*, KPMG LLP

Krausert, A (2018) The HRM-capital market link: Effects of securities analysts on strategic human capital, *Human Resource Management*, **57**, pp 97–110

Kroeber, A and Kluckholm, C (1952) Culture: A critical view of concepts and definitions, *Peabody Museum of American Archeology and Ethnicology*, **47**, pp 1–60

Kryscynski, D, Reeves, C, Stice-Lusvardi, R, Ulrich, M and Russel, G (2018) Analytical abilities and the performance of HR professionals, *Human Resource Management*, **57**, pp 715–38

Kuron, LKJ, Lyons, ST, Schweitzer, L and Ng, ESW (2014) Millennials' work values: Differences across the school to work transition, *Personnel Review*, **44**(6), pp 991–1009

La Cerra, P and Bingham, R (1998) The adaptive nature of the human neurocognitive architecture: An alternative model, *Proceedings of the National Academy of Sciences*, **95**, pp 11290–94

Larsen, HH and Brewster, C (2003) Line management responsibility for HRM: What is happening in Europe? *Employee Relations*, **25**(3), pp 228–44

Larsen, R and Buss, D (2018) *Personality Psychology: Domain of knowledge*, McGraw-Hill Education

Lawler, EE (2017) *Reinventing Talent Management*, Berret-Koehler

Lawler, EE, Levenson, A and Boudreau, JW (2004) HR metrics and analytics: Use and impact, *Human Resource Planning*, **27**(4), pp 27–35

Lawrence, PR and Nohria, N (2002) *Driven: How human nature shapes our choices*, Jossey-Bass

Le Doux, JE (2000) Cognitive–emotional interactions: Listen to the brain, in *Cognitive Neuroscience of Emotion*, ed RD Lane and L Nadal, Oxford University Press

Lee, DY (2016) Design your employee experience as thoughtfully as you design your customer experience, *Harvard Business Review*

Lee, RWB and Yip, JYT (2015) A knowledge management approach to intellectual capital reporting in Hong Kong, in *Intellectual Capital in Organizations*, ed P Ordonez de Pablos and L Edvinsson, Routledge

Legge, K (1978) *Power, Innovation and Problem Solving in Personnel Management*, London, McGraw Hill

Legge, K (2005) *Human Resource Management: Rhetorics and realities*, Palgrave Macmillan

Leonhard, G (2016) *Technology v Humanity*, Fast Future Publishing

Lev, B and Scwartz, A (1971) On the use of the economic concept of human capital in financial statements, *The Accounting Review*, January

Levit, A (2019) *Humanity Works: Merging technologies and people for the workforce of the future*, Kogan Page

Lewin, K (1958) Group decision and social change, in *Readings in Social Psychology*, ed EE Maccoby, TM Newcomb and EL Hartley, Holt, Rinehart and Winston

Lewis, M (2003) *Moneyball*, WW Norton

Lieberman, MD, Eisenberger, NI, Crockett, MJ, et al (2007) Putting feelings into words: Affect labelling disrupts amygdala activity in response to affective stimuli, *Psychological Science* **18**(5), pp 421–28

Littman-Ovadia, H and Lavy, S (2016) Going the extra mile: Perseverance as a key character strength at work, *Journal of Career Assessment*, **24**(2), pp 240–52

Locke, E (1976) The nature and causes of job satisfaction, in *Handbook of Industrial and Organizational Psychology*, ed M Dunnette, Rand-McNally

Lucy, D, Wellbelove, J, Poorkavoos, M and Hatcher, C (2018) *The Management Agenda 2018*, Roffey Park Institute

Luthans, F and Avolio, BJ (2003) Authentic leadership development, in *Positive Organizational Scholarship*, ed KS Cameron, JE Dutton and RE Quinn, Berrett-Koehler

Maak, T, Pless, NM and Voegtlin, C (2016) Business statesman or shareholder advocate? CEO responsible leadership styles and the micro-foundations of political CSR, *Journal of Management Studies*

MacKenzie, MJ and Baumeister, RF (2014) Meaning in life: Nature, needs and myths, in *Meaning in Positive and Existential Psychology*, ed A Bathhyany and P Russo-Netzer, Springer

MacLean, PD (1989) *The Triune Brain in Evolution: Role in paleocerebral functions*, Plenum

Malhhotra, A, Majchrzak, A and Rosen, B (2007) Leading virtual teams, *Academy of Management Perspectives*, **21**(1), pp 60–70

Marr, B (2018) *Data-Driven HR: How to use analytics and metrics to drive performance*, Kogan Page

Maslow, AH (1954) *Motivation and Personality*, Harper & Row

Mayer, JD, Salovey, P and Caruso, DR (2004) Emotional intelligence: Theory, findings and implications, *Psychological Inquiry*, **15**(3), pp 197–215

Maylett, T and Warner, P (2014) *Magic: Five keys to unlock the power of employee engagement*, Greenleaf

Maylett, T and Wride, M (2017) *The Employee Experience: How to attract talent, retain top performers, and drive results*, Wiley

Mayo, A (2001) *The Human Value of the Enterprise*, Nicholas Brearley

Mazutis, DD and Slawinski, N (2015) Reconnecting business and society: Perceptions of authenticity in corporate and social responsibility, *Journal of Business Ethics*, **131**, pp 137–50

McAdams, DP (2012) Meaning and personality, in *The Human Quest for Meaning: Theories, research and applications*, ed PTP Wong, Routledge

McAdams, DP (2019) The emergence of personality, in *Handbook of Personality Development*, ed DP McAdams, RL Shiner and JL Tackett, The Guildford Press

McChrystal, S, Eggers, J and Mangone, J (2018) *Leaders: Myths and reality*, Portfolio Penguin

McClelland, D (1961) *The Achieving Society*, Free Press,

McGregor, D (1960) *The Human Side of the Enterprise*, McGraw Hill

McKinsey Global Institute (2018) *Skill Shift: Automation and the future of the work force*, McKinsey Global Institute

Meaney, M and Keller, S (2017) *Leading Organizations: Ten timeless truths*, Bloomsbury

Mercer (2017a) *Human Capital Scan*, Mercer

Mercer (2017b) *Talent Trends: 2017 global study: Empowerment in a disrupted world*, Mercer

Mercer (2018a) *Diversification: Is there a NEET, not in employment or training, solution to the workforce crises?* Mercer Workforce Monitor, Mercer LLC

Mercer (2018b) *Global Talent Trends Study: Unlocking growth in a human age*, Mercer

Mercer (2018c) *Thriving in an Age of Disruption: Putting people at the heart of change*, Mercer

Mercer (2019) *Global Talent Trends 2019: Connectivity in the human age*, Mercer

Mercier, H and Sperber, D (2017) *The Enigma of Reason: A new theory of human understanding*, Penguin

Meyer, E (2014) *The Culture Map*, Public Affairs

Miao, C, Humphrey, RH and Qian, S (2017) A meta-analysis of emotional intelligence and work attitudes, *Journal of Occupational and Organizational Psychology*, **90**, pp 177–202

Michaels, E, Handfield-Jones, H and Axelrod, B (2001) *The War for Talent*, Harvard Business Review Press

Miles, RE and Snow, CC (1984) Designing strategic human resources systems, *Organizational Dynamics*, Summer, pp 36-52

Miller, R, Williams, P and O'Neill, M (2018) *The Healthy Workplace Nudge: How healthy people, culture, and buildings lead to high performance*, Wiley

Millman, J, Von Glinow, MA and Nathan, M (1991) Organizational life cycles and strategic international human resource management in multinational companies: Implications for congruence theory, *Academy of Management Review*, **16**(2), pp 318–39

Minchington, B (2015) Who must lead employer branding? International waters – employer branding, *HR Future*, **9**, pp 14–17

Mintzberg, H (1983) *Power In and Around Organizations*, Prentice-Hall

Mintzberg, H (1983) *Structure in Fives: Designing effective organizations*, Prentice-Hall

Miralles-Quiros, MDM, Miralles-Quiros, JL and Ariano, IG (2017) Sustainable development, sustainability leadership and firm valuation: Differences across Europe, *Business Strategy and the Environment*, **26**, pp 1014–28

Monbaeva, DB (2018) Building credible human capital analytics for organizational competitive advantage, *Human Resource Management*, **57**, pp 701–13

Montano, D, Reeske, A, Franke, F and Huffmeier, J (2017) Leadership, followers' mental health and job performance in organizations: A comprehensive meta-analysis from an occupational health perspective, *Journal of Organizational Behavior*, **38**, pp 327–50

Moore, K and Birkinshaw, JM (1998) Managing knowledge in global service firms: Centers of excellence, *Academy of Management Executive*, **12**(4), pp 81–92

Mor Barak, ME (2014) *Managing Diversity: Toward a globally inclusive workplace*, Sage

Morgan, J (2014) *The Future of Work*, Wiley

Morgan, J (2017) *The Employee Experience Advantage: How to win the war for talent by giving employees the workspaces they want, the tools they need, and a culture they can celebrate*, Wiley

Morhman, SA (2003) Designing work for knowledge-based competition, in *Managing Knowledge for Sustained Competitive Advantage: Designing strategies for effective human resource management*, ed S Jackson, M Hitt and A Densi, Jossey-Bass

Morrison, R (2015) *Data-Driven Organization Design: Sustaining the competitive edge through organizational analytics*, Kogan Page

Morrison, JE and Fletcher, JD (2002) Cognitive readiness, IDA Paper P-3735 Log: H 02-002087, Institute for Defence Analyses

Mosley, R (2014) *Employer Brand Management: Practical lessons from the world's leading employers*, Wiley

Mullins, L (1985) *Management and Organizational Behaviour*, Pitman

Nadkarni, S and Herrmann, P (2014) Managing strategic change: The duality of CEO personality, *Strategic Management Journal*, **35**, pp 1318–42

Nalbantian, HR (2017) *Navigating Human Capital Risk and Uncertainty Through Advanced Workforce Analytics*, Mercer LLC

Nalbantian, HR, Guzzo, RA, Kieffer, D and Doherty, J (2004) *Play to Your Strengths: Managing your internal labor markets for lasting competitive advantage*, McGraw-Hill

Nardi, D (2011) *Neuroscience of Personality*, Radiance House

National Institute for Health and Care Excellence (2019) www.nice.org.uk/guidance/qs147 (archived at https://perma.cc/74CE-ZQQ8)

National Wellness Institute (2019) www.nationalwellness.org/page/Six_Dimensions (archived at https://perma.cc/ZY57-8FGJ)

Neenan, M (2018) *Developing Resilience*, Routledge

Nellis, J (2017) What does the future hold for Generation Alpha? www.cranfield.ac.uk/som/thought-leadership-list/what-does-the-future-hold-for-generation-alpha (archived at https://perma.cc/QN25-MFW6)

Ng, TWH, Yam, KC and Aguinis, H (2019) Employee perceptions of corporate and social responsibility: Effects on pride, embeddedness and turnover, *Personnel Psychology*, **72**, pp 107–37

O'Boyle, EH, Forsyth, DR, Banks, GC and McDaniel, MA (2012) A meta-analysis of the dark triad and work behaviour: A social exchange perspective, *Journal of Applied Psychology*, **97**(3), pp 557–79

O'Connell (2014) A simplified framework for 21st century leader development, *The Leadership Quarterly*, **25**, pp 183–203

Ochsner, KN and Gross, JJ (2005) The cognitive control of emotion, *Trends in Cognitive Sciences*, **95**(5), pp 242–49

OECD (2019) *OECD Skills Strategy 2019: Skills to shape a better future: The skills implications of megatrends*, OECD Publishing

Offerman, LR and Basford, TE (2014) Inclusive human resource management, in *Diversity at Work: The practice of inclusion*, ed BM Ferdman and B Deane, Jossey-Bass

Ogunfowora, B, Stackhouse, M and Oh, WY (2018) Media depictions of CEO ethics and stakeholder support of CSR initiatives: The mediating roles of CSR motive attributions and cynicism, *Journal of Business Ethics*, **150**, pp 525–40

Ong, M, Mayer, DM, Tost, LP and Wellman, N (2018) When corporate social responsibility motivates employee citizenship behaviour: The sensitizing role of task significance, *Organization Behavior and Human Decision Processes*, **144**, pp 44–59

Ordonez de Pablos, P (2015) Preface, in *Intellectual Capital in Organizations*, ed P Ordonez de Pablos and L Edvinsson, Routledge

Ordonez de Pablos, P, Tennyson, R and Zhao, J (2013) *Intellectual Capital Strategy Management for Knowledge-Based Organizations*, IGI Global Publishing

Organ, DW (1988) *Organizational Citizenship Behaviour: The good soldier syndrome*, Lexington

Orth, U and Robins, RW (2019) Development and self-esteem across the lifespan, in *Handbook of Personality Development*, ed DP McAdams, RL Shiner and JL Tackett, The Guildford Press

Ostry, JD, Espinoza, JAR and Papageorgiou, C (2018) Economic gains from gender inclusion: New mechanisms, new evidence, IMF Staff Discussion Note, SDN/18/06, October

Ouchi, WG (1980) Markets bureaucracies and clans, *Administrative Science Quarterly*, **25**, pp 129–41

Panskepp, J (1998) *Affective Neuroscience: The evolution of human and animal emotions*, Oxford University Press

Parry, E and Urwin, P (2011) Generational differences in work values: A review of theory and evidence, *International Journal of Management Reviews*, **13**, pp 79–96

Pascale, RT and Athos, AG (1981) *The Art of Japanese Management*, Simon & Schuster

Passmore, J (2007) An integrative model for executive coaching, *Consulting Psychology Journal: Practice and research*, **59**, pp 68–78

Peters, S (2012) *The Chimp Paradox*, Ebury Publishing

Peterson, JB (1999) *Maps of Meaning: The architecture of belief*, Routledge

Peterson, C and Seligman, M (2004) *Character Strengths and Virtues: A handbook and classification*, American Psychological Association, Oxford Press

Petrenko, OV, Aime, F and Ridge, J (2016) Corporate social responsibility or CEO narcissism? CSR motivations and organizational performance, *Strategic Management Journal*, 37, pp 262–79

Petrides, KV and Furnham, A (2001) Trait emotional intelligence: Psychometric investigations with reference to established trait taxonomies, *European Journal of Personality*, 15(6), pp 425–48

Pew Research Centre (2014) *Attitudes About Aging: A global perspective in a rapidly graying world, Japanese are worried, Americans aren't*, Pew Research Centre

Pfau, BN (2016) What do Millennials really want at work? The same things the rest of us do, *Harvard Business Review*, https://hbr.org/2016/04/what-do-millennials-really-want-at-work (archived at https://perma.cc/6XYG-Z4SE)

Pfeffer, J (2002) *Managing with Power, Politics and Influence in Organizations*, Harvard Business School Press

Pfeffer, J (2015) *Leadership BS: Fixing workplaces and careers one truth at a time*, Harper Collins

Pfeffer, J (2018a) *Dying for a Paycheck: How modern management harms employee health and company performance – and what we can do about it*, Harper Business

Pfeffer, J (2018b) The overlooked essentials of employee well-being, *McKinsey Quarterly*, September

Phelps, R (2004) Measurement: Why HR must seize the opportunity, *Strategic HR Review*, 3(2), pp 16–17

Phillips, JJ and Phillips, PP (2015) *High-Impact Human Capital Strategy*, Amacom

Phillips, JJ, Phillips, PP and Smith, K (2016) *Accountability in Human Resource Management*, Routledge

Pichler, S, Blazovich, JL, Cook, KA, Huston, JM and Strawser, WR (2018) Do LGBT-supportive corporate policies enhance firm performance? *Human Resource Management*, 57, pp 263–78

Pink, D (2009) *Drive*, Canongate Books

Polach, J (2007) Managing an age diverse workforce, *MIT Sloan Management Review*, 48

Porter, L and Lawler, E (1968) *Managerial Attitudes and Performance*, Dorsey

Porter, ME (1980) *Competitive Strategy: Techniques for analyzing industries and competitors*, Free Press

Porter, ME (1985) *Competitive Advantage: Creating and sustaining superior performance*, Free Press

Porter, ME and Kramer, MR (2002) The competitive advantage of corporate philanthropy, *Harvard Business Review*, 80(12), pp 56–68

Porter, ME and Kramer, MR (2006) Strategy and society: The link between competitive advantage and corporate and social responsibility, *Harvard Business Review*, **84**(12), pp 78–92

Porter, ME and Kramer, MR (2011) Creating shared value, *Harvard Business Review*, **89**(1/2) pp 62–77

Post, C (2015) When is female leadership an advantage? Coordination requirements, team cohesion, and team interaction norms, *Journal of Organizational Behavior*, **36**, 1153–75

PwC (2008a) *Building the Case for Wellness*, PwC

PwC (2008b) *Managing Tomorrow's People: Millennials at work: Perspectives of a new generation*, PwC

PwC (2011) *Millennials at Work: Reshaping the workforce*, PwC

PwC (2018a) *Preparing for Tomorrow's Workforce Today*, PwC

PwC (2018b) *Workforce of the Future: The competing forces shaping 2030*, PwC

Quinn, JB (1980) *Strategies for Change*, Irwin

Quinn, R and Cameron, K (2011) *Diagnosing and Changing Organizational Culture: Based on the competing values framework*, John Wiley & Sons

Rasche, A, Morsing, M and Moon, J (2017a) *Corporate Social Responsibility: Strategy, communication and governance*, Cambridge University Press

Rasche A, Morsing M and Moon, J (2017b) The changing role of business in global society: CSR and beyond, in *Corporate Social Responsibility: Strategy, communication and governance*, ed A Rasche, M Morsing and J Moon, Cambridge University Press

Reilly, P and Williams, T (2003) *How to Get Best Value from HR: The shared services option*, Gower

Reimer, M, van Doorn, S and Heyden, MLM (2018) Unpacking functional experience complementarities in senior leaders' influences on CSR strategy: A CEO-top management team approach, *Journal of Business Ethics*, **151**, pp 977–95

Riordan, C (2014) Diversity is useless without inclusivity, *Harvard Business Review*

Rippon, G (2019) *The Gendered Brain*, Bodley-Head

Robbins, S (1991) *Organizational Behaviour*, Prentice-Hall

Robertson, I and Cooper, G (2011) *Well-Being: Productivity and happiness at work*, Palgrave Macmillan

Rock, D and Grant, H (2016) Why diverse teams are smarter, *Harvard Business Review*, November

Roebuck, C (2014) *Lead to Succeed*, Wordscapes

Roethlisberger, FJ and Dickson, WJ (1939) *Management and the Worker*, Harvard University Press

Roos, J, Roos, G, Edvinsson, L and Dragonetti, NC (1997) *Intellectual Capital*, Macmillan

Rotter, J (1966) Generalized expectancies for internal and external control of reinforcement, *Psychological Monographs*, 80, pp 1–28

Rousseau, DM (1988) The construction of climate in organizational research, in *International Review of Industrial and Organizational Psychology*, ed LC Cooper and I Robertson, Wiley

Ruch, W, Gander, F, Platt, T and Hoffmann, J (2016) Team roles: Their relationships to character strength and job satisfaction, *Journal of Positive Psychology*

Rudolph, CW, Rauvola, RS and Zacher, H (2018) Leadership and generations at work: A critical review, *The Leadership Quarterly*, 29, pp 44–57

Russ, GS, Galang, MC and Ferris, GR (1998) Power and influence of the human resource function through boundary spanning and information management, *Human Resource Management Review*, 8, pp 125–48

Ryan, RM and Deci, EL (2017) *Self-Determination Theory*, The Guildford Press

Salancik, G and Pfeffer, J (1977) Who gets power and how do they hold on to it? A strategic-contingency model of power, *Organizational Dynamics*, 5

Salovey, P and Mayer, JD (1990) Emotional intelligence, *Imagination, Cognition, and Personality*, 9

Sandberg, S (2015) *Lean In*, WH Allen

Sanghera, S (2009) Picking over the bones of human remains: A resource that business does not need, *The Times*, 9 October

Sartre, JP (1965) *Nausea*, Penguin Books

Savitz, A and Weber, K (2013) *Talent, Transformation and the Triple Bottom Line*, Jossey-Bass

Savitz, A and Weber, K (2014) *The Triple Bottom Line*, Jossey-Bass

Schein, E (1990) Organizational culture, *American Psychologist*, 45, pp 109–19

Schein, EH and Schein, P (2017) *Organizational Culture and Leadership*, Wiley

Schmidt, FL (2016) The validity and utility of selection methods in personnel psychology: Practical and theoretical implications of 100 years of research findings, Working Paper, Tippie College of Business, University of Iowa

Schneider, B and Bartram, D (2017) Aggregate personality and organizational competitive advantage, *Journal of Occupational and Organizational Psychology*, 90, 461–80

Schroder, HS, Moran, TP, Brent Donnellan, M and Moser, JS (2014) Mindset induction effects on cognitive control: A neurobiological investigation, *Biological Psychology*, 103, pp 27–37

Schuler, RS (1990) Repositioning the human resource function: Transformation or demise? *Academy of Management Executive*, 4(3), pp 49–59

Seaton, DT, Bergner, Y, Chuang, I, Mitros, P and Pritchard, DE (2014) Who does what in a massive open online course? *Communications of the ACM*, 57(4), pp 58–65

Seligman, M (2018) *The Hope Circuit: A psychologist's journey from helplessness to optimism*, Nicholas Brearley

Seligman, M and Csikszentmihalyi, M (2000) Positive psychology: An introduction, *American Psychologist*, **35**, pp 5–14

Shanks, R, Sinha, S and Thomas, RJ (2016) *Judgment Calls: Preparing leaders to thrive in the age of intelligent machines*, Accenture

Sharma, S, Elfenbein, HA, Foster, J and Bottom, WP (2018) Predicting negotiation performance from personality traits: A field study across multiple occupations, *Human Performance*, **31**(3), pp 145–64

Sheehan, C (2005) A model for HRM strategic integration, *Personnel Review*, **34**(2)

Sherwood, MW and Pollard, J (2019) *Responsible Investing*, Routledge

Shore, LM, Cleveland, JN and Sanchez, D (2018) Inclusive workplaces: A review and model, *Human Resource Management Review*, **28**, pp 176–89

Sial, MS, Zheng, C, Cherian, J, Gulzar, MA, Thu, PA, Khan, T and Khuong, NV (2018) Does corporate social responsibility mediate the relation between boardroom gender diversity and firm performance of Chinese listed companies? *Sustainability*, **10**(10), p 3591

SIF Foundation (2014) *Report on US Sustainable, Responsible, and Impact Investing Trends 2014*, SIF Foundation

Simon, H (1976) *Administrative Behaviour*, Free Press

Sims, CM (2018) The diversity intelligent servant leader: Developing leaders to meet the needs of a diverse workforce, *Advances in Developing Human Resources*, **20**(3), pp 3131–30

Sinek, S (2009) *Start With Why*, Penguin

Sinek, S (2017) *Leaders Eat Last*, Penguin

Sloman, S and Fernbach, P (2017) *The Knowledge Illusion: The myth of individual thought and the power of collective wisdom*, Pan

Smith, M and Smith, P (2005) *Testing People at Work*, BPS Blackwell

Smola, K and Sutton, D (2002) Generational differences revisiting generational work values for the new millennium, *Journal of Organizational Behaviour*, **23**, pp 363–82

Sok, JMH, Lub, XD and Blomme, RJ (2014) Work–home values: The interplay between historical trends and generational work-home values, in *Generational Diversity at Work: New research perspectives*, ed E Parry, Routledge

Sparkman, R (2018) *Strategic Workforce Planning*, Kogan Page

Sparrow, P and Otaye L (2015) Employer branding: From attraction to a core HR strategy, White Paper 15/01, June, CPHR

Sparrow, P, Hird, M and Cooper, C (2015) *Do We Need HR? Repositioning people management for success*, Palgrave Macmillan

Spearman, C (1904) 'General intelligence' objectively determined and measured, *American Journal of Psychology*, **15**, pp 201–93

Stacey, RD (2010) *Complexity and Organizational Reality*, Routledge

Stanford, N (2018) *Organization Design: The practitioner's guide*, Routledge

Steelman, LA and Wolfed, L (2018) The manager as coach: The role of feedback orientation, *Journal of Business Psychology*, **33**, pp 41–53

Stern, W (1965) The psychological methods for testing intelligence, in *A Source Book in the History of Psychology*, ed RJ Herrenstein and EG Boring, Harvard University Press

Stewart, TA and Woods, W (1996) Taking on the last bureaucracy: People need people but do they need personnel? It's time for human resources departments to put up or shut up, *Fortune*

Stewart, JS, Oliver, EH, Cravens, KS and Oishi, S (2017) Managing Millenials: Embracing generational differences, *Business Horizons*, **60**, pp 45–54

Storey, J (1987) Developments in the management of human resources: An interim report, Warwick Papers in Industrial Relations, 17, IRRU, School of Industrial and Business Studies, University of Warwick

Storey, J and Neces, P (2014) When corporate social responsibility (CSR) increases performance: Exploring the role of intrinsic and extrinsic CSR attribution, *Business Ethics: A European review*, **24**(2), pp 111–24

Strauss, G (2001) HRM in the USA: Correcting some British impressions, *International Journal of Human Resource Management*, **12**(6), pp 873–97

Strengthscope® (2019) Say hello to Strengthscope, www.strengthscope.com/strengths-tests-assessments/self-awareness-report/ (archived at https://perma.cc/G4YS-B53Z)

Sveiby, KE (1990) *The Invisible Balance Sheet*, Konrad Group

Swart, T, Chisholm, K and Brown, P (2015) *Neuroscience for Leadership*, Palgrave Macmillan

Sweeney, C and Borthwick, F (2016) *Inclusive Leadership*, Pearson Education

Syed, M (2015) *Black Box Thinking: Marginal gains and the secrets of high performance*, John Murray

Tajfel, H (1970) Experiments in intergroup discrimination, *Scientific American*, **223**(5), pp 96–102

Tang, N, Chen, YJC, Zhou, Z, Chao, CC and Yu, Z (2015) Inclusion and inclusion management in the Chinese context: An explanatory study, *The International Journal of Human Resource Management*, **26**(6), pp 856–74

Tang, Y, Mack, DZ and Chen, G (2018) The differential effects of CEO narcissism and hubris on corporate and social responsibility, *Sloane Management Journal*, **39**, pp 1370–87

Tapai, AT and Lange, D (2016) *The Inclusive Leader*, Korn Ferry Instutute

Taylor, F (1911) *Principles of Scientific Management*, Harper & Brothers

Teece, DJ (2007) Explicating dynamic capabilities: The nature and microfoundations of (sustainable) enterprise performance, *Strategic Management Journal*, **28**(13), pp 1319–50

Teece, DJ, Pisano, G and Shuen, A (1997) Dynamic capabilities and strategic management, *Strategic Management Journal*, **18**(7), pp 509–33

Thaler, RH and Sunstein, RS (2009) *Nudge*, Penguin

Thomas, H, Smith, RR and Diez, F (2013) *Human Capital and Global Business Strategy*, Cambridge University Press

Timms, P (2018) *Transformational HR: How human resources can create value and impact business strategy*, Kogan Page

Tonello, M (2015) Corporate investment in ESG practices, https://corpgov.law. harvard.edu/2015/08/05/corporate-investment-in-esg-practices/#9 (archived at https://perma.cc/6GVZ-KYD8)

Toronchuk, JA and Ellis, GFR (2007) Criteria for basic emotions: Seeking disgust? *Cognition and Emotion*, **21**, pp 1829–32

Towers Perrin (2005) *The Business Case for Workers Age 50+: Planning for tomorrow's talent needs in today's competitive environment*, AARP

Truss, C, Gratton, L, Hope-Hailey, V, Stiles, P and Zaleska, J (2002) Paying the piper: Choice and constraint in changing HR functional roles, *Human Resource Management Journal*, **12**(2), pp 36–63

Tuckman, B (1965) Development sequences in small groups, *Psychological Bulletin*, **63**, pp 384–99

Tuckman, BW and Jensen, MAC (1977) Stages of small-group development revisited, *Group and Organization Studies*, **2**(4), pp 419–27

Tung, R (1981) Selection and training of staff for foreign assignments, *Columbia Journal of World Business*, **16**, pp 66–68

Turnbull, H (2016) *Illusion of Inclusion*, Business Expert Press

Twenge, JM and Campbell, SM (2008) Generational differences in psychological traits and their impact on the workplace, *Journal of Managerial Psychology*, **23**(8), pp 862–77

Tyson, S (1987) The management of the personnel function, *Journal of Management Studies*, **24**(5), pp 523–32

Ulrich, D (1997) *Human Resource Champions*, Harvard Business School Press

Ulrich, D and Dulebohn, JH (2015) Are we there yet? What's next for HR? *Human Resource Management Review*, **25**, pp 188–204

Ulrich, D and Ulrich, W (2010) *The Why of Work: How great leaders build abundant organizations,* McGraw-Hill Professional

Ulrich, D, Brockbank, W, Johnson, Sandholtz, K and Younger, J (2008) *HR Competencies*, SHRM

Unite, J, Shen, Y, Parry, E and Demel, B (2014) Generational differences in the factors influencing career success across countries, in *Generational Diversity at Work: New research perspectives*, ed E Parry, Routledge

United Nations, Department of Economic and Social Affairs, Population Division (2017) World population prospects: The 2017 revision, key findings and advance tables, Working Paper No ESA/P/WP/248

UNPRI (2019) www.unpri.org/pri/what-are-the-princi ples-for-responsible-investment (archived at https://perma.cc/6STE-MLH9)

Vafaei, A, Taylor, D and Ahmed, K (2011) The value relevance of intellectual capital disclosures, *Journal of Intellectual Capital*, **12**(3), pp 407–29

Valuing Your Talent (2016) *Reporting Human Capital: Illustrating your company's true value*, CIPD

Van der Togt, J and Rasmussan TH (2017) Towards evidence-based HR, *Journal of Organizational Effectiveness: People and Performance*, **4**(2), pp 127–32

Verissimo, JMC and Lacenda, TMC (2015) Does integrity matter for CSR practice in organizations? The mediating role of transformational leadership, *Business Ethics: A European review*, **24**(1)

Vishwas Maheshwari, V, Gunesh, P, Lodorfos, G and Konstantopoulou, A (2017) Exploring HR practitioners' perspective on employer branding and its role in organizational attractiveness and talent management, *International Journal of Organizational Analysis*, **25**(5), pp 742–61

Vlachos, PA, Panagopoulos, NG and Rapp, AA (2014) Employee judgements of and behaviours toward corporate and social responsibility: A multi-study investigation of direct, cascading, and moderating effects, *Journal of Organizational Behavior*, **35**, pp 990–1017

Vlachos, PA, Panagopoulas, NG, Bachrach, DG and Morgeson, FP (2017) The effects of managerial and employee attributions for corporate and social responsibility initiatives, *Journal of Organizational Behavior*, **38**, pp 1111–29

Von Hippel, W (2018) *The Social Leap*, Harper Wave

Vroom, VH (1964) *Work Motivation*, John Wiley & Sons

Waber, B (2013) *People Analytics*, Pearson Education

Wade, MR, Tarling, A and Neubauer, R (2017) *Redefining Leadership for a Digital Age*, IMD International Institute for Management Development and metaBeratung GmbH

Walker, J (1978) Linking human resource planning and strategic planning, *Human Resource Planning*, **1**, pp 1–18

Walker, M (2018) *Why We Sleep: The new science of sleep and dreams*, Penguin

Wang, H, Waldman, DA and Zhang, H (2012) Strategic leadership across cultures: Current findings and future research directions, *Journal of World Business*, **47**, pp 571–80

Ward, C, Bochner, S and Furnham, A (2001) *The Psychology of Culture Shock*, Routledge

Watson Wyatt (2001) *Human Capital Index: Human capital as a lead indicator of shareholder value*, Watson Wyatt Worldwide

Weber, KEM (1924) *The Theory of Social and Economic Organization*, ed AH Henderson and T Parson, Free Press

Webster, BD and Smith, MB (2018) The dark triad and organizational citizenship behaviors: The moderating role of high involvement management climate, *Journal of Business and Psychology*, pp 1–15, https://doi.org/10.1007/s10869-018-9562-9 (archived at https://perma.cc/4Q9D-NDK5)

Weick, KE (1995) *Sensemaking in Organizations*, Sage

Weinstein, N, Ryan, RM and Deci, EL (2012) Motivation, meaning and wellness: A self-determination perspective on the creation and internalization of personal meaning and life goals, in *The Human Quest for Meaning: Theories, research and applications*, ed PTP Wong, Routledge

Wernerfelt, B (1984) A resource based view of the firm, *Strategic Management Journal*, 5(2), pp 171–80

White, JE (2017) *Meet Generation Z*, Baker Books

Whiteman, WE (1998) *Training and Educating Army Officers for the 21st Century: Implications for the United States Military Academy*, Defence Technical Information Center

Wilde, J (2016) *The Social Psychology of Organizations: Diagnosing toxicity and intervening in the workplace*, Routledge

Wiley, J and Kowske, B (2011) *Respect: Delivering results by giving employees what they really want*, John Wiley & Sons

Willis Towers Watson (2016a) *The Human Capital Framework*, Willis Towers Watson

Willis Towers Watson (2016b) *The Power of Three: Taking engagement to new heights*, Willis Towers Watson

Winsborough, D and Chamorro-Premuzic, T (2017) Great teams are about personalities, not just skills, *Harvard Business Review*, January

Winters, MF (2014) From diversity to inclusion: An inclusion equation, in *Diversity at Work: The practice of inclusion*, ed BM Ferdman and BR Deane, Jossey-Bass

Wong, PTP (2012) *The Human Quest for Meaning: Theories, research and applications*, Routledge

World Bank Group (2019) *World Development Report: The changing nature of work*, International Bank for Reconstruction and Development, World Bank

World Commission on Environment and Development (1987) *Our Common Future*, Oxford University Press

World Economic Forum (2016) *The Future of Jobs*, World Economic Forum

World Economic Forum (2017) *Realizing Human Potential in the Fourth Industrial Revolution: An agenda for leaders to shape the future of education, gender and work*, World Economic Forum

World Economic Forum (2018a) Annual meeting of the global future councils, www.weforum.org/events/annual-meeting-of-the-global-future-councils-2018/about (archived at https://perma.cc/U69E-9T8M)

World Economic Forum (2018b) *Digital Transformation Initiative: Executive summary*, World Economic Forum

World Economic Forum (2018c) *Eight Futures of Work: Scenarios and their implications*, World Economic Forum

World Economic Forum (2018d) *The Future of Jobs Report*, World Economic Forum

World Economic Forum (2019) *The Global Risks Report 2019*, 14th edn, World Economic Forum

World Health Organization (2019) www.who.int/about/who-we-are/constitution (archived at https://perma.cc/TN9S-LJMY)

Worrall, L, Cooper, C, Kerrin, M, La-Band, A, Rosselli, A, Woodman, P (2016) *The Quality of Working Life: Exploring managers' wellbeing, motivation and productivity*, Chartered Management Institute

Wright, PM, McMahan, GC and McWilliams, A (1994) Human resources and sustained competitive advantage: A resource-based perspective, *International Journal of Human Resource Management*, **5**, pp 301–26

Wright, L (2015) *HR in the Boardroom*, Palgrave Macmillan

Wright, PM and McMahan, GC (1992) Theoretical perspectives for strategic human resource management, *Journal of Management*, **18**, pp 295–320

Wright, PM and Snell, SA (1998) Towards a unifying framework for exploring fit and flexibility in strategic human resource management, *Academy of Management Review*, **23**(4), pp 756–72

Wright, PM and Snell, SA (1999) Social capital and strategic HRM: It's who you know, *Human Resource Planning*, **22**, pp 62–65

Wright, PM, McMahan, GC and McWilliams, A (1994) Human resources and sustained competitive advantage: A resource-based perspective, *International Journal of Human Resource Management*, **5**, pp 301–26

Wright, PM, McMahan, GC, McCormick, B and Sherman, WS (1998) Strategy, core competence, and HR involvement as determinants of HR effectiveness and refinery performance, *Human Resource Management*, **37**(1), pp 17–29

Wright, PM, Dunford, BB and Snell, SA (2001a) Human resources and the resource based view of the firm, *Journal of Management*, **27**, pp 701–21

Wright, PM, Graber, TM, Moynihan, LM, Park, HJ, Gerhart, B and Delery, JE (2001b) Measurement error in research on HR and firm performance: Additional data and suggestions for future research, *Personnel Psychology*, Winter, **54**(4), pp 875–92

Yonck, R (2017) *Heart of the Machine*, Arcade

Zadek, S (2004) The path to corporate responsibility, *Harvard Business Review*, **82**(12), pp 125–33

Zak, P (2017) The neuroscience of trust, *Harvard Business Review*, January–February

Zenger, JH and Folkman, JR (2009) *The Extraordinary Leader: Turning good managers into great leaders*, McGraw Hill

Zhou, Z, Luo, BN and Tang, TLP (2018) Corporate social responsibility excites 'exponential' positive employee engagement: The Mathew effect in CSR and sustainable policy, *Corporate and Social Responsibility and Environmental Management*, **25**, pp 339–54

Zhu, Y, Sun, LY and Leung, ASM (2014) Corporate social responsibility, firm reputation, and performance: The role of ethical leadership, *Asia Pacific Journal of Management*, **31**, pp 925–47

Ziskin, I (2018) HR as orchestra conductor, in *Black Holes and White Spaces: Reimagining the Future of Work and HR with the CHREATE project*, ed J Boudreau, C Lavelle Rearick and I Zoskin Black, Society For Human Resource Management, Loc 2198–2276

Ziskin, I and Boudreau, JW (2011) The future of HR and effective organizations, *Organizational Dynamics*, **40**, pp 255–66

INDEX

7S model of organizations 145–146

Accenture (case study) 259–261
Affect, distinction from emotion 24
affect-labelling 27
affect network 34
agricultural revolution 14
Alderfer's existence, relatedness and growth
    (ERG) theory 83
Alibaba (case study) 252–253
amygdala 27
Ansoff's Growth Matrix 143
anterior cingulate cortex 27
Aramco Overseas (case studies)
    346–348
artefacts 42
artificial intelligence, impact on the future
    of work 15
assumptions 42
attitudes 44
attribution theory 358

Baby Boomer generation 4, 196–198, 203,
    204, 207
banking regulation 3–4
Barclays Bank (case study) 262–264
Baseball, use of data analytics 308
BCG Growth Matrix 143
Behaviour, emotions and 26–28
Behavioural Modification Theory 87
beliefs 42, 43
    influence on learning and
        development 356–358
Beugré, CD 34
bias 67–70
Big Bang 14
Big Five personality dimensions (Costa and
    McCrae) 47
biology 14
Blue Ocean strategy 141–143
Boyer, Pascal 22, 28, 31
brain
    evolution of 16–17
    hard-wired (innate) modules 16–17
    neuroplasticity 21
    soft-wired connections 16–17, 21
    structure 17–21
    terms to describe areas of 19
brain networks 34

capability view of organizations 144–145
case studies
    Accenture 259–261
    Alibaba 252–253
    Aramco Overseas 346–348
    Barclays Bank 262–264
    Hermes 254–255
    Ledcor 257–259
    Monzo 344–346
    Oui SNCF 256–257
    Patagonia Inc 264–266
    Qantas Airways 127–128
    Smurfitt Kappa 125–127
    Tata Group 129–130
    Volvo 342–344
Cattell's 16 PF test of personality 46–47
change, leadership and 111–114
character 60
    developing strengths 63–64
    personality strengths 62–63
    strengths and virtues 60–62
    tools for individual and team
        development 63–64
CharacterScope 63–64
chemistry 14
Clarke, Andy 28
coaching 359–340
cognitive bias 67–68
cognitive empathy 27
Cognitive Evaluation Theory 86, 90
cognitive gadgets 31–34
cognitive intelligence 59
cognitive modules 32–33
cognitive processing, effects of emotional
    arousal 27–28
cognitive reappraisal 27
cognitive revolution 14, 15
cognitive technology 174–178
Colvin, Geoff 15
constructionist view of emotion 24–26
control network 34
corporate and social responsibility (CSR) 4,
    229–232
    ESG investment criteria 233
    impact of leadership 234–34
    responsibility for 238
    stakeholder impact 234–238
corporate climate 226
corporate sustainability 230

Costa, Paul 47
crystallized intelligence 59
cultural anthropology 214–219
cultural evolution 29–31
cultural intelligence 59
culture 212–226
    and the Big Five personality
        dimensions 223–224
    dimensions of 213, 214–219
    eight-scale culture guide 221–222
    expatriates 222–223
    global talent migration 213–224
    motivation and 97–98
    organization culture 224–226
    organizational implications 219–221

dark triad traits 54
data analytics baseball statistics 308
data governance 305–306
decision-making 74–75
    procrastination 77–78
    System 1 and System 2 thinking 75–77
default network 34
demographic trends 4
demographics 193–210
    Baby Boomer generation 196–198, 203,
        204, 207
    Generation X 196–197, 198, 204, 207
    Generation Y/Millennials 196, 198–201,
        204–210
    Generation Z 196, 201–203
    generational trends 196–197
    global trends 194–196
    multigenerational workforce 197–203
    narcissism in different generations
        208–210
Descartes, René 28
discriminatory bias 68–70
distributed ledger technology, impact of 15
diversity and inclusion (D&I) 238–249
    cultural resistance to 248–249
    implementation 244–248
    leadership impact 241–244
    management of 239–241
    practical implications 244–248
    responsibility for 249
Dodd-Frank Wall street reform 4
drive demands 18
Drive Theory 86–87

Eckman, Paul 24
efficacy 55
electricity, impacts of wide availability 15
Ellis, George 16, 17–18, 22, 29, 34–33
emotion
    behaviour and 26–28

classical view 25
constructionist view 24–26
distinction from affect 24
evolution of 21–23
hard-wired modules of the brain
    16–17
types of 23–24
emotional arousal, effects on cognitive
    processing 27–28
emotional empathy 27
emotional intelligence 26–27, 59–60
emotional mind 21–22
emotional regulation 27
empathy 27
employee engagement 311–315
    engagement surveys 311–313
    unlocking 313–315
employee experience 316–322
    employee feedback 321–322
    three contracts and trust 317–318
    vs employee engagement 318–321
employee segmentation 324
employee value proposition 322–324
employees
    fundamental desires 325–327
    giving them what they want 325–327
employer brand 322–325
    employee segmentation 324
    employee value proposition 322–324
    responsibility for brand
        management 324–325
Enactment Theory 151
environment 131–132
    challenges of the business environment
        3–5
environmental, social and governance (ESG)
    investment criteria 233
Equity Theory 88–89
evolution of Homo sapiens 14
expatriates, cultural issues 222–223
Expectancy Theory 89
Eysenck, Hans, personality traits 46

fallacies 67
faulty thinking, types of 66–78
Feldman Barrett, Lisa 24–26
Fiedler's Contingency Model 102–103
financial reward, motivation and 89–90
financial services, regulation 3–4
Five Forces Framework 140–141
Flow, motivation and 94–95
fluid intelligence 59
freeze, fight or flight response 20
Frith, C 22
functional magnetic resonance imaging
    (fMRI) 28

future of learning and development
    350–340
  attribution theory 358
  coaching 359–340
  high-impact learning that lasts 352
  influence of beliefs 356–358
  influence of mindset 356–358
  influence of personality 354–356
  lifelong learning 352–354
  skills 351
future of work 159–191
  alternative/contract workforce 181,
    185–188
  changes in the pattern of work 160–162
  changing jobs 165–166
  changing skills 166–167
  cognitive technology 174–178
  flexible working 181, 185–188
  gaps in leadership perceptions 173–174
  gender issues 189–190
  human – machine augmentation 176–178
  humanity in work 178–180
  leadership challenges 181–189
  loss of jobs 162–165
  on the bright side 190–191
  organizational capabilities 171–174
  people 174–180
  remote working 181–85
  team impact 188–189
  technology impact 162–167
  top 10 at-risk organizational
    capabilities 172–173
  top 10 future organizational
    capabilities 173
  workforce scenarios 167–171
future people management 400–408
  leadership challenges 400–402
  organizing for people management
    403–408
  people management challenges 402–403

Gallup's Q12 survey 311–412
Gardner, Howard 26
Generation X 4, 196–197, 198, 204, 207
Generation Y/Millennials 4, 196, 198–201,
    204–210
Generation Z 4, 196, 201–203
generational differences in work
    expectations 4
global talent migration 213–224
  global talent considerations 213–214
GLOBE project 213–122, 15–219
Goal Theory 88
Goleman, Daniel 21–22, 23–24, 26–27,
    28–29
group culture 70–72

group development 70–72
groups, in and out groups 72–74

Harari, Yuval Noah 14–15
Hermes (case study) 254–255
Herzberg's Hygiene Factors 83–84
Heuristics 67, 68
Heyes, Cecelia 29–34
high-impact learning that lasts 352
Hofstede, Geert 28
  cultural dimensions 213–214
Hogan, Robert, personality tests 47–49
human capital 283
  impact of people management 290–292
  measurement 285–287
  people metrics 288–290
Human Capital Monitor 287
human capital reporting 292–297
  10 core reporting areas 293–294
  future of 294–295
  human capital metrics 296–297
  investor impact 296
human capital strategy 282–284
Human Capital Theory 283
human history
  Big Bang to the cognitive revolution
    14–15
  turning points from the Industrial
    Revolution 15
human resource management (HRM)
    371–394
  current positions on 419–420
  developing a people operating
    model 430–431
  future people function 422–433
  future people management
    challenges 400–408
  HR in the boardroom 398
  people management and 3
  people management framework
    408–411, 422–431
  previous thoughts on 'personnel'
    management 417–419
  shared services 391–392
  strategic HRM 372–377
  structure 390–392
  talent management 398–400
  transformed by the future 420–422
  underlying tension 397–398
  viewed as not strategic 398
human resource management roles
    377–385
  frameworks for HR functional
    roles 378–379
  integrated roles 383–385
  relative roles 377–378

Ulrich model 379–383
view of CEOs and senior leaders
    392–394
human resource professionals
    influence of 385–390
    integrated influence 387–390
    relative influence 385–387

Implicit Association Tests (IAT) 68–69
impression management 53, 54
in and out groups 72–74
inclusion *see* diversity and inclusion (D&I)
information technology impact of the
    development of15
integration, strategic options 143–144
intelligence 58–60
interests 44
interpersonal intelligence 26
investment, ESG criteria 233

Job Facet Theory 85
job satisfaction, personality and 95–96
Jung, Carl 50–51

KPIs (key performance indicators) 289

Leader –Member Exchange (LMX)
    Model 104
leadership 100–123
    challenges of the future of work
        181–189
    challenges of the multigenerational
        workforce 204–210
    change and 111–114
    contingency theories 102–104
    developing a people operating
        model 430–431
    development 121–123
    future challenges for people
        management 400–402
    future of 106–111
    handling relationships 27
    impact on diversity and inclusion
        (D&I) 241–244
    in a VUCA world 108–111
    male and female leaders 117–118
    management and 2, 104–106
    organizational behaviour 115–120
    research 102–104
    selection 120–121
    social responsibility and 234–234
    task orientation vs people
        orientation 118–119
    theories of 102–104
    trait approaches 102
    transformational leadership 119–120

learning and development, future of
    350–340
Ledcor (case study) 257–259
lifelong learning 352–354
locus of control 45–46

Machiavellianism 54
MacLean, Paul 434
McCrae, Robert 47
McGregor's Theory X and Theory Y 84–85
McKinsey 7S model of organizations
    145–146
McLelland's Need Theory 84
Management, leadership and 104–106
management by objectives (MBOs) 288–290
Managerial Grid 103–104
managing emotions 26
Maslow's Hierarchy of Needs
    82–83
meaning in life 55–56
    well-being and 342–343
Millennials *see* Generation Y
mindset
    influence on learning and
        development 356–358
    motivation and 93–94
Mintzberg, Henry
    Organization Model 152–153
    Power Theory 153–154
mirror neurons 69–70
Monzo (case study) 344–346
moods 24
motivation 26–27, 80–98
    culture and 97–98
    financial reward and 89–90
    flow and 94–95
    job satisfaction and personality 95–96
    mindset and 93–94
    need theories 82–87
    neuroscience and 91
    our human and chimp brains 92–91
    overview of theories 81–82
    process theories 87–89
Motivation 3.0 86
multigenerational workforce 197–210
myelination of neurons 21
Myers–Briggs Type Indicator (MBTI) 49,
    50–51

narcissism 54, 208–210
Need Theory 84
NEO-PI test 47
neocortex of the brain 16–17, 20, 28
    emotional mind and 21–22
neurogenesis 21
neuroimaging 28

neurons 16–21
    mirror neurons 69–70
neuroplasticity 21
neuroscience
    male and female leaders 117–118
    motivation 91
    task orientation vs people
        orientation 118–119
    well-being and 341–342
neurotransmitters 17

objectives and key results (OKRs) 288–290
optimal distinctiveness theory (ODT)
    238–239
organization culture 224–226
organization enactment, social
    constructionism and 151
organization paradigm 267–268
organizational behaviour 115–120
    male and female leaders 117–118
    methods of study 115–116
    task orientation vs people
        orientation 118–119
    transformational leadership 119–120
organizational climate 226
Organizational Justice Theory 88
organizations 133–157
    adapting to the VUCA environment
        154–157
    balance of business portfolio 143
    capability view 144–145
    capacity for agility 154–157
    challenges of the VUCA world 138–139
    cultural competency 219–121
    design 147
    developing a business strategy 141–143
    development 148–150
    environmental sustainability issues 138
    external environment 134–140
    impact of political and economic
        policy 134
    internal environment 144–147
    legal/regulatory factors 138
    McKinsey 7S model 145–146
    models to view organizations 145–146
    organization ecology 140
    power structures 153–154
    practical implications of changing
        structures 154–157
    purpose 134–135
    Resource-Based View 144
    social factors 134–137
    Star Model 145
    strategic integration 143–144
    strategic planning 140–144

strategy development approaches
    146–147
strategy direction 143
structures 151–157
technological factors 137–138
Oui SNCF (case study) 256–157

Panskepp, Jaak 23
Patagonia Inc (case study) 264–266
Path – Goal Theory 103
people 1–2
people analytics 302–303
    baseball statistics 308
    data governance 305–306
    research design 303–305
    social sensing technology 306–307
people data 301–302
people development, future of 349–340
people management 3
    impact of 290–292
    see also human resource management
        (HRM)
people management framework 408–411,
    422–431
    people advisors 409–410, 424–425
    people enablers 411, 429–430
    people facilitators 411, 428–429
    people portfolio management 409, 410,
        426–427
    people specializations (embedded) 409,
        410, 427
people metrics 288–290
people operating model 1, 349
people paradigm 131–132
people portfolio management 272–275
people principles 1, 369
people risk
    risk management 275–279
    risk of key talent loss 278–279
    workforce planning 272–279
people technology 299–301
personality
    emergence of 56–58
    influence on learning and
        development 354–356
    job satisfaction and 95–96
    Type A vs Type B 49–50
    types 49–51
personality development 56–58
personality psychology 40–42
personality strengths 62–63
personality traits 44–45
    dark triad traits 54
    multiple personality trait systems
        46–49

personnel management 417–17 *see also*
    human resource management (HRM)
physics 14
Porter, Michael, on strategy 141
Power Dependency Theory 153
power structures in organizations 153–154
procrastination 77–78
prosocial behaviour 27
psychological safety 334–337
psychological well-being 335
psychopathy 54
purpose in life 55–56

Qantas Airways (case study) 127–128

Red Ocean strategy 141–42
regulation 3–4
Reinforcement Theory 87–88
Relationships, handling 27
Resource-Based View of organizations 144
reward network 34
risk control model 276–278
risk management, people risk 275–279
robotic process automation, impact on the
    future of work 15
ROI (return on investment) 288–290

Salovey Peter 26
scientific revolution 14
self-awareness 26, 27
Self-Determination Theory (SDT) 85
self-efficacy 45–46, 55
self-motivation 26–27
self-worth 55
Situational Leadership Model 104
skills for the future 351
Smurfitt Kappa (case study) 125–127
social constructionism 52–53, 151
social enterprises 229
Social Exchange Theory 153
social intelligence 59–60
Social Learning Theory 87
social movements 228–249
social sensing technology 306–307
socially responsible investing 233
socio-analytic theory 51–52
Solms, Mark 16, 17–18, 22, 29, 34–36
stakeholder theory 229
stakeholders impact of CSR 234–238
Star Model of organizations 145
stereotypes 69, 70
strategic human resource management
    372–377
    complexity 375–376
    configurational approach 372–374

contingency approach 372–374
internal environment 376–377
universalistic approach 372–374
strategic workforce planning 270–272
Strengthscope® 63
stress 337–338
    contributors to 338–340
    resilience to 340–341
structural capital 283–284
Swart, T 17, 21, 22, 34
SWOT analysis 140–141
synapses 17–18, 21
System 1 and System 2 thinking
    75–77

talent management 398–400
Tata Group (case study) 129–130
Teamwork, future of 188–189
technology 3
    advent of industrial technology 15
    cognitive technology 174–78
    impact on the future of work 15,
        162–167
theory of mind 33–34
Theory X and Theory Y 84–85
thinking 28–34
    cognitive gadgets 31–34
    cognitive modules 34–33
    cultural evolution 29–31
    evolution of 28–29
    mechanisms of thought 31–34
    theory of mind 33–34
    types of faulty thinking 66–78
Three Core Elements (Towers Watson)
    310–313
Three Faces of Power (Luke) 155
Three Needs Theory 84
transformational civil philanthropy
    230–132
transformational leadership 119–120
triune brain 434
Type A vs Type B personality 49–50

values 42, 43–44, 55
VIA Inventory of Strengths (VIA-IS) 62
VIA Youth Survey 62
Volcker rule 4
Volvo (case study) 342–344
VUCA (volatile, uncertain, complex and
    ambiguous) world 3, 4–5, 133
    challenges for organizations
        138–139
    leadership challenges 108–111
    practical implications for
        organizations 154–157

Watson Wyatt Human Capital Index
    286–287
well-being
    frameworks for 330–332
    meaning and 342–343
    neuroscience and 341–342
    practical implications 344–347
    psychological safety 334–337
    psychological well-being 335

stress and 337–340
wellness and 329–332
workplace design and 332–334
work, future of, *see* future of work
workforce, multigenerational 197–210
workforce planning 267–268
    people risk 272–279
    strategic 270–272
workplace design, well-being and 332–334

From 4 December 2025 the EU Responsible Person (GPSR) is:
eucomply oÜ, Pärnu mnt. 139b – 14, 11317 Tallinn, Estonia
www.eucompliancepartner.com

www.ingramcontent.com/pod-product-compliance
Lightning Source LLC
Chambersburg PA
CBHW042312210326
41598CB00042B/7364